D1006926

THE MEN WHO WOULD BE KING

THE MEN WHO WOULD BE
KING

AN ALMOST EPIC TALE
OF MOGULS, MOVIES,
AND A COMPANY CALLED
DREAMWORKS

NICOLE LaPORTE

HOUGHTON MIFFLIN HARCOURT
BOSTON   NEW YORK
2010

For information about permission to reproduce selections from this book,
write to Permissions, Houghton Mifflin Harcourt Publishing Company,
215 Park Avenue South, New York, New York 10003.

www.hmhbooks.com

Library of Congress Cataloging-in-Publication Data
LaPorte, Nicole.
The men who would be king : an almost epic tale of moguls,
movies, and a company called DreamWorks / Nicole LaPorte.
p. cm.
Includes bibliographical references and index.
ISBN 978-0-547-13470-3
1. DreamWorks Pictures—History. 2. Spielberg, Steven, 1946–
3. Katzenberg, Jeffrey, 1950– 4. Geffen, David. I. Title.
PN1999.D74L37 2010
384'.80979494—dc22   2009042488

Book design by Melissa Lotfy

Printed in the United States of America

DOC 10 9 8 7 6 5 4 3 2 1

For Richard

CONTENTS

———

III. ROCKIN'

IV. CLOSE-UP

The dream is a lie, but the dreaming is true.

—ROBERT PENN WARREN

A NOTE TO READERS

How do you tell the DreamWorks story? Few corporate figures, politicians, or celebrities are more determined to control what's written about them than blockbuster movie director Steven Spielberg, inexhaustible studio executive Jeffrey Katzenberg, and billionaire music mogul David Geffen. These are the men who, in 1994, founded DreamWorks, the much-touted movie studio (the first created in sixty years), where they labored, in varying degrees of togetherness, until recently. Despite the fact that their products depend on publicity and exposure, and that their carefully tended reputations have been created, to a degree, in partnership with the press, all three rejected my entreaties to interview them for this book. These are not peacocks who drop their plumage for Oprah or Barbara, or nearly anyone, particularly when the story doesn't end with them smiling triumphantly as the credits roll.

As the DreamWorks partners know all too well, journalism in Hollywood is a tricky business. It is often a tool to be enlisted "on background," when there is an ax to grind or an agenda to advance. Media relations in Hollywood often involve unspoken trade-offs. If the powerful get buffed and polished, they give: beneficial "friendships," exclusive scoops, trips on the private jet or yacht. But just as easily as VIPs can bestow favors, so can they take them away. When Claudia Eller, a business reporter for the *Los Angeles Times,* wrote that DreamWorks was in less than stunning shape, Katzenberg and DreamWorks marketing head Terry Press met with the *Times'* editor in chief and managing editor, complaining that she treated their company more harshly than others. The point was clear: DreamWorks was not going to take things lying down. To make the point all the more clear, Katzenberg and Press—the latter, at that point, had a close, personal friendship with Eller—stopped speaking to her for several years. DreamWorks' relationship with the press wasn't just convenient, it was necessary. The company, after all, was built on buckets of hype, beginning with its first press conference at the posh Peninsula hotel in Beverly Hills, upon which hordes of media descended to catch the first glimpse of the self-proclaimed Dream Team. As a private company (the animation division went public in 2004), DreamWorks never owed anyone numbers, in the form of balance sheets or quarterly earnings. Its inner workings were always a mystery. So it relied on the press to spin its usually self-glorifying view of its ventures.

Self-aggrandizement was, of course, what one expected from three of the greatest showmen in Hollywood, and if DreamWorks excelled at anything, it was putting on a performance. In its early days, the new venture became famous for its inches-thick press releases and extravagant press conferences—such as the one held in an airplane hangar to announce plans for a state-of-the-art studio (a vision that never came to pass). Spielberg was always front and center as the poster child and a symbol of affability and goodwill. Katzenberg was on hand to explain the brass tacks. And Geffen was a soothing—and intimidating—reminder that an especially demanding billionaire was overseeing the whole operation.

But as the DreamWorks story turned out to be much less than its founders envisioned, all that hype took its toll. By setting the expectations so high, on so many levels—the plan was to be a sprawling, multimedia venture that made better product (movies, TV shows, music) than the rest of Hollywood—it was all but impossible to live up to its promise. Tom Hanks once joked that the inevitable reaction to DreamWorks' first film, given who was behind it, would be: "Is that it?" By the time DreamWorks' live-action studio was sold to Paramount in 2005, the same question could be asked of the entire studio.

There was, certainly, an inspiring nobility in DreamWorks' desire to rewrite the rules. The company's stated mission was to put art first; it was proclaimed the new United Artists, the prototypical inmates-running-the-asylum studio formed in 1919 by Douglas Fairbanks, Mary Pickford, Charlie Chaplin, and D. W. Griffith. But too often the attempt to do more, do *better*, smacked of hubris and egos that had long ago lost touch with reality as mere mortals know it.

· · ·

The power that Spielberg, Katzenberg, and Geffen wield in Hollywood —and their effective demonstrations of it—breeds extreme fear and trembling in a town that thrives on hyperbole and drama. "There's a very strong fear element," confided one insider who has a long history with DreamWorks. Both Geffen and Katzenberg are known to have long memories when it comes to keeping score, and when an enemy is declared, the war is no mere skirmish. Years before onetime superagent Michael Ovitz was toppled from his perch atop the Creative Artists Agency, Geffen told friends he was going to "destroy" Ovitz, with whom he had a tempestuous past. "Watch me," he said.

Ovitz undoubtedly had a hand in his own fall, but Geffen fueled the process, trashing Ovitz for years and creating the perception that he was very damaged goods; the result of these effective theatrics was estimable. As Ovitz himself loved to say of Hollywood: "Perception is everything." Similarly, when Geffen turned on Bill and Hillary Clinton, after years of serving as the former president's biggest Hollywood donor and champion, it was not pretty. Or private. "Everybody in politics lies, but they do it with such ease, it's troubling," Geffen told *New York Times* op-ed columnist Maureen Dowd, whose column was considered—at least where Hollywood contributions were concerned—a watershed moment in the 2008 race for the Democratic presidential nomination, turning things in Barack Obama's favor. Dowd neglected to question her source's own credentials as an arbiter of integrity. Not to mention that some speculated that should Geffen buy the *Los Angeles Times* (a possibility at the time), she would be one of his first hires.

Few people in Hollywood are willing to cross these men, for fear of risking a premature close to a career or some other form of revenge. At one point during my tenure at *Variety,* where I covered the company, DreamWorks felt I was asking too many informed questions—thanks to a certain source whom I regularly called for briefings. Through a semi-elaborate baiting system—referred to within DreamWorks, by some, as a "massive sting"—the chatty source was identified and blackballed by the studio. DreamWorks employees who divulged too much were met with similar treatment. One former executive confided that when too many stories about the company started showing up in the press, Geffen addressed the staff, laying down threats: "I've got phone records," he said. "I'll go through them and find out who's talking. We'll get you." (Granted, talking to the press is verboten at most Hollywood studios, but at DreamWorks, the fact that it is *David Geffen* making threats makes it more chilling.)

Katzenberg made dozens of calls, warning sources not to talk to me for this book, a reality that made telling the DreamWorks story a delicate, difficult process. (At times I wondered who was working harder to make contact with people—Katzenberg or myself.) As a result, many of the more than two hundred people I interviewed only felt comfortable under the veil of anonymity, and even they were anxious. I got used to nervous glances toward restaurant entrances, quick exits.

My attempts to change the minds of the DreamWorks' partners about being interviewed were futile. In one of my few conversations with Katzenberg, he expressed his anger that I had set out to "profit" from his "story"—a saga, mind you, that he has spent years sharing with reporters for the purpose of articles and books that have benefited him enormously. But then, the story of Katzenberg's rise at Disney, where he'd been studio chairman under Michael Eisner, shows him in a far better light than his less-than-sentimental education at DreamWorks.

Well into the reporting of this book, I encountered Katzenberg at the premiere of *Shrek the Third* on a Sunday afternoon in the summer of 2007. He was charming enough about his reticence (perhaps because we were in public, not on the phone), but still firm. Standing in the theater lobby, telling every passing mother and child to enjoy the show, he appeared approachable. When I went up to him and introduced myself, asking, yet again, for an interview, he looked startled for about a tenth of a second and then regained his composure. Digging into the enormous tub of popcorn he was holding, he smiled widely and shook his head: "Not a chance, not a chance." Then he moved on to shake more hands.

One episode in particular stands out when I think about the experience of writing this book. It was a Saturday—a gray, misty spring morning—and I was meeting a source at a restaurant off Pacific Coast Highway. Driving north on the slim coastal strip that outlines the western edge of Southern California, I caught glimpses of surfers in slippery black wetsuits bobbing idly, waiting for the waves. On my right, there was a kitschy Italian restaurant, a dilapidated surf shop, a

KFC—the kinds of places that make much of Malibu seem more like a backwater beach town than a setting for Paris Hilton's beach parties.

I pulled into the nearly deserted parking lot. It was still a few hours before noon. As I got out of the car, I spotted a man walking briskly toward me.

"Nicole?" he asked.

"Yes, hi." We shook hands. "Thanks for agreeing to—"

"Not here," he said brusquely. "Too many people. Come with me."

I followed him as he walked to his car and signaled me to get in. "Damn Malibu," he said. "You can't go anywhere without seeing people."

Starting to feel nervous myself—*What the hell have I gotten into?*—I nonetheless opened the door and got in the car. He pulled back on PCH, and for the next two hours, I listened to my source as we sped along the California coastline—past a dreary, industrial-looking naval base in Ventura County, then back south, past Pepperdine, then north again.

When I was finally dropped off, my head was aching from so much time spent in such a small, tension-filled space. Nearly numb with exhaustion, I got in my own car and drove to Neptune's Net, a fish shack popular with the Harley-Davidson crowd. After ordering a grilled cheese and a Diet Coke, I opened my notebook. For the next hour I sat in an orange linoleum booth, among heavy-metal T-shirts and tattooed arms, reviewing my notes and recalling the trepidation of my source. Driving home, I still couldn't determine what it was I was getting into, but I was overcome with a sense of resolve. There was no question as to whether there was a good story here.

Why bother banging my head against the fortress wall? More than a few people advised me not to write this book, including fellow journalists, who warned me that I'd never eat lunch, dinner, or breakfast in this town again. But with each slammed door, I became more determined. As stated, DreamWorks used the press to its advantage whenever possible. But what about a story without the DreamWorks spin? That's the story I set out to write.

The DreamWorks tale reveals the movie business just as it is, at the industry's highest levels, where its most fleet-footed operators do their thing. At the heart of the book is a mystery. Just what happened, given the massive amounts of money involved, the unprecedented combination of talent, the confidence of so many observers (and the DreamWorks partners themselves)? A glance at the cast reminds us that DreamWorks' team was comprised of three players driven by ambitious self-interest and accustomed to living, first and foremost, according to that self-interest. Spielberg was the center around whom DreamWorks revolved. But his agenda frequently led to imprudent, money-losing ventures (the aforementioned state-of-the-art studio; nonmovie divisions such as video games and arcade centers, which fizzled). Most damaging to DreamWorks' bottom line, the director's most commercially successful films were directed for other studios. Anyone who expected Geffen or Katzenberg to be able to keep him wholly vested in his own company was quickly set straight. A studio head by name, perhaps, Spielberg was always an artist first, and he expected to be treated like one.

Then there was Katzenberg, an ambitious, self-promoting studio executive, who imagined himself as an infallible animation maestro, and whose quest for revenge against Disney (and especially Eisner) after his break with that company too often became a guiding principle at DreamWorks. In 2005, wanting to beat the DVD track record of Pixar's *The Incredibles* (Pixar then had a distribution deal with Disney), Katzenberg overpredicted sales of *Shrek 2* DVDs, leading to class-action lawsuits and a Securities and Exchange Commission investigation of DreamWorks Animation. Both were ultimately dropped, but DreamWorks Animation's stock has yet to fully recover from the debacle.

One of Katzenberg's strengths was running a movie studio, as he had done at Disney and, before that, Paramount. Yet he was exiled from DreamWorks' live-action studio by his partners, who didn't trust his creative instincts (his record in live action was far more mixed than in animation). The live-action studio, it was made clear from the get-go, was Spielberg's turf. To run it, the director relied on his trusted friends, the husband-and-wife team of Walter Parkes and Laurie MacDonald, whose highbrow taste fit with his hopes to win Oscars. But the couple had virtually no studio experience; both were self-proclaimed creative types who were, first and foremost, producers (Parkes was also a screenwriter).

As for Geffen, here was a shrewd operator who, according to his biographer, had tried to buy up his employees' stock before selling his own company. Geffen was relied on as the "business guy." But, having already secured his legacy and wealth (he was a billionaire when DreamWorks was formed), he had no interest in dealing with the innumerable headaches of a sprawling multimedia start-up. He took care of Spielberg's business, tended to investors, and masterminded partnerships and deals. But he rarely appeared fully engaged until things hit rock bottom, or he felt he had been intolerably wronged. (Ask Paramount executives about this phenomenon.)

These were not groupthink guys, or team players. They were lone wolves who came together and locked arms in the face of crisis and catastrophe, but who otherwise tended to their separate fiefdoms. They were performers who knew how to dazzle, rich men accustomed to spending other people's money. They knew how to make the story sparkle, at least from the outside. But what about behind the façade?

People ask: Was DreamWorks a failure? After all, the studio won several Academy Awards—*American Beauty* and *Gladiator* both took home Best Picture. Then there were animated hits like *Shrek,* which was not only wildly successful (the film grossed $484 million worldwide) but artistically groundbreaking. Spielberg's *Saving Private Ryan* is one of his best films, and resulted in a Best Director Oscar. But by the time the live-action studio was sold to Paramount, DreamWorks had shuttered or reduced its nonfilm divisions. The dream of being a huge multimedia venture was over, in part because the economics of the company never made sense. There was always enormous overhead even though there was no reliable supply of revenue in the form of a film library. In 2003, in the wake of its most financially disastrous release, the animated film *Sinbad,* DreamWorks came close to bankruptcy. Paul Allen, the Microsoft billionaire who provided the lion's share of the company's backing (he initially invested $500 million, in 1995, in the company), was called on for help. In 2009 Allen ultimately walked away with an amount estimated at more than $1.2 billion on a total investment of $700 million. Technically, he did not lose money. Nor did he make very much, considering that his rate of return was more in line with a savings account than private equity associated with the likes of Spielberg, Katzenberg, and Geffen. Like so many others, Allen had much, much higher hopes when he signed on to be a part of the dream.

Drawn by the reputations of its principals, and its pledge to be different, employees came in droves to join DreamWorks. They took pay cuts, gave up valuable stock options and the kind of bonuses that are considered standard in Hollywood, in order to proudly serve at a creativity-first kind of place, where there were no job titles and Spielberg sat in residence. Early on, a Utopian environment prevailed. Employees enjoyed the lack of studio bureaucracy: at DreamWorks, if one had an idea, one went and executed it. For a time, it seemed, those ideas were actually judged more for their artistic integrity, as the company attempted to move beyond stale formulas.

But DreamWorks changed, unable to sustain itself according to such ideals. By the end, too many promises were never realized. When the live-action studio was sold, Spielberg, Katzenberg, and Geffen—who had each invested $33 million to found the company—took away $175 million apiece. Employees who were hoping to share in that windfall were disappointed, especially considering Katzenberg's ongoing promise that the troops would ultimately be rewarded for their toil (his justification for DreamWorks' no-bonus policy).

Granted, it wasn't employees who'd ever put money into the company. But, again, the expectation made it feel unfair. There was similar grumbling when certain, but not all, executives profited handsomely in the IPO of DreamWorks Animation, which raised close to $1 billion in its first day of trading. DreamWorks' marketing team, which helped push *Shrek* riches into the stratosphere, was told that it was not technically a part of the animation studio and thus not subject to the same stock rewards. Meanwhile, Katzenberg's stake in his company soared up to $336 million the day DreamWorks Animation went public; Spielberg's and Geffen's each hit $312 million.

The three kings of DreamWorks represent the last generation of Hollywood raised on the visions of Samuel Goldwyn, Louis B. Mayer, and the other outsize, sometimes outlandish, personalities who built Hollywood. Since then, the landscape of the entertainment business has shifted dramatically; the golden age of those colorful men has been replaced by the corporate age, an era in which movies have more in common with amusement parks and video games than the old classics. But the company came to be in an era of plenty, before Enron and Sarbanes-Oxley, the 2002 legislation that cracked down on accounting practices at public companies and that greatly affected

Hollywood, which is mostly owned by New York conglomerates. It was a freewheeling time—eons before the collapse of Lehman Bros. et al.—when money seemed to grow on palm trees. Executives in charge rewarded themselves royally, and got away with it: In 1996 Michael Ovitz was fired from the Walt Disney Company after only fourteen months as its president, and given a $140 million parachute for a job not well done. At Sony, in the early '90s, Peter Guber and Jon Peters became infamous for their pocket-lining prowess.

But the times are changing. Wall Street is not the only industry suffering from a massive hangover. Although the change has gone largely unnoticed by the people who buy movie tickets, fewer dollars are circulating in an industry where agents and executives have, for so long, bumped up budgets by offering astronomical fees for stars. DVDs no longer pay the bills. A hundred million dollars at the box office no longer necessarily signifies a hit. Suddenly, it's not enough to be Spielberg—these days even he's hearing the hitherto unfamiliar sound of the word "no," and has been forced to sustain his company with his own funds—a career first.

An exploration of what occurred at DreamWorks helps us understand how we got from there to this most uncertain time. It's a story of movies, money, and the game of Hollywood as it is played by masters. But most of all it's a candid close-up of the big performers who have made Hollywood into the glorious, awful, magical, and treacherous place it is.

So. Enjoy the show. Turn the page if you want the tale from the beginning.

I

STARTING UP

1

THE EMPEROR IN AUGUST

In "the industry," there are the pictures, and then there is the big picture: the movie-like drama of ambition and retribution that is Hollywood life. In the course of this performance, skinny kids from the outer boroughs are transformed by force of will and sleight of hand into moguls and billionaires. Kings leave the stage against a backdrop of subtle maneuvers. Fathers and sons wage war. Deals and negotiations become dramas staged by players adept at manipulating realities. What motivates them? Of course: money and power. But there is more. They crave the special kind of recognition that comes with ruling their world.

IN THE FALL OF 1994, during the warm, dry months when Hollywood's most ambitious project in decades—a new super-studio called DreamWorks—was in its inception, a monarch was preparing for his bows. For much of the previous half century, Lew Wasserman had been chief of MCA/Universal, the town's most formidable entertainment conglomerate. The onetime theater usher was inextricably linked with the myths and the memories, the scandals and the lore that define Hollywood. His grandeur had both intimidated and inspired. Jack Valenti, former president of the Motion Picture Association of America, would refer to him as "Zeus."

Many of Wasserman's would-be heirs had modeled themselves after the slender man with the bright-white pompadour and signature black-framed glasses. These men had waited in the wings for the old king's inevitable drift from center stage. That moment seemed near at hand. The old guard was fading. For Sale signs announced opportunities. Foreign investors were calling. Ownership had become the obsession. It was not enough now to occupy the corner office; it was necessary to own it, the building, the lot. This was the New New Hollywood. The dealmakers had replaced movie stars as the jet set. Americans consumed box-office rankings with more interest than reviews. *Vanity Fair* and *The New Yorker* gave studio executives' exploits the scrutiny once lavished on Elizabeth Taylor's romances and the latest Kennedy rumors.

At the talent agencies, there were whispers: superagent Michael Ovitz, who had built Creative Artists Agency (CAA) into the ruling talent agency, was now positioning himself for his own starring role. He wasn't the only one.

On the morning of October 10, a rare trio—Steven Spielberg, David Geffen, and Jeffrey Katzenberg—drove up the long driveway off North Foothill Road in Beverly Hills. Their destination: the glass-walled mansion where Lew Wasserman lived with his wife, Edie, Hollywood's first lady. It was located, fittingly, next to Frank Sinatra's old place. Here, where the palms sheltered perfect flowers and the license plate on the white Mercedes roadster read MCA 1, it was almost possible to hear the voices of Old Hollywood, the patter of Bob Hope, the crooning of Bing Crosby. The halls were lined with paintings by Degas and Matisse. But the art most remarked upon by visitors was the portrait of Wasserman by Bernard Buffet, a gift from Alfred Hitchcock.

Walking toward the entrance, the three men would have missed the backyard's ornamental pond, home to hundreds of brilliantly colored Japanese koi, which reliably spawned after visits from President Bill Clinton, for whom the Wassermans had held fundraisers. "You have the same effect on fish as you do on women," Wasserman once told his friend. (Later, when Clinton asked what could be done to get more movies made in Arkansas, Wasserman replied, "Not much.")

The visitors were on a diplomatic mission requiring deference and grace. They hoped to present to Wasserman—godfather, benefactor, friend of popes, mobsters, Reagans and Monroes—their plan for the first new Hollywood studio in sixty years. Wasserman's ways were writ large in this town and few had taken more cues from him than the three men now making their approach. Schooled in the arts of émi-

nence grise, they understood what was to be gained through obser-
vation of and counseling by the elders, the Lears, Prosperos, and Don
Corleones, who tended to exact both obeisance and gratitude in complicated ways.

Wasserman, whose brass knuckles had long been replaced by polished fingernails, was the undisputed Hollywood paterfamilias. Yet
time was finally having its say. Eighty-one years of age, he had been
hospitalized for cancer, but the state of his health was not the only
thing under scrutiny by observers. Once *the* master of the negotiating
table, Wasserman had been slipping since 1990, when he had, albeit
reluctantly, sold MCA to Japan's Matsushita. Call it a disaster—"the
dumb thing I did," Wasserman admitted. It took time for those accustomed to his flamboyant imperiousness to adjust to the fact that Lew
Wasserman and his deputy, MCA president and COO Sidney Sheinberg, were lacking what Hollywood most prized in its patriarchs: absolute control.

Wasserman's guests hoped to inherit part of his legacy. They had
large ambitions that had only recently converged on the idea of creating, together, a company, and their joining forces in this new venture would have a major impact on Hollywood, and major implications for Wasserman. Geffen's and Spielberg's respective music and
film companies, Geffen Records and Amblin Entertainment, were under the MCA/Universal umbrella. Spielberg, who called Wasserman
his "guardian angel," had barely left the Universal lot since, as a college
kid self-conscious about his "schnoz," he'd sneaked past the gate using a briefcase as a prop. Anything vaguely resembling a defection on
Spielberg's part would not be welcome news to the studio. There was
enough trouble with the Japanese.

Picture a sunny California day with Steven Spielberg whizzing through
the Universal lot. His sports car hits a speed bump and he bangs his
head. By the next morning, all the speed bumps on the lot have been
removed. The vignette, perhaps apocryphal, suggests the lengths to
which MCA/Universal had been willing to go to make Spielberg feel
protected and at home. The director was closest with Sheinberg, who
got him his first directing job (on TV's *Night Gallery*), in 1969. But according to Connie Bruck's *When Hollywood Had a King*, the director
maintained that it was Wasserman who had saved him when guest

star Joan Crawford found out he was a first-timer. "I could tell," recalled Spielberg, "that Joan was going to . . . raise hell. Lew had been her manager, he was the one who got the call."

Wasserman told his diva to behave, as it was she who was in danger of being replaced. "From that day on," said Spielberg, "Joan Crawford treated me like King Vidor."

Wasserman, who believed in investing in the best, had been prescient. Since his beginnings, from *Jaws* and *E.T.* on, Spielberg had brought in billions. As a director, he alternated between extraterrestrial fare (*Close Encounters of the Third Kind*), thrill rides (the *Indiana Jones* series), and dramas (*Empire of the Sun, The Color Purple*). As a producer, he offered family fun (*Back to the Future, The Goonies, Gremlins*). His maturation held further magic: the previous year, his movies had won ten Oscars, three for the year's highest-grossing film (*Jurassic Park*), and seven for the most acclaimed (*Schindler's List*). Never had he been more revered.

Spielberg called MCA his "homeland," and so Wasserman and Sheinberg had made it, building a $4 million complex on the Universal lot to house his production company, Amblin. Homey and eucalyptus-shaded, it was modeled on George Lucas's Skywalker Ranch, and was similarly awash in splendid gadgetry. Spielberg, seemingly satisfied and quite productive, rarely left home. His life was as comfortable as his stonewashed jeans; his contracts were off the charts, and included an enormous portion of back-end grosses, a percentage of a movie's ticket receipts. On *Jurassic Park,* he took no money upfront, but received 15 percent of the first-dollar gross, or fifteen cents on every dollar off the top that went to Universal.

No money upfront was risky, but Spielberg flops were rare. *E.T.* and *Jurassic Park* remain among the top twenty of the highest-grossing movies ever. Because of this track record, he and Universal basically split the profits on films he produced. When *Jurassic Park* grossed $914 million worldwide, Spielberg took home about $300 million, as much as Universal. Spielberg also received extraordinary revenues from ancillary rights (namely, home-video profits) and merchandising. And in a deal unheard of anywhere else in Hollywood, he was granted 2 percent of ticket receipts from Universal theme parks, which amounts to $30 million a year.

But so much was changing, for all the men. Spielberg knew that the

Universal of Wasserman and Sheinberg was fading. Yet his own future was still filled with the promise of further ascension.

Sitting in the luxurious den overlooking the sloping backyard, Wasserman listened as Spielberg described a studio of the future that produced movies, TV, music, and more. The perpetual wunderkind was forty-seven years old, bespectacled and with a lightly graying beard. Wasserman took it in, but to him there was presumably something more noteworthy than the new studio. He must have been surprised by Geffen and Katzenberg's seduction of Spielberg, whose interests had never previously involved the risky business of ownership, in an industry of volatile change.

Geffen's involvement with the venture was easier to discern. Like Wasserman, he had started out as an agent. The child of a depressive father and a mother hospitalized for emotional problems after the loss of her extended family in a concentration camp, Geffen was known for his way with talent. The high-voltage currents of artists seemed compatible with his mercurial intensity. He took care of those he represented (Joni Mitchell, Jackson Browne), while screaming down disbelievers and aggressively cajoling the record executives he wrangled into submission. These days, he moved companies (his record label had gone to MCA for 10 million shares of MCA stock, valued at around $545 million). But Geffen had never stopped respecting talent, the soul of the industry, and connecting with those driven souls who possessed it. With the help of Katzenberg he was suddenly in business with the most commercial talent in town: Steven Spielberg. It was a triumphant moment.

Spielberg told Wasserman that he wanted to go beyond formulas and films made to order by marketing departments. MCA was the inspiration, of course, said the director. But MCA was not, at least these days, known for its artistic innovations. Spielberg wanted to go Wasserman one better. He wanted to go everyone one better. He was, after all, Steven Spielberg, accustomed to advancing the game.

The new partners were thinking state-of-the-art, so cutting edge they couldn't quite articulate as yet all that the new enterprise would entail. But it would all come together. Failure wasn't written into the scripts these three worked from. Their falls from grace had been quickly erased from Hollywood's collective memory. They were the glory boys, whose world was part ruthlessly pragmatic, part romance. From themselves they expected, as did many others, only further spectacular feats.

How many callers had Wasserman seen arriving at his gates? Now, here he was, the waning patriarch, shifting into that most unrewarding of roles: benevolent good sport. So he turned up the enthusiasm, taking what was later described as delight in what he was hearing. After being given assurances of the partners' loyalty, and a discussion of MCA/Universal making a distribution deal with the new company, the old tough guy seemed to drift a bit. He showed the men keepsakes, like his drawings by Walt Disney, and began to speak tenderly, nostalgically, about the old days, when defeat was unknown to him, and Hollywood was Hollywood.

2

THE END OF MAGIC

REWIND TO THE MOMENT that many would call the *real* beginning of DreamWorks: April 3, 1994, when Disney president and COO Frank Wells died in a helicopter crash. The beloved executive had served as the mollifying glue (a "marriage counselor," as Katzenberg would put it) between Katzenberg and his boss of nearly two decades, Disney CEO Michael Eisner. With Wells gone, things went sour quickly.

Katzenberg had aggressively angled for Wells's job. When he didn't get it, he was gone.

The departure of the forty-three-year-old Katzenberg, who as Disney Studios chairman was known for back-to-back power breakfasts, air kisses, and animation blockbusters, left Hollywood with the sense of a blood feud. Katzenberg's ouster was like "a man being kicked out of his homeland. It was biblical," remarked a colleague. In the aftermath, Disney was a divided territory. In firing Katzenberg, not only had Eisner pulled off an attention-grabbing power play, he was withholding a multimillion-dollar bonus payment that Katzenberg believed was owed him by contract. Now *this* was high-concept. Katzenberg had not so much worked at Disney as lived the company, seven days a week, for a decade. Now he had been stripped of that identity by the man he had long been driven to please. His own father was distant, complicated. From Eisner, it had always seemed, Katzenberg had been determined to extract what had been missing in that relationship.

Arriving in 1984, after a successful stint at Paramount, where Eisner was COO and Katzenberg head of production, the two had transformed Disney from a has-been studio, where WASPs in pastel cardigans drank gin at lunch and took off early to head for the greens, into a corporation that no longer seemed like an anachronism. Suddenly there were hits, like *Down and Out in Beverly Hills* and *Ruthless People*—movies for grownups, with hip plots and carefully leavened spice quotients. Old favorites—classic Disney films—were repackaged and, for the first time, resold. Share prices rose. New divisions and theme parks opened. Katzenberg had a hand in the company's resurgence, but he'd made his true mark in animation. Because of his passionate, sometimes crazed, commitment, the Disney brand was restored, with *The Little Mermaid, Beauty and the Beast, Aladdin.* And then: *The Lion King.* Released just two months before Katzenberg's exit, the film broke every record for animated films, grossing $700 million at the worldwide box office and contributing another billion-plus in merchandising and ancillary revenues. With this blockbuster, Jeffrey Katzenberg was beginning to look—a bit too much for some—like the king of the Disney jungle.

Alternately lovable and annoying, Katzenberg is the manic, crazy-making kid-brother type. At fourteen, while other mischief-makers at his summer camp tipped over canoes, Katzenberg—who would come to be known as a bit of a cardsharp—dealt out an illegal hand and walked off with the other campers' allowances. Rather than suffer the subsequent punishment of standing by the flagpole, he cut out.

At Disney, there were no flagpoles and no poker. Katzenberg worked feverishly and expected the same dedication from others. He demanded seven-day workweeks, driving his employees hard ("You never knew if he was gonna hug you or kick you," said *Lion King* producer Don Hahn). His proven ability to keep to the bottom line had earned him a reputation for stinginess. But Katzenberg had admirers on and off the lot, including a cadre of hard-driving female loyalists. He was the kind of always-on achievement junkie that Hollywood considered its own breed. But unlike some, Katzenberg actually delivered more than lip service, with seemingly never-ending hours in executive offices and editing suites. And he was quick to thank those who sweated it out with him, even if it meant making three hundred phone calls a day.

"Jeffrey really likes to do things that make people feel good," said Penney Finkelman Cox, a producer who worked with Katzenberg at Paramount on *Terms of Endearment.* "He likes to keep people happy.

He never asks of others what he wouldn't do himself." But so single-minded was he that he had no qualms about bending or blurring inconvenient truths when necessary. "He has no limits about what he'll lie about or say," says a source. "That's really his gift." He liked to think of himself as tough and straightforward, and enjoyed playing the role of cutthroat executive. He once told screenwriter Dale Launer that Disney was the best place to work because "Here, we don't stab you in the back. We stab you in the chest!" Launer came to respect Katzenberg, but at first he flinched.

As CEO of the most recognizable entertainment company in the world, Michael Eisner reaped the benefits of his underling's gung-ho enthusiasm. How high could he make Jeffrey jump? There seemed to be no limits. Smooth and perceptive, Eisner was successful at manipulating Katzenberg's ambition. Yet as the years passed, Katzenberg started proving himself wilier than his boss. The bad days began when the protégé began looking for more—of everything, naturally. After the death of Frank Wells, Eisner's number two, Katzenberg seemed the logical successor.

But that wasn't, as it turned out, how it played out. Even though Eisner had stood on a snowy Aspen street and promised Katzenberg the title *if* . . . he held back. Katzenberg knew there was trouble when, subsequently, Eisner had a heart attack, requiring surgery, and Katzenberg was not among the first to be alerted. During Eisner's recovery, it was CAA's Michael Ovitz he wanted at his bedside. Unlike Wells, who Eisner said "carried a piece of paper in his pocket that said, 'Humility is the best virtue,'" Katzenberg did not do self-effacement. It was always, no matter what, about Katzenberg. He worked for his own glorification, not the team's. Stories about Jeffrey's magic touch were now regularly appearing in the press; the accounts could make it seem that Jeffrey was singularly responsible for Disney's new direction. (Disney publicist Terry Press, an inveterate "Jeffrey Girl," played a hand in this.) The coverage did not sit well with Eisner and Disney's board of directors.

Eisner had legitimate concerns when it came to Katzenberg. The man whom he famously, and rather patronizingly, dubbed his "golden retriever" could—at the beginning, at least—seemingly will movies past the $100 million mark, land any star, cut any deal. But leading a public company required the kind of cool-headed shrewdness that pacified Wall Street. Jeffrey—whom the *Wall Street Journal* described as "creative but unpolished"—was pure Hollywood. Eisner rightly judged Katzenberg's tendency toward self-aggrandizement as anathema to the board of directors, especially Roy E. Disney (nephew of Walt). But Eisner's reluctance to reward his longtime protégé was ultimately considered unfair by many observers.

So came the rebellion, during which Katzenberg—more popular than his boss, around town and with the press—played to the balcony, orchestrating coverage, making certain no one mistook him for the villain. The day he was forced to resign, Claudia Eller, a reporter for the *L.A. Times*, who had been on the Disney lot for a movie screening, was brought into Katzenberg's office by Terry Press. As a stream of shocked executives entered the room offering their condolences, some of them weeping, Eller dictated notes over the phone to her colleagues at the paper. But this was just Act I.

Next move: Katzenberg would strike back, and quickly. It was expected in a town raised on *The Godfather*—parts I and II. Counseling him was his ally and mentor, David Geffen. A shrewd strategist and brutal foe, Geffen had been encouraging his friend's quest for ascension at Disney, and feeding the press in Katzenberg's favor. But Geffen had misjudged Eisner.

Who could say for certain what game Geffen was playing? Here was a cunning *macher* who lived to maneuver all the players on the board according to whatever scenarios he was advancing. "People are always calling him, spilling their guts out," said a source. "There is no deal he is not privy to. [And he uses] every piece of information to further himself and his investments." Waves of change were rolling, and Geffen would ride them—to the bank or wherever his preferred destination. He was following the evolving situation not just at Disney, but at MCA, closely. Wasserman's *job* wasn't what interested him: Geffen, who liked working behind the mirror, had outgrown offices. But if there was going to be a power vacuum, he would help determine who filled it, and Hollywood's future, in which he certainly planned to figure.

CAA's Michael Ovitz, a persistent fly in Geffen's ointment, was getting too big, too full of himself. He had driven stars' prices up to the point that some considered dangerous, and he was starting to broker not just the big deals but the *biggest*. In 1989, after helping Sony buy Columbia, he had attempted to set himself up as that company's new chief executive. These days he was gazing at Wasserman's post at MCA/Universal, a company he'd helped sell to Matsushita. Geffen, who had a large financial stake in MCA, didn't like it.

Katzenberg and Geffen had met years back, when Katzenberg was an assistant to Barry Diller, then chairman of Paramount. Katzenberg had been charged with meeting Geffen's plane at LAX and, sensing that this was not a man inclined to wait for the Vuitton, had whisked him through customs so fast that Geffen blinked—and saw himself. In Hollywood, nothing beats narcissism for inspiring a lasting relationship.

Katzenberg's battle with Eisner punched Geffen's buttons. How many times had Geffen endured his own battles with ungrateful father figures: music moguls Ahmet Ertegun and Clive Davis, Warner Communications CEO Steve Ross. The six-foot-three, ruddy-cheeked Disney chieftain had grown up with silver and suits, boasted about books he had actually read. Geffen sped through memos, traffic, people. He remained the scrappy Jewish kid from Brooklyn's Borough Park who had kept his ambition upfront and his sexual orientation a secret.

If there was a show to come, Geffen, slugging it out in Katzenberg's corner, would rev it up. And the members of the press were waiting to see just when the story would break. "Ever since Jeffrey stepped down from Disney, we'd been hearing rumblings," said Alan Citron, then a reporter at the *Los Angeles Times*. There were hints suggesting that Katzenberg would be moving on to something illustrious, possibly a new company. "It was like, OK, when's the next shoe going to drop? We'd been obsessively chasing the story, concerned we'd get beat by the *New York Times* or the *Wall Street Journal*."

In newsrooms across the country, the chase was on.

3

MR. SPIELBERG WILL SEE YOU NOW

S TEVEN SPIELBERG'S main residence is a warm, bustling manor
awash in iconography, souvenirs from the director's own films
and mementos. Among the kids' toys and baseball caps hang
original Rockwells and Remingtons overlooking treasures such as the
balsa-wood Rosebud sled from *Citizen Kane.*

Jeffrey Katzenberg was not headed there for the tour.

Among Katzenberg's tangled strands of strengths and weaknesses
was a cord of will. "No" was never an option. And on this day in late
August, as he drove to Spielberg's in his black Mustang soon after his
break with Disney, Katzenberg was calling on the personal determination that had so rarely failed him. He had worked with Spielberg
on the wildly successful 1988 film *Who Framed Roger Rabbit,* which
Spielberg executive-produced. And in 1994 the two had partnered in
opening the whimsical submarine-themed L.A. restaurant Dive! Now
Katzenberg wanted to join forces with Spielberg again, in a much
more special union.

The director had already rejected his first overture, just days before.
Katzenberg knew what he was up against. Spielberg's setup at MCA/
Universal was simply too good to be true.

Spielberg's wife, the actress Kate Capshaw, once described her neighborhood, the Pacific Palisades, as "sidewalky," conjuring up the image of young mothers pushing prams. But the Spielbergs' place is a
sprawling estate overlooking the Riviera Country Club where Spencer
Tracy and Katharine Hepburn once teed off (their film *Pat and Mike*
was filmed at the club). Neighbors include Tom Hanks, Tom Cruise,
and Arnold Schwarzenegger. In this setting, Spielberg had achieved a
perfect mise en scène.

After his 1989 breakup with his first wife, the actress Amy Irving (*The Competition, Yentl*), he had wed the blond, petite Capshaw—who had, fittingly, originated as an elementary school teacher (née Kathleen Sue Nail) in Missouri. Their family included five children (two of their own; one each from their previous marriages; and an adopted son). Capshaw relished playing the lead in Spielberg's real-life movie. Unlike Irving, she seemed unfazed by red carpets.

Spielberg was disillusioned by marriage after his breakup with Irving, but Capshaw did what it took to convince him to, again, exchange lifelong vows. She put her career aside and started couples therapy with Spielberg. Realizing that, even more than most famous people, Spielberg kept careful watch over his fortune, she offered to sign a prenup. She even converted to Judaism. "Kate made it clear she'd be a different kind of woman—a supporting, loving, and present wife," one source says. "What Amy was *not*."

Jeffrey Katzenberg also had a marriage of sorts in mind. After driving off the Disney lot for the last time, Katzenberg had set up an office on Maple Drive in Beverly Hills. Inquisitive well-wishers like Ray Stark—discoverer of Streisand, producer of Neil Simon—were unable to divine his next move. Things grew even quieter after Katzenberg started his campaign to secure Spielberg. The dialogue had begun, innocently enough, just after the news broke of Katzenberg's ouster. Friends, such as Barry Diller, had called offering their support.

Spielberg checked in from the Bahamas, where he was vacationing with Robert Zemeckis, a close friend and the director of *Roger Rabbit.* In the background, Zemeckis called out: "You guys should do something together!"

But Spielberg proffered only his encouragement, quoting the last line of *Back to the Future,* spoken by Christopher Lloyd. "Where you're going, you don't need roads," he said in classic Spielbergian style.

"What do you mean *you?*" Katzenberg said. "I'm talking *we.*"

Later, when Geffen called, Katzenberg told his friend that he never wanted to work for anyone ever again. "Well, good. Start a company. Do whatever you want," Geffen told him. "You can do it."

"Should I do something with Spielberg?" Katzenberg asked.

Geffen didn't think twice. "Are you kidding? If I were you, I'd do it in a second."

So Katzenberg started putting it together—at last, *his show.* Slaving away on financial models and a business plan were his new team, which consisted of Sandra Rabins, former head of production and motion picture finance for Buena Vista International, and half a dozen members of Price Waterhouse's entertainment division. Peter B. Frank, the head of Waterhouse, had offered Katzenberg $50,000 of essentially free services toward his next endeavor.

As Rabins and Price Waterhouse ran the numbers, Katzenberg started making house calls.

Katzenberg knew that snagging Spielberg would take ingenuity. Despite his laid-back image, Spielberg was a man who wanted everything—and made sure he got it.

The public Spielberg still recalls the shy kid from a broken home, all "skinny wrists and glasses," in his words. He wears those former insecurities on the brims of his trademark baseball caps. Memories of classmates sneezing "Hah-Jew!" when he passed still seem to linger in his consciousness, along with his recollection of trying to gentilize his nose with duct tape. ("I thought if you kept your nose taped up . . . it would stay . . . like Silly Putty!")

Yet whatever else he may be, Spielberg is an intense power player who cares deeply about financial matters. Says a former agent from CAA, the agency that represents the director: "He's probably the toughest person who ever lived, with the added aggravation that he wants everyone to like it. It's that star thing. He has people around who make his wishes come true before he expresses them. There's a whole phalanx." Sid Sheinberg attested that "there is no better businessman in Hollywood than Steven." And Spielberg affirmed, to the *New York Times,* in 1992: "I *am* a tough negotiator." Not that Spielberg himself liked to negotiate. He hated actually dealing with business matters, preferring to play the role of menschy, likable artiste—the dirty work was left to his team of agents, lawyers, and managers.

As a business partner, Spielberg's name would attract the best of everything, including investors. But he, in turn, demanded the best and was accustomed to getting it. His universe genuflected before him. CAA lived in mortal fear of its star client ever deserting, and would do anything to prevent it. How many decades had passed since anyone had told Spielberg the truth, a commodity his coddlers worked strenuously to keep from him if it was less than reassuring? Amblin had been created to serve its star resident to an almost surreal degree.

Screenwriter Richard Christian Matheson tells the story of a jaunt around the Amblin campus with Spielberg: "Every once in a while, from a rock or a tree, you'd hear, 'Steven, your two thirty is here.' Obviously, there were microphones among the rocks that talk, because you'd hear a voice saying, 'Steven, do you want something?' He'd say, 'Guys, do you want some Popsicles?' And then he would say to nobody, 'Bring us three root-beer Popsicles!' The whole place was obviously tracking his whereabouts."

It wasn't like he'd gone Howard Hughes. But Spielberg had resided within the insular world of the very famous for a very long time. No environment was more conducive to Spielberg's vision of things than his movie sets, where everyone's unwritten job was to intuit what the director wanted even before he did — and to deliver.

"Three to four times a day, I'd be standing right next to him and he'd turn to me with a new idea that was so good and right," said producer Bruce Cohen, who has worked as Spielberg's assistant director. "And then I'd be on a mad scramble, because if anything that is involved — costume, wardrobe, actor, line of dialogue, special effect, prop — that we don't have, now Steven wants them, and do I have them ready?" Says another source, "There's a lot of tippy-toeing around him, a lot of talk of when's the right time to ask Steven, whose people are very protective of his creative process. You know that when he's chewing his hand, it's not a good time. He puts most of his fingers into his mouth and gnaws — that's the sign that he's thinking deeply; a sign not to go near him."

On that August afternoon, as Katzenberg met with Spielberg in his home, it became clear that, despite their differences, they had a lot in common. Both had existed under the aegis of older mentors. Neither had ever felt completely in charge of his destiny. For Spielberg, this truth seemed to touch a nerve, as Katzenberg pitched his version of an exciting new reality. The more Spielberg thought about it, the more enamored he became of the concept of *his* company. Despite his ironclad, Michael Ovitz–negotiated contracts, Spielberg had always essentially been a director for hire, working for one studio or another. By this time, he was the father of a growing household of kids, not to mention Oscars. He was ready to truly become the patriarch. Ownership, as outlined by Katzenberg, suddenly seemed less an option than a responsibility. On another level, he had grown tired of being "the blockbuster guy." *Schindler's List* had proved that he could be just as serious a moviemaker as his longtime friend and rival Martin Scorsese, the critics' choice. For too long he had been marooned in the suburbs, where kids hid aliens in the closet.

Wasserman had had his day. It was now the younger generation's turn to take the helm. People talked of Ovitz as the new king of Hollywood, and yet Ovitz was Spielberg's *agent. He* was the guy who was making the movies that made the money for everyone. It was time to claim what was rightfully his—the position of Hollywood's acknowledged ruler.

One wonders at what point the company that Katzenberg was envisioning for himself became the latest extension of the Spielberg empire. One ponders just how Katzenberg reconciled the fact that Spielberg's own dreams about the venture would inevitably collide with, actually eclipse, his own. Spielberg, meanwhile, had his own issues to resolve.

Somewhere buried in the undercurrents of the conversation was Katzenberg's reputation. The tightfistedness that had become synonymous with Katzenberg could hurt a studio seeking to create long-term relationships with talent, not to mention relations with agencies, including Spielberg's very own. During the Eisner-Katzenberg reign, negotiations between CAA and Disney were high-stakes battles with one side or the other always upping the ante. On one occasion, an ordinarily steely CAA representative was reduced to sobs—her assistant plying her with Kleenex—after an hour of negotiating a writer's fee with Helene Hahn, head of business affairs at Disney and another Jeffrey Girl, known as Attila the Hahn. The brutal haranguing was over just $5,000, but nobody budged. Finally, Disney split the difference, take it or leave it. After hanging up with Hahn, the agent called Katzenberg, a friend, and said that she hoped their relationship was worth more than $2,500. Katzenberg replied tersely: "I have to make many $2,500 decisions every day."

Filmmakers were also insulted by Disney's obsessive thrift, particularly after they had delivered films that profited the studio. After *Good Morning, Vietnam,* Ovitz upped the price for director Barry Levinson's follow-up. Disney demurred, so *Rain Man* went to United Artists and won the Oscar. After the Zucker brothers received no financial *merci* for *Ruthless People,* they, too, left. Screenwriters bristled not just about dough, but about Disney's creative interference.

"The 'Disney Notes' were notorious," said Dale Launer. "They were extensive notes, like thirty to forty pages . . . Jeffrey had a big hand in it."

Then there was Katzenberg's rough-around-the-edges style. If an executive couldn't secure rights to a book, or lost a project in a bidding war, Katzenberg would bellow, "Rip it off!"

Still, Jeffrey's penuriousness had its advantages. It was, after all, his energy and thrift that had been instrumental in Disney's turnaround. Even more importantly, Spielberg knew that in any partnership, Katzenberg would be the workhorse. Sparing him from the business details he so loathed.

Yet Spielberg couldn't ignore that the "homeland" to which he was so attached was threatened. Wasserman was not a young man, and even Sheinberg was approaching an age when, in Hollywood, the winds begin to whisper, *Palm Springs, Palm Springs.* Their corporation was turning Japanese, and the foreigners were not giving their American underlings free rein. Ovitz had masterminded the deal, which had become so deplorable that Sheinberg and Wasserman had scheduled a showdown with Matsushita in Hawaii to discuss a possible buyback. The situation at MCA also reminded Spielberg of the friction and politics inherent in Hollywood corporate culture, making Katzenberg's proposition of building an independent, self-run studio all the more seductive.

Although Katzenberg made substantial headway with Spielberg, he did not land the director that afternoon in Pacific Palisades. Spielberg had more thinking to do: Capshaw, for one, would need convincing. Spielberg once confided to a colleague that "if it wasn't for my wife" he'd routinely direct movies back to back, as he'd just done with *Schindler* and *Jurassic Park.* And how was Capshaw going to feel about him being a studio owner, a job that would demand much more of his already overtapped time?

"I love Jeffrey. But I never want you to become Jeffrey," Capshaw had told her husband. "I don't want you in that lather of workaholism."

When Spielberg assured her that her fears were unfounded, and even said that he would be home every day by 5:30 P.M., Capshaw softened—though she was not placated until Spielberg made it clear to Katzenberg that these stipulations were contingent on his involvement.

Katzenberg, meanwhile, had his own contingencies. He wanted to bring in another partner: enter David Geffen.

4

GEFFEN SLEPT HERE

B Y THE END OF SEPTEMBER, the company was starting to look real. Katzenberg had wrangled not just Spielberg but Geffen. For the moment. There was much to discuss if the partnership was to be finalized. They needed to talk, but in private, something that was impossible in L.A., given the spotlight on Katzenberg since his departure from Disney.

When Katzenberg realized that they would all be in Washington, D.C., for a September 27 White House dinner honoring Russian president Boris Yeltsin, he suggested a summit.

After the dinner, Katzenberg and Spielberg returned to the Hay-Adams Hotel. Geffen, overnighting across the street in the Lincoln Bedroom, was expected later. But after midnight, still no Geffen.

Finally he called, explaining that he'd been held up by the Clintons; Bill could go on all night. "But it's one o'clock in the morning!"

"I don't care!" Katzenberg bellowed. "Get over here now!"

Ten minutes later, the phone rang again: "I can't get over there," Geffen said. The White House was closed for the night; there was no one around to let him out.

"David," Katzenberg began, "you pick up the phone, you dial operator..."

Moments later, another call. A Secret Service agent had advised Geffen that it was best to stay put.

"I'm a hostage..." he told Katzenberg.

So how did the unlikely duo become an even unlikelier threesome? Spielberg may have respected Geffen's flair for making fortunes, but he could not exactly be called one of the dealmaker's acolytes. In producer Julia Phillips's juicy tell-all, *You'll Never Eat Lunch in This Town*

Again, Geffen called Spielberg "selfish, self-centered, egomaniacal, and worst of all—greedy."

And while bringing the strange and satirical off-Broadway musical *Little Shop of Horrors,* about a man-eating plant named Audrey II, to the screen, there had been ugly screaming sessions over the film, which Geffen was producing and Spielberg executive-producing. Spielberg ended up walking off the picture, taking his credit, so valuable to studio marketers, with him.

A different sort of complication existed between the men when it came to Steve Ross, the impresario of Warner Communications in the 1970s and '80s. Both Spielberg and Geffen had admired Ross and counted him as an important adviser in past years. But they showed their feelings in remarkably different fashions.

Ross had become close with Spielberg in 1982, when he was determined to break Universal's hold on the director. To do so, he offered Spielberg $23 million for the video-game rights to *E.T.,* a deal derided by some as ridiculously generous. Ross didn't see it that way. As one former Warner executive told Connie Bruck in her biography of Ross, *Master of the Game,* "Steve's viewpoint was, so what if I overpay by $22 million? How can you compare that to the value of a relationship with Spielberg? And I think he was dead right."

For Spielberg, Ross was an older sophisticate, someone who could take him beyond TV and Oreo cookies. "Steven was a young man, in his early thirties, with no business sophistication," Terry Semel, the former chairman of Warner Bros., has said. "He found Steve, who was much older, so fascinating. Steve Ross was into things we knew only a little about—art, planes, homes." Spielberg had found another father figure, one who also presented a mutually beneficial business bond.

Ross had known Geffen longer; the friendship dated back to the latter's early days in music. Geffen had sold his first label, Asylum Records, to Warner Communications in 1972, where it was merged with Elektra Records. Years later, when he'd switched gears and become a movie executive, it was Ross who paved the way, setting Geffen up in the executive suite at Warner Bros. Yet Geffen's periods of peaceful coexistence with Ross had been punctuated by moments of hostility. Most publicly Geffen had excoriated Ross for Warner's drooping stock in front of other top executives at a companywide meeting in the early 1970s. (He told another executive, "You're a failure! You should quit!")

Geffen's antics caused Warner's general counsel David Horowitz to re-mark, "Who would have the effrontery to treat the chairman in this way?"

Ross had been more predisposed than most to Geffen. He had granted him favorable deals even when they were ill-advised. But in 1989, when Geffen abruptly sold Geffen Records to MCA, severing ties with Warner and Ross, he finally managed to drive Ross past for-giveness.

Geffen's vilification of Ross in the press, even as the older man lay dying of prostate cancer, offended Spielberg, the good son, who re-mained at Ross's side, attending the funeral along with Quincy Jones, Paul Simon, and Barbra Streisand, who sang at the service. Geffen re-ceived no such invitation. Nor was he asked to the less private me-morial—the guest list was several thousand names long—at Carnegie Hall, though he attended anyway.

At the time that Katzenberg came calling, Geffen and Spielberg's relationship suggested that of rivalrous siblings. But their feelings for Ross had also connected them. And as they moved on without those who had previously guided them, it was not incomprehensible that they would look to each other. It would often be said that Spielberg and Geffen came together "over Jeffrey"—an explanation that sug-gests generosity and loyalty to their friend. But both needed the other in ways that transcended Katzenberg.

Spielberg saw Geffen as battle-ready and time-tested. As he con-sidered life without his ties to Sheinberg and Wasserman, he would have seen Geffen as his latest insurance policy. Then there was Spiel-berg's awe at Geffen's wealth. His billion-dollar fortune was quite a bit more than Spielberg's own $600 million net worth. For a man who considered these things with care, for whom, as one source said—"it's *always* about money"—it surely must have pained him that the hot-tempered Geffen outranked him so conspicuously.

Always knowing what buttons to push when it came to getting his way, Katzenberg had needled Spielberg: "If you're so successful, how come Geffen has more money than you?" Kim Masters reported in *Vanity Fair.*

Consider the buttons pushed.

And Geffen's involvement would serve Spielberg in another im-portant way. For years, his closeness to Ross had served as an implied threat to Wasserman and Sheinberg: do the boy right or he'd be gone. In a similar way, Geffen's less-than-loving relationship with Spielberg's agent, Michael Ovitz, made a Geffen association appealing. Ovitz and Geffen would be a check on each other, keep them working for Spielberg rather than using him for their own, sometimes hard to discern, interests. He would have the toughest, shrewdest guys in the business taking care of him *and* keeping an eye on each other.

As for Geffen, Katzenberg's banishment from Disney was not just an opportunity to help a friend—to "give Jeffrey a job"—but to create his own platform, one that would keep him in the game.

Immediate acquiescence, however, was not Geffen's style. First there would be a performance.

"No, I don't want to do that," Geffen had said emphatically when Katzenberg clued him into the fact that he and Spielberg were about to come courting. "What, are you *crazy?*"

"Well, would you at least talk to us?" Katzenberg, ever persistent, prodded.

To which Geffen replied that he was not averse to talking, but: "I don't want to talk to you about *that.*"

Then: "I mean, I'll *talk* to you."

"Why don't you just meet us at Steven's house tomorrow?" Katzenberg suggested. "Come over at twelve o'clock, we'll schmooze, and maybe we can just pick your brain."

"OK," Geffen said. "But I'm not interested in this, Jeffrey."

Why would the newly minted billionaire want to give up afternoons by the Pacific for such aggravation? Geffen had more than lived up to the title King David, bestowed by his Ukrainian-born mother, Batya, a bossy, opinionated force of nature who transformed her skill at corset- and brassiere-making into a business that got her family off government assistance when her depressed, ineffectual husband could not. Her son, who had grown up sleeping on a couch, or tied to his mother with a rope while she slaved, made himself up using her example, supplemented by movie matinees, trips to see the Rockettes, and biographies of Louis B. Mayer. The latter he read in California, where he had followed his big brother, Mitchell, and enrolled at Santa Monica City College. (Though, if anyone inquired, he studied at UCLA.)

Despite his Machiavellian tendencies and ruthlessness, Geffen—

like his mother—also adheres to unflinching standards and his own brand of integrity. Not everyone understands his code of ethics, but he holds to it, punishing violators mercilessly. Geffen's evaluations of people, situations, and deals allow for no gray areas or in-betweens.

"Be careful. David is scary," one attorney advises, without unnecessary elaboration. Scary David, Mad David, and, most of all, Vengeful David stories are plentiful in Hollywood. Those who know Geffen personally do not bother to deny his ability to frighten. But they also add that much of the persona is just that—an act, a façade he uses to get exactly what he wants, fast. His friends claim that Geffen is simply a veteran Hollywood performer, playing the part of a mogul in a highly theatrical world. "People find him so intimidating in the mainstream," said Jeff Yarbrough, former editor in chief of the *Advocate* in Los Angeles. "If you ask about David, it's 'Oh, he's so mean, so nasty, so off-putting.' The truth is, he isn't any of that. That's more a character he plays."

By the time the new company was being discussed, Geffen had beaten cancer, come out as gay, seen friends such as Calvin Klein through financial disaster. He had created Asylum and Geffen Records—groundbreaking labels led, respectively, by iconic acts such as the Eagles and Guns N' Roses. His days were spent flipping through his investment portfolios, fielding interview requests. Everyone wanted the mogul of Malibu, who regularly dialed President Clinton and who flew the world in his Gulfstream IV, perpetually changing destinations as boredom set in. His Beverly Hills estate, the former home of Warner Bros. cofounder Jack Warner, which Geffen had paid $47.5 million for in 1990, was being exquisitely Geffenized with the help of designer Rose Tarlow. But he wanted to be more than a rich, respected fixture; he wasn't chemically suited to sitting on the sidelines. Geffen, his friends say, is determined to stay *relevant*. A new company could keep him in the picture.

And then there was Ovitz.

CAA, which Ovitz had cofounded in 1975 with a group of fellow William Morris dissidents (Michael Rosenfeld, Ron Meyer, Bill Haber, and Rowland Perkins), dominated the town with its superstar client list and "packaging of projects."

Initially, Haber had been the agency's go-to guy, but Ovitz had transformed himself from intense TV agent to intense film lord. His agency's culture bore his imprimatur, but its discipline, the clean professional feel that added reassurance in a business based on incalculables, was inspired by Lew Wasserman's MCA style. Ovitz's Armani-suited "foot soldiers" had drawn their tactics from the old king's army: they traveled together in entourages, dressed in similar shades to signal a united front in crowded rooms. Ovitz's minions delighted in coming across as menacing. They made no bones about the fact that their mission was to conquer and, if necessary, destroy. (If opposed, they would "blow your brains out," as Ovitz warned in a 1989 letter to screenwriter Joe Eszterhas, who had threatened to defect.)

Signing Spielberg, who had up to then operated agentless, had been one of the great coups of Michael Ovitz's expanding career. For Geffen, partnering with Spielberg in a new company would be a way to set his foot squarely in Ovitz's territory. In effect, he would be stealing Ovitz's star client from behind his back.

Ovitz was changing what it meant to be an agent. His reach was broadening into new territories, even beyond the MCA/Universal sale. He'd advised Coca-Cola on branding strategy, and there were further plans for expansion.

Geffen nursed a vivid spectrum of resentments against the CAA chieftain—from the superagent's supposed homophobia to a brouhaha over the first feature film that Geffen produced, 1982's *Personal Best*, which had cost Geffen millions. The latest outrage was Ovitz's moving in as broker on the MCA/Matsushita deal. Geffen wasn't interested in encountering another first-class manipulator operating behind the scenes.

Geffen had done self-help. He had fire-walked with Tony Robbins, read the *Book of Miracles* with Marianne Williamson. But antagonism remained the best restorative. Battling Ovitz kept him hungry. According to producer Howard Rosenman, Geffen fumed of Ovitz: "I'm gonna kill that motherfucker. It may take me years, but I'm going to destroy him. Watch me."

Screw the beach.

Geffen strode into the Hay-Adams at 6:30 A.M. after his nightlong captivity in the Clinton White House. He hadn't been impressed by the Lincoln Bedroom. Lincoln, in his opinion, should have slept at the Mayflower. But he was wide awake, ready to talk, ready to be Geffen.

It was decided that the three would each kick in $33 million to build a multimedia company. The rest—they were thinking billions—would come from investors. For Geffen and Spielberg the contribution was negligible, but not for Katzenberg. Eisner was still withholding the former studio chief's bonus (estimated at more than $120 million). Katzenberg would be forced to mortgage two of his homes to come up with the money.

The rest of the details would be figured out back in L.A.—quickly. It was time to put on a show.

5

THE ANNOUNCEMENT

E ARLY IN THE DAY on October 11, around the time Spielberg and Co. were paying their respects to Lew Wasserman, Alan Citron of the *Los Angeles Times* and his colleague Claudia Eller heard a rumor that there was news dropping on the Katzenberg front. Something was about to break. The confirmation came in the form of a release, faxed at 4 P.M., by Katzenberg's newly hired PR man, Harry Clein.

Prompted by the coy one-page release, which disclosed only that Katzenberg was holding a press conference the following morning, the phones began ringing all over, bringing excited inquiries from the *New York Times*, the *Wall Street Journal*, *Variety*, the *Hollywood Reporter*.

But the mystery was short-lived. Within a few phone calls, Citron and Eller had divined what Katzenberg was up to. Or, at least, who he was up to it with: Steven Spielberg and David Geffen. The mention of Spielberg's name upped the ante. And raised the question: *Why?*

The pressure was on the journalists to get the scoop.

"Everybody was calling," said Clein, who did his best to ignore everything.

Citron and Eller worked the phones nonstop for more details. By day's end they had their story.

"We didn't get anything from the DreamWorks partners," Citron said. "We got it from a lot of little people who had little bits of information."

Jeffrey Katzenberg's home in Beverly Hills, where he lived with his wife, Marilyn, and their twins, Laura and David, was like many in America's most expensive neighborhoods. There was the guesthouse, the swimming pool, the shrubbery carefully attended. But in keeping with his self-styled image of suburban Everyman who chooses Mustang over Lexus and dines at Hamburger Hamlet, Katzenberg's residence was not as eye-catching as the neighbors', with their tennis courts, White House–level security gates, and immigrant squadrons snipping back the bougainvillea. The place lay on the *south* side of Sunset Boulevard—alternately referred to, with slight shudders, as "the flats" or "the slums." This was not the hills, or Bel Air, where the fabulous reside in more untouchable splendor.

Unlike other Hollywood royalty, Katzenberg did not treat his home like a trophy or a personal showcase; it was not jam-packed with museum-quality art or high-tech gadgetry just in from Japan. This was Katzenberg's "business house." (The others, the ones to be mortgaged to pay his way into the new partnership, were a beach place designed by Charles Gwathmey, located near Geffen's, and a ski chalet in Deer Valley, Utah.) It was more about work than family or play. At least according to those who inevitably found themselves sitting around his kitchen at 7 A.M. on a Saturday or Sunday discussing release strategies or faulty story lines.

The décor was white on white, with hard, clean surfaces and no flourishes (aside from a few pieces of African art). The clue to character here was, in fact, characterlessness. No bold statements or rough edges provoked questions of taste. It was like many a Disney product—designed to be inoffensive, if not inviting, to any possible audience.

Visitors are hard-pressed to recall specific details, other than the cleanliness, which observers stress when describing the Katzenberg manse. One guest recalls tracking dirt in on the gray carpet and a maid materializing within seconds. Yet beneath the soft hum of the vacuum and the hissing of sprinklers, an impression was being communicated, reassuring observers that the man of this house was not likely to run up budgets or disappear on tequila-soaked weekends in Puerto Vallarta. The place said: *Conservative, Corporate, Disciplined, No Big Spender.* And, as Michael Ovitz was so fond of repeating, in Hollywood, "perception is everything."

It was here, on October 11, 1994, that Katzenberg found himself watching his fantasies become Hollywood history. What more could he, a man who seemed to crave public triumphs and revenge served boldface, have wished for than to be partnered with these giants? Michael Eisner would be suitably chastened by his former subordinate's spectacular comeback. But Katzenberg was entering terrain of rugged complexity where expectations were huge. Whatever his past experience, partnering with Geffen and Spielberg was bound to be fraught with complications. Katzenberg had already labored under the burden of one difficult man. How would he fare under two even more demanding and self-regarding figures? What about the independence he had hoped for in his new incarnation? Was he trading the possibility of true advancement for momentary one-upmanship?

That evening, there was enough ambition flowing through the Katzenbergs' uncluttered halls to compensate for the absence of Picassos. Spielberg and Geffen were gathered in the home's very white screening room along with Spielberg's lawyer, Bruce Ramer, for whom the mechanical shark in *Jaws* had been nicknamed. Harry Clein was in attendance, too. They were there to discuss the next morning's formal unveiling of their partnership, the still-nameless studio venture. But the mood in the room was not celebratory.

As Clein put it, "the money shot had been given away." The press had been tipped off. The bombshell had been dropped. They had lost the element of surprise, not to mention control, a commodity they always made sure they had.

"Are you sure people are going to come tomorrow?" asked Spielberg, giving voice to his old insecurities. "Why should they? It'll already be in the news."

No worries, Clein assured everyone. People would come. But a tinge of deflation lingered. After all, this *was* show business; the drama mattered.

Everyone was convinced the news had been leaked by Ovitz, whose reputation as a manipulator rivaled even Geffen's and who hadn't been included in any of the company's planning, despite his status as Spielberg's agent. Already, Geffen was making it clear what the new order was going to look like. Having been given no role, Ovitz presumably decided to play the spoiler, just as Geffen had, allegedly, in 1990, leaking the news of MCA's deal with Matsushita. It had been Ovitz's deal, his moment. Welcome to Hollywood.

Arriving twenty minutes after everyone else, Ovitz was not greeted with warmth. As the three partners pored over the press release that would be sent out the next day, officially announcing the new company, he had little to say.

"He was kind of the fifth wheel," said Clein. "Because he wasn't needed. Everything was done without him. So it was like, What's he bring? Why's he coming over? . . . My feeling was that he was there because he felt he couldn't not be there."

Ovitz, meanwhile, had his own secrets. Though no one knew it yet, he had been meeting with Michael Eisner about a job at Disney, the very job that Katzenberg had so hoped to obtain.

"The announcement" was held on the morning of Wednesday, October 12, at the Peninsula hotel in Beverly Hills, the regal emblem of the New Hollywood, a commanding, cream-colored *palais* near the I. M. Pei–designed CAA headquarters. The venue suggested the presence of royalty. "I felt," said Harry Clein, "like I was giving a wedding."

Spielberg, Katzenberg, and Geffen gathered in the green room behind the spacious Verandah Room, where the announcement would be made. Spielberg still hadn't shaken his doubts about the draw.

"Are you sure they'll show up? Look, it's all right here!" he said, waving the *Los Angeles Times*. A front-page story trumpeted the new alliance, quoting an unnamed source who didn't beat around the bush: "They will make history," declared this observer, "by starting another studio."

Geffen, nursing a ginger ale, was sick to his stomach. Not for years had he experienced this kind of crazy. "What a drama queen!" commented an observer, as reported by Kim Masters in *Vanity Fair*.

Katzenberg was rehearsing his lines, pacing back and forth as, outside, the ballroom filled. Beyond the usual throng of reporters, the trio's star power drew Hollywood big shots like International Creative Management president Jim Wiatt and United Talent Agency partner Jim Berkus. These players were not typically on view outside the gilded confines of their headquarters or the clubby exclusivity of the Grill, the power-lunch headquarters off Dayton Way in Beverly Hills. Standing among the ranks of scruffy journalists and cameramen, they looked, with their black Armani suits, perfect haircuts, and chunky Rolexes, like they had just drifted in from some VIP funeral. When Ovitz and his CAA partner Ron Meyer came into the room, Citron steered clear, not wanting to add credence to the rumor that Ovitz had fed reporters the news of the partnership.

At 9 A.M. Katzenberg, dressed in khakis and a blazer, a yellow polka-dot tie against a dark blue dress shirt, and oversized glasses, took his seat at the front of the room, flanked by Spielberg and Geffen, also in khakis.

The men's casual attire belied the anticipatory mood among those assembled as, blinking into the glare of spotlights and clicking cameras, Katzenberg spoke: "There's a pretty giant misunderstanding here," he began. "The reason that we wanted to have this press conference this morning is to announce that the next Dive! restaurant opening will be in Las Vegas on April 15."

A wave of laughter swept the room.

Katzenberg then introduced his partners. "I look at the three of us," he said rather emotionally, "and I figure this has gotta be the Dream Team. Certainly, it's my Dream Team."

Spielberg read a prepared statement: "Hollywood studios," he said, "were at their zenith when they were driven by point of view and personalities. Together with Jeffrey and David, I want to create a place driven by ideas and the people who have them. I regard Jeffrey and David as pioneers. I'd like to be one, too."

Geffen closed the show. "I've always been on my own," he began, "and this is a great opportunity for me to work with partners and start something new and get excited about working once again."

When a reporter asked how they would divide up duties, Geffen quipped, "I'm going to direct *Jurassic Park 2*." Spielberg responded by saying he'd be happy to let Geffen direct if in exchange he could become a billionaire.

Katzenberg, slipping into the sort of hyperbole that would define this day and so many after, announced: "There's an opportunity for us to have a revolution."

Exactly what *kind* of revolution was a matter of conjecture, however.

There was talk of being "different" and "artist-friendly," but few specifics were discussed. Katzenberg's career at Paramount and Disney had been, rather famously, fairly artist-*un*friendly. As for Spielberg, what he actually stood for, personally, beyond virtuoso filmmaking and commercial success, was hard to articulate. The new company was something of a blank slate, reflected in the fact that it didn't, as yet, even have a name.

• • •

Presentation wrapped, there were no champagne toasts. First order of business: the new company needed a home. A development known as Playa Vista (Beach View) was a possible studio site. The 1,087 acres of marshland, located just north of LAX, on L.A.'s west side, had been a headache for developer Robert F. Maguire since his company, Maguire Thomas Partners—responsible for the city's tallest skyscraper, the seventy-three-story Library Tower—took a controlling interest in it in 1989. The site was a hot zone for environmentalists who did not want to see one of the city's last wetlands turned into condos, and a California recession had made any kind of real-estate development a dicey proposition. Maguire was desperate for a star tenant to lure others to the site.

Playa Vista had a cinematic backstory, suitable for press mentions: in the 1940s, eccentric billionaire Howard Hughes had built his infamous two-hundred-ton Spruce Goose—a giant seaplane—in a hangar on the site, after which, he'd taxied it down to Long Beach Harbor and lifted the thing seventy feet in the air for a brief thirty seconds before it bellied back into the Pacific.

To help land a tenant, Maguire had hired ICM chairman Jeff Berg who, upon hearing of the new venture, immediately spread the word about the site. Spielberg excitedly imagined an actual, old-fashioned Mayer-meets-Goldwyn studio—and Playa Vista was conveniently located, close to his home in the Pacific Palisades. So, after announcing their plans for a new studio, the partners sped west toward what they hoped was the place where their destinies would unfold.

After the press conference came nonstop calls—Tom Hanks congratulated Spielberg, Robert Zemeckis phoned from New York, where he was working on the Oscar campaign for *Forrest Gump*. Yet one voice remained deafeningly, defiantly silent. Intending to fix this, Katzenberg dialed Joe Roth, his replacement at Disney. "You get that psycho to call me!" he bellowed, referring, of course, to his former boss. "This is about making things better. So when I stand in front of a hundred journalists, I can say, 'The first call I got was from Michael Eisner.' Which is what I'll do. I'll completely exaggerate what he said."

Later Katzenberg could not remember if Eisner ever managed to pick up the phone. But even absent the man whom Katzenberg, after everything, seemed to envision as some sort of proud father, the lines were humming.

For Clein, the fun was just beginning. "Every weekend I was getting calls," the publicist said. "Something was always breaking over the weekend, and it was usually rumors . . . For months, I was just putting out fires."

The *New York Times,* suddenly no gray lady, kicked up its heels and declared the new union "the biggest merger of talent since Charlie Chaplin, Mary Pickford, Douglas Fairbanks and D. W. Griffith founded the United Artists movie empire in 1919." The *Times* wasn't the only one to weigh in on the news. "Oscar Winners Merging Talents," swooned the *Chicago Sun-Times.* "Merger of the Titans" chimed the *Dallas Morning News.* "Young Hollywood Moguls Take On Industry Giants" (the *Guardian*). And the inevitable, perhaps: "Three Men and Their Baby" (the *Orange County Register*). Over the next ten days, *Variety* and the *Hollywood Reporter* would run twenty stories combined about the new endeavor. A photo shoot was lined up with Annie Leibovitz for *Vanity Fair. Time* would do a cover story.

"Because of the incredible things these guys had achieved, the press got swept up," Citron said. "They were such rock stars. It was like a supergroup had been formed."

With this, Citron says, went the assumption that "supergroups only make good music." Not many people, he recalls, were asking: *How is this going to work business-wise? Do the economics make sense?* Indeed, DreamWorks' unannounced ally that morning was the media. The press was continually fascinated by the personalities firing up the new studio. Hollywood, a town where a lack of charisma can be fatal, was increasingly turning into the territory of anything-but-polyester personalities.

The sense was that the new partnership was a sure bet. As Barry Diller would tell *Vanity Fair:* "To put it in the L.A. context—typhoons, floods, fires, pestilence—these guys are so good, plague couldn't stop them. Investing in them is gold."

DreamWorks was, from day one, a grand stage where the big acts were guaranteed to scheme and scream. The only other company that even came close to topping its cult of personality was Miramax, the scrappy indie turned heavyweight indie whose flair for hip, sexy, often truly innovative fare almost certainly helped inspire Katzenberg, Spielberg, and Geffen's vision of what their studio might become. Miramax was enmeshed in the DNA of studio cofounder Harvey

Weinstein, a sweaty, expletive-slinging tough guy. His fantasies—for himself, perhaps, as much as for his company—were grandiose, never sleep-inducing. Weinstein drew reporters—alternately charming and manipulating them—like an open bar. More polished and pedigreed than Harvey, perhaps, but like him, the newly anointed triumvirate knew how to put on a show.

And isn't that what Hollywood is all about?

6

E.T., PHONE HOME

IF A MOVIE IS EVER MADE about DreamWorks, Walter Parkes, whom one associate describes as "a Shakespearean actor holding forth on the Globe stage," can play himself. At the time of the company's formation, some might have said he already was.

Parkes has the chiseled good looks of a leading man, a Yale diploma, and the kind of overpowering self-confidence that is indigenous to Hollywood. Winding down after a pitch, he is inclined to utter, "I just gave myself goose bumps!" before running his fingers through his million-dollar hair. Director Barry Sonnenfeld has apparently joked that "Walter gets everything because of his hair."

But on that October morning after the press conference at the Peninsula, even the locks of Samson could not have been of help to Parkes. Cohead, along with his wife — the equally suitable-for-casting Laurie MacDonald — of Spielberg's production company, it was up to Parkes to face the folks at Amblin, who were wondering what the news about Spielberg's new endeavor would mean for them.

Parkes stood before his staff in the same screening room where an edgy comedienne named Whoopi Goldberg had once convinced Spielberg that she was perfect for the role of Miss Celie in *The Color Purple.* As the thoughts of those gathered alternated between past and future, Parkes offered no Shakespearean utterances to camouflage the fact that the golden child had bolted.

Bruce Cohen, who had started out as Spielberg's director trainee on *The Color Purple,* was, at this time, executive-producing *To Wong Foo Thanks for Everything, Julie Newmar,* in Nebraska. Feeling nostalgic, he couldn't help but remember the March morning after that year's Oscars, when Spielberg had his retribution for prior Academy snubs by winning not one but ten shiny golden gentlemen, for *Jurassic Park* and

Schindler's List (the latter snagged Best Picture and Best Director). The moment had been exquisite for Spielberg. For nearly two decades, the Academy of Motion Picture Arts and Sciences had thrown shade on the director, evidence of a troubling hostility that vexed him deeply.

Spielberg's career had always seemed a case of too much, too soon. After Sid Sheinberg got hold of his short film *Amblin'*, released in 1968, a seven-year contract had materialized. But, said Allen Daviau, cinematographer on *Amblin'*, "there were always people calling for his blood." Daviau recalls the reaction in L.A. in 1971, when word filtered back over the Atlantic that Spielberg's first feature-length film, *Duel*, was making waves in European theaters: "Ah, well," cynics kvetched. "Give it another week."

The Oscar slights had started in 1976, when Spielberg failed to secure a Best Director nomination for *Jaws*. The omission seemed personal, given the acclaim for the film from critics and audiences, and the fact that *Jaws* was up for Best Picture—a major coup for a blatantly commercial film. It hauled in $129 million, the first time in history that a film crossed the $100 million mark.

So certain had Spielberg been of Best Picture *and* Best Director nominations that he'd invited a camera crew to watch him react as nominees were announced. When it was revealed that his name was absent from the list of directors—which included Milos Forman (*One Flew Over the Cuckoo's Nest*), Sidney Lumet (*Dog Day Afternoon*), Robert Altman (*Nashville*), and Federico Fellini (*Amarcord*)—the cameras captured the director, face in his hands. "I can't believe it!" he exclaimed. "They went for Fellini instead of me!"

It was the beginning of a long cold spell. *E.T.*, *The Color Purple*, and *Empire of the Sun* all failed to win Best Picture Oscars. In 1986, when *The Color Purple* was completely *shut out* of the Academy Awards—winning not a single statuette, despite eleven nominations—Spielberg, who had not been nominated for Best Director, was devastated.

Given this history, in March of 1994, when the Academy finally came around to honoring Spielberg, it was especially delicious. So reverentially did he treat the awards that, on the morning after the show, he asked his staff to gather in the Amblin courtyard, where all the trophies were displayed. "It was this beautiful day, and the sun was beating off [the Oscars]," said Cohen. "We were all there together, and Steven thanked us for being part of the family and for what we had all created together. It was amazing, to the point where you kind of wondered if this was going to end. It was like, This must be the end, because it doesn't get any better than this."

Parkes wasn't being coy in his brief message to Amblin's personnel—some of whom were sobbing—on that dark morning. He simply had little to add to what had been communicated. When the inevitable questions were asked about the future of the company, he honestly said he didn't know. He and MacDonald had themselves only just heard what was up. The night before, they had returned home to a message from Steven and headed to his place. After breaking the news, Spielberg had said that he wanted them to be a part of the proposed venture; they were his most trusted lieutenants and good friends, with whom he socialized in the company of stars such as Tom Hanks and Rita Wilson, Martin and Nancy Short.

Spielberg's intentions were a matter of speculation to the staff at Amblin. There was Geffen; that they knew. There was Katzenberg. Whatever was coming would not be a stress-free affair; there would be politics and control battles, given the competing egos involved. Spielberg's domain had been a kind of haven, where questions of rulership were never an issue: no Amblinite ever had to wonder whose preferences mattered most. Was this new situation—a big-business-to-be built for such an outsize cast—really the best next act for their boss? Did he know what he was getting into? Jealousy wasn't the only emotion Spielberg generated in those close to him. He also aroused feelings of protectiveness. The director's Hollywood life had been filled with guardians and parent surrogates. Were Katzenberg and Geffen up to the challenge?

And what about Spielberg himself? Hollywood fame may be the best way to avoid growing up. Troubling realities and mere practicalities are carefully filtered and subdued. But if Spielberg was to develop as a partner, a would-be Mayer or Goldwyn, if he was to grow into a Wasserman-like role, change was required.

Could Jeffrey, who was more likely than the peripatetic Geffen to be left with working out day-to-day dynamics at the new company, help smooth Spielberg's transition to chief executive? Was he up to the sort of subtleties required? As for Geffen, would he really put in the time?

Worrisome to many observers was the fact that Spielberg's stated intention was to keep working for other studios. It was as if he wanted to simultaneously step forward into larger challenges (of the sort that did not necessarily play to his strengths) while remaining safely rooted in his empire. Something, it seemed, had to give, even for Steven Spielberg.

Steven Spielberg is a complicated man wrapped in a patina of extreme likability. Born in Cincinnati in 1946 — not 1947, as he has sometimes said — to a family he watched split apart, he is the son of Leah, a former concert pianist, and Arnold, a workaholic engineer. The senior Spielberg's disappearance from his son's existence began before the latter's career accelerated. ("I didn't care for *Indiana Jones* and I hated *1941*," the elder Spielberg told the *Wall Street Journal*. "When I told Steven, he said, 'Don't talk to me, Dad.'")

Spielberg's maternal grandparents were Orthodox, but his family was, he said, "storefront Jews" who did not attend temple. The director has spoken of feeling like an "alien" while growing up, always haunted by his parents' eventual breakup, which occurred when he was a teenager. He was especially saddened when the situation repeated itself with his 1989 divorce from Amy Irving, as the couple's adored son, Max, was only four years old.

The director lists his parents' divorce and his own from Irving as the most difficult times of his life. Yet other fissures also stung. Before Parkes and MacDonald arrived, Amblin was run, for nearly a decade, by another husband-and-wife team, Kathleen Kennedy and Frank Marshall, who tended to Steven's day-to-day affairs and were referred to, at Amblin, as the "parents." (Having real-life partners running things added to the family quality that Spielberg so craved in his work life.) Kennedy, in particular, who had started out as Spielberg's assistant, understood that working for Spielberg wasn't just about being able to execute; it was about cushioning him from harsher truths, which some might term "reality." Her style, when it came to getting Spielberg's wishes across to others, was forceful diplomacy. Athletic and scrubbed, she did not throw tantrums or phones — her steely forthrightness was enough. "Incredibly efficient," one source calls her, "one of those steam shovels who just rolls over people." (Frank Marshall, the good cop, is described as "a pussy cat.")

Something else Spielberg appreciated: there were no limits to what Kennedy would do. When a severe hurricane struck Kauai, where *Jurassic Park* was filming, wiping out all communication and leaving the filmmakers stranded in the storm, Kennedy ran to the local airport (streets were blocked by fallen trees) and talked a pilot into flying her to Honolulu, where she arranged for the cast and crew to be flown to safety.

In 1991 Kennedy and Marshall decided to leave Amblin to become independent producers. Although Marshall had directed *Arachnophobia* at Amblin, his ambitions as a filmmaker never seemed to be taken altogether seriously by Spielberg, who, one source said, was once surprised to walk into Marshall's office and notice that he wasn't the only director on site who was being sent scripts.

Marshall left first and set up a production company at Paramount, with the idea that Kennedy would follow. But, according to an Amblin source, Spielberg was so upset over the prospect of her leaving — considering it a kind of desertion — that in retaliation he forced her to delay her departure, causing tension between them. When Kennedy finally did leave, in 1993, the rupture was described within Amblin as "the divorce." Marshall himself denied any friction. "Kathy always wanted to stay as long as she had to, until the transition after *Jurassic Park*. It was all very amicable, and all part of the plan," he said.

The separation would not, in any case, be final, but those who witnessed it may have questioned Spielberg's ability to approach his closest professional relationships dispassionately.

Over the years, sequestered at Amblin, Spielberg had grown accustomed to being the focus of his universe. He could seem strangely wary of the world as most mortals experience it, and his passion for secrecy sometimes suggests near-paranoia. Amblin, with its Southwestern style, has jokingly been dubbed Taco Bell, but to others it was more like the Alamo, a fortress preparing for a siege.

When Michael Kahn, Spielberg's longtime editor, viewed footage in the screening room, a black cloth was draped over the projection-booth window to hide the screen. In Spielberg's office, hanging above his desk, a Plexiglas half-moon kept sound from reverberating so that his phone conversations remained ultraconfidential. When an assistant once asked what the funny thing over Spielberg's desk was, a security guard referred to it as a "cone of silence." Another was told that it "channeled sound waves."

One Amblinite described the company's script department as a "vault." Every document that left the office—scripts, development reports, even memos—was coded, so that should it somehow get into the wrong hands (i.e., someone outside the company), the person responsible for the breach could be identified. When Spielberg wasn't at Amblin, live-cam images were streamed to his home. There were also measures to protect against earthquakes or attacks, as Spielberg believed in being prepared. A never-used motorcycle remained permanently parked at his office so that, in the event of the unthinkable, he had a getaway. Employees were given survival kits including jump suits, gas masks, and other essential emergency gear.

On that fateful morning, Walter Parkes actually had little to say to the Amblin tribe, because so little about the new company had been discussed or decided. Indeed, less than a month had passed since the inspiration had hit. Not many more than a half-dozen meetings between the three players had preceded the press conference.

Which provoked the question: *Why?* Why announce so soon, so much, so *big?*

Lost in the swirl of hype were some of the partners' less auspicious endeavors: Despite his mastery of the music business, Geffen's foray into the corporate branches of moviemaking had been a debacle. In 1975 Steve Ross chose his volatile protégé to cochair the live-action division of Warner Bros. with Ted Ashley. But while Geffen's personality was refreshingly devoid of bullshit, his brashness offended colleagues and filmmakers alike. Clint Eastwood was famously incensed when he was told to cut twenty minutes from *The Outlaw Josey Wales.* Eleven months after his arrival, after a falling-out with Ashley, Geffen was gone. Since then his track record as a producer had been mixed. While he discovered a kid named Tom Cruise and cast him in *Risky Business* and, later, *Interview with the Vampire,* there were also more forgettable pictures, like *M. Butterfly* and *The Last Boy Scout.*

Katzenberg's history was just as checkered when it came to the live-action realm. After his initial success at Disney, Katzenberg's reputation was crippled by two staggering disasters: *Dick Tracy* with Warren Beatty and *Billy Bathgate* with Dustin Hoffman.

Despite the aura, Geffen and Katzenberg were not by any means infallible. No one in Hollywood ever is, whatever their publicists say. But in this case, the studio's creative promise rested with Spielberg.

Yet, the director's motives for becoming involved were the least easy to discern. Those inclined to monitor his doings were bewildered by his desire to give up his unparalleled power and autonomy at Universal and enlist with partners, particularly these intense characters, in what was essentially a start-up business.

"I was surprised, quite frankly, because he didn't need that," said Richard D. Zanuck, who produced Spielberg's big-screen debut, *The Sugarland Express,* as well as *Jaws.* "Steven can do practically anything he wants to . . . and nobody's going to say no to him. I was surprised that he would, coming from that position of strength, want to deal with all of the ancillary attachments and problems and things that go with running an operation."

Producer Mark Johnson, who in the mid-1980s had collaborated with Spielberg on *Young Sherlock Holmes,* had a similar reaction. "I thought it was surprising on Steven's side," he said, "because I thought, *Why* does he want to do this? He's Steven Spielberg. He can do anything he wants. He has a great situation at Amblin, he can make any movie he wants as a producer, as a director. Why does he want to now bring on the whole burden of having to be a company and having profit-and-loss statements and having to worry about so many people? What does it give him that he doesn't already have? I didn't ask him that, because it was an obvious question and he had obviously answered it enough to himself, but I never quite understood it. And I think a lot of people felt the same way. It was like, we understand kind of what David Geffen wants and we understand what Jeffrey wants, but why does Steven want to do this?"

Making that strained morning all the more worrisome for Parkes and MacDonald was their utter lack of interest in being executives at a full-fledged studio. They considered themselves, foremost, filmmakers, artists, creators. Before Amblin, Parkes—an Oscar nominee for writing *WarGames*—had been a screenwriter who went on to produce films—including *Awakenings* with Robin Williams and *True Believer* with James Woods. MacDonald, a former Columbia Pictures executive, eventually became his producing partner. At modest-sized Amblin, they had been able to devote themselves, for the most part, to the creative and producing tasks they preferred, despite their management obligations. At a larger venture, this would be much less possible to pull off.

If Parkes and MacDonald felt uneasy, Amblin employees were even more jittery. Their comfy "campus" on the Universal lot was a cross between Xanadu and Camelot, where all the offices had fireplaces and where there was a game room packed with video games, a masseuse named Julie, and a Jacuzzi. The chef was more than willing to produce a club sandwich or a plate of spaghetti Bolognese to placate any afternoon munchies.

Meetings, often impromptu, took place on couches and in stairwells (this was partly out of necessity; it was hard to get Spielberg to sit still for very long). Pets—including Spielberg's own mutt, Potter—were welcome and even catered to. Mike, who ran the mailroom, doubled as a dog walker. At year's end came a lavish holiday party, for which fake snow was imported. Staffers received bonuses and generous perks from Spielberg: Cartier-Bresson photographs, trips to Aspen, Armani suits, antique watches. Then, as now, Spielberg has an assistant whose sole job is to handle his prodigious gift giving (and receiving).

Amblin was a place no one ever wanted to leave; it kept the rest of Hollywood, with its crass, corporate rituals, at a safe distance. So rigorous in its isolation, it was often referred to as "the Vatican." But now, it seemed, Rome was burning, Geffen was fiddling, and Katzenberg was set to corporatize the place. "It was like, wow. This is real. Amblin is changing," recalled Peter Hirschmann, a production assistant. "Amblin was this Utopia, this perfect place. I thought I was going to spend my whole life there. To have that world turned upside down . . . It was definitely a shock to the system."

Sensing something potentially imperfect, Marvin Levy, Spielberg's longtime publicist, dispersed an internal memo that afternoon. "It was on Amblin letterhead, and it was about how the press conference went," said Hirschmann. "It ended with something like, 'We should all be proud of this place called Amblin.' It was a combination of reassurance at an uncertain time, but it was also supportive of the future."

But Amblin was no longer the future.

7

ANIMATED CHARACTERS

KATZENBERG'S NEW OFFICE at DreamWorks SKG—as the company was finally christened in January of 1995, three months after the initial press conference at the Peninsula (SKG stands for the principals' surnames)—was at Amblin, Dream-Works' temporary base of operations. Geffen's domain was on one side (though he still spent considerable time in his Beverly Hills office), and that of Helene Hahn (one of the first of many Disney arrivals—after an acrimonious parting with Michael Eisner) on the other. In keeping with the balance of power among the partners—one of whom was a little more equal than the others—Spielberg's most spacious lair was upstairs, guarded by a squadron of assistants and littered with iconic pieces of Spielbergalia, including the whip from *Indiana Jones,* the typewriter from *Schindler's List,* and a fireplace mantel loaded up with award hardware.

Katzenberg himself had no time for toys. He was in the process of building his identity anew, slamming the door on the lions and the mermaids. Rather than surrounding himself with memorabilia, Katzenberg hung up World War II propaganda posters espousing the virtues of hard work.

When he wasn't darting off to meetings or multiple meals with potential recruits, he could usually be found in the office of Penney Finkelman Cox and Sandra Rabins, who'd been charged, along with Amblinite Bonne Radford, with building the new animation studio. "Jeffrey kind of moved in," said Rabins, who'd passed on her business-operations duties to former Paramount chief financial officer Ron Nelson when he joined DreamWorks. "The joke was that we could never get any work done because he was always there charging around."

Katzenberg would show up with his lists of things to do and people to call. He'd sit on the sofa and down his Diet Cokes as his longtime assistant, Cynthia Park, placed calls. "He was relentless in his energy for calling people," said Finkelman Cox, a soft-spoken, girlish brunette. "He'd call anyone he knew, he sort of knew, he thought he knew, and pitch them his vision of the world over the phone."

Already, there were believers. The television studio Capital Cities/ ABC was ponying up $100 million in development funds to partner with DreamWorks on television shows—and, in an unprecedented move, ABC was giving SKG a cut of advertising revenues. Prestigious talent was also lining up to do business with the Dream Team. *Family Ties* creator Gary David Goldberg—a pal of Spielberg and Katzenberg—had signed an $11 million, four-year production deal to generate shows for the new studio. His cushy package was an advertisement for DreamWorks' largesse toward artists (a distinct break with Disney's penny-pinching and a signal of Katzenberg's metamorphosis). But it was also testimony to the drawing power of DreamWorks' best marketing tool: Fox Television had actually offered Goldberg a similar deal worth more money, but Fox didn't have Spielberg.

Although Katzenberg's experience in the TV business was limited —at Disney he had overseen TV, but the day-to-day running of the division was left to Disney TV chairman Rich Frank—it became yet another DreamWorks artery that fell under his purview, and yet another unit that he set out to build from scratch. Rather than hire a seasoned executive, Katzenberg would run the division himself. The sense was that his work ethic, plus Spielberg's creative aura (if not his actual labor), would be enough. It didn't seem to matter that, by Spielberg's own admission, his track record in TV was "lousy." Aside from *ER*, which was going through the ratings roof, Spielberg's forays into television had mostly missed the mark in the form of shows such as *Amazing Stories*, *Earth 2*, and *seaQuest DSV*, an underwater thriller series that critics dubbed "Das Bomb."

It was a week after the ABC deal was announced that the company finally unveiled its name. Spielberg, musing over what to call it with Walter Parkes, had taken a piece of Amblin letterhead and written down "The Teamworks Company." He'd then passed the paper to Parkes, who shook his head. "The word 'dream' should be in it," Parkes said, and wrote down "Dreamland." Spielberg then had his *aha!* He snatched the paper back and wrote: *Dreamworks.*

But in keeping with the partners' preferred backroom style, most details surrounding the new company remained locked up tight behind Amblin's high-security gates. Information, it was clear, was on a need-to-know basis, and for the most part, the principals didn't want anyone, especially the media, to know anything at all—at least not until it was time for another carefully orchestrated press conference. When, in late January, *Variety* printed the company's business plan—a document whose pages had been individually coded, so that in the event of a leak, the culprit could be identified—"there was hell to pay," said a source.

The brief envisioned DreamWorks as a vast multimedia empire involved in not just live-action and animated movies, television, music, and interactive games, but TV animation, publishing, theme parks, live entertainment and theater, and merchandising.

As for actual product—what everyone was salivating for—there were few tangibles. Movies wouldn't be ready for some time. The first live-action films—the output would start with three and, by 1999, expand to nine a year—weren't expected for another year. An animated feature wouldn't arrive until 1998. This meant that profits would be years away, too, both for the partners and the employees, who, however, would be given stock in DreamWorks, which, over time, Katzenberg promised, would grow into a sizable reward. DreamWorks' motto was, effectively: "Help us grow, and so will you."

The plan was most definitely to grow, and grow big, with animation planned as DreamWorks' cash cow. According to the business plan, animation would eventually account for over 43 percent of DreamWorks' earnings. In eight years, this would mean $355 million in pretax income, compared to the $230 million that was predicted to come from live-action films; TV and music were expected to generate $65 million and $95 million, respectively. With characteristic swagger, Katzenberg told potential investors that DreamWorks' animated movies would do at least 80 percent of *Lion King* business. Considering that *The Lion King*, whose revenues by now had neared the $2 billion mark, was more cultural phenomenon than mere hit movie, it was one of Katzenberg's more presumptuous claims. And in making it, Katzenberg was again taking the lion's share of credit for the film's success. He had confidence in his ability to replicate that success, or at least come close. At a collective-bargaining meeting with the Animation Guild, he told one guild member matter-of-factly: "I'm the only one in this business who understands feature animation."

When Eisner and Katzenberg joined Disney in the early 1980s, animation had not ranked high in their plan to reinvigorate the company's motion picture division. It was actually Roy E. Disney, ultimately one of Katzenberg's major detractors, who first convinced Eisner and Katzenberg to take a harder look at the department that had given birth to Mickey Mouse in 1928. "That's your problem now," Eisner had uttered as he pointed Katzenberg in the direction of the so-called ink-and-paint building, which at the time housed a clubby, conservative bunch made up largely of evangelicals and Reagan right-wingers.

Katzenberg swept out the antiques and picked up the pace, ordering that *The Black Cauldron,* floundering for over a decade, be edited into submission posthaste. Such tactics might be standard in live action but unheard of with animated films, whose every cel is painstakingly rendered, each requiring days', even weeks', worth of work. The Disney animators—aghast—knew that nothing would ever be the same again. Animation producer Don Hahn described Katzenberg's arrival as "World War III at the studio."

Cauldron elucidated a significant difference between live action and animation: the potential for a studio executive to exert absolute control. With live action, executives are involved in development—polishing scripts, hiring directors and casts. Producers and directors take over when shooting begins (though no project is immune from studio executives' notes, and, in some cases, less subtle interference). Animated films, on the other hand, never leave the building, so to speak; an executive can oversee every single frame of the movie. Katzenberg saw his chance.

He became increasingly involved in the making of each of Disney's animated films. His participation escalated over the next decade as he transferred the live-action model of filmmaking to animation, beginning the process of creation with scripts (rather than drawings and storyboards), by hiring live-action screenwriters to provide them. Katzenberg also became convinced—by way of Geffen, actually, a Broadway aficionado—that the future of animated movies was in musicals, and he set about recruiting a slew of production executives from the theater world. Marking the beginning of a rich and fruitful relationship, Katzenberg hired Geffen's friends, lyricist Howard Ashman and composer Alan Menken, to write music for *The Little Mermaid.* For the first time in Disney's history, the company was employing animation executives with zero history in the medium.

Katzenberg's formula also included signing major actors to voice characters in animated films. Robin Williams played the genie in *Aladdin.* Angela Lansbury and Jerry Orbach had parts in *Beauty and the Beast. The Lion King* was awash in A-listers: Matthew Broderick, James Earl Jones, Jeremy Irons, Nathan Lane, Whoopi Goldberg, and Cheech Marin. Katzenberg made deals in which actors were paid nominal fees to lend their voices—work that typically took no more than a few days in the recording studio.

But if Katzenberg won over stars, he had less luck charming animators. "Some people liked him and some thought he should stay the hell out," said one artist. On more than one occasion, veteran animator Glen Keane had said to Katzenberg: "It's a good thing you can't draw—then there would really be no living with you!"

After his first meeting with a crew of artists from the independent animation studio Pixar—which had a $26 million deal to produce three computer-animated films for Disney—to discuss *Toy Story* (the first of those films), Katzenberg said: "Everybody thinks I'm a tyrant. I *am* a tyrant. But I'm usually right. I will give you a chance, if you think I'm wrong, to change the direction, but *you'd* better be right." The Disney animators confirmed Katzenberg's claim. "All of the people backed up what Jeffrey had said, that you better believe he's a tyrant, there's no question about it, but his instincts are usually right on," recalled Pixar's Alvy Ray Smith. "They had seen instances of somebody sticking to their guns and changing the direction and it worked—but if it *didn't* work, their heads would roll."

The initial perception at Disney had been that Katzenberg had latched on to animation because it was a place to make his mark, and the artists resented this. Yet as the hits started rolling in, the Disney chairman began to earn credibility in the studio. During a storyboard meeting with a group of animators and executives working on *The Little Mermaid,* no one could believe it when Katzenberg got up and, assuming the role of the mermaid Ariel, began prancing around the room in order to convey the tone that he was looking for.

"Jeffrey *became the mermaid*—unashamed and totally submerged in it. He made us totally believe," said Marty Katz, head of physical production at Disney. "It was the first time I ever saw him let go of his persona and become an actor and do something this vulnerable. He was great. From then on, the animators gained more confidence in his ability to understand their process."

But though he was able to work with the artists, there was no mistaking Katzenberg for anything other than the demanding executive whose perfectionism was conveyed in his lintless suits and starched shirts. On the occasions he wore jeans, they were ironed. When he instituted attendance-required meetings on weekend mornings (the origin of his famous edict, "If you're not going to show up on Saturday morning, then don't bother showing up on Sunday"), the animators were incredulous. Disney had become Mauschwitz.

Max Howard, a theater manager turned animation supervisor on *Who Framed Roger Rabbit,* said of his twelve-year stint at Disney (he left in 1995): "It was unbelievably hard to work there. It was amazingly difficult. There were constant changes and always deadlines. It was always: 'Draw faster! Do it quicker!' . . . We were growing the company 20 percent every year. There was constant turmoil and change and growth."

Those who have worked with Katzenberg cite his proven instincts for sensing trouble spots. "Jeffrey is a Hollywood hotshot, but yet there's something about those Hollywood guys, they have a knack for knowing what's working and what's not working," said animator Floyd Norman, a longtime Disney artist. "When you'd pitch to Jeffrey, he'd say, 'Nah, it's not there yet, it's not moving me, it's not happening. Go back and do it again.' You'd show him again, he'd say, 'Well, I hear the lyrics but I don't hear the music.' That means he's not happy; it's still not working. You'd do that until Jeffrey would say, 'Now you've got it.' You need a guy with that kind of movie savvy, a Hollywood gut feeling that the old moguls had."

Yet Katzenberg's input worked best in limited doses, according to several people who have worked with him over the years. Things tended to lose their vision and creative purity when he was omnipresent. "If Jeffrey gets too close, it suffocates the project," Howard said.

"He takes over everything and everybody. He's in editorial, he's here, he's there, he's got an opinion . . ." Therefore, "One of the rules with Jeffrey is that you don't do all the notes."

At DreamWorks, animation was not just Katzenberg's way to make his mark, it was his tool for wielding vengeance against Eisner. Taking down Disney's core animation business (and moneymaker, thanks in large part to Katzenberg) would hit Eisner where it hurt the most. That Katzenberg was using his new company as a revenge vehicle was clear to everyone. "DreamWorks, I mean they are driven," Rupert Murdoch, the chairman and CEO of News Corp., has said. "I mean, they are about the destruction of Disney." And Katzenberg's battle with his former mentor was fast becoming an all-out war, one in which Eisner was not about to roll over. When Geffen had approached Eisner about Katzenberg's unpaid bonus, he had been flatly rebuffed. "He's not entitled to anything," Eisner said when Geffen first suggested a settlement of $60 million.

"This is going to get settled," Geffen warned. "And it won't be for $60 million. Each time, the price is going to go up."

Since then, however, Katzenberg had come up with evidence that he was, indeed, entitled—to tens of millions of dollars: a smoking-gun memo written by Frank Wells that spelled out what was contractually owed him. The scent of litigation was heavy in the air. But before a court date was set, Katzenberg set out to deplete Disney's talent pool. He flattered Disney animators shamelessly and offered money—mid-six-figure salaries, in line with what only Disney's top animators received. Bonuses, in some cases, neared the million-dollar mark. DreamWorks dangled long-term contracts—as opposed to the usual per-picture contracts—and promises of profit sharing.

"He was negotiating to get people from Disney, from a secure, stable thing, so he had to make it worthwhile to take that risk," said Ken Harsha, an animator who came over to DreamWorks from Disney. "Jeffrey did very good to make it as enticing as possible."

"He was out to get the Disney staff," said another one of Katzenberg's recruits. "He had a whole list. John Musker [a Disney animation director] did a cartoon of Katzenberg running down his phone list, phoning all the animators from Disney, reading off the same thing, but putting a different name in place for each call."

Katzenberg left no detail to chance. Prospective hires also met with DreamWorks' star marketing tool: Spielberg. Although he would not play a significant role in animation, the message was clear: at Dream-Works, it was artists who were running the show.

"It was part of the sell," said animator Tom Sito. "He would put you in a room alone with Spielberg. He would say, 'Oh, Steven's here! Wanna talk to Steven?' You'd be like, 'No, really, I gotta get going.' And he would say, 'No, you wanna talk to Steven!'

"'But I've got to get back to . . .'

"'*No!* You *want* to talk to Steven!'"

When DreamWorks' animation division officially opened for business on February 5, 1995, with a staff of ten, four of the company's five artists were Disney alums—that number eventually grew to over two dozen. The original quartet consisted of artists Kathy Altieri, Brenda Chapman, Richard Chavez, and Lorna Cook. Katzenberg had also snagged *Lion King* composer Hans Zimmer, making him the head of DreamWorks' music department.

Disney, for its part, was not dealing well with the exodus. When one artist gave his notice, animation head Peter Schneider exploded: "You're totally without honor!" He took the resignations as a betrayal and stopped speaking to members of the DreamWorks camp. "Peter was pretty angry," said one source. Although Katzenberg's feud was with Eisner, "it was Peter's people who Jeffrey was picking off. It was Peter who took it very personally."

Katzenberg also capitalized on Schneider's missteps. According to Penney Finkelman Cox, when Schneider was quoted in a newspaper article that could be read to imply that Disney animators were more or less interchangeable, Katzenberg made copies and sent it to dozens of animators at Disney. Artists would be *artists* at DreamWorks, he promised, not cogs in a production wheel.

Attempting to stanch the flood, Eisner—who rarely dealt with animators—began calling, saying how much their work meant to Disney. When one animator asked Eisner what drawings in particular he admired, Eisner drew a blank. The animator soon hightailed it to DreamWorks.

Artists were not the only targets of Katzenberg's talent-seeking missile. Throughout the spring and summer of 1995, key members of Team Disney were making their way to DreamWorks, including general counsel Kathy Kendrick; TV animation executives Gary Krisel and Bruce Cranston; marketer Peter Adee; and, at the end of the year, Terry Press, so crucial to Katzenberg's media relations. Press and Katzenberg were practically family. Press's father had passed away when she was young, and when she married Andy Marx (grandson of Groucho), Katzenberg gave her away at a wedding held at his home. The dynamic between the two was described by one colleague as "special—hardcore. They would finish each other's sentences."

Besides being an innovative marketer and genuine movie freak (she had studied film history at UCLA), Press, who had gotten to know Katzenberg on *Dick Tracy*, was able to be candid and tough with Katzenberg in a way that others—particularly other women—were not. "Terry is on the wavelength of certain powerful men, and is unafraid to speak the truth to them in a way they're not accustomed to hearing," said Bill Higgins, of *Variety*, who was close to Press in her Disney days. "It's like a therapist. She says things in a way that makes them want to hear more."

Two people Katzenberg was unable to lure were Dick Cook, Disney's head of marketing and distribution, and Rich Frank, who ran Disney's television division and who was responsible for the immensely successful show *Home Improvement*. Over the summer of 1995, Frank stepped down from Disney, reminding Eisner that his contract stipulated his leaving with his stock options and retirement benefits intact. Eisner threatened to sue. Only when reassured that Frank wasn't heading to DreamWorks did Eisner back down and fork over Frank's $30 million in stock options. The agreement did not extend to other members of the Frank family, however, and Katzenberg hired Frank's son, Darryl, a young executive at CBS, to run DreamWorks' TV division with Dan McDermott, formerly of Fox.

"DreamWorks was building its ranks, and it was a big talent drain out of Disney in almost every department," said one former Disney executive. "Michael and [Disney president] Joe [Roth] were feeling like, as contracts expired, off people went to DreamWorks. It was hard to know in their ranks whom to trust. Information was flowing faster than they wanted it to. They felt they were training everyone to go over and run that company."

• • •

Katzenberg lured people with enthusiasm and promises—Dream-
Works was the promised land—but little in the way of concrete details or job descriptions. The lack of titles at DreamWorks added to
the amorphous quality of what people would actually be doing. It
also caused friction as individuals tried to sort out their responsibilities. In some cases, people hadn't been told that they would be sharing their job with someone else (Katzenberg was a big believer in department "coheads"). But that muddled quality was precisely the
point—DreamWorks employees were encouraged to wear many hats,
and to gravitate toward the job they were most suited for, as opposed
to adhering to the confines of a job description.

This noncorporate interpretation of the workplace lured people in
droves, regardless of the fact that it usually meant a pay cut. (When
it came to executives, as opposed to creative talent, DreamWorks
took a start-up approach to salaries.) For Disney executives, farewell
meant kissing goodbye hefty stock packages at a company that was at
its height. Although DreamWorks gave its employees shares of phantom stock, they were worth little compared to the millions of dollars
that some Disney executives were giving up. Something else Dream-
Works was not handing out was end-of-year bonuses, a standard, and
not insignificant, perk at major studios, which offered bonuses ranging from 30 percent to 50 percent of a studio executive's annual salary.
Katzenberg—so concerned about his own Disney bonus—explained
the policy by saying that DreamWorks was in its infancy, and stressing
that its employees would prosper as the company did, through stock
and other benefits.

This philosophy also extended to filmmakers. One of DreamWorks'
headline-grabbing innovations was its promise to offer gross participation—i.e., a percentage of box-office revenue—to screenwriters,
which had traditionally been reserved for a select group of actors and
directors. The inspiration had come from Walter Parkes, who saw it as
an effort to extend goodwill to fellow screenwriters. DreamWorks was
also setting up a program whereby writers would be contracted to the
studio to work on scripts and share in a gross-profit pool. The pledges
were short on specifics, but the town lapped it up. These were, as it
happened, the good old days.

"The writer deal was a way to differentiate themselves as a different
kind of studio, so people would want to work there," said one agent.

"Psychologically, it was a great move. I can't tell you the number of writers going out with scripts who'd say, 'We gotta go to DreamWorks first, because they give you gross points!'"

Even on non-Disney recruits, Katzenberg worked his magic. Dylan Kohler, a techie-artist prodigy who'd worked on developing Disney's Computer Animation Production System (CAPS) and as a rookie artist on *Beauty and the Beast,* began receiving calls from DreamWorks at his office at Warner Bros.' animation studio. Katzenberg wanted him to run DreamWorks' technology division and offered to double his salary. After Warner's offered to top that, a bidding war broke out, but Kohler decided to stay at Warner Bros. out of loyalty. Two weeks later, he got a message at home. "Look," Katzenberg said. "I know you're not onboard, but I've got this meeting set up, and we need someone to represent us for technology. Would you mind just coming over and sitting in on it?"

Days later Kohler found himself at the Amblin office, sitting next to Spielberg and Ed McCracken, CEO of Silicon Graphics, as Katzenberg poured him a Diet Coke. Spielberg was telling a story about how he'd had access to his own T-1 line in Poland to edit *Schindler's List.* Unfortunately, when the O.J. Simpson car chase wrought nonstop coverage, his satellite link was taken over and his access was blocked.

"I'm thinking, 'So he's editing with a Polish editor over a T-1 line and he knows what that is, so he knows networking,'" Kohler said. "I thought, 'Well, these guys know it.' And I'd just come from Warner Bros. where they were still trying to figure it out. The suits would come over and say, 'Why do we need computers at all? Why are you asking for money?' That sort of thing. So it was amazing."

He was in.

Disney alumni may have been Katzenberg's most coveted prizes, but by the spring of 1995, the main source feeding DreamWorks' animation division was Amblimation, Spielberg's London-based animation studio, which was in the process of being moved to L.A. at the time DreamWorks was announced. After Katzenberg convinced them that they should sign on at DreamWorks, Amblimators—most of whom were French (spawned from Paris's prestigious Gobelins L'École de L'Image) and spoke iffy English—began arriving at DreamWorks in waves. The Amblimation influx meant that DreamWorks finally had a big enough staff to begin work on its first animation feature—the story of Moses and the Ten Commandments, or, *The Prince of Egypt*. The idea had emerged at a brainstorming session between the partners at Spielberg's house. As the three men tossed out ideas for their company's debut projects, Katzenberg talked of hoping to expand the breadth of animation and use the genre to make films about bigger, grander themes. He rattled off titles like *Indiana Jones and the Temple of Doom, Terminator,* and his favorite film of all time, *Lawrence of Arabia.*

"Why not do the Ten Commandments?" Spielberg suggested.

"What a great idea," Geffen said. "Let's do it!" He then cautioned: "But if you do it, you can't tell a fairy tale. You're going to have to go about telling this with a sense of respect and integrity that nobody's done in modern times."

Katzenberg would ultimately embrace the story of Moses on a far deeper level than either Spielberg or Geffen, grafting onto it in an intensely personal way. But he also had doubts. Although an animated film based on the Bible would be monumental and grand, it was far from a guaranteed moneymaker. Indeed, members of the business community were shocked that Katzenberg's first film out of the gate put art so blatantly before commerce. But according to sources familiar with Katzenberg's thinking at the time, he wasn't about to question Spielberg's first pitch for the new company.

It would not be the last "Steven idea" that the director's partners would go along with for fear of upsetting their king.

Another proposed project was based on William Steig's children's book about an ugly but lovable green ogre, *Shrek.* Producer John Williams had optioned the book after his two young sons got enthralled enough to actually memorize the text. Williams brought up the idea of a movie based on the book while meeting with Laurie MacDonald to discuss his new live-action deal. She suggested that Williams pitch it as an animated film to Katzenberg. Katzenberg loved it, but he didn't want to do it traditionally; he wanted to produce it in an "alternative medium." What that was, he wasn't sure. But in the spirit of DreamWorks' search for groundbreaking artistic endeavors, he hired a group of four recent (read: cheap) college graduates, known as the Propellerheads, who were experimenting in 3-D motion-capture animation. They had come to his attention by way of a short test produced and sold to HBO called *American Voyeur,* which revolved around a cigar-smoking, piggish-looking host of a smarmy celebrity talk show. The boorish looks of the host, Harry, bore some resemblance to Steig's green ogre, and his manners were irreverent and smart-ass, which fit with Katzenberg's feel for the tone of *Shrek,* whose script was written by Ted Elliott and Terry Rossio.

In late 1994 when he'd first met with the Propellerheads—J. J. Abrams, Rob Letterman, Loren Soman, and Andy Waisler—Katzenberg explained that *Shrek* was the studio's "low-budget" project. *Prince of Egypt,* which was getting most of DreamWorks Animation's focus and resources, was its "big-budget" film. The idea was to make *Shrek* for under $20 million. Katzenberg was so intent on adhering to modest proportions that he limited the film to no more than seventeen characters.

"When we started, we were the discount production," said Ken Harsha, the first animator hired to work on *Shrek.* This designation immediately cast *Shrek* as the inferior movie at DreamWorks, particularly among what Harsha calls "highfalutin folks from animation uninterested in anything done in CGI [computer-generated imagery] —the drawers, animators, ink-and-paint people . . . A lot of them were purists." The premise of the movie also failed to add luster to its image.

"*Shrek* was essentially the story of the ugliest guy in the world who meets the ugliest woman in the world—they get together and have the ugliest children," said one animator who had actually walked out on the pitch for the movie.

A few months after meeting with Katzenberg, the Propellerheads set up shop, first in the animation facility on the Universal lot, and later a few miles away in their own facility on Grandview Avenue in Glendale. Self-described geeks and hackers, they wore flip-flops and shorts to work and, according to Waisler, would "stare into the computer for eighteen hours straight without getting up, and realize we'd gotten nothing done." Waisler had met J. J. Abrams as an undergrad at Sarah Lawrence, where they were both "pretty dorky—we played a lot of computer games." Letterman had just graduated from the University of Southern California, where he'd produced a CGI film based on the Silver Surfer comic book character. Soman's background was in software.

Looking back at his DreamWorks days, Waisler remarked, "Things were swelling at the time. Everyone wanted to get into business with DreamWorks—tech companies, people. It was sort of a miracle time, watching all of the growth."

As for 3-D motion capture, he said, "Nobody knew how to do this stuff. No one had ever produced ninety minutes of motion capture. We'd produced one minute . . . CGI was being invented every time anyone did anything."

Before landing at DreamWorks, Waisler and his buddies had to sneak into USC, where Letterman was enrolled, at night in order to work on high-speed computers. Now, suddenly, they were being plied with all the latest technology by major software companies, and were being constantly asked: "What do you need? What can we get for you?"

"We were like kids in a candy store," Waisler said.

Saturday Night Live actor Chris Farley had been cast as the voice of *Shrek,* and he was brought in to do voice tests. After going through his lines, he'd break into his own shtick, which was captured on videotape and replayed late at night, when the Propellerheads were slap-happy and brain-dead after so many hours sitting in front of a computer monitor.

"I found [Farley's] wild energy exhausting but really funny," said animator Tom Sito. "He was constantly flushed, bouncing off the walls, sweating heavily and looking like he was about to burst out of his clothes."

Meanwhile, motion-capture tests were done with another actor in order to render a body skeleton of *Shrek.* In motion capture, an actor wears a special "suit" outfitted with sensors on various parts of the body. As the actor moves, his or her motion is transmitted from the sensors into a computer and mapped onto a 3-D model, which becomes the basis for the animated character.

As the months wore on, it became apparent that a cultural and technological barrier existed at DreamWorks when it came to computer-based and traditional animation.

"DreamWorks had a really robust 2-D pipeline," Waisler said. "That's what Jeffrey Katzenberg knew. With 2-D, they knew how to deal with story, technical elements, what they could achieve emotionally."

3-D, however, was in many ways an enigma to DreamWorks executives. "They would ask for something that was hard to do in 3-D, but easy to do in 2-D," Waisler said. "In 2-D, there's a lot of flexibility to characters—an arm can get longer, it's easy to change the shape of a head. All those things are really hard to do in 3-D and cost hundreds of thousands of dollars.

"On the other hand, 3-D has other things that are very easy that don't exist in 2-D, such as shadows and depth of field. A bridge needed to be built between the two. They understood 2-D really well, but they needed to understand the limits of technology."

The Propellerheads' inexperience didn't help, either.

"These guys wanted to please Jeffrey, for him to be happy with them, and so they conceded some of their vision, point by point," said Harsha. "After a while, their demise was that they didn't have a strong vision. And the vision they had didn't align with Jeffrey's vision."

The drama was heightened as new waves of producers and directors came and went—among them Matt O'Callaghan and Kelly Asbury. Katzenberg just couldn't seem to nail down the right team to tackle his "fractured fairy tale"—a term from the old *Rocky and Bullwinkle* era that Asbury invoked. Nobody, it seemed, could crack the film or the tone that Katzenberg was insisting upon: "edgy."

As *Shrek* floundered, its status as the ugly stepchild at DreamWorks was reinforced.

"It was known as the Gulag," said one animator. "If you failed on *Prince of Egypt* . . . you were sent to the dungeons to work on *Shrek*." The assignment was referred to as being "Shreked."

"It was a difficult production," said Harsha. "There was not a script that was locked down. We had a book, we had a tone, and we had Jeffrey's vision for the thing." That was it.

As Shrek's story evolved, so, too, did his appearance. At first he was oafy, with oversize hands and feet and a small head. But he gradually took on more of Chris Farley's characteristics. It had never gone quite like that in animation before. "Chris was a huge influence," said Harsha. "He was the perfect role model." Suddenly Shrek looked "like Chris as an ogre"—a football-player type with a big nose, "funky ears," and "*Tommy Boy*–type hair."

After over a year on the job, in which money was being spent with little to show for it, the Propellerheads were feeling the strain. "We were incredibly burned out," said Waisler. "It was a long, uphill battle."

In addition to the hardships of the project, the dynamics in the group were changing. Abrams, also pursuing screenwriting, had sold his second script, *Regarding Henry,* during the development of *Shrek,* and was spending more time in New York writing. Soman, meanwhile, wanted to get into software. Waisler was feeling the itch to return to architecture, which he'd studied in graduate school. But the group's real death, at least in relation to *Shrek,* came when Katzenberg saw the one-minute test they'd done and was vastly underwhelmed.

In the test, Shrek was cartoony and exaggerated. When a bandit jumps down in front of him as he enters the castle gates, he picks him up and strangles him the way that Homer Simpson might throttle Bart—as his grip bears down, his cheeks blow up Dizzy Gillespie–style and turn a deep shade of purple. Katzenberg wasn't pleased. "It looked terrible, it didn't work, it wasn't funny, and he didn't like it," was the assessment.

Production was shut down and the crew of forty-odd people who'd been assembled to work on the film was dispersed. Several millions of dollars in development costs were written off.

The prospects for DreamWorks' low-budget animation experiment seemed dim.

8

LIVE ACTION

THE SCOPE AND BREADTH of DreamWorks' ambitions reflected the go-go 1990s—a time when the economy was surging, Bill Clinton was in the White House, and a still mysterious resource known as the World Wide Web was about to change everything. But its expansiveness was also a reflection of its resident rainmaker: Steven Spielberg. It was not because of Jeffrey Katzenberg or David Geffen that DreamWorks was getting into the video-game business or mulling over the creation of entertainment centers where families could chow down on hamburgers and zap Space Invaders (what would be known as GameWorks). The company was molded around the ideas and dreams of its resident man-child, the inspiration for DreamWorks' newly unveiled logo: a little boy sitting on the edge of the crescent moon, casting his fishing line into the stars. Whenever a wish materialized in Spielberg's endlessly imaginative mind, it was up to Geffen and Katzenberg to wave their magic wands and make it come true.

Even when Spielberg's partners did not see eye to eye with him—such as over building a studio at Playa Vista (Geffen in particular was skeptical)—they came through for him, understanding all too well that the star that made DreamWorks SKG shine so brightly, that had the media doing somersaults, the investors lining up for lunch in the Amblin dining room, was not what the *K* or the *G* in the company's initials represented but the *S*. Which is why the *S* came first.

Whatever the size of their egos, neither Geffen nor Katzenberg had any illusions about the supremacy of Spielberg's agenda. As Geffen put it: "When we first started DreamWorks, I said to Jeffrey, 'We ought to call this new company the Spielberg Brothers. Anything Steven thinks is important, we want to invest in.'"

The tricky part for Katzenberg and Geffen, however, was not just catering to Spielberg but making certain that he stayed focused. According to Bruce Jacobsen, cohead of DreamWorks' video-game division, Katzenberg was often heard saying, in his sports-talk lingo, "This is a town where the batting average is .210 and where you're profitable if you bat .290. I've got like a .410, and Steven bats .667. My mission in life is for Steven to swing as many times as he can and, with all due respect, I should be taking a few swings at bat, too."

Already, this aim had been somewhat derailed, given Spielberg's insistence on directing for other studios. What Steven wanted also determined how DreamWorks' live-action studio would be run and who would run it—which, to the shock of Hollywood, was not going to be Katzenberg, despite his nearly twenty years of studio experience at Paramount and Disney. At the time when the live-action duties were being divvied up at DreamWorks, Katzenberg's Touchstone track record was being assessed more from its back than from its front end. Everyone had witnessed his losing streak during his twilight years at Disney, when the company started forsaking its live-action formula of simple, accessible story lines and reasonable budgets. Not only were there fewer hits toward the end of Katzenberg's tenure, but they were costly ones, such as *V.I. Warshawski* and *Newsies,* a musical about a singing newspaper boy in the Depression. Eisner had had concerns about the latter movie, but had let Katzenberg go with his gut, which, in this case, misled him terribly: the film lost $42 million. Katzenberg was blamed for all of them, even flops such as *Cabin Boy,* which he'd had major doubts about but pushed through for Eisner's sake.

That Spielberg apparently deemed him not ready for prime time must have come as a shock to Katzenberg, too. Already, he'd begun talking to Touchstone executive Donald De Line about coming to DreamWorks, obviously feeling he was in a position to make such decisions. But it soon became evident that Spielberg would be ruling his turf without any input from his new partners. He'd handed the keys to his cherished kingdom to Walter Parkes and Laurie MacDonald, whom he had convinced to sign on to run the live-action studio by promising them that they could continue to produce movies even as they served as studio executives with management responsibilities. For Spielberg, it was a no-brainer: he believed in the couple, trusted them above anyone, and valued their sophistication, class, and taste.

Where these qualities were concerned, Katzenberg was at a distinct disadvantage.

Moreover, Parkes had recently brought Spielberg in as an executive producer on a film he was producing at Sony, *Men in Black*. A sci-fi comedy starring Tommy Lee Jones and Will Smith with a $90 million budget, the film was planned as a summer "tent pole"—a major event movie that is expected to do big box office and sustain the rest of the year's slate—and if all went accordingly, Spielberg would be in for a windfall. As an executive producer—i.e., doing little more than lending his name to the picture—Spielberg was to receive a generous portion of first-dollar grosses, or a percentage of every dollar the movie made at the box office.

"I'm not saying Steven was *bought*," said one source. "But Walter brought him a very successful franchise that had nothing to do with Steven, at Sony, and he asked Steven to come in on it. That's a good thing."

According to several sources, Katzenberg's exclusion from the live-action studio was mainly about taste, and the perception was that Katzenberg, despite his many strengths, didn't have enough of it to create a pedigreed live-action division that produced both blockbusters and Oscar winners.

"It's hard enough to find fifteen decent movies, of which, you hope, three of them are great," said one insider. "But the idea that both [Touchstone and Hollywood Pictures, Disney's live-action units] were churning out twenty movies a year—and there was nothing but dreck. Jeffrey would probably say it was mandated by their pipelines, but what it really looked like was that Jeffrey had no taste."

Katzenberg's attitude toward moviemaking—cheaper, faster, better—also clashed resoundingly with Geffen's, whose philosophy, à la Wasserman, was to always go for the *best*. (Even if, when it came to movies, his choices didn't always pay off.) According to one source, Geffen, who prided himself enormously in having refined taste, would cringe when Katzenberg talked about movies in terms of "singles and doubles."

"David doesn't do baseball," this person said. "He likes quality. So David sentenced Jeffrey to animation. He said, 'That's what you're good at.'"

• • •

Katzenberg gave no outward indication of being upset by his exclusion from live action, but according to a longtime friend, he was deeply pained. "He'd never admit it, but absolutely," this person acknowledged.

Another source said: "Jeffrey wanted live action. It was an embarrassment to him when he didn't get it." It was Katzenberg who had gotten the ball rolling on the company, after all, and he idolized Spielberg and trusted Geffen to champion his unlimited ascension. Of course, control of animation was unquestioningly Katzenberg's, but live action was DreamWorks' jewel in the crown.

Whatever Katzenberg may have felt, there was no time for self-pity, even had he been inclined toward introspection, which, friends say, he was decisively not. A studio had to be built and movies needed to be made. But first, DreamWorks needed money, and in raising it, Katzenberg's partners played their respective roles: Geffen made the calls, hosted the lunches, got down to brass tacks; Spielberg was brought in when sizzle was required; when a potential benefactor needed to be charmed into signing on the bottom line. To hear DreamWorks tell it, the moneymen were lining up in droves—or, as Spielberg put it to *Time*, it was "like stacking hour over Kennedy airport!" Who wouldn't, after all, want a building named after them at Steven Spielberg's new studio, or a "thank-you" in the credits of his next blockbuster? Even just one trip on Geffen's Gulfstream . . .

Yet the situation wasn't quite as movie-like as the partners were letting on. While it was true that DreamWorks was attracting great interest, tough questions were being asked. One financier who looked at the business plan, which was more of a "book," said, "I remember thinking, *Are you kidding me?* It was a huge undertaking. It was like, really, you're going to do all this—build a brand-new studio, have thirteen businesses, get into merchandising?"

Prince of Egypt also elicited questions, as in, how was an animated movie based on the Bible going to translate into a blockbuster? And because the company had no immediate revenue stream, such as a library—which provides steady home-video and TV revenue even when theatrical releases fall through—or product ready to release, DreamWorks had to hit it out of the park on the very first pitch, to employ a Katzenbergian metaphor.

There were other reasons for skepticism, or at least an understand-

ing that success was not a fait accompli. A chief concern remained
the issue of how three individuals each so powerful in their own right
would manage as a team. "People were afraid that all of the air would
be sucked out of the room," said one financier.

Such concerns caused some potential investors, such as the California Public Employees' Retirement System, the largest public pen-
sion fund in the United States, which had been in talks with Dream-
Works to invest almost $300 million, to back out.

The radically different style of each man was apparent at meetings
with financiers at Amblin. The event inevitably occasioned a buffet
lunch, and a room in which three tables were set up, one for each of
the three partners. The bankers would rotate between them in order
to have face time with Spielberg, Katzenberg, and Geffen.

Recalled one financier: "You'd sit down with David, and anything
you said was wrong. If you said, 'What an incredible career you've
had, you've made billions,' he'd say, 'No, it's such a burden. The more
money you make, the more you have to invest, and you have to stay on
top of those investments.' He seemed like a very lonely, deeply unful-
filled person."

As for Katzenberg, he was "more middle of the road. He's so driven,
he obviously feels cheated. But he'll talk to you, look you in the eye.
Though you can tell he's champing at the bit to give his opinion. But
at least he'll ask. David will never ask.

"When you talk to Steven and tell him you loved *E.T.*, he'll light up:
'Oh, really?'"

Another negotiation that was laden with hurdles was with Microsoft, which DreamWorks was interested in partnering with on a video-
game division, even though Microsoft's game unit was considered
fairly weak compared to its software business. (Apple was the leader in
CD-ROM game titles, which at the time were the dominant game platform.) Still, both sides were eager to get into business together and pair
DreamWorks' creative power with Microsoft's tech savvy. Microsoft's
chief technology officer, Nathan Myhrvold, even spent a week shad-
owing Katzenberg to get a better sense of what made his peculiar spe-
cies run. Myhrvold's findings were recorded in a fourteen-page memo
titled "My Week with Jeffrey: Hollywood on a hundred phone calls a
day," which was dispersed among Microsoft employees and printed in
The New Yorker. An excerpt, as it appeared in that magazine:

He is a master with this particular instrument of communication, which is not surprising given how much he uses it. The stories you read about Jeffrey making 100 to 150 phone calls a day are true . . . His three secretaries have headsets and try to fill any free time during the day with calls — they will keep calling people back or try to arrange times and then when they get somebody put them through to Jeffrey with a brief comment about why he's talking to them. All in all it is a very efficient process . . . Jeffrey calls to check in with people, and they with him, often regardless of need. These phone calls are like the banter people exchange in the halls at work, and last about as long. Jeffrey cruises these virtual halls, and others cruise his, maintaining the network of personal relationships from which the fabric of the entertainment industry is woven . . .

Somebody at DreamWorks told me that in Jeffrey's days at Disney his time was so pressed that they found it necessary to actually rehearse the calls that they wanted to make to Jeffrey in front of a mirror until they got enough points packed into the smallest duration . . . I couldn't help thinking of all of the people who have premeetings to rehearse a review with Bill [Gates]. The big difference is that the message on brevity seems to [have] escaped our folks so far.

But Microsoft, a ruthless dealmaker, had questions about DreamWorks' prospectus. When the software giant performed as thorough a job of due diligence as DreamWorks, with its fortress mentality, would permit, Geffen burst out: "Hey! We're not under DOJ investigation, you know!"

Another issue was trust. A few years earlier, Bill Gates had been approached by Michael Ovitz to drum up a partnership, but Ovitz's game plan had been vague, along the lines of, "Let's just invest money and we'll figure out what we're doing later," according to Bruce Jacobsen, then a member of Microsoft's negotiating team. Gates, perhaps the world's greatest stickler when it comes to detail and strategy, was unmoved by the appeal. He was further turned off, or at least perplexed, when Ovitz took him to dinner at an expensive L.A. restaurant and, in an attempt to impress him, had them seated in the restaurant's kitchen. Not, apparently, Seattle style.

In an effort to convince Microsoft that he was as unslick as any computer nerd, Katzenberg exclaimed, apropos of nothing: "I've been married to my wife for fifteen years!" Despite such proclamations, Microsoft hired its own Hollywood lawyer to level the playing field and address such issues as Spielberg's royalties on video games based on his films; although DreamWorks claimed he always got 35 percent of revenues, Microsoft discovered cases where he had received less.

The cultures of the two companies also collided. During one discussion, Katzenberg was insulted when, after telling Gates that it took four hundred animators to make *The Lion King*, Gates shot back: "Can't you cut that down to forty people and do the rest on computers?"

"Jeffrey misunderstood Bill," Spielberg told *Time*. "He wasn't turning his nose up at creativity; he was putting us to the test, asking very tough questions because he wanted to hear how we would answer them. He was manipulating that meeting."

But perhaps Microsoft's greatest concern had to do with the extent of Spielberg's devotion to the new company. "Steven's commitment ultimately was a handshake with DreamWorks, seeing as he could direct movies for other companies," said Jacobsen. "One question from Microsoft was: Is Steven in it? Or is he just dabbling? Steven being in it was really crucial. [Microsoft] was hoping for *E.T.*"

To reassure its suitors, SKG amped up their three-ring circus of seduction. Spielberg assured the Microsoft team that he was absolutely in for the long haul, as he chatted energetically about his love of video games (including Microsoft's Flight Simulator) and waxed knowledgeable about new technology. Katzenberg gave his amped-up spiel about DreamWorks being a home for creative talent and about his own fascination with animation technology born during his Disney days. Geffen, who was still under contract with MCA, played it low-key, limiting his input to asking pointed questions. At the end of one meeting, Spielberg gave the group a tour of the Shoah Foundation, his nonprofit organization that has collected tens of thousands of video testimonials from Holocaust survivors. Patty Stonesifer—then senior VP of Microsoft's Interactive Media Division and one of Gates's right-hand executives—left in tears. Bill Gates would not be going home just yet.

The Koreans, on the other hand, were close to pulling out. When Samsung offered to plow as much as $900 million into DreamWorks, Spielberg and Capshaw hosted a dinner at their home for Samsung chairman Lee Kun-Hee and more than a dozen other guests. But as business was discussed—through an interpreter—over Chilean sea bass and white wine, Spielberg began to get a funny feeling in his stomach, and not because of the fish.

"The word 'semiconductor' must have been used about 20 times during that two-and-a-half-hour encounter," Spielberg said. "I thought to myself, 'How are they going to know anything about the film business when they're so obsessed with semiconductors?' It was another one of those evenings that turned out to be a complete waste of time."

As for the Samsung executives, they were, rightly, skeptical that they would have any say in creative decisions in the new company, and the talks collapsed.

But a deal was not completely off the table. Lee's niece Miky, the Harvard-educated managing director of One World Media Corporation, an offshoot of Samsung, knew Geffen and was interested in an investment, albeit for a lower amount.

The biggest question facing the troika was MCA, and how, or if, the studio would figure into DreamWorks' distribution plans. Spielberg had given Wasserman and Sheinberg his word that, so long as they were still working at MCA, DreamWorks would be bringing its business, but the men's future was looking more uncertain than ever. After Matsushita rebuffed Wasserman and Sheinberg's offer to buy back MCA, the two quarreling factions had met in San Francisco, but nothing was resolved. In January, another meeting had taken place, this time at the Matsushita headquarters in Osaka, but again, Wasserman and Sheinberg left feeling anxious.

The worst of it was that Ovitz was now in a front-and-center role with the Japanese, who had hired him as a consultant to assess the worth of MCA. No one in Hollywood had any doubts that Ovitz would try to parlay this role into a far more prominent one and make a play for running MCA. When Wasserman heard that Ovitz had been summoned to the meeting in Osaka, he'd shouted: "I've been in this business for sixty years and I'm not going to stand and have my performance evaluated by Michael Ovitz!" With that, he walked out of the room.

If ascension is what Ovitz had in mind, he faced a threat named David Geffen, who would, presumably, do whatever was called for to waylay his bitterest rival. According to *The Operator*, when Geffen sold Geffen Records in 1989, the fact that Wasserman was aging and would soon be in need of a successor had affected his decision to select MCA as a suitor. Now that Matsushita was planning its next move—rumor was, a sale was ahead—Wasserman's place would very likely be vacant. Geffen possessed the golden carrot that could affect MCA's future: Spielberg. DreamWorks' distribution arrangement with MCA was a handshake deal. To firm it up and keep the most successful filmmaker in history (no more so than right now, in the wake of *Jurassic Park*'s $900 million worldwide grosses) from straying, Geffen could, and surely would, use Spielberg to influence negotiations. Geffen's other valuable card was Geffen Records, which MCA owned and which Geffen had been running, though his contract was about to expire. The label was coming off its most profitable year to date, a fact that Geffen was making sure to publicize. The message to MCA was clear: this was not the moment to anger Mr. Geffen.

9

SHOW ME THE MONEY

B ILL GATES WAS not the only Microsoft mogul courted by
DreamWorks as the company wooed its way toward reality.
There was someone else—a man who would prove not only
far more vulnerable to the overwhelming charms of the DreamWorks
trio, but also a far more useful catch. In fact, without him—and his
billions—there would have been no DreamWorks. He was, certainly,
the most unlikely of benefactors. An unrepentant nerd, barely could
he make eye contact with the beautiful starlets who frequently crossed
his path. But he loved stars, movies, and glamour—a "cool chaser"
they called him—and in DreamWorks, he saw not just the brightest
orbs of all, but one, in particular, who could guide him through the
strange, wonderful land he had been waiting, behind the velvet rope,
to enter.

Paul Allen did not know David Geffen well when, in the fall of 1994,
he received an invitation for lunch at Geffen's Malibu home. The two
had met at media financier Herb Allen's Sun Valley summer retreat,
where moguls strut around in shorts and T-shirts and, over roaring
fires and Grey Goose on ice, discuss prospective conquests. Allen,
pathologically shy, hated the annual schmooze fest, though, with a net
worth of $3.9 billion, his VIP credentials outshone most.

Wisely, a few months later, when Geffen was drumming up investors for DreamWorks, he called Allen. The "other" Microsoft cofounder had left the company in 1983 when he was diagnosed with
Hodgkin's disease (since in remission). Now he was plowing billions
into dozens of multimedia and technology companies in pursuit of
what he called a "wired world."

• • •

The pudgy, bespectacled Allen, accustomed to the insularly white-bread, techie world of Seattle, which, in the 1990s, was like a grown-up version of *The Revenge of the Nerds,* couldn't have helped but be smitten, sitting across from David Geffen.

Geffen, in turn, was impressed by a man who outranked him so conspicuously on the Forbes 400 list. However, fortunes aside, Geffen and Allen had little in common. The magnate whom *Wired* magazine dubbed "the accidental zillionaire"—Allen's post-Microsoft investments were scattershot and, in many cases, money losers—spent most of his time in the protective company of his mother, Faye, and sister, Jody Patton, who was also his business partner. Both lived on the grounds of his six-acre, $68 million estate on Mercer Island in Seattle. The property was grandiose and extravagant: there was a full-size basketball court whose walls were lined with original art (Allen was a big enough fan of the game to buy the Portland Trail Blazers); a twenty-seat theater; a pool over which dangled Dale Chihuly chandeliers; a screening room; individual, temperature-controlled rooms for the Maseratis and Lamborghinis; plasma TVs in almost every room; an art gallery worthy of a museum; an indoor tennis court; a library.

But despite the lavishness of the spread, it lacked a vision. According to visitors, it felt more like a desolate bachelor pad, albeit a rather grand one. Some rooms looked almost sterilely corporate, with black leather couches and uninspired furniture; the grounds were not landscaped. Unlike Geffen, who was scrupulously tending to the overhaul of Jack Warner's old estate, where even the shrubbery had pedigrees, Allen was less concerned with, and less versed in, aesthetics.

Geffen also had a social style, and ease, that Allen could not summon. Although Allen frequently entertained actors, rock stars, and other celebrities on his yachts and airplanes, his lack of social graces kept him from truly engaging in the events he, or in some cases his sister, organized.

One of the few times that Allen seemed at ease was when he was jamming to '70s-era rock with his band, the Threads, or talking about sci-fi books or, his true passion, outer space. (A devoted Trekkie, Allen called his investment company Vulcan Ventures.) But he nonetheless craved a part of whatever was considered hot, not just socially but in business. In 1992 he'd invested $100 million in the Palo Alto–based Interval Research Corporation—an eclectic, cutting-edge think tank of engineers, programmers, behavioral scientists, and psychologists in pursuit of the next big thing in technology. The company was considered an heir to the Xerox Palo Alto Research Center, the revolutionary research lab where, in the 1970s, the first PC and laser printer were developed. For Allen, the company was a link to the hottest names in Silicon Valley, and he habitually flew down to attend the group's extravagant parties.

And now Allen was faced with the possibility of being connected to *the most* star-studded company of all. As he and Geffen discussed two of their favorite topics — money and the toys that money can buy — Geffen urged Allen to broaden his art collection beyond the Impressionists (Allen's favorite artists were the old standbys Renoir and Monet; Geffen preferred De Kooning and Jasper Johns). Allen, in turn, urged Geffen to buy a yacht. In the meantime, he offered to lend him his.

Serving to help unite the two was William Savoy, Allen's chief investment adviser, who was equally taken with Geffen. Many observers were bewildered that, in lieu of a team of MBAs, Allen relied solely on the guidance of Savoy, who studied computer science at Atlantic Union College before he was hired by Allen at the age of nineteen (he was now thirty). But Allen needed him; Paul was more into ideas and concepts than nitty-gritty business details. As he had so many times before with individuals who held promise — or some use to him — Geffen took Allen under his wing. He began a process of fluffing him up, improving him, as though he were just another aspiring rock and roller. Offered up were tips like: "Lose the beard" and "Trade in the glasses for a cooler pair." Allen obliged. Geffen also gave Allen three brightly colored shirts that Allen wore nonstop.

"It was just like *Candide*," producer Howard Rosenman said, "in which David played the role of Dr. Pangloss, the sophisticated man who teaches the humble Candide how the world works."

Geffen also began expanding Allen's social circle, inviting him to L.A. and introducing him to Carrie Fisher, Mick Jagger, and Jerry Hall. Allen's previous taste of L.A. had been through Ticketmaster, the L.A.-based ticket retailer in which he'd recently invested and where he hung around the office, wearing his trademark Sears-style slacks and tattered shirt and chatting with the hoi polloi. (Once, he had been mistaken for the IT guy.)

"He's a really sweet guy. He would talk to anyone, even the most junior people. He genuinely seemed to want to just hang out," said one former Ticketmaster executive.

But after meeting Geffen, Allen switched to a more high-profile scene. Suddenly, he was showing up at movie premieres and A-list dinners.

"Suddenly he was in with Geffen, and he changed," noted the former Ticketmaster executive. "He stopped wearing Dockers pants, he trimmed his beard. It was totally a Geffen production!"

In March 1995 Allen became DreamWorks' granddaddy of investors, putting up nearly $500 million in exchange for an 18 percent stake in the company. Allen's investment propelled DreamWorks forward more than any other single event. Spielberg and Katzenberg celebrated by taking their wives to the film *Bye Bye Love*—produced by their friend Gary David Goldberg, who was also directing Dream-Works TV's debut show, *Champs*—and then dining at Dive!

Allen wasn't doing it for the money, at least not primarily, but Geffen assured him that he'd be repaid, and he meant it. ("David's very integrous about those things—*very*," said Rosenman, meaning paying back money.) To prove this, Geffen arranged for Allen to be the first outside investor compensated once DreamWorks generated profits.

Allen had originally agreed to invest a smaller amount—around $350 million—but Geffen came back and asked for more, according to a source close to Allen at the time. Later, given the opportunity to scale back to the original amount, Allen decided to keep his half-billion in place. He had none of the reservations about the Dream Team that he'd had about Pixar, Steve Jobs's digital studio that was about to release its first feature film, *Toy Story,* in partnership with Disney. Allen had talked to Jobs about investing in that company, but had remained unpersuaded. Pixar had been losing money for years as chief creative officer John Lasseter and his crew tinkered away at the revolutionary, but still unproven, new medium of CGI. Not to mention that neither the humorless, black-turtlenecked Jobs, nor the rotund, jolly Lasseter, with his Hawaiian-print shirts, approached SKG star quality.

According to Mike Slade, who ran Allen's software company Starwave, Allen once told him: "I don't get many opportunities to do business with guys like them. Spielberg is about as important as it gets."

Slade scoffed at the portrait of Allen as the "rich rube who comes to

Hollywood and gets fleeced. That's a gross oversimplification," Slade said. "Paul's motivations were more pure. When Paul got a movie theater installed in his house, he'd have 'movie night,' and he wouldn't show *Die Hard,* he'd show Visconti. He's a film buff. That was well before DreamWorks."

Within a week of the Allen announcement, Microsoft also reached a deal with DreamWorks to invest, albeit for a far more modest amount — $15 million — money that would go toward SKG's video-game division, DreamWorks Interactive, which was a fifty-fifty partnership with Microsoft. Although it was one of the few times that Allen had outdone his former business partner — the richest man in the world, worth $15 billion in 1995 — Bill Gates still managed to prevail. *Business-Week* dubbed the union between DreamWorks and Microsoft, "Hollywood's Digital Godzilla."

As for Allen and his half a billion, the *L.A. Times* asked: "Paul Who?"

With money from Allen and Microsoft — as well as $1 billion in bank debt from Chemical Bank, advances from a domestic pay-TV deal with HBO, and other, smaller investments, DreamWorks had $2.7 billion in capital. *BusinessWeek* called it "the costliest startup in entertainment history." Now the only thing needed was product as flashy as the operation itself.

Allen was not the only Hollywood outsider who, having plunked down a considerable amount of cash to be admitted to the land of glamour and glitz, was finding himself at a loss. The next arriviste was a wealthy, dapper businessman with a Van Gogh goatee, who had dabbled in movies (as a producer) and songwriting, but had never been the kind of player whom he so idolized. That is, until one of those idols came knocking.

In early March of 1995, Edgar Bronfman Jr., the thirty-nine-year-old CEO and scion of Seagram, the Canadian spirits company, flew on his Gulfstream IV to the Matsushita headquarters in Osaka. After an interpreter-assisted one-on-one with the company's president, Bronfman flew back to New York. After one more, similarly clandestine meeting, a deal was born. Matsushita sold 80 percent of MCA to Seagram for $5.7 billion. One of the world's most prestigious movie empires was suddenly owned by Canadians. Once again, the man covertly consulting on the sidelines was Michael Ovitz, who had known that Bronfman was looking to push Seagram deeper into entertainment (and that Matsushita was looking to rid itself of the troublesome Americans). Already, Seagram had bought stock in Time Warner. But in 1995, buying wasn't enough; you had to own. Ovitz denied his role in advising Bronfman, even though, at the meeting to close the deal, he sat on the Seagram, not the Matsushita, side of the table.

Ovitz was friendly with Bronfman and, as it happened, owed him a favor. Years earlier, when Ovitz's father had worked as a liquor distributor affiliated with Seagram, Ovitz had called Bronfman and asked him to prevent his father's forced retirement. Bronfman had complied. Ovitz apparently hadn't forgotten.

The move left Wasserman and Sheinberg—strategically kept out of the loop—enraged. Not only had Matsushita done the thing they'd said they wouldn't—sold—but Ovitz had done the thing they'd most feared: gone behind their backs and facilitated another deal. Even worse, Bronfman was courting Ovitz to run MCA, which he renamed Universal Studios. In other words, finally, and completely, Ovitz could very well become the next Wasserman, aka *le roi*. Wasserman, whose opinion of Ovitz had never been high, was outraged, and made one thing clear: if Ovitz was in, he was history. Likewise Sheinberg. And if Wasserman and Sheinberg were out, then DreamWorks—and all those future *Jurassic Parks* and *Schindler's Lists*—was gone too. Things were getting sticky.

As Ovitz prepared for his coronation, he convinced his closest partner at CAA, Ron Meyer, to come with him to Universal, along with as many as twenty other agents. But there were few guarantees. "There were no job descriptions. I guess he said, 'Bill [Haber], you'll run TV. Ron, you'll run movies,'" said a former CAA source. "No one said yes. It was really never fleshed out. Mike had a tendency—he'd say things. 'You come, and you'll come.' But there was never a plan."

Ovitz himself was ambivalent about the move. He seemed torn between wanting to rule the town and anxious about working for an established royal family where he was an outsider.

Ovitz's uncertainty led him to ask for more and more: a package worth about $240 million, one of the most lucrative corporate packages in history. Bronfman would have handed it over, but his father,

Edgar Sr., and uncle, Charles, both older and more pragmatic, said no. What would have been the deal of deals was off—even after *Newsweek* had put Ovitz on the cover, proclaiming him the new king of Universal.

This was, for Ovitz, a humiliating defeat. The agent couldn't close a deal that was all but served up for him. It was also a blow to Bronfman, who looked like an amateur controlled by his elders. With no chairman in place, Seagram stock would take another beating. Seagram had sold its 24 percent stake in DuPont, which had provided more than 70 percent of Seagram earnings, in order to buy MCA. And Seagram stockholders let their unhappiness be known.

Bronfman needed help—and a splashy comeback—and so he turned to the one man he believed could assist him. As he told one former MCA executive, "I consider David Geffen my guardian angel." Geffen, of course, was also one of Spielberg's guardians, and if Bronfman could seal a deal with DreamWorks and say that Spielberg would be part of MCA going forward, stockholders would be appeased. So Bronfman made an urgent call to Geffen, who was at the Mayo Clinic in Rochester, Minnesota, with producer Ray Stark, for their annual physicals. When Geffen heard that the Ovitz deal was off the table, he was incredulous. "You're kidding me, right?" he said. "It'll get put back together."

"I promise you, it will not get put back together," Bronfman said. "But I want to make a distribution deal with you guys. Can we sit down and talk about this?"

Bronfman had talked to Spielberg, Katzenberg, and Geffen about a deal in earlier weeks, but DreamWorks had made it clear that until Bronfman had picked his management team—and they approved—they were not ready to sign. The attempts at negotiation had been prickly at best. At one meeting at Katzenberg's house, Bronfman, having looked at DreamWorks' term sheet, started off the meeting by saying that he would not be able to meet DreamWorks' demands.

Hearing this, Geffen lost his cool. "I have one job in the world now and that's to make him happy!" he said, pointing at Spielberg. "And you're putting me in a position where I cannot make him happy!"

"David, stop screaming," Sheinberg said.

"I'm not screaming!" Geffen yelled.

"You're screaming, David," Sheinberg said.

Then Spielberg chimed in. "David, you know what would make me happy?"

"What?" Geffen asked with a stormy look.

"Stop screaming," Spielberg said.

The meeting ended inconclusively.

Now, with Ovitz out of the picture, and Bronfman feeling desperate, things were rather splendidly in DreamWorks' favor, and they were ready to get serious. A few days after the *Newsweek* cover ran, on Wednesday, June 7, Bronfman Jr., MCA Motion Picture Group head Tom Pollock, and Helene Hahn descended on Geffen's Malibu home to work out the deal. This time, Bronfman arrived with, in lieu of a negotiating strategy, the fervent desire to make it happen fast. Rather than argue, he began by saying to Geffen: "David, you are a fair person. I don't want this to be a protracted, difficult, unfriendly negotiation. Let me tell you exactly what's going to happen. You're going to tell me what the deal is, and I'm going to say yes."

"That's not fair!" Geffen said.

"It's the only way this will work," Bronfman replied.

In less than two hours Geffen designed—and Bronfman agreed to—a deal aggressively in DreamWorks' favor. (A former Universal executive later lamented: "We were hosed.") Compared to the average distribution fee paid by a company financing its own films—15 percent to 17 percent of a film's gross—DreamWorks would pay Universal just 8 percent, sliding to 5 percent. The home-video deal was equally low-ball. Granted, MCA wouldn't be putting up any production or marketing money for DreamWorks' films, so there was technically nothing to lose, but there was also not much to gain unless DreamWorks churned out nothing but blockbusters.

"The deal was not set up to accommodate failure," said one former Universal source. "When you make a bet like that, you secure the bet with terms and conditions, so that if things don't go quite as anticipated, hopefully, you at least break even. That security was not present in that deal. It was kind of like a free fall."

Another critic was Ovitz, who called Bronfman and blasted him for having relinquished so much. (Ovitz also called Geffen, telling him that he'd just congratulated Bronfman.)

Also as part of the arrangement—per Spielberg's wishes—Wasserman and Sheinberg were not brushed aside, at least not entirely. Sheinberg stepped down and was given an incredibly rich production deal at Universal (ultimately worth $130 million) for his company, the Bubble Factory, which allowed him to green-light his own movies. As for Wasserman, he was made chairman emeritus of Universal and was even allowed to keep his office on the fifteenth floor of the so-called Black Tower building on the studio lot. Underlying the generous gestures was the reality that a new era was at hand. Bronfman's intentions were made clear when his team moved downstairs to the fourteenth floor.

Geffen had also arranged for MCA (through Geffen Records) to serve as the distribution arm for DreamWorks Records, which Geffen had put in the hands of Mo Ostin and Lenny Waronker. The two music titans had recently left Warner Bros. when Time Warner, its corporate parent, showed Ostin—now sixty-eight years old—the door, and his number two, Waronker, loyally followed him out. To the rescue came Geffen, who tempted Ostin out of retirement with the opportunity to work at a privately held company where there were no stockholders to please, and where Ostin and Waronker—a former producer who'd nurtured the careers of Randy Newman, Neil Young, and the Doobie Brothers—could operate the equivalent of a mom-and-pop operation, but with tons of cash.

The bad blood that had existed between Geffen and Ostin—they had once had a nasty feud that ended in Geffen lying and telling Ostin's wife of thirty-four years that Ostin didn't love her—was long gone, as it often was with Geffen, who scolded, upbraided, cursed, destroyed, and then came back, after the show, full of love. Ostin seemed to accept this. So he and Waronker signed on, along with Mo's son, Michael Ostin, who'd run A&R (artists and repertoire) at Warner's. Later, Michael "Goldy" Goldstone, an A&R whiz at Epic, who'd discovered the bands Pearl Jam and Rage Against the Machine, joined the trio as a fourth partner at the label. They set up shop in a sleek compound on West Third Street in Beverly Hills.

The addition of more big names to the DreamWorks playlist merited, naturally, more headlines. Yet camouflaged in all of the fuss was a distinct sense that Hollywood's supposedly forward-looking company seemed, curiously, to be looking backwards, considering Ostin's age. "It was like Clinton coming back to office," remarked one DreamWorks Records source. Adding to the nostalgia factor, Dream-Works' first signing was George Michael, the former frontman for the boy band Wham! whose last hit album had been *Faith*, released in 1987. But Geffen believed in him, as he had in many others over the years—Donna Summer, Elton John—even when their careers had seen better days. He wasn't about to change his style. So when George Michael became embroiled in a nasty legal fight with his longtime label Sony, DreamWorks laid down $6 million to extricate him from his contract. It was a hefty expense for a company not yet on its feet, but the message was clear: DreamWorks wasn't kidding around.

With the DreamWorks deal in place, Seagram stock bounced back, and everyone came out beaming, no one more so than Geffen, who, as one source said, "played his cards perfectly and took Edgar."

"David Geffen is about four hundred times smarter than Edgar Bronfman Jr.," this person said. "And he knew how much Edgar needed the deal, with the departure of Wasserman and Sheinberg, who had a hold on Spielberg. And he packed it accordingly."

As for Bronfman: "He was a bit naive. He drank the Kool-Aid."

Perhaps, but he had Spielberg on the lot, a sequel to *Jurassic Park* in the works, and he remained in awe of Geffen, to whom he turned to help him pick a replacement for Ovitz.

Meanwhile, CAA's young guard was less than thrilled with the return of their now deeply mistrusted leader. The man who had said, so often, and with such passion and menace, "If you leave CAA, you're dead," had betrayed them. Now they wanted *him* dead.

With Ovitz out of the picture, Bronfman relied on Geffen's advice on who should run Universal Studios. The answer was Ovitz's partner at CAA, Ron Meyer. A high school dropout and former Marine, Meyer had the rare distinction in Hollywood of being beloved by all. He was genuinely affable and charming—a "regular guy" who went by "Ronnie" and favored jeans and flannel shirts. A true agent, Meyer put his clients (Tom Cruise, Whoopi Goldberg, Sylvester Stallone) first. He knew how to handle outsize personalities, temper tantrums over whose trailer was bigger than whose, and any other meltdown that might occur, at any hour of the day or night. Then there was the fact that Meyer—always good cop to Ovitz's bad—was not known as a tough negotiator. Some say he made even Bronfman look hard-nosed. With no experience running a studio, he would be looking for advice, which Geffen (and Katzenberg) would be happy to proffer.

As it turned out, Meyer had been in the midst of his own career crisis. Tired of being the backup guy to Ovitz, Meyer had his own dreams of ascendancy. Accompanying Ovitz to Universal would have been one possible means to move out and up, and when the deal fell through, Meyer told Ovitz that he was leaving CAA. Hearing this, Ovitz had said: "Well, if it means that much to you, go get the Universal deal back."

Meyer had then flown to New York, and over dinner at Bronfman's Upper East Side townhouse, pleaded his and Ovitz's case. As he talked, Bronfman began to see what it was Geffen was talking about, and realized that the soft-spoken, intelligent man across from him would, indeed, be perfect (and far less expensive than Ovitz) for the top spot. When Meyer concluded, Bronfman said: "If you feel so strongly about it, why don't you take the job?"

Meyer accepted on the spot, even knowing the irreparable harm that would be done to his relationship with Ovitz. For more than twenty years he and Ovitz had worked side by side. Their families vacationed together. Although Meyer was ready to move on, Ovitz was stunned by the news, which he considered a betrayal. Years later, on *Charlie Rose*, Ovitz said about Meyer's move to MCA, "I was very hurt. It was like I went through a divorce."

But even more than a breakup with a friend and business partner, the collapse of the Universal deal "set something in motion," Ovitz said, that could not be undone. The crown that he'd had his eyes set on for so long now, whose weight and texture he could practically feel, remained locked on the other side of the glass. But there were other crowns, and one kingdom in particular that beckoned.

CAA was not the only Hollywood agency in the throes of revolt. In the middle of the night in March 1995, a quartet of brash, rebellious agents at ICM packed up their things, shoved them into the back of a station wagon, and drove down Wilshire to start up their own agency, which they dubbed Endeavor. Not since CAA had been similarly established, in 1975, had anyone upset the Hollywood equilibrium so brazenly. The media was abuzz in a way that rivaled its excitement over DreamWorks. In fact, the two companies had much in common, besides being the red-hot new kids on the block.

Like DreamWorks, Endeavor fashioned itself as an alternative to its corporate-minded competition—CAA, UTA, William Morris. The agency would be smaller, more user-friendly, and reflective of the independent, no-frills (by Hollywood standards) tastes of its founders, Ari Emanuel, Tom Strickler, Rick Rosen, and David Greenblatt, none of whom had second homes in Malibu or drove Ferraris. Emanuel was the son of an Israeli pediatrician who had been active in the Irgun; his brother, Rahm, was an adviser to President Bill Clinton and would go on to become President Barack Obama's chief of staff.

Not long after Endeavor was formed, Katzenberg came by the agency for a chat, stressing the similarities between the two upstart companies. "We're the new guys," Katzenberg said. "We need to work together, help each other."

Soon enough DreamWorks and Endeavor were negotiating a deal for Endeavor's client Jeffrey Lane, who'd cocreated *Mad About You,* to sign a producing pact at DreamWorks TV. In keeping with the spirit of the times, when blockbuster sitcoms such as *Friends* and *Seinfeld* had networks offering, in some cases, tens of millions of dollars in development deals to TV writers, DreamWorks was showering big-name TV writers—*Ellen* cocreator David Rosenthal; *Friends* writers Mike Sikowitz and Jeffrey Astrof; Linda Bloodworth-Thomason and Harry Thomason, the husband-and-wife team behind *Designing Women*—with lavish deals. It was all part of DreamWorks' image as talent-friendly.

Or so it seemed. Endeavor soon found out that DreamWorks shared Disney's parsimonious tendencies. According to a high-level Endeavor source, when Lane developed his first show, *Ink,* about a divorced husband and wife who run a newspaper, which attracted the interest of Ted Danson and his real-life wife, Mary Steenburgen, DreamWorks refused to pay Endeavor its full agency packaging fee. A combination of back-end grosses and a percentage of a show's budget, packaging fees can be incredibly lucrative, and are often what keep the lights on at agencies. (Consider that on a hit show, agencies can make anywhere from $20,000 to $60,000 an episode.) Over time, this adds up. The William Morris Agency has made over $50 million in reruns alone from *The Cosby Show.*

Because Endeavor was still small and hadn't yet built up strong litigation or contracts teams, the agency couldn't fight back, and the deal was finalized as per DreamWorks' wishes. Endeavor, infuriated, swore never to do business with DreamWorks again, a vow that would, over time, prove harmful to DreamWorks. Little did Katzenberg know that in the upcoming years, Endeavor would emerge as the number one television agency in Hollywood. When I spoke with an Endeavor agent in 2008, he was still seething. "Endeavor *hates* DreamWorks," he said, and immediately brought up the story about Lane.

As the heat of August prepared to settle across Los Angeles, the end-of-summer rituals began to take shape: The agencies thinned out, as the town's dealmakers, toting scripts to be read by the pool at the Four Seasons, boarded flights to Maui and Cabo. The maitre d' at the Grill wasn't quite as crazed around lunchtime. This August, in particular, the mood was one of reflection—on what exactly had transpired in the last several months, some of the most tumultuous in Hollywood history. MCA had changed hands once again; a new order was gunning for power at CAA; Ovitz was a lame duck; and Wasserman had officially retired.

It was in this moment of momentary calm and collectedness that, on July 31, Ken Solomon, a DreamWorks TV executive whom Katzenberg had recruited from Fox, received a call at 5 A.M.

"Ken, you're not gonna believe this, but Disney just bought ABC," said Solomon's friend Greg Meidel, the president of Twentieth Television, Twentieth Century Fox's syndication arm.

"What?" Solomon said, speechless.

It was true. After years of doubting the wisdom of acquiring a television network—something Katzenberg had pushed for aggressively at Disney—Eisner had come around. Formidably so: Disney was plunking down $19 billion for Capital Cities/ABC, the very network with which DreamWorks had just signed a $100 million deal to coproduce shows.

The *Los Angeles Times* called the union, the second-largest merger in history, "a landmark merger that creates the largest entertainment company in the world." The *New York Times* described it as a "stunning surprise."

For DreamWorks, it was precisely that. It also meant, as Solomon put it, "peril."

DreamWorks' plans to provide a Saturday-morning block of animated kids' programming for ABC were quashed, as animation was Disney's bread and butter; indeed, it was soon announced that Disney would be providing ABC with a "full slate" of Saturday-morning kids' shows. (Ironically, DreamWorks had just raided two of Disney's veteran TV animation executives to spearhead that now moot effort: Gary Krisel and Bruce Cranston.) As for ABC looking fondly on Dream-Works' other programming, considering the bad blood between Katzenberg and Eisner and the fact that Katzenberg was considering litigation against Disney for breach of contract over the matter of his unpaid bonus, things did not bode well.

While Eisner clearly had bigger reasons for his decision — new Disney executives had been egging him on to make an acquisition, and TV regulations were shifting, making ownership of a network more lucrative for studios — at DreamWorks, there was a palpable sense that at least part of his motive was to draw blood.

"You felt that the motivation to buy ABC was because of Dream-Works," said Max Howard, Katzenberg's former colleague at Disney. "I think, for a while, the purchase of ABC seemed crazy. They paid too much for it.

"Why did they do it?" Howard mused. "Did they do it so they could control DreamWorks, stop DreamWorks from being successful?"

The feud between Eisner and Katzenberg now extended to Dream-Works. It "became a part of our everyday lives," said Solomon. "It was a small, personal company, and Jeffrey was our fearless leader, and we felt that he had been dealt with unfairly, both emotionally, and, I think, practically."

Besides its staggering price tag, the purchase of ABC was historic because it marked the first time that a studio was aligned with a Big Three network, giving Disney a distribution channel for its programming. At that point, only Rupert Murdoch's upstart Fox network was in the position of being able to distribute its own programming, as it was not considered a news network. (The Financial Interest and Syndication, or Fin-Syn, Rules placed a limit on the number of its own shows that a network could buy.) But the Federal Communications Commission was in the process of obliterating those rules. Disney would be able to produce and distribute an unlimited amount of its own content in lieu of other studios' offerings (including that of DreamWorks). The TV business would never be the same. DreamWorks' plans for an independent television studio suddenly looked ill-timed.

Forty-five minutes after speaking with Meidel, Solomon was on the phone with Katzenberg, who had just landed in New York. Katzenberg sounded, amazingly, okay about the merger.

"Don't worry," he told Solomon. "We'll be fine. Our content will rule. We'll make our way. It's not a problem."

Bruce Cranston, whose DreamWorks TV animation division—which had bulked up to a staff of eighty artists and writers—now seemed doomed, received similar reassurances. "Jeffrey's a very can-do kind of guy. He pretty much did not bat an eyelash, at least not publicly," Cranston said. "He said, 'Don't worry, we're gonna sell TV shows.' He was very grandiose—'We'll buy CBS. We'll sell shows to CBS. Don't worry about it.'"

Nonetheless, Cranston said, "A lot of wind came out of the sails at that point."

Publicly, everyone blew kisses. Because DreamWorks had to make it work. Although a clause in its contract with ABC stipulated that in the event of an ownership change, DreamWorks could opt out, it was unlikely that any other network would offer terms that were as generous as ABC's. A hundred million dollars in development funds, plus shared advertising revenue, was unprecedented largesse.

And so, despite the fact that issues of *Los Angeles* magazine, in which Geffen had lambasted Eisner as a "liar" and a "little bit woohoo" to journalist Robert Sam Anson, were still on magazine racks, Geffen cleaned up his act, telling the *New York Times:* "Michael Eisner is a very smart guy, very creative and now sitting on top of the most important media company in the world."

As for the issue of Katzenberg's bonus, he said: "For me it's about, Does Michael take care of his obligations and responsibilities to Jeffrey? If he takes care of those . . . I'm happy to say, let bygones be bygones. We have great relationships with people at Cap Cities, superb. Whether or not these relationships will be able to stay in place at Disney in the future is yet to be seen. We have in our contract the right to terminate . . . If it's bad, we'll leave."

Katzenberg also spoke diplomatically to *The New Yorker's* Ken Auletta, saying that he had to give Eisner credit. "I was his leading critic," Katzenberg said. "Everybody . . . starting with me, was wrong. We were all wrong. And it's not as if we were a little wrong."

The white flag elicited a personal phone call from Eisner to each of the DreamWorks partners three days after the deal was announced.

"Michael," Katzenberg said, in his first conversation with Eisner since his exit from Disney, "my feelings about this are that you and I had nineteen unbelievably great years together. And now we've had ten awful months. Let's not make it eleven."

"Nothing could make me happier," was Eisner's sugarcoated reply. But the show was *so* not over.

10

CULTURE CLASH

A s the contours of DreamWorks began to take shape, a stark cultural dissonance was felt between Katzenberg's Disney recruits and Spielberg's Amblin staff, many of whom—after recovering from the loss of their Shangri-la—stayed on to form the foundation of DreamWorks' live-action studio. It was the Disney worker bees, with their bureaucratic, industrious ways, versus the children from Spielberg's land of milk and honey. Nowhere was the divide more evident than at 9 A.M. on Mondays, at meetings run by Katzenberg in which members of DreamWorks' marketing, distribution, and production teams gathered to talk shop and, in the spring of 1995, surmise about a summer movie scene pitting Val Kilmer (*Batman Forever*) against Mel Gibson (*Braveheart*).

Monday-morning meetings, standard at all the majors, had never existed at Amblin until the arrival of Katzenberg, who was the only DreamWorks partner ever present. For both the Disney and Amblin alumni, it was like observing life from an alien planet. To the shock of Spielberg's camp, not only were the Disney folks awake at the un-Amblin hour of nine, they were *wide* awake, jabbering, writing things down, polishing off second and third cups of coffee. The Disney contingent, meanwhile, found their own jaws agape at the sight of the Amblin folks—led by Walter Parkes and Laurie MacDonald—who sauntered in (a little less punctually) as though they were showing up for a leisurely brunch at the Bel-Air Country Club.

"What you had was this weird mix of the ones of us from Disney, who are hyper, type-A-personality workaholics, with the laid-back, nobody's-here-on-Friday, it's-snack-time-again Amblin people," said one Disney expatriate. "So you put us all in a room, and I remember everyone from Amblin was sort of horrified, I'd say, at the level we worked at. And there was a certain level of us thinking these people were a complete joke."

One Amblin disciple referred to Katzenberg's coterie, disdainfully, as "the Disney memo people." (Company memos were another Amblin anomaly.) "It was like, Oh my goodness! What's happening? We're at Disney!"

More like the Gulag. How else to explain why the Jacuzzi room now housed a copy machine, or that Spielberg's beloved video-game collection had given way to a conference room? Gone, too, were end-of-year bonuses and lavish Christmas gifts. "It was different," said Bruce Cohen, who had left Amblin to pursue a producing career. "The corporate culture had come in. Everyone was watching spending all of a sudden." The blame was thrown on Katzenberg, who was only doing what any prudent businessman would do, and what DreamWorks' investors expected him to do: rein in unnecessary spending.

But what Amblinites considered hell on earth, new arrivals to DreamWorks saw in more celestial terms. The masseuse might be cutting back her hours, but there was still free lunch, a dog walker, daycare, and a dress code that outlawed anything remotely resembling corporate attire, a regulation that the "new," post-Disney Katzenberg adhered to with characteristic ardor. "Next time I see you in a tie, you're fired!" he would yell. Taking a cue from his new partners, he had relaxed his own wardrobe from suits to khakis. There was a big summer picnic that employees and their families were invited to, with face painting and rides for the kids, and a Dickensian Christmas party, also for *tutto famiglia,* complete with fake snow.

Rain Man producer Mark Johnson, one of the first to sign a deal at DreamWorks, recalled how different the environment was at Dream-Works compared to the staunchly corporate Paramount, where he'd previously been based.

"We'd all sit out in the courtyard, and there'd be Steven Spielberg, and there'd be Bob Zemeckis, and you're having this cool lunch in this wonderful situation. It was really amazing.

"There were these young PAs [production assistants], it was their first job in Hollywood, and I wanted to say, 'Enjoy this, because you'll never have this again.' You know, most places, you're in a cinder-block office where you're fighting over a phone and you're lucky if the water's free. Here you are [at DreamWorks], you're going into the kitchen having a candy bar, and you're walking past Clint Eastwood. It just doesn't happen like that anywhere else."

At the animation studio, which was housed in a building near the Lakeside Drive entrance of Universal's back lot, Katzenberg justified spending on creature comforts as a way to lure artists. Here at Club DreamWorks, fresh-baked cookies were served every afternoon —"You could smell the cookies—homemade chocolate chip cookies—through the hallways," said animator Richie Chavez. "Everybody would say: 'Do you smell them? Cookie break!' "—as, of course, were breakfast (bagels and lox), lunch (duck à l'orange), and, on the first Friday of every month, coolers of beer, which were rolled in for a party. Every Monday morning, fresh flowers were delivered for the staff to bring back to their offices and have a whistle-while-you-work kind of day. Terry Press toed the line, mandating that flowers were fine, but they had to be white. This was still a workplace, after all.

"The whole thing was to create a tighter-knit family than we had at Disney," said Chavez. "We were trying to create an identity. It was a bit of a David and Goliath story."

And this would be one well-fed David.

Cutting through the tribal differences of the former Amblin and Disney workers was a unifying sense that something unprecedented—even revolutionary—was at hand, and that they were in the thick of it. Whether they had arrived by default, from Amblin, or because of Katzenberg's wooing, they drank deep of the SKG Kool-Aid, determined to prove that there was, indeed, a third way in Hollywood; that the corporate hegemony of the major studios—with its strict hierarchies, endless variations on titles, VIP parking spaces—could be challenged. In Katzenberg's two-and-a-half-hour Monday-morning meetings, everyone fed off each other's start-uppy enthusiasm, believing fervently that this wasn't simply a job, but a calling. It became clear that the particular synergy of worker bee and aesthete just might produce something powerful.

Something else that the factions shared was the belief that they were not just different from the rest of Hollywood, but special, *better;* that the Dream Team metaphor extended beyond the partners. One former executive called the Monday-morning assemblage "a roomful of the best and the brightest. It was all the A personalities. That's what the three men wanted. They got it."

Another said: "It was the best room to be in. Everyone was smart, funny. We'd laugh and joke around, but we'd get things done. There was a kind of magic."

But was magic enough?

"It was a kind of crazy time in the industry and at DreamWorks," said Glenn Entis, CEO of DreamWorks Interactive. "I'd go to monthly staff meetings, and . . . you'd sit around that table and there's twelve entertainment executives each trying to build up a business from scratch. We had funding, we had DreamWorks' cachet, but we didn't have much else."

Even as the live-action studio morphed from Amblin into Dream-Works, expanding its ranks with new hires and adapting to a more Katzenbergian structure of meetings and schedules, the studio maintained the identity, and elite insularity, of Amblin. This was, there was no question, Spielberg's turf. The fact that, physically, DreamWorks was still based at Amblin added to this perception, and, it was felt, fueled Katzenberg's desire to get the Playa Vista studio built so that Spielberg could be moved to a place that had nothing to do with Sid Sheinberg or *Jaws* or *Jurassic Park*.

As Tony Ludwig, a former CAA agent turned producer, put it, for DreamWorks to evolve it needed a separate space, "even an office building in Hacienda Heights, just to get away from [Amblin], because that's the castle. And no matter, I don't care who you are, you don't live there, you're just the guest every day. You could feel that—that Steven lived there, and you're the guest. And I think that didn't help."

The prince and princess of the castle were Parkes and MacDonald, who, after initial reluctance about giving up "the best job in the world," as Parkes often referred to running Amblin, had come around when Spielberg promised that DreamWorks would be different from other movie studios, as would be the job of running it.

There was also the fact that DreamWorks—which was relying on animation to make most of the money—didn't intend to release as many movies every year as the majors, which subsist on a diet of more than twenty. DreamWorks would be making half that. This modest amount would allow Parkes and MacDonald to continue producing movies, and to operate more or less as they had been in the five months they were running Amblin before DreamWorks was formed.

Unlike Katzenberg, Parkes and MacDonald had no interest in the manic lifestyle of studio executives, who volley between meetings with producers and drinks with agents and see-and-be-seen red-carpet events, only to wake up and do it all over again the next day. Parkes was happiest working out a script problem on his computer, and both he and his wife put a high premium on spending time with their two children. These priorities had been accommodated at Amblin, and Spielberg saw no reason why anything should change at DreamWorks.

From the start, as DreamWorks' other divisions hustled to release product, a distinct lag was felt at live action. As 1995 wore on, no films had been given a green light, despite the fact that the company's business plan called for two live-action releases in 1996, a goal that now seemed impossible to meet.

Part of the problem was that Parkes and MacDonald were busy producing films they'd committed to before DreamWorks was formed—Sony's *Men in Black* and *The Mask of Zorro;* and *Twister,* at Warner Bros. But there was also the experience factor. Not only did Parkes and MacDonald have little experience working at a studio, neither did executives working under them, most of whom were young, in their twenties and thirties, and had either crossed over from Amblin or other production companies. The only executives that came from studios were Nina Jacobson, who'd been a senior vice president of production at Universal, and Bob Brassel, one of Geffen's former romantic partners, who'd proven his savvy at Warner Bros.

The fact that movies were not getting made was a cause for frustration.

"It was excruciating," said one former executive. "It was like, What are we doing?"

Another said: "It was as though we were waiting to pop the cherry. The first movie had to be the *right* movie."

When investors would show up to check in on what projects were coming down the pipeline, "We had nothing to show them," said another source. "*Nada.*"

Katzenberg, who had been building marketing and distribution teams only to have nothing for them to work on (Terry Press was telling her idle marketing staff to "Go home! Be with your friends! Redecorate your house!"), was starting to boil. According to several sources, the situation came to a head at a company retreat held at Shutters, the seaside resort in Santa Monica, where Katzenberg—waiting, wisely, until the controversy-averse Spielberg left the room—laid into Parkes. "Where are my movies, Walter?"

Underlying Katzenberg's frustration must have been the feeling that, were he in charge, this issue would not exist. Although Katzenberg himself (still) never expressed anger over it, people close to him frequently brought up that he had been wrongly "pushed aside" from live action by Spielberg.

Geffen used more colorful language, directed at senior executives: "Why the fuck is that [project] not happening?"

As executives mumbled excuses, Parkes, in his unflappable way, reminded Katzenberg that DreamWorks was about quality, not quantity; that he and MacDonald weren't about to start shoving movies down a pipeline just for the sake of doing so. (Spielberg was also behind this philosophy, having pledged to the press: "If we can't find ten good movies a year, we won't make five good ones and five bad ones. We want quality over volume.") Although no one said it, it was clear that the DreamWorks way was not going to be the Disney way.

Katzenberg wasn't one to raise his voice in front of dozens of executives. He kept his cool. But the tension between him and Parkes did not go away. On another occasion, when Katzenberg told Parkes that DreamWorks really should have a tent-pole summer movie on its release schedule, Parkes replied: "If this is the kind of place where you need to have a big summer movie, well, maybe, I'm not the right person for the job."

Whether or not Parkes was the right person for the job was beside the point. Spielberg thought he was the perfect person for the job, and that was all that mattered. For a man who, as one insider says, "falls in and out of love with people," Spielberg was enamored of his friends, who had filled the painful hole left by Kathy Kennedy and Frank Marshall.

It wasn't hard to see why. Parkes and MacDonald were, quite simply, dazzling. Beautiful, smart, sophisticated, they were Hollywood's Barbie and Ken, only more polished, more urbane, and brainy. They also had that thing that everyone in Hollywood tried, paid, and worked so desperately to have: taste. "You had to try to keep your jaw off the table," remarked one person who's been in meetings with the couple. "They were always beautifully dressed, they were chic, and they were good talkers."

Parkes, in particular, delighted in holding forth on subject after subject with erudite charisma. He was bookish and cultured, but in a boyish, even at times, nerdy, way that made him accessible to an Oreo-cookie-lover like Spielberg, who shared Parkes's love for movies and passion for storytelling. Here was someone who, like Spielberg, was inclined to jump up and high-five over a really cool scene in a script and natter endlessly over the brilliance of *Alien*. When it came to film, they shared a language, even if their interpretive tools were differ-ent—Spielberg spoke with his camera, Parkes with words.

"They complemented each other," said screenwriter Scott Frank, "because Steven works from the outside in—what, physically, is it go-ing to feel like, look like? And Walter works from the inside out, so the conversation begins more with the character."

If Parkes thought in terms of script and language, Spielberg thought in terms of visuals and emotion. Once, after a monster movie came out and bombed, a colleague asked Spielberg what he thought went wrong, expecting him to say something about the story or the direct-ing. Instead, Spielberg put his hands across his nose, flattening it out. "They should have made it look more like a cocker spaniel," he said. "Like this! And it should have had a sparkler on the end of its tail."

It was actually a very good note. The monster wasn't likable enough.

Parkes came in handy when Spielberg, as he was wont to do, would spontaneously blurt out a scene he'd just thought up but didn't know what to do with, as it didn't fit into the narrative of whatever film they were discussing. No problem. Parkes could easily figure out a way to contextualize it by adding a new subplot here, deepening a character there. Unlike most, Parkes wasn't afraid to get in the ring with Spiel-berg and spar over ideas. He also had no trouble telling the director that some of his ideas were harebrained or, worse, lowbrow.

"Walter wasn't afraid to bully Steven," said one insider, "with every-thing—his looks, his ideas."

Said another observer: "If an alien from space landed in a room with Steven and Walter, it would think that Steven worked for Walter."

Soon after Parkes and MacDonald arrived at Amblin, movies that reflected Spielberg's more adolescent sensibility — a film about "trees that attack"; or one about a Brinks truck filled with cash that crashes in a poor neighborhood (Spielberg was intrigued by the morality questions raised by the scenario: is it OK to steal money if you have none?) — began disappearing from Amblin development reports. For Spielberg, who wanted to stretch beyond the confines of the "blockbuster guy" stereotype, Parkes was someone who could prod him along. Like Kathy Kennedy, Parkes also understood that playing bad cop came with the territory. Spielberg's reluctance to deliver bad news (such as firing a writer or director) was well known.

However, Parkes's flamboyance, and his often self-serving sermons — he preached "the Gospel of Walter," as one person put it — made him a polarizing figure. Not everyone was charmed when Parkes would preface his comments by saying, "Speaking as the only WGA [Writers Guild of America] card-carrying member in the room." When, in meetings with screenwriters, he would refer to the structure he'd used in *Sneakers* (a Robert Redford film he'd cowritten and produced), writers would begin imagining their own structures, in which Parkes did not make it to the third act.

But Hollywood is a town where the ringing endorsement of a major player makes up for all shortcomings. And in Spielberg, Parkes had the biggest player of them all. One studio executive recalled being in a meeting with Spielberg, Parkes, and other studio honchos to discuss an Amblin film. Spielberg had remained distinctly unmoved by what anyone said until Parkes spoke. "Steven was like, 'Walter's right, Walter's got the most brilliant idea.' I was falling off my chair, sitting there, thinking, What kind of crazy world is it that Steven Spielberg is talking about how great Walter Parkes is? Everything he said, Steven was wildly enthusiastic about."

No one could miss the Freudian implications of the relationship between the nerdy boy-man who had, growing up in unkind suburbia, wanted "to be a gentile with the same intensity that I wanted to be a filmmaker," and this chiseled golden boy.

"Walter Parkes is Steven's idea of what he should have been — East Coast–educated, upper-middle-class family, good-looking guy, right wife the first time, not the second time," explained Tony Ludwig.

MacDonald was even more the real, genteel deal—"the ultimate shiksa goddess," as one studio head has said. She was in the mold of Spielberg's other polished, buttoned-down female protectors: Kennedy, Capshaw, Bonnie Curtis, his assistant turned producer, and Stacey Snider, president of production at TriStar, with whom Spielberg—who had no interest in Katzenberg's coterie of tough-cookie types—was also close. Spielberg let his appreciation for MacDonald be known, and in meetings in which MacDonald was, frequently, the sole female battling males and their egos, Spielberg would make a point of soliciting her opinion, making it clear to all that she was a member of his inner circle.

Unlike her husband, MacDonald was all business, no-nonsense; a straight-shooting foil to her pontificating partner.

"Laurie is a great reality check," said Frank, who recalled that while he and Parkes were writing the ABC series *Birdland*, "Walter and I would go off on a tangent and think it was really good. Then we'd talk to Laurie about it, and she would be, sort of, 'Wait, this doesn't work for X, Y, and Z reasons.' She can smell when an idea's not working or a character is wrong. She has a good instinct for that." MacDonald acknowledged this. "I do have good instinct," she has said. "I seem to know the right moment when you have to close the deal—though often I send Walter to do it!"

Like Parkes, she was most interested in filmmaking. During her stint as a vice president of production at Columbia, MacDonald had been frustrated by how little time there was to invest in individual movies, as executives ran themselves ragged trying to keep up with the dozens of projects that were in various stages of development and production. After four years, she'd quit and turned to producing, where it was possible to nurture one or two films at a time.

MacDonald's style was to downplay, deflect. In meetings, she tended to look down studiously at her notes, before squinting up from behind stylish eyeglasses perched on her perfect nose and succinctly delivering the verdict. She was no wallflower, but she measured her moves. Forceful but discreet. Smart but unpretentious. And the ideal partner for Parkes, whom she was willing to let run the show, until he needed a good reining in. "Oh, Walter!" she would say, affectionately rolling her eyes when Parkes would get a bit too carried away with his own hype.

MacDonald kept things real in other ways, making family a priority, and insisting that no matter what her and Parkes's work schedules were like, someone would always be there for their two children. At the kids' private school, she was just another mom, dropping the kids off or showing up for a function. She never made a show of it or played up her connection to Spielberg, behavior that was the norm in the elite environment of the Los Angeles private-school circuit, where the pristine Jaguars and Benzes line up every morning like the valet line at the Four Seasons, and where everyone is connected, by birth or otherwise, to someone famous.

Walter Parkes first came to Spielberg's attention over *WarGames*, the 1983 Oscar-nominated film that he wrote with Lawrence Lasker, his friend from college. The film—about a young boy who nearly starts World War III by playing a video game—naturally warmed Spielberg's heart. Not long after it was released, he invited Parkes and Lasker over to Amblin to discuss collaborating. When they left the meeting, Lasker recalled Parkes telling him: "Steven's very comfortable with us because he knows we don't want anything from him."

Parkes and Lasker were soon hired to rewrite *Peter Pan*, a film Spielberg was developing (unrelated to *Hook*, which he would later direct), and given an office at Amblin. Nothing ended up happening with the movie, but the same could not be said for Spielberg and Parkes, who, having discovered their "shared language," became friends, a relationship that was enabled by the fact that MacDonald and Capshaw traveled in the same social circles. Back in those days, being buddies with the most successful director on the planet was not taken for granted, and one source recalled that when Parkes and MacDonald—who by now had teamed up as producers—were first invited to visit Spielberg's East Hampton estate it was "a big deal."

It was on one of these heralded visits that Spielberg made the couple an offer that few could have refused. It was over the summer of 1993, while the two couples were watching *The Apartment* at Spielberg's Long Island lair. When Parkes launched into a sharp, detailed analysis of the movie, Spielberg had an epiphany.

"My God!" he said. "You should be running my company!"

Walter Parkes grew up as Walter Fishman next to Lucille Ball's. At Beverly Hills High, where he went as "Wally," Walter stood out as a little cooler than the other kids. He got As, seemingly without effort.

He played junior varsity basketball and was the lead guitarist in a rock band. And while everyone else sported polyester permanent-press slacks and button-downs, he cultivated a Beatles-ish look, wearing paisley prints, trench coats, and ascots.

In 1969 he entered Yale as Walter F. Parkes, adopting the name of his stepfather, with whom he was close. He majored in anthropology, but his first love was still music, and he fit in classes around local gigs with his new band, the Rockets. After Yale, he went on to graduate school at Stanford, where he studied documentary filmmaking. Fame, or a taste of it, came rather quickly—in 1975, the documentary he made about a group of American neo-Nazis, *The California Reich*, received a special mention at the Cannes Film Festival. Then came a profile of Parkes and his collaborator, Keith Critchlow, in the *Los Angeles Times*, in which the twenty-four-year-old Parkes was described as "perfect" for Hollywood. "He bristles with asides, interruptions and ambition that stick out like porcupine quills."

Critchlow seconded this, when I spoke to him years later, calling Parkes a "performer." While making their documentary, Critchlow said that Parkes "had a way of filling a room and, just sort of by his DNA, setting the agenda for the meeting and doing most of the talking."

When Parkes moved to L.A. and began writing scripts with Lasker, he was introduced to MacDonald through another screenwriter, Steve Zaillian, whose sister-in-law had roomed with MacDonald at Sonoma State. On their first date, they dropped by the *WarGames* set, but were kicked off. She eventually moved to L.A. and began her Hollywood career, working her way up to an executive gig at Columbia Pictures. In 1983, just three months after they'd first met, she and Parkes exchanged vows in a ceremony held at Parkes's childhood home in Beverly Hills. Parkes had moved on to producing and was having success—he and Lasker produced the Robert De Niro and Robin Williams film *Awakenings*, and *True Believer*. In 1990 his wife left Columbia to produce as one-half of Parkes/MacDonald Productions.

The live-action studio could have gotten off to a swifter start had Spielberg jumped into the director's chair, an act that would have delighted no one more than Katzenberg, who'd built DreamWorks' business plan around the idea of a Spielberg blockbuster every few years.

But Spielberg was taking a break, keeping his word to Capshaw, who was pregnant again (bringing the Spielberg-Capshaw brood up to seven). During DreamWorks' first year, Spielberg spent his time reveling in his enormous and multifaceted new playground: meeting with screenwriters to talk about movies, advising the animators working on *Prince of Egypt,* reviewing the architectural plans for Playa Vista, brainstorming about DreamWorks' restaurant-arcade business.

One area where he was particularly involved was DreamWorks Interactive (DWI). Now—like his rival and friend George Lucas (whose gaming company, LucasArts, Spielberg had consulted for)—he didn't just get to play games, he got to make them. The man who had worked his way up to level 15 of MechWarrior, and was a masterful practitioner of the subtle but precise wrist movements demanded by Microsoft Flight Simulator, was in heaven.

"Steven would brainstorm with us at our offices fairly frequently in those days," said Noah Falstein, a DWI game producer. "Sometimes we'd talk about a game as a reference and he would say he hadn't seen that game, so we'd give him a copy and he'd come in the next day talking about level 5 of the game. The next day he'd come in and talk about level 7. We could see the progress he was making . . . He was probably putting in five to six hours a day playing video games."

DWI, the joint venture with Microsoft (Patty Stonesifer, senior vice president at Microsoft, was a special consultant at the company), was made up mainly of Microsoft alumni, who gave up lucrative stock packages to move from Seattle to L.A. and be part of the coolest entertainment company in the world. "When I left to do Dream-Works Interactive, I thought, Wow, what a unique opportunity," said Alan Hartman, a game producer at Microsoft. "I knew it was going to cost me money. Microsoft stock was already going up. But I'd made money, I was happy. I was given a signing bonus by DreamWorks to compensate for some of the lost stock options. I went in with my eyes wide open."

The company was set up first in whatever office space was available in the animation building on the Universal lot (game producers found themselves in rooms wallpapered with *Prince of Egypt* storyboards), then in the Oakwood Apartments, a corporate housing complex (favored by child actors and their families) located on Barham Boulevard, across the street from Universal. The hope was to marry DreamWorks' creative talent with Microsoft's technological prowess to make video games for PCs and consoles, some of which, though not all, would be tied to DreamWorks' movies.

Besides playing games, Spielberg was pitching them, and in one meeting, he said: "Look, games are sort of one-trick ponies. You guys are good at playing the adrenaline card. But if you go to a movie complex, there are all sorts of movies—R-rated movies, comedies, thrillers. If we want to take games to the next level, we need to think about how to crack out of the shell. We need to come up with a game that has a different emotion. What about a comedy game? Or a game that elicits sympathy, where you feel bad if a character dies?"

Spielberg then went on to outline the loose concept of a game—called *That's Life*—that hinged on the basic interactions and decisions made during the course of a regular day (taking out the trash, making lunch, going on a date). To the producers, whose idea of entertainment was blowing things up, Spielberg might as well have proposed making a video game based on *The Bridges of Madison County.* "We listened with a little skepticism," said Falstein. "Nobody had done anything close to that before." Stumped, the producers consoled themselves over after-work drinks, but no one dared argue with the Master that a game based in the everyday world, where you played your very mortal self, was cockamamie. (At this point, *The Sims*, which would take this premise and run, becoming one of the best-selling video games of all time, was years off.)

"We couldn't shake the nervousness that we were making a game that was really only appealing to people like Steven Spielberg, who are so famous that they never have to go to the grocery store or wander around in the streets," said Falstein. "We joked that we'd charge a million dollars a copy and sell the game to him and Bill Gates and George Lucas."

To help the producers wrangle with such foreign elements as emotions and relationships, Spielberg suggested they hire an expert to write the script.

"Let's get Nora Ephron on the phone," Spielberg said one day. And so, in one synergistic, Hollywood-glazed moment, suddenly the relationship guru of the silver screen and writer of such tearjerkers as *Heartburn* and *When Harry Met Sally . . .* was writing a video game.

A few weeks later, Hartman and Peter Hirschmann, who'd been a production assistant at Amblin before joining DWI as a story editor, boarded a plane to New York to meet with Ephron and Spielberg, who was vacationing at his summer home in East Hampton. (Ephron, conveniently, had a home across the street.) It was the Fourth of July weekend, and when the men landed at JFK late in the evening, fireworks blazed across the skyline. They spent the night at a hotel in Queens that was surrounded by chainlink razor wire, and the next morning they were picked up by a town car that whisked them out of one of the seediest parts of New York to one of the most elegant. Spielberg's and Ephron's neighbors included designer Calvin Klein and financier Ron Perelman. The members-only Maidstone Club was down the street.

The first stop was Spielberg's, who welcomed his guests and gave them a tour of Quelle Farm—his peg-and-beam Pennsylvania farmhouse that had been transported and rebuilt on the lip of Georgica Pond on Long Island's south shore. "It's kind of a Stickley museum in here," Spielberg said, as he led them through rooms jam-packed with turn-of-the-century Americana and Rockwells. When the tour was over, Spielberg grabbed a cup of coffee from the kitchen and led the men across the street to Ephron's.

Over lattes in Ephron's living room, the group discussed *That's Life* and the challenges of interactive media—for instance, the necessity of multiple story lines that can interact, or play back and forth, with each other.

"It was actually a really good meeting," said Hartman. "But I think it was tough for Nora as a storyteller to wrap her head around branching story lines."

Back in L.A., the producers kept up their dialogue with Ephron, but as time went by, her next movie was beckoning (she was directing John Travolta in *Michael*), and she seemed to be losing interest in writing what could potentially be a two-thousand-page script.

Hartman said that although Ephron was consistently a good sport, "I don't know how much of that was because it was something that really appealed to her. I never got the feeling she was dying to do this. But when Steven Spielberg calls and says he has a project he wants you to help with, people fall into line."

That's Life was put on ice, but a Spielberg game that gained more traction was *Normandy Beach*, based on the Allies' invasion of Normandy during World War II. The game was yet another eyebrow-raiser, considering that the World War II theme was then virtually unheard of in the games business, whose biggest consumers were teenage boys, not war vets. The game was code-named *Beach Ball* in order to protect its premise, and Spielberg spoke enthusiastically to the producers about his visions for it, giving them a list of World War II movies—including *Tora! Tora! Tora!*, *Battleground*, and *The Longest Day*—to watch as homework.

Spielberg's father had fought in World War II and he had always been fascinated by stories about the war and its history, not to mention all the weaponry and combat gadgets. A few years earlier, when Spielberg was collaborating on the LucasArts video game *The Dig*, Falstein visited Spielberg at his home office and saw three books piled on top of one another on the director's desk. On the bottom was *Schindler's List*, by Thomas Keneally; in the middle was *Jurassic Park*, by Michael Crichton; and on top was the manual to the LucasArts game *Secret Weapons of the Luftwaffe*.

"*Secret Weapons of the Luftwaffe* was well thumbed and dog-eared, while the others looked brand-new," Falstein said.

Spielberg's role at DWI, as it was throughout the company, was limited to creative areas. The business of actually running the division was left, on the DreamWorks end, to Katzenberg, who found himself trying to make sense of a business he knew little about, as he simultaneously tried to kick that business into gear, quickly. The goal was to have video games on the shelves by Christmas of 1996, a remarkably quick turnaround time, considering that games can take years to produce. And the anticipation was that those games would make money.

"They had very, very ambitious goals for the amount of money they thought DWI should make," said Daniel Kaufman, co-COO of DWI, without offering specifics. "We had to get product out."

By the fall of 1995 DWI's debut slate was narrowed to four titles, including another Spielberg brainchild called *Someone's in the Kitchen!*, a kids' game in which players could whip up dishes (following recipes supplied by Spielberg's housekeeper) in a fantasy kitchen outfitted with singing appliances and a dog, TasteTester, that either keeled over in mock death or barked his head off in response to the finished product; a riddle-solving Claymation game for adults, *The Neverhood*; a title based on R. L. Stine's popular kids' book series *Goosebumps*, which included live-action sequences starring Jeff Goldblum and Isabella Rossellini ("Welcome to DreamWorks," Kaufman mused); and another educational kids' title, *Cooper McCue Breaks Through!* The games were all CD-ROM titles for Windows 95.

As per the DreamWorks formula, the games weren't just ambitious, they were costly. The development cost of *Someone's in the Kitchen!* was an estimated $2 million—more than twice that of anything else on the market.

But first there was the matter of getting the games out on time, an issue that became rather prickly in one meeting with Katzenberg over when the *Goosebumps* title would be ready to ship in order to have it on store shelves by the end of 1996. Katzenberg was stunned when he was met with noncommittal answers from the producers.

"Why the hell don't you know when exactly we can ship?" Katzenberg asked, according to Kaufman. He then launched into a lecture on *The Lion King,* a film on which he said he'd worked with hundreds of animators, had had hundreds of millions of dollars on the line. Still, he emphasized, "When I said it was gonna be in the theater the last Friday in June, then you could spend your five bucks, park your butt in your seat with a bucket of popcorn, and the movie would come on the screen. *You* just need to make *that* happen."

"Our answer was, yeah, that's neat, but software doesn't work that way," said Kaufman. "In a film, if you're running behind, you can throw a lot more animators on it and catch up. Microsoft has a phrase: Nine women, one month, no babies." In other words, it's a matter of time, not numbers.

What Kaufman and his colleagues were trying to explain to Katzenberg, obviously, is that software is a relatively unpredictable medium, where more people or more money doesn't necessarily result in a faster-made product. Because of this, software products in general are more loosely tied to their anticipated release dates, a phenomenon that is unheard of in the movie business, where movies are released regardless of whether, say, an ending seems tacked on or dialogue isn't entirely polished.

"In software, you don't know how many lines of code [the game] is, it might just have a bug," Kaufman said. "Ten more engineers doesn't necessarily solve the problem . . . We were trying to explain that to Jeffrey and it was difficult for him. He was not happy."

11

THE UNTHINKABLE OCCURS

K ATZENBERG HAD NO TIME for more headaches. And the dispute with Disney about his unpaid bonus was mutating into a real migraine. Then in September 1995, on the heels of Disney's purchase of ABC, Eisner named his successor to Frank Wells, i.e., his number two at Disney. His name was Michael Ovitz.

DreamWorks' two biggest personal nemeses were now in partnership, commanding the company that was DreamWorks' main professional nemesis. Who said this wasn't war?

It had all happened speedily. Eisner's interest in Ovitz had been re-piqued when he heard that Ovitz was in talks with Seagram to run Universal. Ovitz at Universal was not good for Eisner at Disney: Universal was the only other major studio with theme parks. Eisner knew Ovitz too well to want to compete with him. So he'd reignited the courtship. As reported by James B. Stewart in *DisneyWar*, he invited Ovitz to lunch at his home and put it to him plainly: "Why would you want to go to Universal when you could come to Disney as my partner?"

Both men were wary of what, exactly, a "partnership" would mean. Ovitz was no low-profile Frank Wells. And Eisner's difficulty sharing any amount of performance space was, by now, well known. But both were in need of splashy rebooting. Ovitz's ill-fated dealings with Seagram had left him with zero credibility at CAA. And since Katzenberg had left Disney, the company was hemorrhaging executives. Meanwhile, although Eisner's heart condition had stabilized, Disney's board was nagging him to name a successor. He needed to act. And act big.

From the minute he moved his Picassos into Wells's old office in the Team Disney building, installed the Calder mobile above his desk, knocked out a wall to create a balcony, and had the room properly feng shuied (a $2 million renovation), Ovitz's attention was directed squarely at the Dream Team. Eisner wanted him to solve the animation problem. Too many artists were jumping ship, heading not just for DreamWorks but other studios as well. Following *The Lion King's* billion-dollar bonanza, nearly every studio in town was scrambling to set up animation units. Warner Bros. was in on the act, having poached Disney's Max Howard, who'd overseen the construction of its animation studios in Florida, as president of its fledgling animation division. (Disney retaliated by suing Howard—unsuccessfully—alleging that he had misappropriated "trade secrets" and committed "fraud.") Fox had just finished building a $100 million animation facility in Phoenix and was at work on its first feature, *Anastasia.* Under the supervision of Amy Pascal, Turner Pictures was also preparing to churn out animated features.

The efforts to build talent pools at the competing studios drove prices higher, and suddenly animators—a traditionally scruffy, modestly compensated lot—were blinged out with high-powered attorneys, new cars (the parking lots at Disney and DreamWorks could have passed for that of the Four Seasons), and mortgages on designer homes in the Hollywood Hills. Artists who'd never before seen a $100,000 paycheck were now making triple, even quadruple, that amount. Animation stars such as Glen Keane, who'd drawn the title character in *Pocahontas,* were suddenly hauling in $1.5 million a year.

The animators took full advantage, playing offers from various studios against each other in an effort to drive up their salaries. After receiving an offer from one studio, an animator would call up another studio and set up an interview, get a higher offer, then do the same at another studio—by the end of the process, his or her original salary would have tripled.

"It was an extraordinary bubble. It was a moment," reflected Max Howard.

No one was more persistent than Katzenberg, who wasn't just shelling out dough, but locking artists into long-term contracts.

"To his credit, Jeffrey was very tenacious at trying to romance these people," Ovitz said. "And it is not difficult to shake the relationship of a creative person. And Jeffrey was expert at it . . . we were in a constant fight with DreamWorks at the beginning."

In response, Eisner issued a Whatever It Takes edict, shelling out as much money in salaries and re-signing bonuses as was necessary to keep artists from leaving, in some cases threatening to sue over breach of contract. Yearly bonuses were also introduced.

"I do recall people opening their bonus envelopes and jaws dropping," said Disney animator Floyd Norman. "Some people thought it was an accounting mistake."

In June of 1995 — the same month that Disney's latest animated feature, *Pocahontas,* was on its way to grossing a strong but unspectacular $141 million domestically (another film Katzenberg had overseen, with even greater attention than *The Lion King*) — Eisner spoke to Disney's Orlando-based animation group, opening his comments by asking if he should talk about projects or just pass out bonuses.

But as the exodus to DreamWorks and other studios continued, Eisner brought out the big guns. He turned to Ovitz, the master of talent relations, asking, "Can you save this? Can you handle this? Can you save that?" as Ovitz would later recall.

Ovitz did what he always did in these situations: he seduced, and he spent. He began meeting one-on-one with key animators and encouraged them to display their art in the Disney commissary. And he threw a party at his Brentwood home for the artists (Eisner frowned when he saw the bill), where he led them on "tours" of his art collection.

As a result of Ovitz's charm offensive, and a few dollar bills thrown their way, Disney top artists Keane, Andreas Deja (who'd drawn the characters of Jafar in *Aladdin;* Gaston in *Beauty and the Beast;* and Scar in *The Lion King*), producer Don Hahn (*Beauty and the Beast; The Lion King*), and the team of John Musker and Ron Clements (who directed *Aladdin* and *The Little Mermaid*) all remained put at the studio.

But others, especially younger artists wanting to be at the top of the food chain, succumbed to the seduction. Animators such as James Baxter (who drew Belle in *Beauty and the Beast*), Will Finn (the artist behind the macaw Iago in *Aladdin*), Duncan Marjoribanks (who created the villainous Governor Ratcliffe in *Pocahontas*), and Don Paul, the visual-effects supervisor on *Pocahontas,* were all DreamWorks employees by the end of 1995.

An even more pressing issue for Ovitz was Katzenberg's threat to sue Disney for breach of contract, which he called a "hot-button issue." He began addressing the problem soon after being installed at the company. Ovitz was many things, but he was above all an agent, a talent handler, and a fixer, and he knew that the money dispute between Katzenberg and Disney could have devastating results, particularly if it went to court.

In October, at the wedding of ABC president Bob Iger to newscaster Willow Bay, in Bridgehampton, Long Island, Ovitz—dispatched to the event by Eisner, who declined the invitation in an effort to dodge Katzenberg, who he knew would be there—made a point of seeking out Disney's former studio chief. Two weeks, he told him. He would resolve the bonus situation within two weeks.

Based on testimony that Ovitz would later give, he was determined, for many reasons, to avoid a public showdown. But it took persistence on Ovitz's part to bring Eisner around to the idea of at least opening up a discussion with Katzenberg.

Ovitz soon arranged to meet Katzenberg in the reception area of St. Joseph hospital in Burbank, across the street from Disney, so that the meeting would not attract attention. Over Diet Cokes and Fritos, Katzenberg made his case, calmly but firmly, stating that, according to his contract, he was owed a percentage of the profits of the films he'd worked on while at Disney. He said that money wasn't the issue; he simply wanted Eisner to honor his word. As Ovitz listened, he thought Katzenberg sounded reasonable. He said he thought they could work something out. Before leaving, Katzenberg instructed Ovitz to conduct any future negotiations on the bonus issue with Geffen.

When Ovitz reported the conversation back to Eisner, the Disney CEO wasn't pleased, but he agreed to settle for up to $80 million. Ovitz then met and spoke with Geffen several times, with Geffen making it clear that Katzenberg wanted $100 million—the amount that Eisner had warned him he'd be giving up by leaving Disney early. A compromise was reached, with both sides agreeing to $90 million. But when Ovitz relayed this to Eisner and his attorney and confidant Sandy Litvack, briefing them for forty-five minutes on his talks with Geffen, Eisner apparently had a rather severe change of heart. "I don't want to settle," he said bluntly.

There was nothing Ovitz could say to change his mind. The most powerful man in Hollywood, the man who could convince anyone, hammer out any deal, bring a client from tears to triumph, had been as effective as a wet noodle trying to jimmy a lock. Which is more or less what his old rival said when Ovitz relayed the news. "This isn't the old you," Geffen said. "You could close anything. You could get it done. Now you have no credibility."

For Katzenberg, for whom Eisner's obstinacy cut to the bone, this wasn't business, this was personal, intensely so. "This is just the beginning," he told Ovitz. "You have no idea what you're in for."

Neither knew then just how right he would turn out to be.

Nowhere was the spirit of DreamWorks more fully expressed—and challenged—than in the plans for Playa Vista. The sprawling grounds of the "studio for the twenty-first century" were envisioned as a film-making paradise, representing a new Hollywood golden age.

"We were going to have bungalows for producers," said Sandy Rabins, who worked on the architectural plans for the new studio. "We'd look at the layout and be like, Bob's [Zemeckis] going to be here, Gary's [David Goldberg] going to be there. It was designed like a big, Cape Cod–style ranch on a lake." (Rabins had already been charged with making Goldberg comfortable at his temporary office on the Universal lot, where she had a basketball court built for him and outfitted his office with a fish tank.)

"In the early days, DreamWorks was all about *people*," Rabins continued. "The sense was that all our friends were going to be here."

Spielberg, more than anyone, had been taken with the site on which he envisioned a completely state-of-the-art, creative showplace —MGM for modern times. When talks had commenced, Katzenberg had been put in charge of making them come to fruition. Geffen continued to question the rationale behind the enterprise. To him, the most business-savvy of the trio, there was not much sense in expending so much capital when DreamWorks could operate just fine as a virtual studio, with office space and borrowed sound stages across the city. But Spielberg wanted it—badly. So Geffen didn't push, and Katzenberg got to work.

Katzenberg had already commissioned an $85 million animation campus in Glendale—cozily situated a stone's throw from Disney—so he was less invested in Playa Vista. But the belief was that building Spielberg his own physical studio would give the director more of a creative stake in the company. It would make the DreamWorks dream real—and maybe keep Spielberg working more at home rather than for other studios.

But even for someone as driven as Katzenberg, Playa Vista came with daunting challenges. Environmentalists out to preserve the property's marshlands pitted themselves against the City of Los Angeles, which saw in the studio a way to create jobs and spike tax revenues at a time when the city was coming off the worst recession since the 1930s. When the city prepared an unprecedented package of tax breaks and incentives worth over $70 million to woo DreamWorks to Playa Vista, the opposition began firing off letters to the *L.A. Times.* One city councilman called the city's concessions a way "to make a lot of rich guys even richer."

Suddenly, the DreamWorks partners, who prided themselves on their liberal causes and, in the case of Spielberg, maintained a staunchly Mr. Nice Guy image, found themselves in the uncomfortable position of being perceived as evil corporate creeps setting out to bulldoze fragile habitats and oust frogs and other wetland creatures from their homes. In December of 1995, DreamWorks hosted the second most memorable press conference of its history. It was a dreary, rainy afternoon, but it was another DreamWorks Announcement, and so everyone came: hundreds of reporters; California governor Pete Wilson; *Titanic* director James Cameron (who was checking out space at Playa Vista for his production company); and George Clooney.

Spielberg, in a black leather jacket and baseball cap, was beaming. "When we decided to form a movie studio, I realized we had to have a physical studio," he told the rapt crowd. "The legacy of Warner Bros., Universal, MGM, Paramount, Disney, and Columbia has a direct connection with the real estate upon which rests their moniker." Later, the man who was always, like E.T., wanting to go home—which, until now, had always meant Universal—referred to the prospective studio as "our identity" and "our own homeland."

To appease environmentalists, who were protesting the development with signs reading "DreamWorks Wake Up" and "Spielberg Phone Home 2 Stop This Project," Spielberg said, "I also welcome every frog in Los Angeles to please come to Playa Vista. When the wetlands are complete, you have a home here, too."

Spielberg had big plans for his new residence. The twenty-acre "entertainment campus" would have a movie theater, a commissary, and fifteen movie and TV sound stages. There would be writers' buildings, the kind in which *Sunset Boulevard*'s Joe Gillis and Betty Schaefer worked side by side. Everything would be state of the art, with up-to-the-second computer technology and a fully digitized postproduction facility. As for his lake, it was no fishing pond, but an eight-acre body of water that would have to be built from scratch and that would be two-tiered—with a small waterfall splitting it in two—to keep boats (i.e., Spielberg stalkers) from trespassing.

Opponents of DreamWorks' plans loathed the lake more than other features, seeing it as land that could otherwise be used for housing or office space, and because it would be fenced in, it would be of no benefit to the public. But to the studio's future tenants, the lake was yet another promise of amazing things to come. A miniature architectural model of Playa Vista was exhibited at Amblin, and executives would stop by and marvel.

Recalled producer Mark Johnson: "They showed me where my building or villa was going to be, and where my boat would be to go over to the main building. It was like, Ooh! This is nice!" he said. "There was a dock. You could walk, but you could also get in your boat and go to the main building or go to the postproduction building or whatever. They were really grand dreams."

12

GEORGE IN SLOVAKIA;
JEFFREY IN EXTREMIS

———

WALTER PARKES HAD SAID there were "little problems." "Little problems that I don't want to become big problems."

But when producer Mark Johnson and screenwriter John Lee Hancock arrived in Slovakia, where DreamWorks' first live-action film—*The Peacemaker*—was shooting in June of 1996, Johnson said, "I feel like the door of the plane opened, and we walked into a buzz saw."

George Clooney was in meltdown mode. Having signed on to star in a film that Spielberg had personally requested him to headline, he now found himself in godforsaken eastern Europe in the middle of a very troubled production. One of many issues was that Parkes, a producer on the film, had taken to rewriting the *Peacemaker* script. When Parkes's rewrites would arrive by fax from Los Angeles, Clooney would be sent into conniptions.

"I can't believe this! He doesn't know what the hell he's doing!" the actor fumed, according to more than one report from the scene. "Had I known then what I know now, I never would have signed on for this movie!"

It is unorthodox in Hollywood for studio heads to send in script changes. But to Parkes, he was simply applying his skill-set as a screenwriter, which was all in keeping with the DreamWorks ethos of: we're all artists here. To Clooney, to have a "suit"—regardless of his pedigree—assuming the responsibilities of "talent" was wrong.

Whatever it might be called, there was nothing peaceable about *Peacemaker*. Clooney, still best known as the hunky star of TV's *ER*, and most comfortable on the small screen, was jittery. Meanwhile, Nicole Kidman, who had just finished working with Jane Campion on *Portrait of a Lady* and who now found herself on the set of an action thriller, was still behaving like the high-spirited Jamesian heroine she had portrayed, insisting that director Mimi Leder shoot dozens and dozens of takes.

Help, in the form of American studio executives, was thousands of miles and multiple time zones away, in Los Angeles. When calls from the set would come in to DreamWorks, they were like SOS flares. "I did get a phone call at 3 A.M., saying that 'We're in war, you've got to get up and solve the next plan of battle,'" said one DreamWorks source.

Parkes would have gone to Slovakia himself to deal with the no-longer-little problems, only he was busy producing *Men in Black* (its own special nightmare; Parkes and director Barry Sonnenfeld were at each other's throats) in New York. Besides, Clooney might have done something most un-Clooney-like had Parkes shown up in person.

With *Peacemaker*, which began shooting in May of 1996, the live-action studio's cherry was finally popped. The project had originated when investigative journalist Leslie Cockburn, who knew Parkes from Yale, had sent him a treatment for a story she and her husband, Andrew, were working on for *Vanity Fair*, about the high-stakes game of nuclear-arms smuggling in the former Soviet Union. From the start, *The Peacemaker* had been a chaotic production. Needing to be in theaters by the end of 1997 (a year later than DreamWorks had originally planned), it had been rushed into production even though its script was considered problematic. One issue was that the character of Dr. Julia Kelly (played by Kidman) — a brilliant, Russian-speaking White House wonk, who was the strait-laced foil to Clooney's wisecracking frat-boy Army officer — was underdeveloped.

"There wasn't much there," Leder lamented. Even in the final version, "there could have still been more there, even though Nicole brought much conviction and strength to her character," she said. But Leder had rolled with it, quipping, "Scripts are for sissies," as she headed off to Europe to shoot, not only her first feature (up to that point she had directed only for television, with credits that included *ER* and *China Beach*), but her first action movie.

"It was a joke, as in, who would need a script, going to eastern Europe to shoot a movie?" said a former DreamWorks executive. "The idea was that she was this tough broad who didn't need a script."

People at DreamWorks had another saying for how *Peacemaker* was getting made: "Fire, aim, ready!"

Kidman at that time was best known as the better half of Tom Cruise, who was then at the height of his fame. As such, she was more famous than Clooney. When the two actors walked through the streets of Bratislava, he was frequently mistaken for Kidman's bodyguard (according to a source close to Clooney, he was annoyed at how upstaged he was by the ethereal-looking Australian).

Even before arriving in Slovakia's capital city—a location producer Branko Lustig had chosen in order to keep *Peacemaker*'s production budget at $53 million—things were going backwards. Because Clooney only had limited time to film before returning to *ER*, his scenes had to be shot first, meaning that Leder had to shoot the very last scenes of the film—which involve Clooney and Kidman desperately trying to reach a ticking bomb—first.

"It's not how I wanted to shoot my first movie—to shoot the end first," Leder said. "Because the actors are racing through the streets of New York, and they're going, you know, they have to go at an extremely high voltage, high pace, so their acting, on the meter, is way up here. It's really high—it's a thousand percent. And they kept saying, 'Am I too high? Is it too over the top?'"

Parkes had been on the set then, bouncing back and forth between *Peacemaker* and *Men in Black,* which had its own challenges. Sonnenfeld, an eccentric ball of nerves who has been described as "openly neurotic," and Parkes were so at odds that "they weren't speaking," according to one person who worked on the film.

A month after shooting began in New York in May, *Peacemaker* moved to Bratislava, where things went from bad to worse. One of the first scenes Leder had to shoot was an eight-minute sequence called Demolition Derby. Among other things, the scene required blue screens, pyrotechnics, and luxury automobiles screeching through the cobblestone streets of the city and, eventually, blowing up. Leder had gone over the scene on storyboards numerous times before, but that didn't change the fact that she was a novice director facing a very complicated scene, with studio assistance five thousand miles away and a crew that seemed to speak every language but English. Not to mention that it took nearly a week to look at dailies, because the film had to be sent to Munich to be processed, and then sent back.

"Everyone had just arrived in Slovakia and was adjusting to time zones and really bad food and a less than perfect hotel, all that kind of stuff, and we're dropped into one of the toughest sequences," said editor David Rosenbloom. "Now we have a completely new crew and they're speaking a different language and there's all the special effects involved, with flipping cars and stunt work. It was really challenging. That was pretty tough for Mimi. Those were definitely her dark days."

"If we could have had everyone speaking the same language, that would have been a miracle," said Clooney. "I would have learned Slovakian if we could all have spoken it. There was Croatian and Slovakian, and we had a French crew. So it was tricky, because, you know, we're blowing up bombs and you want to make sure everybody is off the bridge. You know? 'Get off the bridge! We're going to be blowing up that bridge now!'

"'*I'm on the breedge!*'" he exclaimed in a mock French accent.

Not exactly what anyone had imagined when they'd signed on to make DreamWorks' first feature. Clooney had been asked to star in the film by Spielberg himself, who'd sent him a handwritten note saying, "This is our first project for DreamWorks. I wanted to know if you'd like to do it."

"Yes!" was Clooney's response, without even reading the script. He framed Spielberg's note and hung it on the wall of his home.

The actor had caught Spielberg's attention on *ER*, the highest-rated show in television, which Amblin produced. Once, on the set, Spielberg had been watching Clooney perform on a monitor, when he'd tapped the screen and said, "If you stop moving your head around, you'll be a movie star." With *Peacemaker*, he was offering to make that happen, paying Clooney $3 million, and clearing his schedule for him. (Clooney had been preparing to star in *The Green Hornet* at Universal, but the film was languishing, and a word from Spielberg extricated him, landing Clooney another $3 million, seeing as his *Green Hornet* deal was pay-or-play; i.e., you get the money, even if the movie doesn't get made.)

In initial conversations, Spielberg had floated the idea that he might direct *Peacemaker* himself (something he often does before he commits to projects; those who have been around long enough know not to take these flirtations too seriously). When Leder was hired, Spielberg told Clooney that he'd still be very involved in the making of *Peacemaker*, and that he would even direct second-unit action sequences, according to a source close to Clooney.

The choice of Leder—whose work on *ER* had also impressed Spielberg—caused some surprise in Hollywood, where everyone had been anticipating more big-name announcements when it came to DreamWorks' first ever film. "There was disparaging talk around town of how this big movie studio's first movie had a TV star and a TV director," recalled one agent. "People were surprised that they had hired Mimi. They felt that they could have gotten a much bigger director."

(In fact, DreamWorks had first approached *In the Line of Fire* director Wolfgang Petersen, but he'd passed.) Leder was acutely aware of the scrutiny she was attracting. "I think Steven probably had a lot of resistance," along the lines of " 'What, are you crazy?' I can only imagine what people thought about his decision to hire me," she said.

"I had a lot of experience; I had been directing in TV for ten years before I did my first feature. And I won an Emmy for directing 'Love's Labor Lost,' one of the big episodes from *ER* in its first season. And I'm sure people were saying, 'Why aren't you hiring a very big, established film director?'"

When Spielberg asked if she was up for *Peacemaker*, Leder said, "I was stunned. I said to him, 'Why do you think I'm the right person to direct an action movie? I don't direct action.' And he said to me, 'Yes, you do. You direct it every day on television.' Now who could resist that?"

The arrival of Johnson and Hancock brought great relief to the *Peacemaker* set.

"We were kind of on our own," said Rosenbloom. Leder "was really happy to see them. Mark provided great comfort to Mimi."

A routine developed whereby Johnson, Hancock, Leder, Clooney, and Kidman would sit down and hash out ideas for how to make the script work better. Then Hancock would go back to his hotel and write, and his changes would be faxed to L.A. for approval.

Sometimes, however, what came back from L.A. was not what Hancock had written. When Clooney realized this, and confronted Hancock about certain new changes to the script, Hancock insisted he'd made the tweaks at the last minute.

Clooney didn't buy it.

"OK, John, here's the deal," he said. "I'll do this scene if you can look me in the eye and tell me that this is a scene you wrote.

"Or," he continued, "that this is a scene you think we should do."

Hancock couldn't do it.

While *Peacemaker* was filming halfway around the world, back in L.A., DreamWorks' live-action unit was finally kicking into gear after its belabored start. Over the summer, a slate of films was announced, including—at long last—Spielberg's next projects, featuring a World War II drama, *Saving Private Ryan,* and a film about the true story of the African slave ship *Amistad.* The rest of the lineup, however, seemed anticlimactically reminiscent of Amblin—a big-screen version of Dr. Seuss's *The Cat in the Hat;* a comedy about a rogue rodent, *Mousehunt;* and one about a talking parrot, *Paulie.* Still, it was an occasion for an announcement, and DreamWorks staged another dog-and-pony show, this one on a Universal sound stage, where Spielberg and Paul Allen geeked out like teenage boys, playing a mockup of a video game (at one point, they crawled behind the monitor to check out the wiring); Geffen played host to investors; and Katzenberg gave a presentation on *Prince of Egypt.* He also noted that he'd just come back from one of his male-bonding vacations with other Hollywood types to Africa, where he kept getting calls from Michael Ovitz about his lawsuit against Disney. (Star litigator Bert Fields had advised his client to bring a satellite phone to the bush.)

Katzenberg had hoped to settle the matter out of court, but nothing Ovitz could say or do could convince Katzenberg that there was any hope of making headway with Eisner. In April 1996 he filed a breach-of-contract suit against Disney, claiming that he was owed more than $250 million (a tad more than the $90 million Geffen and Ovitz had settled on, only to have it rebuffed by Eisner) in bonus on all profits of films he'd developed at the studio. "If Frank Wells were alive, this never would have happened," Fields told the *L.A. Times.* Herbert Wachtell, a prominent New York attorney who was also part of Katzenberg's team, also commented, making the case that the "contract [terms] expressly requiring Disney to pay Mr. Katzenberg the profit-sharing in question are as clear and unambiguous as they can be."

Eisner had pushed Katzenberg too far. The previous January, at a funeral wake for Don Simpson, the bad-boy producer of such iconic '80s films as *Flashdance* and *Top Gun* (made by Simpson and his producing partner Jerry Bruckheimer under Eisner/Katzenberg at Paramount), all of Hollywood's biggest names—Barry Diller, Michelle Pfeiffer, Will Smith, Warren Beatty—had packed into the fabled dining room at Morton's, in Beverly Hills, to honor Simpson, who died of a drug overdose. When Katzenberg spotted Eisner, he approached him cordially, determined—as he always was—to move things forward. Once face-to-face, Katzenberg broke the ice with a lighthearted comment. "Well, he's happy tonight," he said, referring to Simpson, who loved a good party.

The attempt couldn't have fallen flatter.

"Jeffrey," Eisner said, looking disgusted. "He's *dead.*"

With that, the conversation was over.

Then, a few months later, Eisner had set up a meeting with Katzenberg to discuss DreamWorks' TV deal with ABC. The conversation was to take place at Eisner's ski chalet in Aspen. Katzenberg cleared his schedule, hoping that he would have an opportunity to discuss the issue of his bonus in a reasonable manner. Only, the meeting never took place. A day before it was scheduled, Katzenberg received a call saying that Eisner had to cancel. Furious, Katzenberg picked up the phone and dialed Ovitz: "He can't do this to me anymore."

With the army of DreamWorks behind him, Jeffrey went to work preparing for his biggest battle, one that showed no sign of being anything less than nuclear. He amassed an A-list legal team consisting of Fields, Wachtell, and Bonnie Eskenazi. Helene Hahn and other members of DreamWorks' legal and business affairs division were on the case as well, crunching numbers and counseling their boss. "I've found my love, and it's animation . . . and litigation," Katzenberg joked to *Newsweek*.

Producing his first animated film for DreamWorks, *The Prince of Egypt*, Katzenberg was fueled by feelings of anger and injustice that felt as biblical as the movie itself. He dove in like a man possessed. Or really, really pissed off.

"Jeffrey is not a very spiritual man, but *Prince of Egypt* is about as close as he may ever get," said Penney Finkelman Cox, who produced the film with Sandra Rabins. "He really believed in that movie like he believed in any religion. His work is religion and for four years, *Prince of Egypt* was his religion."

Katzenberg practically moved into the animation studio, throwing himself so passionately into the making of *POE*, as it was known, that the filmmakers joked he was the film's "personal trainer." He sat in on pitch meetings (where artists pitch sequences of a film, scene by scene, using sketches pinned up on corkboards); he worked with the animators on scenes, such as the one in which young Moses and King Rameses II (in the movie, Moses is Rameses' adopted sibling) mischievously drop water balloons out of a palace window (Katzenberg had performed similar acts on passersby from his apartment on Park Avenue while growing up in New York City). He weighed in on the most minute of details, pointing out, say, that the queen's mouth was "way too big," according to one artist. He cajoled the actors, trying to get Val Kilmer (the voice of Moses) to whip it up more in the recording studio. (Kilmer's habit was to read his lines sitting motionlessly in the dark booth while smoking a cigarette.) To show the animators the level of emotion he wanted in a scene where Moses crumples against a wall and dissolves into tears, Katzenberg slammed his own body into a wall.

But what really drove Katzenberg was the Bible story itself. With minor creative liberties, *Prince of Egypt* told the story of how Moses, after discovering he is Hebrew, broke away from the older, domineering Rameses and followed God (God, in this case, being Steven Spielberg). The similarities were lost on no one. One of the animators even drew a cartoon depicting Katzenberg as Moses, confronting Eisner as Rameses. The caption read: "Let my people go!"—an allusion to Katzenberg's raid of Disney talent. Like his biblical forebear, Katzenberg had endured the hardships and challenges of a journey that ultimately led him to the promised land, i.e., DreamWorks, a place free of corporate shackles, full of lavish perks, and where he, finally, had the freedom to rule. If at one time Katzenberg had been the Zion King (as Disney artists had joked), he was now the Prince of Egypt. And he was preparing his return to the throne. It wasn't just Eisner he was out to show this time. His energies were also directed toward his "friends" who had engineered his second exile—from DreamWorks' live-action studio: David Geffen and Steven Spielberg.

Katzenberg was determined to show that his partners had it wrong, that he was as much a creative maestro as an executive powerhouse; i.e., that he could make, not just commission, art. He wanted respect, of the sort that Spielberg and other "talent" got. And with *Prince of Egypt*, he was going to show that he deserved it.

POE might as well have been called the un-Disney movie, which was, of course, largely the point. Katzenberg outlawed talking animals. The Hebrew and Egyptian characters in the film were realistically drawn: historical details were accurate thanks to extensive research and a trip to Cairo. The film's tone was sophisticated, grown-up. Emotions were expressed with nuanced depth: when Moses and his people emerge from the Red Sea and the waters close upon the Egyptians, the Hebrews don't jump for joy or break out into song; rather they weep, crumble, smile wearily. There were quicker cuts from scene to scene, a technique borrowed from live-action filmmaking. The whole look of the film was something that could not quite be called cartoony. For visual inspiration, the artists had studied the painterly visuals of David Lean's *Lawrence of Arabia*, nineteenth-century illustrator Gustave Doré's Bible woodcuts, and Monet, all of which were reflected in moody Egyptian vistas.

Everything was deliberate, and everything was about dynamiting Disney traditions. Katzenberg even went so far as to pin up character designs from *Prince of Egypt* on the wall, next to those from his alma mater. When he led visitors on tours, he pointed to the drawings to stress how DreamWorks was advancing beyond Disney's technique.

"He'd give these tours and talk about how we were making a break with Disney," said DreamWorks' cohead of technology, Dylan Kohler. "He'd show the different proportions of noses. Or say, 'Here's how Disney does heads, and here's how we do heads. Look how much longer these faces are!'"

"This movie would not have been appropriate had I been at Disney. In no way, fashion, shape, or form would this fulfill the mandate of the Disney fairy tale cartoon," Katzenberg said, adding that comparing Disney films to *POE* was like comparing "apples to submarines."

Katzenberg's war cry was infectious, and the artists, many of whom themselves came from Disney, joined in the rally. "*Prince of Egypt* was our first project, we were putting the flag on top of the mountain," said visual-development artist Paul Shardlow. "It was nothing Disney would have done. We all felt the call to stick it to Disney."

But Katzenberg's feelings toward Disney were complicated. While he undeniably detested Eisner, he had adored the Walt Disney Company, for its history, might, and all-American brand. He had always loved taking trips to Disneyland, even if he just whizzed through in less than an hour. He adored hearing about new rides that Disney's theme-park designers, the Imagineers, had cooked up. (After his departure the Imagineers had sneaked him into the park to test out a new ride.) Infused in this love was a belief that Disney people were better than everyone else—hence his muscular poaching efforts. Wherever possible he wanted Disney artists on his movies.

"He *had* to have Disney writers write the *Prince of Egypt* script," said Finkelman Cox. And so the *Pocahontas* writing team of Susannah Grant and Philip LaZebnik was hired to write the screenplay; Hans Zimmer, who'd scored *The Lion King,* wrote the music to the film; and Stephen Schwartz (another *Pocahontas* alumnus) provided the lyrics. Codirector Brenda Chapman was a Disney veteran, and her partners Simon Wells and Steve Hickner were Amblimation émigrés who had worked with Katzenberg on *Who Framed Roger Rabbit.*

Katzenberg also continued the quest for celebrity voices that he'd begun at Disney, stepping it up a notch so that the cast list for *Prince* read like the seating chart at the Governors Ball: Kilmer (*The Doors* and *Batman Forever*) and Ralph Fiennes (*Schindler's List, The English Patient*) voiced the biblical boys, and the supporting cast included Sandra Bullock, Jeff Goldblum, Michelle Pfeiffer, Helen Mirren, Steve Martin, Martin Short, Danny Glover, and Patrick Stewart.

Aware of the potential for controversy given the film's subject matter, Katzenberg took a proactive stance, soliciting expert views on how the story should be portrayed. He and Finkelman Cox, who was in charge of the outreach effort, went on the road, meeting with hundreds of religious leaders, scholars, clerics, and even a kabbalah expert. They went to the Vatican (twice), sat down with staunch conservatives such as Jerry Falwell and Pat Robertson (the artists refused to come to work those days), and conferred with members of Harvard's Divinity School.

The torrent of opinions led to lengthy discussions on issues ranging from what God's voice sounded like to what kind of hair Moses had. (A meeting over the latter issue lasted six hours as the artists studied various hairpieces.) As to the Almighty's pipes, after a bunch of ideas were tossed (that God sound like a woman or like many people talking at once), in the end the higher power spoke in the voice of whoever addressed him. This meant that God mostly sounded like Val Kilmer.

If DreamWorks was advancing the game with traditional animation, Pixar—and by extension, Disney, which had a distribution arrangement with the company—had been first out of the gate with computer-generated imagery, or CGI. Pixar's *Toy Story* was the first feature animated film in history that was not hand-drawn but made by computer graphics. A stunning success when it was released in the fall of 1995, the film grossed $191 million domestically on a minuscule budget of $30 million. (Terry Press, who'd been at Disney when the film was released, had overseen its marketing campaign, which included a three-story-high *Toy Story*–themed attraction in the historic El Capitan Theater in Hollywood.) The *New York Times* gushed that owing to its "exultant wit" and "distinctive voices," *Toy Story* was an "aural and visual delight," as well as "the sweetest and savviest film of the year." In the wake of *Toy Story*, Disney renegotiated its three-picture deal with Pixar, becoming a fifty-fifty partner with the studio on its next five films, though Disney retained the rights to merchandise and any sequels.

Katzenberg was no stranger to *Toy Story*. While he was at Disney, he'd negotiated the distribution deal between Disney and Pixar, and he was the only one at Disney who believed the film wasn't a lost cause when other executives were arguing that it be scrapped. After one early viewing, when the film was universally declared a "mess" by both Disney and Pixar executives, Katzenberg lobbied on behalf of the film, suggesting that one way to salvage it would be to rework the relationship between the film's two main characters, the cowboy Woody and the space-toy astronaut Buzz Lightyear, so that they were buddies. Katzenberg had urged Pixar creative head John Lasseter and his team to watch some of the most iconic buddy movies of all time: *48 Hrs.*, with Nick Nolte and Eddie Murphy, and *The Defiant Ones*, the 1958 classic starring Tony Curtis and Sidney Poitier.

When Katzenberg segued to DreamWorks, he kept in touch with the Pixar gang, keeping them separate from Disney—at least at first. When Lasseter and Andrew Stanton, an artist and screenwriter on *Toy Story*, traveled from Pixar's base in Emeryville, California, to L.A. to do postproduction work on *Toy Story*, they stopped by Katzenberg's new office at Amblin. The meeting was friendly, and Katzenberg chatted about what DreamWorks was up to, asking in turn what Pixar had in the hopper. Lasseter and Stanton told him about a bug movie—a humorous, reverse twist on the Aesop fable about ants and grasshoppers, in which, rather than the lazy grasshoppers learning from the industrious ants, the ants are the victims, forced to liberate themselves from the tyrant grasshoppers who steal their food every year. When Katzenberg asked them when the film would be released, Lasseter said Thanksgiving of 1998. Katzenberg noted that that was when *Prince of Egypt* was scheduled for release.

In March of 1996, when Lasseter received a Special Achievement Award at the Academy Awards for his pioneering efforts in CGI, Katzenberg sent him a chocolate Mr. Potato Head (one of the characters in *Toy Story*) with the note: "You've Got a Friend," referring to the movie's theme song.

The success of *Toy Story* was a wake-up call within the animation industry that CGI was more than just an experimental new format. Here, it seemed clear, was a compelling filmmaking tool that, despite the carping of animation traditionalists, had staying power. *Toy Story* was the first major sign that CGI was no longer a sideline player. "It showed a wealth of possibilities," said David Silverman, a director for *The Simpsons,* who would go on to work at both DreamWorks and Pixar. "And if you had any sense at all, you realized it was only going to get better."

Katzenberg, an ardent devotee of traditional animation, was nonetheless perceptive about CGI's promise. In the spring of 1996, DreamWorks bought a 40 percent stake in Pacific Data Images (PDI), a special-effects and computer-animation house in Palo Alto. The plan was for DreamWorks to simultaneously produce traditionally animated films in L.A., and CGI films up north. Add to Katzenberg's hectic schedule weekly flights on the DreamWorks jet up to San Francisco. (The plane was actually Geffen's Gulfstream IV, turned over to DreamWorks, which paid for maintenance and operating expenses.) The trips were utterly efficient. Katzenberg would leave at 7 A.M. and be back in L.A. in time for lunch.

The flight was less than an hour and a half, but to executives at DreamWorks, it was a valuable, and rare, amount of uninterrupted time to spend with Katzenberg. "Executives would find excuses to go to PDI," said one insider. "There would be a little struggle, sort of a test of who got the seats. It was really about having a conversation with Jeffrey. DreamWorks is a cult—the cult of Jeffrey Katzenberg. People who do well there really work hard for Jeffrey's favor." The Dream-Works jet was one place to curry it.

Then again, being on a plane with Katzenberg was only about one thing: work. "When I would go on airplanes with him, it was torture for me, because he'd want to do work," said one former DreamWorks employee. "If it wasn't about work, there'd be uncomfortable silences."

At Disney, executive Marty Katz had once tried to knock out Katzenberg—who was taking medication after hurting his neck exercising—with painkillers on a flight from London to L.A., but it had no effect on the robo-exec, who "was still working, and writing, and reading," by the time Katz gave up and went to sleep. When they landed in L.A., Katzenberg suggested that his colleague cancel his car service and accompany Katzenberg back to the office. "I said, 'What do you mean?'" Katz recalled. "'We've been flying nonstop for thirty-six hours! I need to go home, change, go to sleep!'"

The DreamWorks source said that being on a plane with Spielberg was more laid-back. "You get on a plane with Steven Spielberg, and he'd ask about your family, your life . . . I would get to know more about Steven, and he'd get to know more about me than Jeffrey ever would, and I'd only see him three times a year."

During one expedition up to PDI, Katzenberg announced Dream-Works-PDI's debut production. The project had been pitched by Nina Jacobson, a live-action executive at DreamWorks, who sold Katzenberg on the idea of making an ant film, specifically: "a nonconformist in a world of conformists—and the lead would be Woody Allen." After Katzenberg described the project, there was a confused silence. Everyone in the room was well aware that Pixar was at work on *A Bug's Life*. Finally, one PDI employee raised his hand and addressed the elephant in the room.

"Um," he began. "Does it bother you that Pixar's also doing a film about ants?" he asked.

Katzenberg didn't skip a beat. "No!" he said with a mixture of diplomacy and force. "In fact, I think it's great, because ours is gonna be better!"

When the news got back to Pixar, Lasseter was shocked. Feeling completely betrayed, he picked up the phone.

Katzenberg "hemmed and hawed," according to Lasseter, and "started talking about all this paranoid stuff—that Disney was out to get him . . . He said he had to do something. That's when I realized it wasn't about me. We [Pixar] were just cannon fodder."

In a company meeting, Lasseter laid into DreamWorks. "It was pretty mean-spirited," said a former Pixar employee. "There was a lot of nasty stuff about Jeffrey and PDI."

Katzenberg was hardly above borrowing ideas. But in the case of *Antz*, evidence disproves that he was, in fact, ripping anything off, although there's no denying that he was clearly aware that Pixar was making *A Bug's Life*.

Screenwriter Zak Penn—who wrote the original treatment for *Antz* with Jacobson—was in New York City with Jacobson the day they settled on the story for an animated movie that Jacobson had come up with. According to Penn: "Nina and I went to this little park in Battery Park City where they have all these little creatures—it's like a sculpture garden in a kids' playground, where there are all these tiny little creatures made out of bronze that are on the ground, and the kids can play with them. And we thought it was so trippy, and *Antz* kind of rolled out of that."

Penn, who grew up on the Upper East Side block where Woody Allen lived, and who was a devoted fan of the filmmaker, suggested the main character be based on Allen. He also suggested contrasting Allen's outspoken, individualistic persona with a repressive, Orwellian ant colony.

"I think it's possible that Jeffrey *did* want to do something to compete with the Pixar movie," Penn admitted. "But the idea of doing a Woody Allen movie in an ant colony—Orwell and Woody Allen are my favorite things."

Whatever the film's origins or motivations, Pixar ultimately had the upper hand, as *A Bug's Life*, which had been in production for some time, was due for release in November of 1998. DreamWorks planned on releasing *Antz* the following March.

Nonetheless, *A Bug's Life* would still be competitive with *Prince of Egypt*, also due out in November, a fact that greatly concerned Katzenberg given the untraditional nature of his film.

Katzenberg's anxiety, doubled with his desperation to win, reportedly compelled him to call Lasseter and ask him to move the release date for *A Bug's Life*, so that *POE* would have an open run. In exchange, Katzenberg said, he would stop production on *Antz*. Lasseter refused, as did Steve Jobs, Pixar's CEO.

"Jeffrey called us and asked us to convince Disney to delay the release of *A Bug's Life* beyond the holiday 1998 season because that's when he wanted to release *Prince of Egypt*," Jobs said. "He said if we did that, he would kill *Antz*. And we said, 'Don't go there.'" (Katzenberg denied making any such calls.)

Katzenberg was going to have to find another way to protect *POE*, which he did by moving its release up a month, to December 18. Disney retaliated by moving its remake of *Mighty Joe Young*, a kids' movie about an ape on the loose in Hollywood, to the same month.

Meanwhile, production on *Antz*, which was written by Chris and Paul Weitz, raced forward. "We'd get up at five in the morning and get on the DreamWorks jet with Jeffrey, who was already on his tenth can of Diet Coke. He was up!" said Paul Weitz, recalling the trips.

Not only was Katzenberg awake, but he was "very specifically addressing lines of dialogue. 'Line 7D, I think we need a third alternate on that for when we go to record with Gene Hackman,'" said Chris Weitz. "And we'd be cringing as this tiny jet zipped along."

Said Paul: "He weighed in on every single part of the process . . . I remember him giving us notes on the size of the pupils of the ant characters. He's really detail-oriented. I do believe he's respectful to the director of animated films, but at the same time, if you read David O. Selznick's old memos about *Gone with the Wind*, they're voluminous. Jeffrey would not have been outdone by Selznick in his attention to detail."

13

THE NOT SO LONG GOODBYE

B Y THE END OF 1996, as DreamWorks was still a year away
from releasing any films, Disney's own film division, now under the stewardship of Joe Roth, was enjoying a strong year
with live-action "event" pictures (Roth had no interest in Katzenberg's
"singles" and "doubles" philosophy) such as *101 Dalmatians*—starring Glenn Close in full diva drag as Cruella De Vil—the biggest hit
of the holiday season, and *Ransom,* a Mel Gibson thriller: both made
$136 million. Disney's animation unit was also powering on Katzen-
bergless, even if it was beginning to show signs of vulnerability—*The
Hunchback of Notre Dame* managed to squeak by the $100 million
box-office bar, but it was no *Lion King*.

But despite the rosy reports in the *Hollywood Reporter,* one Hollywood buddy story in particular was not going according to script.
"The first day I got to Disney, nothing was like Michael Eisner said
it would be," Michael Ovitz would divulge years later, to *Vanity Fair's*
Bryan Burrough. "The day I went there, [top Disney executives] Steve
Bollenbach and Sandy Litvak refused to report to me"—as had been
stipulated in Ovitz's contract. "Michael, instead of backing my play,
said, 'Do you want to back out now?' I said, 'Michael, I've already left
CAA. What might you be smoking?'"

Eisner had regretted his decision almost as soon as he'd made it,
irritated by how much of an—*surprise!*—agent Ovitz was. Always,
it seemed, he was spending money, and always, Eisner felt, he was in
search of a big, splashy deal to announce. Some he pulled off, such
as signing Martin Scorsese and his next two pictures to Disney for
$11 million. But most other deals he tried to make were rebuffed. Dis-
ney did not buy the management company Brillstein-Grey Entertain-

ment. Or the L.A. Lakers. Or the record company EMI. And without deals, Ovitz was, well, average. Deals were his forte. He didn't seem to grasp the more subtle complexities of running a media behemoth. Nor was he winning points with colleagues. In meetings, he would hand out copies of his bible—Sun Tzu's *The Art of War*—and say: "Read this. It will help you understand *me*." And at a company retreat in Orlando, he refused to get on a bus transporting everyone to an event, insisting on being chauffeured in his own car, even though the destination was ten minutes away—and even Eisner was on the bus. When other top executives badmouthed him behind his back, Eisner abandoned him, withholding turf and responsibilities.

The press—less intimidated by the former agent now that he seemed that most un-Ovitzian thing: vulnerable—was also gunning for Ovitz. Scathing stories ran in *Vanity Fair, Newsweek,* and the *New York Times.* After Ovitz courted Jamie Tarses, NBC's number two programming executive, to run ABC—Tarses was the hottest up-and-comer in television, associated with hits such as *Friends, Mad About You,* and *Caroline in the City*—stories ran alleging that Ovitz had urged Tarses to threaten a sexual-harassment lawsuit against NBC West Coast president Don Ohlmeyer, so that NBC would release her from her contract. (According to *DisneyWar,* Tarses' boyfriend at the time, TV producer Robert Morton, who was also a client of Ovitz's, told Ovitz that Tarses was already contemplating such an action.) Ovitz would deny this, but *Time* ran a story in which Ohlmeyer, believing Ovitz was the source of the leak, called Ovitz "the Antichrist."

Eisner was beside himself over the press coverage (stories also ran in the *New York Post* and *New York* magazine), all the more so when he received a letter from General Electric chairman Jack Welch (GE owned NBC), complaining about ABC's behavior. As DreamWorks watched this drama unfold, Geffen couldn't stay on the sidelines. "Apparently, Don Ohlmeyer thinks more highly of Michael Ovitz than I do," Geffen remarked to reporters. As Ovitz was no longer Spielberg's agent, there need be no attempt at diplomacy. Geffen took the gloves off, going after Ovitz in the press with the same vitriol he'd been, up until now, reserving for Michael Eisner.

Ovitz became aware of the target on his head when rumors about his family began making the rounds of the Hollywood gossip circuit. According to *The Operator,* believing Geffen was the source, Ovitz called Barry Diller and asked for advice.

"Now I hear he's going around town saying terrible things about my children," Ovitz said. "How can I make this guy stop?"

In a subsequent conversation with Diller about Geffen, Diller jokingly remarked that if Ovitz wanted Geffen to stop the badmouthing, he should just threaten to smack him. Later, Ovitz phoned Geffen. He wanted to sit down and talk; work things out. Presumably relishing the idea of a good mano a mano confrontation, Geffen invited Ovitz to lunch at Amblin.

But on the day of the appointed meal, whatever illusions Ovitz had of letting bygones be bygones were immediately shattered. Almost as soon as he took his seat in DreamWorks' private dining room—a small, rustic space, combining unassuming elegance with *Robinson Crusoe* simplicity—Geffen laid in, lambasting Ovitz for seemingly every wrong he'd ever committed against Geffen, all the way back to the fiasco over *Personal Best* in 1982.

Ovitz sat, stunned. For a while he didn't say anything, he just listened to Geffen's tirade. Then he delivered his own lecture: "You're so smart, so bright, so aggressive," he told Geffen. "I wish to God you could take all your venom and turn it into something positive.

"Your whole life is negative. It's not enough for you to win. You have to have everyone else do poorly around you. They have to do badly. I don't get that."

Then, recalling Diller's advice, he threatened to beat Geffen up if Geffen didn't stop saying negative things about him and his family.

Geffen was shocked. "If you so much as touch me, I'll have you arrested," he said simply as he got up and left the room. Lunch was over.

Back in his office, Geffen began working the phones madly, telling everyone that Ovitz had threatened him. Diller commented that Geffen was "so insane over the moon that he frightened me." Diller was so afraid of further provoking Geffen's wrath that at first he did not confess to him that he'd been the one who'd inspired Ovitz's threat.

But Geffen was the least of Ovitz's problems. By late 1996, the situation with Eisner had deteriorated, despite various overtures by Ovitz. "I don't have a job," he'd said plaintively over dinner with Eisner on one occasion. "Just give me something to run." He sent Eisner a seven-page handwritten letter outlining his grievances. But the epistle did nothing more than further irritate Eisner. By now, Eisner was telling the Disney board that Ovitz had to go, even as he professed to reporters, and on *Larry King Live*, that things between the two couldn't be peachier.

The charade didn't last long. By December, Ovitz stepped down, in a "mutual" agreement with Disney. The obits ran fast and furious in the press, which, after years of being manipulated by Ovitz, relished the moment. Unnamed sources, all "top executives" and "veterans," declared that yes, it was true: the king was dead. The man who had risen so high so fast had, Icarus-like, plummeted just as quickly. The storm of media coverage surpassed even that reserved for Katzenberg's splashy exit, but there was a kicker: in a move that redefined the term "golden parachute," the ousted Ovitz was being astoundingly compensated for fourteen months of nothing. Between stock options and cash, Ovitz looked to walk away from Disney with $140 million, according to the terms of his contract. The arrangement "transcends wretched excess," wrote economist Robert Samuelson in the *Washington Post*. Others put it less poetically. Even more staggering, in the wake of Ovitz's departure, Eisner signed a new ten-year contract that included stock options worth $770 million. The media's response, succinctly echoing that of the general public's, went: *WTF??*

At DreamWorks, the news of Ovitz's bitter end did not spark condolences. Geffen's arch-nemesis had been toppled. The idea that Ovitz would inherit the throne left behind by his—and everyone else's—idol, Lew Wasserman—a thought that not very long ago seemed all but inevitable—had proved preposterous. If Geffen had been thinking for years now that Ovitz needed to learn a lesson, the fates apparently agreed.

But it was Katzenberg who had the most reason to gloat. For if Disney was paying Ovitz $140 million for having screwed up, Katzenberg's demand that he be paid $250 million for a decade's worth of stellar service suddenly sounded reasonable, almost quaintly so. It was almost starting to look easy—just put that beautiful, round number—*a hundred and forty million*—in front of a jury, and watch!

A fate that Katzenberg had less control over was that of DreamWorks, which had still produced very little that the public could actually touch, see, or hear. What had been released had proven disappointing. The TV debut *Champs* had arrived in January of 1996, but was canceled. A second offering, the cop drama *High Incident*, was picked up again, though only—it was believed—because of Spielberg's involvement as executive producer. Then there was the music: George Michael's *Older,* though not a complete disaster, was no *Faith.* On top of it all, negotiations for Playa Vista were bogged down in bureaucratic red tape and lawsuits—the studio of the twenty-first century looked years away, and even that was optimistic thinking. What's more, with a hefty overhead of eight hundred employees, and money being funneled into a myriad of ventures beyond just moviemaking, DreamWorks was blowing through its $2.7 billion in capital at a rate of $400 million a year. By 1998, it was predicted that the company would have burned through $1.3 billion of investors' money.

The media was beginning to ask questions, to wonder if the dream was just that—never to become a reality. *Forbes* described Dream-Works as "the richest and most hyped baby in the history of the entertainment industry," but noted that "the kid hasn't yet learned to walk." "Plenty of Dreams, Not Enough Works?" questioned a *BusinessWeek* headline.

Geffen pooh-poohed the notion that DreamWorks was off-course. "This is a marathon, not a sprint," he told Ronald Grover at *BusinessWeek.* "Watch where we are at the end of the race. I would rather die than fail." He also pointed out that "Geffen Records lost money in every quarter for its first six years. Then in 1989 it was worth $500 million."

It would have been the perfect moment for Spielberg to swoop in and save the day. Only, he didn't. In the fall of 1996 Spielberg announced that his long-awaited return to the director's chair would be to make *The Lost World,* the follow-up to *Jurassic Park.* For Universal.

Considering that Spielberg had thus far been reluctant—with the exception of *Indiana Jones*—to make sequels to his films, saying that some were simply too perfect as they were (*E.T.*) and that some, such as *Jaws,* were too demanding, production-wise, to revisit, this decision was remarked upon and noticed. Spielberg claimed that his reason for changing course with *Jurassic Park* was that he thought of it as a less sacred work; that it wasn't as masterful when compared to his other showcases. With fans writing letters, begging Spielberg to wreak more Mesozoic havoc, he acquiesced. What Spielberg downplayed in his reasoning were the dollar signs dancing off in the distance. CGI dinosaurs might be ignoble, but they were lucrative, and Spielberg looked to earn more on this film than the $300 million he made on *Juras-*

sic Park, with his newly raised directing fee (15 percent of first-dollar gross up to 17.5 percent).

DreamWorks might have to wait for Spielberg movies, but not too long. Like an Olympic athlete coming off an intense recovery period, Spielberg was recharged. The dervish was about to start whirling, and *Lost World* was just the beginning. Both *Saving Private Ryan* and *Amistad* were being readied so that Spielberg could segue seamlessly from one to the other. If all went as planned, he would direct three movies in twelve months. Or do what it takes even the most highly experienced directors several years, even decades, to do. Then he could toss off his baseball cap, light up a cigar, revel in the fact that he was, indeed, all that.

When asked once by *Variety* editor in chief Peter Bart about his penchant for jam-packed work schedules, Spielberg replied: "It's a question of retaining one's perspective. When I focus on one project alone, I tend to obsess on every scene. I shoot something and I fall in love with my own work. On the other hand, when I juggle several projects, that helps me keep a sharp sense of perspective. If I stop what I'm doing to go to a meeting about a script, I find myself wrestling with those problems and then, when I return to my own movie, I see it all in context."

On a more subconscious level, he added: "There's also the other possibility . . . that I'm simply an insecure Jew, that I always was and always will be."

Spielberg's return to the director's chair meant that he was less focused on DreamWorks, although he was still, in his manic, multitasking way, a presence at the studio. Screenwriter Adam Rifkin recalled a meeting with Spielberg at Amblin in which he bound into the room from the set of *Lost World*—parts of which were shot on sound stages at Universal—"all excited about a sequence that he'd just shot that he said went really well," and then, without skipping a beat, launching into a pitch for *Small Soldiers,* a languishing-in-development Amblin film that he wanted Rifkin to revive for DreamWorks.

As Spielberg described the movie, Rifkin said that he entered the zone he tends to enter when an idea, or several, enthralls him. He walked around the room, animatedly gesturing with his arms, acting out parts of the film, even speaking in the characters' voices.

After this performance, Rifkin said, "Steven looked at me with an incredible expression of not really knowing what my answer was going to be, and asking me did I think it might be something that I might be interested in writing for him . . . I couldn't believe that he actually didn't just know that I would be thrilled to do it."

Spielberg's ingenuousness at such moments often went against expectation. He once said to a colleague: "I had dinner with Bruce Ramer [his lawyer] last night, and found out that his wife, Madeline, works for [CBS chief executive officer] Les Moonves. Madeline has the ear of Les Moonves! Can you believe that?" (As though forgetting that he had the ear of all of Hollywood.)

Sometimes after reading a script, he would ask, with childlike wonder: "Can we get this?!" as though it had slipped his mind that Steven Spielberg could get any script, any day.

"Sometimes he forgot his power," said one insider. "Other times he was very aware of it and used it."

Some areas of the company felt his absence now that he was reengaged with his own art. No longer was he stopping by to play video games and brainstorm at DreamWorks Interactive. DreamWorks' TV animation group, already severely crippled by Disney's purchase of ABC, also felt a deficit of Spielberg's attention. Bruce Cranston, co-head of the division, recalled pitching cartoons to Spielberg while he was on the set of *The Lost World*.

"It was an industrial stage, a rainy set—the scene where the BMW goes over the cliff—and I was, literally, on a shooting break, pitching him," Cranston said. "Water is falling all over my storyboards, I'm standing in mud, and I don't completely have his attention. When you're a director, you've got five hundred people onstage, everyone's looking at you for instructions—and I'm trying to pitch shows. It was absolutely horrible."

While Spielberg was busy directing, Cranston said, "he was unavailable. He was torn between getting things done for DreamWorks and for Universal. It was just very tough."

At times, the group would have to push ahead without Spielberg's blessing, which created a new headache when, Cranston said, "We'd show him shows after we'd [sold them to networks], and he'd say, 'I don't want to do that.'"

Cranston then had the unenviable job of having to go back to networks and renege on a deal, to the anger and disbelief of network executives.

As the media circled, all the more so with the news that Spielberg's first directing gig was for Universal, not his own company, Dream-Works employees buckled down, drew closer together. Outside criticism only fueled employees' sense of purpose, the collective desire to prove everyone wrong. The media's, and everyone else's, skepticism and doubts bound employees—whatever their ancestral differences (Amblin or Disney)—tighter together as a tribe; a tribe that was under attack by naysayers who were waiting, practically salivating, for DreamWorks to fail.

This spirit of solidarity was amply on display at an impromptu gathering that took place at a dive bar on Wilshire Boulevard in Santa Monica around this time. (Having the event at Spago would not have fit the Gap-casual ethos of DreamWorks.) Proving that DreamWorks' parties were not about stilted conversation and cheese cubes, but artistic expression and lettin' it all hang out, Terry Press got up onstage—barefoot and wearing overalls—and belted out a Linda Ronstadt number. Walter Parkes jammed on his guitar with his band. And David Sameth, head of creative advertising, sat down at the piano and sang along to a little ditty he'd written about Playa Vista.

It was an amazing night, and employees went home feeling a distinct sense of togetherness and pride in their company. But they also felt something else. Underneath all the camaraderie was a call to arms, a determination to prove the critics wrong. As one person put it: "Fuck those people! We're gonna win!"

II

ROLLING

14

OF MEN AND MICE

WALTER PARKES had another announcement. The scene was the Amblin screening room, and it was the fall of 1996, the day before the cast and crew of *Mousehunt*, which pit Nathan Lane and British comedian Lee Evans against a rogue rodent, were to head north to shoot in an old Victorian home outside Yosemite National Park. *Mousehunt*—an Amblin-style film that Spielberg had loved, Parkes had bought, and now everyone felt had gone off the rails—had been rushed into production (Dream-Works had only bought the script that spring) in order to open by the end of 1997. Still a year behind schedule, but not a day more: the film was due out on December 19.

As the film's director, Gore Verbinski, and producers Tony Ludwig, Alan Riche, and Bruce Cohen took their seats, a wave of anticipation swept through the group, which also included assistant directors, cinematographers, the camera crew; everyone who would have a hand in making the movie happen. After months of preparation—and no shortage of battles with DreamWorks—finally, the big day had arrived. Tomorrow, they were off.

When Parkes entered, he did not look about to raise a toast and wish everyone a bon voyage. As he walked up toward the front of the room, he stopped short of stepping onto the stage, halting, instead, on the stairs leading up to the platform. So began the "Walter Parkes show," as Ludwig called it.

"Walter said, 'You think I'm going to wish you well and hope that everything goes well. I'm not. I don't think you're ready to make this movie. I don't think this movie is any good. I think this was a big waste of money, and I think that all of you are going off on an adventure of folly.' And he walked out," as Ludwig recalled.

A studio source doesn't recall Parkes being quite so harsh, and said that his message was more along the lines of, "We have a problem here. People are seeing very different movies, and we need to see the same movie. I'm worried." But whatever words were used, Verbinski—who not very long ago had felt like the luckiest thirty-two-year-old in the world, having been hired off of a commercial in which frogs croak out the name of a beer, to direct for the most star-studded movie studio in Hollywood—was crushed by what he called "the anti–pep talk."

He and Parkes had been butting heads over the creative direction of *Mousehunt* for weeks. Parkes and DreamWorks wanted *Home Alone* with a mouse; Verbinski was giving them broody and artistic. Neither man had been reticent about his feelings, and both got to know rather quickly of what stuff the other was made.

"You just have to know Walter," Verbinski said of Parkes's speech. "That's just his demeanor. We were expecting, 'OK, you start shooting tomorrow, win one for the Gipper.' I have never been more disappointed in my life. I just remember it was incredibly negative."

When, in February, Parkes had called up Alan Gasmer, an agent at William Morris, and told him, "I want to buy a mouse," Gasmer had been sure he'd misheard him.

"You *do?*" Gasmer had replied, amazed that DreamWorks, with all its talk of being nontraditional and high class, was interested in what was essentially a *Tom and Jerry* romp.

When news spread about DreamWorks' purchase, the joke around town was that Katzenberg jumped for joy: "We've got our mouse!"

"The whole idea was that Katzenberg was buying a mouse to launch against Disney," said one source. "They were thinking of spinning it off into cartoons."

To direct the film, DreamWorks hired Verbinski—in the 1990s, young directors coming off commercials were the equivalent of the 1970s film-school brats. Michael Bay, Spike Jonze, and David Fincher were among the up-and-comers who had made their names with eye-catching thirty-second spots and music videos. Verbinski's Budweiser commercial with the croaking amphibians had won a prize at Cannes and received four Clio Awards. His reel had set Spielberg and Parkes to pondering what this kid could do with a mouse.

Born Gregor Verbinski, the director had grown up near San Diego, the son of a nuclear physicist. As a teenager, he devoured Kafka and Black Sabbath and played guitar for punk bands.

In his meeting with Spielberg and Parkes, he stunned them by citing *Harold and Maude* and *Brewster McCloud* as inspirations for *Mousehunt*, a family comedy. "I was talking more about my fondness for theater of the absurd," Verbinski said. "I thought I was talking myself out of a job. So I think that put them back at first. They were like, 'What? You don't want to use a CG mouse?'" (No. He wanted to train real ones.)

But Spielberg and Parkes liked his swagger, and first-time directors were in keeping with the company's stated mission. As Parkes often reminded the press, DreamWorks was a place for either superestablished filmmakers or newbies—anyone but the dreaded "middle."

A week after his introductory meeting, Verbinski got the call, and embarked on what he called his "Hollywood briss": "You're never the same after your first one."

As *Mousehunt* prepared to shoot, Parkes and MacDonald were consumed with their own producing duties, which they did not take lightly. Even when *Men in Black* was in postproduction, Parkes was pitching new scenes, inciting Barry Sonnenfeld to squeal: "But Walter! The movie's coming out in *six weeks!*" The couple was also doing their best to keep on top of the handful of DreamWorks movies moving forward.

Already, Parkes's incessant intrusions were causing filmmakers to question DreamWorks' "artist-friendly" credo. The stories of meddling were multiplying. DreamWorks' own definition of "artist-friendly" wasn't turning out to be about "See you later," but about the people at the company never letting go of the creative process, whether it was Parkes rewriting scripts or Katzenberg's "invisible director" tendencies on animated films. As DreamWorks saw it, this sort of participation added creative value that was more valuable than the crass notes offered by traditional studios, where heads of marketing weighed in on what characters and stories were the most "sellable" to the public. Filmmakers were going to have to get used to it.

In the meantime, sparks would fly. When, not long before shooting on *Mousehunt* began, Parkes and MacDonald were shown some design sketches, they flipped. *Home Alone* it was not. Instead of jeans, T-shirts, or any version of the Banana Republic 1990s they envisioned for the film, Verbinski had selected 1940s-style costumes, courtesy of an old Italian tailor on Hollywood Boulevard who had made suits for the dapper old Hollywood star Adolphe Menjou. There were spats, top hats, frilly blouses. Adding to the moody, slightly surreal quality, Verbinski had hired Linda DeScenna, responsible for the hauntingly dreary world of *Blade Runner,* as the film's set decorator. The film's palette was brown and brooding, like a Depression-era period piece. Calls started coming in from Parkes. "Why is everyone wearing hats? What time period is this?" he asked Verbinski.

The studio was "a little freaked over his vision," said Riche. "Some of the clothes that he originally chose were frightening to them."

Other decisions also disturbed Parkes, whose attention was now fully focused on this movie gone wild. "I continued to push this relationship between the [main characters] as individuals who are trying to live up to the legacy of their father," said Verbinski. "I don't think that was important to the studio. They were like, 'Make sure you get the *Tom and Jerry* stuff in there.'"

The tension between Parkes and Verbinski mounted, and no one missed it. Ludwig said that, in arguments, whenever Verbinski would mention provocative films like *My Beautiful Laundrette,* "Walter would take out his barf bag."

Things got so bad that Verbinski walked off the picture twice, and called up Spielberg to ask him to "Get Walter off my back."

But Verbinski, as strong-willed as Parkes, "never acted like a first-time director even when he was one," according to one source. He took on Parkes. He even admitted to liking the antagonism between them. "Walter and I always had that relationship; I think it's healthy," he said. "We're not afraid to dig our heels in."

To the filmmakers, Parkes played the heavy, but, according to sources, Spielberg was equally perturbed over what was going on with *Mousehunt.* But Spielberg hated doling out bad news and remained above the fray. As one DreamWorker put it: "All of us played the bad cop for Steven. You never let Steven take the hit — *ever.*"

Spielberg especially hated confrontations with directors, the only Hollywood creatures he saw as his equals, Ludwig said, "only next to himself and well above anybody else at the company." Katzenberg has joked that Spielberg sees producers as "dead weight." But directors, like Spielberg, were artists, to be coddled, encouraged, and protected.

Aware of this, Ludwig and Riche would encourage Verbinski to take their grievances to Spielberg, knowing that the good father would not say no to an eager protégé who just wanted respect for his vision. Whatever Spielberg was saying behind the scenes, the strategy worked.

"Whenever we had a beef with Walter over the script, Gore would walk out sulking and whining, and then we'd turn to Gore: 'What do we do now?' He'd say, 'I know, I know what I've got to do.' And he would literally walk into Steven's office and get what he wanted."

Later, when *Mousehunt* went before test audiences, it wasn't just Spielberg and Parkes who had questions. Geffen weighed in. "What is that crazy oompah music?" Geffen asked Verbinski, his face two inches from the director's, as they flew back to L.A. on the Dream-Works jet from a disastrous screening in Northern California. Geffen may have been at something more than his usual irritation level, given that DreamWorks Records had yet to produce a hit and was taking a beating in the press. Under Ostin and Waronker, the label was combining old reliables (which were turning out to be not so reliable after all) with esoteric acts such as Henry Rollins and Forest for the Trees. Tasteful and, in the latter case, edgy, perhaps. But neither was producing hits that justified the spending. Nor were the choices creating a sound or statement distinguishing DreamWorks Records from other labels.

Perhaps Geffen could make more headway with Verbinski's score, which, at this point, he hated. Geffen didn't care that the polka-like ditties had been created by Bruce Fowler, Frank Zappa's trombonist. His advice: "You need to get rid of your editor and fire your composer!"

The preview had gone terribly. Clocking in at two hours, *Mousehunt* was way too long. People had walked out. On the plane, Verbinski slunk into his seat, depressed and "wanting to slit my wrists."

But after unleashing his tirade, Geffen softened, became more of a nurturing father. "This is your first preview, isn't it?" he asked.

Verbinski nodded.

"Don't worry," Geffen said, offering more reassurances, but still insisting that the music had to go. The next day he called Danny Elfman, the award-winning composer who'd scored the Tim Burton films *Pee-wee's Big Adventure* and *Corpse Bride.*

Spielberg and Parkes then worked with Verbinski to trim the film down by twenty minutes, and DreamWorks had one of the most offbeat mouse movies Hollywood had ever seen. No one would ever mistake it for a Spielberg movie. More like a Coen brothers film, finding its humor in the dark and the warped, nowhere more so than in the performance of Christopher Walken as the grim exterminator.

Despite progress on the moviemaking front, by the summer of 1997, the company was officially a joke. At Herb Allen's summer mogul retreat, a gag gift was given to Geffen and Katzenberg, who both attended, called "the DreamWorks doll." The joke was that when you wound it up, nothing happened. DreamWorks was Hollywood's longest-awaited blockbuster. Only one TV show had survived, and still no movies had been released.

Playa Vista remained an elusive dream. DreamWorks and the developers, Maguire Thomas, facing financial difficulties, had ceded the property to a new alliance, dubbed Playa Capital Company. This brought negotiations back to square one, at which point DreamWorks increased its demands. The company wanted more free land in exchange for the tax credits and marquee value they were bringing to the project. The developers were outraged, and finding themselves in over their heads when dealing with the likes of Geffen and Co.

"When they wanted something, they used every conceivable lever point to make it happen," said one person who was involved in the negotiations.

Said another member of Playa Capital: "DreamWorks used their political connections. We were like Cub Scouts showing up at a Hells Angels meeting. They owned the public show. They had enormous political clout and they were not afraid to use it."

While Katzenberg was overseeing the minutiae of day-to-day negotiations, firing off letters to the California Transportation Commission, asking for assurance that improvements related to Playa Vista would be taken care of on schedule, Spielberg was "drifting in and out of it all," said one source. But if anyone was going to put a good face on the messy controversy, and assure the public that DreamWorks was not out to bulldoze precious wetlands, it was do-gooder in chief Steven Spielberg. At a fence-mending lunch with environmentalists and community leaders at Amblin, Spielberg chatted warmly with his guests, saying that he, too, lived on the West Side and that the last thing he wanted to do was disturb the peace. He reiterated his dedication to preserving the wetlands habitat and to forging a relationship between Playa Vista and the surrounding area—even working with Loyola Marymount University (just up the hill from Playa Vista) to form a joint theatrical or film program.

"He gave a very sincere, believable description of his vision of this beautiful village with walkable streets—narrow streets, tree-shaded, people living and working in the same place," said Adi Lieberman, who was then an aide to City Councilwoman Ruth Galanter. "By virtue of who he is, he had a great ability, he did a great job of pitching stuff. You could just see, by the end of it, everyone's concerns had all melted away, they were all ready to put a second mortgage on their house to make this happen."

The environmentalists were less charmed by Saint Steven, and continued to publicly voice their outrage, with protests at DreamWorks movie premieres, "Dance of the Frogs" performance pieces on the Santa Monica promenade, and even a two-page ad in *Daily Variety*, which warned the entertainment community: "Although you have hired well-respected environmental consultants to work on this project, placing a development this massive on and around a wetlands ecosystem is not environmentally sound—no matter how many recycling programs it has."

In the face of the controversy, Hollywood dropped its usual eco-conscience, more fearful of crossing Spielberg, Katzenberg, and Geffen than spoiling precious wetlands. The one exception was Martin Sheen, who led a group of demonstrators to block the entrance of the Playa Vista headquarters, chaining the main doors closed for two hours. Other demonstrations took the form of activists chaining themselves to bulldozers on the development site, and one man who staged a hunger strike, refusing to eat until he got a meeting with Spielberg—he didn't; instead, he was sent to the hospital.

The anti–Playa Vista contingent was having better luck in court. Although the first phase of construction at Playa Vista had been approved, those opposed to the development filed more lawsuits, claiming that sufficient environmental analyses had not been completed at the site. Two in particular, which were at the federal level, were succeeding in slowing down the DreamWorks dream considerably.

Adding irony to insult over the summer of 1997—and more upsetting than any windup doll—the two biggest films of the season were Spielberg's made-for-Universal sequel *The Lost World* ($618 million world-wide gross) and *Men in Black* ($589 million). DreamWorks might not be making money, but Spielberg—who took in over $125 million on *Men in Black* for doing little more than lending his name to the film—and Parkes were rolling in it.

The biggest trouble spot was the live-action studio, where Parkes and MacDonald's novice stripes were showing, and where the couple was struggling to keep up with the noncreative aspects of studio management. There were just not enough movies. DreamWorks' resistance to following in the footsteps of the major studios with full production schedules was starting to seem less noble than wrong-headed. However formulaic the studios' system might be when it came to building a slate—based on the notion that X number of summer tent poles were needed every year, coupled with Y number of cheap comedies and Z number of gross-out flicks—the system produced product, which is something that DreamWorks was in desperate need of.

Recognizing that a solution was needed, Katzenberg suggested bringing in another executive to deal with the things Parkes and Mac-Donald were less interested, and less versed, in. When Bob Cooper, the president of TriStar Pictures, was fired from his post in March 1997, Katzenberg asked him if he wanted to work at DreamWorks. Two days later, Cooper—who had also worked at HBO—was hired.

Cooper had come to Katzenberg's attention during a problem involving *Amistad,* the first film Spielberg was directing for DreamWorks. HBO, as it happened, turned out to also be developing a film about the slave ship. When Katzenberg, trying to clear the path for Spielberg, called Cooper, he encountered a man cut from his own cloth. Katzenberg was impressed by Cooper's crafting of a savvy deal—HBO would stop production only if DreamWorks' movie would be made in association with HBO, and Spielberg would commit to producing movies for HBO (later, DreamWorks also gave Cooper a producer credit on *Amistad*). Cooper was known for his taste, having overseen such upscale films at HBO as *Barbarians at the Gate* and *The Josephine Baker Story.* At TriStar, he'd worked with James L. Brooks on *As Good As It Gets,* and with Parkes and MacDonald on *The Mask of Zorro.* That he also had a reputation as being combative, and not at all in the Dream-Works laid-back mold, gave some at the company pause. Nevertheless, when Katzenberg recruited Cooper, he told him: "This will be your last job. This is family."

DreamWorks also signed more producers in an effort to jolt live action. One of the most celebrated was Cameron Crowe, the rock journalist turned writer-director. *Jerry Maguire,* which he both wrote and directed, had become one of the biggest hits of 1996. It boasted that rare combination of stupendous box-office draw ($273 million worldwide) and critical acclaim (five Oscar nominations, with a Best Supporting Actor win for Cuba Gooding Jr.). *Maguire* had been the shining light at Sony, which released the film. In its wake the studio had thrown everything but the company jet at Crowe in hopes of getting him to sign a producing deal. But Sony didn't have Spielberg, and when DreamWorks offered, Crowe chose the studio where he believed he would have not just a rich deal and a sweet office (an ultramodern space in Santa Monica), but a real creative mentor.

But the most vaunted producer deal was made with Spielberg's buddy Robert Zemeckis and his company, ImageMovers, which was to be DreamWorks' Amblin—i.e., its prime supplier, coming up with three to five films a year. If Zemeckis and his crew delivered, DreamWorks' worries would be over. Katzenberg could stop hounding Parkes, who with MacDonald could come up for air. Spielberg could feel like a good friend. But despite the warm feelings all around, sources say that both Geffen and Katzenberg had concerns about the price of signing one of Hollywood's hottest and most expensive directors—Zemeckis's latest blockbuster, *Contact,* grossed $100 million that summer. But Spielberg didn't see it in financial terms, he saw it in terms of loyalty and support.

Although the two shared a brotherly rivalry (Spielberg won a round when he got his Oscar first, for *Schindler's List;* Zemeckis caught up a year later with *Forrest Gump*), their relationship ran deep. Zemeckis had come to Spielberg's attention with an award-winning student film he made while at USC, which Spielberg thought was "spectacular." It had, said Steven, "police cars and a riot, all dubbed to Elmer Bernstein's score for *The Great Escape.*" Being a few steps ahead of Zemeckis in the Hollywood game, Spielberg took him under his wing, executive-producing his first two films. When the latter, *Used Cars,* bombed and put Zemeckis in director jail, Spielberg saw to it that the failure wouldn't keep Zemeckis from directing a time-traveling adventure movie called *Back to the Future* at Universal. Sid Sheinberg had his doubts, but Spielberg assured him that if there was any trouble, then Spielberg would step in and direct the movie himself.

During the to-and-fro with Sheinberg, "Steven was there for Bob," said one source. And now, with his brand-new company, Spielberg was there for Zemeckis again, with a lavish production deal that went so far as offering ImageMovers a so-called "put" deal, whereby Image-Movers could actually green-light its own films, even without Dream-Works' approval. Zemeckis's producing partner, Jack Rapke (until then his agent at CAA), would be receiving a generous seven-figure salary from DreamWorks.

Although Spielberg's rationale escaped Geffen and Katzenberg, for Spielberg it came down to one thing: "It was important to Steven to get Bob into the *family*," as one person put it. And in this family, where Spielberg played the good father, Geffen and Katzenberg often found themselves in the role of black-sheep brothers.

DreamWorks actually did have one treasured property by 1997, albeit a relatively modest one. *Spin City* debuted on ABC in the fall of 1996 as the season's third-highest-rated show. It wasn't the breakout hit that both DreamWorks and ABC (which, in its first year under Disney ownership, with Jamie Tarses at the helm, was struggling) had hoped for, but it held on strong enough to be picked up for another season, which was more than could be said for DreamWorks' other TV launches. Both *Ink*, with Ted Danson and Mary Steenburgen, and *Arsenio*, which starred the late-night talk show host Arsenio Hall as a newscaster, were costly and quickly canceled. Spielberg's cop show, *High Incident*, was equally short-lived. In the case of *Ink*, Danson and Steenburgen had been unhappy with the show's first four episodes, at which point they insisted that the pilot be scrapped and a new producer (*Murphy Brown*'s Diane English) be brought on to completely rewrite and reshoot, a decision that resulted in an additional $4 million in production costs for CBS.

But *Ink* still did a quick fade. *Arsenio* was even more tumultuous. Hall, accustomed to the freeform format of a talk show, had trouble remembering his lines. As reported in the *New York Observer,* during taping, he blew up at writer David Rosenthal. "Why don't you get your dick out of your ass and write me some fucking jokes?" he yelled. Rosenthal burst into tears and walked off the show. After debuting on ABC in the spring of 1997, *Arsenio* was pulled off the air to be tweaked, but it never returned.

Both *Ink* and *Arsenio* demonstrated the pitfalls of Katzenberg's strategy of going after stars and then trying to build shows around them. It is a formula that, when applied to movies, tends to have far better results. Television executives put the TV failure rate anywhere between 80 percent and 95 percent: for every *Seinfeld*, the networks spend hundreds of millions of dollars on dozens of shows that quietly expire. In this light, DreamWorks' record wasn't so out of the ordinary, or unexpected. But for a studio lacking any syndicated hits or long-running cash cows to fall back on—such as *Wheel of Fortune* and *Jeopardy!*, which mightily sustain Sony Pictures TV—it was costly. Rather quickly, television was becoming DreamWorks' biggest financial drain.

DreamWorks' syndicated efforts were also falling flat. After protracted negotiations with Maury Povich and his wife, Connie Chung, to partner on a news-oriented talk show, not enough local networks were interested. Povich opted to continue with *The Maury Povich Show*. Two years in, the division's only success was a set of syndicated specials with Olympic Games historian Bud Greenspan that aired during the 1996 Summer Olympics in Atlanta.

But *Spin City* was a ray of light, a sign that Katzenberg's belief in the comfortable familiarity of stars wasn't misplaced. After *Champs* came and went, Katzenberg became convinced that what Gary David Goldberg—and DreamWorks—needed was a reunion with Michael J. Fox, who'd portrayed America's favorite yuppie-in-training on his *Family Ties*, one of the biggest shows on television in the 1980s.

There was only one problem. Goldberg and Fox had grown estranged in the years since Mallory, Alex, and the rest of the clean-cut gang had gone off the air in 1989. After a decade of togetherness, there had been tension, of the usual Hollywood sort. Goldberg, who had originally written Fox's character—Alex P. Keaton—as a minor role (the focus of the sitcom was intended to be the parents, not the kids), had rewritten the show after tests showed audiences loved Fox's character.

"In some ways, Gary was probably very thankful to Michael, but on some level there was resentment," said one source. "Fox became a bigger deal than Gary."

But Katzenberg had no concern for a petty ego contest. Without telling Goldberg, he called Fox and told him that Goldberg wanted nothing more than to reconnect and work on another series with him. Fox's post-TV movie career, which included films such as *The American President* and *Life with Mikey*, was not quite soaring; he didn't hang up the phone. Katzenberg then called Goldberg and said the same thing about Fox—that the actor was dying to work with him again.

"I didn't think it was underhanded or unbusinesslike," said Bill Lawrence, who wrote *Spin City* with Goldberg. "Truly, those two guys seemed to need a bridge."

But even with the glimmer provided by *Spin City*, the industry wasn't doing DreamWorks—an independent television studio without the built-in distribution system of a network—any favors. All across Hollywood, studios were aligning with networks, putting independent sellers like DreamWorks at a distinct disadvantage. After all, networks' first choice would be to buy programming from in-house production companies. In 1995, the same year Disney acquired ABC, Paramount launched the UPN (United Paramount Network) and Warner Bros. created the WB network.

Forced to deal with this new reality, Katzenberg was already beginning to scale back DreamWorks TV's ambitions, making fewer high-profile deals with stars. He called the shifting landscape "the most dramatic and traumatic that the entertainment business has faced in twenty-five years. There's been an extraordinary consolidation into a handful of companies where production, distribution, and delivery systems are all under one roof and there is very, very little shelf space." He said that though he believed "a great show could get on the air . . . and that was the only thing that mattered," at this time, there is "no access for someone who is solely a production company without a pretty strong affiliation . . . Going solo like we were with Connie and Maury is not possible."

Said DreamWorks TV executive Ken Solomon: "Up until that moment in time on the calendar, there was this never-ending Möbius strip of debate over whether content or distribution was the answer. On the heels of what Fox was doing was the moment when the scales really tipped toward verticalization. If you didn't own some form of distribution it would affect your ability to scale as a company, to grow in size . . . In hindsight, there's no question it had a gigantic effect on the evolution of [DreamWorks TV]."

But for now, DreamWorks would forge ahead, despite the liability of not having its own means of distributing TV shows. After all, they could still *make* shows—better, they believed, than anyone else.

And then, finally, there were films . . .

By the time Walter Parkes made his way to the front of Mann's Chinese Theatre on the evening of September 23, 1997, the crowd that had gathered for the Los Angeles premiere of *The Peacemaker* was palpably restless. The screening was delayed by over fifteen minutes, and Hollywood crowds do not like to wait, even when they've been plied with cocktails, as had this particular audience. Impatience turned to shock when Parkes said something unexpected—that Spielberg had been in a car accident on the way to the premiere and would not be able to make it to the screening. The news caused a collective gasp in the audience.

"Don't worry, it's just a fender-bender," Parkes said, trying to make light of the fact that DreamWorks' biggest star was not going to be on display at DreamWorks' biggest night to date. He then went on to introduce the film.

But no one was listening to the host. Instead, a wave of whispers ("I hope he's OK!" and "Oh my God!") swept through the cavernous room, reverberating off the gilded Eastern exotica that covered the auditorium's ceiling and the aged chandelier dangling like a gigantic earring.

It was the second no-show for Spielberg, who as a result of the accident—which, as it turned out, was somewhat more dramatic than a fender-bender—had been taken to the hospital with a sprained shoulder. The night before, he'd been absent from *Peacemaker*'s New York premiere, held at another storied theater, the Ziegfeld, having attended Princess Diana's funeral (accompanied by Tom Cruise and Tom Hanks), in London.

In New York, where buff men in tight black T-shirts handed out "DreamWorks"-embossed champagne flutes to guests such as Herb Ritts, Penny Marshall, Fran Lebowitz, and Gregory Hines, Spielberg's presence came in the form of a congratulatory note, signed, simply, "Steven."

"Steven? Steven who? Steven Seagal?" someone in the audience joked when the note was read by Parkes.

At the L.A. premiere, the absence of Spielberg, and the circumstances leading to it, lent an uneasy vibe to the night—one guest recalled feeling the "bad energy." It was a major letdown. For what seemed like so long—too long, in the opinion of many—the anticipation had been building toward DreamWorks' first major release. Even before the film went into production, Radio City Music Hall had requested to book it. At a meeting of field publicists for *Peacemaker*, Terry Press distributed shoulder-strap briefcase bags emblazoned with the film's title. "Hold on to these," she advised her troops. "They *will* become collectors' items."

In the weeks leading up to the release, Nicole Kidman and George Clooney—*The Peacemaker*'s unlikely counterterrorism team, pursuing nuclear-bomb smugglers in the former Soviet Union—did a series of media appearances, including one on *Larry King Live*, where the conversation veered from Clooney's recent antipaparazzi remarks—made in the wake of Princess Diana's death—to Kidman's marriage to Tom Cruise. When King inquired about how involved the DreamWorks "big guns" had been in the making of *Peacemaker*, Clooney showed his real acting chops, and joked: "Nicole banned them from the set."

The day after the L.A. premiere, Spielberg had recovered enough from his injury to attend another opening, for *The Locusts*, an Orion film starring Kate Capshaw. Standing on the red carpet, he vividly recounted the car accident to *L.A. Times* society reporter Bill Higgins: "We were pushed out of the intersection, spun 90 degrees, air bags went off, glass shattered, the car filled with the acid smell from the air bags and the horn stuck, which is a cliché I would never have put in a movie."

The Peacemaker was released on September 26. It beat out *The Edge*, written by David Mamet and starring Anthony Hopkins and Alec Baldwin, and the urban drama *Soul Food*, to emerge number one at the weekend box office. But it was met with mixed reviews, and went on to gross an unspectacular $41 million. Perhaps nothing could have lived up to the overhyped expectation with which the movie was met, but there was still a sense of disappointment, not just that the film wasn't an out-of-the-ballpark blockbuster, but that it did not seem to be attempting to be anything more than a slickly produced formula thriller.

Parkes himself, when I interviewed him years later about the movie, used the word that everyone had *hoped* DreamWorks' first film would be. "In some ways, *Peacemaker* was kind of the opposite of movies we tend to make now," Parkes said. "I think *Peacemaker* is a really well-made movie and has a few people who became movie stars, and it has a fabulous director. But the idea itself wasn't particularly strong. It wasn't *special.*"

"First one in, first one out," Katzenberg said, wildly reversing gears from his usual over-the-moon rhetoric. "It's not like we had a choice of twenty things and picked this because it's some statement or something."

15

SLAVES TO THE RHYTHM

I F THERE WAS A FILM that was going to be a statement, that was going to be "special," and that DreamWorks was counting on to define, once and for all, what exactly it was all about, and what it meant, exactly, to have Steven Spielberg as your star pitcher, well, in 1997 that film was on its way. *Amistad* was to hit theaters before the end of the year. Because the movie was envisioned as his follow-up to the serious achievement of *Schindler's List*, Spielberg was putting not just his imagination, but his heart and soul, into this one—the true story of a slave uprising aboard a Spanish slave ship, and the Supreme Court case that ensued when the Africans were tried for murder.

Spielberg was even dedicating the film to his and Capshaw's two adopted African American children, Theo and Mikaela (the latter of whom was born while Spielberg was in the early stages of *Amistad*). "I felt very strongly that this is a story they should know about," Spielberg said. "And my other children should know about it, too. It was a very emotional story to tell. My hair started standing up on the back of my neck during the first week of shooting, and it got a little tired of standing by the end of it." It was another epic *kvell* on the heels of *The Lost World*, which Spielberg had neatly tossed off almost as soon as he'd started it (shooting had begun in September of 1996 and wrapped a week before Christmas). Hundred-million-dollar productions Spielberg took in stride.

But *Amistad* was something else.

Spielberg was truly invested in the film. This one mattered to the director, perhaps too much. He had started working on the script with screenwriter David Franzoni, Parkes, MacDonald, and producer Debbie Allen (the former choreographer and *Fame* starlet). Allen had been trying to make the project—based on the 1974 book *Black Mutiny*, by William Owens—for years. When she'd brought it up to Parkes and MacDonald, whose kids carpooled with hers, their interest was piqued. As was Spielberg's; during script meetings, he was like an eager schoolboy, lapping up history lessons.

"The nice thing about Steven is, there's what Plato, or somebody, described as 'truth given' and 'truth discovered.' Religions have truth given. In other words, there's no discovery, they just know it all," said Franzoni, who'd originally been hired to write a screenplay about the *Amistad* story for Warner Bros. (When Spielberg expressed an interest in making the movie, Warner Bros., which was not very far along in development, backed off, and DreamWorks hired Franzoni.) "That's how I characterize most studios, and how I expected Steven to be. But Steven was very much truth-discovered. We would all sit there and try to figure out how to do it. I remember it was one of the finest experiences . . . We'd talk about the civil rights movement, we'd look at old pictures. We'd try to make it real."

Spielberg would scribble notes in the margins of Franzoni's screenplay: "Take me here!" "Take me there!" "Take me here!"

He became particularly excited about a reference to the fact that when the Marquis de Lafayette returned home to France after fighting with the Americans in the Revolutionary War, he brought with him a case of dirt. The reason? Even if he was buried in France, Lafayette wanted his casket to be laid in American soil.

"Steven wanted to know all about that," Franzoni said. "He wrote in the script—'Find out about this! What's the story? Is this true?' "

But, say people who witnessed the production, cutting through Spielberg's enthusiasm was a growing nervousness as *Amistad* became more of a reality. He had the politically correct rhetoric down pat. "Comparisons between black slavery and the Holocaust are essential," he told a reporter who visited the set. "You can't look at history selfishly. To paint an honest picture of man's inhumanity to man you also have to look at the American internment of Japanese during the Second World War, the Armenian slaughter, gay-bashing, the entire Native American—you know—tragedy. You have to look at every aspect of intolerance."

Perhaps Spielberg was too wrapped up in the weighty burden of his responsibility as history teacher. And, unlike *Schindler's List, Amistad*

wasn't *his* history, and he had experienced less than satisfactory results tackling this material before. A decade earlier, *The Color Purple* had been attacked by some critics, who felt that Spielberg had ro-
manticized the Old South, reinforcing Pap and Jim stereotypes, and
making an ugly part of American history feel a little too good. "*Gone
with the Wind* of 1985," they'd called it. These memories came back
to Spielberg, making him appear, to some, cautious with *Amistad,* a
movie that "definitely represents some competing forces in Spielberg's
brain," said one source. "I saw him fall in love with the Africans, the
African story, during the shoot. But he had been burned by *The Color
Purple,* so he very much pushed to describe [*Amistad*] as an *American*
story, not a black story." Said another DreamWorks source: "I don't
think Steven was ever comfortable making *Amistad.* He seemed out of
his element."

Others, however, denied this. Franzoni said Spielberg was "completely charmed" while making the film, and that he was so committed to portraying the story's harsh history that he didn't flinch when it
came to the violent and bloody scenes aboard the slave ship.

Still, in rewrites of Franzoni's script by Steven Zaillian (who'd written *Schindler's List*), the film broadened its focus from Joseph Cinqué,
the leader of the slave rebellion, to include the plight of Roger Sher-
man Baldwin, the young white attorney who represents the slaves.

Casting had also been a less effortless process than Spielberg was
accustomed to. To play John Quincy Adams, who initially argued the
case before the Supreme Court, he wanted Anthony Hopkins. But
Hopkins was busy with *The Mask of Zorro,* an Amblin project that
Parkes and MacDonald were producing. Spielberg's next choice was
Paul Scofield, but Scofield passed on the role. As for Baldwin, Spielberg's choices included Sean Penn and Daniel Day-Lewis. When they
demurred, the role went to Matthew McConaughey, who accepted.

During casting sessions, Spielberg appeared "vexed," according to
one insider. "He was insecure about not being able to get great actors.
He had done *Schindler's List,* but he was still considered the blockbuster guy."

Determined to land Hopkins, Parkes flew down to the *Mask of
Zorro* set in Mexico and showed the actor the *Amistad* script, offering
to shorten his *Zorro* schedule so that he could do both films. Hopkins
accepted.

Spielberg had more luck casting Cinqué, which went to a thirty-three-year-old African man who'd gone from sleeping on the streets of Paris to modeling for Herb Ritts, and who now was looking to break into movies. Spielberg welcomed Djimon Hounsou to Hollywood.

Meanwhile, others at DreamWorks were also worried, for different reasons. DreamWorks marketers were concerned about the commercial prospects of a historical courtroom drama with no big stars other than its director. The marketing department was already calling *Amistad* "the spinach movie." As in: good for you, but not exactly mouthwatering fare. And surveys were proving them right—even African Americans (the film's target demo) were failing to ignite over the "wig drama," regardless of whose story it was or who was directing it. But Spielberg didn't want to know, according to sources. When Terry Press, Jeffrey's truth-serum girl, laid the less-than-cheerful facts in front of him, he wouldn't listen. He didn't want to hear that *Amistad* just might not make the kind of history—at the box office and on the awards circuit—that he had in mind.

Like Katzenberg, her mentor, Press was more concerned with the end result than how pretty the process was, or whose egos were bruised along the way. At Disney, she had taken on Warren Beatty—insisting he do TV interviews for *Dick Tracy,* even when he refused—and won.

Press did not do nicey-nice. For her, the desired end always justified the means, even if that meant throwing cold water on Steven Spielberg's outsize expectations. Because she was so often right, she was highly respected; her loyal cadre of subordinates—including Mike Gottberg, Mitch Kreindel, Diana Loomis, Chip Sullivan, and Michael Vollman (known as Press's "out box")—thought of working for Press as being enrolled in a kind of killer graduate school in movie marketing. This was a woman, after all, who could name every Best Picture–winning film since 1928. But she could be a brutal instructor.

In one publicity meeting, when someone referred to something as being "ironic" in a way that Press felt was rather *mor*onic, she laid in.

"That is *not* ironic. Do you even know what irony is?" she snapped.

She then proceeded to go around the table, asking each executive, "Do *you* know what 'irony' is?"

Each answer was derided as incorrect, as Press grew visibly more irritated. "I don't think she was disgusted as much as disappointed," said one person, who was not amused by the exercise.

Another executive's first introduction to Press was when she called and announced herself by saying: "Who do I have to fuck to get a script around here?"

When it came to dealing with Spielberg, Press didn't dial it back or tiptoe, as most people did in their encounters with the man whose last three movies alone had grossed nearly $2 billion. *Amistad,* she told the director, was not lining up to be *Schindler's List 2.* Press's comments were perceived to reflect not just her own opinion, but that of Katzenberg, who would never dare challenge or confront Spielberg, particularly on a creative issue. "Terry was Jeffrey's mouthpiece," said one observer. "She did Jeffrey's dirty work, so he could look like the good guy." (When Press talked to reporters, as she was famous for doing, she also represented Katzenberg's views, as she had for so long at Disney.) On *Amistad,* Katzenberg remained silent. His protégée did not.

According to several sources, Spielberg was particularly upset when Press informed him that she didn't think *Amistad* was a strong Oscar contender. Crushed, the director told Press that she wasn't working hard enough, that marketing wasn't doing its job. He made it clear that he didn't want to hear reality; he just wanted to be told that everything would be fine.

A chill set in between Spielberg and Press, whose reputation as Jeffrey's Girl was firmly cemented within the halls of Amblin.

But Press's opinion was the least of Spielberg's problems when it came to *Amistad,* which became the center of a very public, and nasty, controversy two months before its release, when author Barbara Chase-Riboud slapped DreamWorks with a $10 million copyright-infringement suit, claiming that *Amistad* had "shocking similarities" to her 1989 historical novel *Echo of Lions.*

Studios, and the people who make their movies, are routinely sued for "stealing" ideas, never more so than when the movies are made by high-profile filmmakers and likely to result in a jackpot of riches. Spielberg had been no stranger to such lawsuits, and not long before had been slapped with one over *Twister* (which he subsequently lost). His vulnerability to these sorts of legal actions is one reason why the script departments at his companies are so highly guarded and why he registers every idea, every pitch, with the Writers Guild, sometimes several a day.

Most of the legal threats never make it very far, but this was not the case with *Amistad,* which immediately made headlines. It called to mind the famous Hollywood plagiarism case between humorist Art Buchwald and Paramount over the origins of the Eddie Murphy hit movie *Coming to America,* which evolved from a pitch that Buchwald had made to none other than Jeffrey Katzenberg. Buchwald won the suit, which had also involved Helene Hahn, who'd testified on behalf of Paramount in the case. Bringing it all full circle, Chase-Riboud had hired Pierce O'Donnell, who'd represented Buchwald and written a book about the case, as her lawyer.

But DreamWorks had its own, bigger gun: Bert Fields, Katzenberg's lawyer in the lawsuit against Disney and the attorney considered the most aggressive and clever in Hollywood. Fields fought back with characteristic flair, not only denying Chase-Riboud's claims by saying that she'd written a novel, not history, which was open for all to interpret. Fields contended that *she* had committed plagiarism, by lifting from *Black Mutiny* while writing her book.

As the barbs flew back and forth, the contretemps seemed destined to continue. Ultimately, Spielberg was forced to give a deposition, in which he said he'd never read *Echo of Lions,* even though, he admitted, it had been submitted to Amblin, in 1988, by Jacqueline Kennedy Onassis, a friend of Chase-Riboud's. (Amblin passed, at that time, on the project.) David Franzoni also claimed he'd never read the book. According to a detailed motion filed by O'Donnell, which was summarized in *Variety,* the *Amistad* project that Franzoni had been working on for Warner Bros. was called *Echo of Lions* and was based on Chase-Riboud's book. According to Franzoni, he'd only been told about the book after he was hired to write the script, when a Warner Bros. executive asked him if he was interested in reading it. Hearing that the book was fiction, he declined. Even so, the coincidence made some DreamWorks executives nervous.

Spielberg just wanted it all to go away. Here he was, having come to the end of a project he'd gone into with such noble intentions—to make it for the *kids,* for *history*—and it was all blowing up in his face.

Suddenly he was seen as the evil Hollywood potentate taking advantage of an innocent African American woman, all in the name of cinematic glory. (The language used in the suit conjured images of slave owners exploiting slaves—Chase-Riboud wanted "reparations" from DreamWorks.) Because this was Spielberg drama, the press was all over it. Every day brought a new story, op-ed piece (in the *New York Times, USA Today*), or headline. *Time* referred to "Steven Stealberg," which deeply distressed the director. "Steven was in tears this morning," Geffen told *The New Yorker* on the day that the *Time* article ran. "It's awful. Disgusting. The film is forever tainted by this lawsuit."

In the face of disaster, the DreamWorks partners were called from their corners into united action, and each assumed their respective duties. Geffen was in his agent role, at Spielberg's side, counseling him and offering reassurance. Katzenberg had been dispensed to clean the whole mess up (through Fields), though Spielberg would have liked him to have done it more quickly. (A federal court in L.A. denied an injunction motion that would have prevented the film's release pending trial, and *Amistad* opened nationally on December 12.) And Spielberg tried to keep his head held high and the name of DreamWorks unsullied.

But the movie also brought out tensions between the partners. Geffen had never understood why such a downer of a film was being released over the holidays. And while he might be by Spielberg's side when it mattered, for occasions he felt were less momentous, he opted to retreat back into billionaire mode. Instead of attending the film's Washington, D.C., premiere, he went to Acapulco; he reluctantly attended the L.A. opening, even though he would have preferred to "go home, watch a movie, and go to bed." When Terry Press needled him for being willing to fly to D.C. to attend a dinner with Chinese diplomats, Geffen said, "There's a big fucking difference between going to the premiere of a movie" and a dinner with dignitaries.

"What the hell do I have to be in Washington for? You don't need me," he said. "Let Jeffrey be there with Steven. I was there with Jeffrey last time."

When *Amistad* was released, it garnered only so-so reviews, and grossed just $44 million. It cost $70 million to produce and market. Not only was Spielberg depressed, DreamWorks' backers were nervous. According to one source, Geffen and Katzenberg were frustrated over what was a "vanity project" for Spielberg. *Amistad* wrought "tension on all levels, because, the truth of the matter is, if Steven Spielberg hadn't directed *Amistad,* it'd be an after-school special," said one source.

But no one was more upset than Spielberg, who took responsibility for the film's fate by declining to accept his director's fee on the movie. Even Spielberg's kids couldn't muster enthusiasm for the film. "They walked out of *Amistad,*" Spielberg said—a confession he could only bring himself to make many years later, to Roger Ebert. "I lost my whole family. All my young kids, you know. I wouldn't ever show them the middle passage and I didn't let them see the very beginning, and they were bored by the legal stuff. They left."

As the Christmas holidays arrived, DreamWorks wasn't a jolly place, and not just because there wouldn't be any imported snow that year. On December 19 *Mousehunt* opened, along with the not-so-little *Titanic,* which would become, and remain for a dozen years, the highest-grossing film of all time, bringing in $1.8 billion in worldwide ticket sales. DreamWorks did its best to make light of the fact that it was completely capsized (subsequent posters for *Mousehunt* featured a sinking ship in the background and a mouse rowing away, with the tagline: "It was the mouse"), but there was nothing amusing about *Mousehunt*'s opening weekend. When producer Alan Riche, in Micronesia on a scuba-diving trip with his wife, got the news that *Mousehunt* grossed just $6 million its first weekend, "I was sitting there, four thousand miles away, ready to slit my throat," he said.

Through word of mouth, the film picked up in subsequent weeks and went on to gross $61 million. It was hardly the kind of showing DreamWorks had hoped to make as its first year as an operational film studio came to a close. The final nail in the *Amistad* coffin came in February, the same month Chase-Riboud and DreamWorks settled their differences out of court for an undisclosed sum (a little too late; by now, *Amistad* was declared dead). When the Academy announced its Oscar nominations, as Terry Press had predicted, *Amistad* was shut out of the major categories, receiving just four nominations. (Not even Hounsou, whom DreamWorks made a strong push for in the Best Actor category, was recognized.) Once again, *Titanic* triumphed, garnering fourteen nods, more than any film in nearly half a century (tying with 1950's *All About Eve*).

It was not a time of plenty or happiness. Most eerily, also in February, Spielberg was accompanied by bodyguards to the Santa Monica courthouse to testify against a stalker who'd been caught trying to enter the director's Pacific Palisades home the previous summer, armed with a "rape kit," including razor blades, duct tape, and handcuffs. It was the nightmare Spielberg was always preparing for—the horror scenario that was too awful to even be put in any of his films, and the reason he chose to live in lockdown mode, even at Amblin. The thing that not even David Geffen, or any number of highly paid handlers, could protect him from. Testifying before a jury, months after he'd first learned that he was the target of a very warped, and dangerous, mind, Spielberg was apparently still badly shaken.

As reported in the *Chicago Sun-Times*, he testified: "The razor could have been used for . . . you know. The threat was very real to me. It is still real to me," he said. "No one before has come into my life to do me or my family harm. I really felt, I still to this day feel, I am prey to this individual."

In the wake of the scare, Amblin became even more impenetrable. Spielberg "trusted his team and that was about it," said Jill Overdorf, who at the time was a chef at DreamWorks' animation studio. Spielberg "was very closed-door and wary about who was allowed on campus at Amblin. There was a significant amount of security on-site . . . If you wore a chef's coat, and you were not a face that was seen all the time, you had to be escorted in from the gate. There was a certain level of paranoia."

Spielberg could be forgiven if he began to question the course he'd steered for himself with DreamWorks. *Amistad* had revealed risks to the director both professional and creative. And now this uncharted territory was posing personal risks as well.

On another legal front, Katzenberg's suit against Disney was also heating up over the summer of 1997. In June, L.A. Superior Court Judge John Ouderkirk ordered Disney to turn over key profit records so that Katzenberg's claimed bonus could be calculated. In September, two mock juries voted in favor of Katzenberg; a key factor in their decision, the smoking-gun memo written by Wells, which stated that

Katzenberg had a stake in 2 percent of Disney revenues even after he left the company.

Katzenberg and Eisner's war also raged on other fronts. For thirty years, Disney had been content to rent the land in Glendale where Disney Imagineering was based. But in June, the studio announced that it was buying up the ninety-six acres known as the Grand Central Business Center near Katzenberg's planned animation campus. Indeed, although Disney preached "expansion" as its motivating force, the move was interpreted by DreamWorks as a means of preventing Katzenberg from geographically expanding his animation empire and ensuring that Disney was still, at least physically, the domineering presence in the area.

Another salvo was launched from the Magic Kingdom in DreamWorks' direction when Eisner announced that Disney was planning a theatrical rerelease of *Beauty and the Beast* for November of 1998 — the same month Katzenberg's pet project, *Prince of Egypt*, DreamWorks' debut animation release, would hit theaters. To Katzenberg, the move was personal, and he called up his former boss to plead his case — a story he recounted to animators at DreamWorks. "Look," Katzenberg said, "I know we have our differences, but *Prince of Egypt* is an important film. Please don't kill it just because you can."

Katzenberg wasn't just going to take a hit, however. He had a counterattack of his own in mind. Immediately, he put in a call to Dylan Kohler, who was attending a meeting in San Jose with Sun Microsystems along with his fellow technology coheads Bill Villarreal and Rob Hummel. Kohler excused himself to take Katzenberg's call, which lasted all of thirty seconds.

"If you know anyone at Pixar, go after them!" Katzenberg barked. "We need to get those guys, we need to hurt them."

Kohler did know people at Pixar whom he'd worked with at Disney on the CAPS project, but they refused to budge. Unlike potential recruits at other companies, they weren't even interested in using DreamWorks to up their salaries.

For a few weeks, raiding Pixar became a priority at DreamWorks. In the end, the effort was fruitless. Pixar was on the rise in a major way, and not even Jeffrey Katzenberg could offer enough money or incentives to convince Lasseter's disciples to defect. Pixar, it was clear, was no Disney.

But Katzenberg kept trumping Disney on the legal front. In November, Disney—amazingly, given Eisner's stubbornness—agreed to settle with Katzenberg for $117 million. The concession might be a coup for Katzenberg, but it wasn't enough. He said he was owed more money. Disney refused to pay another penny, and so it was determined that the case would go to trial.

Katzenberg wasn't thrilled about the idea of his life at Disney being put on public display, but he realized that a trial was necessary in order for justice, as he saw it, to be served.

16

SAVING SPIELBERG

———

WHEN THE LIGHTS WENT UP after the first screening of *Saving Private Ryan*—reserved for Spielberg and a small coterie of friends and filmmakers—the reaction was not typical of a Spielberg debut. "It was a tiny screening room, everyone was separated by two to three seats, and when the film was over, my jaw was on my chest, everyone was stunned," said Robert Rodat, who wrote the film's script. "Nobody said anything for a little while."

Matt Damon, who played James Francis Ryan in the film—the private who would be saved—was still riding high on his *Good Will Hunting* Oscar. He was sitting next to Rodat. As the credits rolled, he looked over and, wordlessly, patted the writer on the leg.

"It wasn't a congratulatory pat," Rodat said. "It was a pat of—Wow, that was intense."

As the group—which also included Spielberg, Robert Zemeckis, and producer Mark Gordon—stood and emptied out into the hallway, the silence persisted. Only when Rodat was out of earshot of Spielberg did he dare breathe, and say the unsayable: "Holy shit! How are they going to sell this baby?"

"We were worried," Rodat said. "We were afraid the headlines would say: 'Too Violent. Don't See It.'"

There was reason to worry. The first twenty-four minutes of the film, which re-created the D-day battle scene on Omaha Beach, was so unflinchingly violent that when the film was screened for a group of veterans, one man had a heart attack and had to be rushed to a hospital (he recovered).

As originally written by Rodat, the scene had been twelve minutes long, with the action commencing only after the Allies had landed on-shore and ascended the fog-swathed cliffs. But Spielberg had something more immediate in mind. He had wanted the audience to feel the carnage and violent fury in the very first shots, before the Allies' boats even landed on the beach. To maximize the drama, he wanted the scene to last for close to half an hour.

Spielberg hadn't actually rewritten the scene, but had come up with the sequence visually, in his head, and then dictated it out to Marc Haimes, a young executive at DreamWorks, in a rush of ideas and images. The scene had then been storyboarded out and shot. Scott Frank (*Get Shorty*), who did rewrites on *Saving Private Ryan*, recounted the situation for *Variety* editor in chief Peter Bart, for his book *The Gross*, which chronicles the making of the movie: "When I heard how Steven intended to shoot the first twenty minutes, my first reaction was, hell, the story is irrelevant. If he could deliver those twenty minutes, you could run a Buick commercial for the rest of the movie."

When Frank arrived on the set in County Wexford, Ireland (Spielberg likes to have writers on hand during filming, in the event that an idea strikes), in July of 1997, Spielberg was in the midst of the opening sequence, and pumped: "He's telling me the whole D-day sequence. He's in the middle of shooting, and he's saying, 'They're gonna come up the beach there, come out of the boat there . . .' He had the whole thing in his head," Frank said.

As usual, Spielberg was multitasking with a vengeance; when the crew broke for lunch, he would retreat into his tent and edit *Amistad*. "He's cutting *Amistad* on a Moviola, showing me clips from the film," Frank said. "It was like film school. I'd go in my trailer, rewrite scenes, then every once in a while, I'd come back out and watch him blow things up."

Spielberg was in heaven. He once said to a colleague, "I grew up with my mother and my sister. I loved making *Saving Private Ryan*, because it was a bunch of guys—it's all about male bonding!"

Although Spielberg was wound up, the atmosphere on the set was "all business," said Rodat. "Steven is surrounded by competent people, real professionals. He's clearly in control. People are not fooling around." No one can afford to, seeing as working for Spielberg means being able to think on your feet. Rodat recalled Spielberg preparing to shoot a scene with Tom Hanks and "trying to set up the shot, figuring out where he wanted Tom . . . He said, 'I want the camera here.' He looked at the ground, there was a fake shell hole, four feet deep. Looking at it, he said, 'How can we put the camera in that?' Ten seconds later, five guys with shovels showed up and finished filling in the shell fifteen seconds before the camera started rolling. He never told them to fill in the hole."

The complexity and danger of the shoot added another level of intensity to an already ultraserious undertaking. "I remember a day when these burning guys came out of a landing craft," Rodat said. "It was really intense, like a dozen or so stunt guys wearing fire suits were in the landing crafts and then an explosion lights and all these guys are on fire all at the same time, with Tom Hanks in the foreground. It was an incredibly complex shot. One guy was assigned the fire extinguisher for each of the stuntmen, and everybody prepared for the shot all day long. It was beyond dangerous. You could've lost twelve people in one shot. Everybody was really serious. The stuntmen were focused.

"They did the shot, the fire control guys put out the burning stuntmen, finally the stuntmen raised their hands, said, 'OK.' There were maybe a hundred people there. A third of them were weeping. It was this weird combination of what happened at Omaha Beach and the depiction of it."

The filming of *Ryan* may have been intense, but the director was on comfortable turf here, especially coming off *Amistad*. World War II was a favorite subject that Spielberg had grappled with over the years, in *1941, Empire of the Sun,* and *Schindler's List.* It was also the frequent terrain of one of Spielberg's favorite filmmakers, Lewis Milestone, whose fluid camerawork (in *All Quiet on the Western Front, A Walk in the Sun,* and *Pork Chop Hill*) the director admired and, to a degree, sought to imitate. Spielberg saw *Saving Private Ryan* as his own contribution to the genre, an important film for Americans and also for himself, as he considered it an homage of sorts to a man who aroused in him many conflicting feelings: his father, a World War II veteran who'd been a radio operator aboard a B-25 bomber during the Burma campaign. Spielberg's father had dropped out of his life when he was young, and never showed himself to be much of a fan of his son's earlier films. With *Saving Private Ryan,* Spielberg had a chance to fix his "daddy damage," as one person put it, once and for all.

Spielberg's partners at DreamWorks were less concerned about the motives, Freudian or otherwise, driving Spielberg. They just wanted the movie made and released. Coming off its inauspicious debut year, which was followed by another letdown in early 1998—*Paulie,* the movie about the talking parrot, grossed just $26 million—Dream-Works needed a swift turnaround. Katzenberg was putting the final touches on *Antz* and *Prince of Egypt,* but they wouldn't be ready until the end of the year. As for other live-action prospects, *Deep Impact,* an $80 million end-of-the-world thriller (director Mimi Leder's follow-up to *The Peacemaker*), was due out just before *Ryan,* in May. That film had been troubled, and Spielberg had confessed to one DreamWorks executive that it was sure to bring "more bad publicity" to the new company. DreamWorks—and especially Spielberg—was making a difficult adjustment to the new media environment it found itself in.

So concerned was Spielberg about *Deep Impact*—a screening of the film at Paramount, which was coproducing the movie, had been so disastrous that executives walked out mumbling "straight to video"—that he was taking footage home at night and coming back in the next morning with notes for Leder. Walter Parkes was also in on the rescue effort, working with Leder in the editing room and rewriting the film's final scene, a monologue voiced by Morgan Freeman. Even Geffen weighed in, giving suggestions to producer Richard Zanuck: "Go for the gut, go for the emotions!"

But Geffen had bigger problems to worry about than tweaking a movie. He and Spielberg were in a tiff over *Memoirs of a Geisha,* Arthur Golden's best-selling novel. Spielberg wanted to turn it into a feature film and direct for Sony after *Saving Private Ryan* (Sony owned the rights and was eager to get things moving with Spielberg). When Spielberg said he wanted to make the film in Japanese with non-Hollywood actors, his own studio—i.e., Geffen and Katzenberg—balked, fearing another *Amistad.* But most troublesome was Spielberg's generous directing fee. (If the film was made, because of Spielberg's involvement, DreamWorks would come in as a cofinancier.) The situation wrought such tension that the three men stopped talking for a period. When word got out that trouble was brewing, one person inquired about the matter to Katzenberg, who said coolly, "We're handling it."

With relations between the partners fraying, rumors swirled that DreamWorks needed a bailout and saw one in Edgar Bronfman Jr., whose legacy at Universal was going down in the history books as one of the more painful. Since the especially undistinguished deal with DreamWorks, Bronfman had done his share of what many considered to be foolish deals. Not only had he sold most of Universal's domestic cable TV assets to Barry Diller's HSN Inc. (since renamed USA Networks), he had paid more than $75 million for half of the production arm of the fabled management company Brillstein-Grey, not seeming to get that it was the management entity, not the production one, that was worth something. Hollywood was shaking its head. Bronfman had cut Universal's chairman and CEO, Frank Biondi, out of the deal with Diller, only telling him about it afterward. As Universal faltered—the film division hadn't had a hit since *The Lost World*—Bronfman was unceremoniously firing key members of his management team, as well as the heads of marketing. The press was all over it. The worst came in May, when he shared with Connie Bruck his feelings about Hollywood, in a profile in *The New Yorker:* "It's a dumb town."

Hollywood might be many things, dumb among them, but it was never dumb on the record, never dumb in *The New Yorker.* Within days the *d*-word was swiftly redirected, at Bronfman in the *Los Angeles Times.*

One person who remained uncharacteristically mute was Geffen, who, it was perceived, was approaching that moment when it was time to cash in on his relationship with the beleaguered Seagram scion. Three years after DreamWorks had come to Bronfman's aid by signing a splashy distribution deal and delivering Spielberg, it was time for payback. As one executive told Bruck: "Everyone is saying the ultimate rescuer of DreamWorks is Edgar. He's like a piñata. Hit him and money comes out." The rumor even landed on the *New York Post*'s page 6, where it was reported that high-level talks were going on between Universal, DreamWorks, and Barry Diller's USA Network about joining forces. Everyone denied the talk, and nothing came of it, but the idea that DreamWorks was struggling was not so far-fetched. With still little product to show for itself, DreamWorks had burned through more than a billion in start-up funds. There was talk of shuttering divisions, of making DreamWorks a little less multimedia empire, a little more plain old studio.

For the time being—until Katzenberg's promised animation engine kicked in—*Saving Private Ryan* looked like the company's best bet—or at least, it had. After the Friday-afternoon screening, Rodat called up his agent, Devra Lieb, of the Hohman, Maybank, Lieb agency, and said: "Dev. It's like—*whoa*."

Robert Rodat had first come up with the idea for a World War II movie in 1995, while spending the summer with his wife and children in the town of Keene, New Hampshire. That summer, when his wife gave him a copy of historian Stephen Ambrose's book *D-Day: June 6, 1944; The Climactic Battle of World War II,* he dug in. As Rodat read the Ambrose book, he became fascinated by the story of the Niland family, whose four sons went off to fight in World War II. As related by Ambrose, after three of the young men were killed, the Army organized a mission to rescue the fourth brother, so that not all of the Nilands would be lost to history quite so soon. (In fact, only two brothers were killed, a detail that Spielberg would correct.)

"I had just read one hundred pages describing furious violence, and all I could think of was: How did they snatch that guy out of there?" Rodat recalled. His next thought was, "Think of that poor bastard's mother," which was followed by, "Hey! *I've* got a mother." Now the story gained poignance. Sensing there was something there, he rattled off his ideas to his wife, finally asking: "Is this a movie?"

Rodat had first met Mark Gordon, a prolific television and film producer whose credits included both *Speed* films, when they'd worked together on a TV biopic about Jack the Ripper. Gordon loved Rodat's idea and promptly took it out to every studio in town. All passed except for Paramount, where Don Granger, an executive, loved it. "Stay here," he instructed Rodat after he'd finished his pitch, and left his office to grab John Goldwyn, Paramount's president of production. When Goldwyn—grandson of movie pioneer Samuel Goldwyn—heard the idea, he bought it on the spot.

Rodat turned in his first draft of the script to Paramount in January of 1996. Since the studio had first expressed enthusiasm in Rodat's pitch, however, it had bought two other World War II movies, both of which had major stars attached. Bruce Willis was interested in starring in *Combat!* Arnold Schwarzenegger was attached to *On the Wings of Eagles*. Paramount said that it wasn't going to make all three; Rodat and Gordon grew nervous.

"We were screwed because we didn't have a star," Rodat said. "Mark's attitude was, 'Look, we're going to get it made sooner or later; there's no way it's not getting made, but who knows how or when.' It didn't look good."

Gordon decided to take things into his own hands. He gave a copy of the screenplay to Carin Sage, an agent at CAA, and to a handful of directors. Richard Donner (*Lethal Weapon*) and Bob Zemeckis passed, but Rob Cohen, who was in postproduction on a film at Paramount, was interested. Over a dinner meeting, Cohen and Gordon enthusiastically discussed the script, and by the end of the meal, it seemed like an easy match.

But the next morning, as Gordon was about to call Cohen's agents to start negotiating, he received a call from CAA partner Richard Lovett. "Don't make an offer yet," Lovett instructed. "I can't tell you why, but we may have some big news by the end of the day."

Gordon was mystified. Twelve hours later, at eight o'clock in the evening, as Gordon was finishing up work at his office, Lovett called again. This time he was less coy. Tom Hanks, he said, was interested in *Saving Private Ryan* and wanted to discuss it over lunch. Lovett instructed Gordon to "make [Hanks] feel comfortable with the project. And don't tell anyone that he's interested." (CAA operates according to the belief that silence is always the best policy.) Gordon couldn't believe what he was hearing. Tom *Hanks?*

Over lunch, Hanks spoke thoughtfully about the lead character he would play: Captain John H. Miller, who, in the aftermath of the D-day invasion, leads a dangerous mission across enemy lines in France to find a soldier, Private James Ryan, after all three of his brothers have been killed in combat. Hanks talked about how the mission would have affected his character, and how he would understandably feel ambivalence toward Ryan, given how ungrateful he turned out to be, seemingly indifferent to the hardships that Miller and his troops had endured on their journey to find him. Hanks also said that if he were to play Miller, the character would have to be softened. He preferred a more nuanced soldier who was less defined by stereotypical macho ticks, like cigar chomping and hurling foul-mouthed orders at his underlings. He introduced the idea of a "citizen-soldier" as opposed to a born-and-bred Army man—someone who wasn't a career soldier and who, more than anything, just wanted the war to be over so that he could go home and resume his normal life.

Gordon listened attentively. Things couldn't have been going any better. Or so he thought. Suddenly, Hanks broke off his train of thought and said—"What would you think about Steven Spielberg directing this?"

Gordon didn't know what to say. "Well, yeah," he replied, struggling for words. Then he mustered up something more definitive: "That sounds like a good idea."

Unbeknownst to Gordon, Sage, who had given the script to Hanks, had also pitched the project to Spielberg, when he had come in to CAA for one of his update meetings. More typically, CAA agents met with Spielberg at Amblin; on the occasions when the director graced the stately premises of the agency's intimidatingly sleek headquarters, there was a big to-do. On those days, agents—who met with Spielberg around a conference table in a meeting room—were particularly well-versed in what projects were set up where around town and the ins and outs of the most interesting material. Of those projects, they selected one or two that Spielberg might fancy, and pitched them with relish and efficiency (everyone knew Spielberg had a short attention span), each taking their turn as they went around the room doing their best to wow their star client. Even so, no one was very hopeful—Spielberg famously never made movies based on pitches from agents. On Spielberg's most recent visit, Sage had brought up *Saving Private Ryan*. Spielberg listened quietly as she explained the narrative, smiling faintly. When she finished, he politely said that he would be sure to read the script.

Devra Lieb knew something was up when she was having lunch one afternoon with her partner, Bayard Maybank, and two Paramount executives, Michael Hackett and David Solomon, at Ca'Brea, an Italian restaurant in the Miracle Mile section of L.A. Both of the executives looked like cats who'd swallowed canaries—all atwitter, about what they wouldn't say.

"You have no idea what's going on," Solomon said, smiling. "When you go back to your office, call Mark Gordon."

"They were giddy, practically vibrating at the table," Lieb recalled.

Lieb did as she was told and dialed up Gordon, who said: "Dev, OK, who are the biggest actor and the biggest director?"

Lieb knew right away. *Mission: Impossible* had come out in May and grossed over $450 million worldwide. "Brian De Palma and Tom Cruise," she replied, referring to that blockbuster's director and star.

"No, you ass!" Gordon said good-humoredly.

"OK, who?"

Gordon paused. "Dev—Steven Spielberg and Tom Hanks want to make *Saving Private Ryan*. DreamWorks and Paramount are going to make it. It's happening."

Sherry Lansing, president of Paramount Pictures, received the news as she was driving home on a Friday evening after a long week at work. Lansing had been grappling with the battle of the World War II pictures (Spielberg's as well as the projects starring Bruce Willis and Arnold Schwarzenegger)—what she considered a "high-class problem," considering that they were all strong scripts. But none had emerged as the front-runner. It was a quarter to seven as she was navigating the windy road up Benedict Canyon. Suddenly her phone rang. It was Lovett.

Lansing answered with her perennial cheerfulness.

"Sherry," Lovett began in his low-key but utterly businesslike manner. "How would you like it if Steven Spielberg and Tom Hanks did *Saving Private Ryan*? How does that sound to you?"

"He said it, like, literally, Do you want the mustard or the ketchup," Lansing recalled. "I just said, Yeah, that'd be just fine."

"OK," Lovett replied succinctly. "Well, I think we can make that happen."

Indeed, he could, no matter what it took. *Variety* reported that CAA had been "moving mountains" to make Spielberg's and Hanks's deals. If *Saving Private Ryan* got made with the two stars, it would be as much CAA's accomplishment as anyone else's, seeing as it was the first film that the agency had "packaged" for Spielberg since Michael

Ovitz had signed him as a client. (Although CAA technically only represented Spielberg, and not DreamWorks, the two were one and the same at the agency. "We had DreamWorks up the ass at CAA," said one former CAA agent. "It was 'Steven Spielberg said this, Jeffrey said that, David is killing us about that.'")

When Lansing arrived at her home, the phone was ringing. It was Jonathan Dolgen, Paramount's chairman. "Did you get the call?" he asked.

"It can't be real," Lansing said, by now beginning to realize what, exactly, Lovett's words had meant. "This can't possibly be true."

Lansing was accustomed to the protracted negotiations that were practically required when it came to landing stars on the caliber of Spielberg and Hanks and negotiating their contracts. There was no way a deal with either, much less both, could have come together so quickly and smoothly.

The next morning Dolgen called again. "It's true," he said. "David Geffen called me and asked how we could make the deal."

When Lansing finally allowed herself to believe the news, "You heard a scream so loud," she recalled.

To determine how the studios would divvy up domestic and foreign distribution rights, Geffen and Viacom chairman Sumner Redstone resorted to a coin toss at the Beverly Hills Hotel. Whoever won would receive the more desirable domestic rights. Redstone called "heads." DreamWorks called "tails." It was tails.

But for all of the cork popping over a Steven Spielberg–Tom Hanks production, the deal was less a cause for celebration in its nitty-gritty details, both for Paramount and DreamWorks. Both Spielberg and Hanks were demanding 20 percent of first-dollar grosses. To keep *Ryan*'s budget down to a modest $65 million, Spielberg and Hanks were willing to lower their upfront fees, but they were standing firm on back-end. After a month of haggling between CAA and Paramount, the stars agreed to lower their back-end a smidgen to 17.5 percent each. Even so, the deal was better for the stars than for DreamWorks or Paramount, with 35 percent going out the door to the big names.

Over the summer of 1996, while Spielberg was in the Hamptons, a series of script "deconstruction" meetings was held with Spielberg, Rodat, and others. In one meeting, Rodat, Hanks, Parkes, and producers Gordon and Gary Levinsohn were gathered in Spielberg's home office in L.A., while Spielberg was videoconferenced in on a large TV screen from Long Island.

"What are the key outtakes?" Spielberg asked from three thousand miles away. What the director wanted to know was what scenes Rodat had tossed aside and discarded while writing.

Rodat cleared his throat before addressing the projection of Spielberg's face.

"Well," Rodat said, "I thought Miller should die."

In Rodat's initial script, Captain Miller, the character Tom Hanks would play, had died at the end of the movie. But Paramount executives had insisted that killing Miller off was too much of a downer. So Rodat had rewritten the ending so that Miller lived—a plot point he'd never liked.

"You bet he's got to die," Spielberg replied without hesitation, his voice crackling a little over the transmission.

Spielberg's words—which may as well have been sent down from the heavens accompanied by a thunderbolt—rendered Rodat ecstatic. On any movie, the director is God, but never more so than on a Spielberg film, where what Spielberg says overrides all else. With Miller taken care of, the conversation next segued to the title character, Private Ryan.

"I'd seriously considered that he was a prick when they found him and thought of spinning around on that, making the soldiers question their motivation," said Rodat. "But it ultimately didn't work for me. Ryan is supposed to represent America."

Tom Hanks weighed in with the notion that Ryan be incapacitated when Captain Miller finds him—a bandaged-up, mysterious figure, a "nonparticipatory MacGuffin," said Rodat.

During the discussion, in which everyone was throwing out ideas, "deconstructing and considering really radical things," Rodat said, Spielberg was the evenhanded moderator.

"Steven was doing the Kennedy leader thing—asking questions but not making decisions," said Rodat. "He was letting us fight it out."

Afterward, Rodat went home and incorporated the notes in his script. The backstories of the secondary characters were scaled back, and the tone of the film became more earnest. In Rodat's initial script, the dialogue between the soldiers had been more flippant and irreverent—Spielberg wanted that gone.

"Talking to my father and the guys with whom he served, there was always a degree of black humor," Rodat said. "I was always struck by the odd combination between the seriousness with what happened to them and the lack of seriousness with which they talked about it. They were young men. I tried to capture that in the script."

In the new draft, "humor as an escape from anguish was used less. The spectrum of emotions became somewhat narrower," Rodat said.

A dose of Spielbergian sentimentality was also added via the two sequences that bookend the film, showing James Francis Ryan as an elderly veteran visiting the cemetery at Normandy with his family years after the war. The scenes were Spielberg's idea and were, he said, in honor of World War II vets. Parkes and Scott Frank had tried to talk Spielberg out of the prologue and epilogue, thinking they were unnecessary, but Spielberg felt strongly about their inclusion.

Parkes was also involved in shaping the script, and, as was his custom, he would board out the film on three-by-five-inch cards pinned up on a bulletin board (a process that drove some writers mad) to study the story and see how it hung together.

Spielberg's tendency is also to work with multiple writers, and in the fall, Frank Darabont, who'd written *The Shawshank Redemption,* was hired to do a rewrite of Rodat's script.

"Steven tends to use writers like paintbrushes," remarked James V. Hart, one of a number of screenwriters who worked on Spielberg's *Hook.* On that film, he said, "The joke was that everyone in town who had his fax number was writing for it."

Darabont spent several months on *Saving Private Ryan,* dramatically reimagining the script. Then, two weeks before *Ryan* was to begin shooting, in July of 1997, writer Scott Frank was brought on. "The mission for me was to delineate the characters—make one guy more religious, make one guy a writer," said Frank. "I was also executing various research odds and ends, story ideas that Steven had. During shooting, he would say he wanted a scene where they were all cleaning their guns, or where they were stepping on cow patties because they knew there were no land mines there. He comes up with tons of ideas while shooting."

Rodat also returned as things went into overdrive in the days before cameras rolled. "It was intense. Those were twenty-hour days. I was writing pages as fast as I could, sending them over [to Spielberg] every day."

Besides receiving notes from Spielberg, Rodat was also getting input from Captain Dale Dye, a retired Marine officer who'd served three tours of duty in Vietnam and who had been hired as a military consultant on *Saving Private Ryan.*

"He would send me these incredibly long, well-put-together tech documents, saying 'This guy wouldn't say that. This weaponry is wrong. This is the tactic in this case,'" said Rodat. "I was incorporating those and then talking to Steven constantly, maybe every night or two we'd have long telephone conversations, then I'd crank out more pages."

Meanwhile, Ian Bryce, whom Spielberg had brought onto the project as a line producer, had scouted locations in the U.K. and Ireland to fill in for the beaches of Normandy and the French countryside. It was showtime.

As *Ryan* gained steam, however, two people who were becoming marginalized in the process were producers Mark Gordon and Gary Levinsohn, who were learning what it meant to be part of a Steven Spielberg movie when you weren't part of the family. Although Gordon had been instrumental in getting the film off the ground, once *Ryan* switched into production mode, he was not included in the day-to-day making of the movie. Spielberg's chosen producer was Bryce. Bonnie Curtis, Spielberg's former assistant, also joined the film as a coproducer.

Gordon's being exed out came as a blow. According to one source, Gordon "desperately" wanted to be more involved in making *Ryan;* however, "that was not an option."

When Terry Press first viewed *Saving Private Ryan,* her reaction was along the lines of Rodat's. *Holy shit. How am I gonna sell this baby?* No one spoke for thirty minutes! There were virtually no women in the film! And the running time was nearly three hours—concerns she aired with her staff. No matter how brilliant, how artistically triumphant, this was no heart-warming *M*A*S*H* episode. On top of all this, Spielberg, in the aftermath of the *Amistad* debacle, was feeling particularly vulnerable. Having been stung by the press coverage on that film, his self-protection mechanisms were on high alert. Spielberg was always secretive about his films, and paranoid about footage being leaked early, but on *Saving Private Ryan,* he played it even more close to the vest than usual. Marketers working on the teaser trailer were only given a few frames of the film, along with some lines of dialogue and a shot of Tom Hanks. There was so little footage to work with that the teaser ended up being made in slow motion in order to eat up time.

When Press asked Spielberg for another shot, the one where the Ryan brothers' mother, seeing a car winding up the road to her home, falls to her knees, evoking Andrew Wyeth's Christina, understanding that it's an Army official bearing the worst possible news, Spielberg refused.

As in her dealings with the director over *Amistad,* Press held her ground, knowing that if you argued your point cohesively with Spielberg, he often came around. "Steven, this is a movie about war. I guarantee, if you give me this shot, women will come. This is the mother's experience of what this—war—is all about. It's important people see this."

Spielberg and Press continued to butt heads, but eventually the director relented, and was pleased when, after the spot aired, he received a call from someone outside of DreamWorks, saying how great that scene was. But Press's work was just beginning. A much bigger issue she needed Spielberg to come around to was the idea that he needed to get out in the world and sell his picture. The film needed to be presented as something more than just a World War II movie; that would get the veterans in, but what about thirteen-year-old boys, the most sacred demographic of all? Press knew that nothing could sell *Saving Private Ryan* better than Steven Spielberg. She wanted him to go on the road and personally present the first forty minutes of the film to audiences. But Spielberg hated to campaign. Hated dealing with the press, and hated the idea that he *had* to sell himself or his movie. Not only did it not seem necessary (this was Steven Spielberg, not some kid from USC's graduating class), it was crass. Spielberg adhered to the philosophy that artistic works should speak for themselves, and hadn't taken a film "on the road" since *Raiders of the Lost Ark.* He despised the hype and the self-promotion.

When Press broached the subject, she was, predictably, shot down. And so she enlisted Marvin Levy, Spielberg's longtime press representative, as well as Katzenberg, in her cause. Finally, Spielberg gave in. He would go on the road for *Private Ryan*.

In May, two months before *Saving Private Ryan* was released, for the first time in a long while, the fates seemed to—at last—be smiling down on DreamWorks. *Deep Impact,* despite its laughable early screening, despite Spielberg's fears of disaster, was the company's first hit, grossing an impressive $140 million, thus beating the summer's most anticipated blockbuster, *Godzilla.*

The mood at the studio dipped once again in early July, when *Small Soldiers* proved a disappointment, grossing $54 million, spoiling Spielberg's dreams of a mega toy-merchandising opportunity. But then, suddenly, it was July 21, the night of the worldwide premiere for *Saving Private Ryan* at the Mann Village Theatre in Westwood, a grand, spire-topped 1940s Spanish-mission-style theater.

If ever there was a time for Spielberg to shine, and to signal the kind of turnaround that his studio was so desperate for, it was now. He seemed to know it. That night, wrote Peter Bart in *The Gross,* "was clearly Steven Spielberg's moment . . . unlike other such events this summer, [it] had the pomp and excitement of a true celebration. This was a premiere that Hollywood insiders actually *wanted* to attend. All of the principal streets of Westwood were blocked off as hundreds of stargazers lined up for a glimpse of Tom Hanks, Sylvester Stallone, Rene Russo, Bill Paxton and others. In a tribute to Spielberg's charisma, more filmmakers were in attendance than at any premiere within memory—the likes of James L. Brooks, Rob Reiner, Oliver Stone and Penny Marshall."

Before the premiere, a private party was held at the Geffen Playhouse, where a grinning Spielberg found himself caught up in a whirl of congratulatory backslaps and air kisses. In between talk of World War II, he spoke about his new anticancer, fruits-and-vegetables-only diet, prescribed by Goldie Hawn. "You've got to squeeze and mix your own fruit juice," he advised. "You can't delegate that task to anyone else."

Spielberg, in top form, personally introduced the film. Though he looked his typical unassuming self, even slightly diminished standing before the crowd of fourteen hundred, his words negated any sense of smallness.

He began by saying that "D-day was nothing less than the pivotal moment of the twentieth century"; that it wasn't just about warfare, but about "saving Western Civilization."

And with that, the lights went down.

For DreamWorks, the lights effectively came up when opening weekend box-office grosses came in for *Saving Private Ryan* a week later. The film opened to an impressive $30 million. Over the next several weeks it would total an even more impressive $216 million in the U.S. Worldwide, it wound up making $481 million.

If *Deep Impact* had suggested an about-face, *Saving Private Ryan* confirmed a new dawn, both for DreamWorks and Spielberg. Validation was in the air. The studio's critics now faced a film that Janet Maslin, in the *New York Times,* called a "soberly magnificent new war film, the second such pinnacle in a career of magical versatility."

In *Newsweek,* David Ansen wrote: "Spielberg has taken Hollywood's depiction of war to a new level . . . The truth is, this movie so wiped me out I have little taste for quibbling. When you emerge from Spielberg's cauldron, the world doesn't look quite the same."

But Geffen, naturally, summed up the significance of *Saving Private Ryan* more sagaciously than any film critic. The film, he said, meant, "We don't have to take any shit for a while."

Maybe. But the reality under the glowing reviews and strong box-office numbers was a bit troubling. Because of Spielberg's and Hanks's generous deals, and the fact that revenues were being split with Paramount, DreamWorks only received about $40 million of the film's true net—or close to what DreamWorks had put up to make the film. It would not be the first time Spielberg's profits would outsize those of his studio.

Eight years after buying the old Jack Warner estate in Beverly Hills, Geffen finally moved in. Having done the heavy lifting of schmoozing investors and getting DreamWorks up and running, he'd returned to a more comfortable autopilot setting. He was spending time with John Seabrook, who was writing a profile of him for *The New Yorker;* hanging out with Bill Clinton, who was finding in Geffen a more hip

Hollywood host than Lew Wasserman. The two men had grown so close that, on a recent trip to L.A., the president had asked to stay over at Geffen's Malibu home. Geffen hadn't been able to put him up, so he'd offered him Katzenberg's pad, just a few houses down the beach, instead. After the sleepover, Clinton had called Geffen and said, "How come Jeffrey's house is so much nicer than yours? I thought he was the one who doesn't have any money." Geffen had replied: "Well, 'broke' is a Hollywood term!"

But Geffen's relationship with the president of the United States was no different than his relationships with everyone else in his life. The ever-critical mogul was starting to see flaws in Clinton, weaknesses. When the Democrats lost control of Congress in 1994, Geffen felt Clinton was to blame, and he was disheartened by the president's "don't ask, don't tell" stance on gays in the military. But what really pushed him over the edge was the Monica Lewinsky scandal, which broke in January of 1998, and which "drove David up the wall," according to a source. In Clinton, Geffen was beginning to see a man who was not being led by his convictions, who was more about political expediency than a real belief in the issues, and who was putting his own interests before those of the country. And to Geffen, whom friends describe as a "political purist," an uncompromising idealist, there was nothing worse. Geffen still stood staunchly by Clinton, publicly saying that Clinton's private life was his own business, and raising more money for him than anyone else on the Left Coast—nearly $20 million during his time in office. But there were signs that the honeymoon would not last.

Geffen's new home was the new focus of Geffen's always-searching life. The sprawling property, tucked among a sea of freshly planted sycamore trees, was what the $80 million animation studio in Glendale—also ready to be inhabited—was to Katzenberg. This personal castle, with its neoclassical columns, sweeping staircase, art deco screening room, billiard room, gym, pine-paneled library, and collection of Pollocks, Rauschenbergs, and De Koonings, represented a passage of sorts—a physical upgrade from mogul to king. Jack Warner's office and dressing room had been left completely untouched; in the latter room, Warner's hairbrushes and tonic bottles were lying on a table, as though the new owner were expecting a ghost.

Geffen seemed comfortable. The company was doing better, so he proudly showed off his new home to friends and began hosting dinner parties there, inviting former superagent Sue Mengers, Barry Diller, and even manager turned producer Sandy Gallin, a close friend with whom he'd been in a year-and-a-half silent feud. On a professional level, Geffen's new address meant that he was less present at DreamWorks, where, during the company's start-up years, he had been at least a semiregular presence, often seeming to enjoy being in the thick of things as the company got up and going. But Geffen's new home was his new headquarters. He took all of his meetings, even with DreamWorks executives, there.

As Geffen retreated into his personal quarters, the perception of him as a godfather figure, of someone who stage-managed from afar, grew. Nine times out of ten, sources asked to describe Geffen's role in the company gave some variation of: "He's the behind-the-scenes guy—he swoops in and hammers out the deals, fixes the problems." Most executives at DreamWorks, even those at a high level, could count on one hand the number of times they had ever even seen Geffen over the course of several years.

On days when Geffen actually showed up at his DreamWorks office, a ripple of excitement and intrigue was sent through the employee ranks. However the rich man's role might be described, it was clear that he had no interest in being the "hands-on" guy. In *The New Yorker,* Seabrook observed: "Geffen's job at DreamWorks did not seem to take up an inordinate amount of his time." With Katzenberg putting in all the sweat equity, Geffen was free to "work with investment bankers, play devil's advocate, and float."

Part of his godfather role, one that did take up an inordinate amount of time, was the business of advising—and not just Katzenberg and Spielberg, but a horde of other artists and executives who found themselves in a pinch or otherwise were in need of steely, remorseless guidance. One such person was George Michael, who in April was arrested for demonstrating "lewd" behavior in a public restroom in a Beverly Hills park. Although Michael hadn't been happy with DreamWorks' handling of his last album, *Older,* he knew there was no one better at crisis management than Geffen. Indeed, Geffen orchestrated a public relations offensive, arranging for Michael to appear on Maria Shriver's news program *Dateline NBC* a few days after the incident. More significantly, Michael had decided to finally come out and admit that he was gay. The singer's career had been built on the image of a hunky ladies' man who wore tight jeans and who understood, as he wrote in his song "Freedom '90," "But when you shake your ass / They notice fast." The admission could potentially hurt his following, making his decision to talk truthfully about his sexuality all the more meaningful. In the end, Michael ended up ditching the date with Shriver in order to break the news faster on CNN. But even so, Geffen had once again come through for a friend in need, business squabbles momentarily forgotten.

Older wasn't the only struggling DreamWorks Records release. By 1998, only two of the label's releases had gone platinum — *Older* and the original cast album for *Rent*. And only one other, Chris Rock's *Bring the Pain*, had sold more than five hundred thousand units. But despite its sluggish sales, the label was faithfully living up to DreamWorks' promise to put art first. Indeed, Michael had been the only big-name, blatantly mainstream signing. After its first wave of signing alternative, left-of-center acts, Geffen's label kept up the serious-seeming feel, securing artists such as the Eels, Henry Rollins, Rufus Wainwright, and Elliott Smith, who'd gained acclaim (and an Oscar nomination) for songs that appeared in the film *Good Will Hunting*. They were artists unlikely to become huge stars, but their music, often critically acclaimed, inspired dedicated cult followings. With Mo Ostin and Lenny Waronker, this was all that mattered. DreamWorks wasn't putting pressure on its artists for immediate monster albums. True to the old strategies, the company looked to be thinking long-term, second, third, or even fourth albums. In 1998 such thinking was an anomaly. As the record business was consolidating, coming under increased pressure from corporate parents, the music business was all about the instant hit.

One music veteran who, fearing the wrath of Geffen, spoke on condition of anonymity, summed it up. "Lenny and Mo's thing was to develop artists, and it ran counter to how the industry was thinking. The new attitude was: concentrate on today's hit today; worry about tomorrow, tomorrow. It was incredibly short-range thinking."

The contrast between the attitude at DreamWorks and other labels was so bold as to be almost unfathomable. "DreamWorks was so blatantly artist-friendly that everyone was looking at them like, you can't keep this up. When are you going to sign the straight-out hit band?" said one manager. Still, DreamWorks stuck to its guns. One band, Ours, discovered and signed by Michael Goldstone in 1997, did not release its first record for DreamWorks until 2001.

Nurturing, however, meant spending, something that DreamWorks Records was doing rather freely. There were the requisite perks (people at Geffen Records referred to DreamWorks Records as "Snack Works" due to its well-stocked pantry), and also the money that went toward backing and promoting artists who were not—yet, anyway—producing hits. In many ways, DreamWorks was spending along the lines of a major record label, even though it was only releasing a quarter, or less, the amount of records that majors typically release.

By the fall of 1998, Geffen was concerned about just how freely money was flowing, and he brought in Jim Walker, the former CFO of Geffen Records, to look after the label's finances. One of the first things Walker did was cancel the annual Christmas party, earning him the nickname "the Grinch" among employees. But when Ostin's wife, Evelyn, heard about the change in plans, she arranged for the festivities to be held at the label's offices, paying for the catering herself. Walker also clamped down on business expenses, assigning budgets to projects and instituting overall cutbacks.

"There was less crazy spending," said one former employee. "We stopped spending ridiculous amounts of money on projects that didn't deserve it."

Fiscal extravagance aside, Ostin and Waronker's focus on quality —and doing whatever it took to achieve that quality—won the label praise for its integrity and taste, and in 1998, three DreamWorks re-leases—Smith's *XO*, Wainwright's eponymous debut, and the Eels' second album, *Electro-Shock Blues*—were singled out by veteran music critic Robert Hilburn. Writing in the *L.A. Times*, Hilburn called Smith's album "one of three absorbing collections from DreamWorks—a run that suggests label chiefs Mo Ostin and Lenny Waronker are recreating at DreamWorks the same kind of focus on quality artists and long-term career building that they used in the '70s and '80s to make War-ner Bros. the world's most respected label."

Hilburn called Wainwright a "singer-songwriter with a musical vi-sion elegant enough to embrace Noel Coward and Cole Porter"; the Eels were "a Los Angeles rock band whose songs offer the kind of unflinching look at desolation and death that is at once harrowing and inspiring." But even Hilburn couldn't help but ask, "Will a focus on careful career development still pay off in a pop world that, from conglomerate board rooms to radio station programmers to consumers, seems interested only in the short term?"

17

BUG WARS

I N JUNE OF 1998, just as Disney released its latest animated feature, *Mulan* (another non–*Lion King*, it grossed $120 million), Katzenberg had news: he had pushed up *Antz*'s release date to October—five months earlier than originally planned, and a month before *A Bug's Life,* Pixar's insect movie, was scheduled for release.

The decision had been made months before, after Spielberg and Geffen saw a cut of the film and felt that it was strong enough to push. Wanting to not only beat the enemy, but take the enemy by surprise, Katzenberg had instructed everyone involved in the schedule change to keep it quiet. Not even DreamWorks animators in Los Angeles were told that DreamWorks had jumped to first place in the bug race. But animators and visual-effects engineers were working around the clock, and new bodies were brought onboard, to get the movie finished.

"Everybody was working more hours," said animator Noel McGinn. "We were trying to get as much out as possible . . . Everyone was complaining, and it was hard, but at the same time there was such an excitement about getting the film out—a feature film that was our own —that people were OK with it in the end."

According to company sources, the news didn't filter back to Pixar until not long before the official DreamWorks announcement.

Everyone at Pixar was furious, most of all John Lasseter.

"For Jeffrey, it's all about himself and all about getting the work done. But John is a bighearted guy," said a former Pixar employee. "He has a parental attitude and the heart of an enthusiastic kid. I think in his case [what Katzenberg did] really hurt him, and he'd never forgive Jeffrey. He takes those things very personally."

Publicly, DreamWorks dismissed the notion that the date change was spurred by competition with Disney. But within DreamWorks there was no questioning Katzenberg's motivation. According to Sandy Rabins: "There was no doubt. We set out to beat *Bug's Life* to the box office."

Katzenberg was jubilant, as he was about any maneuver that put Disney at a disadvantage. One day he brought in a poster showing the rainbow-striped Apple logo with an *Antz* ant standing on top of it triumphantly. He displayed it prominently and boasted that he'd sent a copy to Steve Jobs.

Generally, there was excitement at PDI about beating the competition to the punch. At the wrap party for *Antz*, PDI cofounder Carl Rosendahl sang a song he'd written about the superiority of red ants over blue ants. (*Antz*'s ants were red; the ones in *A Bug's Life* were blue.) However, for most at DreamWorks/PDI, Disney/Pixar was not seen as the enemy. Many staffers at Pacific Data Images had friends at Pixar, and felt not so much animosity toward Lasseter and his crew as a healthy professional competitiveness. When a finished reel of *Antz* was mistakenly sent to Pixar from a printing company, animators screened it before returning it to PDI. One Pixar artist e-mailed a friend at PDI, noting dryly, "It looks too brown to us."

But Katzenberg's tactics rankled. One former Pixar artist described the studio's feelings toward DreamWorks in an e-mail: "Generally, DreamWorks was seen very negatively at Pixar. Katzenberg, in particular, was the bête noire . . . The promulgated self-image of Pixar was one of commitment to quality work based on story and character. DreamWorks was a bugaboo that was taken to exemplify the wrong way to approach the work. Opinion about Katzenberg's understanding of animation was low. As time went on, this contradistinction between the two companies took on the flavor of accepted wisdom. There was very much the sense of 'us and them' with 'us,' Pixar, occupying the moral high ground."

Katzenberg saw it as "us and them" as well, and he was more than willing to cede Disney the high ground if it meant being able to upstage his former employer. In Glendale, he had built the most luxurious animation studio the world had ever seen. Amenities included a koi pond, olive trees, and an eight-hundred-car garage outfitted with a helipad. And, like most of Katzenberg's grander gestures, the new complex thumbed its nose at the competition down the street in Burbank. Disney's newly built animation facility, completed in 1995, had been met with vocal disdain by animators, who complained that, despite its pedigree (it was designed by Robert A. M. Stern) and playfulness (a three-story version of the star-and-moon-spangled sorcerer's hat worn by Mickey Mouse in *Fantasia* lorded it over the entrance), it was dark and cold, with narrow, walled-in spaces not designed with the needs of animators in mind.

By contrast, Katzenberg's new studio, despite its splendor—the new campus was Mediterranean in theme, with a piazza and five "villas," and oaks, Italian cypresses, and alders—was created, very specifically, to encourage work. Weatherproof electric plugs were decorously landscaped into the area surrounding the koi pond, lest anyone peacefully gazing out at the water suddenly have the urge to fire up their laptop. Free breakfast and lunch was also provided in the "creative services" building, meaning no one would have to leave campus to eat. Katzenberg, who saw to it that a TCBY machine was installed (his favorite kind), used the cafeteria to further his I'm Just One of the Guys identity. "Jeffrey loved to go through the line, he did not want special treatment," said Alicia Ojeda, a former executive chef at the facility. "A lot of people who worked for him would get all crazed—'Oh, Jeffrey's coming, we need to do something really nice.' But he'd show up and say, 'What are we having today? Pizza? Great!'"

But with all three partners now operating out of separate fiefdoms, the physical cohesion that existed when DreamWorks was first formed was diminished. Katzenberg, of course, remained in constant contact with Geffen by way of the phone, and he made a daily stop at Amblin in the morning. Employees knew he was on the premises because his Mustang would be idling in the driveway at eight o'clock. Katzenberg would have been there for hours but, prior to his planned departure, an assistant would pull the car around and rev it up so that Katzenberg could literally just jump in and hit the gas.

Katzenberg had had a hard time getting Geffen to come out and look at the new animation building as it was being constructed—Geffen remained devoutly disengaged from details surrounding DreamWorks that were not part of the big picture—but he managed to ensnare the mogul's presence, along with Spielberg's, for the campus's opening tour. Most of the animators had never set eyes on Geffen before; some asked for his autograph. Geffen did not mask his surprise at what Katzenberg had accomplished. "You know, I haven't really been paying attention to what's been going on over here," he told the group, "but—holy shit!" (No mention was made of another campus across town that was eons away from any ribbon-cutting ceremony.)

On a macro level, the new campus made clear that DreamWorks' animation division was no longer a small, communal enterprise. Four years into its run, the studio was now fully operational, with a 2-D and 3-D pipeline, and a mandate to produce two films every eighteen months—a far more accelerated schedule than that of either Disney, which generally produced one animated film a year, or Pixar, which took up to two years between releases. A beast had been built, and now it would have to be fed.

Antz, released on October 2, made $90 million in the U.S., about as much as it had cost, thanks to high-profile voice talent supplied by Woody Allen, Sharon Stone, Sylvester Stallone, and Dan Aykroyd. No longer were actors always agreeing to make animated films on the cheap, as a "fun" side project that their kids would enjoy. And with more studios in on the act, and willing to do anything to advance their films, they paid up. Yet even if DreamWorks beat Pixar to the box office, already it was suffering in comparison. Critic Kenneth Turan wrote in the *Los Angeles Times* that *Antz* "halfway works, but unlike the computer-generated *Toy Story,* there is no magic in the air, and *Antz* ends up more impressive than embraceable."

In the weeks leading up to the release of *A Bug's Life,* Pixar unleashed its own stream of attacks at DreamWorks.

"Jeffrey stole my idea," Steve Jobs bluntly said in interviews. "We were just disappointed he didn't choose to make a film with an original idea. We're just making the best film we know how to make—which is a different film than he chose to make.

"In the end, copycats don't usually win," he lectured. "To be leeching off other people's creativity doesn't serve you well in the long run."

In the end, Pixar had the last word in the dispute. *A Bug's Life,* which was released on November 25, made $162 million in the U.S. and a total of $363 million worldwide—a touch over what *Toy Story* had made three years earlier (though *A Bug's Life* had cost far more to make than that film). To that, there was nothing Katzenberg could say.

• • •

Meanwhile, over at the live-action studio, in the wake of *Saving Private Ryan*, a far smaller, seemingly inconsequential film was gaining traction, more despite DreamWorks than because of it. *American Beauty* had first come to the company's attention in March of 1998, when a "hot" spec script by TV writer Alan Ball was given to live-action executive Glenn Williamson by producers Bruce Cohen and Dan Jinks. (Since leaving Amblin, Cohen had joined forces with Jinks, who worked as a theater marketer in New York before turning to movie producing, and started up a production company.)

Prior to grabbing the collective attention of Hollywood, Ball—a tall, dry-humored Southerner—had been toiling away for years in the New York theater world. When one of his plays, *Five Women Wearing the Same Dress,* caused a bit of a stir, DreamWorks had considered optioning it. But it hadn't happened, and Ball was forced to keep his "real" job, as a graphic designer at *AdWeek*. By 1994 he'd had enough, and moved out to L.A. to work on sitcoms. But while the money was good, Ball felt creatively starved, never more so than during what he called the sitcom's formula "moments of shit," the feel-good, tie-everything-together flash of insight where a character learns something and the episode ends. The project he turned to wasn't entirely new. He'd come up with it years before and had tried to turn it into a play, but had ultimately abandoned it, shoving it in the proverbial drawer. The inspiration had come from a graphic novel he'd come across in New York that spoofed the tabloid headlines of the time—the saga of Amy Fisher, the "Long Island Lolita" who attempted to murder the wife of her older lover, Joey Buttafuoco, by shooting her in the head.

In Hollywood, Ball started playing around with the Amy-Joey theme when he came home at night from his loathed TV job. "I would come home at like two in the morning and I would sit down at my computer and start working. Certainly, the screenplay to *American Beauty* is fueled by a lot of rage," Ball said.

Indeed. Etched with sharp, noirish dialogue, the screenplay turned on its head—and proceeded to bludgeon—the Beaver Cleaver–esque notion of suburban bliss through the meltdown of Lester Burnham, a blandly responsible husband and father who gets no respect at home or at his dead-end job, and who deals with middle-aged disillusionment by begging his neighbors for pot and fantasizing about his high school daughter's best friend. In the opening voiceover, Burnham deadpans: "My name is Lester Burnham. This is my neighborhood. This is my life. I'm forty-two years old. In less than a year I'll be dead. Of course, I don't know that yet. In a way I'm dead already."

When Jinks handed Williamson the *American Beauty* script, he recalled telling him: "This is maybe the best script we've read in our lives. You *have* to read this. And it's important that you read it yourself. This is the kind of script that, if you rely on coverage, it's going to sound like a bad TV script."

The next day Williamson, having read *American Beauty* the night before, walked into Bob Cooper's office and began excitedly describing Ball's script to DreamWorks' new head of production. Midway through his explanation Williamson stopped and said: "You just have to read this," and handed Cooper the script. (Cooper had a rule that if he was told "You have to read this," he wouldn't ask questions and would just read.) Cooper was about to leave for Cabo for a vacation, but he brought the script with him.

When a few days went by and Williamson hadn't heard back from Cooper, he gave a copy of *American Beauty* to Laurie MacDonald. "I remember being in Laurie's office," Williamson said. "She had real reservations about the script. She talked about *The Ice Storm*, another movie about a dysfunctional family, and how it hadn't done well. But she did say, 'If you feel strongly about it, I'll show it to Steven.'"

As for Walter Parkes, who at the time was busy with a big period film called *Gladiator*, he also had concerns about the film. Though he thought the script was beautifully written, he wondered how the studio was going to sell such a dark movie, and was disturbed by a scene in which Lester Burnham has sex with his teenage daughter's best friend.

When Cooper returned and discovered that Williamson had already gone to Parkes and MacDonald, he was furious, telling Williamson, "You just made my job a lot harder." He had loved *American Beauty*, but would now have to go over his superiors' heads in order to lobby Spielberg, who, he felt strongly, would like to read it.

When Spielberg read the script, he called for a meeting with Cooper and Parkes, saying he wanted to make the film.

American Beauty got made due to "Bob walking into Steven's office and saying, 'You've got to buy this,' and Steven reading it and loving it," said director Sam Mendes. "And Kate [Capshaw], as well, had a big part in it, because she read it, and loved it. Steven told me, 'Kate loves it! I love it!'"

The situation with *American Beauty* did not help Cooper's relationship with Parkes, who was not relinquishing the reins of the studio even as he was caught up with *Gladiator*. Just to purchase a script, Cooper had to get Parkes's approval, which was rarely forthcoming. There had been times when Cooper had all but hired a director only to have Parkes hire someone else, forcing Cooper to rescind his offer. Katzenberg's comment that DreamWorks was "family" was proving greatly ironic.

According to DreamWorks sources, Parkes did not trust Cooper's taste, feeling that it was too "HBO"—i.e., small and esoteric.

DreamWorks, after all, was an insiders-only club. On the outside it seemed welcoming to all. But in truth, membership did not come easily. There were rules and codes to be adhered to. And while Katzenberg may have chosen Cooper for initiation, no one else was prepared to vote him in.

Partly, it was a style issue. There was perhaps no way the professorial Parkes would ever be warmed by Cooper, who could be brash and combative—before coming to Hollywood, Cooper had been a mob prosecutor in Canada, where he'd hosted a *60 Minutes*–like TV show. Or vice versa.

As one agent said, "If you have Walter and Bob together, they kill each other. Both are smart guys, and they both think they know more than anybody else . . . Walter's a writer. Bob used to be a muckraker on TV in Canada. Do the math."

But a deeper problem, in the eyes of many, was that Cooper was a threat to Parkes's relationship with Spielberg, as the *American Beauty* episode had demonstrated. When Cooper would say things like, "Well, I talked to Steven about it, and he loved it," Parkes looked visibly irritated.

Not that the Parkes-Spielberg relationship was in danger of being breached in any way. The two men and their wives still vacationed and socialized together as families, and Spielberg was still very much smitten by Parkes, even seeming desperate for his approval.

Offhandedly, Spielberg once remarked to a colleague, "Walter will never approve of anything I do," a line that, coming from the most powerful man in Hollywood, was a great shock.

One source described the relationship as like that of a student intent on getting straight As and a teacher. Spielberg would do anything for a pat on the head, and was always delighted to receive one.

"He likes to be told that he had a good idea, and thanked for having the idea," said the source.

At the same time, Parkes had a way of preying on Spielberg's insecurities, "unraveling things for him and making him have doubts he didn't have before," said one former DreamWorks employee.

Never was this more true than while discussing a script, when Parkes would bring up his concerns and point out ways the story wasn't working. Distressed, Spielberg would say, "What should we do?" Inevitably, Parkes would suggest himself as the savior, and offer to sit down with the writers and reword things.

Ball and the producers became aware of Spielberg's feelings about *American Beauty* when, the day after he had read the script, they ran into him outside the front entrance to Amblin.

"We were having this conversation, and all of a sudden I saw Steven walking out of the building," said Jinks. "I knew Steven just a very little bit, but Bruce knew him very well, so I sort of elbowed Bruce, and Bruce looked up and said, 'Steven, this is Alan Ball, he wrote *American Beauty*, the script you read last night'—hoping that Steven actually had read the script. And Steven lit up, and said what a pleasure it was to meet Alan Ball, and what a pleasure it was to read the script, and then he got very specific, talking about moments in the script, scenes, ways to cast it, potential directors."

The assiduousness with which Spielberg read scripts stood out in Hollywood, a place where, as Marty Bowen, a former senior literary agent at the United Talent Agency, said, "most directors don't know the names of the writers who won an Academy Award."

But Spielberg "read everything. He knew every writer," Bowen said. "I've been in a room where he could tell you the difference between the second and third draft of a script by a writer he knew and liked, and you never knew he was even looking at the project. That level of attention is staggering."

At DreamWorks, Spielberg was so expedient about reading scripts that Parkes and MacDonald would sometimes instruct their staff not to tell the director when a script was in, so that they would have time to read it themselves first. Once a script was in Spielberg's hands, he'd inevitably call hours after he'd read it, brimming with thoughts and ideas.

Ball, who'd assumed that Spielberg would hate *American Beauty* and think it too dark, was thrilled to hear that the director was a fan, and even more delighted when, at one point in the conversation, Spielberg turned to him and said, "Why haven't I heard of you?"

When Ball explained that he'd been working in TV, Spielberg said, "Well, you should be doing movies, and you should only be doing your own movies."

"I just kind of said, 'Thank you,' " Ball recalled. But for him, that was it. He went home and called Andrew Cannava, his movie agent at UTA, telling him that he didn't care what studios were offering the most money (USA Films was also interested in the script), he wanted *American Beauty* to be made at DreamWorks. The following day, UTA sold *American Beauty* to DreamWorks for the bargain-basement price of $250,000.

From then on, *American Beauty* was the little movie that no one was paying attention to, at least beyond the people in business affairs, who were adamant that the film be made for not a penny more than its shoestring budget of $12 million.

"It was an interesting time at DreamWorks," Mendes said. "*Saving Private Ryan* had just come out and really kick-started the studio in a sense, even though it was not entirely their movie [it was a coproduction with Paramount]. And *Gladiator* was on the block, ready to go. They were concentrating on these thundering, great epics. We just slipped under the radar."

"People were kind of just ignoring us," said Ball, who remained involved with the film during production. "It was like, 'Oh, that's that little movie that Steven likes.' I don't think they ever expected it to be anything big."

American Beauty was so under the radar that Katzenberg referred to it as a "Spielberg hobby."

Sam Mendes wound up directing the "hobby." In L.A. from his home in London, he had been taking meetings in the wake of his American theater debut, a leather-heavy rendition of *Cabaret*, starring the late Natasha Richardson as Sally Bowles. The musical had been imported from London's Donmar Warehouse, which Mendes, who was the theater's artistic director, was transforming into the West End's most cutting-edge, talked-about venue.

Mendes first came across the *American Beauty* script at the home of his agent, Beth Swofford. He glanced at it before departing for a round of meetings, including one with Spielberg, who'd just seen *Cabaret.* As Mendes sat in Spielberg's office, he was convinced someone was playing a joke on him when no one showed up. But then, in came Steven.

"'Hi, how are you? Nice to see you. Loved your show. You should make a movie. Let's make a movie!'" Mendes recalled Spielberg saying. "Just like that. In his inimitable way. You know, energy, big smile, baseball cap." During their chat, Spielberg brought up projects, among them *American Beauty.* "Steven said, 'It's this mad, surreal black comedy—kind of crazy,'" Mendes said. "Everyone who pitched it described it the same way . . . this mad, surreal black comedy."

At the end of their chat, Spielberg gave Mendes a copy of the script. "Read it, read it!" he said. "You want to do that, we'll make that!"

On the plane back to New York, Mendes finally read *American Beauty,* thinking to himself, "This isn't mad at all. It's completely normal," Mendes said. "I thought it was poetic and heartbreaking and very funny."

Mendes had grown up in London, the only child of an academic father and a mother who was in publishing and later wrote children's books. His parents separated when he was young, a situation that introduced "a certain amount of upheaval" and "displacement" in his life, he said. These feelings resonated with him as he read the *American Beauty* script, as did his memories of films he had gobbled up at the local art-house cinema while at Cambridge, such as Wim Wenders's *Paris, Texas* and David Byrne's *True Stories*—features he remembered for their ability to transform ordinary American suburbia into strangely mythic landscapes.

When he landed, Mendes immediately called Swofford: "I really want to do this film."

Unfortunately, so did some other, bigger names than Mendes, including Mike Nichols and Bob Zemeckis. Whatever Spielberg had said about making this movie, it wasn't quite so simple. Mendes would have to audition, and so he found himself back in L.A., in a pitch meeting with Cooper, Parkes, and MacDonald.

"I'd expected they'd ask me, 'Who do you want in [the movie] and how do you want to shoot it?'" he said. "I had prepared answers to those questions. But they asked me stuff like, 'What do you think the movie is about?' These big questions! And what they're looking for is an answer that they already possess. They know that they think—because they've all sat in a meeting about it two weeks earlier—that it's about 'imprisonment.' So what they're looking for is the word 'imprisonment'! But all I'm saying is, 'Well, it's about sexuality, it's about longing, it's about the suburbs . . . '"

Mendes was convinced he'd blown his shot at Hollywood, but the next day Cooper—who was worried that Mendes had never directed a film before—called Swofford and said, "Look, we liked him very much. But we don't think he was quite in top form. We'd like to see him again." By this time, Nichols and Zemeckis were both tied up, and DreamWorks didn't want to wait. As Spielberg said later, Dream-Works "is like a large child, and it always needs the big suck. I went to my partners and said: 'We can't wait for those other guys. We need the eggs!' Did you ever see *Annie Hall*? Well, DreamWorks needed the eggs."

In the subsequent meeting, a well-rested Mendes gave a more memorable performance, and got the job. The only condition was that it was not a very high-paying one. He received $150,000, the Directors Guild minimum, which after taxes and commissions came to $38,500.

"I didn't give a shit what I was being paid," said Mendes, "I would have done it for nothing, in fact. In fact, I would have paid them to do it, I wanted to do it so much."

Mendes knew exactly whom he wanted as the film's leads: Kevin Spacey and Annette Bening. Yet DreamWorks' choices ran more mainstream: Bruce Willis, Kevin Costner, and John Travolta to play Lester Burnham. Holly Hunter and Helen Hunt for Carolyn Burnham, Lester's wife. Says Ball: "They brought up some big A-list movie star names to play Lester and I was like, shoot me. Pick up a gun and shoot me in the head right now. They were all fine actors, just not people who should be playing that role."

Still untrained in Hollywood protocol, Mendes was so excited over the prospect of Bening that he arranged a meeting with her, unbeknownst to DreamWorks, and offered her the role. When Bening's agent telephoned Cooper and said the actress would love to star in the film, what kind of offer was DreamWorks willing to make, Cooper turned blue in the face. He called Mendes and yelled: "She hasn't been offered the part!"

Mendes also met with Spacey (with DreamWorks' blessing), who was in London receiving rave reviews for his performance in Eugene O'Neill's *The Iceman Cometh* at the Old Vic. One night after the show, the two men met at a pub around the corner from the theater. A few days later, Spacey was phoning the director, saying, "I think I can do this."

By this time, DreamWorks had come around to both Bening and Spacey, so long as they would cut their fees. The studio wasn't kidding about a $12 million budget.

Shooting was scheduled for December. To help Mendes prepare, Spielberg offered up some sage advice: "Wear comfortable shoes."

For Katzenberg, *Antz* was just a warm-up. The real test, Katzenberg's true coming-out party, was *Prince of Egypt:* his baby, his creation, his post-Disney opus. Four years after embarking on his follow-up to *The Lion King,* the movie, which he was far more intimately involved with than anything he'd ever done at Disney, was ready. Katzenberg didn't even attempt to play it cool. "Do you know how big the Pentagon is?" he said to the *Washington Post*'s Lloyd Grove in early December. "Is that the biggest building in Washington? Well, let me just assure you, there's not enough square footage there to contain my anxiety. I'm just completely hysterical!"

No wonder. "Jeffrey sort of lost his perspective and built *Prince of Egypt* into something that became hard to handle," observed Penney Finkelman Cox. According to DreamWorks, the film's budget was $75 million. But competitors said, and insiders confirmed, that $120 million was more like it. Then there was the $30 million for the TV spots. Wal-Mart (which Katzenberg had personally pitched, traveling to the megastore's headquarters and preaching the Word of Jeffrey to four thousand employees) was pushing the film through a promotional package that included two tickets to the movie, a storybook, and a movie CD. DreamWorks Records produced not one but three *POE*-inspired soundtracks—pop, country, and "inspirational"—an unprecedented undertaking made all the more monumental by the stars DreamWorks had lined up for the project (Whitney Houston, Mariah Carey, Amy Grant, Faith Hill, Toby Keith, etc.). With stars came drama, and the music-video shoot of "When You Believe," a duet sung by Carey and Houston, caused a diva showdown when Houston, whose limo was the first to arrive at the shoot, refused to get out until after Carey had arrived. Houston's publicists were frantically calling up DreamWorks: "Whitney's in her car but won't get out!" A similar tantrum erupted over which singer had the bigger dressing room.

Most ballsy of all, Katzenberg was opening *POE* on ten thousand screens in forty countries. Traditionally, Disney opened its films in the U.S. and then took a year or more to dub the films and open them globally. *POE* was already dubbed into a dozen different languages and was going to launch simultaneously around the world. "Nobody's ever opened in 85 percent of the world at the same time," Katzenberg boasted. Clearly he was no longer whistling to the tune of a nice double.

At the premiere of *The Prince of Egypt*, a dapper affair held at UCLA's Royce Hall, even Geffen showed up. Spielberg, dressed in a dark suit, brought the wife and kids. Camera crews thrust mikes into the faces of Val Kilmer and his Moses predecessor Charlton Heston. Less noticed by the press were Katzenberg's parents, who'd flown in from New York for the affair. Katzenberg was not close with his parents, and he rarely saw them. His father, a former stockbroker, is described as cold and distant and was competitive with his son. Katzenberg seldom talked about his parents—or anything that was personal in nature—but his paternal void was evident to those close to him, and made his drama with Eisner, and his relationship with elders like Geffen and Spielberg, all the more resonant.

But if the Prince of Hollywood had expected the kind of praise and validation from them that his other "parents" were lavishing on him that night—Spielberg was telling reporters how proud he was of Katzenberg for having "brought this baby into the world from its inception four and a half years ago" (as UCLA students screamed from behind barricades, "Do you need an actress for your next movie?!")— he was bitterly disappointed. After the screening, in a rare display of vulnerability, he confided to a DreamWorks executive that his parents hadn't said a word to him about the movie. The son who was forever looking for recognition from a father still couldn't get any from his own.

Happily, the DreamWorks family were a less withholding bunch, and on the night of *Prince of Egypt*'s release, a party was planned to celebrate what was certain to be a momentous evening. How could it be anything but? Katzenberg had never worked harder on a movie in his life. It was "surely, without question, nothing close and without a doubt," he said, his biggest challenge to date. A bungalow was rented at the Beverly Hills Hotel, where the plan was for champagne to be quaffed as box-office numbers were phoned in by DreamWorks' distribution head Jim Tharp.

But as the evening wore on and Tharp delivered his reports, the champagne quickly lost its fizzle. Director James L. Brooks, who had been invited to the tally party by DreamWorks' music head Hans Zimmer, did his best to cheer up the group—which included Zimmer, Rabins, Finkelman Cox, and *Prince of Egypt* codirectors Brenda Chapman, Steve Hickner, and Simon Wells. Don't give up so fast, he counseled, this is Hollywood. But no amount of pep talk could disguise the fact that *Prince of Egypt* was no *Lion King*.

"By the end of Friday night, you knew where you were going to land," said Finkelman Cox, who referred to the evening as "that dark Friday night of the soul." She continued: "It didn't take very long to know you weren't going to change the world . . . Luckily, it was early enough, so we kept drinking."

Katzenberg, having heard reports from earlier time zones earlier in the day, hadn't even bothered to show up for the party. He knew where things were headed: by Sunday, *Prince of Egypt* grossed just $14 million.

Over the weekend, Katzenberg made his customary thirty-second phone calls to the hundreds of people who had worked on *Prince of Egypt* to say, "Congratulations. The movie opened great, and we're really proud of it." But what the callers heard in Jeffrey Katzenberg's voice was not joy.

In the end, *Prince of Egypt* was not an outright flop. DreamWorks kept it in theaters longer than usual, and in the end it made $101 million in the U.S.; worldwide it grossed $218 million. This came as no surprise to most observers, who understood from the very beginning how limited the commercial prospects were for a film about the Bible. So had Katzenberg. But he was, by nature, a reflexive visionary. He couldn't help but hope to defy the odds. And even if he'd wanted to on this one, there was no way he would have ever challenged a film that had been conceived by Steven Spielberg.

"If you look back at his record, even on lesser movies, if Jeffrey willed something to work, it *worked!*" said Tom Sherak, former head of the Fox Filmed Group. "He used to take movies that nobody would have taken and willed them to go over $100 million. I'll never forget, we used to sit around at Fox and say, 'How'd he get to that number?'"

As for *POE,* Finkelman Cox said, "Jeffrey really believed that this movie would touch people in a way that nothing had done up to that point. He was smart enough to know that a Bible story could never be a *Lion King,* and there was never enough humor to make it *Lion King,* but he thought it would be much more successful and much more compelling to people. He thought people would really just yearn to see this kind of quality storytelling."

Thus, when the movie underperformed, there was "incredible sadness," Finkelman Cox said. "Even though Sandy [Rabins] and I used to talk about not allowing ourselves to buy into Jeffrey's hype, you can't help but want that hype to be true. He's only telling you what you want to happen. You never didn't want what he was selling. Everybody wants what he sells!"

For another DreamWorks visionary, a ray of hope was on the horizon. In December, *Saving Private Ryan* received five Golden Globe nominations, the first real sign that redemption, of the Oscar variety, might be at hand. And a year after *Amistad,* there was nothing Steven Spielberg wanted more.

That year, there had been a sense of inevitability about a Spielberg Oscars sweep. None of the other films that were generating buzz at that point—the period drama *Elizabeth,* starring Cate Blanchett; Roberto Benigni's fantastical Holocaust picture *Life Is Beautiful;* and Terrence Malick's own World War II ode *The Thin Red Line*—had the ambition and scale of Spielberg's opus.

As Oscar consultant Tony Angelotti said: "At the time, you had this juggernaut that was *Private Ryan.* It had come out in the summer and been this gigantic hit. The sense was that Steven Spielberg was back, and nobody perceived anything other than that it would win."

But then, just before the Christmas holidays, a stir was elicited from the direction of Miramax, Bob and Harvey Weinstein's rough-and-tumble indie house, which had been dominating the Oscars—with films such as *The English Patient, Il Postino,* and *Good Will Hunting.* It was never a pretty battle; Harvey Weinstein was an aggressive and cunning opponent, and had written every trick in the book when it came to bullying Academy members into votes and other studios out of them. Beware the hapless competitor that found itself in Harvey's path.

In this year's race, Miramax's front-runner had been *Life Is Beautiful.* That is, until, in mid-December, executives at Miramax first saw a cut of *Shakespeare In Love,* a wry, romantic comedy, written by Marc Norman and playwright Tom Stoppard, about how a down-and-out, penniless Will Shakespeare turned his career around with *Romeo and Juliet.* The film was awash in accomplished actors, including Miramax's First-Lady-to-be Gwyneth Paltrow, Dame Judi Dench, Geoffrey Rush, and Joseph Fiennes, the kid brother of *The English Patient's* Ralph. At the film's premiere, audiences "went through the roof," according to Angelotti, and gushing reviews started flooding in. Suddenly, Miramax began shifting its resources from *Life Is Beautiful* to *Shakespeare In Love.* Weinstein was even more hell-bent this year, given that he was a producer on *Shakespeare;* i.e., if the film won Best Picture, Weinstein would be in possession of an Academy Award, and the acclaim that went with it.

Over at DreamWorks, which until now had been feeling rather complacent about Spielberg's return to the podium, nerves were unsettled. The whiff of a threat wafted over and into the halls of Amblin. Terry Press reached for her armor.

18

HARVEY BABY

I DO NOT WANT YOU to get in the mud with *those people*," Spielberg said to Terry Press, pronouncing the last two words with crisp disdain.

The "people" in question would be Miramax, aka Harvey Weinstein. It was February of 1999, and Press had just received a phone call from a journalist claiming that Weinstein had a squadron of publicists on the Miramax payroll who were going around town slamming *Saving Private Ryan,* saying that only the first twenty minutes of the movie really worked. The Oscars were less than a month away, and Miramax and DreamWorks were in a tight race—*Shakespeare In Love* was up for thirteen Academy Awards; *Saving Private Ryan,* eleven. What had once seemed a sure thing was now suddenly in question. The villain was Harvey Weinstein, Menace to Society, whose in-your-face style stood for everything that DreamWorks—with its A-list names, its cushy quarters, its low-voiced decorum—was not. The new kid on the playground was being circled by the scrappy, cunning school bully. On the sidelines, bets were already being placed as to whose penny loafers were about to end up in the dirt.

When Press heard what Miramax was up to, her first thought was: *I want to rip the shit out of them.* She had been laboring so hard—nearly a year now—trying to sell Spielberg's film, one that she felt nearly as protective of, at this point, as Spielberg did. It had been a long road. So carefully had she packaged *Ryan* so that audiences would look beyond the violence. She'd even gotten Spielberg involved with publicity. And now this, this Harvey, this ... schmuck.

Soliciting Oscar votes was nothing new—in 1955, before her Best Actress win for *The Country Girl,* Grace Kelly had been trotted all over town. And in 1968, the fact that *Doctor Dolittle* was one of the year's biggest, and costliest, embarrassments didn't stop Twentieth Century Fox from screening the film for Oscar voters for sixteen straight nights, plying them with prime rib and champagne. The result: nine nominations, including Best Picture.

By the 1990s, free food and booze was a quaint concept when it came to winning over members of the Academy. Thanks largely to Weinstein, Oscar campaigning was now a blood sport in which "flood the zone" was the overriding strategy. Studios weren't so much asking for support as coercing Academy members into giving it, with glossy publicity materials and screener tapes sent directly to members' homes, full-page ads in the trades, nonstop wining-and-dining opportunities with the stars. Weinstein even made personal calls to voters.

Weinstein had set the standard when it came to "everything from having screenings hosted by actors, to having talent show up at every premiere, to really working the entertainment columnists about how to cover an Oscar campaign—to cover it as a horserace or a political campaign," said Mark Gill, former president of Miramax's L.A. operations. "Naturally, when you're doing that, there are going to be stories about your candidate. All those things have become commonplace now. For example, publishing a special book about your movie and not only sending it out to trade-paper recipients but accidentally dumping about one hundred thousand in West L.A. coffee shops—most of that was Harvey."

Such tactics earned Miramax's *My Left Foot,* a small, obscure film starring Daniel Day-Lewis, a Best Picture nomination in 1990. By 1992, Weinstein had perfected his formula, muscling the controversial *The Crying Game* into the Academy's consciousness and earning it several nominations, including Best Picture. Ever since, Miramax had been in the Best Picture race consistently every year—winning many of them.

The details might not be pretty, but Miramax's success story was a classic Hollywood tale, a modern-day version of what the Mayers and Thalbergs had done back in the day. The two brothers from Queens, Harvey and Bob, who'd fallen in love with Fellini and Truffaut as teenagers, had started out as concert promoters in upstate New York, before scraping together a business acquiring obscure foreign films, Americanizing them, and distributing them in the U.S. The Miramax story, in effect, was the inverse of the DreamWorks story.

Based in New York, not Los Angeles, Miramax had started off as a legitimately cash-strapped start-up, with nothing going for it but its founders' wits and overpowering desire. The boys had no manners to speak of, no fancy education (both were college dropouts), but they were such good Jewish boys that they named their company after their parents, Miriam and Max. Miramax flourished in the 1990s, leading the indie movement charge with edgy films such as *Sex, Lies, and Videotape, Trainspotting,* and *Pulp Fiction.* But even after Disney bought the company, which had expanded into production, in 1993, Harvey and Bob remained staunch outsiders, more hated than loved. Harvey, in particular, was Hollywood's bête noire, an unapologetic bully who used his six-foot, 250-pound frame to full effect, screaming, gesticulating, threatening, and driving even those filmmakers he championed when no one else would to madness. To work for Harvey was to submit to Harvey, whose proclivity for film editing earned him the moniker Harvey Scissorhands. But whatever his gross foibles, Weinstein was a passionate, and consummate, showman, who knew how to get things done. And whatever Weinstein's own reputation, Miramax was a shining beacon of artistic integrity, a company that was synonymous with taste and quality, whose films were distinctly unsullied by Hollywood.

Never was Harvey Weinstein in grander form than in the months and weeks leading up to the Academy Awards, when he and his company went into overdrive. The kids from Queens showed the Hollywood slicksters how it was done.

Shoring up Miramax's marketing and publicity staff were "Oscar consultants" such as PR man Tony Angelotti—considered the king of the tribe—who worked from the outside, building buzz in the media and schmoozing Academy members. Then there was Weinstein himself, who drove Gwyneth Paltrow—who was not yet *Gwyneth Paltrow,* but whom Weinstein was determined to make so by winning her an Oscar—so hard to promote *Shakespeare In Love* that her agent at CAA, Kevin Huvane, had had to intervene.

"When you have a small company with a showman at the helm, you use the press to mitigate advertising dollars," explained Angelotti. "Harvey did that masterfully. No interview was too small . . . No dinner was too small to go to, no lunch was too small. Nothing was too unimportant. He just wouldn't give up. He never gave up. Everything was of deadly importance. If someone was perceived to have fallen down on the job, there was a call from Harvey: '*What the fuck am I paying for?*'"

DreamWorks also saw itself as a studio that did things better than the rest of Hollywood. But unlike Miramax, DreamWorks wasn't about fighting for awards—or anything. A strong sense of entitlement existed at the studio, born from who was behind it. For the Dream Team, winning was a given, regardless of what tricks Harvey had up his sleeve—and what exactly those were was becoming more clear.

Weinstein was making an aggressive bid to the Screen Actors Guild, selling *Shakespeare In Love* as a film by and for thespians. It was a wily strategy. The acting branch of the Academy is by far the organization's largest Oscar-voting bloc. In 1999, of the fifty-six hundred Academy members, more than thirteen hundred were SAG members.

"Harvey made the Academy feel like *Shakespeare In Love* was a classic," said veteran publicist and Academy member Dale Olson. "He made it so it was almost criminal not to vote for it. He said, 'This is the kind of thing that's never been done before.' It was like it was *Gone with the Wind*—the biggest platform picture ever made."

But what drove Press over the brink were the claims that Weinstein was orchestrating a whisper campaign against *Saving Private Ryan*, insisting that once the Allies got over the cliffs of Normandy, the movie turned into sentimental schlock. Weinstein portrayed *Saving Private Ryan* as a "war story, about a bunch of guys who get killed," said Olson. "Part of the whole Harvey campaign was, he kept saying, 'Art instead of war!'"

Weinstein denied such talk, claiming that he and Katzenberg were "old friends." (It had been Katzenberg who'd lobbied hardest for Disney to acquire Miramax.) Weinstein also did not buy it that Press was remaining as white-gloved as she claimed. Especially after a March article in *New York* magazine by entertainment writer Nikki Finke, which claimed that *Shakespeare In Love* was "two hours of Elizabethan froth" and that Weinstein was responsible for mafia-like maneuverings in his quest for a golden statuette.

"Miramax," Finke wrote, "pays a fleet of ultraveteran Hollywood publicists (who also happen to be Academy members) . . . not to generate press coverage but to schmooze their prominent Academy colleagues. As cronies of the Academy's graying voters, they are paid not just during the five-month Oscar season but nearly year-round—a practice unheard of elsewhere in the industry."

She also wrote that Miramax was outspending everyone in its quest for glory; that while "true independents might spend up to $250,000 on an Oscar campaign; the majors, $2 million," Miramax was "estimated by competitors to have spent at least $5 million on its campaign for *Shakespeare In Love*."

DreamWorks denied any foul play, but by now the showdown between Miramax and DreamWorks was news, and the *L.A. Times* ran an article describing the contest as being characterized by excessive spending and "colored by alleged behind-the-scenes sniping." In the story, Weinstein, again, pled innocence: "They're trying to take old friends and make it seem like we're enemies. I was strongly bothered by any inference that I would say anything against *Ryan*. I took great umbrage at anyone saying that I told a critic that the movie was running out of steam. I think Steven is our greatest living filmmaker. Why would I want to say anything negative?"

Speaking on behalf of DreamWorks, Katzenberg said that Weinstein was "running a tough, competitive campaign" and that "we've felt compelled to supplement the original plans we had put in place."

As for relations with Miramax, he said: "There's no animosity."

But others begged to differ. "It was nasty," said one member of the Miramax camp.

If Miramax had a war room, DreamWorks had a makeshift bunker, filled with a cabinet of Disney alumni, most of whom had never before mounted an Oscar campaign. The Disney motto was profit, not prestige. Never in the company's entire storied history had any movie received a Best Picture Oscar.

Speaking for Press and the rest of her ex-Disney staff, one source said, "We were universally naive. We figured that the movie would speak for itself, that we didn't have to actively sell it, promote it, spend major money." Thus there was no schedule or timetable for how and where marketing dollars should be allocated; no strategy for courting certain voting blocs of the Academy—not just the actors, but smaller groups such as the cinematographers and costume designers. There was no sense that this was a campaign, a contest that was about much more than merit alone. Observing the *Saving Private Ryan* effort from his perch at Miramax, Gill said, "They did all the things that were customary at the time. They did trade advertising, a little bit of publicity, other things. I remember thinking at the time, 'They're covering the basics and that's the extent of it.'"

Spielberg, meanwhile, was adamant about maintaining the film's creative integrity. Time and again, Press had begged the director to try and see things her way, according to former executives. "You don't have to campaign," she said, "but you really need to get out there." But this time, Spielberg held his ground, convinced that wining and dining the A-listers, working the Bel Air circuit, dropping by the Motion Picture and Television Fund retirement home (which housed former Hollywood *machers,* many of whom are Academy voters) for tea was crass nonsense. At Press's request, he'd done the rounds promoting the film's release. But he'd have nothing to do with hawking the film for a little gold man.

Whether or not Press and her team had jumped in the mud, Dream-Works had upped its spending in the weeks leading to the Oscar ceremony, and by the time the big night rolled around, on March 21, there remained a conviction across the land that the night would belong to Spielberg; that all of Weinstein's maneuverings didn't change the fact that *Saving Private Ryan* was the kind of epic film that the Academy loved, and that it was about a subject that was near and dear to the hearts of many of the Academy's aging members. Spielberg's buddy Harrison Ford had even been selected to present the award for Best Picture.

"The whole thing was set up like a coronation," said Gill. "Even the producer of the Academy Awards thought he had a wonderful photo op."

As the night wore on, things were going as planned; Spielberg picked up the Best Director award—a sure sign that *Saving Private Ryan* had a lock. "Am I allowed to say I really wanted this?" Spielberg said, looking trim and natty, his beard freshly clipped. He then thanked Capshaw and all of the kids, Hanks, families who'd lost children in World War II, and, finally, his father, to whom he dedicated the award.

By then, *Ryan* had won five Oscars; others were for cinematography, effects, film editing, and sound. Miramax had won five, including a Best Supporting Actress award for Dench, and Best Original Screen-play. When the scales tipped toward Miramax and Paltrow was named Best Actress, one Miramax executive thought: "Oh boy, this is going to make for an even *crazier* night."

And then it was time for the verdict. Harrison walked onto the stage, opened the envelope, and said three words. Only they weren't *Saving Private Ryan;* they were *Shakespeare In Love.*

The audience let out a collective gasp. Ford did not look up from the card; his expression was morose. Moments later, an elated Wein-stein and a flock of four other producers flooded the stage. To Press, Ford's words seemed to travel across the auditorium "like a ball of fire" to engulf her. "It was," she said, "a nightmare."

Spielberg politely smiled and clapped, but he was furious at hav-ing lost by what he considered dirty means, and when the ceremony was over and it came time to head backstage and do press, an act that would mean following Harvey and his procession, Spielberg refused to go.

Doing press—i.e., addressing the hundreds of journalists and pho-tographers who arrive from all over the world to cover the Oscars—is a traditional part of Oscar-night proceedings, and when the Academy heard that Spielberg had refused to participate, they were not happy. DreamWorks publicists were booed in the parking lot, and the follow-ing day the Academy contacted DreamWorks to complain.

Although Press felt that she had been wronged by the system and that Miramax had won by unfair tactics, she put on her game face and, after the ceremony, personally congratulated Weinstein. As she had made her way toward him, her eyes met Katzenberg's and she muttered: "Never again!"

The loss "drove Terry for the future," said Olson. "She could not live with the fact that *Private Ryan* did not get the Academy Award, and she was determined from that time on that whatever Dream-Works films came up that were qualified, she was going to get behind them and make sure that they got the right attention."

To Miramaxers, the perception that DreamWorks was a sore loser only confirmed their feeling of the new studio's sense of entitlement.

"*Bugsy* was definitely supposed to win [Best Picture]. So was *Reds.* They didn't—it happens," said one Harveyite. "But because it hap-pened to DreamWorks at a time when they were riding a crest, and to

Spielberg personally—our kingmaker—it had to be considered foul play . . . They couldn't just sit back and say they lost."

Such cool-headed logic had no effect on the *Saving Private Ryan* team. Producer Mark Gordon, for one, felt like he'd been socked in the stomach. "Everybody was stunned when we didn't win," he said. "I was sort of walking around in shock."

Spielberg did not linger at the Governors Ball, the gala dinner that directly follows the Oscars, where emotions run from exultant to funereal, and where the flowing champagne meets everybody's needs. Instead, he made a beeline for the DreamWorks-Paramount afterparty at Barnaby's restaurant, where the mood was decidedly sullen.

Press had "that pale, haunted look of too-much-stress-not-enough-statues," wrote Sharon Waxman in the *Washington Post*. "Katzenberg . . . looks even shorter this evening."

DreamWorks publicist Mitch Kreindel confided to the reporter that the Academy's Best Picture choice "was classic middlebrow."

"You know what this just shows?" he said. "The academy is not"—he paused—"stretchable."

Even non-DreamWorks guests at the party were versed in appropriate feelings toward a certain movie about a certain playwright.

"I hated *Shakespeare In Love*. I walked out," declared actress Julie Delpy—momentarily a Miramax turncoat, despite her history of working for Weinstein—decked out in diamonds-on-loan and a strapless black lace dress. "I never got why the movie was so great."

Gordon said of his post-Oscar festivities: "I didn't stay long. I went to the party and then I went home to bed. Steven said he was sorry he didn't bring it home. He won Best Director and so I think he was disappointed for all of us—and surprised."

Alas, there would be no photo of a triumphant, Oscar-clutching Spielberg with Harrison Ford on the stage of the Dorothy Chandler Pavilion. Instead, the next morning the *L.A. Times* ran a photo taken at the afterparty of Spielberg, Ford, and Katzenberg sitting joylessly around a table, "looking like they had just learned that the family dog had died," said Gill.

The Miramax afterparty, at the Polo Lounge, was a much gayer affair. Weinstein's court, a mélange of mainstream and indie stars— Quentin Tarantino, Wes Anderson, Ryan Phillippe, Reese Witherspoon, Chris Rock, and Mariah Carey—were body-mashed under the outdoor patio's cascading bougainvillea—golden statuettes glinting under the lights as *Shakespeare* winners snaked their way through the crowd. When Robert Welkos, a reporter for the *L.A. Times,* showed up, he remarked, "Well, I hope you guys are happy. I just came from the DreamWorks party, and it's like a fucking funeral over there."

Unfortunately, in the wake of the *Private Ryan* loss, Spielberg could take little comfort in DreamWorks' fortunes. There were two more live-action flops: Neil Jordan's *In Dreams,* with Annette Bening; and *Forces of Nature,* starring Sandra Bullock and Ben Affleck. And still only one TV success, *Spin City.* And there were still not enough movies to justify DreamWorks' nearly $200 million yearly overhead and fifteen hundred employees. In 1998, the company's first full year of film revenue, which saw a loss of nearly $200 million on revenue of $1 billion, the studio had released four live-action movies. Just six were planned for 1999, or a third the amount that the majors released. The arrival of Bob Cooper hadn't helped. He and Walter Parkes were still like oil and water, neither liking nor trusting each other.

Since Cooper had come to DreamWorks in the fall of 1997, he had only been successful in getting two films green-lighted—*American Beauty* and *Galaxy Quest.* He'd also given Spielberg a copy of *Meet the Parents,* a comedy that Universal was developing. After reading it, Spielberg had called up Edgar Bronfman Jr. and arranged a cofinancing deal. Rumors that DreamWorks might merge with Universal on a larger level were rekindled, and once again Katzenberg was asking where his movies were, more forcefully now; this wasn't a request, it was a major problem. And so a vow was made to double production going forward. But Parkes and Spielberg were resistant. They hadn't signed on to oversee a factory. Not that it was a factory Katzenberg was asking for—just the diet of nine movies in 1999 that had been originally agreed to; instead, that year there would only be six. And just what *had* Spielberg signed on to? By 1999, it was much more clear than it had been in the heady initial stages of blue-skying with his two new partners. What was less clear was what this would mean for Spielberg going forward.

In April, Kim Masters wrote a story in *Time,* claiming that Spielberg was "growing weary" with his enterprise and might be creating an escape vehicle for himself "in case the need arise" by reviving the Amblin label. It was the first time Spielberg's devotion to his company had been so publicly called into question, and the story so rattled the adobe walls at Amblin that DreamWorks responded—even Spielberg went on the record—in the *L.A. Times,* denying the charges. "The very idea that responsible publications, like *Time* magazine, have rumored this fiction that I have grown weary of DreamWorks is false and damaging," Spielberg said. Even Spielberg's lawyer Bruce Ramer chimed in, saying, "In the thirty years I've known him, I've never seen Steven happier."

Soon after the article, Spielberg, Katzenberg, and Geffen had a very public lunch together at the Glendale animation studio, where they sat in the courtyard outside the cafeteria, looking like the most contented three media titans in the world.

As DreamWorks hit rough waters, corners were being cut—first-class air travel was banned; the spouse and kids were no longer invited to the Christmas party—and divisions slimmed down. A chunk of GameWorks, which had only set up a fraction of its intended one hundred luxe video arcades, had been sold to Sega Enterprises. TV animation was told in March that it would be officially off the books in January of 2000. The department had been doomed after Disney's purchase of ABC, but it also suffered from a lack of attention from Spielberg, whose filmmaking duties kept him AWOL as the division's creative head.

"We did a prime-time show for the WB called *Invasion America,* and I remember the only creative meeting with [Spielberg] on that show was over the telephone, with me and the story editor," said Bruce Cranston, cohead of TV animation at DreamWorks. "It was just awful. You can't make a show like that. We'd send him the script and he'd send back notes, but the notes were never in person."

But bypassing Spielberg didn't work, either. "The stuff we were selling, I'm sure you're aware of the selling season—with animation, the networks have to make those decisions early to give you the time it takes to get the shows shot. Sometimes we were selling things without Steven's blessing, because he was off somewhere making a movie. Afterward, he was very clear, 'No, I don't want to make that show.'"

Cranston accepted some of the blame, saying, "I don't think Steven ever really liked our work. I hate to speak for him, but I don't think it was something that ever really turned him on." Cranston said that Spielberg had seemed much more comfortable working with the TV animation team at Warner Bros., where he'd made the *Tiny Toon Adventures* series in the early 1990s. But the DreamWorks group, many of whom were Katzenberg connections from Disney, were new and different, they weren't part of Spielberg's family; the chemistry wasn't there.

Spielberg seemed inaccessible to the team. "With Jeffrey, you could argue all you wanted and you wouldn't be afraid. But with Steven, it was just such a going-to-see-the-wizard experience," Cranston said. "You'd walk down the long corridor and be nervous. I never got past the feeling of, Oh, we're going to see *Steven*."

And so after four years TV animation was shuttered. "When push came to shove, and money was tight, we were one of the first things to go," Cranston said.

Another division to go, and another one that had originally been championed by Spielberg, was DreamWorks Interactive, whose initial mission—to make CD-ROM content—was upended by the shift in gaming to the Internet and to consoles such as PlayStation and Nintendo 64. Lacking its own branded console (Xbox was still a few years off), Microsoft had little interest in games such as *Medal of Honor* (Spielberg's World War II game, originally titled *Normandy Beach*), which utilized a Sony platform (PlayStation), and it became a more removed partner in the venture.

DWI had also taken a huge hit when the costly *Jurassic Park: Trespasser*, billed as "the digital sequel to *The Lost World*" and developed by Seamus Blackley—a physics expert who would go on to cocreate Xbox—at a cost of $12 million, or four times what games typically cost, was a major bomb. DWI's Peter Hirschmann called *Trespasser* the company's "Vietnam." It had taken four years to develop.

With Patty Stonesifer now back in Seattle running the Bill & Melinda Gates Foundation, DWI began looking for a potential buyer.

Meanwhile, Spielberg and Katzenberg's pre-DreamWorks partnership, the submarine-themed restaurant Dive!, proved a bit too true to its name and submerged for good, closing its doors in January.

DreamWorks was changing. Having hit the five-year mark, its days as a family-style company, where everyone hung out in the courtyard and ate cookies, were over. It was now a corporate animal more in need of hits to stay alive. As divisions were shut down in order for the company to stay alive, the mood changed. "Things got a little less fun," said Penney Finkelman Cox.

DreamWorks "was moving beyond the small, family thing into more of a professional, big studio," said DWI co-COO Dan Kaufman. "My first summer there, there was a big picnic out somewhere near Calabasas. It was great. It was all families, there were little kids. As the company got bigger, there were multiple movies, all that stuff became tougher to do."

If Spielberg's investment in DreamWorks was shaky, Katzenberg's attention was being even more diverted. In the months leading up to his breach-of-contract trial against Disney, which began in April, Katzenberg became something of a nonentity at DreamWorks. The lawsuit "took him out," said one source. "He and Helene [Hahn] were not present." The company's entire legal and finance teams gave themselves over to crunching numbers for their boss, drawing them away from their DreamWorks duties. "We were more affected by the team that was assembled to work on the lawsuit," said Sandy Rabins. "They were a hundred percent pulled away from their jobs . . . I mean, every department, every area, their expertise was pulled in . . . It affected the company."

For the most part, Katzenberg kept his mouth shut about the trial, cleanly separating it from his work life. To most DreamWorks employees, the only visible evidence of what was going on was revealed on days when Katzenberg showed up in a suit before heading off to a hearing. "I likened his preparation for his lawsuit to somebody preparing for the Olympic Games," said Max Howard, who stepped down as president of Warner Bros.' feature animation division in June of 1998 and became an animation producer at DreamWorks. "That man was in training."

Confidence was not an issue. Katzenberg went into the trial to win.

"He took it all in stride," said director David Silverman. "I remember him working on [the lawsuit]. He'd be on the bus going somewhere—whatever function we were traveling to—and he'd be going over papers." Naturally, Katzenberg continued to be advised on the matter by Geffen. Spielberg was less involved in the suit than Geffen, but he also supported his partner. "I think Steven had an emotional reaction to what he perceived as Jeffrey being treated wrongly," said one DreamWorks source, who pointed out that in the early days of DreamWorks, Spielberg and Katzenberg were very close.

Katzenberg's absences began eating into *The Road to El Dorado,* a Bing Crosby/Bob Hope–style buddy story about a pair of two-bit conmen (voiced by Kevin Kline and Kenneth Branagh) who set out for the Lost City of Gold after acquiring a map showing its location. Katzenberg had come up with the idea for the movie, but from the beginning, it was a troubled enterprise; *Prince of Egypt,* as the studio's shining debut, had received superior resources and talent. Virtually everything about *El Dorado*'s production was out of whack. The producers were bickering. Elton John's score was no *Lion King.* (In one session, when storyboard sequences were edited together and viewed, accompanied by dialogue and a soundtrack, a visual-effects artist said that he didn't like the film's music, and Katzenberg grumbled, "Well, tell that to Elton John!")

Directors David Silverman and Will Finn had to be replaced. When Finn left, following an argument with Katzenberg over the film's creative direction, he wrote Katzenberg a letter hoping to reconcile their differences. But after reading the letter, Katzenberg looked up and said: "OK. Who else we got?" As one source said: "You don't quit Jeffrey. If you do, he closes the door behind you."

Katzenberg was another problem. Before he became distracted by his trial duties, he was maddeningly hands-on with the film, changing its creative direction midway through production from sophisticated and adult looking (à la *Prince of Egypt*) to comedic and cartoony. Frustrated, the artists had staged an intervention. In one meeting, character animator James Baxter, a normally shy and bashful Brit, stood up to his boss in front of the other artists and told him to back off.

"You don't know what you're doing," Baxter said. "You're too involved. You're losing the respect of the artists."

Katzenberg, who respected Baxter, had seemed to listen. For a few weeks, at least, he kept a greater distance from the production. But soon he was back to his old habits.

As usual, there was a race with Disney, which was in production on its own animated film with a New World setting, *The Emperor's New Groove.* Katzenberg made his wishes clear: beat them. "It was really a race, and Katzenberg wanted ours out before theirs," said Marc

Lumer, a visual-development artist on *El Dorado*. "We didn't know exactly what they were doing, but we had the impression it was going to be very similar. Whoever came out second would face the impression that they copied the other."

From Disney's perspective, Katzenberg was once again swiping an idea—Roger Allers and Matthew Jacobs had been developing *Emperor's New Groove*—originally called *Kingdom of the Sun*—at Disney long before DreamWorks was formed. Whether Katzenberg was aware of the film while he was at Disney is hard to prove, but Disney smelled a conspiracy.

As a last-ditch effort to avert the trial over Katzenberg's bonus, Disney board member Stanley Gold contacted Geffen, who agreed to meet with him at his Malibu beach house. After listening to Geffen chart out Katzenberg's point of view on the matter of his bonus and on how he'd been mistreated by Eisner, Gold told Geffen that the most Disney would offer to settle for was $30 million. Geffen plainly replied that he'd take $150 million—$60 million more than he'd proposed to Ovitz four years earlier. When Gold said he'd like to agree to Geffen's figure but doubted he could get Disney's approval, Geffen said: "Stanley, let me assure you, it will cost you more the next time."

The trial began on April 26, with a dozen journalists sitting in the front row, pens hovering hungrily over notepads.

As events unfolded, the trial revealed itself to be better than scripted entertainment. There was much discussion of Project Snowball—the study that had been commissioned to determine just how much Katzenberg's contractual 2 percent bonus would amount to if he left the company. There was Eisner's insistence that he was unaware of the project (even after Fields handed him a "Project Snowball" memo with his initials on it). The climax, as it were, began when Fields turned to subpoenaed notes taken by Eisner's biographer Tony Schwartz and began grilling Eisner on his personal feelings toward Katzenberg.

"Did you consider yourself the cheerleader and Mr. Katzenberg merely the tip of your pompom?" Fields asked.

"No," Eisner replied.

The journalists in the front row, who up until now had looked ready to nod off, perked up and scribbled in their notepads.

There were a few more back-and-forths before Fields said: "Did you tell Mr. Schwartz that you hated Mr. Katzenberg?"

The journalists froze, pens held motionlessly an inch above paper.

"In one conversation when he pushed me on things that Mr. Katzenberg had [done], I did say that," said Eisner.

"You said, 'I think I hate the little midget'?"

The reporters now looked ready to fall over in their seats. Many laughed. Then pens were madly put to work.

Eisner looked uneasy. "I think you're getting into an area that . . . is ill-advised. I don't think it's productive, Mr. Fields, to ask what he was referring to that prompted that response. It was completely private . . ."

"Didn't you say on more than one occasion that you hated Mr. Katzenberg to Mr. Schwartz?"

"I probably did hundreds and hundreds of hours of interviewing with Mr. Schwartz . . . Probably out of humor. Out of gross unpleasantness. I did not hate Mr. Katzenberg. I still do not hate Mr. Katzenberg. We had a very long and fruitful relationship. There were things that I'm sure that I did that provoked his dislike and hatred of me and vice versa at any one moment in time. But to characterize it as me hating him is absurd and is going down a direction that I think is not in your client's best interest or mine . . ."

Fields continued his questions. "Did you say to Mr. Schwartz, 'I don't care what he thinks. I am not going to pay him any of the money'?"

"I would say again, in anger I said that."

Satisfied, Fields sat down. He had made his point—that Eisner was never willing to pay Katzenberg a dime, regardless of whether he was owed it. The judge ordered a break and the journalists sped into the hallway to call up their editors. As noted by Nikki Finke in *Salon,* the "normally staid" Helene Hahn "could not stop giggling as she burst into what looked like a jig."

Things were, rather quickly, going Katzenberg's way, and after court he'd head over to DreamWorks, where he appeared visibly exhilarated and pumped up. For the first time he ventured to speak publicly about the lawsuit, and would amuse members of the *El Dorado* team by re-enacting what he perceived as Disney's missteps in court.

"You wouldn't *believe* what mistakes they made today!" he'd say jubilantly, and then provide a blow-by-blow of the day's drama. "He *really* shot himself in the foot when he said that," he would crow. And then: "Can you *believe* he said *that?*"

Like any good legal drama, the trial did not drag out interminably, and Judge Paul Breckenridge Jr. swiftly ruled in Katzenberg's favor, finding the evidence "inescapable" that Disney had breached Katzenberg's contract and owed him his bonus, plus interest. As to just how much Katzenberg was owed, that would be determined in further proceedings.

After the verdict was announced, Geffen called Gold: "I told you so."

The next day the two men met at Geffen's new mansion in Beverly Hills. As he'd warned, Geffen told Gold that the cost of settlement had now gone up higher—to $200 million.

Negotiations continued the next day at the Four Seasons Hotel, where Katzenberg and his lawyers gave Gold a presentation on the value of Katzenberg's bonus and how much interest had accrued. But afterwards, when Gold met with Eisner and Sandy Litvack, he was unable to persuade them to settle. When he told Geffen, Geffen repeated once more that the number was only going to go higher.

More proceedings followed in May and lasted until the July Fourth weekend, when Gold again met Geffen at his beach house. By this point he was no longer interested in negotiating; he wanted a deal. A number was agreed upon: $275 million.

When Geffen triumphantly called Katzenberg with the news, Katzenberg was strangely underwhelmed. "I'd always expected something that began with a three," he said. Then he picked up: "Okay, I'll take $280 million," landing on a number that was $5 million higher than Geffen had agreed on.

"Jeffrey, you can't do this to me!" Geffen said, clearly annoyed. "I've given my word."

But Katzenberg, feeling rather confident in light of the past few months, refused to back down. In the end, Geffen said he'd pay Katzenberg the extra $5 million out of his own pocket.

But there was no need for Geffen to cough up any of his own funds. Disney agreed to pay $280. The sum was a whopping $190 million more than Ovitz and Geffen had agreed on back in 1995 and meant that Katzenberg was no longer the poorhouse partner in the SKG alliance. Of course, he was far from qualifying for the billionaire's club, in which both Geffen and Spielberg were comfortably ensconced. But one thing was certain—he would never again have to mortgage his homes to come up with his initial DreamWorks investment.

But if Katzenberg felt vindicated by his triumph over a man who had so cruelly, and publicly, hurt him, people close to him say that he never really dealt with the emotional toll that Eisner had exacted from him. He never sat down and processed what it meant that the man he'd served so loyally all those years thought of him as the tip of his pompom. Process, after all, was not in Katzenberg's nature. When Geffen once suggested he see a therapist, Katzenberg responded, "Why?" In this case, he had won. What was there to talk about?

Then the bottom dropped out on the thing that had represented more promise of things to come, where everything would start going, finally, as planned. In July, DreamWorks pulled out of Playa Vista. Spielberg's kingdom-to-be, his Xanadu, was dead. Once again, Geffen had told them so. For years, Playa Vista had been the pot at the end of the rainbow. Practically, it would mean that DreamWorks would for once be united, that music and movie and TV executives would all be working under one roof, or at least on one campus—not to mention the three partners. A brand-new, high-tech studio might have even tempted Geffen to drive in from Beverly Hills, and as Finkelman Cox said: "When the campus went away, so, too, did some of the glue that held Steven, Jeffrey, and David together. It meant they would never share offices."

But more significant was its symbolism. "When Playa Vista fell through, it had a huge impact on the sense of momentum, and morale, at DreamWorks," one person told me. "For so long people had been talking about, 'When we build a new complex, things will be totally different.' For so long, it had been *the thing.*"

Spielberg felt the loss of Playa Vista most profoundly; he "wanted to cry," he said, when Playa Vista fell through. "It was so, so sad when that part of [the plan] didn't come into play. I really wanted—more than Jeffrey, more than David—I was pushing to have a homeland, to really have a base of operations." The new studio was intended to accommodate Spielberg's entire Hollywood family. And now, that family would remain dispersed.

For Spielberg's partners, the real concern was that they had lost one of their biggest incentives in securing Spielberg's fidelity to Dream-Works. Playa Vista had been like a giant dose of Ritalin for the kid with the roving attention span. Now they were going to have to come up with a new drug.

And fast.

III

ROCKIN'

19

UNEXPECTED BEAUTY

W HEN SAM MENDES saw the first day's dailies for *American Beauty,* his first thought was: "Rubbish."

It was the scene in which Kevin Spacey drives up to a burger joint, sees a Help Wanted sign, and applies for a job. Only, the way Mendes had originally shot it, Spacey walked into the restaurant, which slowed the sequence down considerably. But even if Spacey had been tap dancing, it wouldn't have helped. The lighting was all off, the costumes wrong. Most troubling, the drama itself felt . . . undramatic. Pedestrian. Boring. The scene needed to be rewritten, restaged. Everything needed to happen *faster.*

That night Mendes went home and tried to sleep off his concern. It didn't work. At half past midnight he called producer Dan Jinks. "Dan," he said, "sorry to wake you. But I'm so depressed. The dailies are terrible."

Even Jinks, a preternaturally positive producer, had to agree. "I know," he said quietly.

As the two men talked, Jinks offered his support and said he'd talk to DreamWorks and see if he could arrange for more shooting days. Not that he wanted to—that was the sort of question that, almost unfailingly, yields an unpleasant-at-best response. Jinks couldn't help but anticipate a confrontation.

Surprisingly, there was none. The next day Bob Cooper stopped by the set—the film was shooting at Warner's ranch, located a mile from the Warner Bros. lot in Burbank—and told Mendes he could have more time. But he looked worried. "Are you going to keep doing this on this movie?" he asked.

"No," Mendes said. "I'm getting it now. Give me a couple more days and I think I'll be where I want to be."

Apparently, that wasn't enough. Cooper told Mendes that Spielberg had taken a look at his dailies and wanted to talk to him. "Why don't you come with me over to Steven's house to chat this weekend?" Cooper said.

"Sure," Mendes said, having no idea what awaited him there.

Thus far, Mendes and his little movie had been squeaking by mostly unnoticed at DreamWorks. When shooting began, in December of 1998, Parkes was busy with *Gladiator*. Aside from the initial suggestion to cut the teenage sex scene, he hadn't offered as much as a note or rewrite on the *American Beauty* screenplay. It was so uncharacteristic of him that one DreamWorks executive said to *Beauty*'s screenwriter, Alan Ball, "You know, it's normally not like this."

But now Mendes was suddenly on Spielberg's radar. When he arrived at the great man's Pacific Palisades home the following Saturday, he found Spielberg chipper and gracious. As he led Mendes into the living room, where Cooper was already seated, he said, grinning, "I love watching first-time directors. It's like watching someone lose their virginity."

Having broken the ice, Spielberg got down to business. "I just want to say, I have faith in you, you're great at composing shots," he began. "But sometimes you're not holding your shots long enough. There are times when you can cover a whole scene in the master [shot]"—the establishing shot that holds all of the subjects in view. The master shot is used to set up a scene before the camera zooms in on close-ups or cuts in from various angles.

"If the master's good enough, if you compose it well enough, if there's tension in it, you can hold a master for a long time," Spielberg said. To demonstrate his point, Spielberg whipped out a copy of *Dr. Strangelove* and popped it into the VCR. He fast-forwarded to the war room scene—in which the master shot is held for five unwavering minutes.

"Look at what [Stanley] Kubrick does with this scene. The reason these masters hold so long is the lighting," Spielberg said, pointing to the klieg-like rays of light that bore down on the characters from an unseen, overhead source.

During his "half-hour tutorial," as Mendes called it, Spielberg offered other tips. Watching the scene Mendes had shot of Annette Bening's character having a mini-meltdown, slapping herself and weeping after not being able to sell a house, Spielberg suggested that Mendes zoom in on Bening's face.

"You should push in on that scene," he said.

The suggestion reflected a Spielbergian way of handling emotion: amping it up and not letting it go. It was Spielberg's "moral bossiness," as *New York Times* critic A. O. Scott once wrote. "He tells you how to feel," leaving "you . . . usually powerless to resist his manipulations."

Mendes saw what he was going for, but it wasn't his style. "That's a different way of making a film," he said politely.

"OK, OK," Spielberg said, not pushing the matter.

"I was very determined to hold the camera still and observe her," Mendes said when I spoke to him, years later. "Steven was completely fine about it. He knows what he likes and what he doesn't like, as do I. On that scene, I was holding back a lot, and I still do, trying to observe people in situations without spoon-feeding the audience as to what they should feel."

Mendes's return to the set was far smoother than his shaky start, and as shooting continued over the next several weeks, he was, happily, left alone. Although Cooper stopped by and occasionally gave notes, and Glenn Williamson remained a cheerleader, other executives felt more the way Katzenberg did, that *American Beauty* was a lark—cute, quirky, perhaps, but by no means a moneymaker and therefore not worthy of more than a passing nod. One day, Mendes overheard one executive who'd dropped by the set say to his colleague, "Let's just shake hands with Kevin and get outta here."

This attitude did not help producers Cohen and Jinks, who were dealing with the reality that *American Beauty*'s budget was slowly creeping upward, to $15 million. The budget was a "giant struggle," said Jinks. "We were constantly going to them on our hands and knees, saying, 'Look, we need more money to do this.' There were people at DreamWorks who were nervous the movie was not going to do business."

When shooting wrapped in February, Mendes was eager to get back to London and return to his duties as artistic director at the Donmar. He knew that editing *American Beauty* in London, not L.A., would mean another bump to the budget, and he feared DreamWorks would insist he not go. He was thus pleased and relieved when Spielberg gave him his blessing. And so, for the next ten weeks, he holed up in an editing room, completely cut off from Hollywood.

Mendes's habit, as it emerged, was to do extensive work in post-production. He cut entire scenes, including the trial sequences that bookended the film, showing Jane, the Burnhams' daughter (played by Thora Birch), and her boyfriend, Ricky (played by Wes Bentley), going to court, and jail, for the murder of Lester Burnham. "I change a lot in post," Mendes said. "And *American Beauty* was fundamentally different" in its edited form. "That was the biggest change between what I shot, and what the final movie was, of everything I've done."

The change was so dramatic that when Ball, Cohen, and Jinks flew to London in April to look at Mendes's cut, they were speechless after the screening. Ball, in particular, looked ready to kill himself. "Why'd you take so much out? And where's the trial scene?" he asked.

Mendes took a deep breath. "I'm going to shock you—because I think *more* needs to come out."

Ball's face turned stonier.

"I was just shocked because I didn't expect it," Ball recalled later. "But that was the only time there was any sort of bristling between us."

Mendes tweaked the film further and, the next day, screened it again for the producers and Ball. This time they began to see where Mendes was coming from.

Not so Kevin Spacey, when he saw the film a few weeks later in New York.

"Where's the flying sequence?" he said when the lights went up, referring to a dream sequence in which his character soars through the air. Spacey had spent a day and a half working with blue screens and wires to create the effect. Now it was on the cutting-room floor.

But the reaction of Conrad Hall, the film's cinematographer, was the most explosive. "It's a disaster!" he cried after seeing the movie.

Mendes tried to reason with him. "Please. Just watch it again tomorrow."

Hall agreed, grudgingly, and when he saw the film a second time, he lightened up somewhat.

The real test came in July of 1999, when *American Beauty* was screened for Spielberg at Amblin. At the time, Spielberg was working with screenwriter Scott Frank, and he invited Frank to watch *American*

Beauty with him. (Spielberg liked to screen movies with an audience, whether it was his kids or friends or other filmmakers.) Mendes, who had flown in from London for the occasion, was sequestered off in an Amblin office with Cohen, Jinks, and Williamson, waiting to be summoned when the film was over.

Two hours later, they got the call, and proceeded to stumble over themselves down the stairs to the director's sanctuary. Inside, Spielberg, who was still in his seat, was beaming. Before Mendes had a chance to gauge his fate, Spielberg said: "You've made a masterpiece. Don't change a frame of it."

"You know," he went on, "I watched this the way I normally do— like, this is my studio and my film, and I should be taking notes. That lasted about thirty seconds."

"Steven was completely on the ceiling," Mendes told me. "He was incandescently excited. That's when I thought, 'Oh, wow . . .'"

"I knew nothing about *American Beauty*," said Frank. "And I remember sitting there with Steven, watching the movie, and both of us just saying, 'Wow. Oh, wow,' and laughing. When the lights came up, Steven was unbelievably effusive about how much he loved it. He told Sam how it reminded him of when he saw *Forrest Gump*. All I kept thinking was: it would be good to be Sam Mendes right now."

The next day *American Beauty* was screened for Parkes, MacDonald, distribution head Jim Tharp, Terry Press, and the producers, all of whom seconded Spielberg's reaction. (Parkes had caught on during filming that *American Beauty* was something special, and had sent Mendes a card saying: "What becomes clearer and clearer every day is that we're seeing the birth of a major filmmaker.")

Although Press had concerns—sources say she worried that not only was *American Beauty* too dark, but Spacey and Bening compounded the film's noir quality—she realized that, if it was handled right, this was the kind of movie that could do great things. But it was already July. The Cannes Film Festival, which would have been an ideal launch, had already passed. Press would have to work fast.

The first order of business was to preview the film and get a sense of how it played with audiences. Spielberg, a vocal opponent of previews (he never did them on his own films), had already insisted that testing *American Beauty* was unnecessary. But Press, still reeling from the *Saving Private Ryan* Oscar debacle, was leaving nothing to chance.

"Look, let's strike a deal," Mendes recalled Press telling him and

Spielberg. "We'll preview it, but we won't do the cards"—whereby test audiences write down their reactions to films—"and we won't do focus groups. Sam, you can talk to the audience afterwards and see what they say. That'll be it."

And so it was that Mendes found himself sitting in the back row of what Katzenberg referred to as the "giant preview blowjob house," aka the Block, a thirty-screen movie megaplex in Orange County. Katzenberg's appellation stemmed from the fact that films tended to always test well at the Block, even ones that went on to be bombs.

Katzenberg did not accompany Mendes and Press to his favorite movie biosphere, but he did register his pleasure with the movie, which he'd seen shortly after Spielberg's viewing. One day, while Mendes was dubbing, Katzenberg called. Characteristically, he was in motion. "I'm pulling the car over," Katzenberg said, "because I want to tell you—you just made the studio."

Mendes was floored. "Wow, thanks very much," was all he could muster. One never knew what a Katzenberg bullet-call had in store.

"That was a great movie. I'm really thankful to you," Katzenberg continued. "I don't know where it came from, I was barely aware it was being made. I take no credit. But I just wanted to say thank you." And with that, he hung up.

At the Block screening, after the lights came up, Mendes made his way to the front of the theater and faced a crowd of five hundred people. Few directors enjoy hearing their films picked apart by total strangers, and Mendes, who was beginning to feel sick, was no exception.

"So," Mendes began tentatively. "Who likes it, then?"

About 20 percent of the crowd raised their hands.

Shit, Mendes thought to himself. What was the point of such humiliation?

But he held his ground. "Well, then, who didn't like it?" he asked.

A pair of hands shot up. Mendes waited for more, but none were raised.

"What else is there?" he asked, thoroughly bewildered.

At that, someone in the back row yelled out, "Ask who *really* likes it!"

"Okay, who really likes it?"

As arms shot up throughout the house, Mendes smiled. Then he chatted with the audience about specific scenes—what bits felt too long, which ones were boring, etc.—notes that he would take back to the editing suite. Afterward, as he and Press headed back to L.A., he said, "Wow, this movie might really play." But Press, in her supremely no-nonsense way, wasn't about to indulge in wishful thinking.

"Terry was thrilled, but she's always about putting the next foot forward," said Mendes. "Her attitude was, 'Well that's all very nice, but we've got to go do *this* now.'"

There was reason to be cautious; *American Beauty* certainly wasn't a marketing no-brainer. Dark and difficult, it had no huge stars. But never had Press been so determined to will success to happen. She went Katzenbergian: do or die.

It came as little surprise to anyone when, that same July, Cooper was fired. By now it wasn't just Parkes who was making life difficult. Helene Hahn was calling, questioning deals he had made. And in April, even the press weighed in. In the *L.A. Times*, Claudia Eller wrote that questions "continue about the status of Bob Cooper, who has assumed a low profile at DreamWorks since being recruited by Katzenberg two years ago." Two months later, Parkes delivered the news that it was over. The perennial good guy, Spielberg took the condemned man out to lunch and thanked him, effusively, for his work.

But the vacancy was a problem. Parkes and MacDonald were, if anything, more caught up in producing than ever before. They needed help managing the studio. By now, both Nina Jacobson and Bob Brassel, the only executives who had come to DreamWorks with any real studio experience, had left. Everyone else was deemed too green.

Katzenberg, now free and clear of the legal dispute with Disney, suggested himself. "You guys think this is so hard. It's not—it's easy! Let me do it," he said. He was determined to put things right at the studio, whose pipeline was still parched. With *Gladiator* sucking up so much of Parkes's time, few films were being readied for the future. And there had been two more stinkers. In May, *The Love Letter* starring Kate Capshaw seriously missed the mark. And in July, the big summer horror flick *The Haunting* made only a little more than it had cost to produce—$90 million. Eviscerated by critics, it hardly seemed the kind of daring art that DreamWorks had promised in its early days.

Adding to the embarrassment was another horror film, *The Blair Witch Project*, released by Artisan Entertainment a few weeks before *The Haunting*: with its clever, mockumentary concept and a shrewd Internet campaign, the $60,000 film had turned into a $140 million blockbuster. Terry Press, visiting on the set of another DreamWorks project, had gamely offered her two cents on *The Haunting*, saying, "It's a piece of shit, but at least I did *my* job." (A solid marketing campaign helped the film open to an impressive $33 million.) Others at the studio also kept their distance. Katzenberg was the only executive to show up at the L.A. premiere and was the only one to offer support to director Jan de Bont following a disastrous preview. "Jeffrey was the one who always called me," de Bont said. "Because I was so depressed, afterwards . . . He would call and say, 'Don't worry. We're going to make it.'" Almost: *The Haunting* didn't wind up being a total write-off; it did well in DVD, and made another $85 million overseas.

Katzenberg had no illusions that he, or anyone else, would ever be able to truly rule the studio, given Spielberg's closeness with Parkes. But by now he was desperate enough to play along, kicking his ego to the side and agreeing to pick up Cooper's slack by coming in under Parkes and MacDonald in the pecking order. This arrangement quelled any fears that Katzenberg would push through fare that wasn't up to DreamWorks' snuff. "I'm an employee—I work for them," he told *Daily Variety*, in reference to Parkes and MacDonald. Then he admitted that the situation would probably cause people to "question our sanity." It did just that.

The studio that had installed producers to run its lauded live-action division had now placed one of its partners, a man who had more experience running a studio than anyone at the company, in a subordinate role.

Even to outsiders, it was clear that that's where Spielberg and Parkes felt he belonged. "I think Jeffrey was a little underrated there," said de Bont. "I don't think he was seen as a very creative person . . ." While working on *The Haunting*, de Bont said, the attitude from Parkes and MacDonald was, "'Oh, it's only Jeffrey.' They were never really taking him too seriously—his opinions, his suggestions. Yes, [his ideas] were different, but to me they always made sense. And they were, quite often, less contrived."

Because of this, DreamWorks felt disunited, de Bont said. "It was a little separated. It was really Walter and Laurie and Steven and then everybody else. They were so tight. And if people are such close friends, it's really hard to get in between, because they'll always stand up for each other."

Katzenberg was also excluded from the meetings that took place every Thursday morning at Spielberg's house to discuss creative issues at the live-action studio. "He never went," said one source. "That's just the way it was."

Parkes's feelings toward what Katzenberg was doing at the animation studio were clear when he would show up to screenings of animated films. "Walter would rest his head in his hand and slump in his seat, like he was bored or asleep," said one source.

Katzenberg never openly expressed resentment over his exclusion from the live-action studio or Parkes's role there, but it seemed to come across through the actions and attitudes of his loyalists. Terry Press, who remained very much an unofficial Katzenberg publicist at DreamWorks, was, at times, openly disdainful toward Parkes. At one DreamWorks premiere, one journalist recalled talking to Press when Parkes came over to chat. When he turned to leave, Press dramatically rolled her eyes. The journalist felt the opinion did not belong just to Press but to Katzenberg.

His arrival at Amblin was like a shot of caffeine to development executives accustomed to Parkes's meandering, pontificating ways. With Katzenberg running meetings, it was "like bam, bam, bam. 'We're doing this, we're doing that—done,'" said one executive. "The next day, all the things he'd said he'd do were done."

Katzenberg's edict was simple: Get Movies Made—Now. Immediately, he was on the phone with Tom Pollock and Ivan Reitman, producing partners at the Montecito Picture Company and old friends. Pollock, former chairman of Universal, had once been Katzenberg's lawyer. As it turned out, Montecito did have a picture for Dream-Works—*Road Trip*, a college-humor comedy developed for Todd Phillips, a young NYU film-school grad who'd come to Montecito's attention by way of Reitman's son, Jason, who had seen Phillips's documentary *Frat House* at Sundance. *Road Trip* would be cheap to make —it had a budget of $16 million—and because it was not the type of film that interested Parkes, Katzenberg had no problem pushing it through.

Katzenberg went after big names and wangled them into working on the cheap. One of his first projects was *The Mexican,* an indie-style entry revolving around a feckless, small-time crook sent south of the border on a gangster mission. When his girlfriend gets kidnapped, there are car chases, tequila shots. Produced by *Pulp Fiction* producer Lawrence Bender and directed by Gore Verbinski, it had been kicking around in various incarnations for some time since DreamWorks outbid Miramax for the rights. Verbinski was looking to cast Owen Wilson and Renée Zellweger and "go make a little movie," he said. Katzenberg thought otherwise, called Verbinski, and said: "Julia Roberts wants to meet you." Roberts's casting was followed by the signing of Brad Pitt; Katzenberg had convinced both stars to work far below their typical rates.

"We tried to keep the indie spirit and made it for very little," said Verbinski. "Everyone took massive [pay] cuts. Everyone knew it was this ragtag-priced movie with this legend at the core of it. Julia, to her credit, said, 'Let's do it.'

"By the time we were shooting in Mexico, in Real de Catorce, where the only way to get there is through this mile-and-a-half-long tunnel into town, DreamWorks was a bit like, 'Whoa, we can't send Julia there,'" Verbinski continued. "There were security concerns, so I think they upped the budget for security. But the shooting budget stayed the same. They spent six times that on marketing."

Katzenberg was back in singles and doubles land, and anything that smacked of overpriced was scratched off the slate. Projects in development, such as *Paradise Falls,* a $100 million fantasy film about the first angel murdered in heaven, were put into turnaround (the rights offered up for sale to other studios in exchange for the cost of development), with Katzenberg making it clear that big-bucks projects belonged elsewhere. One agent recalled talking to Katzenberg around this time: "The vibe was that DreamWorks wasn't in the business of making big movies; that DreamWorks wasn't Warner Bros. The vibe was that money was tight."

Katzenberg might have been $280 million richer after his Disney settlement, but it hadn't affected his style. Trained at the most frugal institutions in Hollywood — Paramount and Disney — Katzenberg splurged only when absolutely necessary (typically to lure or placate talent). Otherwise it was tight reins, assiduously clutched.

"That is who Jeffrey is," said one source. "He was a real studio executive. And when you make those cheap Touchstone comedies at Disney, the mentality is: can you do it cheaper? It's ingrained in who he is. Even as a senior executive," this person continued, "Jeffrey almost acted like it was his money, even though it was stockholder money, or the company's money."

In contrast, "Steven has never spent his own money, it's always somebody else's money. So, with somebody else's money, you probably don't think about [lavish expenses]. But I don't think Jeffrey ever got to that level. Because he was never talent."

And DreamWorks' own talent was the one thing Katzenberg could never control. Spielberg's list of non-DreamWorks directing commitments was growing. In addition to Sony's *Memoirs of a Geisha*—which remained a contentious issue between S, K, and G—Spielberg had signed on to direct a film called *Minority Report* for Twentieth Century Fox. The project had come to his attention during postproduction work on *The Haunting*, when he and de Bont were routinely flying up to Industrial Light and Magic, which produced the special effects on the film. De Bont gave Spielberg a script to read that he'd been developing for years with screenwriter Jon Cohen.

Based on a futuristic Philip K. Dick short story, "The Minority Report," it was set up at Fox for de Bont, but Fox executives had made it clear that green-lighting the project depended on de Bont landing a star. Tom Cruise's name had been mentioned and, knowing that Spielberg had a relationship with the actor, de Bont asked his friend to intervene. After reading the script, Cruise was interested but wanted Spielberg to direct. The men had been longtime friends and neighbors but had never collaborated. Fox, naturally, swooned. In the new configuration, de Bont was a producer on *Minority Report*, which he said he didn't mind, seeing as it meant that the movie would actually get made.

Minority Report became a Fox-DreamWorks coproduction, though unlike the studios' previous partnership deals, Fox wasn't willing to give up the domestic rights, after feeling burned on *Titanic*, which it developed but which became a coproduction with Paramount, with the latter studio winding up with the domestic distribution. Fox chairman Bill Mechanic was not about to lose again on another property with blockbuster potential.

Mechanic agreed to split the movie with DreamWorks but only on the condition that Fox get half of another Spielberg movie (as opposed to a DreamWorks movie) in the future. The last issue was budget. As Mechanic and Geffen ran the numbers, it became clear that the project didn't make sense for either studio—unless Spielberg and Cruise cut their rates. When neither one would, Geffen called Mechanic and told him to kill the movie. "It's the right message for us to send to Hollywood," he said.

Geffen then spoke with Spielberg and eventually talked him into reducing his fee. Cruise did the same. Then Geffen went back to Mechanic and presented a complex deal in which both studios would split the film's worldwide distribution ancillary rights. Yet, even with slimmer paychecks, Spielberg and Cruise would together make as much as thirty-five cents on every dollar made.

Minority Report and *Geisha* made it clear that Spielberg's personal directing gigs were becoming a habit. The director's interests were supplanting those of DreamWorks. Katzenberg's mission of getting Spielberg up to bat as often as possible was now becoming a matter of getting him up to bat for DreamWorks at all. And that was proving more and more difficult.

On the animation front, another problem was at hand. *The Road to El Dorado,* the company's next animated release, was, as one source put it, "genuinely troubled."

Making *El Dorado* had been nothing like the collaborative, feel-good experience of *Prince of Egypt.* Directors had come and gone, the creative direction had done several 180s, and Katzenberg, consumed with his lawsuit against Disney, had been an erratic, but no less controlling, presence.

Now, just months before the film's March 2000 release date, executives feared that the problems showed. "The original notion of the dreamer and the schemer, or of the Bob Hope and the Bing Crosby, and the girl in-between, and the road picture, which I loved, wasn't coming to fruition," said Penney Finkelman Cox. "All the characters sounded alike, they felt alike."

Originally, Katzenberg had envisioned *El Dorado* as looking as sophisticated as a live-action film—he'd coined the genre "animaction" and was planning to release *El Dorado* as a PG-13 film. Then, he'd changed his mind, wanted it more broad. Then he swerved back again to realism. Swearing and steamy love scenes were folded in. The character of Chel (voiced by Rosie Perez), the saucy love interest of the lead characters Miguel and Tulio, became so much of a hoochie mama that she had to be toned down. Partly this was due to the influence of codirector Eric "Bibo" Bergeron, a Frenchman whose notions of sexuality were a tad too European.

"Chel was too sexual," said one artist who worked on *El Dorado*. "Someone in HR said, 'I find this sexist.' We had to have Rodolphe [Guenoden—Chel's supervising animator] change the design so her crotch wasn't so out in the open, so it was a little more subtle."

Ultimately, even Katzenberg agreed that things had gone too far. New orders were given to scale it back. Chel became less of a sexpot (she retained her curvalicious caboose), the language was cleaned up, and the rating was softened to PG from PG-13.

When Finkelman Cox had voiced her concerns about *El Dorado* to Katzenberg, she said he wouldn't listen, believing fervently in the *El Dorado* screenplay, written by Ted Elliott and Terry Rossio, his "star" writers, who'd crafted the smash hit *Aladdin* at Disney. "When Jeffrey believes in something, it's really hard," Finkelman Cox said. "He will put his faith in a person and he will believe what they tell him because he really wants to believe in that person. He believed in, he loved Ted and Terry. He adored them. They could do no wrong. If Ted and Terry said it was blue, it would stay blue, even if it was closer to lavender."

But *El Dorado*'s problems went way beyond the script. "It was broken," said one artist. "Very broken." Many of its issues were endemic to the animation process as it was evolving at DreamWorks, a process in which inexperienced directors and producers were hired to serve under the aegis of Katzenberg, and movies were made according to groupthink instead of in the service of one artist's vision. The system was markedly different from that at Pixar, where, although artists, directors, storyboard artists, and even "the janitor," as writer-director Pete Docter once joked, weighed in on a film while it was being made, ultimately all creative decisions were up to the director. Even John Lasseter's opinions were not the final word, if the director felt otherwise. Pixar's process was also kept pure by the fact that films were nurtured by the same core group of people from start to finish. Directors were not hired and assigned to a project, but were generally the ones who came up with the project in the first place, and who also worked on the script.

On *El Dorado*, directors Will Finn and David Silverman, who had never directed a feature film before, were replaced by Bergeron, an Amblimation artist, and Don Paul, who was yanked from his post overseeing special effects. Producers Brooke Breton and Bonne Radford were also inexperienced.

Katzenberg may have been giving people a chance to break in, but most people viewed the strategy more cynically. "Jeffrey puts people in positions that complement him, or, who do it the way he wants them to do it. And he values that higher than he values creative ability," one source said.

According to artist Paul Lasaine, "If you're not eye to eye with [Katzenberg] on a project, then there's no point in fighting it, because he is the final word there. If you're not in synch, just go ahead and move on."

Ellen Coss, a producer who has worked at DreamWorks, defends Katzenberg's process, however. "A lot of people complain about Jeffrey's involvement and say that DreamWorks is not a happy place for a director," she said. "But Jeffrey has the audience's back, that's what it comes down to . . . He understands what an audience wants, whereas sometimes a director doesn't. Directors can want to be too much of an auteur and can get very caught up in their own vision . . . DreamWorks is not a place for an auteur. It's definitely moviemaking by committee there."

Freed from the competing duties that had occupied him during *Prince of Egypt*, when DreamWorks was in its start-up phase, Katzenberg was more than the final word on *El Dorado*, he was *the word*, even when he wasn't up to speed on things because of his involvement in the Disney lawsuit. "He's a control freak," said one source. "If you think of how that plays out creatively on a movie . . ." said one former artist, who complained that Katzenberg would order changes and overhauls late in the game, because he hadn't been following the film's progress.

"When you've already signed off on the look of this thing, the style of this thing, to come in and go, 'I don't like the way it looks.' People are going to suffer because of that," says the source. "People are going to have to work extra hours, because he either didn't attend meetings often enough, or he's just yanking our chain to show that he's boss . . .

That's the day-to-day with Jeffrey, that's the frustration you're going to hear from people, and that's how it manifests itself in production. It was wasteful."

The same charges had been lobbed at him at Disney, but they were exponentially more evident at DreamWorks, where animation wasn't one of Katzenberg's jobs, it was his primary job.

Complaints about Katzenberg's control-freak ways had been brought to his attention once at a company retreat, where one of the group activities was to—anonymously—write down a list of Katzenberg's strengths and weaknesses. Employees eagerly filled a whiteboard with a long list of their frustrations. When Katzenberg read through them, he didn't get angry, or defend himself. "That's the truth!" he said. "That's me!"

"'Duly noted!'" was "what Jeffrey said when he didn't want to respond to something," said one source, who said he was "good-humored" about the exercise. "He did so much with a smile. He could get away with so many things, because he had a smile on his face."

It was at one of those retreats—at the La Quinta resort in Palm Springs, over the summer of 1997—that an intervention of sorts had been staged by Finkelman Cox, Sandy Rabins, and Ann Daly—the former head of home entertainment at Disney who was now managing DreamWorks' animation studio—to try and get Katzenberg to see the folly that was *El Dorado*. According to sources at the retreat, the three women arranged to have breakfast with Katzenberg one morning to discuss the film's problems. But breakfast was short-lived. After a case was made that *El Dorado* desperately needed a creative reassessment, Katzenberg curtly responded, "You're wrong," and left the table.

Whether it was the pressure and frustration of having his vaunted second act not pan out as quickly as hoped, or a sincere vexation, Katzenberg, it seemed, was changing. A few years into DreamWorks, his legal victory over Eisner having filled him with a confidence even more supreme than usual, Katzenberg was no longer the more collaborative Jeffrey he'd been during the dawn of DreamWorks, and particularly during the making of *Prince of Egypt*. Memories of his hard-charging Disney days were returning. The "New Jeffrey," as one person put it, "was gone. He was really gone."

20

THE BATTLE FOR OSCAR

S DALE OLSON LISTENED to Jeffrey Katzenberg, Terry Press, and members of DreamWorks' marketing department discuss strategy for an *American Beauty* Oscar run, he kept his mouth shut. Olson, former president of the venerable Rogers & Cowan publicity agency, where he'd worked on more than 150 Academy Awards campaigns, knew a thing or two about how to win over stodgy Academy members. But being the new kid, he politely waited before raising his hand to speak.

"You're doing it all *wrong*," said Olson, who has a roundish face, bright-white hair, and brown, Lew Wasserman–esque glasses. (Spotting them from across the Universal cafeteria, Wasserman had shouted: "Mine are *black!*") "You have to try to not think like a studio. You have to think *smaller*—that's where the voters are." Olson then proceeded to explain his strategy.

When he'd finished, Olson held his breath. Surely Katzenberg would snap or Press would shoot back a clever rejoinder. More than likely, he'd be asked to leave.

But after several interminable seconds, Katzenberg finally spoke. "You know, he's right," he said, settling back in his chair and motioning for Olson to continue.

Olson then mapped out in detail his plan for how *American Beauty*, due out in a few weeks, could reclaim the Oscar crown from Miramax, a year after Harvey Weinstein stole the show.

"I was new, and so I could be bolder," said Olson, who had observed that Press's staff seemed hesitant to challenge their fiery leader. "They were a great team, but when Terry would say something, they all jumped," he continued, describing Press as "fierce."

"Her whole mien . . . she's so *definite,* so strong," Olson said. "She can just make you wither, until you're fortunate enough to get to know her." Months before Olson had been recruited, to work on *American Beauty*—a first, for DreamWorks—Press had begun laying the groundwork for the film's September 15, 1999, release. She wasn't going to get in the mud, but she was determined to never again be outmaneuvered by Weinstein—or anyone else. She was willing to try new things, having learned the hard way. And with *American Beauty,* a film Press adored and believed in along with everyone else at the studio, there were going to be no rookie missteps, despite the race with the clock. No one at DreamWorks had seen the film until July, when most studios are well into awards campaigns. Media outlets had already planned their coverage of the fall film season, when studios begin unleashing Oscar hopefuls. When the *Los Angeles Times* published its fall movie preview in August, there was no mention of *American Beauty.*

In the past, Press might have gone into overdrive, screening *American Beauty* for as many members of the media as possible, to build fast, furious buzz. But she held back, treating *American Beauty* like a precious gem to be shown selectively and with care. In August, she arranged a private screening for the *New York Times'* Bernard Weinraub, and set up a chat between him and Sam Mendes.

In the meantime, creative advertising head David Sameth came up with an iconic and sexy image to build the marketing around—a photograph of a young woman's nude belly, across which she holds a single red rose. Written underneath were the words: ". . . look closer."

Weinraub's piece appeared on September 12, on the front page of the Arts and Leisure section. Titled "A Wunderkind Discovers the Wonders of Film," the glowing profile of Mendes and his film included flattering quotes from Spielberg, Kevin Spacey, and Annette Bening, and appeared to be saying go, go, go. "It *almost* reviewed the movie, which was quite out of character for the *Times,*" Mendes said. "So people were slightly uppity about it, slightly pissed off that this thing had been written. But they were also intrigued—what is this movie?"

The story ratcheted up the buzz ignited at the Toronto International Film Festival, where *American Beauty* premiered the day before to a thundering standing ovation. Over the years, Toronto had grown into a major event, on par with Sundance. Like that festival, it had be-

come chic, inundated not just with small, arty films—that year's selection included Woody Allen's *Sweet and Lowdown;* Miramax's *The
Cider House Rules;* and indie darling Kevin Smith's *Dogma*—but
also with limos and glittering swag. Toronto's timing made it an Oscar springboard. And the night of the *American Beauty* premiere, the
O-word was oft uttered.

"*American Beauty* is expected to win Oscar nominations, and Kevin
Spacey is walking on eggshells, aware he's given a strong performance,"
observed Roger Ebert in the *Chicago Sun-Times.* Still, Ebert couldn't
help but wonder: "Will the academy find this material too dark for
nominations? Oscar likes to put on a happy face."

When *American Beauty* walked away with the coveted People's
Choice Award in Toronto, one of the only awards bestowed at the
noncompetitive festival, any lingering doubts about Oscar prospects
were quashed. Now the games *really* began.

Oscar consultants were hired—in addition to Olson, indie film
marketer Nancy Willen, and Bruce Feldman, who'd worked at Universal and PolyGram Films—to take a more grass-roots approach and
reach out to local radio, colleges around the country, and cable TV.
Basically, to work it more like Miramax did. But even as critical reception grew, the question remained: Would *American Beauty* play? And
make money? Producers Bruce Cohen and Dan Jinks had already been
warned not to expect audiences in small towns or overseas. Expectations stayed low, but reviews glowed. In the *New York Times* Janet
Maslin wrote: "*American Beauty,* directed with terrific visual flair . . .
strikes an unusually successful balance between the mordant and
the bright." In *Variety,* Todd McCarthy reaffirmed: "*American Beauty*
is a real American original. Multilayered, bracingly resourceful and
tweaked to push its many brash ideas to the edge and beyond, this
independent-minded feature represents a stunning card of introduction for two cinematic freshmen, screenwriter Alan Ball and director
Sam Mendes."

The film was given a platform release, opening on just sixteen screens
around the country, all in major cities. The plan was to gradually
open in more theaters as word of mouth spread. The system—new to
DreamWorks, which until this point had taken all of its distribution
cues from Disney and Universal—was in marked contrast to releasing

blockbuster movies, which open "wide" in as many theaters as possible in order to garner big first-weekend grosses. (*Saving Private Ryan*, for instance, opened on nearly twenty-five hundred screens.)

Given its small, initial portal, it came as a surprise when *American Beauty* grossed $861,531 over its first weekend, or an impressive $53,845 per-screen average. Katzenberg, avidly watching the numbers, upped the number of screens for the following weekend from a planned 100 to 429. Marketing dollars also spiked. "Overnight, DreamWorks doubled, quadrupled the spend on it," said Mendes. "Katzenberg basically started marketing it like *Forrest Gump*, but skillfully. In other words, the marketing spend of a major movie as opposed to a specialty-division movie. He monitored it every week, as they do, and it just kept going. So they kept spending."

DreamWorks bought twice as many ads in *Variety* and the *Hollywood Reporter* than all the other studios, including Miramax. *American Beauty* kept grossing, and growing, eventually playing on 1,990 screens, an extraordinary number for a so-called small film. "It came on really strong and fast after its opening," said Miramax's Mark Gill. "It had great critical response and went from being barely on the radar to being a phenomenon . . . It happened really fast."

By February of 2000, *American Beauty* had grossed $74 million, almost quintuple what it cost to make. And when Oscar nominations were announced, the film received eight nods, narrowly beating out both Miramax's *Cider House Rules* and Michael Mann's *The Insider* (Disney) by one nomination. Another Disney release, M. Night Shyamalan's *The Sixth Sense*, was up for six. Press had triumphed: so far. The race was still tight, with no clear front-runner.

Miramax, of course, could never be underestimated. That *Cider House Rules*, which had never been considered a heavyweight contender, had emerged with so many nominations was testament to Weinstein's prowess. *American Beauty*'s darkness was still an issue for the Academy, which tended to like big and beautiful, not small and quirky. The *New York Times* would only allow that it was the "narrow betting favorite in Hollywood."

If Press had been on overdrive, she shifted into warp speed. Over the next four weeks, DreamWorks spent more than $774,000 on *American Beauty* trade ads, making even Weinstein—who spent $350,000 on *The Cider House Rules*—look like a slacker. The mission, accord-

ing to Olson, was to sell *American Beauty* as the movie that was "real,"
that was about "us." A "story that everyone could identify with," was
Olson's line. No one was allowed to sit on the bench when it came to
preaching this gospel. Said Mendes: "Terry got on the phone and said,
'You need to come out here . . . you need to meet some people, you
just need to be around. You need to be aware . . . that this is potentially
a huge deal for us, and if it wins any awards, it's a huge box-office
boost and it's an enormous deal for the studio. And I think we've got a
chance.'"

And so, for the next three months, Mendes found himself "sitting
in places like this"—he gestured around the white, clapboard inte-
rior of the Shutters hotel café, where I was meeting with him—"for
months!" He recalls, rather miserably: "It went on forever. And you're
not really doing anything, you're just talking about the movie, ped-
dling the myth of the film. You go sort of insane."

Spacey was caught up in the same nonstop PR machine, a fate that
the pregnant Bening was spared. Says a source: "Spacey went *everywhere*. He was at the motion picture home serving tea."

Other studios took note of DreamWorks' push, particularly Miramax, which recognized itself in DreamWorks' emboldened effort.
"For *American Beauty*, DreamWorks went through the entire Miramax playbook," said Mark Gill. "That campaign was relentless."

Rivals were less diplomatic, cattily sniping about DreamWorks'
shameless working of the "gay circuit" in an attempt to accumulate
votes, capitalizing on the fact that a number of people involved in the
film—such as Ball, Jinks, and Cohen—were openly gay.

Justin Falvey, a senior executive at DreamWorks TV, liked to say that
DreamWorks was "too good for TV." It was a particularly Dream-
Worksian sentiment—no one had ever accused anyone at the company of suffering from an inferiority complex. It was also a way of explaining, or at least justifying, why so many of the studio's shows got
canceled—the tally now included Gary David Goldberg's *Battery Park*
in addition to Peter Mehlman's *It's Like, You Know . . .*—and why it still
only had one legitimate hit: *Spin City*. By Falvey's logic, it's not that
DreamWorks was making bad shows, the shows were just too smart,
too savvy to drive up ratings. However arrogant, the claim wasn't entirely off-base.

It's Like, You Know . . . about a dyed-in-the-asphalt New Yorker transplanted to the silicone valley of Los Angeles, received high marks from critics who appreciated the show's *Seinfeld*esque acerbic cynicism. An early sign that the show might be pushing the limits of mainstream television a little too aggressively was the first line of the pilot, when the character of Lauren Woods (played by A. J. Langer, hailing from *My So-Called Life*) responds to the question of how long she's been living in L.A. by saying: "Well, nine months, but the first month was a total wash, you know—I lost my wallet, I didn't have a car, I had to get an abortion . . ." ABC insisted on killing the line and, ultimately, the show.

In September of 1999, DreamWorks rolled out another debut designed for the Too Good for TV category: *Freaks and Geeks*, an eccentrically appealing journey into the tortured existences of slightly-on-the-outside '70s teens. Unlike the rosy-cheeked, deeply earnest *Dawson's Creek* and *Felicity*, *Freaks and Geeks* was angst-ridden and rough around the edges. Most of the previously obscure cast members had been selected by the show's creator, Paul Feig, and producer, Judd Apatow, who were intent on using "real-seeming" teenagers as opposed to what Apatow called "kids who can do Froot Loops commercials." The writing was no insult to the intelligence and actually veered toward the believable: the characters talked as their counterparts on the other side of the screen did. They never seemed to actually be trying to get a laugh. Bad things that happened were not resolved in the third act.

Freaks and Geeks' fresh, edgy unconventionality clicked with critics. *Time* called it "the best fall drama aimed at any demographic." *Rolling Stone* gushed: "Stunningly funny and moving." A cult following was instantly born among smart, discerning twenty- and thirty-somethings. It all seemed to be going so perfectly. And then . . .

Feig had come up with the idea for *Freaks and Geeks* in 1997, when he was touring his independent film, *Life Sold Separately,* around colleges in the Midwest. Depressed by it all, he found himself holed up in miserable motel rooms, alone. He'd blown his $30,000 savings to make the film. He'd been fired from his acting role on *Sabrina the Teenage Witch.* Back in L.A., no job was waiting. *Maybe he could clerk in a bookstore?* Instead, he decided to write a TV pilot about his maladjusted youth. "I always said, I really want to do something . . . that was really about my friends, the world that I knew," Feig said. "When I saw *Welcome to the Dollhouse* [the Todd Solondz film], I said, 'Oh my God, somebody actually did it, somebody actually made that darker tone real, where the archetypes aren't so stereotyped.'"

Ally McBeal and *Felicity* had piqued his interest. Here were shows using the hour platform to mix comedy and drama in quirky ways. "So all of that was swirling around in my head, and I was like, maybe now's the time to do my high school show. And just out of nowhere the term 'Freaks and Geeks' came into my mind. I had 'freaks,' because we used to call burnouts 'freaks.' We never used the word 'geeks'—that was too modern. We were either nerds or whatever else. But I was like, 'What rhymes with freaks?' And it just popped into my head."

When he'd finished his script, Feig sent it to his friend Apatow, who'd recently signed a TV and film deal at DreamWorks. Apatow was the hottest name in comedy that no one outside Hollywood had heard of. His reputation came from writing for the offbeat sketch-comedy series *The Ben Stiller Show,* and HBO's *The Larry Sanders Show.* Both series were revered by people who considered themselves "real" comedy connoisseurs. Apatow had also produced and rewritten *The Cable Guy* for his friend Jim Carrey.

Apatow and Feig met in the mid-1980s, following fast times at USC. Both were orbiting the Ranch, a "piece of shit" house in the Valley, a place where a lot of comedians were congregating to hang, smoke, chug coffee, and play poker. The nebbishy, bearded Apatow had been a comedy overachiever for forever or at least since his adolescence in Long Island, where he'd hosted a high school radio show that featured—thanks to his mom's job at a comedy club—interviews with majors such as Jay Leno, Jerry Seinfeld, John Candy, and Garry Shandling. At NYU, Apatow had boosted his credentials further by rooming with Adam Sandler.

Feig's trajectory had begun outside Detroit, where he had grown up at least slightly off-center, worshiping Woody Allen and Steve Martin. Hollywood had not beckoned, but the summer after his freshman year at Wayne State he'd landed a job as a tour guide at Universal Studios. He got the job because he was funny, at ease in front of crowds. But his looks—he was pale, slight of build, and less than radiantly complected—caused concern. Before he started, he was ordered to spend hours sitting outside in the sunshine, because "They didn't want some white, pasty kid with acne standing up in front of people," Feig said.

Apatow was younger than most of the guys at the Ranch, but he and Feig bonded over their similarly deranged senses of humor. One particular tape (this was pre-Internet, when underground comedy traveled via VHS), of what seemed to be a rather harrowingly demented woman doing standup with a laid-in laugh track, sent them into spasms. "He and I thought it was hilarious," Feig said. "We just couldn't get enough of watching it . . . Everybody else felt dirty watching it because, they're going, 'You're just making fun of this person, she's almost retarded or something.'"

Feig, who at the time "couldn't pull my life together," was impressed with how "in charge" Apatow was for someone so young. Here he was, booking comedians for a club and volunteering for the HBO show *Comic Relief.* When some elder Ranchers gave Apatow a hard time, Feig told them, more presciently than he could have ever guessed: "You guys better be cool to him, because he's gonna run the town someday."

When Feig sent his high school script to Apatow, he loved it, and sold it to DreamWorks. NBC then snatched it up, but it was January 1999—way past the TV-development period for that year. Yet, because NBC was happy with Feig's script just the way it was, they agreed to jam production in order to have episodes ready for the fall. At their first meeting with NBC brass, Feig and Apatow had agreed that there was one thing they were holding firm on: they were not going to cast Hollywood-type actors in *Freaks and Geeks.* Having once played a nerd in a propeller beanie on *The Facts of Life,* Feig loathed all the tired conventions of alienated TV kids—the tape on the glasses, the calculator in the pocket, the hiked-up polyester pants.

"I remember saying to Judd, 'We cannot do a show where they're gonna make us cast good-looking kids and dress them up as nerds . . . We're not going to make them cartoon characters.'" Apatow and Feig prepared for the type of creative battles that victims of network television tell of around campfires fed by script pages. But NBC, at an apparently laid-back moment, gave its blessing to cast as they saw fit. With casting director Allison Jones, they searched the country for new forms of unconventionality. "You have to . . . see a thousand guys and look for the weird kid and see which one you can teach to act," explained Apatow. "They have to be characters."

One by one, the cast filled out. The asparagus-thin, Coke-bottle-glasses-wearing Martin Starr; the lumbering, goofy Jason Segel; the vulnerable but in no way a knockout Linda Cardellini. And then came . . . Seth Rogen. "When we found Seth, we both thought we'd found God," said Feig. "My jaw hit the table," he recalls, when, in Vancouver, Rogen walked in and started reading. "So funny, and so . . . He had this weird voice, and he was kind of oddly confident. The first speech he read was this nerd speech, it was about kung fu, like 'I can do kung fu,' and it's all kind of goofy. And then he read the stoner one, which was about how to grow pot . . . It was like . . . oh my God, he's perfect! He just cold-read it. He ended up getting cast from that."

In some cases, the kids were unique enough to inspire Apatow to begin tearing up the script and re-creating characters based on the kids who had come through the doors, a process that had Feig, an admittedly persnickety and self-protective writer, "freaking out." But he tried to chill, knowing Apatow's reputation for guarding the creative process at all costs. Once, when an executive at Fox had offered him notes on *The Ben Stiller Show,* Apatow fired off a memo: "I'm not changing anything. Now what happens?" (What happened was this: the show was killed.)

Wisely, DreamWorks and NBC kept their distance, creatively, from *Freaks and Geeks,* despite the money being spent ($1.5 million per episode) and the unorthodox style of everything taking place around them. Director Jake Kasdan described the visual philosophy as based on "uncosmetic decisions." "The close-ups are looser than you'd expect—there's a little too much space, and the kids are kind of awkward in the frame—and we used a very cool palette as opposed to most network dramas, which are very warm, and everyone's incredibly pretty and healthy looking . . . On *Freaks and Geeks* everyone's face is sort of like . . . light blue."

Katzenberg swung by the set one day and slung compliments. Soon Spielberg would be sneaking in to stealthily check out the first episode. Afterward, he wrote Feig a letter telling him he loved what he'd seen and calling the show the most honest portrayal of high school he knew of. Delighted, Feig framed the letter and hung it on his wall. When Apatow heard about the communiqué, he fumed: "I can't believe *you* got the letter from Spielberg!"

The trouble-free development process soon slammed to a halt:

when *Freaks and Geeks,* which was to debut in September, was slotted at 8 P.M. on Saturdays, aka the "death slot," Apatow and Feig started drawing up their wills. Adding to the crepe hanging was the fact that Garth Ancier, who ran programming at the WB, had been made president of NBC Entertainment, replacing Scott Sassa, who had been all about "Go forth and do your thing." Ancier saw everything differently.

Feig got his first taste of Ancier at the upfront presentations—when the networks present their fall lineups to much schmoozing and free-flowing booze in New York City—when he introduced himself to the new man in charge. According to Feig, Ancier simply looked at him and said, "Just deliver the goods, man. Deliver the goods. You don't want to end up like this guy," he continued, pointing to a fellow next to him who looked like a caricature of a hapless schlub.

Driven by those rapturous reviews, *Freaks and Geeks* did well on opening night. Then ratings dropped precipitously. Things got worse as NBC put the show on a succession of hiatuses, making way for sweeps season and the World Series. When ratings stayed at cellar level, the suits lost all pretense of interest or patience. "They started to panic and their notes were getting a little more nervous—'Should you do this? Should you do that?'" Feig said.

To Ancier, the product of boarding school and Princeton, the show seemed to represent an alternate, alien, and unappealing universe. Over lunch with Apatow, he brought up the episode when Sam (John Francis Daley), the show's seminal loser, is asked to have lunch with Cindy (Natasha Melnick), the leggy cheerleader he adores, only to get the news that she digs someone else.

"There are no victories, man! Your show has no victories!" Ancier told Apatow.

In March, the show's breathing became extremely labored: *Freaks and Geeks* was "relaunched" (for the third time) on Monday nights, pitted against ABC's *Who Wants to Be a Millionaire,* a low-budget ratings ruler. Within a month—no *Freaks,* no *Geeks.* Apatow got the call. "I'm screaming and half crying," he told the *L.A. Weekly's* Robert Lloyd of his chat with the less-than-human-seeming Ancier, "saying every single thing I ever wanted to say to him . . . And he's a hard person to talk to, because he's one of those people who does not confront you, so you could say anything and he'll just go (sympathetically) 'Yeah, I know, yeah.' So it's no fun even to let it all go. He sounds like he's made that call a thousand times . . . For all I know he's on a speakerphone and there's someone else in the room and they're giggling. I know it doesn't bother him. So it's just a terrible moment."

Fans of *Freaks and Geeks*, who tended to lurk on Internet chatrooms and truly cherish their moments of actual identification with commercial entertainment products, saw red. And charged. "Do you have blind chimps making your programming decisions?" questioned one such *F&G* fanatic online. "Are you guys high? No more NBC for me after the last episode airs." Fans were adamant—and organized; they even banded together and bought an ad in *Daily Variety* (at a cost of $3,746) that read: "The fans cared enough to get together and pay for this ad. Now doesn't that speak for itself? . . . GIVE *FREAKS* A CHANCE!"

All kinds of observers felt that *Freaks and Geeks* had been "dicked around," according to one former DreamWorks executive, who said that some NBC executives actually later admitted, publicly, that they should have kept the faith a bit before moving in for the kill.

DreamWorks may have been willing to bet outside the box in television, but the bets were costly and the losses were racking up. Like all the studios, DreamWorks was throwing money at writers in the hopes that just one hit would stick to some wall somewhere. But other TV studios—especially those owned by conglomerates—had much deeper piles of dough, and TV was in flux in a major way. With the advent of cheaper-to-make reality TV and game shows, and fleeing advertising dollars, the justification for insane spending was fading. Still, DreamWorks stuck to its belief that good, smart material would prevail.

In late 1999, DreamWorks Interactive was sold to video-game goliath Electronic Arts (EA), continuing DreamWorks' painful diminishment. In its last year, the company had begun to turn a profit, but too little, too late. DWI employees who had joined up from Microsoft were not just jobless; they had to face missing out on a significant payday at their old home. Microsoft's stock (which they'd given up) had soared over the previous four years.

The sale was finalized in February, just as DWI's latest game, the Spielberg inspiration *Medal of Honor*, was taking off. Rather mightily—*Medal of Honor* would not only foster a new genre, World War II video games, but go on to be one of the biggest-selling titles ever. By 2007, the franchise had sold over 31 million units, generating nearly $1 billion in revenue, all of which went to EA. (Had the game been based on the *Saving Private Ryan* license, DreamWorks would have also had a stake.) Looking back, COO Glenn Entis called DWI "an impressionable youth—a new shiny thing. Everyone had ideas about how it should work, how it should be. But at the end of the day, you had to create a profitable business."

But DreamWorks and all things digital hadn't parted company entirely. Dot-com mania was sweeping the nation. Twenty-six-year-olds were becoming insta-millionaires. It was perhaps inevitable that DreamWorks would want in. Here was an industry where money could be made overnight in an initial public offering, give or take a solid business plan, and that spoke directly to Spielberg's inner geek. This was the guy, after all, who had a T-1 line way back when. When Netscape initiated the Internet boom back in 1995, raising $2.2 billion its first day as a public company, Spielberg had brought in the press release announcing the news to the guys at DreamWorks Interactive, remarking how "cool" it was. Four years later, with the bubble wildly expanded and tech IPOs in headlines daily, DreamWorks wanted to move, as did many others in Hollywood.

It became "a bit of a land grab," said David Bloom, reporting on the tech boom in L.A. for the publication *Red Herring*. "It was like the Oklahoma Sooners—Oh my God, there's free land, we have to grab it!" Paul Allen was, at last, witnessing his wired world becoming reality. By 2001, Allen said, people would no longer be dialing up to their AOL accounts, but connecting via broadband (i.e., high speed). The delivery system for broadband, he believed, was cable—not satellite, the prevailing wisdom earlier. During the previous year Allen had spent more than $20 billion buying up cable companies, including his flagship-to-be: Charter Communications. Almost overnight, Allen was the fourth-largest cable operator in the U.S. and, for content, he was scooping up Internet companies. Enter DreamWorks with a proposal for an entertainment dot-com. See Allen pledge $50 million for a 50 percent stake in what would become Pop.com.

Allen had no interest in being actively involved—which is exactly how DreamWorks preferred it. Being the Dream Team's biggest

backer meant showing up for presentations and glamorous Hollywood events, such as movie premieres, the *Vanity Fair* Oscar party,
or a Spielberg movie set. Geffen was charged with managing Allen,
whom he hovered around like a "secret service agent," said *Variety*
party columnist Bill Higgins. "If anyone wanted to go up to Paul, it
was clear that you had to go through Geffen," who seemed to be pro-
tecting Allen—and DreamWorks—from himself. ("Like when I bring
my mom to a premiere," said a source, "but tell her she can't talk to the
talent.") Geffen's buffering of Allen was not just to keep competitors
away. It was also, presumably, to make sure that Geffen remained Allen's primary source of information about DreamWorks.

Sources say that Allen had become concerned about DreamWorks'
balance sheets. But not exceedingly so. "To Paul, DreamWorks wasn't
about making money. He was ready to give it a long ride," said one
person who knows Allen. "The only time he worries about things is
when they make him look bad. If a bad investment makes him look
foolish, then he cares. If someone tells him he looks stupid, then he'll
turn on it, get rid of it. But only then."

However, "when he turns, he turns *hard*."

Pop was actually the brainchild of Ron Howard, one of the biggest directors in Hollywood (*Parenthood, Apollo 13*) and one-half of one of
the biggest production companies in Hollywood, Imagine Entertainment. The other half was Brian Grazer, a high-energy, spiky-haired
surfer who prided himself in knowing *everyone* (an assistant *cum* cultural attaché rounded up names and forged introductions to people
like *The Tipping Point* author Malcolm Gladwell and Frank Wilczek, a
Nobel-winning expert on particle accelerators). Grazer flipped when
he heard tech geek Howard going on about using the Web as a platform for inexpensive, experimental entertainment, or "pops": short
films, streaming video, performance art, etc.

When Spielberg, a longtime friend of Howard's, heard about Pop,
he flipped, too. While Spielberg and Howard gushed ideas, Grazer
and Katzenberg became designated implementers, despite the fact
that they were far less Web-savvy than their partners. (Katzenberg
"searched" the Internet by having his staff "record" Web pages onto
a videotape, which he then popped into a VCR. He replied to e-mails
by fax. Grazer had to ask his assistants to pull up Web pages for him.

Underlings also printed out his e-mails so he could read them on paper.)

In October, Pop.com was announced to enormous fanfare: a revolution was at hand. Grazer was flying all over, meeting with potential contributors and partners, such as *Interview* editor Ingrid Sischy, *Vanity Fair* editor Graydon Carter, and artist Jeff Koons. And then there was the Imagine and DreamWorks' Hollywood roster: Mike Myers, Steve Martin, Ben Affleck, Matt Damon, and so on. Katzenberg and Grazer went to all the agencies, pumping Pop, comparing the Internet to what MTV had been twenty-five years earlier. Spielberg called it a "large, fertile field." "You can harvest all sorts of spinoffs, just from whatever germinates," he said. "It could be a book, a piece of music, a movie—who can say?"

It was a good question. Not anyone at DreamWorks, or anywhere else, for that matter, could necessarily define exactly what they were setting out to do. Or what limitations they were facing with a platform—the Internet—that was not yet fully mature. Allen's prediction concerning full broadband access within a year was far from certain. Timing would matter quite a bit, considering that the types of content Pop would carry—streaming videos, short films—would require quick, uncomplicated access in order to download in a user-friendly manner. (Via dial-up, a short film might take eight hours to download.) But tough questions weren't part of the dot-com mentality. "All of these guys were ahead of their time, but most were not sufficiently concerned about a sustainable business model," said reporter David Bloom.

In March of 2000, just months after America Online met Time Warner and wed to the tune of $200 billion, Pop.com held a launch event at the Chateau Marmont during the Yahoo! Internet Life Online Film Festival. The party was far more opulent than those of any of the other companies playing host at the Chateau. DreamWorks/Imagine rented out one of the fabled hotel's biggest bungalows—more of a house, actually—and handed out fruity cocktails by the pool, along with "tchotchkes with striking graphics and uncertain utility," said Bloom. Most impressive of all, the stars themselves showed up, or at least some of them—Howard, Grazer, and Katzenberg—who chatted with young Netheads hawking streaming shorts.

A new era was at hand. The Chateau, formerly ground zero for

Hollywood bacchanalian behavior—Jim Morrison had leapt from the roof; John Belushi had overdosed here—was now playing host to squeaky-cleans whose drugs of choice were venture capitalism and portfolios. As Red Bulls were passed around, DreamWorks executives gulped and then raised up the cans to toast another relatively "risk-free"—or at least entirely bankrolled—investment whose upside was the chance to make history. What could possibly go wrong?

21

NOBODY'S BITCH

THE NIGHT OF THE OSCARS, March 26, 2000, David Geffen was curled up in a green leather booth at Morton's, where *Vanity Fair* hosted its annual Oscar party. "Don't stand there!" he yelled to a woman blocking his view of the telecast. Best Original Screenplay was about to be announced, and Geffen was hoping like hell that Alan Ball won. When the envelope was opened, and Ball's name was announced, Geffen lurched forward and said, "*Yeah!*" in what was more an emission than a burst of enthusiasm. Then he fell back into the booth, spent.

As noted by Frank DiGiacomo in the *New York Observer*, Geffen might have graced the party with his presence knowing that, finally, DreamWorks would have something to celebrate. But he was still strictly Geffen. Although flanked by a newly single Jane Fonda (now separated from Ted Turner), Fran Lebowitz, and Barry Diller, he was not into revelry. "His face," DiGiacomo wrote, was "an angular relief map of power," which "conveyed only the importance of winning."

Over at the Shrine Auditorium, seated in the "surreal" and "terrifying" thick of things, as he called them, Alan Ball wasn't having much more fun. To keep it together, he periodically dipped into a flask of scotch tucked into his tuxedo pocket. When his name was called, "I went up there and I was out of my body. I had prepared a speech . . . but, there's that big monitor at the back that starts flashing '15' [seconds remaining], '14.' I'd be lying if I said I wasn't glad that I won an Oscar . . . But I wouldn't put it on my list of most enjoyable experiences."

Until Ball's win, the Seventy-second Annual Academy Awards had been mostly about *The Matrix*, the Wachowski brothers' gadget-palooza starring Keanu Reeves in a black leather duster and shades.

The film had swept most of the minor, technical categories. *American Beauty*'s only other prize up to that point was for cinematography (Conrad Hall, who had last won in 1969, for *Butch Cassidy and the Sundance Kid*). For once, Miramax was low profile. *The Cider House Rules* won Best Adapted Screenplay (John Irving) and Best Supporting Actor (Michael Caine). But this was no replay of *Shakespeare In Love*, something Harvey Weinstein had known nine days earlier, when he'd called Katzenberg and told him: "Congratulations. You saw the playbook and outplayed us." He then inquired, pointedly, what movie DreamWorks would be hawking for next year's Oscars.

When Best Actor was up, Geffen again leaned in for what would be a close call. Denzel Washington had been an early favorite for his turn in Norman Jewison's *The Hurricane*, about the life of boxer Rubin "Hurricane" Carter. But—it was Spacey!

"*Yeah!*"

Geffen was starting to loosen up.

Best Actress was a wash—Annette Bening lost out to Hilary Swank in *Boys Don't Cry*. No utterances from the green leather booth.

Then Best Director. Spielberg himself opened the envelope, and when he did, he smiled the smile of a proud parent, and everyone knew who'd won: Mendes.

"*Yeah!!*"

Geffen was almost . . . pumped.

And then: Best Picture. Now Geffen "looked like he was strapped into a NASA rocket sled," wrote DiGiacomo. He was pressing "both of his hands against his forehead as if to keep his skull from exploding."

American Beauty.

"*YEAH!!!*"

In lieu of embracing Fonda to the point of cracking her skin-tight metallic sheath, Geffen politely clinked glasses and then darted off, dodging past Viacom CEO Sumner Redstone, actress Selma Blair, and socialite Lynn Wyatt as he made his way to the exit. When DiGiacomo caught up with him outside, all Geffen would give was a pursed, "I'm thrilled."

Over at the Shrine, emotions were free-flowing. Bruce Cohen and Dan Jinks stormed the stage, thanking Mendes, Ball, and "everyone at DreamWorks from Glenn Williamson to Steven Spielberg"—a line rumored to not have gone over well with Walter Parkes. As the producers walked off, they were embraced by Mendes, Spacey, and Spielberg amid an explosion of camera flashes. "Everyone was clutching the Academy Award," Mendes said, "and Steven, who was visibly bursting with pride, said"—echoing Katzenberg's words—"'I just want to say, you've just made the studio.'"

Then the group was ushered backstage to do press. This year, Spielberg was among them.

Later, at the DreamWorks post-Oscar party in a rose-petal-festooned Spago—where Geffen had headed after the Morton's dash—a still-glowing Spielberg, accompanied by Parkes, approached *American Beauty*'s young director.

"We've got something for you," Spielberg said as he handed Mendes a gift: a check for a million dollars. "Thank you," he said. And meant it. DreamWorks, at last, had an identity. It wasn't Warner Bros. or Fox, nor was it Miramax. It was its own thing, somewhere in between, original, different. All the adjectives tossed out ad infinitum back in '94 finally meant something. Finally, there was such a thing as a DreamWorks movie.

Vases containing five red roses—in honor of each of the Academy Awards won by *American Beauty*—were displayed throughout DreamWorks the day after the Oscars. But at the animation studio, they did little to improve the feng shui. Less than a week later, Katzenberg's *The Road to El Dorado* crashed into theaters, performing miserably. Grossing just $12 million its first weekend, it was more of a bomb than even *The Prince of Egypt*. And there was no airbrushing the disappointment by holding the movie in theaters to juice its grosses. Unlike with *POE*, DreamWorks couldn't blame the Bible for not setting audiences on fire. This was pure, unadulterated Bad News. Having cost over $95 million to produce, plus millions more to market, *El Dorado* made just $50 million.

Katzenberg was stunned. *El Dorado* had been his inspiration. He'd believed in the film, despite the naysayers. And now, he didn't seem able to accept that it was a failure, that he had been so, so wrong. It was too much.

And so Katzenberg started slamming doors and crossing off names. Not even Elton John, who'd produced such magic on *The Lion King*, was spared. "If you look at the promotions surrounding *El Dorado*,

Jeffrey was always talking about Elton John. The feeling was, Elton John's a winner. He doesn't write songs to lose," said one source. "But when the *El Dorado* soundtrack went down like a lead balloon . . . Elton was out. They brought in Bryan Adams to do the soundtrack on *Spirit* [DreamWorks' next animated film]. Either you're a winner or you're a loser. That's Jeffrey."

Katzenberg deflected criticism; he remained in denial that he bore any responsibility for the film's failure. Instead, he pointed to the filmmakers, saying that they should have made him more aware of *El Dorado*'s problems. He blamed his involvement in the Disney lawsuit, seeming to forget how, early on, he'd been criticized for being too hands-on. "He would not accept the blame for *El Dorado*," said one source. "He blamed the deposition and said he wasn't there enough. But that didn't go down. He did his job, just after hours and on weekends . . . He was a hundred percent there, every step of the way."

This was not the Katzenberg who had once gone out of his way to make DreamWorks a creative and collaborative place full of goodwill. Beyond the failure of *El Dorado*, many people believed the change was due to Katzenberg's victory in court, and the validation that the win had wrought in the number two, who was now very much a number one. "Once he won the lawsuit, he started to believe that he was untouchable, that it was his way or the highway, that his opinion was the only one that mattered," said one source.

Katzenberg didn't seem to know how to handle, or how to justify, things going so terribly off-course with *El Dorado*. Having prevailed against Eisner, he expected to prevail at DreamWorks, just as he had promised investors and his partners. Worse, when the media weighed in, it was clear that the story line had changed. Katzenberg was no longer being viewed in the context of the hard-done-by subordinate. There was no longer a villain, a job that he was being screwed out of, money withheld that was rightfully his. Now he was the guy who'd gotten his revenge. And his partners made Eisner look like a lightweight.

Nor was there any patience left for DreamWorks to work out its start-up quirks. The honeymoon was long over, and reporters drilled in. The most aggressive story, by Claudia Eller and James Bates in the *L.A. Times*, pointed out that the failure of *El Dorado* had ramifications for the Dream Team. "Many in Hollywood believe," wrote the reporters, "that the [animation] division will make or break the company" and that "without the cavernous pockets of DreamWorks' billionaire backer Paul Allen, the studio's animation business might well be on the ropes." In other words: DreamWorks "might well" be on its way out of business.

The story recalled Katzenberg's prediction, way back when, that DreamWorks' animated films would replicate, or at least come close to replicating, the commercial success of *The Lion King*. The article went on to point out that the combined grosses of DreamWorks' first three animated films—*Antz, The Prince of Egypt*, and *The Road to El Dorado*—did not come close to matching *The Lion King*'s $783 million worldwide gross, let alone its gargantuan licensing and merchandising intake.

When the story ran, Press and Katzenberg were irate, feeling that it made unfair presumptions. The issue was personal as well as professional: Eller and Press were extremely close friends. The two women socialized together, and Eller had even hosted a baby shower at her home for Press, when she had been pregnant with twins. The women were similar creatures—brash firebrands unafraid to speak their minds. They were also alternately tough and nurturing; a combination that worked brilliantly with the kings who rule Hollywood, so many of whom are hard-charging bullies with paper-thin skin. When Katzenberg was at Disney, Eller had been one of his closest media allies and had written many flattering articles. But Eller called it like she saw it. And the way she saw it now, DreamWorks was in trouble.

"I think it hurt everybody," said Finkelman Cox. "Everybody was mad at Claudia. It was a wrench for her and Terry. I don't remember if anything that negative had been written about DreamWorks before that."

The *Times* story did not overstate the case. Allen's billions were no luxury option. He was called on to supply a billion-dollar credit line to stanch the financial bleeding from *El Dorado*, which rocked the company more severely than any single event in its history. Years later, when from a more objective standpoint, Katzenberg could be more honest, he called the *El Dorado* fiasco "like nothing I've experienced in twenty years. I've never had anything like that." It was "more humbling and humiliating than anything else." The following spring and summer were "a tough six or nine months," he said. "I was sweating."

So were others at the studio, on whom it was dawning that this was no fluke, that something was constitutionally off: "I think that was the moment, for me, when I started to feel nervous—when *El Dorado* was released and didn't do well," said artist Paul Lasaine. It was the first major sign, added art director Richie Chavez, that "the market wasn't embracing us."

The market was actually threatening to leave DreamWorks in the dust. In 1994, the year the studio was formed, four animated feature films had been released in theaters; by 1999, that number had more than doubled, thanks to the efforts of studios like Warner Bros., Twentieth Century Fox, and Miramax. Not only were there more animated movies, but computer animation was beginning to look like the future.

In November of 1999, Pixar had released *Toy Story 2,* which grossed $477 million worldwide, making it the second-highest-grossing animated film behind *The Lion King.* The theory that computer animation was merely a flash-in-the-pan fad was losing its legs. As the shift in thinking took root, studios started cutting back on traditional animators. In 2000 DreamWorks downsized to 324 artists from 500 a year earlier. Long gone were the days of million-dollar signing bonuses and years-long contracts. Animator Floyd Norman recalled returning to L.A. in 2000 after working up at Pixar on *Monsters, Inc.:* "I began to see a real shift in the industry. Prices were falling. So much talent was available that studios no longer had to . . . offer top salaries."

By 2000, the animation studio had shed its cozy, family-like proportions, from the days when artists huddled together in the old Lakeside Drive building on the Universal lot. There may have been fewer artists on the payroll, but with more movies, the studio needed more administration and management. As a result, some of DreamWorks' early, idealistic innovations were being cast aside, such as the no-job-titles policy, which had proven not so much democratic as confusing. To the outside world, no titles meant that it was not clear who was in charge of what. Within DreamWorks, it meant that employees stepped on each other's toes and that there was no clear reporting structure, which led, according to one former employee, to the establishment of "empires"—i.e., self-created hierarchies. Katzenberg didn't necessarily mind this; when he was confronted about it, he replied, "I like empires. It means that people are passionately trying to accomplish things."

The lack of titles also created an ostensibly flat reporting structure in which there was Katzenberg and there was everyone else, a situation that caused its own set of headaches for managers who felt usurped when Katzenberg would go directly to an executive under them instead of through the chain of command. While employees appreciated that, unlike most CEOs, Katzenberg was readily available and would return every phone call and agree to any meeting, regardless of the employee's stature, the situation also gave rise to a cult-like environment in which a big part of surviving was playing up to the cult's king.

"Everybody had access to Jeffrey—there was very little in between," said Bill Villarreal. "Because of that, [DreamWorks] became a very political place. Because, of course, when you have access to the top guy, you're going to play yourself up and . . . it became about self-promotion." But something else that was chipping away at the hitherto free-'n'-easy culture and giving way to a more rigid ethos was the very real pressure that the studio was under. As DreamWorks' other divisions—from music to TV to video games—failed to hit their strides, animation (the company's presumptive cash cow) was ever more under siege.

Katzenberg didn't bend, but bore down deeper, committed to winning the way he'd always planned he would—by making compelling story-driven movies that were good no matter what the platform—old- or new-style animation. He wasn't dismissing CGI—*Shrek*, which had been sent up to PDI after *Antz* was released, had finally found its footing in CGI and was readying for release. Yet he remained staunchly devoted to the art form he'd fallen in love with, and been schooled in, at Disney. He still tossed out the well-worn sound bite about rereading Frank Thomas and Ollie Johnston's book *The Illusion of Life: Disney Animation*—a book he considered his "Bible"—every year while on vacation with his family in Hawaii.

Once, during a trip up to PDI, animator Noel McGinn bluntly asked Katzenberg why he wanted to continue with 2-D when CGI clearly offered more possibilities.

"I would never, *ever* give up on 2-D. Never," Katzenberg replied.

"He was basically affronted by the whole idea," said McGinn.

And so, he plowed onward, never considering moving the next two 2-D films in DreamWorks' pipeline—*Spirit* and *Sinbad*—over to the CGI pipeline. Good storytelling, not spectacular graphics, was the thing, he always said.

• • •

The financial troubles wrought by *El Dorado*—which considerably dimmed the rosy blush left by *American Beauty*—coincided with another wave of partnership talks, this time between DreamWorks and Pop.com ally Imagine Entertainment. The idea, as it was fleshed out informally with lawyers and Paul Allen's people, was that Imagine would be melded into DreamWorks, with Brian Grazer overseeing the studio, Katzenberg staying put running animation, and Ron Howard coming aboard as a content provider, directing and producing movies. It would be a win-win for everyone. DreamWorks' recurring problem of never having enough movies would be solved. Grazer and Howard would become business owners, not just highly paid producers who worked for studios.

Despite their differences—the boyishly affable Ron Howard versus the slightly maniacal Brian Grazer—both men were radically ambitious. And to both of them, the idea of owning something bigger than Imagine was tempting. Imagine was a very successful company, but it was also a place where, essentially, a studio backed in a truckload of money. Although Grazer and Howard received enormous salaries and a high percentage of first-dollar grosses, they didn't own the company. And they wanted to own. And own big.

There were questions, of course—namely, just how equal a partnership it would actually be, a detail significant in the event DreamWorks were sold. And could the various players, used to competing for projects, truly get along? This issue was already becoming a problem at Pop.com, where, one executive told *Time,* "We'd go through the slate of projects and Steven would like this, Ron would like this, Jeffrey liked this, and Brian liked this."

But that was the least of the problems at Pop, which would have been more aptly called Implode.com. By the spring of 2000—when Pop was supposed to launch—there was no actual Web site in sight. Nor was there any clear timetable for when engineering issues would be resolved. Or the building of hundreds of different Web applications.

Not that this stopped anyone. Practically overnight, there were 125 people on the Pop payroll, all of whom showed up for work every day in a Glendale warehouse that had housed the early *Shrek* animators. Inside, on the stage where the Propellerheads had once supervised motion-capture tests, couches and beanbag chairs were set up for gatherings. A piano and Ping-Pong table were propped nearby. Lunch was delivered daily, and, on Friday afternoons, party food and beer were rolled in.

"Pop was a very *busy* place for a company without a Web site," said Phillip Nakov, cofounder of CountingDown.com, a site bought by Pop. "Between production, design, writers writing things, people shooting things, making shows, editing shows, acquiring content . . . There was a lot of activity." But Mike Kelly, founder of Undergroundfilm.com, which Pop was in the process of acquiring, was more dubious. "They had a lot of people working there," he said. "Everybody had an assistant. I just couldn't identify what they were doing."

That was a mystery hard to penetrate. Pop's CEO, Kenneth Wong, another Katzenberg hire from Disney, where he'd worked at Imagineering, had no experience in the Internet and seemed clueless as to how to get Pop up and running. An architect with a background in management construction, Wong was accustomed to Disney's rigid bureaucratic structures. He was hardly an entrepreneurial Internet pioneer who thought in terms of overnight growth and profitability. Wong's number two was another tech newbie: Dan Sullivan, a twenty-seven-year-old Wharton grad who had overseen business development at Imagine.

One Pop employee called Wong the "cheerleader in chief"; someone who was good at team spirit and talking the talk, but who had more trouble with the meat of it all. There were meetings, inspirational speeches, and bonding activities, but as for meaningful work getting done: not so much.

In the dot-com spirit, Pop's compensation model was all about stock—the plan was to build the company quickly and then make millions, if not billions, in an IPO. Employees were paid in stock, as was the talent being wooed to make content—a model that was especially pleasing to the frugal Katzenberg. The only problem was that there was so *much* stock—Pop was incorporated with 250 million shares—that it wasn't ever likely to be worth very much.

"Having raised money and incorporated a company, I remember looking at the number of shares and thinking, Lord, that is an astronomical number," said Kelly. "A lot of people probably thought they were getting a buck a share, that the company would go public and they'd be selling for $40 a share. But if the hundreds of millions of shares are, when you go public, ten shares to one or something, it's sort of misleading, and I think that was the purpose—to mislead."

Some balked. When the stock situation became clear, the deals with A-list talent, always a part of the plan, fizzled. (Pop had even established a star tier system, which broke down actors and filmmakers that Pop hoped to hire into A, B, and C lists. Each category was allocated different stock paydays. A-listers included Mike Myers, Eddie Murphy, Steve Martin, and Jim Carrey. Jerry Seinfeld was B team. And MTV prankster Tom Green a hapless C-lister.) When this "list" was leaked via reporter Chris Petrikin in Inside.com, agents bristled. Pop was now a foe.

From the Pop point of view, it was agents who were "pigs at the trough," said one source. "Everybody was in the roaring dot-com mindset, where any agent thought they had a viable name that could change the face of the Web." Mike Myers's agents asked for the most and, when Pop didn't give it, they discouraged their client from doing work for Pop. Not that he especially wanted to—Myers was already in an ugly feud with Imagine over the film *Dieter,* based on Myers's black-turtleneck-clad, Teutonic "Sprockets" character on *Saturday Night Live.* Myers, a longtime friend of Brian Grazer, had just finished filming *How the Grinch Stole Christmas* for Imagine, which Ron Howard directed. Next, he was supposed to turn to *Dieter.* Only, at the last minute, he balked, saying he didn't like the script—a dubious claim, seeing as he'd written it with his longtime collaborator Michael McCullers.

As reported in *Time,* lawsuits flew back and forth between Universal, Imagine, and Myers, who was seeking $20 million in damages, claiming Universal had been "thug-like," "outrageous," and had demonstrated "reckless conduct." Imagine, which claimed $30 million in lost profits, called Myers "egomaniacal," "irresponsible," and "selfish."

In the midst of the drama, Katzenberg, who knew a thing or two about legal mudslinging, was brought on to broker peace. But he wasn't exactly an indifferent party. Myers was Katzenberg's star voice talent on *Shrek,* and he didn't like seeing his name sullied.

Katzenberg assumed the role of Myers's agent, calling up Universal chairman Stacey Snider, saying, "You don't know what you're doing! You're not handling this the right way! There's no way to win this!" according to a source. More diplomatically, he brought Myers to a Lakers game that he knew Grazer was attending. It didn't do much good.

Both Grazer and Myers were "major grudge holders," said one source, and neither was about to budge.

Katzenberg called on Spielberg to help, but it was Jeffrey who finally made the save that pleased both Imagine and Myers and benefited DreamWorks. The proposal was for everyone to join forces on a Mike Myers film—*The Cat in the Hat*, specifically, a project that had been languishing in Amblin development hell for years. One of the problems in getting the film off the ground was the difficulty of getting the blessing of the Theodor Geisel (aka Dr. Seuss) estate. But Imagine had an in, having just come out of *How the Grinch Stole Christmas*. And with Imagine's involvement with *Cat*, boom: rights granted. Everybody got a movie, everybody was happy.

Except, that is, Pop.com, where, still, nothing was happening. Meanwhile, Grazer and Katzenberg, who had each been clocking in as much as thirty hours a week on Pop, were by now smelling failure and started pulling back.

As for Spielberg and Howard, Pop's biggest cheerleaders, they were being sucked back into directing projects. Spielberg was preparing to shoot *Artificial Intelligence: A.I.*, having put *Minority Report* on the back burner. Like so many things at DreamWorks whose creation was owed to Spielberg's interest and enthusiasm—DreamWorks Interactive, TV animation, GameWorks, not to mention Playa Vista—Pop was ultimately abandoned by the director when his ever-shifting attention was captured by something that looked like more of a winner.

And then the real bottom fell out: in April, the NASDAQ collapsed. The Internet gold rush was over. Dot-coms had gone from bubble to bust. San Francisco, the bust's epicenter, was being deserted by entrepreneurs turning out the lights and putting their names on the months-long U-Haul waiting list. Suddenly, the prospect of Pop ever going public and making a gazillion dollars was as likely as Katzenberg turning into Steve Jobs.

Pop reacted with typical Hollywood denial. With Spielberg, Allen, and Geffen as protectors, Pop was immune. *Right?* "We were aware of the Internet bubble bursting, but felt we were insulated because we were a privately held company," said Nakov. "We had Vulcan [Paul Allen's] funding, we felt we were insulated from everything going on in the rest of the world."

The attitude at Pop could best be summed up by a contest that Wong, who always tried to maintain a certain campy cheer, organized to choose the company's logo. In the spirit of Everyone's Ideas Are Important Here, he sent around a memo, urging all to help determine the catchphrase that best defined the company.

The winner, by a landslide, was: "Nobody's Bitch."

When the Internet bubble burst, that attitude kicked in: Screw you, we will survive! But outside the insulated walls of the Glendale warehouse, Pop was becoming a lightning rod for reporters hungry for the next dot-com bust story. Sensing something brewing or busting, *Entertainment Weekly* and Inside.com were among the news organizations taking a look.

Screenwriter Scott Frank had been working with Spielberg for a long, difficult year on the script for *Minority Report,* when he walked into Spielberg's office in the fall of 1999 and was told by the director: "We're in a race. I'm writing *A.I.,* and whichever script gets done first, I'm gonna make." Frank did not take the news as an occasion for optimism. He had a good idea who was going to win this race, and he was not surprised when, in the spring, Spielberg decided that *A.I.* was his next film, leaving *Minority Report* in a sprawling, 180-page state of chaos. After months of struggling through the script, with the help of Spielberg and Parkes, *Minority Report*—a futuristic thriller in which a special "Pre-Crime" unit enlists "Pre-Cogs" to foresee crimes before they take place—remained a conundrum.

Besides its being a complicated story, Spielberg had told Frank that he was uncomfortable with mysteries. And in *Minority Report* there was not one, but two mysteries, one of them being why the protagonist (which Tom Cruise had signed on to play) himself is identified as a pre-criminal.

At one point, Spielberg, Parkes, and Frank had decided to give up, but Cruise remained an enthusiast so they'd stumbled on. Then, with Cruise's schedule delayed with *Mission: Impossible II,* and Spielberg having fallen harder for *A.I.,* whose script he'd rewritten himself (after taking over the project from Stanley Kubrick when Kubrick died of a heart attack), *A.I.* it was. Frank lost all hope in *Minority Report* ever making it to the screen. "I thought the movie was dead," he said.

Years earlier, Spielberg had confessed to Geffen, while aboard the DreamWorks jet, that *A.I.* was the best project he'd ever read. Only it wasn't his. Kubrick had been working on it since the 1970s, but had been stalled over how to pull off the high-tech elements in the futuristic film. The project was loosely based on a 1969 Brian Aldiss short story, "Supertoys Last All Summer Long," about a robot boy and his struggle to become real. Kubrick had enlisted Spielberg's help, when he was considering using special effects to create the boy-robot instead of casting an actor.

Spielberg and Kubrick discussed the film at great length over the years, engaging in marathon phone calls between L.A. and London, where Kubrick lived, during which the only times they would break would be to go make sandwiches and then come back to the phone. Kubrick even insisted that Spielberg install a fax machine in his bedroom so that he could receive Kubrick's sketches and outlines any time of the day or night. Paranoid that anyone wise up to what they were doing, Spielberg kept the fax in a locked closet, to which only a very few people had a key.

When Kubrick passed away, Geffen swooped in, on cue, and negotiated with his pals at Warner Bros., Bob Daly and Terry Semel, to arrange for Spielberg to pick up where Kubrick left off. A deal was reached whereby Spielberg would not just direct *A.I.*, but write it (taking his first screenwriting credit since 1982's *Poltergeist*), using Kubrick's script, notes, and drawings as a guide.

DreamWorks, meanwhile, was faced with the reality that yet again their star player was getting up to bat for another team. Although DreamWorks was brought on as a coproducer on *A.I.* and would handle foreign distribution, Warner Bros. had the more enticing role of releasing the film in North America. Once again there were murmurs that Geffen and Katzenberg weren't keeping their boy on a tight enough leash.

Spielberg's hopscotching between projects was tolerated by the studios—everyone got on line to be in the Spielberg business—but there was a greediness to his behavior that did not go unnoticed. For instance, with *Geisha*, even if Spielberg couldn't get around to it yet, he wasn't going to let anyone else step in. Ron Bass, the original writer of *Geisha*, told the *Washington Post*, "Columbia [Pictures] said to Steven many times, 'If this is something you've lost interest in, tell us. Lots of other directors would want to [direct].' He said, 'Absolutely not. I'm directing it. I just don't know when.'"

"Steven's like a hungry kid," said one Hollywood veteran. "He can be naughty, such as with *Geisha*, where he kept it for a long time while he made other movies."

Spielberg was also making mischief with *Harry Potter*, a franchise that Warner Bros. was desperate to get going before Christmas and have out the following year, now that J. K. Rowling's books had become a global phenomenon. Nothing would delight Warner Bros. more than to pair one global brand (Spielberg) with another. Only, Spielberg wasn't sure he wanted to direct the movie, and took his time deciding. As he hemmed and hawed, the clock ticked. Executives at Warner Bros. ground their teeth, but did the only thing they could do: wait, for several grueling months, while their would-be tent pole remained unmade.

Spielberg's interest in *Harry Potter* also upset his friend and protégé, director Brad Silberling (he directed *Casper* at Amblin), who was originally attached to direct the film. When new management came in at Warner Bros., Silberling was put on ice, though he only found out about Spielberg's involvement in the project when Spielberg called one day to say he was thinking of directing *Harry Potter*. Spielberg made no apology for the fact that he was considering taking over what had been a dream gig for Silberling, who had already begun mapping out how he wanted to make the movie. Granted, it was Warner Bros.' decision as much as Spielberg's, but Silberling was nevertheless hurt, according to a source. Such was the price of being friends with Steven Spielberg.

In the end, Spielberg "passed" on *Harry Potter*, or so he liked to say. In reality, the talks fell apart when Spielberg and Warner Bros. came to a creative impasse: Spielberg wanted to combine more than one of the *Harry Potter* novels into one movie, with the intent of making one of the greatest movies of all time. Warner's wanted to stick to just one, saving the rest for sequels down the road. Spielberg then asked to be a producer on the film, believing that, during his talks with Warner's, he'd helped the studio solve some of the film's creative issues. But Warner Bros. didn't think Spielberg had been indispensable. Nor did it care to give away 50 percent of *Harry*'s grosses on a Spielberg producing deal.

Nor did Silberling, alas, wind up with the job, which went to Chris Columbus, the director of the blockbuster *Home Alone*.

Meanwhile, DreamWorks' own live-action studio was hanging in the balance. Would *American Beauty* prove to be just a fluke—the first and last "DreamWorks" movie—or was it just the beginning of something more lasting, something great?

The next test was *Gladiator*, which had millions more of DreamWorks' resources tied up in it, and which, unlike *American Beauty*, was doing anything but flying under the radar. If it failed, it would make *The Road to El Dorado* look like a very minor misfortune.

22

SWORD FIGHTS

———————

YOU MOTHERFUCKER. I will kill you with my bare hands."
"Hello?" Branko Lustig said, confused and barely awake; it
was, after all, 3 A.M. in England.
"You motherfucker," the speaker repeated.
"Who's on the phone? *Who is this?*" Lustig demanded.

When Russell Crowe identified himself, the genuinely terrified
Lustig, one of the producers of the about-to-be-filmed *Gladiator*,
hung up and called Steven Spielberg in Los Angeles.

"Steven," he said. "I'm leaving. Russell wants to kill me."

Having survived a concentration camp, Lustig was not taking
chances.

Crowe, not yet *Russell Crowe*, but still just another *verkakte* Australian coming off a sleeper (*L.A. Confidential*), was sour because he believed DreamWorks was low-balling his assistants on their per diems.
Rather than raise this grievance at a mundane daylight hour, Crowe
opted for a more dramatic statement, a tactic not unknown in these
parts. The actor's recent behavior had been erratic, like just about
everything else on the project. One of the screenwriters, falling into
the everyday hyperbole of dazed moviemakers, described the Dream-
Works production as "an epic struggle in every sense."

Back in L.A., DreamWorks executives were panicking, even more
so than usual. Uncertainty—approaching apoplexy—over the *Gladiator* script was delaying the shoot. The budget was ticking upward.
Time waits for no movie, despite the faces of Spielberg and the others
that hovered like Macy's balloons in the besieged minds of their employees. Filming absolutely had to begin within a month—it was now
January 1999—if the picture was to be released in May 2000.

Gladiator had been built from the ground up to become a shining

DreamWorks venture. Never before had the company put so much capital—more than $100 million—into a picture. The Crowe Situation had devolved into the Crowe Crisis days before, after the latest round of edits in the still-in-progress script, which did not yet have a workable ending. "We had a bunch of different versions [of the ending]," said producer Douglas Wick. "In one, Russell escapes [from slavery] and comes back with an army, and is reunited with his dog."

Walter Parkes and Laurie MacDonald had flown in from L.A. to convene at Shepperton Studios, director Ridley Scott's brick-and-ivy-appointed production grounds in Surrey, England, where *Alien,* among others, was filmed. From the second of Crowe's uncombed arrival at a fraught script conference, it was clear that he was not in the best of moods or shape. He appeared to have barely survived what must have been a long and very recently ended night.

"The character doesn't make sense now," Crowe remarked bitterly. "I don't understand why he's doing what he's doing."

Gently, Parkes began to explain that the latest edits improved the film, that they made Crowe's character, a general in ancient Rome, less of a brute, thus justifying the gargantuan number of human lives to which he lays waste. But the brawny actor, who would become known for the kind of short fuse that leads to flying telephones—wasn't hearing it. He was the Artist, shouldering the burden of Integrity. He stood abruptly and left, rendering those gathered speechless.

"Do you think he went to the bathroom?" Parkes asked hopefully, peering over his reading glasses. This seemed unlikely. More realistically, the lead actor of DreamWorks' most treasured blockbuster-to-be had just walked off the picture.

Screenwriter David Franzoni originally pitched *Gladiator* to Spielberg himself. The director warmed to the notion of a movie about gladiator fights at the Colosseum after Franzoni, not without savvy, shared his secret. The story was, at the end of the day, not really about those old Romans, but about Hollywood.

"I believed it was about things, it was about who we were," Franzoni said. "The Oliver Reed character was Mike Ovitz. Ted Turner was Commodus. CAA represents the gladiators. This is how I pitched it to Steven. The Colosseum is Dodger Stadium. This is about *us.*"

Of such inspirations are green lights and big budgets born.

"*Yeah,*" Spielberg had said.

Since then, the higher-ups at DreamWorks had intensely monitored the film's development, guiding the script rewrites, and bringing onboard Scott, whose credits ranged from the cultishly beloved sci-fi film *Blade Runner* to the Go Girrrl empowerment picture *Thelma and Louise*. But who, more recently, had struck out with films such as *1492: Conquest of Paradise* and *White Squall*.

No one had been more active than Walter Parkes, who had been even more hands-on than usual. Battles with Scott over the script were described by one bystander as "hellacious."

Laurie MacDonald had done her part, making sure all the men making this very manly picture didn't wipe out the women. "Often, Laurie was the only woman in story meetings," said Wick. "One time, when we decided to kill off Connie Nielsen's character in the first act, Laurie—who had left the meeting—came back and said, 'Hey, nice work, guys. You just got rid of the only woman.'"

If Crowe's intention was to walk off, he was either too hung over or too ambivalent. Scott, who had gone off to hunt for him, found the actor in his car, brooding. "He was anxious," said a source. "He was carrying a $100 million movie in which he says, 'My name is Maximus Decimus Meridius' and wears a skirt."

Scott did what he could to mellow Crowe, reassuring him enough so that the director thought he might actually join the rest of the cast for a read-through of the detested script. The atmosphere at the sound stage where this would occur was decidedly festive. Still adorned with the set dressings of whatever had last been shot there—*The Canterbury Tales,* from the looks of the place—the space was festooned with vaulted ceilings, elaborate scrollwork, and long, medieval-style tables.

In the midst of this fantasia, Oliver Reed, the predictably outrageous English actor (*Oliver!, Women In Love*) who had been cast as Proximo, the head of the gladiator school, was regaling a group including actors Joaquin Phoenix and Connie Nielsen, as well as Franzoni and another writer, John Logan, with chapters from his wanton history. Particularly memorable was his tale of a trip to a Vermont jail after getting into a bar brawl following a rugby match. (Reed, a famously inveterate boozer/ladies' man, once described his ideal mate as "a mute nymphomaniac whose father owns a pub.")

Yet beneath all the ribaldry was the unspoken question of what had become of the movie's star: it was becoming harder to gloss over the leading man's absence. Though Reed's spirits did not, according to Franzoni, fail for an instant. "He's like, 'Oh my God, they jumped me, it wasn't my fault!' We're having a great time, but we're waiting for Russell. Russell's not appearing."

Finally, Crowe materialized—unrepentant and sans affability. If Scott's pep talk had any effect, it seemed to have lodged deep in the actor's subconscious. Crowe played along, but refused to summon a scintilla of good humor. He didn't so much recite his lines as growl them in a deranged accent that flitted between indeterminate continents of origin. More absurd was Reed's delivery. Even though his lines were as long as haiku, he filled them with dramatic flourishes. Having recently renounced drinking, he said that the only thing he was chugging was lemonade, but the question was just what he was mixing in the stuff.

"*My oold frrriend,*" he read, puckering his lips and rolling his *r*'s with all the pomp of a seventeenth-century thespian.

Crowe, in turn, chewed up monologues, spitting out each and every poisonous syllable.

Logan, who had lovingly crafted many of these lines, watched in horror. He scrawled four words on a piece of paper: "Kill me! Kill me!"

A month later, after filming in England, the shoot moved to Ouarzazate, Morocco—a town near the Sahara Desert, where Hollywood has traditionally gone for its sword-and-sandal needs (*Lawrence of Arabia* was filmed in the area). Crowe's mood did not improve. Twice he had walked off the set. Even when he was supposedly having "fun," Crowe was a puffy pain. After challenging members of the crew to a foot race, and losing, he would mutter for days, "I would have won, but I can't run in the sand in sandals."

But the thing that most vexed him, that unleashed his not-so-inner fury, was the script. Still. Even after his memorable performance in England, Crowe remained an unhappy camper, experiencing near seizures as his character was shaped, and reshaped, by the writers and then faxed back in L.A. for Parkes's approval. "Russell was getting his lines at such a late date that he had built up a real irritation factor," Ridley Scott said. "So at that moment, when you get that irritated, anything that comes through the door, he's going to get pissed off with." From Crowe, there was a lot of: "I'm not gonna say this shit. It's shit. It's stupid shit. Why should I say this? Why can't we have it the way it was this morning?" according to Bill Nicholson, the designated on-set screenwriter. (Franzoni had dropped in on the set and gotten roped into working by Scott, while visiting with his family.)

Never were Crowe's spirits more in flux than when he was to read the climactic "And I will have my vengeance, in this life or the next" scene, in which his character, Maximus, removes his helmet and reveals his identity. It was only the most seminal line in the entire movie, and yet Crowe was convinced that it was ridiculous—overwrought puffery that no man would ever be caught dead saying, least of all a brawny, sword-carrying killer standing under the unrelenting African sun. Scott was one of the few people who seemed to understand Crowe, that underneath all that volatility was a very scared actor who needed to feel safe. Rather than blow up at him, Scott waited until the tantrum subsided. Then he agreed to shoot the scene the way Crowe preferred.

After doing the take, Crowe still looked dissatisfied. "Let me see the other script again," he said to Scott, referring to the loathed revision. After studying the page stonily, he shrugged. "Well, we might as well try it."

And so the scene was reshot. Everyone agreed it was brilliant. Everyone, that is, but Crowe. "Russell, what's the problem?" Scott asked, finally showing a hint of exasperation. "It worked."

"It was shit," Crowe repeated, "but I'm the greatest actor in the world and I can make even shit sound good." And with that he marched off.

At times, however, not even Scott could control Crowe. Even during brief periods of calm, the actor would end up blowing up. Once, Crowe invited Scott and Franzoni out to his villa for dinner to discuss, of course, the script. Although everyone else, including Scott, was staying in a hotel in Ouarzazate, Crowe had his own mansion, located about an hour away, near the Algerian border. "It was out in this area where all these Moroccan generals had built mansions and created an artificial lake, so it looked like Westlake or Thousand Oaks," said Franzoni.

After being dropped off by their driver, Scott and Franzoni were greeted by one of Crowe's many assistants, who handed them each a glass of wine.

The hospitable vibe lasted but briefly. Before long, "Russell and Ridley start yelling at each other" about the script, Franzoni said, a confrontation that ended with Crowe yelling, "Fuck you, get outta here! I'm going to bed!"

The two men were kicked out, and stranded—the driver wasn't due back for two hours, and no one's cell phone was working—in the midst of North African suburbia.

According to Franzoni, while they waited for their ride, they did the obvious thing: "We break into the rec room of some general's house, he's not there, and we played pool and Ping-Pong all night."

Six thousand miles away in L.A., Parkes had done his best to control the chaos. More than any other DreamWorks film to date, Parkes was entrenched in *Gladiator*.

If Parkes's skill, as screenwriter Zak Penn describes it, is "recognizing material that can get nominated for an Oscar and shepherding it in that direction," he'd found the perfect vehicle with *Gladiator*, which he always saw in the most lofty, epic terms.

"I remember saying to Walter, 'Yeah, it's a revenge movie,'" Penn said. "I said, 'It's *Death Wish* in ancient Rome.' And he's like, 'No, it's not. It's a movie about politics and this and that.' I said, 'Well, there are speeches about politics, but fundamentally, this guy's wife gets killed, the guy goes and almost kills himself, goes back and kills the guy who killed his family . . . There's nothing to be ashamed of, it sounds like a cool action movie.'"

But Parkes disagreed, and he'd made it his mission to prove that he was right; that *Gladiator* was in fact much more than just a cool action movie. In the early stages of development, as Franzoni's script was being worked on by Logan, he'd written a twenty-page treatment giving his take on things. He and Wick, who'd helped develop Franzoni's original pitch into a script, had gone to enlist the services of Scott, toting an enormous neoclassic painting to serve as a pitch. It had worked. Scott had studied the painting—which featured a gladiator standing in the middle of the Roman Colosseum, triumphantly astride his defeated opponent as he looks up to see the emperor's verdict—and then pointed at it, saying, "I can do *that*."

Though DreamWorks was still nervous about a $100 million so-called sword-and-sandal picture—a genre that, since *Ben-Hur*, had become a parody: Roddy McDowall in robes and Roman cuffs in *Cleopatra*. And so, Universal was brought in to cofinance the film.

As the script problems persisted, Parkes had been in constant communication with Wick and Scott, no newbie director who was going to be "puppeted," as one person put it, by Parkes, as so many other directors at DreamWorks had been. Moreover, Scott appreciated Parkes, recognized that he had good ideas, and was willing to go back and forth with him creatively, a sometimes combative process, as each man argued for his version of changes to the screenplay. It was the very best version of being in the ring with Parkes, whose more intellectual storytelling instincts complemented Scott's visual strength. The situation was also helped by the fact that there was a script "committee," as Wick called it, which vetted all the tweaks, meaning no one person could hijack the script.

"There was constant arguing, but it was a healthy version of combat," said Wick. "It was the best team sport I've ever played on, despite the tensions. It was a bunch of kids shoving in the sandbox, but it was the most constructive version of that."

At one point when a friendship between screenwriter Franzoni and Crowe was sparked by their mutual love of motorcycles, DreamWorks got nervous, fearing that Crowe would use the relationship to have his way with the script, which was exactly what started happening. "I got along with Russell," Franzoni acknowledged. "Russell did not believe in the movie. He was scared. But I couldn't disagree with him. I thought he was very lucid in his concerns about where the script was going. It wasn't one of those cases where somebody's out of their mind. He was right. We'd be on the set in the morning, and he'd have these ideas. The thing with the guy who stabs with two swords and cuts his head off—that's all Russell's idea."

In April, the production had moved to Malta, where the gladiator fight scenes would be shot in a full-scale replica of the Colosseum that had been built; or, rather, a third of it had been built—the rest would be added digitally. Now there was a new problem that was much more serious than a script. An actor was dead.

Bill Nicholson, who by now had returned to England, heard the news when he received a call from Parkes. "Oliver Reed died two hours ago," Parkes said. "Get on a plane and go back to Malta and create a new ending."

Sometime since the script read-through, when Reed proclaimed he was sticking to lemonade, he'd apparently traded it in for more lethal stuff. In Malta, on his days off he would head to a local pub in the city of Valletta in the morning and stay until the afternoon. He became something of a fixture—a gregarious bloke who amused the locals and the British naval officers who frequented the place, and who never let anybody buy him a drink, even when they figured out that he was the guy from *Oliver!*

On one of these days, after twelve double rums, Reed had a heart attack. On the ambulance ride to the hospital, Reed had another heart attack, this one fatal.

"We were seeing dailies of Oliver, thinking, 'What an extraordinary performance.' Ollie looked so tan and so great," said Parkes. "And we were just talking about the fact that Oliver Reed has come back—an amazing actor is suddenly going to have a rebirth in his career. That was a Friday, and then Saturday morning I got the phone call that he had died.

"You first take in the human loss and then, much too quickly, the producer takes over and you say, 'That's terrible. How much of this have we shot and how are we going to deal with this?'"

How it was dealt with was that Nicholson rewrote the script so that Reed's character, Proximo, dies earlier in the story. For scenes he absolutely had to be in, editor Pietro Scalia combined footage of Reed that had already been shot with CGI effects to create new material. In some instances, a body double acted out the scenes, and a digital mask of Reed's face was mapped on to the actor's face in the editing room.

A year later, in the spring of 2000, *Gladiator* was finally ready for release. On opening night, Friday, May 5, Parkes, MacDonald, Wick, and his wife, Lucy Fisher—who'd recently stepped down as vice chairman of Columbia-TriStar to join her husband as a producer—packed into a car to check out theater lines, a ritual in Hollywood that provides the first glimpse of what will be either a very good, or a very unpleasant, weekend.

As they drove into Westwood, the UCLA village where *Gladiator* was playing, no one had any idea what to expect. Now that all was said and done, DreamWorks and the filmmakers felt they had a strong action movie on their hands, one that would surely attract teenage boys in droves. But they worried that women would be turned off by all the blood and violence, and would stay away. In postproduction, Scott had chopped away some of the brutality and played up the love-story element of the film, but there was no escaping the blood and guts in *Gladiator.*

Terry Press, high on her *American Beauty* victory, had done her part, with what was now characteristic chutzpah. In addition to a strong, traditional marketing campaign—an onslaught of billboards, radio, and TV (including a costly Super Bowl ad), double-truck ads in the *New York Times* and the *L.A. Times,* etc.—Press had screened *Gladiator* to Harry Knowles, the founder of the popular movie fan site Ain't It Cool News, and two hundred of Knowles's friends.

A pudgy movie geek with long, curly red hair who lives in ragamuffin bachelor quarters in Austin, Texas, Knowles—or "Harry"—is universally feared by Hollywood movie studios. Ain't It Cool News has incredible influence among Hollywood's most sought-after demographic—teenage boys—as well as an alarming number of "spies" who seem to be on all Hollywood sets at all times, gathering behind-the-scenes intel and posting it on the site. If Ain't It Cool smells a turkey, it says so, months before a film is released, muddying the film's reputation and causing migraines for marketing executives in L.A. On the other hand, if Ain't It Cool likes a movie, it provides the kind of word-of-mouth buzz that is impossible to buy.

Press was correct in guessing that *Gladiator* was the kind of movie that would fall into the latter category. "This is the Ridley Scott that we fanboys and girls drool over," Knowles began, in a review that was posted on February 25.

Later in the piece, he wrote, "When Russell Crowe says, 'I will win the crowd. I will give them something that they have never seen before.' The utter shiver of coolness that goes through you is . . . electric."

With the help of Knowles, *Gladiator* received a strong Internet push months before its release. Press had other tricks up her sleeve, such as making a deal with Wells Fargo, which aired the *Gladiator* trailer on the screens of six thousand ATM machines around the country.

But now was the real test. *Gladiator* had been built. Would audiences come? Reviews, so far, were mixed. Although Crowe's performance was praised, critics were less enthusiastic about other aspects of the film. "*Gladiator* suggests what would happen if someone made a movie of the imminent extreme-football league and shot it as if it were a Chanel commercial," wrote Elvis Mitchell in the *New York Times*, taking a swipe at Scott's early work as a commercials director.

In the *L.A. Times*, Kenneth Turan wrote: "*Gladiator* delivers when it counts—but then and only then. Like an aging athlete who knows how to husband strength and camouflage weakness, it makes the most of what it does well and hopes you won't notice its limitations." *Variety*'s Todd McCarthy, however, gave the film a rave review. "After a virtual absence of 35 years, the Roman Empire makes a thrilling return to the bigscreen in *Gladiator*. A muscular and bloody combat picture, a compelling revenge drama and a truly transporting trip back nearly 2,000 years, Ridley Scott's bold epic of imperial intrigue and outsized heroism brings new luster and excitement to a tarnished and often derided genre."

As Parkes and Co. cruised by the theater, their worst fears were confirmed. People were showing up—this was good—but they were virtually all male. And not just boys, but men. *Real men.* "They were almost like motorcycle gangs," recalled Wick. "These thuggish males. We were shocked." The next night, Saturday, another drive-by excursion proved more promising. Now there were women standing in line to buy tickets. Not a lot, but some.

In the end, *Gladiator* triumphed. After opening to a solid $34 million, the film went on to gross $187 million in the U.S. and even more overseas, totaling $457 million worldwide. Though, like *Saving Private Ryan*, the riches would be split with another studio, in this case, Universal. In hindsight, the decision to share *Gladiator* was "a big mistake," said Branko Lustig. "But there is a proverb: You cannot fuck and be a virgin at the same time."

The success of *Gladiator* was followed with more good news at the live-action studio. Virtually the entire summer lineup—the first time that DreamWorks *had* a summer slate—performed so strong that Dream-Works wound up being number one at the box office for the season, beating out Disney, which came in second, and Paramount, whose *Mission: Impossible II* was the top-grossing summer movie—*Gladiator* was the second highest.

The other films bolstering DreamWorks' bottom line were the

Robert Zemeckis–directed ghost thriller *What Lies Beneath,* which grossed $155 million; and Todd Phillips's comedy *Road Trip,* which took in $68 million on a budget of $16 million. And an animation collaboration with the British Claymation company Aardman—*Chicken Run*—was hailed by critics and made $106 million. Although Woody Allen's *Small Time Crooks* wasn't a big moneymaker—it grossed $29 million worldwide on a budget almost as high—Allen received more praise than he had in recent years and the film was seen as a mini comeback.

At least so hoped DreamWorks, which made a deal to release Allen's next three comedies. Katzenberg, who'd worked with Allen at Disney, on *Scenes from a Mall,* and, more recently, when Allen lent his voice to *Antz,* had forged the deal, which was less about financial reward than the prestige of being in business with Allen. "Of all the people I've worked with, he's the one who impressed my mother the most," Terry Press once said.

But of all the movies, *Gladiator* represented a crowning triumph —the third film in three years, following *Saving Private Ryan* and *American Beauty*—that validated DreamWorks as being, whatever its financial ills and Internet travails, a pedigreed film company that specialized in high-end fare with commercial appeal. DreamWorks' original claims of setting out to be different—and, it was implied, better—than the rest of the Hollywood studios were not just ringing true but were seeming like a lasting proposition. If *American Beauty* had "made" the studio, *Gladiator* patented the studio more lastingly as a success.

Someone who should have been thrilled, even gloating, was Parkes. With *Gladiator,* he'd shown Katzenberg that not only could he deliver a summer movie, but he could deliver a finely crafted summer movie, one that already was receiving early Oscar buzz. (He could take less credit for the slate, seeing as Katzenberg had been responsible for half of it: *Chicken Run, Road Trip,* and *Small Time Crooks.*) And he'd shown how his intensive approach to guiding movies at Dream-Works—which, in this case, was essentially producing the movie—did not always end disastrously with filmmakers.

But although DreamWorks' position was looking increasingly solid, Parkes and his wife were reassessing their relationship with the studio, according to sources close to the couple. Five years in, they were exhausted. The start-up demands of running the studio and simultaneously acting as producers on movies had taken their toll. And what was obvious to everyone else was just as obvious to them: they were not cut out to run a studio. They couldn't break out of thinking like producers, not studio executives, and meticulously focusing on one film at a time as opposed to an entire slate. As a result, DreamWorks' pipeline was dangerously thin. When there *was* a robust lineup of films—in 2000, for the first time ever, DreamWorks released ten live-action films—it was short-lived: only five films were on the 2001 slate. Parkes and MacDonald simply couldn't keep up.

With their five-year contract about to expire, Parkes and MacDonald made a decision: they were going to step down and go back to producing. There was only one problem—at the prospect of yet another one of his family members abandoning him, Spielberg said, No way. And he was willing to do whatever it took to keep them in the fold. And so he came up with a proposal: What about if the couple got to produce movies at DreamWorks, even as they continued to run the studio? Then would they stay?

It was quite an offer. Unprecedented, in fact. To be able to run Steven Spielberg's company *and* produce—and be compensated for—their own films. "Isn't it a direct conflict of interest?" asked one studio head turned producer. "As a producer, you fight for movies, no matter what. As a studio executive, you have to represent the interests of the studio. I've been on both sides. In a way, those responsibilities are mutually exclusive. It's just an untenable tightrope to walk."

It was unorthodox, to be sure. It was also, quite possibly, the most amazing deal ever crafted in Hollywood, combining power and creative freedom—and the potential to become very rich—in a way that would never have passed muster at a public company checked and balanced by board members. But unorthodox was the DreamWorks way, never more so than when the idea came out of Spielberg's imaginative head. Helene Hahn might be angry about it (as many suspected), though when she was confronted by one executive who was dumbfounded that either she or Katzenberg could have signed off on something that was so, as this person believed, "bad for DreamWorks," she dutifully defended the policy.

As for Geffen and Katzenberg, whatever reservations they may have had took a backseat to keeping their main man happy. Just as they'd gone against their better instincts and agreed to Bob Zemeckis's rich ImageMovers deal (which, as of yet, had produced just two films for DreamWorks, one of which was *What Lies Beneath*), and to pursuing money- and resource-sucking projects such as Playa Vista and Dream-Works Interactive, they again gave Steven what he wanted.

But even while the deal was justified by DreamWorks' status as a private company that wrote its own rules, no one was blind to the questions it would raise, and so ground rules were established. For one, it was agreed that Parkes and MacDonald would never green-light their own movies. That would be left up to Spielberg. In other words, at least in theory, movies that Parkes and MacDonald pro-duced would be subject to the same questions of merit and financial prudence as any other potential film.

It was another example of the way that at DreamWorks, what was good for the people who worked at the company was frequently put before what was good for DreamWorks, the company. Once, when I was talking to a former executive, he explained the attitude at the stu-dio, as proselytized by its founders, as: "We are fulfilling our destiny. We want you to stay here and fulfill your destiny with us. And as long as your agenda fits with ours, we're cool."

Placating any doubters was the understanding that the arrange-ment would be temporary. Parkes and MacDonald still wanted to shed their studio duties, and while this was a fabulous interim ar-rangement, they didn't want it to be long-term. It was agreed that at some point in the relatively near future someone would be brought in and Parkes and MacDonald would step down.

Around DreamWorks, Parkes and MacDonald's new contract was described as "the deal of the century." Everyone knew Spielberg cher-ished Parkes, would do anything for him, but this was a new level of largesse. On a practical level, executives worried that they would now have even more trouble getting Parkes interested in their projects, now that he'd have more incentive to focus on his and his wife's. For it was no secret that Parkes was a hard sell when it came to ideas that didn't come out of his own, pedigreed head, or that appealed to his not-so-catholic tastes. Desperate executives had even come up with tricks to try and spark his attention, the underlying theme being to *make it about him.* In a technique they called "the assist," they would pitch an idea and refer back to something he'd brought up in the past.

E.g.: "You know how you were talking about X? Well, this is a *lot* like that, in that . . ." Or: "This is a more mainstream version of X." They were appeals founded in narcissism, and, very often, they worked.

When he was interviewed by *Variety* about the new deal, Parkes admitted that it was "unconventional," but said that now that Dream-Works was working with more experienced directors, such as Bob Zemeckis and Cameron Crowe, who didn't need (and wouldn't put up with) as much studio meddling, there was more room for him and MacDonald to jump in and make movies themselves. As for the effects he thought the change in course would have on DreamWorks, Parkes said, "I don't think things are going to change much."

Others weren't so sure.

23

SHREKED

At the animation studio, Katzenberg was still feeling the sting of *El Dorado*, but underneath his layer of flop sweat there was a small but growing sense of hope. For up at PDI, the movie once dubbed "the Gulag," whose name had been used as a verb to describe the most degrading humiliation there was—to be "Shreked" was to be exiled to the lowest caste at the animation studio—was starting to look like something other than a misguided mess.

How had it happened?

Not overnight. *Shrek* had stumbled along lifelessly for quite some time. Ted Elliott and Terry Rossio cranked out three thousand pages of material in the process of writing an original script. Three years in, they dropped out and were replaced by Joe Stillman (*Beavis and Butthead Do America*) and Roger Schulman (*Balto*). Several directors, including Henry Selick (*The Nightmare before Christmas*), gave *Shrek* a stab but were ultimately replaced by two first-time directors: Andrew Adamson, a PDI special-effects director, and Vicky Jenson, a storyboard artist.

Working in their favor was that they weren't appendage-swinging auteurs who would freak out at Katzenberg's intense surveillance.

Or at least that's how it appeared. Katzenberg would be sorely mistaken about Adamson, a tall, transplanted kiwi with silky blond hair that fell in straight, straw-like shafts well past his shoulders, who, until *Shrek* came along, had been toiling in obscurity at PDI.

"When Andrew was first brought on, Jeffrey didn't think he would be a strong personality," said one PDI source, who described Adamson as soft-spoken and gentle, but possessing a lashing dry wit and rock-like will. And as his confidence grew, so, too, did those latter qualities.

As *Shrek* continued on its tumultuous evolution from a thirty-two-page children's book about an ugly green ogre into a ninety-minute movie, at the center of it all were Katzenberg and Adamson "butting heads over ideas," said one source. "They weren't furious, they just had competing visions of the way the film should go . . . I think Andrew had a very clear idea of how the film should evolve, how it should work . . . Jeffrey didn't intimidate him in the same ways Jeffrey intimidated people who came from inside DreamWorks. A lot of that came from the PDI story department, which hadn't been indoctrinated by DreamWorks' ways. They still had a Bay Area irreverence toward authority."

The biggest arguments were over just how far *Shrek* should push the envelope when it came to appealing not just to children but to adults. Katzenberg wanted both demographics, but he found some of Adamson's suggestions a bit too outrageous. Take the scene suggesting a twitter of sexual excitement on Lord Farquaad's part when he sees Princess Fiona's image in the mirror. Before the scene cuts away, Adamson thought it would be funny if the blanket on the bed rose ever so slightly. Katzenberg ultimately acquiesced, but stood firm on other arguments. When Adamson suggested laying the headbanging Guns N' Roses song "Welcome to the Jungle" over the scene in which Shrek is chased by villagers, Katzenberg, whose taste ran more toward crooning ballads, said: No way.

"Andrew was good at making Jeffrey feel comfortable taking these risks," said the source. As such, he was unlike any director who had preceded him at DreamWorks, and *Shrek* began to take on a life of its own that felt fresh and irreverent. Helping Adamson's cause was that *Shrek* was being made up at PDI. Although Katzenberg flew up regularly, he was not the daily presence that he was on films made in L.A.

"Jeffrey was very, very involved with *Shrek;* there wasn't a frame of that movie that he wasn't in the cutting room to see," said Penney Finkelman Cox. "But the advantage you had at PDI is that you had five days without him in your face. So he might come up and tear everything apart, which he does, but you still had five days of breathing room [during which] you could actually make a real impact."

It was also Adamson's innovation to push storyboard artists Cody Cameron, Chris Miller, and Conrad Vernon to spike up the level of humor among the fairy-tale creatures—Pinocchio, the Three Little Pigs (who, for no apparent reason, speak in a German accent), and Gingy, the gingerbread man—and help the movie find its creative tone.

"OK," Adamson would tell the artists, "everybody come up with three funny ideas for the fairy-tale characters."

The artists became so integral to the process that, after having provided "scratch" voices (temporary voices, used before dialogue is recorded by the actual cast) for several fairy-tale characters, they ended up lending their voices to the actual film.

"The one thing Andrew did was, he recognized that his real creative geniuses were around him," said Finkelman Cox. "He was the one that zeroed in on the Conrad, Chris, and Cody grouping, and pulled them into the process. He found comedy through the artists ... The beauty of that movie is Andrew Adamson getting all the board artists to do the best they could have ever done, with him as the guiding light."

Mike Myers, who had stepped in as the voice of Shrek after Chris Farley's death, and Eddie Murphy, who voiced Shrek's sidekick, Donkey, also upped the funny ante.

Adamson said of Murphy: "You'd pitch him a sequence and you'd show him the pages, and he'd read it very quietly, just kind of to himself. And then he'd step in front of the microphone and just—bam!—instantly, [it's] Donkey. He'd come up with stuff we'd never even imagined. He'd take a single-beat joke and turn it into a three-beat joke. Sequences got longer because his jokes were so good."

But *Shrek*'s real heart and soul lay in its characters and the way in which they evolved from William Steig's book of crudely drawn creatures. "At the beginning, Shrek was a very angry guy," said animator Noel McGinn. "He was constantly badgering Donkey, putting him down all the time, there was no heart to it. For us animators working on it, it was like, This guy is not very likable."

But over time, Shrek's "super scary" qualities were toned down, McGinn said.

Shrek also evolved into a more lovable character when Myers came onboard. Shrek lost the *Tommy Boy* hair and doofy expression and took on bushier eyebrows and a squarish face. Myers also inspired Shrek's character.

"Mike created a very interesting character, a Shrek who has a sense of humor that's not good, but it makes him happy," said screenwriter Terry Rossio. But perhaps Myers's most notable contribution was

Shrek's Scottish brogue. After originally recording the film in his own Canadian accent, he later decided he needed to add something more. He wanted Shrek to sound more vulnerable and decided to go with "the Scottish accent of somebody who's lived in Canada for twenty years."

Seeing as a third of Myers's scenes had already been animated before Myers adopted the accent, Katzenberg was reluctant to start over. Rerecording all of Myers's lines would mean reanimating the mouth movements and facial expressions for those scenes—a process that would cost $4 million. Katzenberg—and Adamson—were also worried that a Scottish burr was too similar to Myers's voice in the comedy *So I Married an Axe Murderer* (in which Myers plays Stuart Mackenzie, a Scottish coffeehouse poet), not to mention his portrayal of the Scottish henchman Fat Bastard in *Austin Powers*.

But Myers was convinced, and Katzenberg was willing to do whatever it took to make *Shrek* work. He brought himself to, as he put it, "choke out a yes."

On top of the characterization challenges, there were enormous technical obstacles, as DreamWorks set out to make the most advanced CGI picture to date. When the PDI crew from *Antz*—which segued from that film to *Shrek*—asked how much harder *Shrek* was going to be, Adamson told them: "Five to ten times."

In *Shrek,* there were humans, or in the case of Shrek himself, humanish bodies and faces to animate, which meant creating a system that would make the characters move and speak in a realistic manner. To do this, PDI developed tools known as shapers that essentially recreated the way that layers of muscles, skin, and clothing interact with each other and move.

According to *Shrek* production notes, this is how it works: "Essentially, the skull of the characters is formed in the computer and covered with computer re-creations of the actual muscles of the face. The skin is then layered over and programmed to respond to the manipulations of the muscles as would a human face, complete with wrinkles, laugh lines, and other imperfections. Hundreds of controls are wired into the face like human nerves, enabling the animators to go far beyond the speech phonemes for the correct lip synch."

The result was that Shrek and his cronies appeared incredibly vivid and lifelike. When Shrek grinned, wrinkles formed around his eyes. When he frowned, creases deepened between his eyes. When he moved, his cotton tunic changed shape to reflect that movement.

The mostly male animation crew had a hard time with Princess Fiona, who ended up looking a little too rigid and thin-hipped, but she was realistic enough that the first time Cameron Diaz, who voiced Fiona in the film, saw herself in digital form, she ran out of the room screaming.

"It's so weird!" she exclaimed. "It's like seeing my sister, but it's not my sister! It's somebody I know, but it's not somebody I know. I'm hearing my voice, but it's coming out of her, not me."

PDI also further developed its Fluid Animation System, which had been created for *Antz,* so that not only do water and other liquids look real in *Shrek,* but so do more viscous substances, such as mud and lava.

Whatever its technical achievements, the narrative subtext of *Shrek* was pure Katzenberg. The film was essentially one big Fuck You to Disney. No one missed the long-faced Lord Farquaad's resemblance to Michael Eisner. And in a reverse insider joke—given Eisner's "little midget" comment that became public during the trial—Farquaad was designed to be very, very short.

"Farquaad is short because Jeffrey insisted he be short," said *Shrek* co-screenwriter Ted Elliott. "I could postulate that maybe it was Jeffrey making fun of himself. I think to some extent he's also making fun of who he had to be at Disney."

Then there was the kingdom of Duloc, with its kitschy, Disney-landesque spires, cobblestoned streets, and kids' attractions. But Duloc was no cutesy theme park—it was cold and militaristic, and overrun with menacing, black-hooded men.

The most blatant spoof on Disney was the way *Shrek* took a whole population of familiar fairy-tale characters, many of which were from the Disney family, and subverted them in irreverent ways. When Snow White is presented by the Magic Mirror as an "eligible bachelorette" to Farquaad, he is told that she "lives with seven other men" and "is not easy."

"Just kiss her dead, frozen lips and find out what a live wire she is," booms the Magic Mirror. "Come on. Give it up for Snow White!"

The movie's wiseass aesthetic marked a drastic departure from Disney films. Indeed, *Shrek* marked the first time that Katzenberg's philosophy of appealing to both kids and adults was thoroughly, and effectively, realized. The tone he had long sought for the film—edgy—was finally realized.

In early August, Ken Wong showed up at Pop and asked everyone in the company to gather round. Everyone expected another go-get-'em speech as they filed into the large open area in the warehouse *cum* office where such meetings were held.

What had inspired this particular conclave was a story in that morning's *L.A. Times.* It was a particularly harsh look at Pop, stating that "nine months after five of Hollywood's most powerful players combined to create an online entertainment site, Pop.com is foundering so badly that certain partners are seeking a graceful way out before it has aired a single show."

Addressing bad press had become a sort of ritual at Pop, as it had occurred with more and more frequency since the Internet bust, when Pop's own fortunes began a relentless slide. By the summer of 2000, there was still no launch date in sight, and now, as the *Times* story rightly stated, DreamWorks and Imagine were looking for a graceful escape. Pop had been in talks to merge with the Web sites Atom Films and iFilms for months, the idea being that by acquiring already existing Web sites, Pop would be able to launch faster. But now, the talks with those companies were more urgent, and they were less about building up Pop than letting it go. A "merge" would be a way for DreamWorks and Imagine to exit a company that had burned through $7 million in start-up cash with virtually nothing to show for it. By now, even Paul Allen was asking questions.

The sense within the company was that the media was playing hardball because it was SKG, and there was an element out there that wanted the mighty moguls to fall. "Along the way there'd be stories that came out that didn't really have much to do with anything," Phillip Nakov said. "I almost feel—I know this from personal experience in this business—that everyone was just holding their breath for [Pop] to fail."

But on that early-August morning, Wong didn't launch into an explanation or analysis of the doomsday *Times* story. He responded to it, rather, by hanging up a piñata, taping on the name of the reporter, Greg Miller, who'd written the story, and proceeding to smash it to a papery pulp. Then he let others take a whack. Oddly, Wong didn't seem visibly upset. It truly did feel more like a game, an almost Scientological exercise in excising, or at least denying, the reality imposed by the outside world. "It was like a high school pep rally that was oblivious to the reality of our situation," said one former Pop employee. "It was like the violinist performing on the deck of the *Titanic* going down."

And the ship was, most certainly, sinking. By the end of the month, the plug was pulled on Pop for good, proving that no amount of wishful thinking, nor the protective power of SKG, nor even Paul Allen's millions, could keep the enterprise afloat.

Nakov, who would retain his connection to DreamWorks via CountingDown.com—which became DreamWorks' online presence —received the news over Labor Day weekend. "I got a call at 9:30 in the morning on Saturday from Jeffrey," he said. "He called to let us know there was going to be an announcement made the following Tuesday that Pop was not going to launch. He wanted to give us a heads-up that we [CountingDown.com] were going to be kept around."

After the announcement by Katzenberg, "Most people were in shock," said Nakov. "I just remember being very nervous; I think I just went out for a smoke." Soon madness settled in. Executives began running around, ripping up contracts so that artists and filmmakers would be able to take their projects elsewhere and not have it in writing that their rights were owned by Pop.

If the media had been hounding Pop in the months and weeks leading up to its fizzle, when it really did go under, the press went haywire, zeroing in like buzzards on a carcass. Another bold misfire from SKG. *This* was news.

But despite all the bluster, Pop was one of the more minor Internet disaster stories, having lost just $7 million, in comparison to the tens, and in some cases hundreds, of millions of dollars lost by the multitudes of dot-coms caught in the technology bust. Pop's loss was a drop in the bucket compared to, say, the $60 million that was soaked up by the Digital Entertainment Network, a high-profile Hollywood dot-com that produced a few dozen online TV episodes before it went belly-up. As for Paul Allen, the cost of Pop was nothing compared to the $250 million he lost on the Interval Research Corporation, which he had finally shut down months before. And both DreamWorks and Imagine had certainly seen more disastrous results just from a single movie that bombed. More than anything, Pop was a symbolic failure. Its trajectory—what went right, what went wrong—contained elements of so many DreamWorks endeavors. There was the hype, the hubris of a new, never-before-seen entity. There was the star power of not just SKG but Imagine. There was the initial, though not lasting, enthusiasm of Steven Spielberg. There was the sweat and toil of Katzenberg. There was the remove of Geffen—and Allen, who yet again ponied up the funds. There was the absence of any real business plan or truly experienced people selected on the basis of something other than a prior history with Disney. There was money that was freely spent. There was the untimely shift in the market; the belief that the broadband revolution was right around the corner.

At the same time, it can't be denied that Pop was ahead of its time, as would become clear when, years later, the video-sharing Web site YouTube became one of the hottest Web sites in the world. Allen's prediction that by 2000 the world would be interconnected via high-speed Internet was off by a few critical years. But the essence of his idea was correct. Once again, DreamWorks had trouble synchronizing the dream and the reality.

As Pop was coming undone, so, too, was the relationship between DreamWorks and Imagine, and talks to merge were written off. The failed experiment left a bad taste in the principals' mouths, a sense that a partnership maybe wasn't their destiny after all. According to reports at the time, Ron Howard and Brian Grazer chafed at not being made equal parties in the company with Spielberg, Katzenberg, and Geffen. They were not convinced that, if the company was ever sold, they would receive a substantial share of the riches. But the overriding reason for Grazer and Howard's reluctance was the amount of debt DreamWorks had accrued over the years, which was close to $1 billion. Having lived through an unhappy spell when Imagine was briefly taken public (Howard and Grazer wound up buying their company back), Howard and Grazer didn't want to go through that again. They decided to remain small, but secure, as a production company funded by a major studio. And so DreamWorks went looking for a cash infusion elsewhere, smelling opportunity in what was transpiring right in its own backyard, where, for the third time in a decade, Universal was changing hands.

DreamWorks' designs were evident on a hot night in July at the premiere of Imagine's *The Nutty Professor II: The Klumps,* where Katzenberg was working the French—one, in particular, Jean-Marie Messier, the dapper, buttoned-down chairman and chief executive of the multimedia conglomerate Vivendi. After the screening, Katzenberg, a heat-seeking missile in action, had cruised over to where Messier was sitting and plunked himself down in the empty seat beside him, where he remained for the next thirty minutes.

There was much to discuss. DreamWorks' distribution contract with Universal was up for renegotiation, just as Universal's own future was about to be decided yet again. Messier was in talks with Edgar Bronfman Jr. to buy Seagram and Co., a $34 billion stock purchase that would unite Universal with Vivendi—the onetime water utility company that owned half of pay-TV giant Canal Plus and had a hand in publishing and cellular phones—to create the second-largest media company in the world, after the newly formed AOL Time Warner. Bronfman was, understandably, ready to quit Hollywood, or at least so prominent, and potentially vulnerable, a role in it. Since his arrival five years ago, when he'd been determined to shed his reputation as a rich dilettante, he'd done little to alter that perception. Universal's film division was still mostly struggling, with a few shining exceptions, such as *Erin Brockovich* and the high-grossing *American Pie.*

For DreamWorks to go beyond being just part of the new enterprise, for it to secure $250 million in equity from Universal—which the always bold Katzenberg and Geffen were proposing—Katzenberg had some talking to do. The afterglow of *Gladiator*'s box-office triumph hadn't yet faded, but the overall picture of the last five years was less dewy. Without any major Spielberg or animated blockbusters, and with a generally uneven track record, DreamWorks had accounted for less than 10 percent of Universal's bottom line. Yet, when it came to draining resources and energy from Universal executives, who had to cater to Spielberg and listen to Geffen's ranting and Katzenberg's nitpicking, DreamWorks took up a far larger percentage of Universal's time. "They're very labor intensive," one Universal executive said. "They suck a lot of time and emotional energy."

DreamWorks, with its steroid-level pride—"It's what happens when you work at a place where Steven Spielberg, Jeffrey Katzenberg, and David Geffen are in love with you—you're convinced you're better than everyone else," noted one producer—had never been the *appreciative* child. Case in point: just a few weeks earlier, at Herb Allen's summer mogul retreat, Katzenberg had first buttonholed Messier, presenting him with a list of everything Universal was doing wrong, as Kim Masters reported for Inside.com. One of his biggest gripes was that the studio had bungled the home-video release of *Prince of Egypt* and had come close to doing the same with *Saving Private Ryan*. The impression was that Katzenberg was positioning himself as Universal's savior—i.e., the one who should be running things at the studio, a suggestion that had been made by Geffen to Bronfman before, according to a Universal source. When word of the episode filtered back to L.A., Universal executives were furious, especially CEO Ron Meyer, who was trying to make a good first impression on his new boss.

When Claudia Eller wrote about Katzenberg's behavior in the *L.A. Times*, noting that "with his trademark lack of subtlety," Katzenberg was "working overtime cozying up to" Messier, DreamWorks suspected that Meyer was Eller's source. This led to a chilly spell between SKG and Universal, even though Geffen and Meyer had just gone to the Mayo Clinic together for their annual checkups.

The *L.A. Times* story infuriated DreamWorks and sent Eller's already damaged relationship with the studio to an even chillier place.

Infuriated by the article, Katzenberg and Terry Press paid a visit to the *Times*, bringing a stack of Eller's pieces about DreamWorks—which they complained were relentlessly negative—and presented them to the *Times'* editor, John Carroll, and managing editor, Dean Baquet.

If Katzenberg was trying to get Eller fired—as Eller believed (a DreamWorks source denied that that was the goal)—it didn't work. As one of the paper's prized business reporters, Eller wasn't going anywhere. But her relationship with DreamWorks was over. From then on, no one at the company would speak to her. To Katzenberg, it was pure betrayal. Eller had "quit" him, and so he slammed the door on her, hard. As of the writing of this book, the relationship had still not fully healed.

The issue became public months later, when the *Times* ran a series of articles about entertainment coverage in Hollywood. The story was a self-examination, of sorts, about how the *Times'* coverage, long criticized as being "soft," was hardening up. In it, Eller was singled out as one of the paper's most aggressive reporters, though her critics complained that she went easy on those she liked (such as Disney's Joe Roth) while bullying her enemies. Press and Katzenberg, both interviewed for the article, claimed that DreamWorks belonged to the latter category—citing the Messier story.

The *Times* story elucidated the ramifications of crossing Dream-Works in the media. Rarely does friction between a reporter and a company become a news story in its own right. Eller told her newspaper that she'd also written critical articles about Katzenberg while he was at Disney but that, since he went to DreamWorks, she'd written "more tough pieces . . . that were warranted." Of Katzenberg, she said, "He wants to control the press," adding that reporters who didn't write what he liked were "shut out."

Vivendi's response to DreamWorks' overtures was a crisp, monosyllabic *non*—something that would have been unimaginable five years before, when players like Bronfman weren't just willing to get into business with the holy triumvirate, but were happy to let Geffen dictate the terms.

Everything was different these days. SKG was not at all as untouchable as it had been in the past. The entertainment business was both ballooning and fracturing at the same time, and being independent and unaffiliated was getting harder to defend—and to pull off. Especially for three company heads who couldn't justify their company's enormous overhead. After a robust 2000, DreamWorks was looking ahead to a year that seemed frighteningly thin in terms of planned film releases. The company may have astutely pulled out of Playa Vista, but it was still no nimble player. By year five, it had racked up $1 billion in debt, according to a source with knowledge of Dream-Works' finances. And now, DreamWorks needed to find a new distribution partner. And fast.

Despite the pileup of cancellations DreamWorks TV was enduring in mid-2000, the mood at the studio remained, if not exuberant, then stubbornly upbeat. Spielberg was producing a reality TV show for NBC, *Semper Fi*, about the grueling process of enlisting in the U.S. Marines. (A military consultant, Dale Dye, was on the case, presumably ordering the writers to drop and give him fifty every morning.) Spielberg was also producing two ambitious miniseries—the World War II–themed *Band of Brothers* with Tom Hanks for HBO, and *Taken*, for the Sci-Fi Channel. But what most imbued the studio with a sense of security was the fact that *Spin City* was about to go into syndication, a development that could result in $250 million for DreamWorks over five years. Everyone at the company was conscious of this milestone. As one former executive said, "The attitude was, 'Well, *Spin City* is paying our bills now.'"

Spin City was, every way you looked at it, a kind of charmed property. Not considered a *great* show along the lines of *Seinfeld*, it was, without a doubt, a very good, solid show that persistently held on in the ratings, generating between $2.5 million and $3 million an episode. Indeed, nothing seemed to shake it, even when Michael J. Fox left the series for health reasons (in 1998 Fox announced that he'd been diagnosed with Parkinson's disease) in January of 2000. Still, *Spin City* had hit the one-hundred-episode mark, the magic number that means a show is eligible for syndication. Fox's last episode, an hourlong special that aired on May 24, was a poignant farewell. In the teleplay written by former show-runner Bill Lawrence, who'd left *Spin City* after its third season, Fox's Mike Flaherty leaves city hall after a mob scandal. The swan song drew the largest audience in the show's history and went on to win two Emmys.

Fox's exit was a significant blow to a show that was effectively built around him as an actor and whose popularity was largely driven by his presence. As Lawrence said, "No matter what you call *Spin City*, it's a Mike Fox show." Thus DreamWorks' initial response was to cancel the series, a sentiment that also came out of loyalty and respect for Fox. But from a business perspective, there was reason to push ahead. Research showed that *Spin City*'s supporting cast was popular with viewers, particularly since the recent addition of Heather Locklear as a new campaign manager and love interest of Fox's. Any further episodes would mean more syndication dollars, regardless of how well they did in the ratings. So DreamWorks began brainstorming for replacements for Fox. Among the suggestions were Matthew Broderick, Denis Leary, and Charlie Sheen. In the end, Sheen—who'd forged a relationship with Gary David Goldberg while making the pilot *Sugar Hill*—was selected, despite some reservations about his off-camera behavior (he'd been treated for drug and alcohol abuse). In the weeks leading up to that summer's TCA (Television Critics Association) press tour, executives from DreamWorks and ABC fretted about how Sheen, who was scheduled to speak on a *Spin City* panel, would go over with the press. But their worries proved needless.

Indeed, when Sheen made his debut that fall, ratings went up, not down. Lured by curiosity, and the new sex appeal that Sheen introduced to the series as New York's new deputy mayor Charlie Crawford (in his first episode he's shown in bed with a flight attendant), viewers tuned in. When, on one occasion, *Spin City* managed to beat out the popular *West Wing* in the ratings, DreamWorks was all the more certain it had made the right decision to soldier on.

DreamWorks Records was also hitting its stride, having discovered the thing that had so far proven elusive: a breakout hit. Her name was Nelly Furtado.

When Marc Ratner, a promotions executive at DreamWorks Records, first met the singer-songwriter, he made one thing clear. "The harder you're willing to work, the better chance we have," he told her. In his head, Ratner was assessing the challenge that lay ahead of him: "We have to become *that buzz.*"

Ratner knew that turning Furtado—a twenty-one-year-old unknown artist from Canada whose music was an unusual blend of pop, hip-hop, and Brazilian bossa nova—into the It artist of the moment was no easy task. So he told Furtado to pack her bags. For the next six months, starting in the summer of 2000, Ratner, Furtado, and her manager traveled around the country playing miniconcerts at local radio stations. It was Loretta Lynn for a new millennium, with Furtado singing and playing the guitar in front of a group of radio programmers sitting around a conference table (Ratner did his best to improve the acoustics by hooking up a PA system).

"I knew that the way to do it was to take Nelly on the road," Ratner told me over the phone from Maine, where he now lives. "And to [DreamWorks'] credit, [DreamWorks Records coheads] Lenny [Waronker] said, Mo [Ostin] said, 'Do it.' Then, Johnny Barbis [head of promotions at DreamWorks Records] came in and gave me the open checkbook to go do it. Nelly worked really hard. We just went out there and did it. That was the beginning."

Indeed. Having completed the first round of performances, Furtado then returned to various stations to play before a larger group of the stations' listeners. This time, she graduated from conference rooms to rented hotel suites.

The first sign that the old-fashioned, grass-roots campaign was paying off came one night in Des Moines, when Furtado stopped in a

7-Eleven and saw that she was mentioned in the latest issue of *Rolling Stone*. It was official: she had that buzz.

And by 2000, DreamWorks Records needed just that—a big break-out act. Although by this time the label had established its reputation as a nurturer of interesting talent, none of its acts garnered enormous followings. Waronker could have been speaking about virtually all of DreamWorks' artists when he once said of Elliott Smith: "We're try-ing to expose the music however we can expose it with the notion that at some point the audience will catch up." But by 2000, the audiences still weren't catching up. The closest DreamWorks had come to tap-ping into a wider audience was with the rap-rock group Papa Roach and the rock band Powerman 5000, both of whose albums had gone platinum, but neither of which was quite a household name.

The hope was that Furtado, who was DreamWorks' first real pop artist, would earn that distinction, and so they were pushing her like hell. Another artist the label saw as a potentially huge pop act was Kina, a Tina Turner–like belter, whom Waronker was particularly im-passioned about and whom DreamWorks was prepared to put huge resources behind. Like Furtado, Kina was sent on the road six months before her debut release, playing small clubs with a seven-piece band all over the country. The vision for Kina changed, however, when Benny Medina, the legendary manager of Mariah Carey, Sean "P. Diddy" Combs, and Jennifer Lopez, took on Kina as a client. This de-velopment occurred when Ostin and Waronker were having lunch at Sushi Roku in West Hollywood, when who should walk in but Med-ina, who'd worked with Ostin and Waronker at Warner Bros., where he'd overseen the label's urban division. The DreamWorks group had just been discussing how Kina could benefit from a powerhouse man-ager, and when they mentioned this to Medina, who'd sat down next to them, he perked up. Later that week, Medina went to a show of Kina's at the Mint Club, was blown away, and signed her.

With Medina onboard, the plan (though not the resources) for Kina changed overnight. Suddenly, she was positioned more as a hip-hop artist, with a marketing campaign geared more toward generat-ing street-level buzz. Still, by the time Kina's debut album was released in July of 2000, that buzz had become a deafening roar. *Interview* pro-claimed her "the about-to-be-massive Kina" who "brings rockstar magnetism to her humble tales of 'Girl From the Gutter' made great."

· · ·

Before Furtado signed with DreamWorks in March of 1999, she was being chased by a number of bigger labels, such as Epic, Elektra, Interscope, and Jive. But she went with DreamWorks because of its reputation as an artist-friendly company. While the other labels were talking about making Furtado into a Britney Spears–type pop diva and partnering her up with more commercial producers, DreamWorks said that Furtado could pursue whatever kind of music she liked, and that she could continue to work with her two longtime Canadian producers. DreamWorks (which was offering less money than its competitors) sealed the deal by flying Furtado and her manager, Chris Smith, out to L.A. and driving them over to Geffen's Beverly Hills manse, where Geffen did what Geffen does best.

"It was a life decision for her, but Geffen made it sound simple: she had to join DreamWorks," said Beth Halper, an A&R executive who had first listened to Furtado's demo tape and convinced the label to go after her, despite some reservations that Furtado would never catch on beyond the college circuit.

The meeting at Geffen's was interrupted when Geffen's chiropractor showed up. "Do you want an adjustment?" Geffen asked his prospective clients. They accepted; a month later they also accepted DreamWorks' offer.

In the fall of 2000, Furtado's debut album, *Whoa, Nelly!*, was released. Despite the mini road show, however, sales were disappointing. Still, DreamWorks kept at it, continuing to tour Furtado around radio stations, booking her on TV and arranging interviews with print media, and giving her a strong push on MTV. The strategy was counterintuitive to the prevailing wisdom in the record business, which by this time stated that (as in the film business) a lackluster opening boded ill for the future and that it was wisest to give up and direct energies elsewhere. But Ostin and Waronker were not interested in the prevailing wisdom. To them, once the decision was made to support an artist, that support never waned.

This wisdom did not, however, extend to all acts. Within the record business, promoting an urban act is more akin to promoting a film. A lot of money is generally spent up-front in order to generate strong word of mouth on the street—this means spending to make the *right* music video, to make the *right* remix. If sales aren't high within the first week of a record's release, the game is generally over. So, unfortunately, it was in the case of Kina. When her debut album did not make the splash DreamWorks had anticipated, she did not receive the Furtado-like push. Not long afterward, she and DreamWorks split ways.

By 2000, the realities of the record business had grown grim. In the wake of President Clinton's signing of the Telecommunications Act of 1996, which eliminated the cap on how many stations a company could own in a single market, independently owned radio stations had been devoured by a small number of media powerhouses, such as Clear Channel and CBS Radio. The corporatization of radio meant major cutbacks in an effort to streamline operations. As a result, Ratner explained, "Whereas you used to have a program director, and a music director, and a full-time disk jockey twenty-four hours a day, and a weekend staff, and a marketing director—all that went away. They cut back people, and those who remained became so overworked that they didn't have the time to get into the music as much as they wanted to. You [now] have a program director running four stations, who comes in to a meeting and says, 'What's on the chart that I haven't heard yet?' That's all he has time for."

As Alec Foege wrote in his book, *Right of the Dial: The Rise of Clear Channel and the Fall of Commercial Radio,* "As radio groups got larger, they demanded less and less creative input. Radio executives became far more interested in quantitative research than in the opinions of any one programmer, regardless of that person's level of experience."

For this reason, selling someone like Furtado, who didn't neatly fit into the genres that were defining the new era—bland, lowest-common-denominator categories such as pop and easy listening—became virtually impossible, without the extra oomph of bringing her around and literally forcing programmers to listen. Most record companies didn't have the time or interest in such gestures (which Ratner described as "very grueling"). But at DreamWorks, where there were fewer acts and a greater interest in developing those acts over the long term, such nurturing was an accepted practice.

Another development that had rocked the music industry was the advent of Napster, in 1999. Suddenly music downloads were available online, free of charge, which sent CD sales plummeting. Napster was eventually sued by several recording companies and artists for copyright violations, and the service shut down, but it paved the way for other file-sharing services that were harder to control. With or without Napster, online music was here to stay. And until the introduction of iTunes and other online pay services, which were a few years off, record companies were not profiting off the Internet.

It was a fumbling time, as companies sought out the new, still very much undefined path. In the midst of the uncertainty, DreamWorks did not abandon its core philosophy even as it took baby steps onto the Internet, signing deals with companies to create online music videos and creating a site where artists could submit their work. The label continued to push Furtado, who, by the end of 2000, was in the midst of a genuine breakthrough. Sales of *Whoa, Nelly!* were up to about twelve thousand copies a week from just four thousand when the album was first released. That number would quadruple over the following year, and in 2001 Furtado would take home a Grammy Award for Best Female Pop Vocal Performance for her single "I'm Like a Bird."

The new century looming ahead, DreamWorks barreled forward, for better or worse, firm in its belief that what had worked in the past would work in the future. Ostin and Waronker's tenets—that the artist comes first; that slow and steady wins the race—still reigned at the company, even as the surrounding landscape took on a drastically new hue.

24

ROCK AND ROLL

W**HAT IS THE NAME** of your fucking movie? I can't fucking market a movie that doesn't have a name!"

It was Terry Press calling. Cameron Crowe still hadn't decided what to call the film that DreamWorks was releasing in September of 2000, on the heels of its *Gladiator*-gilded summer. Crowe was the writer-director of films such as *Singles* and *Say Anything . . .* whose debut screenplay, *Fast Times at Ridgemont High,* graciously bestowed on cinema history the genre of surfer-stoner (in the character of Jeff Spicoli, as brought to the screen by Sean Penn). Crowe had been working on his new film ever since he'd arrived at DreamWorks as one of the studio's "big-name" talent deals three years earlier. Crowe didn't mind Press's bullying, according to a source close to him. He appreciated that she was one of the few people in Hollywood who said what she thought.

But Press's needling didn't change the fact that Crowe was genuinely vexed about what to call his film, which was based on his years as a teenage music critic for *Rolling Stone.* Even as the film began shooting in May 1999, it remained nameless, listed on DreamWorks production charts as simply "Untitled Cameron Crowe." Crowe, who in his early forties was still boyishly unassuming, with floppy brown hair and a slightly doughy face, was so desperate for ideas, he'd held an on-set contest asking for title suggestions. At one point, he considered calling it *Untitled.* That had a nice ring to it, he thought, and fit in with the film's musical theme.

The film was his follow-up to *Jerry Maguire,* which had grossed $273 million worldwide, been nominated for five Oscars, and positioned Crowe as the next James L. Brooks, a director who combined

poignancy and humor on a large—and very lucrative—scale. Everyone around the world had fallen in love with Tom Cruise's turn as
an amped-up sports agent. Naturally, DreamWorks was hoping that
Crowe's new film would have a similar effect and that it would go
down as the next entry in the company's roster of defining films.

To executives at DreamWorks, the lack of a title was yet another
mysterious detail surrounding a movie that had been veiled in secrecy from the start. Crowe's tendency was to hole up and write, never
showing anyone any pages of his scripts until they were completely
finished. On his new film, Crowe had been even more close-guarded,
as its subject was so personal. Even the soundtrack to the film was a
soul-baring exercise—Crowe and his wife, Nancy Wilson (one-half of
the band Heart), wrote many of the film's songs.

In the end, Crowe decided to call his movie *Almost Famous,* a title
that spoke to the bittersweet sentiment of what it's like to be so very
close to celebrity and yet so very far away. This is the feeling experienced by William Miller, Crowe's wide-eyed alter ego in the movie,
who finds himself transfixed by a world spinning dizzily on a triple
axis of 1970s-era sex, drugs, and rock 'n' roll.

The original draft of *Almost Famous* clocked in at 172 pages, or
about 50 pages longer than your typical screenplay. At Warner Bros.,
say, or Paramount, such a tome would inevitably elicit the order "cut!"
from a senior vice president of something or other. But at Dream-
Works, Spielberg loved every page of Crowe's script. His only instruc-
tion, in fact, was to not let anyone touch it—a comment that became
a sort of protective mantra for Crowe during production, whenever
executives tried to get involved and suggest changes. Spielberg's proc-
lamation kept even Walter Parkes at bay, a dynamic that, according to
a source, "created tension between Walter and Cameron. Walter likes
to pride himself in being Steven's right-hand man. He doesn't like it
when someone else inserts themselves between them."

DreamWorks exerted more muscle when it came to casting. When
Brad Pitt—whom Crowe desperately wanted to star as Russell Ham-
mond, the spaced-out lead guitarist of the fictional band Stillwa-
ter—wanted more than the $10 million DreamWorks was offering for
the role, the studio refused to budge. (Pitt had just received twice that
figure to star in David Fincher's *Fight Club* at Fox.) Geffen was called
in to mediate—he knew Pitt from *Interview with a Vampire* and Crowe

from his music days—but to no avail. In the end, the role went to Billy Crudup, a rising star. The rest of the cast included newbie Patrick Fugit as Miller; Kate Hudson as the sunny groupie, or "Band-Aid," as she describes herself in the film; and Frances McDormand as Miller's mother—who, when she drops her fifteen-year-old son off at a Black Sabbath concert, yells out the window of the family station wagon: "Don't take drugs!"

The latter casting decision caused some intrafamily tension between the Spielbergs and the Hankses, because Rita Wilson, Tom Hanks's wife, let it be known that she wanted to play Miller's mother. No one was quite sure how Wilson had got hold of the script, but it was suspected that Kate Capshaw had something to do with it. Spielberg did not apply pressure to cast his wife's friend, but it became a sticky situation when McDormand landed the role, and for a while there were fewer Spielberg-Hanks yacht trips.

Almost Famous began shooting just as Katzenberg stepped into what would be a brief stint running the live-action studio. By the time the film was released, he had returned his focus to the animation studio. *Almost Famous* was not a troubled production, but it caused a great deal of angst on all sides. For one thing, no one at the studio could understand why a "Billy Crudup movie"—with no major star and no special effects—was costing $60 million. From the studio's point of view, it should have cost half that. (In fact, it wasn't Crudup that was costing money, but the rights to music from legendary acts such as Led Zeppelin and the Allman Brothers Band, an A-list crew, and thousands of extras needed for concert scenes; Crowe's production-company overhead was also included in the budget.) There was also concern about Crowe's filmmaking process, which was to shoot an abundant amount of footage and edit it down during postproduction; in some cases, scenes had been shot with music to which DreamWorks did not have the rights. Spielberg, in particular—who edits in his head, leaving almost nothing for the cutting-room floor—thought Crowe was being wasteful and undisciplined, according to several sources. Throughout production, DreamWorks executives would give Crowe a list of scenes that they thought should be cut. In response, Crowe would make up his own list and cut those.

Pressure from DreamWorks, and from himself, made Crowe a bit of a wreck during the shoot, to the point that he told Michael Grillo,

DreamWorks' head of physical production, to stop coming to the set. Grillo's participation was just too nerve-racking for Crowe. Something else that was stress inducing was the idea of having executives weigh in on his movie (the first cut of which was four and a half hours long) after Crowe finished shooting. Thus, before anyone at Dream-Works was allowed to see the finished product, Crowe held a "friends and family" screening. As it happened, Mike Myers, who was doing voice work on *Shrek,* attended the exclusive screening, after which he reported back to Katzenberg and Geffen what he liked and didn't like about the film. The fact that the DreamWorks partners were hearing about their movie from an actor not even involved with the film did not win much love for Crowe.

Relations were smoothed when executives were finally given a glimpse of the film and were relieved to discover that Crowe had made a sweet and soulful coming-of-age story with endearing performances and a bass-heavy soundtrack. Still, the movie was too long, and Katzenberg spearheaded an effort to chop forty minutes of footage.

Crowe recognized that the film needed to be cut and that segments involving the characters' backstory were weighing the film down. When the original version had been test-screened, he said, "By the end, people were exhausted. The whole point of the movie was veering off the rails." But the trimmer version took away some of the film's breadth. In his original version, he said, there's "more of everybody's point of view—or more of a God's-eye view. You see all the lives. But when we cut it down, you basically see the kid."

Crowe ultimately lived with the edits, but it wasn't easy. "It's a personal thing," he said, "but the reason I wanted to make the move is the image of Kate Hudson's character dancing in the trash of the arena. It should have gone on longer, and that's my mistake—I cut it short. The whole battle when you're editing a movie is like when you're writing a piece: an editor says something isn't moving your piece along, and you go, 'Wait, that's the most important thing about it.' Someone will say, 'You're running behind. Do we really need Kate Hudson dancing in the trash?' These are the things I go to war over."

At the time *Almost Famous* was released, the three most frequently used words in the DreamWorks lexicon were *American Beauty* and *Gladiator.* These were the films that were held up as the templates of what

a DreamWorks film was, and each represented a particular formula
— the small, nuanced indie-like film; the big, swashbuckling epic — that
the studio applied. As for *Almost Famous,* it fell into the former category and was given what was known at the studio as the *"American
Beauty* treatment." That meant it was rolled out on a platform release,
opening on just 131 screens with the hope that audiences would grow
as word-of-mouth praise spread. (At its widest, the film was released
on 2,262 screens.) But unlike *American Beauty,* audiences for *Almost
Famous* did not grow, at least not very much, despite its being one of
the best-reviewed films of the year. In the end the movie made just $32
million, or half its production budget.

According to sources, Crowe was not happy with either Dream-
Works' distribution or marketing approach — he felt that the *"Gladiator* treatment" would have been a more appropriate way to approach
his movie; in other words, treating *Almost Famous* like a big, commercial movie and opening it, and selling it, as a wide release. There was
also a sense that *Gladiator,* which, by the fall, was essentially receiving a full-on second marketing campaign in the run-up to the Oscars,
was — still — consuming the studio's attention. At one test screening of
Almost Famous, Terry Press was heard on her cell phone saying, "It's
our best shot for the Academy Awards." She was talking about *Gladiator,* not *Almost Famous.*

DreamWorks executives say that it was aggressive in its marketing of *Almost Famous,* giving it the same push as *What Lies Beneath* —
which grossed a hefty $291 million worldwide — and doing things
such as holding 425 word-of-mouth screenings. But there were challenges. Unlike *Jerry Maguire,* which had the advantage of having one
of the biggest stars in the world — Tom Cruise — the biggest star of
Almost Famous was Crowe. In lieu of Crudup, Hudson, or McDormand's names — all respected actors but hardly considered major stars
at the time — posters for the film read: "By the writer-director of *Jerry
Maguire.*"

Whether or not Crowe's complaints were just sour grapes, *Almost
Famous* left him disillusioned with DreamWorks, and so, when his
contract was up, he left. By the time *Almost Famous* was released, he
was already in negotiations to reunite with Cruise on *Vanilla Sky* at
Paramount, where Cruise had his deal. Executives at DreamWorks
were "pissed," according to one source. "Their attitude was that they'd

given him this lavish deal, out of which all they got was one movie, and now he was ditching them."

Spielberg's low-key role at the company also apparently figured in Crowe's departure. Given that the DreamWorks pitch was all about "the opportunity to work with Steven Spielberg," directors and screenwriters were often disappointed to discover that "working with Spielberg" often meant working at a studio that Spielberg ran. It was, perhaps, unrealistic to think that someone as high profile and thinly stretched as Spielberg would be able to spend quality time with filmmakers, but that was the inevitable expectation.

Spielberg still championed filmmakers, and his blessing turned, overnight, a no-name actor or director into the most sought-after talent in Hollywood. He still read scripts and weighed in on dailies, and even provided tutelage, as he had with Sam Mendes on *American Beauty*. He still lit up cigars with fellow directors (something Kate Capshaw wouldn't let him do at home). But DreamWorks was far from being a Steven Spielberg mentorship program, in part, because, as one person said, "Steven is afraid to be seen as a director interfering with other directors." Out of respect, he let them do their thing. But if that was the reality, his partners, and DreamWorks executives, often oversold his role.

"His name was trotted out a lot more than he was," said one screenwriter. "'Steven thinks this. Steven wants you to do this.' It was a bit of the way they could get you to do things. The ideas of Steven were always present in the room, but Steven wasn't always present in the room."

By 2000, another DreamWorks selling point that didn't pan out was that screenwriters would be rewarded with gross points—something that had earned DreamWorks praise as a revolutionary studio when it was first announced. "After Jeffrey and Steven said it was going to be this fabulous back-end, when it came, it was a net back-end—garden-variety net back-end," said one attorney. "Adjusted gross after break-even, basically . . . There's nothing special about it. It may be slightly better [than other studios] in that you may get $10,000 from it, if you have a picture that does a billion dollars."

It wasn't for lack of trying—Spielberg and Parkes both championed the idea that screenwriters should share in the overall profits of their films. But by the time the details of the compensation strategy crossed Helene Hahn's desk, the deal was so watered down as to be meaningless. It was another Amblin-style vision that was at odds with a company that took so many cues from Disney.

It was also another example of DreamWorks not living up to the ideal as it had initially been presented to Hollywood. One writer who worked on films at the company in the early days told me: "I think some of us had this vision that DreamWorks would be what people had talked about United Artists being . . . where it's really a conglomeration of artists—where artists are as much a part of the family as the employees are—but it just isn't true. It's just another studio, really . . . That's the thing, I think, that was the most frustrating to people—they had this vision of this artist-driven company where it would be like a safe haven for other artists, but instead it was just another studio."

As a result, some early DreamWorks disciples began packing up and leaving. A few months after Crowe left, producer Mark Johnson signed a deal with the independent production company Intermedia, having found making movies under Parkes and MacDonald to be a grueling, and nearly impossible, process. Johnson had an especially bitter taste in his mouth after his experience on *An Everlasting Piece,* a movie that was released in December of 2000 and that resulted in one of the producers suing DreamWorks—claiming that the studio had dumped the film when it came to its marketing and release. (Dream-Works denied the allegations and the case was settled out of court.) He had also been disappointed by DreamWorks' marketing of *Galaxy Quest,* which he'd produced. But he was most upset about the process of getting films made at DreamWorks. Parkes and MacDonald, Johnson said, "didn't approve anything. It was impossible for me to develop things with Walter.

"Nobody was succeeding there," he continued. "You'd hear it from everybody—everybody who had deals there was really, really frustrated." The sentiment was, indeed, repeated by others I spoke with, who said that Parkes was chasing talent away and giving the live-action studio a negative reputation. Producers would find their scripts developed interminably and then not go anywhere. And those were projects that got a preliminary go-ahead; many more were flatly refused. Producers grew accustomed to being told "Walter doesn't like the concept" or "Walter's not interested" or "Walter wants to put a new writer on it."

As for writers, "The big thing at the time was, you can't work at DreamWorks because you're going to be rewritten by the guy who runs the studio," said one.

"It was more than just rewriting," this person said. "Walter really developed a script like it was his project. He had a tendency to not only rewrite but also to make people feel like they weren't empowered. He would tell people what to do a lot. Whereas Steven [Spielberg] doesn't . . . Because he didn't see himself as a studio executive, he saw himself more as a producer; he saw himself as a creative partner."

Around town, Parkes's reputation had become that of "the arsonist and the fireman," as one A-list director put it, meaning that he simultaneously created problems and pitched himself as the best one to solve them.

Parkes incited further rage when, in front of screenwriters, he and MacDonald would ask their precocious preteen son what he thought of a script. As one agent spewed: "It's narcissistic to a degree of narcissism that I couldn't possibly fathom! They're meeting with a writer who's getting paid hundreds of thousands of dollars a week, and they defer to their son!"

Parkes and MacDonald shrugged off such reactions, considering it typical hyperbole. They could even point to times their kids' insight had paid off. While screening footage for the ending of *Men in Black*, the couple's eleven-year-old daughter had wandered into the room and asked, "What's that?" When MacDonald explained that "that" was the film's menacing monster, the budding development girl replied, "He's cute. He looks like Audrey." Audrey was the family cat. MacDonald called director Barry Sonnenfeld, who had the creature redesigned.

"When a child can do it, you know it's not a business you need to take too seriously," MacDonald said.

Screenwriters' complaints about meddlesome forces are, of course, as old as the movie business itself. Producer David O. Selznick was famous for his pages-long memos on *Gone with the Wind*, a film he rewrote extensively, often composing scenes the night before they were shot. And Irving Thalberg and Darryl F. Zanuck were known for being heavy-handed with all aspects of production, driving screenwriters — and others — to madness.

Some writers admitted to liking Parkes's involvement, and the way he served as a sparring partner when it came to figuring out script issues. He was smart, and held the bar up high when it came to what was good enough. He was also willing to work doggedly to get a script into shape. "It's a horrible experience to feel like someone wants to open things up, and change the whole movie. Walter does that a lot, and it can be infuriating. But if you hang on, his process ultimately makes the movie better," said screenwriter Scott Frank.

On *Minority Report*, Frank said, "Walter was jumping in, trying to figure it out. It was a difficult story, we were trying to meld the sci-fi, cold aspect with more emotional things, and trying to make it fun. There were myriad challenges with that movie. It was so hard to write. And Walter hung in there. Steven was very involved, obviously, but Walter functioned as a producer of that movie. I never would have written anything nearly as satisfying if I didn't have Walter. I gave him pages, drafts, I was calling him up, saying I was stuck. He'd say, 'Come over, have lunch, let's talk about it.' We spent hundreds of hours on that script."

Parkes, Frank emphasized, "*does the work,*" something that could not be said of every producer. In the midst of rewriting *Minority Report*, Parkes had to fly up to visit the set of another DreamWorks movie. Frank came with him, and would work with Parkes in his trailer during whatever free time he had. After flying back to L.A., the two men were so caught up in the script that when the DreamWorks jet landed at Burbank, they both stayed in the plane, working furiously on the tarmac.

"That's the way Walter was; we were not getting off until we'd solved a major problem."

But there still weren't enough movies at DreamWorks. And if producers were blaming Parkes, DreamWorks executives pointed to other reasons. If the material that was being submitted to the studio was so good, why wasn't it going on to be made elsewhere, they wondered? They also note that while most studios have up to two dozen, or more, producer deals, DreamWorks had a fraction of that, due to its boutique size.

The problem, according to these executives, was that there were not enough big producer deals supplying movies. And hence, there were not enough movies.

Because of the cozy relationship between Spielberg and Zemeckis, the latter's company, ImageMovers, was receiving the bulk of the studio's production funds. Therein lay the problem. The more Dream-Works spent on ImageMovers, and the more ImageMovers wasn't making movies, the more resentment built up between the two companies.

Zemeckis, himself, wasn't so much the issue. He'd made *What Lies Beneath* (though DreamWorks executives were quick to remark that that film had been given to him by Spielberg) and brought Dream-Works in on the big Tom Hanks vehicle *Cast Away*, at Fox. But Image-Movers was supposed to have been about more than just Bob Zemeckis movies. That's why his former CAA agent, Jack Rapke, was being highly paid as part of ImageMovers' deal: to drum up material. And that's why DreamWorks had gone out of its way to make things pleasant for ImageMovers, even building the company a Tuscan-style villa on top of a hill overlooking Amblin, after Playa Vista fell through. Mark Johnson, who occupied space on the first floor of the building, along with the Shoah Foundation (ImageMovers got the whole upstairs), described the building as "bigger than a villa" and "really, pretty impressive." But under the deluxe surface, Rapke was miserable. None of the projects he pitched to DreamWorks was getting made, let alone accepted. "Years and years were going by, and nothing was happening," said one source, who said that Rapke was feeling "a lot of anxiety."

DreamWorks felt no more love for Rapke, or the projects he was submitting. "Jeffrey hated Jack. And Jack hated Jeffrey," said one source, who once overheard Katzenberg say, "I don't understand it. Jack was such a great agent, and he's such a lousy producer."

As far as DreamWorks was concerned, the only thing valuable about the ImageMovers deal was Bob Zemeckis; everything beyond "Bob Z" was extra padding, and a waste of money. "There was a lot of resentment and anger," said one DreamWorks source, describing the ImageMovers deal. Though, ironically, Spielberg—the reason the deal had been forged in the first place—had no idea things were growing so ugly. Clearly, it was not a subject anyone wanted to broach with him. But just how much longer it could be tolerated "for the sake of Steven" was the question. ImageMovers' deal wasn't up for another two years, but that was starting to seem like a very long time.

25

GOLDEN GLOW

I F THE *AMERICAN BEAUTY* Oscar campaign was all about building buzz slowly through word of mouth, and coyly engaging the
Academy's attention, the campaign for *Gladiator* was anything
but subtle. "*Gladiator* was marketed like Bill Doll used to market movies," consultant Dale Olson said, referring to the old-time press agent
who invented what was unapologetically known as stunt advertising,
and who once said, "We plan the publicity before we buy the property." (He was actually quoting the producer Mike Todd, with whom
he worked for decades.) When Doll, whose other clients included
Federico Fellini, Judy Garland, Ringling Bros. and Barnum and Bai-
ley Circus, and Silly Putty, was marketing *Around the World in Eighty
Days*, in 1957, he threw a party for eighteen thousand guests at Madison Square Garden; festivities included free booze, gifts for everyone,
and performing elephants. The night ended up being a debacle, but as
Doll said afterward, "Nobody's ever forgotten it."

DreamWorks had its own version of colossal parties that nobody,
hopefully, would forget. In November, *Gladiator* had been "show-
cased" at a weeklong run at a movie theater in Century City (located
in West L.A., the home of most Academy members) where, every
night, the film was introduced by one of the film's principals, from
Russell Crowe to director Ridley Scott, who was satellite-beamed-in
from Morocco, where he was shooting his next film. When Dream-
Works took out double-truck ads (at a cost of about $75,000 each) in
the *L.A. Times* to announce the screening, competitors' jaws dropped.

"They were spending *insanely*," one rival said. "Those ads were advertising a movie that was playing in *one* theater." (Normally, a double-truck ad promotes a movie that's playing in dozens of theaters.)
"Basically, they were doing a whole, second marketing campaign."

"The biggest asset on *Gladiator* was what it was—a picture that a vast number of people went to theaters to see," said Olson. "It was a big picture, and we emphasized its size and bigness. It was the first epic since *Ben-Hur*. We did everything to show its size." At the center of *Gladiator*'s second three-ring circus was Terry Press, who, it was clear by now, had not just matched Weinstein's Oscar high jinks, but was elbowing him out of the honor of owning awards season. Indeed, the name "Terry" now elicited as much shock and awe (and bitter sniping from rivals) as "Harvey" had five years earlier. Within the Academy, Press and Weinstein had become so notorious, and so synonymous with pushing the limits when it came to Oscar campaigns, that their tactics were referred to as "The Terry Rules" and "The Harvey Rules."

In 2000, however, it was Terry's rules, and Press herself, who was on top. For the second year in a row, Weinstein was coming up short on Oscar movies. The only Miramax film that even stood a shot was *Chocolat*, a fanciful picture in which Juliette Binoche wins over a stuffy French town with her confectionary arts. The film was considered sweet, no pun intended, but had received mixed reviews and ultimately seemed too slight to be a real awards contender. Not that Weinstein wasn't trying to muscle it into greatness. After screening the film at the United Nations, he'd wangled endorsements from Jesse Jackson and Abraham Foxman of the Anti-Defamation League, who praised the film for its anti-prejudice message. As recounted in *Down and Dirty Pictures*, when Lisa Schwarzbaum of *Entertainment Weekly* was quoted in *USA Today* calling Foxman a "flack" for the movie, Weinstein grew enraged and called Schwarzbaum's editor to complain. He also cornered Schwarzbaum at Sundance, and threatened: "I can make life difficult for you."

Press had her own tactics, some of which drew rebukes from the Academy. When DreamWorks, in its effort to send subliminal messages to Academy members, made a TV spot for *Gladiator* featuring a golden statuette in the background, the Academy ordered that the spot be removed and docked DreamWorks four of its designated twenty Oscar tickets.

But if DreamWorks was successfully selling *Gladiator*, the studio was having more trouble with Crowe, who, having smiled for the cameras, was now resistant to being paraded all over town in a quest for more awards. Having just wrapped another film, *Proof of Life*, Crowe was eager to return home to Australia and not have to schmooze Academy members and journalists at cocktail parties.

"They kept asking him for more, and he kept pushing back," said one source. "He was basically being a surly SOB."

The situation worsened when Crowe's romance with Meg Ryan on the set of *Proof of Life* blew up in the press, where the hero of *Gladiator* was suddenly the home-wrecker of America's sweetheart couple. (Ryan announced that she was leaving her husband, Dennis Quaid.) Desperate to airbrush *Gladiator*'s star marketing tool, Katzenberg was called on to intervene, and he told Crowe, "Look, we need you. We can't do this without you. This is your movie."

When Crowe was in Rome doing publicity for *Proof of Life*, Katzenberg called him on his cell phone. Crowe was on the way to the airport, but Katzenberg didn't care.

"Stop the car," Katzenberg instructed. "Turn around and go back to the Colosseum and take a picture of yourself in front of it."

Crowe did as he was told, and DreamWorks was delighted when the photo made it onto the AP wire and showed up all over the media.

When the Oscar nominations were announced in February 2001, DreamWorks dominated, with *Gladiator* racking up twelve nominations. The only film that even came close to that number was Sony Pictures Classics' Chinese-language martial arts fantasy, *Crouching Tiger, Hidden Dragon*, directed by Ang Lee, which nabbed ten. But seeing as everyone assumed that *Crouching Tiger* would win for Best Foreign Language Film, *Gladiator* became the movie to beat.

But in the coming weeks, as the never-ending, pre-Oscar-awards shows unfolded, *Gladiator*'s fate became less certain. At the guild awards ceremonies, the movie was practically shut out. The Directors Guild of America chose Lee for *Crouching Tiger* over Scott. The Screen Actors Guild gave its top honor to Benicio del Toro of *Traffic*, Steven Soderbergh's kinetic drug-world tapestry that was released by USA Films. And the Writers Guild went for Stephen Gaghan (*Traffic*), and Kenneth Lonergan, who wrote the indie darling *You Can Count on Me*. Only the Producers Guild chased *Gladiator*.

"We lost a few awards early on, and so we didn't expect to win," said producer Douglas Wick. "It looked like it would maybe tip the other way, to *Traffic*."

DreamWorks' luck turned at the Golden Globes, where *Gladiator* won Best Drama. Icing was added to the cake when *Almost Famous* beat out *Chocolat* in the Best Comedy/Musical category, a fact that drove Weinstein wild. (Adding to his fury was the fact that Binoche lost out to Renée Zellweger in *Nurse Betty*.) After the ceremony, Weinstein gathered his publicity troops in the lobby of the Beverly Hilton Hotel for a public flogging.

Despite a Globes victory (and another at the British Academy of Film and Television Arts), by the eve of the Academy Awards, no one at DreamWorks was willing to assume anything. The memory of *Saving Private Ryan* was still resonant. An upset was never out of the question. As Press told the *Los Angeles Times:* "I do not think anyone goes into the Oscars expecting a sweep. That would be moronic."

On the long-awaited night of March 25, by the time Michael Douglas stepped forward to announce the big winner of the night, DreamWorks was no closer to any kind of assuredness. *Gladiator, Traffic,* and *Crouching Tiger* had each won four awards. Crowe had won Best Actor, but *Gladiator*'s other wins were in more minor categories, such as costume design and special effects.

"We were just sitting there thinking, 'Who the hell knows?'" David Franzoni said. "We weren't waiting to go up."

When Douglas—who, as a member of the *Traffic* cast, had somewhat of a bias—opened the envelope, he did a double take.

Then: "*Gladiator!*"

Wick, Branko Lustig, and Franzoni rose out of their seats, stopping to hug Crowe as they made their way up to the podium.

For Press, the night was even more a vindication than the previous year had been. Not only did DreamWorks take home the night, but for the first time in years, Miramax walked away with zero statues. Someone who seemed to have complicated feelings about it all, however, was Parkes.

"One of Walter's greatest bitternesses is that he didn't get any credit on *Gladiator*," said one source, who said that Parkes, who received an executive-producer tag on *Gladiator,* "was producing that movie." Thus, when he wasn't made a producer (which would have meant an Oscar), "he felt ripped off. He got nothing, no credit. He never said anything, but after that movie I noticed a difference in him. He was more focused on getting recognized for the work he'd done."

(Others, however, scoff at this notion, saying that Parkes was simply doing his job as head of the studio. A very good job, certainly, but not that of a filmmaker.)

Parkes and MacDonald's new deal to produce movies for Dream-Works in a more official capacity would assure that this happened—and it was no coincidence that the deal was signed the same month that *Gladiator* was released.

Later in the night, at DreamWorks' own party, hastily organized at Dominick's in West Hollywood once it was clear the night could be called victorious, Press waltzed in carrying the next day's edition of *Variety* with the *Gladiator* headlines. Wick and his wife, Lucy Fisher, were late because their limo driver had mistakenly driven them to the airport. Geffen was wandering around in a T-shirt and jeans. Katzenberg was already talking about *Gladiator 2*. Crowe—who was flying back to New Jersey the following morning to return to the set of *A Beautiful Mind*, another Universal-DreamWorks coproduction—showed up after midnight for a quick appearance and then headed back to his hotel room for a more private soiree. And Spielberg was all aglow, thanking everyone in sight.

"Steven was fantastic," Franzoni said. "He said, 'Look, you know the reason we're all here is because of you.' I said, 'Well, thank you. But, you know, Steven, let's give credit where credit's due. Nobody would have made this movie but you.' And he said, 'Well, that's because we're insane.' I said, 'Yeah, I realize that. You have to be insane to be an artist.' So there were some really good vibes."

The following summer, having traded in his uniform of white T-shirt, dark V-neck sweater, and khakis for a tuxedo, Jeffrey Katzenberg slipped into his seat at the Palais des Festivals, which serves as the epicenter of the Cannes Film Festival. Poised between the glittering blue waters of the Mediterranean and the bustling Croisette—Cannes' main drag—the Palais is where the world's most admired filmmakers have been paid their respects after winning the Palme d'Or award, perhaps the only piece of hardware as prestigious as an Oscar. In 1960 the golden, frond-shaped statuette was awarded to Federico Fellini for *La Dolce Vita*; in 1967 Michelangelo Antonioni's *Blow-Up* was anointed; and in 1979 it was Francis Ford Coppola's *Apocalypse Now*.

Now, on the evening of May 12, 2001, DreamWorks' latest animated movie, *Shrek*—a cartoon about an ugly, insecure green ogre who lives in a swamp—was competing for the golden palm. As Katzenberg sat in the darkened theater, he knew he was either going to be the laughingstock of the most famous film festival in the world or its most unlikely hero. And this time it would be more personal than ever—*Shrek* was the first film Katzenberg took a full producer credit on. Katzenberg was partly reassured by the fact that Thierry Frémaux, Cannes' new artistic director, had confidence in *Shrek* and had selected it for the festival after screening it in January—the first time an animated American film had been chosen since 1953, when *Peter Pan* screened on the Riviera.

Frémaux, a forty-year-old progressive-minded Frenchman, was looking to do away with criticism that films at Cannes were inaccessible and esoteric. To this end, in the last year he'd traveled to Hollywood twice to meet with executives at major studios. The result: not only was *Shrek* screening on the Riviera; so, too, were American films such as Baz Luhrmann's *Moulin Rouge!*, David Lynch's *Mulholland Dr.*, and Joel and Ethan Coen's *The Man Who Wasn't There.*

But unlike those films, all of which had serious artistic cred, albeit of the Yankee sort, *Shrek* was a cartoon. With a lot riding on it. While DreamWorks' live-action studio was basking in its second-in-a-row Oscar win, the animation studio was still recovering from *El Dorado*. Six years in, Katzenberg had yet to prove he could reignite animation as he had at Disney.

As the theater quieted and *Shrek* flashed up on the screen, the audience of four thousand cineastes was immediately alerted that this was not your standard Cannes film. Digitally animated mud splattered across the screen, forming the word "Shrek" as the boppy rock song "All Star" by Smash Mouth blasted into the cavernous room. When the paunchy green ogre made his debut, he demonstratively picked a wedgie before plunging into a pond of water and letting out a flatulent explosion. He then smiled dreamily and, Austin Powers–like, rested his pinkie on the corner of his mouth.

Seated with Katzenberg in the audience were Mike Myers, codirectors Andrew Adamson and Vicky Jenson, and producer Aron Warner, who later recalled, "As soon as Shrek jumped in the water and farted, I know I put my head in my hands."

"Here we are, sitting in tuxedos and evening gowns, wearing borrowed jewels, and everyone's watching Shrek take a poot in the water," said Jenson.

But Katzenberg's mind was on other things. As the movie rolled, he noticed that *nobody was laughing.* "For the first ten minutes—nothing," Katzenberg recalled. "My heart was thumping, my forehead was breaking out in a sweat. I said to myself, 'They're going to burn the place down.'"

Eventually, the crowd thawed and began to ease into the picture. There were some chuckles, and then heartier laughs. By the end, the audience had been completely won over and stood up for a standing ovation—a rare triumph at Cannes.

Katzenberg had come to Cannes and conquered. He would not be a laughingstock, after all. *Shrek* was instantly lauded for its technical advancements in CGI and for its story mixing heartfelt warmth with hip humor. Critic Roger Ebert, mostly disappointed with the American offerings, wrote in the *Chicago Sun-Times* that *Shrek* was a "delightful animated feature from DreamWorks" that "generated great enthusiasm from audiences, who were surprised at the way it layers its story with elements of satire."

If Cannes was any indication, when *Shrek* opened a week later, on May 18, Katzenberg's comeback—after years of a faltering post-Disney existence—would be confirmed.

Considering how Katzenberg and Co. would come to dominate the Croisette in subsequent years, the *Shrek* entourage was relatively small. Myers was the only talent on hand. There were no crazy publicity stunts, no outrageous parties of the kind the studio would become famous for in later years.

Another reason the *Shrek* contingent was so lean was that certain people who'd been involved in the film, such as Sandra Rabins and Penney Finkelman Cox, were no longer at DreamWorks, having left the studio following a falling-out with Katzenberg. The blowup had occurred when Katzenberg told them that after *Shrek*, he wanted them to produce *Sinbad*, a traditionally animated version of the Arabian Nights tale. By this point, seven years into DreamWorks, Rabins and Finkelman Cox were still holding on to their dream of producing live-action movies together, seeing as they'd fulfilled their duty of helping Katzenberg build up the animation studio. That had always been the agreed-upon deal—they'd help build animation and then, in return, Katzenberg would let them go produce live-action movies. But Katzenberg, whatever he'd said, no longer saw it that way; he wanted them to stay at the studio and keep making animated films, *Sinbad* among them.

"Jeffrey gave us an ultimatum," said Finkelman Cox. "He said, 'You have to step in and produce *Sinbad,* and I want you to give up your live-action deal because you can't be tweeners' [i.e., produce both animated and live-action films]. Originally, he said we could be tweeners."

Feeling that Katzenberg hadn't kept his promise, the women decided it was time to step down. (To fill the void, Lance Young, a live-action executive at Warner Bros., was hired as head of creative development at the studio, and Bill Damaschke, a Disney alumnus who had been at DreamWorks since 1995, was promoted to head production.)

The fact that Rabins was leaving (Finkelman Cox stayed on to work on *Over the Hedge,* an animated film that had been pitched by her husband, screenwriter Brian Cox) was a significant rupture, considering that Rabins had been one of Katzenberg's most trusted lieutenants for so many years, and had been a key person in getting DreamWorks up and running. According to one source, "Jeffrey only cared about three people: Helene [Hahn], Terry [Press], and Sandy—and talent, whom he respected. It gave him an ounce of humanity. He didn't care a thing about anyone else."

But however much Rabins's leaving hurt Katzenberg, he saw it as a betrayal—especially when, months later, she was hired by Sony to start up an animation division at that studio, where Finkelman Cox would join her. And as he dealt with any betrayal, he cut the women off. There were no warm goodbyes, no thank-yous—and no plane ticket to Cannes.

Shrek grossed $42 million its first weekend—the biggest ever for a DreamWorks movie. It would go on to haul in $267 million in the U.S. and $484 million worldwide. *Shrek* might not quite be *The Lion King,* but it was close enough. Reviews were rapturous.

In the *L.A. Times,* Kenneth Turan called *Shrek* "a gleeful piece of wisenheimer computer animation" that is "all comic attitude, all the time. Casual, carefree, consistently amusing, it plays a lot like the earlier *Aladdin*."

Variety's Todd McCarthy called *Shrek* "an instant animated classic . . . for animation fans to cherish as well as one that non-enthusiasts can enjoy." The movie became not only Katzenberg's biggest, and most profitable, DreamWorks animated movie, it was DreamWorks' biggest, most profitable movie to date. Unlike live-action hits such as *Saving Private Ryan, Gladiator,* and *Cast Away, Shrek* was not sharing profits with other studios. Furthermore, there were no gross players to pay out—Myers, Murphy, and Diaz had been paid modest upfront fees ($350,000 each), though Katzenberg rewarded them all with bonuses the weekend after the movie opened. Myers and Murphy each received $12 million. Diaz, a lesser star, got around $5 million. The film wrought so much green for the company—which had bled through $115 million in 2000, thanks to *The Road to El Dorado*—that, for the first time in DreamWorks' history, executives received bonuses. (Laurie MacDonald, who'd brought the property to the company and passed it on to Katzenberg, received an extra, *extra* something in her paycheck.) As more than one person remarked, "*Shrek* saved DreamWorks."

Naturally, a sequel was green-lighted, though this one would be a bit more costly. To keep his stars onboard, Katzenberg paid Diaz, Murphy, and Myers $10 million each for what would amount to about a week's worth of voice work.

For people at PDI, the bonuses went a small way toward compensating them for their own unhappiness when in February of 2000 DreamWorks bought out Carl Rosendahl's majority-stake interest in the company and renamed the studio DreamWorks/PDI. The sale left many people in Northern California disgruntled. Employees felt that Rosendahl had undervalued PDI and sold it to DreamWorks for too low a price, which in effect devalued stock shares. According to one high-level source, Rosendahl sold PDI for about $38 million. From the PDI perspective, the company was second only to Pixar when it came to CGI feature animation, and at the time, Pixar was valued to be worth over $1 billion.

"It was kind of a slap in the face, really," said animator Noel McGinn. "A lot of people were very upset about it. A lot of these guys were programmers, and in Silicon Valley they could have gone to work for another company that had real stock and become a millionaire.

"We were worth what Pixar was worth. We had a production team as good as any in the business." (In 2006 Pixar would be sold to Disney for $7.4 billion.) PDI executives blamed the deal on Rosendahl, saying he was in over his head when it came to bargaining with players like Katzenberg, a situation not helped by the fact that he was eager to sell his company and move on.

"Valuations are a really difficult thing to do," Rosendahl said in response to the criticism. "We had a third party come in [and determine the price]. You know, Pixar had a record—they'd released films that were out there . . . I stand by it. It was a fair valuation."

The purchase of PDI affirmed Katzenberg's confidence in CGI in general, and in *Shrek* in particular. But at the same time, Katzenberg was not yet willing to throw in the towel on his first love: traditionally drawn animation. The studio still had two 2-D animation releases in the pipeline—*Spirit* and *Sinbad*—and despite the debacle of *El Dorado*, Katzenberg remained a devoted supporter of the traditional art he'd been schooled in at Disney.

To Katzenberg's delight, as *Shrek* continued to power through the summer—outperforming everything in its wake, including live-action blockbusters like Paramount's *Lara Croft: Tomb Raider* and Universal's *The Mummy Returns*—Disney was drowning in it.

Just months before, Michael Eisner had predicted that Disney's Jerry Bruckheimer/Michael Bay World War II epic *Pearl Harbor* would be "the biggest movie of the summer." Accordingly, Disney had spent tens of millions of dollars marketing the movie—one stunt was to fly a hundred journalists to Hawaii to attend the film's premiere aboard a hulking Navy ship, whose decks were flanked with lei-draped stars such as Ben Affleck, Jennifer Garner, and Alec Baldwin. Despite all the Hawaiian-style hoopla, when *Pearl Harbor* opened on May 25, it proved a disappointment. Having cost $150 million to produce and tens of millions of dollars to market, it went on to gross $198 million in the U.S. and $449 million worldwide. Big, perhaps, but not the biggest.

Disney's animated offering for the summer of 2001—the traditionally animated *Atlantis: The Lost Empire*—was also a letdown when it came out on June 8. Having cost $120 million, the film grossed $84 million in the U.S. and $186 million worldwide. Needless to say, it was no *Shrek*.

Adding to the turmoil at the Mouse House, Peter Schneider, Katzenberg's erstwhile colleague turned rival, who'd segued from running animation to overseeing Disney's film studio when Joe Roth left in January of 2000, was stepping down, having decided to return to work in theater in New York.

DreamWorks wasn't just trouncing Disney, the studio was trouncing Hollywood, as *Shrek* continued to rack up grosses, officially becoming the top-grossing film of the summer.

If Katzenberg was to have a post-Disney coronation, a moment when he was glorified not for his past but for his present, it was now. *Shrek* shut up the naysayers who'd watched, with dwindling confidence, as Katzenberg tried to find his footing, his identity, really, with non-Disney movies such as *The Prince of Egypt* and *El Dorado*. Until now, it had been out of his grasp. But no longer. Even within DreamWorks, Katzenberg's status was elevated. Animation was now the company's breadwinner and, as such, Katzenberg was given more leeway. From *Shrek* onward, Spielberg, as well as Parkes and MacDonald, tended to weigh in less on Katzenberg's animated films. "In the early days, pre-*Shrek*, Steven would go to screenings of animated films with Walter and Laurie," said one former DreamWorks employee. "When *Shrek* hit, Jeffrey was able to distance himself" from the live-action brass.

But even with Katzenberg's biggest, by far, success since Disney, he wasn't jumping on the tables, the way he had back in *Lion King* days. Katzenberg had always been controlled about his emotions, to the point of seeming rather emotion*less*. Even during the legal drama with Eisner, he'd kept himself together.

One colleague of Katzenberg's recalled how cool he had remained during the trial, even when Eisner made his famously disparaging remarks about his former underling. "I would be so devastated that I'd given twenty years of my life to this guy, and he saw me as this thing on his pompom," this person said. "I would have gone home and I probably would not have been able to leave the house.

"But Jeffrey doesn't process that kind of stuff. He operates in such control; he will not let himself get really down, and he won't let himself get really high. Even after *Shrek,* it was more like, 'Yeah, this is great. Thanks.' No extreme."

Another company that did well by *Shrek* was Universal, which had re-upped its distribution arrangement with DreamWorks in April, just before *Shrek* was released. The renewal of vows with Universal had been a surprising, eleventh-hour development, considering that a year earlier Universal's parent company, Vivendi, had made it clear that it had no interest in continuing its distribution relationship with SKG.

DreamWorks had subsequently approached other suitors, finding only one that was willing to forge a partnership: Warner Bros.

But at the last minute, the deal stalled. According to DreamWorks, the point, or person, of contention was Warren Lieberfarb, then head of Warner's video operations. When it was clear Lieberfarb was not going to give Katzenberg as much control as he wanted over Dream-Works' home-video releases, Katzenberg and Geffen had a change of heart.

In the midst of haggling with Universal brass, Katzenberg gave a strategic interview to *Le Figaro*—Vivendi's hometown newspaper—saying that there had been a "huge misunderstanding" between Universal and DreamWorks, and made it clear that, despite talks with other studios, DreamWorks remained open to other suitors.

The plant was effective—the story reached Vivendi Universal co-chief executive operating officer Pierre Lescure, who said, "When I read what Jeffrey said about [Universal], I thought it was a pity not to renew the deal."

Amends were soon made on the home front, as well. On the Friday before the Easter weekend, Katzenberg and Universal president and COO Ron Meyer had breakfast at the Bel-Air Hotel, where Katzenberg aired his grievances with Warner's and told Meyer things didn't look good.

"What are the terms of the deal?" Meyer asked.

When Katzenberg told him, Meyer realized they were much lower than what DreamWorks had originally proposed to Universal, and he said, "I'll make that deal."

Over the course of Easter weekend—unbeknownst to Warner Bros. —Universal and DreamWorks huddled in their attorneys' offices and hammered out a deal in which Universal loaned DreamWorks

$250 million and agreed to distribute the studio's movies overseas and its home-video releases around the world for another five years.

For the first time in the Academy Awards' history, a new category had been added to the 2002 Oscar race: Best Animated Feature. Katzenberg himself had led the charge to create the category. It wasn't hard to understand why: an Oscar win not only boosted box-office grosses, but justified success like nothing else in Hollywood. No one understood this better than Katzenberg, who had never been directly responsible for a golden statuette. For all of DreamWorks' Oscar wins—*Saving Private Ryan, American Beauty, Gladiator*—none were films that had Katzenberg's creative stamp. This was not the case, of course, with *Shrek*.

The only thing that stood in Katzenberg's way was Pixar, seeing as, by the end of 2001, *Shrek* and *Monsters, Inc.* had emerged as not only the top-grossing animated films of the year, but the best reviewed. (*Shrek* finished the year as the third-highest-grossing film of the year, after *Harry Potter and the Sorcerer's Stone* and *Lord of the Rings: The Fellowship of the Ring*.) A showdown was an absolute certainty.

As Katzenberg was riding high on *Shrek*, the live-action studio was striking out again, the afterglow of *Gladiator*'s Oscar triumph having quickly faded. In June, Spielberg's eagerly awaited *Artificial Intelligence: A.I.* (which was released by Warner Bros. domestically) missed the mark, grossing $78 million in the U.S. on a budget of $100 million. Although Spielberg was given props for making a creatively brave film and for moving beyond his comfort zone in an effort to embrace Stanley Kubrick's original vision, even executives at DreamWorks had feared early on that the two-and-a-half-hour-long movie was "a mess," according to one. But, per protocol when it came to Spielberg, they'd kept mum, fearing upsetting him with unpleasant news.

Critics were sharply divided over the film. *The New Yorker*'s David Denby called *A.I.* "an extraordinarily accomplished movie, but a failure."

A *New York Times* article posed the question: "Is it the worst movie ever made?" Although the *Times'* reviewer, A. O. Scott, called *A.I.* "the best fairy tale—the most disturbing, complex, and intellectually challenging boy's adventure story Mr. Spielberg has made."

What no one was conflicted about was that, business-wise, *A.I.* was very much a failure. Spielberg's noble desire to push himself in a more nuanced, personal, and sophisticated direction was continuing to hurt DreamWorks' bottom line.

In TV, Mr. Spielberg was having better luck. When *Band of Brothers,* his and Tom Hanks's World War II collaboration, was released in September, it garnered rave reviews and ranked as HBO's second-most-watched show after *The Sopranos,* despite the fact that viewership was hurt by the terrorism attacks of September 11. HBO had rolled out the red carpet for the maestro: *Band of Brothers'* production budget was $120 million (twice what *Saving Private Ryan* had cost), plus another $15 million in marketing. It was all deemed worth it, when the series was a hit.

Parkes and MacDonald had failed to keep up the momentum after a robust 2000: *A.I.* was one of just five films on the 2001 live-action slate. Adding to the drought, *Road to Perdition,* a $90 million epic directed by Sam Mendes, which was dripping with A-list talent (Tom Hanks, Paul Newman), was being held for a 2002 release. Originally planned as a 2001 film, *Road* was put on the back burner out of deference to *A Beautiful Mind,* the Ron Howard–directed, Universal-DreamWorks coproduction based on the life of the mathematical genius John Nash, played by Russell Crowe, which was due out in December.

The fluctuating fortunes of the live-action studio drew interest from observers, not so much because it was uncommon in Hollywood, but because such highs and, especially, lows were more problematic at a studio that was not buoyed by a corporate parent or a steadfast revenue stream. As Peter Bart wrote in *Variety,* "Has DreamWorks really been managed for profit or for more exotic aims?" Referring to the *Gladiator* Oscar win, he went on to ask, "Amid all its glory, has DreamWorks quietly lost its way?" Bart was referring to the company's up-and-down film slate and the fact that, six years in, most of its ancillary ambitions had been curbed. He also remarked that, "DreamWorks still runs counter to the conventional wisdom about show business. It controls no vast library, no theme parks, no global distribution mechanism. At a moment in time when everyone obsesses about the wafer-thin profits of the film business, DreamWorks essentially remains a pure film play."

In response to such questions, *Shrek* was the most resounding answer DreamWorks had produced yet as to why it was too early to count the studio out. Despite a dim live-action slate, at the end of 2001, *Shrek* pushed DreamWorks' revenues past the $2 billion mark for the first time in its history. Profits exceeded $100 million and debt dipped below $200 million from a high of almost $1 billion. DreamWorks might be a pure film play, but it was suddenly a very lucrative one.

IV

CLOSE-UP

26

THE MOTORCYCLE DIARIES

IT IS NOT UNLIKELY that Michael De Luca was the first Dream-Works employee to say, upon being asked in the middle of a meeting why he looked so tired: "Courtney Love and Winona Ryder came over last night at 2 A.M., and I couldn't get them to leave."

For the thirty-six-year-old De Luca, scenarios involving beautiful divas, at hours when most studio executives were tucked beneath their six-hundred-thread-count sheets, were just another day in the life. To DreamWorks' live-action executives, almost all of whom were male and in their early thirties, De Luca's life was fabulous and envy-inspiring: when he arrived at DreamWorks in June of 2001 as president of production under Walter Parkes and Laurie MacDonald, it was like a rock star had driven through the Amblin gates. Fittingly, De Luca drove through them on a motorcycle.

De Luca, a Hollywood wunderkind who'd made his name at New Line Cinema, where he'd become president at age twenty-eight, was DreamWorks' latest solution to the perennial problem of not enough movies. Geffen had first called, and then Katzenberg had wooed, the dark-haired boy wonder—who, in his trademark uniform of blue jeans and black T-shirts, looked like a new-age Fonz, only buffer—after he'd been fired from New Line following a sixteen-year stint. Overnight, the hot-hot De Luca, who'd championed artistically daring filmmakers such as Paul Thomas Anderson (*Boogie Nights*, *Magnolia*), and realized that the TV comedian Jim Carrey was a movie star, casting him in *The Mask*, went cold with Warren Beatty's *Town & Country* and *Little Nicky*, with Adam Sandler. In January of 2001—to much shock in Hollywood and tears at New Line—he was fired.

De Luca at DreamWorks wasn't the likeliest of unions. De Luca's taste was alternately edgy and übercommercial, neither of which quite fit the DreamWorks' mold, which, at its best, was about being prestigious. De Luca's personal style was also a bit wilder than those who worked at the family-oriented DreamWorks, with its daycare center and resident dog walker. De Luca, who'd famously been involved in an *in flagrante* fellatio incident at agent turned producer Arnold Rifkin's pre-Oscar party, wouldn't be needing either service. Terry Press's comment when she heard about the new hire was: "I wonder if we'll have to tell him there's no happy hour here."

But De Luca was a beloved figure around town and with artists, something that DreamWorks badly needed in the live-action studio, given the frustration over Parkes. His sensibility, which Katzenberg told him he "loved" and "needed" at DreamWorks, would complement those of Parkes and MacDonald, who were busy producing big-budget prestige pictures. Katzenberg, meanwhile, was ready to hand over the reins of the live-action studio. Many felt that, unsurprisingly, given his ultraefficient nature, Jeffrey had grown frustrated during his short stint at live action. In the beginning, he'd say in meetings, with willful enthusiasm, "Let's try and get Walter and Laurie to do *this!*" But eventually he gave up and was ready to pass on the responsibility of ironing out the studio's dysfunction.

Katzenberg was also presumably ready to beat it out of live action given that, though he'd been successful in getting more movies made, they included some rather major flops. There had been the lackluster *The Mexican*, and the even bigger money-loser *The Legend of Bagger Vance*. Another dud, *Evolution*, had also been made on his watch, though Parkes had been involved in that film, laboriously working on several drafts of its script.

When Katzenberg had called on De Luca to take over, De Luca had his own reservations, specifically "the Walter issue," as one source put it. He wondered just how much power he would actually have, given Parkes's controlling style. (Others approached to run the studio, such as Warner Bros. president Jeff Robinov, demurred on that very basis.) The Bob Cooper experiment had been a failure, even if good movies had come of it. But Katzenberg had assured De Luca that it was only a matter of time before Parkes and MacDonald stepped down. After a year, the couple would be transitioning out of the executive ranks.

It all sounded reasonable. And the fact of the matter was that De Luca was less "hot" these days, and no one else was calling with a job.

New Line was offering him a $100 million production deal, but staying on at the studio in a less exalted producer role seemed wrong. So he said yes to Jeffrey.

Not that he wasn't excited to work at DreamWorks. One producer friend of De Luca's said that he was "starry-eyed and eager to work at a place that had promises of greatness—there was the idea you'd be working with the single most talented filmmaker in the world."

The idea of De Luca at DreamWorks sent shock waves through Hollywood. No one could help wonder how the guy who held court at Chaya Brasserie—New Line's virtual commissary, where the leggy waitresses all fawned over the coolest studio exec in town—would mesh with his new home, and especially with Parkes, given their divergent styles. Besides the obvious superficial differences between the two—one person described the contrast as a "shot of Jäger" versus a "shot of milk"—De Luca's approach was nothing like Parkes's. Willing to fight like a dog to get a director hired, or a movie green-lighted, once all the pieces were in place, De Luca begged off. He let filmmakers do their thing. *Austin Powers* producer Jennifer Todd recalled working with De Luca on the Vin Diesel thriller *Boiler Room* at New Line, and how, after calling him on a Friday to make a plea for a green light on the movie, De Luca got back to her the following Monday.

Todd recalled: "He called me and said, 'Are you going to be there 24/7?' I said, 'Yeah.' 'And the director's not going to fuck up?' 'No.' And he said, 'OK, you can make the movie.' And the next time he got involved was in post [production]."

Furthermore, executives under Parkes understood their boss's narrow taste range and knew better than to even bother trying to pitch him a lowbrow movie. As one former executive said to me, "If you brought up a genre action movie in a meeting—forget it."

And now, the guy behind not just *The Mask*, but *Rush Hour* and *Austin Powers* was moving in. The town held its breath.

By the time he took the job at DreamWorks, De Luca had dialed back his life quite a bit. Friends say that his expulsion from New Line had a serious effect on him, and he was determined to turn over a new leaf. Things hit a low when he received a DUI and had his license revoked, meaning that he had to travel either by motorcycle or black town car—a mode of transport that only enforced his rock star image.

De Luca had always been laid-back, but at DreamWorks, he gave off an even more mellow vibe. Now, instead of heading out to clubs or parties in the Hollywood Hills after work, he went home and worked out with his yoga instructor, named Happy, and personal trainer.

When producers stopped by his new office, they assumed they'd walked into the wrong room. Unlike his New Line lair, which one producer described as "totally rock 'n' roll"—the place was more like a college dorm, with posters of movies (*Menace II Society*) and grunge bands (Cold), and a littering of *Austin Powers* toys—De Luca's Dream-Works office was sparklingly spartan, with two coffee-table books decorously arranged on a low table that was so clean you could have eaten off of it. It didn't seem in any way reflective of the guy who'd once said, "Some days, I feel like P. T. Barnum, but with a better circus. And bad days, I feel like Fatty Arbuckle, but with better lawyers."

At DreamWorks, De Luca spoke regularly with Katzenberg, in some cases pitching projects to Katzenberg and Parkes simultaneously. He communicated less with Spielberg (and even less with Geffen), but when Spielberg discovered that De Luca shared his obsession with sci-fi and fantasy movies, he would call to rhapsodize, say, about a *Twilight Zone* episode. De Luca would pick up immediately on what Spielberg was describing, and chime in—"Oh, yeah, episode 23!"

Spielberg also liked that having De Luca at DreamWorks occasioned visits from filmmakers such as Paul Thomas Anderson, and when the *Boogie Nights* writer-director stopped by De Luca's office, Spielberg swung by and sat down for a lively chat. But whatever interests the two men shared, it was clear to De Luca that only one person at DreamWorks had Spielberg's ear, and that was Parkes.

As De Luca settled in to his scrupulous new quarters, Parkes and MacDonald were busy with a number of films they were producing under their new contract, such as the $80 million sci-fi film *The Time Machine*, a particularly troublesome project whose director, Simon Wells, was ultimately replaced by Gore Verbinski.

Then there was *The Ring*, based on the Japanese horror film *Ringu*, about a cursed videotape that upends the lives of a single mother (played by Naomi Watts) and her son. The film had been brought to the studio in January of 2001 by executives turned producers Roy Lee and Mike Macari—Macari had passed on a copy of the Japanese film to DreamWorks executive Mark Sourian, who'd watched it with Lee at

Sourian's West Hollywood apartment. They were scared out of their minds by the time the credits rolled—"We were like two kids watching the movie," Lee said. "And at the end, when [the spirit] comes out, we literally jumped out of our seats."

The next day Sourian had driven the film over to Parkes and MacDonald's house to watch it with his bosses; when the film was over, Parkes, sensing something special, ordered Sourian to buy it, which DreamWorks did, beating out Disney, for $1 million. Neither Lee nor Macari had producer experience at that point (Lee would go on to make his name as the "Asian remake guy," producing films such as *The Grudge* and *Dark Water*, but *The Ring* was his start), and so Parkes and MacDonald became the producers and the movie was barreling forward.

Partly as a thank-you for stepping in on *Time Machine*, Verbinski—in the director doghouse after *The Mexican*—was asked to direct by Parkes and Spielberg, who still believed in him.

What Parkes didn't love about *The Ring* was, at least at first, Naomi Watts. Parkes derided her as "a TV actress" when she was first proposed by Macari's producing partner, Neal Edelstein. Edelstein had just produced David Lynch's *Mulholland Dr.*, which had caused a stir in Cannes but hadn't yet been released in the U.S. DreamWorks had already made offers to Jennifer Connelly, Drew Barrymore, and Gwyneth Paltrow, all of whom passed. (Paltrow said she couldn't do it because she was dating Luke Wilson and wanted to spend Christmas with him in Texas.)

It wasn't until *Mulholland Dr.* was released in theaters, in late October, and Watts began receiving critical attention, that Parkes came around, and Watts was hired.

Besides *The Ring*, Parkes was also working with Scott Frank on the *Minority Report* script, and butting heads with Sam Mendes over the creative direction of *Road to Perdition*, a $90 million Depression-era mobster film that Parkes thought should adhere more to its pulpy roots (it was based on the graphic novel by Max Allan Collins), but which Mendes wanted to be more polished and highbrow.

The project had been submitted to DreamWorks by Dick Zanuck—Spielberg's longtime producing pal—and his son Dean, also a producer, who'd first come across Collins's graphic novel in a pile of scripts that he'd taken home for his weekend read.

"I put it in my bag and read it that weekend, and as soon as I put it down, I told my wife, 'Something special's going to happen with this.' I could feel it," said Dean, who is tall and blond, with a square jaw and the wavy-haired good looks of a surfer.

Dean next contacted his father, who was shooting in Morocco. Zanuck père was also intrigued by the material, especially by the father-son story that existed below the surface of the film's more shoot-'em-up gangster elements. He wrote Spielberg, who got back to him in two days. "I like this," he said over the phone, "I think we should develop it. Call Walter and make the necessary arrangements."

With Spielberg's blessing the project sped ahead: screenwriter David Self was hired and turned in a draft, which Parkes brought with him while he and MacDonald were on a yacht with Tom Hanks and Rita Wilson. When Parkes was fifty pages in, Hanks asked if he could take a look. Parkes handed the screenplay over, and when the actor finished reading it he announced he wanted to star in the movie.

Next, Parkes sent it to Sam Mendes, who was also very quickly involved.

Unaware of these transactions, the Zanucks, back in L.A., were worried. They'd sent Parkes the script three weeks earlier and still hadn't heard back. "It was very unusual, because Steven is especially known for, the next day, [giving you] handwritten notes, detailed thoughts on a draft. And we didn't get any of that," Dean said. "We got nothing from Walter. We confirmed that they got the script. We didn't know what was up, it was kind of an uncertain period."

Finally, Parkes called. "We've got a movie. Sam and Tom want to do this," he told the Zanucks.

"For producers, that's the dream," Dean said. "You've got Sam off his Academy Award, he's the hottest director in town, and Tom, of course, is just an amazing actor . . . When you have Sam and Tom, they're just like magnets. Paul Newman came to the table, Jude Law, and all the best technical crew hopped on." (Including cinematographer Conrad Hall, who'd collaborated with Mendes on *American Beauty*.)

And so DreamWorks had what it hoped would be a follow-up to *Gladiator* and *A Beautiful Mind*—a big, lavish production that would do great things at both the box office and the Oscars.

Dean Zanuck said that on *Road to Perdition*, which Parkes signed onto as an executive producer, "Walter was very helpful in the pre-production period. There's a lot of talk about Walter and Laurie . . . But what we experienced was a guy, a very smart guy, who had a lot of good ideas for this piece and was trying to help get it made." At the same time, he added: "If you're submitting [a movie] to Walter, you're inviting another producer on—that's the Catch-22."

On all the films he was working on, Parkes was characteristically hands-on. Script meetings on *The Ring* would go on for eight hours—lunch would be catered by the DreamWorks chef—during which Parkes would scrupulously break down the script, discussing theories and concepts that seemed lifted from a graduate seminar. A Dream-Works memo from an August 10 script meeting between Parkes, Mac-Donald, Sourian, Verbinski, and screenwriter Ehren Kruger goes on for pages, and includes nearly thirty subheadings of topics discussed: "The Spectral Presence," "Samara's Projected Daguerreotypes & Early Video," and "Rachel & Aidan Driving Home" ("Address Aidan's per-ceptiveness. Does he read the subtext of Rachel's actual questions and ask a question in return that addresses her state of mind?").

The process may have been grueling—Parkes and Verbinski were, again, going at it—but it seemed to be working. By the end, the script had an airtight, near-perfect story structure. In postproduction, how-ever, Parkes pushed Verbinski over the edge when he insisted on testing his own cut of the movie, in which the first twenty minutes of the film were lost. The final version of *The Ring* was a compromise—Parkes's cut remained (it had tested well), but some parts of Verbinski's ver-sion were added back in.

With Parkes tied up deconstructing scripts, De Luca got to work. His mandate was simple: make more movies, broaden the slate. So he pur-sued his New Line strategy, going after smaller, art and genre pictures. *Old School* was Todd Phillips's follow-up to *Road Trip,* a comedy that the Montecito Picture Company had been developing about a group of middle-aged guys intent on recapturing the fun and recklessness of their youth by forming a fraternity. Appealingly low-budget—$26 mil-lion—it fell into the category of films that De Luca could oversee (anything under $30 million). Even so, its budget was a battle. A big sticking point was the cost of Vince Vaughn, cast along with Will Fer-rell, then a tall, goofy regular on *Saturday Night Live.*

Vaughn had won critical acclaim for his turn as a fast-talking hipster in *Swingers,* but he wasn't considered a commercial star, and DreamWorks balked at his $2 million fee. (The cost of Ferrell, who received $1.2 million, was less of an issue.) But Phillips was adamant: no Vaughn, no movie. In the end, the producers found ways to trim the budget and Vaughn was in. But money remained a sticky topic, and Phillips felt much like the *American Beauty* team had felt years earlier — that their movie was being made in spite of an executive's support (in this case that of De Luca), not because of it.

Other projects De Luca jumped on were the family comedy *Surviving Christmas,* and *Biker Boyz,* another inexpensive film that flew well below Parkes's interest radar. Although De Luca wasn't taking on what seemed like major pictures, his arrival had sent a much-needed message to the community and inspired some who'd sworn they'd never return to DreamWorks to reconsider, such as Barry Levinson, who had no interest in making another DreamWorks movie after *Everlasting Piece.* But with De Luca's assurances — the two had worked together on *Wag the Dog* at New Line — he signed on to direct the satirical comedy *Envy.*

Though De Luca was moving forward on certain films, it became clear that his sensibility was not always going to fly at his new home. When he proposed that DreamWorks release the next *Terminator* — the Arnold Schwarzenegger, *I vill be baack* franchise financed by Intermedia — it was quickly shot down, despite De Luca's prediction that the film could make at least $80 million at the domestic box office and that the new T-X Terminator was "kick ass."

Part of De Luca's interest was in getting a franchise going at DreamWorks, which, somewhat astoundingly, had never made a sequel. In Hollywood, franchises such as *Spider-Man* are bread and butter to their respective studios. Even Miramax was in the franchise business.

People outside DreamWorks began to get the sense that De Luca's rein was not going to be so free when, not long after he arrived at the studio, he, Parkes and MacDonald, and senior live-action executives made the rounds at all the major talent agencies. The point was to introduce De Luca as the studio's new president, and to talk up DreamWorks. At each agency, the team met in a conference room with about thirty to forty Hollywood agents.

But if the agents had thought that DreamWorks' new head of production was to be the special honoree that day, they were mistaken. As De Luca and the other executives waited outside, Parkes and Mac-Donald began with a presentation of the movies they were producing and told agents that they could be commissioned as producers. Only when they were finished did De Luca and the rest of the troupe come into the room to talk about DreamWorks.

"It was unbelievable," recalled one agent who was in attendance. "You let them all wait outside, because you want to talk about your agenda. And then, when you're done with your personal business, you open the door and let everyone in to say, 'Here's what's going on.'

"The writing was on the wall, right there. [Their] agenda was first, and Mike was an afterthought. I would have been mortified."

DreamWorks sources say, however, that the event was an example of Parkes and MacDonald's naiveté when it came to how to conduct oneself in Hollywood. They wanted to reach out to agents and ask them to submit material directly to them. It wasn't just to benefit them — part of their job, after all, was to scour for material for Spielberg. If anything, they were, apparently, attempting to create a kind of church and state separation between the rest of the studio and themselves. But whatever their intentions, the episode went down as the latest example of Parkes and MacDonald's self-interestedness, and yet another way in which Parkes was "deaf to how he's perceived," said one DreamWorks source.

When Jeffrey Katzenberg announced that Robert Redford had agreed to star in the military drama *The Last Castle,* he said, "That's the good news and the bad news."

Redford was, famously, a mixed bag. He was, of course, Redford — the Sundance Kid, the Natural, one of the President's Men. But on set, he could use his golden locks and perfect features to excuse behavior that would never be tolerated by anyone of lesser beauty. For one thing, he operated on what was known as "Redford Time," which pushed the limits even of what passed as acceptable in Hollywood, where to show up anywhere on time was to appear unimportant, a lesser player in the game. Redford wasn't minutes late, he was hours late, to lunches, dinners, camera calls.

The Last Castle, which came out in the fall of 2001, was one of the last films commissioned under the Katzenberg reign at the live-action studio. An expensive ($72 million) production, *The Last Castle* was green-lighted, in the spring of 2001, when a writers and actors strike was threatening to bring Hollywood to a standstill. So Katzenberg pushed the movie ahead at full speed, ordering executives to "Get this movie *made!*" Also problematic was the fact that another Redford film was coming out in November—Universal's *Spy Game*. DreamWorks wanted *Last Castle* out early enough to give that film room to breathe.

The result was that Rod Lurie, a West Point graduate and onetime film critic, whose experience was limited to two small films (one of them was *The Contender*, which DreamWorks had acquired and released), was left to churn out a big-budget film, with a major headache of an actor, in seven months.

Even before cameras rolled, Redford was having his way with *The Last Castle*, which, as originally written by David Scarpa, told the story of a beleaguered prison warden, Colonel Winter, who finds himself in over his head when his military prison is overtaken by the megalomaniacal, Pattonesque general Eugene Irwin, who proceeds to organize a prison uprising. The villain in the film was Irwin, whom Redford was playing, and the sympathetic "access character" was Winter, played by James Gandolfini.

"In the script I wrote, General Irwin was a Clint Eastwood type, a darker-shaded character," said Scarpa. "At first he seems like a John McCain, he seems very heroic, and the colonel he's up against is a bureaucrat. But over the course of the movie, the general is gradually revealed to be delusional, and the colonel, the bad guy at the start, eventually becomes the good guy."

According to a source involved with the film, when Redford signed on, he expressly said he was interested in playing against type as a dark antagonist. However, during development, he became more uncomfortable with the way General Irwin was portrayed, and over the course of rewrites by Richard LaGravenese—a screenwriter with whom he had worked on *The Horse Whisperer*—Redford's character became the film's hero and Gandolfini's character became unsympathetic. (Screenwriters Graham Yost and Bill Nicholson also worked on the script.) Sections of the screenplay that delved into Colonel Winter's family life, portraying him as a compassionate Everyman, were entirely cut, while scenes depicting the torture and brutality inflicted on inmates by Winter—and, by extension, the U.S. military, which he represented—were added. The shift in story line caused the U.S. Armed Forces, which had originally supported the film, leading the filmmakers on a tour of Fort Leavenworth for research, to withdraw its involvement.

"It was a clear case of the star taking control," said one person involved with the film. "[Redford] became the creative locomotive on the project."

Facilitating this was Lurie's inexperience. Word was getting out that he was ill-equipped to be making such a large-scale film. Barely a week into shooting, Lurie had come a hair's breadth from being fired when DreamWorks was unhappy with his arty, indie style. So he quickly changed course. Then he had to contend with Redford, of whom one source said: "On the set, in post, it's all about Bob. As long as you agree with him, he's charming and affable. But as soon as you're anything different, suddenly you're vilified, you can't be trusted, you're part of the studio system that's corrupt. You're demonized."

Lurie professed nothing but love and admiration for Redford, denying any contention. Others were more dubious. Once, in postproduction, after Lurie cut down a scene in which Redford carries huge rocks back and forth as a form of punishment, Redford confronted the director. The actor, who appears shirtless in the scene, had prepared for the sequence for weeks, training and working out with weights. (One person snidely referred to it as his *Bridge on the River Kwai* moment.") While shooting the scene, he had asked for several takes, intent on getting it just right. But when Lurie screened the footage, the scene dragged on for nearly twenty minutes.

"I don't get it, where's my rock-carrying scene?" Redford asked. When Lurie explained his rationale for the cut, Redford grew angry and stormed off.

(Gandolfini, who's also known to possess prima donna tendencies, grew similarly outraged when one of his monologues—the speech, he said, that made him want to do the movie—was trimmed.)

Meanwhile, Parkes was sending pages that he'd rewritten to the set to be shot the following day. In some cases, Parkes's notes were impossible to execute. For instance, he suggested staging a mass prison escape in which the prisoners literally tear down the prison walls. Considering that *The Last Castle* was shot at a real prison, the Tennessee State Penitentiary in Nashville, with a historical legacy—it was where

James Earl Ray was held after he killed Martin Luther King Jr.—tearing down the walls was not happening.

"Walter had a lot of radical ideas that he was suggesting when we were already shooting," said one person on the set. "They were challenging because they were coming from the head of the studio. There would be long conversations, then he would fly down and try to come to some sort of compromise. There wasn't a purity of vision on the film."

After a whirlwind, twelve-week shoot, *The Last Castle* wrapped in late June. Almost impossibly, and with the assistance of two editors—one who worked on dialogue and one who worked on action sequences—Lurie had a rough cut to show DreamWorks a month later. Now there were less than two months to test and edit the film and have it in theaters. Lurie and the DreamWorks crew, which now included Katzenberg and Press, began shuttling back and forth on the DreamWorks jet to San Diego for test screenings. At one of the first screenings, a reel broke fifteen minutes in, causing a fifteen-minute pause in the proceedings.

During this interruption, Katzenberg marched out of the theater and announced to Lurie: "The movie's great, but you're going to have to shorten the action sequences. I can tell you, you've given them too much."

"But Jeffrey—" Lurie began, thinking to himself, *How can he say that after seeing just a snippet of film?*

"Rod," Katzenberg interrupted. "It's gonna work."

Katzenberg also predicted the movie wouldn't test higher than 80 percent, "because the lead character dies at the end and people don't want to see that."

"So the polls come back, 77, 78—he was exactly right," Lurie said. "When people write down what they don't like: Redford dying. Jeffrey knew *exactly* what was right and what was wrong with the film."

Redford, who had already begun to withdraw from the movie during postproduction, unhappy about how the film was being edited, refused to do press for *The Last Castle*.

"When he saw it was being turned into an action movie instead of a character drama, he thought it was being cheapened and trivialized, and he stopped cooperating," said one source.

Making matters worse, Redford lambasted DreamWorks in the

media. In an interview with Sydney's *Sun-Herald,* he griped about a change in the film's ad campaign that occurred following 9/11. Then he went on to say that he never saw the finished film and to slap Dream-Works for "jamming [*Last Castle*] into release way early," an act, he said, that was "unfair to the director and the film."

"None of the actors thought the movie should have come out that soon," Redford said. "The director should have been given a little more time to complete the work."

Lurie seemed surprised when he was told about Redford's comments.

"He did see the finished film," Lurie said. "He means he didn't see it with color timing. I've had nothing but good conversations with him."

ImageMovers' relationship with DreamWorks had gone from bad to worse, but Robert Zemeckis's production company remained bound to the studio until the end of 2002. *Cast Away* and *What Lies Beneath* remained ImageMovers' only DreamWorks films. Meanwhile, Dream-Works (Spielberg aside) was still resentful of how much money the director's friend's company was getting in terms of overhead and development funds.

The situation reached a head when, for the first time, Rapke employed the clause in ImageMovers' contract that allowed the company to "put" a film to DreamWorks—in other words, force Dream-Works to green-light a movie. When Katzenberg refused, Rapke was furious. Not only was Katzenberg reneging on a deal, but, per Image-Movers' contract, the company was not able to shop the project to other studios.

According to sources, a blowup ensued, with Katzenberg insisting on restructuring ImageMovers' deal so that it was much leaner, and in line with more traditional production deals. He also wanted, essentially, to lose Rapke. Zemeckis finally agreed to a slimmer deal, one that was no longer exclusive to DreamWorks, though Rapke stayed.

To all involved (except Spielberg, who was still out of the loop as to what was transpiring), it was clear that DreamWorks was no longer the best fit for ImageMovers, and Zemeckis and his colleagues began quietly looking for a new deal. It didn't take long before Warner Bros., eager to be in the Zemeckis business, opened its arms. The deal got so far along that ImageMovers was looking at office space on the Warner's lot when Spielberg got wind of what was going on and "went ballistic," according to one source.

Katzenberg was then dispatched to ImageMovers' villa to make amends. For a full hour, he sat with Rapke behind closed doors, receiving a verbal mauling. Rapke must have been enjoying—at least a little—the satisfaction of seeing the man so desperate to get rid of him in supplication mode. "We want you here," said Katzenberg, trying to calm Rapke, according to a source with knowledge of the conversation. Besides offering goodwill, Katzenberg also expressed reassurance that things were going to change at DreamWorks for the better.

Katzenberg then sat with Zemeckis in his office for another hour, saying more or less the same thing, but in a less charged setting. Zemeckis did not scream or curse.

In the end, Katzenberg's mission was successful. He had fixed another problem for Spielberg. ImageMovers remained at DreamWorks —at least for now.

27

HARVEY II

O N   T H E   N I G H T   O F   J A N U A R Y   20, 2002, Universal chairman Stacey Snider was feeling rather pleased. Universal and DreamWorks' coproduction *A Beautiful Mind* had won several awards at the Golden Globes, including Best Drama. Long ridiculed in Hollywood for being a less-than-serious awards show, the Globes had gained more credibility over the years, and was now considered one of the most reliable prognosticators when it came to the Academy Awards. (People were also willing to admit that it was a lot more fun to drink, eat, and mill around on the smoking patio during the Globes ceremony than remain in their seats during the stuffy Oscars.) That *A Beautiful Mind*, which since being released on December 21 was on its way to grossing nearly $200 million at the U.S. box office and had received strong reviews, should do well at the Globes was not altogether surprising. Considering its star (Russell Crowe), director (Ron Howard), and Important Subject Matter—the story of John Nash, the schizophrenic Nobel laureate mathematician—the film was what's known as "Oscar bait." But even so, its win at the Globes provided no shortage of joy for Snider, considering what it meant for the film come the "real" awards ceremony in March.

A petite blonde who was always immaculately composed down to her perfectly pedicured toenails and Prada handbag, Snider was one of the most powerful women in Hollywood, having risen through the "D-girl" ranks to become president of TriStar Pictures and then chairman of Universal in 1998, under Universal president Ron Meyer. At both TriStar and Universal, Snider had worked closely with Spielberg, who trusted her enormously. Like Kathy Kennedy, she was a "Steven Girl," a member of his select inner circle. Spielberg had even asked

Snider to run Amblin, back before Walter Parkes and Laurie Mac-Donald took the job. Though she demurred, the two remained close friends and allies over the years.

Like many of the most visible women in Hollywood, Snider's rise had been assisted by powerful men, and not just Spielberg. Her early success came as a development executive for producer Peter Guber, who brought her with him to Sony when he became head of the studio with Jon Peters in the early 1990s. Known as being tenacious and astute with material, Snider was always prepared and rarely seen without an enormous bag bulging with scripts.

Her first stop of the evening, once the Globes were over, was Universal's party at Trader Vic's, the Polynesian-themed restaurant in the Beverly Hilton, which serves as the Globes' headquarters every year (the ceremony itself is held in the hotel's ballroom). Afterward, Snider moved on to CAA's post-Globes party at the nightclub Muse, where her glowing mood darkened at the sight of Harvey Weinstein lumbering toward her. Miramax's own Best Picture hopeful, Todd Field's *In the Bedroom,* had lost Best Drama that night, and Weinstein was not happy. But what had really set him off was a story he'd been told would be running in the *New York Post* the next day, claiming that Miramax had been badmouthing *A Beautiful Mind* and saying Nash was an anti-Semite. This was arguably the most potent charge one could lob in Hollywood, given the industry's disproportionately Jewish population. Weinstein was convinced the story had been planted by Universal and DreamWorks.

As Weinstein neared, Snider braced her five-foot-two-inch, 105-pound frame. The Miramax chairman raised a jabbing finger: "You're going to go down for this! Get your house in order. And clean up your act! Or otherwise we will!"

Snider held her ground under the ambush. Later, she recalled, "He was yelling. He was very angry. He wouldn't come down from it. Usually, you can say, 'Let's relax, let's talk about this, we can figure this out.' He just kept going."

Weinstein was convinced that Terry Press, specifically, was behind the *Post* story. Universal, in his opinion, was also a culprit because of its alliance with DreamWorks on the Golden Globe–winning picture. Finger-pointing abounded. Universal and DreamWorks were convinced that Miramax itself was behind the mudslinging campaign against

Mind—which claimed that the film glossed over less glowing aspects of Nash's life. (The studios were also suspicious of the *Moulin Rouge!* camp—namely Fox and director Baz Luhrmann's representatives.)

Weinstein, in turn, felt that DreamWorks was doing its own mud-slinging, and badmouthing Miramax to reporters, such as the *Post's* Nikki Finke. The lobs were constant and ferocious, made all the more so by the media, which was eager to jump in and chronicle every jab. The Internet, which, unlike three years earlier, during the *Saving Private Ryan* versus *Shakespeare In Love* face-off, was a major medium, and a major voice, in the Oscar race, speeding up the timetable in which information was dispersed.

The next day, Snider called Katzenberg. She wanted him to know that Weinstein was in attack mode; she also knew that Katzenberg and Weinstein were friends—"Hollywood friends," at least. After hanging up with Snider, Katzenberg called Weinstein. "You can't work this way," he said. "You are endangering my friendship and you must apologize to Stacey." The two men had a series of charged conversations over the following twenty-four hours. At one point, Katzenberg said to Weinstein: "I'm sick of you always pointing the finger at Terry [Press]. You think if it's raining outside, it's Terry's fault."

Weinstein said that he was paranoid about Press and was certain it was she who'd spoken to the *Post.*

When Katzenberg said Press had told him that she hadn't spoken to Finke in six months, Weinstein didn't buy it. This caused Katzenberg to shoot back: "You are speaking about somebody who's family to me. So you better think before you call her a liar."

According to former Miramax sources, Weinstein wasn't trying to win a Best Picture Oscar for *In the Bedroom,* though of course that would be nice. Although the film had been a festival darling and was popular with the press, which loved talking to the enigmatic Todd Field, Weinstein had no illusions: what mattered to him was that *In the Bedroom* be *nominated* for a Best Picture, which would propel its box-office grosses. After all, a successful awards season "could mean the difference between a movie grossing $5 million at the box office and grossing $20 million." And that $15 million was worth fighting for.

The bloodshed had begun back in December, when Internet sensationalist Matt Drudge had posted a story on the Drudge Report claiming that Nash's sexual interest in men—addressed in Sylvia Nasar's biography of Nash, upon which *Mind* had been inspired but was not officially based—had been "deliberately left out of the movie!" (Actually, the book chronicles several adolescent crushes that Nash had. Based on the book, Nash might be termed "bisexual" or, most fairly, beyond conventional categorization.) The day after the story in question was posted, Nash's sexuality was discussed and debated on the morning talk show *The View. A Beautiful Mind* was also taking a beating on FoxNews.com, where columnist Roger Friedman (who'd worked at Weinstein's short-lived *Talk* magazine) was routinely drubbing *A Beautiful Mind* while fawning over Miramax's Oscar contenders.

The day after Christmas, *USA Today* weighed in with a piece titled "It's Beautiful, But Not Factual," in which Crowe was quoted as saying, "What I would consider to be the most interesting parts of [Nash's] life are not going to be part of our movie." The story went on to say that the timing of Nash's schizophrenia was inaccurately depicted, and that the film left out his supposed bisexuality. When Press read the story, she told people that it made her cry.

As the Oscars neared in March, Drudge picked up the anti-Semite thread, writing: "Some Academy members are discovering shocking Jew-bashing passages found in the book on which the movie is based!"

When he read this, Brian Grazer, who produced *A Beautiful Mind,* thought, "We're dealing with a man who's been schizophrenic for forty years, and now you want to load him up in a wheelchair and push him onto the 405 Freeway? It's so antithetical to the point of the movie, which is to help destigmatize mental disability . . . It's so fucked up."

Unbeknownst to Miramax, or anyone else, Universal came close to throwing gas on the fire when an interview between Nash—who was otherwise being kept from the media for fear of what might come out of his mouth—and *60 Minutes'* Mike Wallace was arranged. Wallace had struggled with bouts of clinical depression and was known to sympathize with Nash. In one sequence of the program, Wallace interviewed Nash's son, John Charles Martin Nash, whose own schizophrenia had led him to step down from a professorship at MIT. When Wallace asked him why he was no longer teaching, he replied: "Because of the Jews!" The Nash camp said it was his mental illness talking, but it left Universal fearing it was surely all over. Luckily, the sequence was cut from the program, which ended up being, as predicted, a love letter to the Nash family.

Another tactic Universal was pursuing was talking up Howard, who was viewed as a more commercial than awards-worthy director. Howard believed that the reason his *Apollo 13* didn't win Best Picture was because he hadn't been nominated as Best Director, and so the cast of *Beautiful Mind* was instructed to always mention what an "actors' director" Howard was in interviews.

Even the *L.A. Times*' Patrick Goldstein's column on the unseemliness of the campaigning incited attacks. In response, Miramax's publicists sent Goldstein a ten-point defense of their tactics—the first letter of each point spelled: D-R-E-A-M-W-O-R-K-S.

The reality was that DreamWorks had very little input on the marketing and Oscar campaigns for *Mind,* given that it was the film's international distributor. But, an aggressive and territorial partner, it had not been completely relegated to the sidelines, either. According to Universal sources, when Katzenberg and Press didn't like one of the trailers Universal had made for the film, which pushed *A Beautiful Mind* more as a thriller than a drama, they complained to Grazer, championing another trailer that stressed the romance between Nash and his wife, Alicia (Jennifer Connelly).

As attacks on *Mind* heated up, power plays became beside the point. What mattered more was that the movie needed to be protected. Universal, less experienced in gritty Oscar campaigning, relied heavily on DreamWorks to help fend off bombs.

Press had developed a relationship with Crowe during *Gladiator,* which paid off when Crowe, almost on cue, became a public relations nightmare in the midst of the Oscar race. Following his Best Actor win at the British Academy of Film and Television Arts Awards in February, Crowe exploded at the show's TV director, pinning him up against a wall and spewing obscenities at him because he had edited his acceptance speech. Press was brought in to clean up the mess and arranged for Crowe to make a public apology. Even so, Universal was certain Crowe had blown his shot at an Academy Award and prayed that the damage wouldn't spread to the other filmmakers.

When the Oscar nominations were announced on March 12, *A Beautiful Mind* received eight nominations (including Best Picture, Best Director, Best Actor, Best Adapted Screenplay, and Best Supporting Actress) compared to *In the Bedroom*'s five (Best Picture, Best Actor, Best Actress, Best Adapted Screenplay). *Amélie,* Miramax's French-language film starring the Audrey Hepburn look-alike Audrey Tautou, also received five nominations, and *Iris,* another Miramax entry, picked up acting nominations for Judi Dench, Jim Broadbent, and Kate Winslet.

The real winner at this stage, though, was New Line's *Lord of the Rings: The Fellowship of the Ring,* which trounced the competition with a whopping thirteen nominations in categories across the board, from technical achievements to directing (Peter Jackson) to acting (Sir Ian McKellen). If there was a race, it was between *Rings* and *Mind,* with *Moulin Rouge!*—which received eight nominations—as the wild card.

The advantage *Mind* had was that it was the type of film the Academy loved—a sweeping drama with heartfelt performances that was in no way, shape, or form small. Still, *Rings* was a not insignificant threat. The last time a film that was nominated in thirteen categories did not go on to win Best Picture was in 1966, when *Who's Afraid of Virginia Woolf?* lost out to *A Man for All Seasons.* On the other hand, *Rings* was a fantasy film, a genre not typically favored by the august members of the Academy. The race was on.

For Katzenberg, the 2002 Oscar race was about one word: *Shrek.* The showdown this time was with Pixar's *Monsters, Inc.* for Best Animated Feature. (The other nominee was *Jimmy Neutron.*) Besides being another Disney versus DreamWorks race, the runoff between DreamWorks and Pixar also demonstrated the utter domination of animation achieved by these two companies by 2002.

DreamWorks hadn't pushed *Shrek* for Best Animated Feature—that, Press and company assumed, was a given. Rather, they were gunning for more lofty honors. "For Your Consideration" ads for *Shrek* that ran in the trades touted Mike Myers, Cameron Diaz, and Eddie Murphy for their acting chops, suggesting their vocal contributions to *Shrek* were on par with, say, Jim Broadbent's performance in *Iris* or Kidman's in *Moulin Rouge!* A Best Picture nomination for *Shrek* was not impossible. Press had pulled it off before at Disney with *Beauty and the Beast,* the only time an animated film has ever received a Best Picture nomination. In the end, however, *Shrek* was selected in just two categories: Best Animated Feature and Best Adapted Screenplay.

Before anyone could relax, a new dilemma was presented. Should *Shrek* win, who would accept the award before the tens of millions of Oscar viewers? The issue was murky, seeing as there was no acceptance precedent for animated films. On live-action titles, producers accepted. Directors, after all, competed in their own category. But animated films only had one category. So who should claim the glory?

According to Academy guidelines for the new Oscar category, no more than two people could accept the award, and they must be "the key creative talent most clearly responsible for the overall achievement." Given the work he'd invested in *Shrek*, Katzenberg felt that he should accept the Oscar. But when Geffen heard this, he balked. Press also advised Katzenberg that it was a bad idea. Ever concerned about Katzenberg's public image, Press feared that were he to accept the Oscar, it would confirm claims by some camps that Katzenberg was a credit grabber. More seriously, if word of his intentions got out, *Shrek*'s chances might be diminished.

The conversations with Press and Geffen were hard for Katzenberg. "The one thing Jeffrey wants and hasn't been able to get is an Academy Award," said Sandy Rabins, who had become aware of the dilemma when she received a call one day from Katzenberg, whom she hadn't spoken to since her exit from DreamWorks.

"It was a rainy day and I got an emergency call to run out there, to the Glendale campus," said Rabins, who, as an executive producer on *Shrek*, had to sign off on forms submitted to the Academy. "Jeffrey said, 'You need to get here, we have to talk about this—talk about who's taking the award.'" Considering the weather—and the subject—getting in the car and driving across town from Sony's Culver City campus, Rabins said, "was the last thing I wanted to do."

When Rabins arrived, she walked into a meeting packed with DreamWorks' top brass. The mood of the room was somber. Press started things off by saying that in light of a recent, unflattering article about Katzenberg, it was an especially bad time for him to be in the spotlight accepting an award. "Terry's speech was like, 'Jeffrey's been screwed and he can't [accept the Oscar],'" said Rabins. "She was kind of defending him, on the one hand—in the way that only Terry Press can do—and on the other hand, saying, 'He can't have it.'"

The discussion then turned to who *should* get the Oscar, if not Katzenberg.

"There was a big conversation then if we should go to (codirectors) Andrew [Adamson] and Vicky [Jenson] or not," said Rabins.

Given the number of people who had been involved in the film over the course of its life, the decision-making process was not simple. The most obvious choice, to many, was Adamson. But some felt that he was already getting too much credit for a movie that was, by definition, a collaboration. In the end, producer Aron Warner was designated the would-be Oscar bearer.

At Pixar, which was mounting its first-ever campaign, there was already a feeling that *Shrek* would be difficult to beat. Even before Tony Angelotti, whom Disney had hired as an Oscar consultant, was shown *Monsters*, he warned Steve Jobs and John Lasseter that *Shrek* was a substantial threat. *Time* critic Richard Schickel had declared it the best film of 2001. Even Jobs conceded that *Shrek* was "a juggernaut."

"Still," Jobs said, "that doesn't mean we can't give it our best effort."

Despite all the weeks of warfare leading up to the Oscars, by the time the Academy Awards weekend rolled around in late March, DreamWorks and Miramax were, at least for appearances' sake — or at least in the Hollywood sense of the term — friends. Weinstein had even showed up at Russell Crowe's room at the Bel-Air Hotel waving his Oscar ballot. "See! I'm voting for you!" At Miramax's annual pre-Oscar fete — a cross between a night of follies and, according to the singer Sting, a "bar mitzvah" — at the uncompromisingly hip Mondrian Hotel on the Sunset Strip, Katzenberg and Weinstein went so far as to dress up like gladiators (a reference to another DreamWorks Oscar movie) for their skit. The gag was this: in light of all their Oscar sparring, the men were receiving anger-management counseling from Snider (played gamely by Christina Applegate). But to onlookers — including Cameron Diaz, Benjamin Bratt, and Ethan Hawke and his then wife, Uma Thurman — the sketch was baffling and shocking. Jaws dropped as Katzenberg and Weinstein rolled through this montage of R-rated jabs:

> SNIDER (channeled through Applegate): First it was *Saving Private Ryan* and *Shakespeare In Love,* and now it's backbiting about *A Beautiful Mind!*
> WEINSTEIN: I swear on the life of my driver, I never said any of it! (Big cheer from crowd.) But Nash was gay, wasn't he?
> KATZENBERG: Hey. Looking at you in that outfit, you oughtta know. (pause) I bought your company.
> WEINSTEIN: Yeah. In 1993 with Michael Eisner's money.

KATZENBERG: Lucky for you, back then he still had some.

WEINSTEIN: Not that you ever saw any of it.

KATZENBERG (to Applegate/Snider): Does it turn you on when he talks dirty like that?

WEINSTEIN: Jeffrey, if you're looking for a three-way, call Barry Diller.

KATZENBERG: Barry, I begged him to take that out. Honest to God, I begged him.

WEINSTEIN (similarly breaking character): Michael, Jeffrey made me put that line in, I swear.

APPLEGATE/SNIDER: Enough. Now look. This isn't about you . . . This meeting is about me. This weekend is about me. The Academy Awards are about me. It's all about me.

Applegate/Snider then explained that she was the daughter of a child psychologist and a marriage counselor and that, borrowing their techniques, the two men should cuddle teddy bears and make up. Not that anyone for a second believed that Katzenberg and Weinstein were truly allies.

"Whenever [Weinstein and Katzenberg] got together in an electric atmosphere, there was a lot of ill will," said one insider. "Harvey looked at Jeffrey as the guy who saved him from oblivion, when Miramax was not doing well financially. But once Jeffrey left Disney, he didn't look at Harvey as the guy he raised, he looked at him as the competition. Those two guys are the most highly competitive executives that live."

The mood at the actual Oscar ceremony was affected by the memory of 9/11, which was still relatively fresh, even for those wearing strapless Vera Wang (no one was immune from security checks). Tom Cruise opened the show by discussing the terrorist attacks. Later, Kevin Spacey asked the audience to stand in a moment of silence for the victims of 9/11. A tribute film to New York City made by Nora Ephron was shown and introduced by another New York dignitary, Woody Allen, a staunch East Coaster who famously never attends the Oscars and who received a standing ovation. "Thank you very much," he responded. "That makes up for the strip search."

Allen's surprise appearance had been orchestrated by Press, who'd flown to New York to personally appeal to the director. The night became all the more historic when Halle Berry and Denzel Washington received Best Actor awards, for *Monster's Ball* and *Training Day*. It was the first time that two African Americans had simultaneously won best acting Oscars. Adding to the poignancy was that Sidney Poitier, the first—and only, until now—African American to win a Best Actor award, also received a Lifetime Achievement Oscar.

Nothing could upstage the sight of Berry, Poitier, and Washington clutching their Oscars amid tears. Still, when Nathan Lane—who'd provided the voice of Timon in *The Lion King*—announced the Best Animated Feature category, Katzenberg was on the edge of his seat. A moment later, when Lane pronounced the monosyllabic word *Shrek,* Katzenberg was out of it, on his feet, hugging everyone in sight.

In February of 2002, a month before DreamWorks' third straight Oscar victory, Judd Apatow wrote a note to television critics begging them to write more "about our little show," as well as to "pray for us." This time, the little show in question was *Undeclared,* Apatow's sophomore series for DreamWorks TV, which was a sequel of sorts to *Freaks and Geeks,* though this time his posse of anti-Socs had matriculated into the halls of higher learning. *Undeclared* had debuted in the fall of 2001 on the Fox network. Like its predecessor, the show was pure Apatow: unvarnished, funny-smart, and populated by underdogs. "It was like *Freaks and Geeks 2,*" said Joel Madison, a writer and consulting producer on the show.

Even before Apatow was pleading for more coverage for a show that was tanking in the ratings, there had been trouble, as Apatow's creative method, or lack thereof, clashed with the network. On *Freaks and Geeks,* Apatow and show creator Paul Feig had written a few characters based on the actors playing them. But on *Undeclared* Apatow was writing virtually the entire show around the kids as they were cast. As a result, until all the actors were lined up, there was no script. When Gail Berman, president of entertainment at Fox, would call Apatow in a panic and say: "We need to see outlines! We need to see pages!" to Berman's disbelief, Apatow would say that he wasn't done casting yet.

Even when there *was* a script, Berman was unimpressed.

"Judd does what he calls 'vomit passes,'" said Feig, who brainstormed with Apatow about *Undeclared* in the early stages but then went off to pursue a show of his own he was developing. "He just blurts everything out. It's kind of all there, but it sort of needs to be cobbled together still . . . And the networks just can't handle that because they're used to everything that's put in front of them being finished and polished . . . You can tell them a million times, 'No, this is just a document,' but they can't process that."

Apatow's casting choices weren't winning him any more points with Fox, which refused to cast Seth Rogen—Apatow's muse and alter ego—as the lead. After long, drawn-out battles, Apatow finally relented, casting Rogen as a supporting character and hiring him as a writer on the show. Apatow's next choice for the lead was Jay Baruchel, a reedy nineteen-year-old from Montreal who looked like he could last about two minutes, tops, in the ring with Woody Allen. This occasioned more fights. When Berman asked to know more about Baruchel, who had little acting experience, all she was told was that he was "this kid." (In the end, Apatow won the round and the kid was cast.)

Tension grew between Apatow and Fox, which prided itself on being "edgy" and "sexy." When Sandy Grushow, head of programming at Fox, told Apatow that he wanted *Undeclared* to be raunchier, à la *American Pie*, Apatow complained sorrowfully that, "They want me to be the Spice Girls and I want to be the Pixies."

When *Undeclared* debuted in September, *Spin City* remained DreamWorks TV's only success story, and the show that was paying most of the bills. The hope was that *Undeclared*, along with Dream-Works' other fall launch—*Off Centre*, a comedy for the WB by *American Pie* directors Chris and Paul Weitz—would join *Spin City* in the syndication-bound-series stratosphere. At first, this looked feasible, or at least not impossible: *Undeclared* was instantly lauded by critics as a breath of fresh air.

But when ratings didn't match reviewers' enthusiasm, Fox began treating *Undeclared* like a prickly pear, airing it sporadically and running shows out of order. Being put through the ringer for the second time in a row, Apatow was losing his patience, as well as his mind. In December, when *Time* ranked *Undeclared* number three in its top-ten list of the best things on television in 2001, saying that it "takes the eccentric sensibility of *Freaks and Geeks* and applies it to smart, sharply observed coming-of-age stories of self-discovery, romance and beer,"

Apatow was all the more convinced that Fox was doing him wrong. In a fit of frustration, he framed the glowing review and scribbled out a note to Grushow, who had pulled the plug on him once before (*The Ben Stiller Show* had also been at Fox). The note succinctly thanked Grushow for, once again, fucking him in the ass.

When Apatow called Justin Falvey, who was now running Dream-Works TV with Darryl Frank (Dan McDermott had left to pursue screenwriting), and told him what he'd done, Falvey panicked.

"Judd! Are you crazy? You can't do that! They'll cancel the show!" Falvey said, and dispatched a PA to go intercept the package.

Around this time, Apatow was also on the receiving end of incendiary attacks. Wanting to have Topher Grace, who starred in another Fox comedy, *That '70s Show,* guest star on *Undeclared,* Apatow reached out to the show's producer, Mark Brazill. When he didn't hear back, Apatow e-mailed. Brazill replied by e-mailing him a scathing note, accusing him of having once stolen an idea from a pilot he had made for MTV and using it in *The Ben Stiller Show.*

"There's a saying, 'I forgive but I don't forget. And I don't forgive,'" Brazill wrote in what became an infamous e-mail exchange. "So, now you know. Although I kind of think that you already did." After Apatow wrote back and denied that he had ever done such a thing, saying "I am not a thief of ideas. I'm sorry you believe differently," Brazill fired off another note. This one said, "Personally, I feel you've made a career out of being a sycophant to [Jim] Carrey, or [Garry] Shandling, or Roseanne. When you weren't . . . you were stealing from lesser known comics or leeching off other people's ideas . . ." The note was signed, "Get cancer. Love, Mark." In a later e-mail, Brazill told Apatow to "die in a fiery accident and taste your own blood."

Brazill eventually apologized to Apatow and peace came—sort of. When Brazill sent Apatow a gift basket, Apatow warned, only half-jokingly, "Don't eat that."

By February, things were looking grim for *Undeclared,* and Apatow knew it. As a last-ditch effort, he sent his SOS letter to critics along with the show's final episodes. *Undeclared* wasn't canceled just then—it managed to eke out an off-and-on-again existence for a few more months. But by the spring it was off the air. (*Off Centre* was also ultimately axed.)

By mid-2002, the fate of DreamWorks TV, too, was looking questionable. *Spin City* had fallen in the ratings, and after a full, six-year life, was canceled by ABC, leaving DreamWorks bereft of its only hit show. Adding to the blow, *Spin City*'s second cycle of syndication revenue wasn't as high as DreamWorks had anticipated. So much for the notion that everyone could sit back and relax because *Spin City* was paying the bills.

In recent years, DreamWorks TV had gradually been cutting back. Publicity, business affairs, casting, and production had all been downsized; everything, in fact, had been trimmed except the creative department. But with the studio's deal with ABC about to expire in the summer, even Katzenberg knew it was time to get realistic. In August it was announced that DreamWorks was transitioning from an independent studio to a smaller, more traditional production studio with a first-look deal at NBC. The network would be taking care of DreamWorks' overhead and would receive a majority ownership stake in shows it chose to develop; i.e., future riches from a *Spin City*–type hit would be lining NBC's coffers, not those of DreamWorks.

Announcing the news, Katzenberg said: "The world has changed. The networks have a much, much stronger hand and are a much stronger force in the development and production of shows for air. You can stick your head in the sand and ignore that at your own peril."

A few more *Spin City*s would have likely prevented a change in course. Greater success in television, more so than almost any other division, would have gone a long way to buoying DreamWorks' bottom line, and perhaps could have changed its ancillary-division-dumping trajectory. Instead, DreamWorks TV scaled back and became a traditional production company.

Lest anyone think this setback was anything more than a minor business adjustment, going forward, Katzenberg said, the live-action studio—with Mike De Luca now onboard—would produce between ten and twelve films a year, up from seven to eight, and the animation studio would now be making two to three pictures annually.

Still, there was curiosity as to how stable the company was. The live-action studio was swinging misses again—*The Time Machine,* though split with Warner Bros., was a disappointment (it grossed $56 million U.S. on a budget of $85 million), as was Woody Allen's *Hollywood Ending.* In May, Katzenberg's latest (traditionally) animated film, *Spirit: Stallion of the Cimarron,* also failed to live up to expectations, grossing $73 million in the U.S. and just $122 million worldwide. The experience put him back in the underdog position with Eisner when, a month later, Disney's *Lilo and Stitch* (also a 2-D film) made $145 million in U.S. box-office grosses and $273 million worldwide.

The failure of *Spirit* and the success of *Shrek* should have signaled Katzenberg that CGI animation—and hip, unearnest storytelling—was the way of the future. In March, Twentieth Century Fox had entered the digital fray with *Ice Age*, a celebrity-studded (Ray Romano, John Leguizamo) CGI film about a group of wisecracking, prehistoric creatures that grossed $176 million domestically and $383 million worldwide. But Katzenberg remained unmoved. He refused to turn his back on 2-D projects and was still very much considered a "2-D guy." During the promotional campaign for *Spirit*, Katzenberg waxed amorous about the virtues of old-school animation, saying: "It's the difference between an e-mail and a handwritten letter. Whether it's from a loved one or a friend or even a boss, God forbid, there's an emotion that comes through a handwritten letter. There's something that human beings do when we create on a piece of paper, we put something of ourself into that."

Katzenberg, it was clear, was going to keep putting himself into the medium that had made him.

28

WHAT SINBAD WROUGHT

TWO YEARS AFTER Walter Parkes and Laurie MacDonald signed their "deal of deals," in which they were treated, and compensated, as DreamWorks' biggest in-house producers, the effect of that deal was being felt. Of the eight films that DreamWorks was releasing in 2002, the couple produced four (*The Time Machine, The Ring, Catch Me If You Can,* and *Minority Report*) and executive-produced two (*Road to Perdition, The Tuxedo*). Parkes and MacDonald also produced (and Spielberg executive-produced) the follow-up to *Men in Black* for Columbia Pictures, which was one of the summer's big-event movies.

Parkes and MacDonald now worked primarily out of their new home in Santa Monica, a stone's throw from the bluffs overlooking the Pacific. As befitting the couple, the manse was decorated by L.A. designer Michael Smith (future decorator to the First Couple, the Obamas; his Hollywood clients included Dustin Hoffman and Rupert Murdoch) according to the comfy-classy aesthetic of the Spielberg residence, another Smith commission.

"The house literally rendered me speechless. It was beautiful," said one visitor who has seen many a Hollywood spread. Yet again, when it came to style and effortless class, Parkes and MacDonald had it over the rest of the town in spades.

For executives at DreamWorks, Parkes and MacDonald's new arrangement meant spending a lot more time in the car, for the couple now took all of their meetings at their home. Some executives were making the hourlong commute from Studio City to Santa Monica three to four times a week. "The option was, you could miss the meeting or go drive out," said one former executive, who said that an added frustration was that Parkes and MacDonald frequently canceled or rescheduled appointments at the last minute, while people were en route.

Parkes and MacDonald told friends, and even people at Dream-Works, that they desperately wanted to step down and focus only on producing. "I think Walter and Laurie were split," said one source. "They truly wanted someone to take over for them, and they truly *didn't* want someone to take over." Michael De Luca couldn't quite step in. As directed, he was busy making lower-budget genre pictures of the sort favored by New Line, where there was not such deep pride in the Brand. DreamWorks didn't seem to entirely trust its newest employee, an outsider who had his own quirky style. De Luca didn't like carrying a cell phone and so couldn't always be reached. He feared flying and so was loath to take airplanes. Within months of his being hired, De Luca discovered that DreamWorks had reached out to Nick Stevens, a comedy agent at UTA, who represented Jim Carrey, Ben Stiller, and Jack Black, to talk to him about joining De Luca in a partnership role at DreamWorks. The talks never went anywhere, but De Luca was not pleased.

The impossibility of a Parkes–De Luca partnership, given their radically different sensibilities, came into full view when De Luca showed interest in making a comedy written by Will Ferrell and his *Saturday Night Live* writing collaborator, Adam McKay—*Anchorman: The Legend of Ron Burgundy,* about a politically incorrect 1970s-era newscaster—which Judd Apatow was producing. To sell Parkes, De Luca set up a pitch meeting at DreamWorks with the filmmakers and Ferrell. The tall, goofy comedian, then unknown outside his *SNL* work, showed up wearing an enormous blue cowboy hat. He was Will Ferrell being Will Ferrell. But Parkes was not amused. When the meeting was over, he told executives that Ferrell was not a movie star. Dream-Works passed.

In a way, the summer of 2002 was a replay of the summer of 1997, when *The Lost World* and the first *Men in Black* were released—i.e., when DreamWorks players were doing very well by non-DreamWorks movies. When *Men in Black II* came out over the Fourth of July weekend, it went on to rack up $140 million domestically and $441 million worldwide. Spielberg's deal was greatly diminished from the first film, though he still received 7.5 percent of first-dollar grosses in exchange for essentially lending his name. *MIB II* was one of the most alarming examples of how big blockbusters increasingly seemed to serve stars more than studios—in order to get Will Smith and Tommy Lee Jones to return for a sequel, Sony gave each actor a $20 million payday in addition to huge gross points.

Minority Report was Spielberg's latest attempt to ambitiously stretch beyond the traditional blockbuster confines. The film, he said, was his first foray into film noir. *Variety*'s Peter Bart noted that with all its heady discussions about self-determination and predestination (interspersed with scenes of Tom Cruise sprinting like Carl Lewis), it made *Blade Runner* (another dreary, psycho-techie homage based on a Philip K. Dick story) play like *The Sound of Music*. Roger Ebert, and other critics, gave Spielberg more props, calling the film "an awesomely virtuoso futurist thriller." Box office—$132 million domestically (and $358 million worldwide)—was not so awesome when you factored in the film's $102 million budget and Spielberg's and Cruise's sizable gross deals. Spielberg and Cruise took home an estimated $70 million or more, while Fox and DreamWorks wound up with about $20 million each, at best.

DreamWorks' other big, and very costly, summer movie, *Road to Perdition,* another Fox coproduction, also opened to respectfully mixed reviews, and grossed $104 million. Sam Mendes's second film was no *American Beauty.* DreamWorks might be making the kind of films that made the company proud, but profitability was still a vexing issue.

Another blockbuster that summer came in the form of an article by Bryan Burrough in the August issue of *Vanity Fair.* In the article, Michael Ovitz attributed his Hollywood demise to a "Gay Mafia" led by David Geffen. More than a decade after Geffen had vowed to his friend Howard Rosenman that he would "destroy" Ovitz—"watch me"—Ovitz was very much destroyed. Or, as Burrough wrote, "Michael Ovitz is ruined." After plowing more than $150 million of his personal fortune into what was to be his own dream company and a rival to CAA—the Artists Management Group—he was forced to sell the company for a piddling $12 million. His reputation as the Most Powerful Man in Hollywood had long since been replaced by Hollywood's Most Hated. And Geffen and his ilk were largely responsible, Ovitz believed.

The most telling sign of just how depleted Ovitz was, was his decision to speak so candidly to Burrough. The man who had wrapped himself in myth, who had built his reputation on his image—the *perception* of who Michael Ovitz was—had come out from behind the curtain. Never had he appeared so mortal. Geffen, who was of course quoted in the story, reacted with his own characteristic candor.

"Oh, please. A Gay Mafia?" he said. "This is so crazy. This is insane. I think he needs a psychiatrist. It's so paranoid, and so crazy, and so irresponsible, and makes him look like such a nut. It's beyond crazy. On a scale of 1 to 10 crazy, it's 11 . . . He's made a fool of himself, and he's made a huge failure of his life. To say you've been brought down by the Gay Mafia and its allies is as crazy as anything I've ever heard in my life."

Geffen didn't stop there. He called Burrough a minute after the interview. "Did I mention his extraordinary homophobia?"

And with that, the crown was officially passed. For those who had watched the uneasy dance between Geffen and Ovitz over the years, who always knew one had to be toppled, that the throne would not sustain two kings—and especially not *those* two—the duel was over. It was a far less dramatic finale than the chorus would have hoped for, although Ovitz's on-the-record reference to a "gay mafia" was not bad copy. The press, naturally, went crazy, and Ovitz was called out of the shadows to make a public apology when he realized just how much worse he'd made the situation. Meanwhile, the question rising in everyone's minds was: Who would be next? Geffen would need a formidable foe. It's what kept life interesting. It would only be a matter of time, everyone seemed to know.

Ironically, the year's most profitable film that year was its least assuming candidate for that honor. *The Ring,* after grossing an underwhelming $15 million its first weekend (causing more criticism of marketing), based on strong word of mouth, the following weekend, with an added 500 screens, grossed $18 million, an unusual turn of events. It would ultimately make $129 million domestically and $249 million worldwide. DreamWorks not only had a surprise hit, it had its first live-action franchise. Plans for *The Ring 2* were quickly set in motion. Unlike so many other of the studio's films, there were no major stars taking a chunk out of profits, and the budget had been kept to a modest $48 million.

When the Oscar race heated up, Miramax squarely boxed Dream-Works out of the picture for the first time since 1998. There would be no mudslinging between the two camps this year. The only contretemps had been a skirmish over the release dates for Miramax's *Gangs of New York* and DreamWorks' *Catch Me If You Can*. When Weinstein plunked down *Gangs of New York* on December 25, the day *Catch Me If You Can* was to open, Katzenberg went into a rage. Ultimately, Weinstein blinked and moved his movie to an earlier date in December.

This year was Miramax's most triumphant to date. When the Oscar nominations were announced in February of 2003, Miramax—exerting even more campaign muscle than usual, particularly on behalf of *Gangs of New York* (Harvey had publicly promised he'd win an Oscar for director Martin Scorsese)—racked up forty. Nominees included *Chicago,* based on the Bob Fosse musical; *The Hours,* an adaptation of Michael Cunningham's novel, starring Nicole Kidman as Virginia Woolf (a coproduction with Paramount); and *Frida,* starring Salma Hayek as the Mexican artist Frida Kahlo. The press, which had called Miramax down for the count the previous year, when the studio was trounced at the Academy Awards, was eating its words.

DreamWorks' showing paled considerably in comparison. Both *Road to Perdition* and *Catch Me If You Can* were excluded from all the major categories. *Road* received six nominations for art direction, original score, cinematography, sound, sound editing, and supporting actor (Paul Newman), and *Catch Me If You Can* nabbed just two, for music and supporting actor (Christopher Walken). Spielberg and Hanks were noticeably snubbed.

When the actual awards ceremony rolled around, *Gangs* failed to win even one Oscar. Instead, it was *Chicago* that ruled, winning Best Picture and five other statuettes, and reconfirming Hollywood's faith in movie musicals, a genre that hadn't been considered viable in decades until the ascendance of *Moulin Rouge!* the year before. *Frida* also took home two Oscars, and Kidman won Best Actress for *The Hours.*

This time, Terry Press couldn't cry foul play. DreamWorks had, for the first time in years, simply been shut out. Fittingly, there was no DreamWorks Oscar party, whereas Miramax had two—in addition to its traditional Oscar Eve party at the Mondrian, it held a bash for six hundred people the night of the Oscars at the St. Regis Hotel.

• • •

The weekend was not revelry-free, however. That year Katzenberg instituted the Night Before party, held at the Beverly Hills Hotel—a no-press event that raised money for the Motion Picture and Television Fund's retirement home for elderly members of the entertainment industry. For years Lew Wasserman had been the organization's biggest fundraiser and spokesman, and sometime before, he had recruited Katzenberg to reach out to younger members of the industry. He seemed to know the end was near, and he wanted to pick his own successor, seeing in Katzenberg the drive and passion of a leader. In June, when Wasserman passed away at the age of eighty-nine, Katzenberg inherited his role as the fund's leading light.

Wasserman's passing was akin to a national holiday in Hollywood. His memorial service, held in the Universal Amphitheater, drew more than three thousand attendees, who came to mourn the death of the man who was considered by all to be the last of the Old Hollywood moguls. President Clinton spoke, saying of Wasserman, "He helped me become president. He helped me stay president. He helped me become a better president." Spielberg called Wasserman "a living time machine to that golden era."

Nearly a decade had passed since Spielberg, Geffen, and Katzenberg made their pilgrimage to Wasserman's home to ask for his blessing to build a new studio. To move forward on their own and, fueled by models and dreams of the past, forge a new future in Hollywood. So much—Hollywood itself—had changed since that fateful day. So much had been learned. Would they have done it all the same way, knowing what they knew now?

Sinbad: Legend of the Seven Seas, due out in July of 2003, was Jeffrey Katzenberg's most extreme experiment yet. He called the film "our attempt to do an homage to Steven Spielberg. It is meant to be *Indiana Jones* in animation." The traditionally animated project—which followed the adventures of the seafaring mischief-maker from the *Arabian Nights* tales, had no musical numbers and no animals that talked. Sinbad's sidekick, a dog named Spike, did nothing more than drool a bit. As for Sinbad, he was no imaginatively shaped Shrek—he was all chiseled jaw-line and perfect pecs, much like the man who provided his voice: Brad Pitt.

However, in the months leading up to *Sinbad*'s release, even Katzenberg was having doubts about his once fervent philosophy that animated films should, in effect, be live-action films, only drawn. He was also feeling nervous about his still-not-total commitment to CGI. With the astronomical success of *Shrek,* not to mention that of Pixar (which was about to launch another CGI sensation into the marketplace: *Finding Nemo*), clinging to 2-D was feeling more and more like a losing proposition, and not just at DreamWorks. In November of 2002, Disney's traditionally animated *Treasure Planet* bombed so extravagantly that Katzenberg's former kingdom announced an estimated $74 million pretax write-off on the movie. Disney animation head Thomas Schumacher stepped down and hundreds of artists were laid off.

Starting to panic, Katzenberg began reversing course on *Sinbad,* trying to push it in a more fanciful, less "adult period piece," as he'd called it earlier, direction. "All of a sudden Jeffrey decided to change the art direction [on *Sinbad*] and make it more cartoony," said artist Paul Lasaine. "So it was way back to square one on a lot of things, even though you had a whole team of artists that were already rolling."

But even with these changes, in the wake of *Shrek, Sinbad,* which had been put into production four years earlier, felt like a throwback. When opening box-office grosses came in, they weren't just bad, they were comical. Over five days, *Sinbad* made just $6 million (half as much as *El Dorado* had made over half as many days). One DreamWorks executive recalled being incredulous, certain that the number must be from the first *afternoon.*

"It was a complete and total rejection of the marketplace," this source said.

The magnitude of DreamWorks' stumble was underscored by Pixar, whose *Finding Nemo,* a snappy underwater film about a lost clownfish whose father (voiced by Albert Brooks) searches for him with the help of fish friend Dory (Ellen DeGeneres), went on to become the highest-grossing animated film to date. Released just a few days before *Sinbad,* on May 30, it grossed $339 million domestically and $864 million worldwide.

Katzenberg may have had a hunch that *Sinbad* was doomed, but he wasn't prepared for just how doomed—the movie would lose $125 million. Initially he pointed his finger at marketing, telling Press and her staff: "We all have a piece of ownership in this movie. Own up to what was your mistake."

Ultimately, however, not even Katzenberg could deny that *Sinbad's* problems went beyond its ad campaign. Speaking at a Monday-morning staff meeting, he said, "We made a weak movie. Marketing didn't sell it, but we didn't make a strong product. Everyone has a cross to bear. There is failure to share." Executives were grateful that he was acknowledging his own hand in the disaster—something they felt he hadn't done when *El Dorado* bombed. Something else that was different about Katzenberg's reaction this time around: he wasn't getting over it, at least not as quickly as he had after previous disappointments. When *Prince of Egypt* let him down, Katzenberg had simply forged on, asking: "What's next?" But in the days and weeks after *Sinbad*—which went on to gross an abysmal $26 million at the box office—Katzenberg stewed. He even stopped speaking to Press for several weeks.

"*Sinbad* was a low point," said one former employee. "Jeffrey didn't recover ... He used to dance on tables and get so excited. He lost a lot of enthusiasm. There was a lack of levity."

Sinbad was a wake-up call in other ways, too. Katzenberg's love affair with 2-D animation was officially over. Katzenberg said goodbye to the medium that had made him.

Some say there was Katzenberg before *Sinbad* and there was Katzenberg after *Sinbad*. The same could be said of DreamWorks. If *El Dorado* had rocked the company, *Sinbad* came close to capsizing it, and in its aftermath, DreamWorks was nearly bankrupt. The animation studio would hemorrhage $189 million in 2003 (compared to the $115 million lost in 2000, the *El Dorado* year). According to the business model Geffen had established for DreamWorks, $300 million needed to always be on hand in order to keep DreamWorks liquid. In 2003 that $300 million was not available. Paul Allen was called on for another infusion. He gave it, but not as freely as in the past; this time, in exchange for a $300 million commitment, he demanded more ownership in DreamWorks, bringing his stake up to 24 percent (initially, he owned 18 percent of the company). Thus, even if his money wasn't drawn upon, he would increase his overall return in DreamWorks.

Sinbad was like an enormous domino that crashed down, setting other pieces in motion and sending out reverberations throughout DreamWorks. In the fall, the company's last nonfilm division was cut loose—DreamWorks Records was sold to Universal for $100 million. The label had never managed to produce enough big, commercial acts to support itself—and its lavish spending wasn't working in an environment built around breaking acts fast and moving on to the next thing. Furthermore, without the ballast of a deep-pocketed corporate parent, the label couldn't withstand the changes that had swept over the music industry over the last several years, from the rise in online music and corporate-owned radio to the growth in the DVD and video-game market, which further hurt CD sales.

The sale of the label was pure Geffen, who had finagled the deal in tandem with General Electric's purchase of Universal studios from Vivendi earlier in the year. (Like the Bronfmans, the French found Hollywood as foreign as a Starbucks Frappuccino.) Because the new owners of Universal wanted a guarantee that what they were buying included the rights to distribute Steven Spielberg's movies overseas, and DreamWorks' animated movies all over the world, Universal and DreamWorks re-upped their distribution deal for another five years. As part of that agreement, Geffen slipped in an added clause—that Universal buy DreamWorks Records, even though GE was not buying Universal's music assets. (DreamWorks' Nashville division, which was having success thanks to country superstar Toby Keith, was not part of the deal.)

The end of DreamWorks Records was also the final chapter for Mo Ostin and Lenny Waronker, two of the most beloved music executives of the twentieth century, who had shaped not just the music, but the way making and selling music was conducted for decades in the music industry. Driven by love rather than profits, Ostin and Waronker put the music before all else, a practice that inspired a devoted following among both artists and executives.

The sale was also Geffen's swan song, and with it, the man who had nurtured Laura Nyro, Joni Mitchell, and Jackson Browne—and, even if he hadn't loved the music, championed Guns N' Roses and Nirvana—closed the door on the business that had made him one of the richest men in the world. And, in Hollywood, the most feared.

The sale cut one of Geffen's primary ties to DreamWorks, and some felt that without that link, he became an even more distant partner in the company. But one of Geffen's friends downplayed the significance of the break, saying that it had no effect on his role, seeing as "he left the music business in his mind long ago."

• • •

Over at the live-action studio, no one felt the post-*Sinbad* crunch more than Mike De Luca, who was now, because of the financial situation, being even further reined in. When De Luca sent things to business affairs for approval, they were sent straight to Parkes. "I was told each and every deal had to go through Walter, despite what was in my contract," he would later tell the *L.A. Times'* Patrick Goldstein.

The blurry lines of power frustrated agents and producers, who complained that it wasn't clear who was in charge at DreamWorks, and therefore who should be approached with projects. But most of all it was frustrating to De Luca. Not only had he been stripped of the autonomy he'd enjoyed at New Line, he found himself at a studio where his creative sensibilities were increasingly at odds with those of the other major players. One by one, he had watched as projects he'd lobbied for—including *Sideways,* the latest film from *Election* writer-director Alexander Payne; *21 Grams,* directed by Alejandro González Iñárritu (*Amores Perros*); and Roland Emmerich's global-warming tent pole, *The Day after Tomorrow*—went to other studios because he'd been unable to convince his superiors as to their worth. It wasn't just Parkes who lacked enthusiasm; in the case of *Sideways*—a project De Luca said he would "fall on my sword for"—Spielberg didn't think Paul Giamatti was a movie star.

If Parkes and MacDonald were cracking down, they had their reasons. Having tried to be more hands-off when De Luca first arrived, the films that the new head of production *had* pushed through—*Head of State* and *Biker Boyz*—were disasters. And worse than losing money, which they did, they threatened to tarnish the sacrosanct (and Spielberg-endorsed) DreamWorks brand.

The bottom line was that the films De Luca had been able to make didn't fit in at a company that hung its identity on Oscar-winning films such as *American Beauty, Gladiator,* and *Saving Private Ryan.* Tension between De Luca and Parkes was kept at a low boil, never exploding into screaming matches or slammed phones. This was, after all, DreamWorks. Those who raised their voices did so at their own peril. But nobody missed the two men's mutual disdain. "Walter seemed unimpressed" by De Luca, said one insider. "You could tell by the way he'd take a while to get back to him, not respond to material he pitched, and pass on projects. He was never mean or rude. Arrogant, maybe." Meanwhile, friends of De Luca's say that he was grumbling about Parkes, and feeling undermined. "At first he was disdainful of Walter and his style when Walter wasn't around. Then he was really sarcastic. Then he gave up," said one.

De Luca did not win any points for himself when he arranged a screening of New Line's spring break movie *The Real Cancun* in the Amblin screening room. During the scene in which a frat boy pours a cup of his urine on a bikini-clad babe who's been stung by a jellyfish, in walked Spielberg. He sheepishly turned around and walked right out.

De Luca's days at DreamWorks were not without bright spots, however. When *Old School* was released in February, it was an immediate hit, grossing $75 million, or three times what it had cost to produce. It went on to make another $143 million in DVD sales. Even before *Old School* was released, DreamWorks executives realized that the movie was a fun, risqué romp and that both Ferrell and Vaughn had turned in winning performances. Ferrell, in particular—even Parkes would admit—was the film's breakout star, and *Old School* sent him steadily en route to being one of Hollywood's most sought-after actors. Never again would he receive less than $1 million to star in a movie—within a year, he'd be making twenty times that.

That Ferrell was not just funny, but very funny, was nothing new to his managers, Jimmy Miller and Eric Gold, nor to Judd Apatow, who for years had been collaborating with Ferrell and a number of other funnymen, including Vaughn, Ben Stiller, Jack Black, Owen Wilson, and Adam McKay, who'd met years earlier in various comedy venues, such as *SNL* and *The Ben Stiller Show*. But studios had been slow to come around to the group's brand of post-ironic, at times juvenile, humor, and for years Apatow's feature projects had been turned down. But with *Old School,* the so-called frat pack was baptized into Hollywood. New Line fast-tracked its comedy *Elf,* starring Ferrell as an overgrown Santa's helper. And when it came out and grossed $173 million (on a budget of $33 million), Ferrell was officially the hottest comedy star in Hollywood. DreamWorks reversed its decision about *Anchorman: The Legend of Ron Burgundy,* the film that had inspired Parkes's slight against Ferrell. But it cost the studio—having sent the film into turnaround, DreamWorks now had to enter a bidding war to win back the movie, at a cost of $4 million.

De Luca grew increasingly tired of struggling for control—and respect. By the time *House of Sand and Fog,* a film that De Luca had set up at DreamWorks, was released in December, he was "receding into the woodwork," according to one director. By the end of the year, friends were saying that De Luca would likely be gone when his contract expired in June.

De Luca could not have been warmed by Spielberg's comment in an *Esquire* article by Kim Masters that said he was grateful for Parkes and MacDonald's work at the studio and "to some extent" that of De Luca. Though the most telling quote of all was when Spielberg called 2003—the biggest hit of which was *Old School*—"our first shitty year."

As DreamWorks weathered its most unstable period to date, one looming concern was that, in just two years, Paul Allen could begin cashing out his millions. To pay him back, DreamWorks was going to need money. Someone was going to have to come up with it.

In October of 2003, Bill Savoy was fired as Allen's investment chief. For more than a decade, Allen had put his trust in Savoy in pursuing an investment strategy that now seemed an extravagant disaster. Due to the crash of the tech market, and investments that were ill-timed and, in many cases, ill-advised, Allen's fortunes, which had once shot up to $30 billion, making him the second richest man in the world, had now tumbled down to $18 billion. Although the Microsoft co-founder could often seem indifferent to his losses when they stemmed from causes, or companies, that he was passionate about, Bert Kolde, Allen's college roommate at Washington State University and chief operating officer of Allen's home-entertainment company Digeo Inc., said that the ordeal was "a crucible" for his friend.

Allen himself admitted to *BusinessWeek,* "I've been through the fire in the last few years."

Replacing Savoy was a team of more than two dozen MBAs, many of them with Ivy League credentials. Allen also elevated his sister, Jody Patton—a far more cynical voice in regards to Allen's investments than Savoy had ever been—to CEO of Vulcan Inc. And he became more active in how and where his money was being spent.

Savoy hadn't been the primary reason Allen invested in Dream-Works, but he was *a* reason, and certainly a big reason that Allen had stayed in for so long. Savoy was as much a believer in the company, and as smitten by Geffen, as Allen was. Vulcan's new investment strategy was to cut losses and diversify, and, accordingly, Allen began dumping dozens of slumping investments and writing off many more. In a few months, his portfolio was down to just forty companies, from one hundred. DreamWorks was not excluded from the new scrutiny.

"My sense was that the old Vulcan management thought of [the DreamWorks] deal as a talent relations deal for Paul Allen to be friends with Steven Spielberg, and Steven Spielberg's friends, and David Geffen," said one former DreamWorks executive. "When [Allen] cleaned house . . . the new people came in and said, basically, 'Paul, you don't need to have a billion-dollar investment in DreamWorks to be friends with Steven Spielberg.'"

Another insider involved with the financial dealings between DreamWorks and Allen said, "In the early years, we were always hearing 'Paul's great.' But in later years . . . suddenly we were hearing about 'those Vulcan people' and how difficult they were being. There was a lot of stress amongst everyone, a lot of wear and tear. Paul was less great then."

"Those Vulcan people" were asking tough questions. In one meeting with DreamWorks executives, a Vulcan investment manager told Katzenberg that, having reviewed all of Vulcan's passive investments, DreamWorks was at the bottom of the list in terms of its return.

Everyone at DreamWorks was well aware that Allen could begin cashing out his investment in 2005. An initial public offering had always seemed like a likely solution. By 2003, spinning off the animation studio as a public company was already being discussed, timed to the release of *Shrek 2* the following year. Even so, sources say that DreamWorks didn't expect Allen to actually call his option and demand out. When he did, it set in motion marathon phone sessions between Geffen and Katzenberg, who were now faced with the reality that an IPO wasn't just a wise precaution, it was being forced. Katzenberg responded to the news by saying to Geffen: "If he wants war, we'll fight!" according to a source with knowledge of the conversation. The situation had to be handled with kid gloves, and Geffen set about advising his partner as to how to proceed.

29

NAKED IN PUBLIC

ATZENBERG WAS in coronation mode. The man who, a decade earlier, had gotten a job out of the formation of DreamWorks would now be getting his own company out of an IPO. Katzenberg would now be officially on his own—if *Shrek* had bought him his freedom, *Shrek 2* was about to buy him his independence. An IPO would also earn him a lot more money. Ten years after he'd had to mortgage two homes in order to keep up with his superwealthy partners, Katzenberg's own wealth had increased considerably—according to *Forbes,* he was now worth $800 million. But he was still paces behind his billionaire-club buddies. Geffen's worth was estimated at $4 billion, Spielberg's at $2.5 billion. An IPO would help close the gap.

As the CEO of a publicly traded company, the erstwhile golden retriever would, more than ever before, be on par with Michael Eisner. He would also become an even more direct threat to his onetime homeland, Disney—and to Disney's distribution partner Pixar, then the only publicly traded animation company on Wall Street.

The timing couldn't have been more delicious. Whether it was irony or karma, while Katzenberg was preparing for his crown, Eisner was being deposed. In March of 2004, the Disney board stripped him of his chairman title (he remained the company's CEO), and 43 percent of shareholders voted to oppose his reelection to the board. Eisner was under fire for a myriad of reasons, among them ABC's faltering ratings, stagnant stock, and Eisner's blundering renegotiation efforts with Pixar, whose contract was about to expire. Steve Jobs openly blamed the inability of the two companies to come to terms squarely on Eisner. Suddenly, Disney was in a position to be stripped of its most reliable supplier of animated movies.

Eisner was acutely aware of what was going on with his neighbors in Glendale. At a conference in June, he said that he found it "a little embarrassing" that DreamWorks had a sequel to *Shrek* that summer while, "for whatever reason, which I am not getting into, we don't have the same announcements." (The remark was aimed at Pixar, which, with the exception of *Toy Story*, had not moved ahead on sequels to its other hits.)

One can only imagine the triumphant cackle that emanated from across the street as a result of this admission.

If the IPO hinged on anything, it was *Shrek deux*. Like the first *Shrek*, the film was being counted on to overshadow the company's otherwise unimpressive performance. Just how unimpressive that was became clear over the summer, when, for the first time in history, financial information about DreamWorks was disclosed in a filing with the Securities and Exchange Commission in preparation for the IPO. The results were not pretty. Only in 1999 and in 2001 had the animation studio made a profit, of $4 million and $3.6 million, respectively. Every other year, the studio had drained cash.

Granted, the animation studio had drastically changed course from its early days, through its embrace of CGI and its focus on broad comedies à la *Shrek*, as opposed to adult-themed epics. *Shrek 2*, the hope was, would go a long way in proving that, as would *Shark Tale*, which was due out in October. (For the first time, DreamWorks was releasing two animated films in one year, a schedule more accelerated than any other studio—Pixar took years-long hiatuses between films.) That fall, DreamWorks was also launching the first-ever CGI television show—*Father of the Pride*, about a white lion who stars in the Siegfried and Roy act in Las Vegas, a great favorite of Katzenberg's. Katzenberg was over the moon about the show, crowing to anyone who would listen that it could "change television." In some ways, this was already proving true: NBC was paying a whopping $2.5 million to produce each episode, making *Father of the Pride* one of the most expensive TV shows in history.

Considering what was riding on it, the launch of *Shrek 2* was nothing short of colossal. Naturally, it premiered at Cannes. But this time it wasn't just Mike Myers who showed up on the Croisette to compete against Pedro Almodóvar's *Bad Education*, Jean-Luc Godard's *Notre Musique*, and Wong Kar-wai's *2046*. This year, Katzenberg brought a posse of more than a hundred people that included not just the stars from *Shrek 2* but those lending their voices to *Shark Tale* (footage of which was being shown at the festival). Antonio Banderas, Cameron Diaz, Eddie Murphy, Julie Andrews, Angelina Jolie, Will Smith, and Jack Black were just some of the stars put up in the ritzy Hotel du Cap for several days of nonstop wining, dining, and promoting. There was a *Shrek* party at La Napoule, a mock castle located a few miles west of Cannes. The stars of *Shark Tale*—Will Smith, Angelina Jolie, and Jack Black—were paraded around the harbor aboard an inflatable shark; for a climax, Black dove into the water. Rumor has it that when Jolie resisted getting on the boat, Smith leaned in and whispered: "Do you ever want to star in a movie that makes over $100 million? *Get on the fucking fish.*"

Shrek 2, which was again directed by Andrew Adamson, this time with Kelly Asbury and Conrad Vernon, was as witty and visually powerful as the first film. After being warmly received in Cannes, it went on to gross $441 million in North America and $919 million around the world, displacing *Finding Nemo* as the highest-grossing animated film of all time.

Shark Tale, which was due out in October, was a different story, and one of the most chaotic productions to date. The film had originated as an under-the-sea mobster movie with Martin Scorsese and Robert De Niro. But when Will Smith was cast, the film took a more urban, hip-hop turn. Story lines were tossed aside and then brought back; multiple writers were hired to do punch-ups; whole animated sequences were scrapped (to much expense). Katzenberg, of course, was right there in the middle of it. The tailspin environment meant that everyone was working around the clock; at one point T-shirts were made up that bore the Katzenbergian slogan, "If you're not going to come to work on Saturday, don't bother coming on Sunday." Scorsese's blowfish character—a tough boss—was featured on the shirt.

An early screening of the film for an audience of school kids had gone over disastrously: the kids didn't think it was funny. Afterward, according to one source, "Jeffrey was freaking out."

"He was like, 'We have a problem.' He called everyone into the room, and was basically like, 'You're not leaving the room until this is solved.'"

Katzenberg's orders were clear: "Make it funny."

Naturally, it was noted that *Shark Tale* was an awful lot like another fish movie—Pixar's *Finding Nemo*—and, naturally, Pixar cried foul. But DreamWorks denied the charge. "We wouldn't have done *Shark Tale* if we knew *Finding Nemo* was that far along," said one former DreamWorks employee. "When we found out about *Finding Nemo*, we were in production. And we weren't happy about it." There was even a discussion about scrapping *Shark Tale* to avoid a showdown, but at that point the movie was too far along.

In the end, despite its troubled history, Katzenberg was able to will *Shark Tale* to gold. Reviews were awful, but it still hauled in an enormous $47 million its opening weekend. (This figure was helped by the fact that Katzenberg opened the movie on more than four thousand screens, another extravagant gesture.) The movie went on to gross $160 million domestically and $367 million worldwide.

And so, the stage was set.

In preparation for the IPO, DreamWorks had reorganized its ranks. By now co-COO Ron Nelson had left the company, having given up on trying to curb DreamWorks' profligacy. ("Ron got tired of the kids, and having to say, 'Cut it out,'" said one source. "He didn't feel the [Dream-Works] partners were letting him do what was responsible.") His position was filled by Kris Leslie, who had worked under him for many years. Also gone was co-COO Helene Hahn, whose work schedule at DreamWorks had scaled back in recent years. Since marrying in 1999, she had been spending more time at her home in Park City, Utah, only working in L.A. two days a week; the other days, she communicated with Katzenberg via satellite. When the decision to go public was announced, Hahn retired, on less than cozy terms with Katzenberg, who had not told her that he and Geffen were recruiting Rick Sands, COO of Miramax, to replace her. Sands would also take over Katzenberg's business responsibilities at the live-action studio, seeing as once the animation studio went public, Katzenberg would be legally prevented from devoting more than 10 percent of his time to live action.

The top three executives under Katzenberg at DreamWorks Animation, as the "new" studio would be called—who would steward the studio on its journey from private to public—were Ann Daly, who was promoted to chief operating officer; Leslie, who became chief financial officer; and Kathy Kendrick, the studio's general counsel. Katzenberg, who would assume the role of chief executive officer at the studio—in exchange for a salary of $1 a year—lacked CEO experience. To make up for this, he appointed former Pepsico chairman Roger Enrico as chairman of the animation studio's board. Other board members included Geffen and Starbucks chief executive Howard Schultz. (Spielberg opted out of a board seat because he didn't want to disclose his personal financial information, but would serve as a "consultant" to the company.)

Enrico set about trying to mentor Katzenberg, proffering the advice that to do well in business, you have to be flexible and willing to adapt. To make his point, he told Katzenberg to show up at a meeting wearing his watch on his other wrist, just to see how it felt.

But Katzenberg needed more than just metaphorical inspirations involving timepieces. For there were still major questions surrounding DreamWorks' transition from a private to a public company. Take the *Shrek* franchise away, and the animation studio, which had a valuation of $2.75 billion, had almost nothing but big money-losers. While DreamWorks and Pixar—the company Katzenberg most liked to compare DreamWorks to—might be leading the animation competition, they were, by no measure, equals. Pixar, which had the most flawless record in the motion-picture business, period, had a valuation of $3.7 billion, no debt, and more than $500 million in cash. Furthermore, *Father of the Pride,* which debuted in August, was stumbling in the ratings and on the verge of being shelved by NBC for the fall sweeps. The show was a grandiose, and costly, flop, and took away some of DreamWorks Animation's, and Katzenberg's, credibility. (When Roy Horn—of Siegfried and Roy—was mauled by a white tiger while *Father of the Pride* was in production, a macabre shadow had been cast over the show.)

Then there was Katzenberg. While the company was preparing to go public, Geffen had advised him to bring on a creative head of the studio—someone along the lines of Pixar's John Lasseter. But Katzenberg refused, deeming himself the creative maestro of the studio. It was his Achilles' heel: it wasn't enough to be the most talented, hardworking studio executive in Hollywood; he also had to be seen as a creative powerhouse. But with a company that would be accountable to stockholders and under very public scrutiny, this trait wouldn't just be an annoyance to animators, it could very well be a liability.

Katzenberg would be needed to run the company—lead the board, communicate with investors—and make sure good movies were being made. Not be the one actually making the movies. As his track record at DreamWorks proved, Katzenberg making the movies was a very mixed bag.

Katzenberg was about to step into the role for which Eisner had deemed he wasn't fit. Was he now? He had eight years more experience. And as much, if not more, drive.

This was evident when, in the wake of *Shark Tale*, Katzenberg and Enrico embarked on a seventeen-city road show to talk up Dream-Works Animation to Wall Street investors. Over the course of twelve days and eighty-seven presentations, Katzenberg gave the sales pitch of his life—by the end of the campaign, the offering was fifteen times oversubscribed—a feat he accomplished with characteristic tirelessness. On the last day of the tour, everyone was burned out, ready to return home—everyone, that is, but Katzenberg.

"We're done, there is nobody else to see, and Jeffrey's saying, 'There's got to be somebody else to see,'" said Enrico. "He just loved it. We said, 'Jeffrey, you're done.'"

Geffen, meanwhile, was griping that DreamWorks Animation's ticker symbol was going to be DWA and not SKG—which, for legacy reasons, he preferred. At one point he exploded, "I'm not going to vote my interest if it's not SKG!" Eventually, he backed down.

The live-action studio was going through its own transition over the summer of 2004, albeit a far less auspicious one. Unsurprisingly, when Mike De Luca's contract was up in June, he left to become a producer at Sony.

Meanwhile, more of his movies were bombing, and further sullying the sacred DreamWorks brand. Neither *Win a Date with Tad Hamilton!*, nor *EuroTrip*, nor *Envy* managed to even make $20 million; all received abominable reviews. *Envy* was considered such an embarrassment that Ben Stiller refused to do publicity for the movie, and DreamWorks did not hold a premiere. Even *House of Sand and Fog* had underwhelmed, grossing just $13 million and failing to redeem itself at the Oscars, earlier in the year, where DreamWorks was, for the first time in its history, completely shut out. (There was so little faith in *Sinbad* that it hadn't even been submitted.)

But it wasn't only De Luca who was drawing criticism. None of those movies even opened well, suggesting that marketing wasn't doing *its* job. However much of a stinker *Envy* was, it starred two of Hollywood's biggest comedy stars, around whom a publicity campaign could have lured audiences to the theater before negative word of mouth spoiled its run. Or so production executives charged. Marketing's defense was along the lines of: "Have you *seen* the movie?" As in: good luck.

Terry Press and her team took another hit when *Collateral,* a Michael Mann film starring Tom Cruise and Jamie Foxx, opened to just $24 million, when it had been tracking to open as high as $45 million. Through strong word of mouth, it went on to squeak out over $100 million, but a Cruise-Foxx picture was expected to do far more than that. Worse, Spielberg's next film—*The Terminal,* starring Tom Hanks and Catherine Zeta-Jones as star-crossed lovers stuck in an airport—grossed a wobbly $77 million domestically.

When it did double that overseas (where marketing was handled by UIP), Press again was blamed. (After Parkes, who produced *The Terminal,* saw a cut of the film, he'd told executives, "Well, it looks like our dry spell is over.") But *The Terminal's* problems went beyond marketing. Even before the film was released, Spielberg was uncharacteristically uncertain. He even resorted to testing the film—something he hadn't done since *Jaws*—and shooting two endings.

Meanwhile, Katzenberg was anxious about the film's cost, which sources say was far more than the $60 million DreamWorks claimed. The set alone—a replica of Charles de Gaulle airport—had to be constructed in the middle of the Mojave Desert because in the wake of 9/11 it was impossible to shoot in airports. Beyond the set, which was partially paid for by corporate sponsors that set up "shops" in the terminal (though not as many as Katzenberg had planned), Katzenberg fretted over the cost of Spielberg's transportation—he was flying to the set in a Sikorsky S-76 helicopter. When Katzenberg appealed to Geffen for help, he was told, "That's your problem."

The Terminal took a critical drubbing and occasioned one of *Variety* editor in chief Peter Bart's famous "memos." After acknowledging that Spielberg served as the "apex" of "cinematic royalty," and that "no Hollywood filmmaker has ever been wealthier, exercised more power or traveled in more exalted circles," Bart weighed in.

"Is it possible that Sir Steven is suffering a case of the middle-age blahs?" he asked. "Has the man who always makes magic somehow misplaced his wand?"

Over the next several months, Bart was badmouthed within the gates of Amblin.

By the time De Luca left the company, the job of president of production at DreamWorks was referred to internally as "the putz job." Having watched both Cooper and De Luca suffer so miserably, the position seemed like nothing more than a joke. When De Luca left, it was Adam Goodman's turn. Having learned that outsiders simply didn't work at DreamWorks, the studio turned to one of its own.

Though virtually unknown outside DreamWorks, Goodman, who was thirty-two years old, was a consummate DreamWorks insider. He'd started as an assistant at the company when it was first formed. A hard and driven worker, he'd quickly moved up the ranks over the years, ascending not just to an executive role, but to the most coveted executive role of all—that of "Spielberg's guy." As such, Goodman oversaw all of Spielberg's projects, read material for him, and was his general go-to person. Having grown up at DreamWorks, Goodman wasn't flashy. He dressed in jeans, button-down shirts, and white sneakers. But he was a savvy operator, the possessor of a Katzenbergian understanding of the importance of details—the thank-you note sent promptly after a meeting; the Christmas gift that wowed—and of relationships, both obvious and less so. In addition to people like Spielberg, Katzenberg, and Parkes (as well as Cooper and De Luca), Goodman had forged a relationship with Kristie Macosko, Spielberg's assistant *cum* gatekeeper, whose fearsome reputation (according to one former assistant, Macosko was accomplished in the art of "shutting your ass down") kept most people at a safe distance. Goodman felt no such trepidation and would frequently stop by Macosko's desk to chat, or join her outside for a smoke.

Goodman's track record in films wasn't all that impressive—he'd worked on *Head of State* and *Surviving Christmas*. But he was one of the few people at DreamWorks who looked at the big picture and recognized weaknesses. Taking a cue from his wife, Jessica, an executive at Warner Bros., he began making competitive development reports, tracking what movies other studios had in their pipelines. Though standard at other studios, the practice was new to DreamWorks, and impressed higher-ups, none more so than Spielberg.

In his new role, Goodman was feeling the heat. The live-action studio's pipeline was dry, and it was on Goodman's shoulders to produce a slate, seemingly overnight, for the upcoming years. Katzenberg was calling, asking where the movies were, as was Geffen, who for the first time in DreamWorks' history was playing an active role in the live-action studio now that Katzenberg was tied up with animation full-time. Geffen was less of a micromanager than either Katzenberg or Parkes. His style was to give people enough rope with which to either swing or hang themselves, while offering constant, priceless commentary. ("I hate this fucking movie business — do whatever you want!" he might say to Goodman.) But he also offered support, backing Goodman when he believed in a project. Even so, when Geffen called, everyone noticed that Goodman's face paled by a few shades.

Adding to the stickiness of the situation was that Parkes and Mac-Donald weren't totally out of the picture at first. Despite this, Goodman charged ahead. He was determined to divest the studio of any latent institutional complacency — the sort that creeps in when Steven Spielberg is your masthead — and to whip his staff into shape. He pushed them to work the town more and be better informed about what projects were out there. For the first time, executives were being held accountable. When a film went to another studio, there wasn't just a pat on the back and a "Better luck next time" — which had been the standard protocol at DreamWorks — there was hell to pay. (This happened when the next Will Ferrell film, *Talladega Nights,* landed at Sony.)

Having never received any real tutelage in how to manage — Parkes and MacDonald had been his only mentors — Goodman was green, and somewhat naive when it came to leadership. When, as a result of the pressure he was under, he yelled and made threats, other executives and agents were not charmed. (In Hollywood, making a scene is more forgivable when you have experience under your belt.)

But it couldn't be denied that things were happening, or that Goodman was, as he was telling agents, "trying to make DreamWorks an easier place to do business." Within days of being promoted, Goodman — who was working closely with executives Marc Haimes and Mark Sourian — had plunked down a million bucks for a spec script about cloning, called *The Island.* He smelled a Spielbergian-type tent pole, and, after reading it, he sent it to his boss, who at the time was in Japan on the set of *Memoirs of a Geisha*. When Spielberg approved, Goodman signed off on it, even though Parkes and MacDonald—who were on a flight back to L.A. from India—had not. Goodman had the script waiting for the couple at their home when they arrived. When Parkes finally called, he admitted the script was good, though he was apparently irked that Goodman had proceeded without him.

Spielberg found it more than good. He wanted to make it, and he knew whom he wanted to direct it: Michael Bay, the director of *Pearl Harbor* and *Armageddon*. That Spielberg, who normally handled special-effects blockbusters himself, thank you, wanted Bay to direct *The Island* was slightly odd, especially considering that Bay was a mainstay at Disney, where he and producer Jerry Bruckheimer were the studio's resident blow-up guys. Bay was also the most commercial director in Hollywood. Now he was working at . . . DreamWorks? Even Goodman admitted at the time: "Michael Bay was as foreign to DreamWorks as anything was to DreamWorks."

But soon enough, Bay received the million-dollar phone call. Spielberg was on the line, telling him he was talented, and that he'd just read the perfect script for him. Within hours, *The Island* script showed up on the doorstep of Bay's $5 million Bel Air manse.

"I want you to read it tonight. I've got to have an answer right away," Spielberg had instructed him. Bay did as he was told, staying up until 3:30 in the morning reading. By the time he'd finished, he'd made up his mind. "I think the scene that really hooked me was when they execute this pregnant woman," Bay said.

Goodman had his first tent pole. Bay had his first DreamWorks movie, which was also his first non-Disney movie other than *Bad Boys* and its sequel—something that must have delighted Katzenberg, who'd been the one to recommend the director to Spielberg in the first place.

Bay was reminded that he was breaking with his past when he was chatting with Bruckheimer over the phone, discussing weekend plans. Bay was about to hang up, when Bruckheimer said, "So. I hear you committed to something."

Bay sputtered a noncommittal response. "Yeah, but, I mean, nothing's definite. It's just—"

"Just so you know," Bruckheimer broke in. "We passed." And with that, he hung up.

The plan was for *The Island* to serve as a 2005 summer release, along with *War of the Worlds,* a coproduction with Paramount. This meant that the film—which would require complicated sets, special effects, and big money—would have to be made in just over a year's time—a frighteningly short window. It was going to be, as one source put it, "microwaved."

Over the next several months, Goodman and his crew worked quickly to round out the slate. There was a huge sense of urgency. One agent recalled getting a call from a panicked Goodman, who yelled: "I've got to fill these five writing assignments!"

The upcoming slate, when it was revealed, adhered to a practical—and traditional—model of combining big and splashy (*The Island*) with small and economical, such as *Dreamer,* a father-daughter story starring Dakota Fanning and Kurt Russell; and *Red Eye,* an airline thriller that Parkes dryly described as "an hour and a half in coach." Who knew where things were headed, but for the first time in a long while, the live-action studio was moving. The only question was: at what expense? When DreamWorks shelled out $1.25 million for the rights to *Baywatch,* the TV series made famous by the combination of Pamela Anderson and a red Speedo, observers noticed that Dream-Works was veering away from the *American Beauty* business.

"That, to me, was the final straw," said producer Dean Zanuck. "When they optioned the rights to *Baywatch,* I thought . . . They're just like everybody else now. I don't think they would have touched [that project] back in the day."

Early on the morning of October 28, 2004, Spielberg, Katzenberg, and Geffen arrived at the New York Stock Exchange for DreamWorks Animation's first day of trading. It was a historic day, marking as it did the first IPO for a Hollywood studio since 1997, when MGM became a publicly traded company. It was also a symbolic day for DreamWorks, echoing the partners' initial debut, ten years earlier, at the Peninsula hotel. But there were differences. This time, the three men were not dressed in khakis and casual shirts. They were wearing dark suits and perfectly knotted ties. They looked older, too; ten years showed on their slightly gaunter faces. Katzenberg was looking more like Geffen, with his hair trimmed ultra-close to his scalp.

Something else that had changed was that this day was all about

Katzenberg, who, along with Roger Enrico, rang the opening-day bell. Only afterward did Spielberg and Geffen, grinning ear to ear like proud parents, join him at the podium. No longer was Katzenberg the grateful protégé. In 2004, the stage belonged to him.

One thing that hadn't changed in a decade, however, was the sensational response generated by the trio. With the stage set by Google—which had gone public in August and, over the course of two months, more than doubled its valuation to $47 billion—DreamWorks similarly pleased Wall Street. DreamWorks stock, set at a bold $28 a share, soared up nearly 40 percent on its first day of trading, closing at $38.75 and raising a massive $812 million. Because of the strong showing, the so-called green shoe option was exercised—in which the underwriters sell more shares—causing DreamWorks' proceeds to shoot up to $900 million. DreamWorks Animation's valuation blossomed to $4.09 billion, just shy of Pixar's $4.56 billion.

Once again, the media turned somersaults: "Dreamy Start for DreamWorks" (CNNMoney.com); "Street Cred for D'Works cartoon IPO" (*Daily Variety*); "Animated Magic: DreamWorks Heads $howered in Stock Windfall" (the *New York Post*).

Individually, Spielberg and Geffen each saw paper profits of $86 million, boosting the value of their 8 million shares each to $312 million. Katzenberg's stake soared up $93 million to $336 million, making him, officially, and at long last, a billionaire. Paul Allen, whose stake soared up to $1.3 billion, made $60 million from selling some of his shares.

If SKG had reason to celebrate, behind the scenes, a number of high-level employees were disappointed that the IPO meant far less for them. It was, instead, just making a bunch of already rich guys richer. Leading up to the IPO, Katzenberg had promised senior executives jackpots of between $5 million and $10 million when the animation studio went public. But when stock prices were unveiled, just days before the IPO, the numbers were not quite so high. The ballpark was a value of more like $2 million vested over five, and in some cases seven, years. Furthermore, they were in the form of options, not grants, making them far less desirable, and valuable, should DreamWorks' stock plunge.

According to a DreamWorks source, Katzenberg explained the discrepancy by saying that he had had to give more stock and grants to board members than he had originally thought.

The marketing department was particularly upset when they were told that because they were technically part of the live-action studio, they were owed less stock. Virtually the entire department had been there since the very beginning, having come from Disney, where they'd given up lucrative stock plans.

The situation was compounded by how much the principals and other top officers at DreamWorks Animation were receiving. Ann Daly's package, in particular, caused an uproar—Daly's combined shares of vested and unvested stock translated into a $9.5 million payday.

"What Ann got really stood out," said one source, who said the IPO caused "tension and unhappiness."

Disgruntlement over stock allotments is par for the course when companies go public (numerous employees felt Steve Jobs hadn't done them right in Pixar's IPO), but at DreamWorks, the situation wasn't just about an IPO, it was about ten years of promises from Katzenberg that everyone's hard work and sacrifice (lack of bonuses, for one) would one day be repaid. An end-of-the-rainbow payoff had been expected from day one. Everyone from executives to screenwriters had been told from the beginning that, as the company grew and prospered, so too would its employees.

Even without any stock drama, the bifurcation of the live-action and animation studios marked a fork in the road, an end to a journey that had begun so momentously in 1994.

As one employee put it: "DreamWorks was now two companies, there was a different vibe. We'd been a company for eight years, and suddenly half your siblings are different from you." Going forward, it was clear, nothing would be the same. With DreamWorks Animation now its own, freestanding company, the purpose that had brought S, K, and G together in the first place—to rescue Katzenberg from his post-Disney exile—was gone.

"The thing people always forget about DreamWorks is, it was created to give Jeffrey a job," said one insider, who believes the most popular interpretation of the Why DreamWorks Was Formed story. "Steven can work for whomever he wants; Geffen's richer than rich, he doesn't need a studio. The basis for the company was Jeffrey. And once Jeffrey had his own animation studio, it was almost like the reason for the company to exist, didn't exist anymore."

30

IN A SNICKET

O N MAY 18, 2005, Walter Parkes and Laurie MacDonald graced the cover of *Variety*, looking as gorgeous as ever. Parkes, now fifty-four years old, was wearing a dark suit and a crisp, white shirt, unbuttoned at the collar. He was deeply tanned, and his movie-star looks were still vibrantly in place. Next to him, MacDonald was ever the blond, patrician queen. The story, titled "Dream Team Takes Flight," marked the end of the duo's reign at DreamWorks—they were, finally, stepping down to become producers. The decision was described as "mutual," and so it was. The couple was never more eager to leave their studio responsibilities behind—as they had been asking to do for years—having been bathed in increasingly negative, even shrill, publicity in recent months.

The whole town was up in arms. One producer described a meeting of several big-name producers, including Brian Grazer, Jerry Bruckheimer, and Saul Zaentz, during which, when "Walter's name came up, it was devastating how many people were angry. I mean, really angry, at just, sort of, the arrogance and the idea that this guy could be running a studio and then appropriate other people's movies, and the only way you could get a movie made was if Walter became a producer on it, and so forth."

The accusations were harsh, and permeated Hollywood. Yet, looking over the couple's producing credits, virtually all of the films they produced, they developed from the ground up—such as *Catch Me If You Can, The Time Machine, The Terminal,* and *The Lookout.*

In some instances, where they were said to have "glommed on," there were behind-the-scenes details that made the situation far more complicated than at first glance. For instance, Parkes was accused of becoming a producer on *The Kite Runner*, based on the novel by Khaled Hosseini, only after it became a best-selling book. Yet William Horberg, who set up the film at DreamWorks, had an arrangement with Parkes whereby he shared in Parkes's first-dollar-gross deal when Parkes executive-produced his films. Thus it was in his interest to partner with Parkes, and he approached him about the film early on (even if Parkes at first had reservations because the film was small and would be made with subtitles). As for *The Island*, Parkes and Mac-Donald were not interested in producing the film (action movies were never their thing), but were encouraged by DreamWorks—Adam Goodman, for one, seemed to want help dealing with Michael Bay —and agreed to do it.

In some cases Parkes and MacDonald became producers, or executive producers, on films that they did not themselves bring to the studio, but put time and effort on, such as *The Tuxedo* and *Road to Perdition*. When *Gladiator 2* was discussed (the film has never been made), Parkes asked to be a full producer on it. The logic was that he and MacDonald deserved it; they weren't simply attaching themselves, they were being fairly rewarded for their work.

The situation was encouraged by executives working under Parkes and MacDonald. "Walter didn't love the child unless the child was his," said one. "So the strategy for setting up material was to get Walter and Laurie to take ownership. Nine times out of ten, that meant getting them to come on as producers."

To outsiders, however, the fact that Parkes and MacDonald could jointly oversee and produce films, including those that were brought in by other producers, was simply wrong. And by 2005, resentment over the unorthodoxy of the situation had become a resounding roar in Hollywood. Parkes and MacDonald themselves showed signs of being weary of their situation and the outrage it was causing. When Kim Masters wrote a stinging piece about the couple in *Esquire*, Parkes is said to have been devastated.

Then there was the issue of how much money Parkes and Mac-Donald were making in their hybrid roles. It wasn't just producers who were angry. After 2002, when Parkes and MacDonald produced the bulk of DreamWorks' movies—a year that, according to studio sources, they made more money than DreamWorks (this issue was apparently brought up at a meeting at the live-action studio)—people at DreamWorks felt that the couple was profiting too handsomely at the expense of their company. As one former employee, who was especially disturbed, said: "Walter and Laurie backed a Brinks truck up to this company! . . . And they felt entitled to it!"

The issue also seemed to be getting under Spielberg's skin. Although he'd come up with Parkes and MacDonald's producing arrangement in the first place, for the man to whom it was never not about money, it must have been unsettling that his underlings had learned *so well* from him—Spielberg, after all, prided himself enormously in his contracts with studios, in which he generally walked away with more dough. To have his friends now replicating that model with *his* company was believed by many to be the last straw.

By the time of *Lemony Snicket's A Series of Unfortunate Events,* a film that Parkes and MacDonald were producing for DreamWorks and Paramount, which was due out in December of 2004, the bloom was off the rose between Spielberg and his onetime favorites.

The film had originated at Paramount, where it was initially being produced by Scott Rudin and directed by Barry Sonnenfeld. When they dropped out over budget issues, Paramount chairman Sherry Lansing asked Parkes and MacDonald, who she knew were fans of the project, to come onboard as producers, which they did, bringing in DreamWorks as a partner.

Lemony Snicket was another movie where Spielberg was called in to mediate between Parkes and an unhappy director, in this case Brad Silberling. When Parkes insisted that his own cut of the film be tested against Silberling's, Silberling called on the Big Guy. Though, according to a source, Spielberg didn't come to Silberling's rescue as he'd hoped. "I think Brad wanted Steven to step up and say, 'Leave Brad alone.' And I don't think he did." Even so, Silberling apparently used the occasion to tell him bluntly that Parkes was hurting his studio more than helping it.

The whole making of the movie, which starred Jim Carrey as the sinister and eccentric Count Olaf, had in every way lived up to the unfortunateness of its title. Executives at Paramount were nervous about its cost ($160 million) and fretted that it was too dark, and Carrey, a notorious prima donna, was at his worst, griping about having to wait around in heavy prosthetics and makeup; insisting on multiple takes (one person who worked on the film joked that five thousand feet of film was used to capture a scene of Carrey walking out the door); and prone to capricious mood swings. After insisting that he had to fly to London to try on wigs for his role, and after this had been arranged and a private jet was waiting for him on the runway, Carrey suddenly announced that he didn't want to go after all. Unlike his costar Meryl Streep, who was staying at a hotel in Downey, California, where *Lemony Snicket* was being shot, driving around in a rented Prius, and rhapsodizing about what great chicken dinners she was having at night, Carrey was staying at his home in Malibu and being helicoptered to the set every day.

If, by the time Parkes and MacDonald stepped down, Spielberg's feelings toward them had cooled a few degrees, they were not by any means kicked to the wayside. Unlike Katzenberg, when Spielberg moved on, he did not cast off. Loyalty was his thing. Parkes and MacDonald were *family;* they'd just been moved a few seats down the table. Their new producing deal was incredibly generous, and included a new, ultra-posh office in Santa Monica. They were still lined up to produce movies for the studio, including *The Ring 2* and *Just Like Heaven,* with Reese Witherspoon, as well as *Sweeney Todd* and *The Kite Runner.*

But it was clear that the coveted status of "Spielberg's favorite" had been passed on, or more accurately, passed back. Old wounds healed, Kathy Kennedy was now fully back in the circle and producing Spielberg's next two films, *War of the Worlds* and *Munich.* Spielberg and Kennedy had also been working together (unsuccessfully) to develop *The Talisman,* based on a Stephen King short story. There were also revived talks about *Lincoln,* a biopic based on the Doris Kearns Goodwin book *Team of Rivals* that Spielberg had been dying to make with Liam Neeson. The switch was subtle but symbolic for those who studied the moves at Amblin as though it was the Royal Court.

Spielberg was ready, perhaps aching, to return to his comfort zone. After so many years of topsy-turvy fortunes, and a recent dry spell, both for him and his company, he seemed ready to return to the familiarity he'd known at Amblin. Not just with Kennedy, but with the movies he was making. *War of the Worlds* was no attempt to stretch in any erudite or socially conscious or highbrow direction. It was a great big action movie starring Tom Cruise. There would be crazy special effects. A big-ass budget. And otherworldly creatures interacting with

American suburban types . . . There was no way it wouldn't result in a global ka-*ching*. Not that Oscars weren't still on the always-striving director's brain. *Munich* would take care of that. But he was ready, for the first time in quite a while, for *fun*.

In the months and weeks leading up to *Madagascar*'s May 27 release, Katzenberg was on the move—in New York City, England, Vegas—and everywhere talking up *Madagascar*. (He also threw in plugs for *Wallace and Gromit: Curse of the Were-Rabbit*, DreamWorks' second animated film of the year, due out in the fall.) There was a lot riding on *Madagascar*. The studio was planning a secondary, $600 million stock offering in the wake of its release. The primary beneficiary of the offering would be Paul Allen, providing his largest payback yet. Katzenberg needed *Madagascar* to be big, and so, as always, he talked. But at DreamWorks, the feeling was that while *Madagascar* was stronger than *Shark Tale*, it was no *Shrek*.

While making the push for *Madagascar*, Katzenberg's attention was diverted to another movie. After *Shrek 2*, DVDs had flown off the shelves (the title was the highest-selling DVD of 2004). But sales slowed considerably in the new year. Loads of product were being shipped back. Considering Katzenberg's predictions that *Shrek 2* DVDs would go on to sell 55 million copies worldwide—an estimate later shown to be more than 30 percent higher than the subsequent sales—this was worrisome. Katzenberg's optimism was fueled by his desire to beat Pixar, whose film *The Incredibles* was positioned to become the highest-selling video release of 2005. Not wanting to be outshone, he upped the number of *Shrek 2* DVDs that were sent out, ordering his troops to "Ship it! Ship it!" "Jeffrey was pounding everyone relentlessly," said one source. "He wanted that DVD in every store, every gas station . . ."

Aware of the debacle, Katzenberg, for once, didn't talk. At least not until 8 A.M., on Monday, May 9, the day before DreamWorks was announcing its first-quarter earnings. At this time he briefed a group of insiders that *Shrek 2* DVD numbers were off by 5 million; *Shrek 2* had not met its target of selling 40 million copies.

The first whiff Wall Street got of this was when the news was leaked to *Newsweek,* which ran a Web exclusive saying that DreamWorks was about to announce earnings that were "as unattractive as its star character Shrek." When, hours later, this proved the case, and DreamWorks revised its full-year earnings projection from $1.88 a share down to $1.00 to $1.25, DreamWorks' stock plummeted to an all-time low of $30.70. Katzenberg's credibility, and that of his company, also took a dive. Overnight, DreamWorks went from darling to disaster. The DreamWorks Animation stockholders—many of whom were employees—were left with worthless options.

Even Katzenberg couldn't spin this one. "I've been sent to the shed and given a good lashing," he told the *L.A. Times.* "*Shrek 2* is still a blockbuster, and it is unfortunate that we have stubbed our toe in a way that has created the reaction it has. But . . . the fundamentals of the company couldn't be stronger."

DreamWorks canceled its secondary offering, leaving Paul Allen in the lurch. Even when *Madagascar* was released to strong numbers—it grossed $193 million domestically and $532 million worldwide—it was nonetheless dubbed a failure of sorts because it didn't live up to expectations of being a *Shrek* redux.

More drubbings followed in quick succession. In June, six class-action lawsuits were filed against DreamWorks accusing the company of misrepresenting *Shrek 2* DVD sales (they were later dismissed in court). In July, the SEC launched an investigation into insider trading. That same month, DreamWorks announced that earnings for the second quarter would also be down (in part because *Shark Tale* DVD sales were also soft). The stock sank even lower, to $27 a share, a dollar less than its offering price. (Pixar also revised its future earnings due to slow sales of *The Incredibles* DVDs, causing its stock to drop.)

After years of robust growth, DVD sales were slamming to a halt due to an oversaturated, and maturing, market. Unlike the days when *Shrek* had been released on DVD, three years earlier, by the time the sequel hit the market, DVDs did most of their business in the first six days. There were simply too many titles for any of them to have legs; realizing this, retailers such as Wal-Mart and Best Buy shortened the amount of time they devoted to promoting each title. As a result, sales slacked off significantly after the first week of release.

Katzenberg was visibly shaken. This was a disaster of mammoth proportions, on display for all the world to see. Other top officers were also jolted, their inexperience in heading up a public company now painfully clear.

"The people running DreamWorks come from a creative background, not the corporate financial sector," said David Baker, a principal at the investment firm North American Management Corp. A DreamWorks insider blamed this on Katzenberg, saying, "Jeffrey doesn't want strong people around him, because he wants to be the creative force of that company. He doesn't even want strong financial people around him, and that's one of the reasons the company took such a dive when they went public."

And where had Geffen been? His own skill-set, as a masterful deal-maker, not a CFO, was coming into acute focus. A game of blame heated up. Geffen thought Ann Daly should step down, according to sources, but Katzenberg instead reconfigured the management structure so that Enrico took on more responsibility and Daly, Kendrick, and Leslie were all effectively demoted. Going forward, Daly would be solely responsible for overseeing film production and home video.

In early August, appearing at a media presentation at Glendale of *Wallace and Gromit* and *Flushed Away*, not even his crisp ensemble of khakis, white button-down shirt, and seemingly brand-new white Adidas sneakers could hide the fact that Katzenberg appeared harried and frayed. With stock offerings on hold, there was pressure to come up with another way of paying back Allen. And this time, Allen wasn't being shy or tongue-tied in making his demands. The Microsoft billionaire seemed to have learned something from his Hollywood apprenticeship. The disaster at the animation studio wasn't just going to be affecting Katzenberg. Spielberg, too, was gonna be feeling it.

31

NO WHITE SUITS!

I DON'T KNOW WHAT'S GOING to happen with this one. I really don't." Michael Bay was being astonishingly candid about *The Island*, just a few weeks before its July 22, 2005, release. He was also being astonishingly un–Michael Bay. Where was the swagger, the hotheadedness, the supreme confidence? Where was the guy who said, "I always say, 'F—— the critics!'"? He was being remarkably humble in interviews. He sounded nervous. At a media screening of *The Island* held at the decorously staid Academy of Motion Picture Arts and Sciences in May, the guy looked practically sick. The special effects on the film weren't finished, and Bay wasn't pleased that pesky journalists were getting a sneak peek at his work in progress. The six-foot-three macho prima donna, with the square jaw and the ice-blue eyes, showed up to the screening unshaven and looking like he hadn't slept for days.

"This is a director's worst nightmare," he told *Variety*. "I even consulted the DGA [Directors Guild of America] contract to see if I could get [the screening] canceled."

Whatever was going to happen with *The Island*, canceled was not one of them. Not even pushed back, although DreamWorks was desperate to do just that—anything to buy more time for a movie that had been put together in just nine months and that was causing no shortage of headaches in the weeks leading up to its release. But there was no way to move *The Island*. Warner Bros., coproducing, had the next installment of *Harry Potter* coming out in November. *The Island* was stuck in July.

To Bay, it was a miracle that he and his movie had even made it this far. For a long stretch, *The Island* seemed dead in the water. After shelling out a million bucks for the script, DreamWorks had balked at the film's initial $130-million-plus budget, refusing to grant Bay a green light until he shaved down costs. Easier said than done. Talent wasn't costing much—the film's leads, Scarlett Johansson and Ewan McGregor, were young and not yet major stars. But effects and sets were lavish. There was a $7 million "concept car," a "proper birthing room," and oodles of expensive, showy gimmicks. Still, DreamWorks was toeing the line at $120 million, and not a million more. When Bay came in at $122 million or $124 million, Spielberg, Parkes, and Mac-Donald (Parkes was producing, and MacDonald executive-producing, the film) gave him a resounding no. Bay began worrying for his movie.

"I thought *The Island* was going down about four or five times," he said. "There were points where the studio would say, 'If you can't cut $1 million here, we're out.' I thought to myself, 'They are $9 million in, could they do that?'"

With time running out, Bay reached out to Warner Bros. to come on as a partner, trimmed down the number of expensive action scenes, and cut product-placement deals with companies such as Budweiser and Microsoft.

In October, a whirlwind eighty-three-day shoot got under way in Los Angeles, Detroit, and a former space shuttle factory in Downey, California. With cameras rolling, pressures only multiplied. One day, Bay had no completed sets on which to film. On another, he learned that the film's construction crew had been fired after an accounting scandal. Special effects weren't completed until two weeks before the film was released. A new scene had to be shot at the last minute, with one actor (McGregor) in London and one (Sean Bean) in L.A.

The actors, meanwhile, were being run ragged. McGregor was nearly dispossessed of his family jewels, thanks to endless hours spent on a jet-propelled motorcycle with Johansson clinging to his back. Though that was nothing compared to running through miles of sewers, being suspended by wires sixty feet above the ground, hanging on the backs of speeding trucks, and being subjected to exploding helicopters and cars.

"When I got home from the first day of work, I could not walk," Johansson said. "I was crippled."

What was going on on the set was nothing compared with the

drama behind the scenes, which one DreamWorks source likened to "the kindergarten yard run amok."

Early on, Terry Press made it clear that a sci-fi movie with no stars that was being released in the middle of the summer with an incredibly rushed time schedule was not going to work. In an e-mail to Geffen, Press wrote: "I have no idea how to market this movie."

She wasn't the only one. A good eight months out, creative advertising head David Sameth, who normally knocked trailers out of the park, was stumped. How could you make a trailer about a film that was essentially two different movies? There was the first half, when McGregor and Johansson are at a cloning facility, which has a sci-fi, *Logan's Run* feel. Everyone is wearing white suits (a detail that Press loathed; in meetings, she would cry, "No white suits!"). But then they hopped on motorcycles, and suddenly *The Island* was very Michael Bay–feeling, a sexy, sweaty, on-the-run road movie. The fact that no one involved with the movie could articulate what the film was about in less than two sentences only confirmed the problems at hand. That a film called *The Island* was missing that particular geographical feature was yet another inanity.

Adding to the chaos, Bay was withholding footage, making it impossible to move forward on art. When Bay would explode and say things like, "Where the hell's my trailer?" DreamWorks marketers would reply, "Well, Michael, you have to give us your film first."

Adam Goodman and other production executives, hearing it from Bay, would also come down on marketing.

When posters and other key art were created, Bay—who categorically hated everything he was seeing—wouldn't approve them, causing further delays. He told the *L.A. Times* that in the poster for *The Island*, Johansson looked like "a porn star." And though it was Bay talking, he didn't mean it as a compliment.

The situation between the director and marketing became more combustible when Warner Bros., which was handling international marketing, entered the picture. Not only was Press not enthused, but Bay was playing the studios against each other. In his estimation, Warner Bros. won.

In one meeting, after Sue Kroll, head of Warner Bros.' international marketing, showed Bay a mockup of a poster for *The Island* made on specially treated silver paper (which was later deemed prohibitively expensive), the director went wild. Turning to the DreamWorks executives in the room, he said, "*You* guys don't know what you're doing, but Warner Bros. is the best! DreamWorks — *you suck!*"

The whole thing was a tragicomedy. Geffen, who was dragged into things because he was now overseeing live action, was "going crazy" in meetings, only assuaged when the discussion turned to *Dreamgirls,* his pet project. DreamWorks was adapting the Broadway musical (which Geffen produced) into a feature film.

A month before *The Island* came out, Parkes and MacDonald left for a three-week holiday in Italy. That left Goodman in charge, and, as one person put it, "You don't cut your teeth on Michael Bay."

But the real fireworks were between Goodman and Press, a showdown that people had seen coming for a while now. Ever since Goodman took over as president of production, executives noticed that Press was dismissive. In a meeting about the Reese Witherspoon movie *Just Like Heaven,* when Goodman suggested an idea, Press snapped, in front of a roomful of executives: "When you have a vagina, you can tell me how to market this movie!"

Executives claim that, to Goodman, Press was a somewhat antiquated warhorse from Disney who only knew how to sell certain types of movies (upscale films such as *American Beauty* and *Gladiator*). DreamWorks' recent track record — the weak openings of De Luca's films, as well as films like *The Terminal* and *Collateral* — supported his case. Goodman made no secret about how unimpressed he was with DreamWorks' minimal Internet presence. Press's bedside manner, or lack thereof, also needled the new president.

The criticism of Press was that her ego went beyond what was appropriate for a head of marketing. In short, she behaved too much like "talent."

It was the same charge that had always been lobbed against Parkes and MacDonald, and struck many as a systemic problem. "The failed part of DreamWorks is talent being in management roles," one person told me, a sentiment echoed by many others.

The marketing department was no more enthralled by the new regime or its movies. Parkes and MacDonald had made respectable, often very good, movies. In their absence, the upcoming releases ranged from decidedly commercial to crass. The original script for *Norbit*, an Eddie Murphy comedy written by Murphy and his brother, was so lewd and raunchy, according to one source, that "it could have gotten DreamWorks arrested." The film had been wallowing in development for years; the only reason for not killing it was to keep Murphy happy.

The internal tension at the studio was felt by everyone, nowhere more so than at the Monday-morning meetings. Where once the "best and the brightest" of Amblin and Disney had come together for a morning of creative riffing and laughter, there was now a brittle atmosphere and divided camps. Katzenberg, Parkes, and MacDonald were all gone. Those who were left didn't like each other. "Toward the end, the meetings changed," said one source. "The vibe changed. Things were crumbling . . ."

But the summer was off, anyway, to a good start. *War of the Worlds* grossed a hearty $234 million domestically and $591 million overseas (half of which, of course, went to Paramount, not to mention Spielberg and Tom Cruise's back-end deals). The only collateral damage was Spielberg's relationship with Cruise, whose devotion to the Church of Scientology had reached a new fervor. A Scientology tent offering religious literature and "assists"—massages administered by Scientology volunteers—had been set up on the set of *War of the Worlds*, and Cruise had invited studio executives involved with the film on a four-hour tour of three different Scientology facilities. A Scientology contingent was present at the film's premiere, and Spielberg privately expressed his frustration at how Cruise—who was in the midst of a media meltdown, best remembered for his behavior on Oprah's couch—was using his press opportunities to talk about his church and his new love, Katie Holmes, instead of touting *War of the Worlds*. "If he spent half the time he talked about *that*, talking about the movie . . . !" Spielberg fumed, insinuating that however well *War of the Worlds* had done, it could have done better with some PR help from Cruise. But the biggest offense occurred when, upon hearing that one of Spielberg's relatives received prescription drugs, Cruise had Scientologists, who don't believe in them, picket outside the office of the doctor who was prescribing them. Spielberg and Capshaw were furious.

By the time *War of the Worlds* came out, Spielberg was already deeply enmeshed in his next project—a highly secretive film about the massacre of Israeli athletes at the 1972 Summer Olympics in Munich. The film was being made Spielberg-style: while *War of the Worlds* had been in postproduction, the next film—still unnamed—was prepping for release at the end of the year.

And then came the reality check. In July, *The Island* lived up to everyone's worst fears and opened—or, rather, didn't—to an anemic $12 million, one of the most humiliating openings of the summer. *The Island*, which cost $120 million, would gross $35 million domestically. Overseas, it fared better, grossing $162 million worldwide. But there was no way around just how bad things were. Geffen was so spooked that he cut short a Mediterranean vacation aboard his yacht to fly home.

Although he was "not happy," he "was the voice of reason after *The Island*," said one source. "David was fair to everyone. He said, 'You can blame marketing for this, you can blame the movie for that . . .' He rapped everyone's knuckles equally." One person he gave a little more support to, though, was Terry Press. When production weighed in with their complaints, Geffen made it clear that as long as he was making movies, Press would market them. In her defense, he held up the e-mail that Press had sent him months earlier about *The Island*.

Jeffrey's Girl was David's girl, at least for now. But the bigger question was, was she Steven's? Especially given her relations with Goodman and the fate of *The Terminal*. The relationship between Spielberg and Press was "a fascinating love story," according to one source. "There were times when he worshipped her, and thought she was the smartest person on earth. She would tell him things that no one else could." But in the wake of *The Island*, this wasn't one of those times.

In the lead-up to the October release of DreamWorks Animation's *Wallace and Gromit: Curse of the Were-Rabbit*, a noticeable shift was evident in Katzenberg's behavior. As *Variety*'s Ben Fritz pointed out, he was, for once, "soft-pedaling one of his films." Having learned the harsh lesson that Hollywood hype doesn't play well on Wall Street, Katzenberg was perfecting a new skill: the art of the down-sell.

With *Wallace and Gromit*, a stop-motion Claymation film painstakingly crafted by Nick Park and his creative team at Aardman Animations, this wasn't hard to do. In fact, it was almost in keeping with the film's distinctly British (humble, self-deprecatory) tone, which was in turn in keeping with that of the popular duo of Wallace, a cheese-loving inventor, and his trusted mutt Gromit, whose eyes and nuanced facial movements conveyed whole soliloquies of expression.

Unlike *Chicken Run,* the first collaboration between DreamWorks and Aardman, *Wallace and Gromit* was made with virtually no input from Katzenberg or any other DreamWorks executives. Park had stipulated that arrangement. As a result, Katzenberg "fairly much left us to it," he said. Having lived through the American invasion on *Chicken Run,* Park was not interested in a repeat. As one former DreamWorks employee put it, "Jeffrey Katzenberg and the British are about as antithetical as anything you can imagine . . . [Aardman artists] went to tea at 2:30 in the afternoon, and Jeffrey was like, '*What?*'" Katzenberg was also bewildered by the amount of time it took to make clay animation movies, in which artists molded by hand each and every character and prop's movement. *Wallace and Gromit* took five years to make. The process bore no resemblance to the quick mouse clicks used to edit CGI films.

Yet, whatever Katzenberg was saying about lowering financial expectations on *Wallace and Gromit,* he was nonetheless hoping that American audiences would make the charming British characters into Mickey Mouse–like icons. But in the hands of Aardman, *Wallace and Gromit* was quaint and distinctly English. The characters spoke in arch English accents; the film's main voices were provided by British actors Ralph Fiennes and Helena Bonham Carter, who spoke through plastic lips, the better to convey the aristocratic intonations of her character, Lady Campanula Tottington. As the London *Times* put it, *Wallace and Gromit* "is as English as apple-scrumping, walking widdershins and losing on penalities."

Though critics swooned, the film made just $56 million at the domestic box office (half what *Chicken Run* grossed). Better performances abroad helped the film's worldwide gross rise to $192 million. Ultimately, DreamWorks took a $4 million write-down on the film, and when fourth-quarter revenues were announced, the studio took a $656,000 loss on revenue of $81 million.

Katzenberg needed to turn things around. Dramatically. So, in December, he gave up his title of president of DreamWorks Animation (he was still CEO) and appointed board member Lewis Coleman as the number two man at the company. It was an overt attempt to placate Wall Street. Coleman was a pure businessman, having served as chief financial officer, vice chairman, and chief credit officer of Bank of America. He had no creative cred whatsoever, and that was exactly the point. *Variety* quoted one analyst saying of Katzenberg's propensity to hype: "It's like he doesn't realize we write it all down, we remember what he said."

Even with the change in lineup, however, DreamWorks' stock was still in a slump. Katzenberg was going to have to do more than bring in new faces to win back Wall Street's trust.

A month earlier, in November, Bob Wright, the chairman of NBC Universal, had flown from New York to Los Angeles to meet with Geffen to discuss buying DreamWorks' live-action studio. This was the proposed solution to raise money for Paul Allen in the wake of DreamWorks Animation's canceled secondary stock offering. It was the Final Solution, one that had seemed all but inevitable all these years, but that now, finally, was happening.

The irony was glaring: the studio that had been formed as Hollywood's most artist-friendly shop was now in talks with NBC Universal owner General Electric—seller of lightbulbs and refrigerators, and one of the most famously thrifty conglomerates in the world. The anti-suits were about to be gobbled up by the biggest suit of them all. Ron Meyer had initially brought up Universal buying DreamWorks, when Geffen was telling friends he thought it was time to sell. For Meyer, DreamWorks would provide Universal with an in to the CGI animation business. And acquiring the live-action studio would pad Universal's slate just as the studio's international distribution partnership with Paramount, United International Pictures, was about to dissolve. Universal was planning to build its own international distributor, but would need product to fill the pipeline. Of course, there was also the allure of having Spielberg as resident artiste.

At first, Wright and General Electric CEO Jeffrey Immelt had been reluctant, but Meyer was a good talker, and his arguments made good sense. Eventually, he'd brought them around, and talks between the two companies had commenced.

Geffen was optimistic. The talks leading up to the meeting with NBC Universal had progressed rather smoothly, give or take haggling over points related to Spielberg's desire to retain the autonomy he enjoyed at DreamWorks, where it was in his power to green-light movies. There was a feeling of inevitability to the deal. How many times over the years had Geffen and Meyer discussed potential mergers between DreamWorks and Universal? A marriage just seemed *right*. Not only because of Geffen and Meyer's friendship, but because Universal had been where Spielberg had grown up. How he longed for his old, stable home turf.

But quickly into the meeting, which took place at Geffen's Beverly Hills mansion, it became clear that Wright had not come for a friendly chat. Given the recent performance of *The Island*—as well as *Just Like Heaven* and *Dreamer,* which also lost money—Wright said that NBC Universal no longer felt that DreamWorks' price tag of $1.5 billion, plus the assumption of debt, was worth it. Having run the numbers—something for which NBC Universal owner GE was famous—the standing offer was $100 million less.

In fact, it wasn't Wright who opposed the deal, but Jeffrey Immelt. He'd studied applied mathematics at Dartmouth, gotten his MBA from Harvard, and was a numbers guy. And, quite simply, the DreamWorks numbers didn't add up. GE was hardly frugal or shy about making a commitment. The company invests $14 billion in all sorts of industries and acquisitions every year. But after looking into the matter, DreamWorks had showed only a 15 percent rate of return for GE, much lower than the typical 20–25 percent benchmark that GE typically adhered to in such deals. There was also the question as to the value of DreamWorks' library, which, though it included acclaimed films such as *Saving Private Ryan, Gladiator,* and *American Beauty,* contained many more less-distinguished movies, such as *Biker Boyz* and *Head of State.*

Immelt would later say, on *Charlie Rose,* that the DreamWorks deal "was not the deal we needed to do financially." "I'm totally the bad guy here," Immelt admitted. "Bob [Wright] did a great job. Ron [Meyer] did a great job. And, ultimately, I was the guy that just didn't think it was the right place to put $1.6 billion at this time."

Immelt, showing he was more versed in Hollywood game-playing than he got credit for, added that his decision had nothing to do with Spielberg, whom Immelt called "the definitive name in the industry—this is a hero . . . I would [never] do anything to be disrespectful of him. I know who he is and what he means."

When Rose asked him if the situation had been "like Lincoln and his cabinet, where there were eight yeses and one no, but the no was Lincoln's," Immelt said, laughing: "It may not have been eight, but it was close to that."

One person who was not laughing was Geffen, who was infuriated. As he saw it, GE had reneged on its word—behavior that was, when dealing with Geffen, incendiary. Later that afternoon DreamWorks' attorney Skip Brittenham contacted Wright and called off negotiations.

Meanwhile, across town at Paramount, the news that Universal and DreamWorks were no longer canoodling was intriguing to Brad Grey, the veteran talent manager who eight months earlier had replaced Paramount's longtime chairman Sherry Lansing. Grey had been hired by Viacom co-COO Tom Freston, a friend with whom Grey often vacationed. (Geffen was credited with helping Grey get the job.) His mandate was to give Paramount—which over the years had become known as spendthrift and hit-free—the jolt it desperately needed. Hollywood's oldest studio, which had given the world *Chinatown, The Godfather,* and *Beverly Hills Cop,* was now making films such as *Jackass: The Movie*—Paramount's most profitable movie in 2002.

As one-half of the venerable management agency Brillstein-Grey Entertainment, Grey was hardly an unknown commodity. Not only had he famously managed Garry Shandling during *The Larry Sanders Show* years (a relationship that ended in a $100 million lawsuit in which Shandling claimed that Grey had "triple-dipped" into Shandling's career earnings), and Brad and Jen (pre–Angelina Jolie), but he was a producer of the hit show *The Sopranos.*

Even with such pedigree, however, Grey's lack of experience as a movie executive had made his hiring a somewhat surprising one. Typically, studio heads were plucked from the studio executive ranks (with a few exceptions, such as Meyer). They came to the table with long-lasting relationships with filmmakers, and movie business know-how. Grey had a helping of the former but very little of the latter. Even so, he played it like the seasoned player he was. Though barely five and a half feet tall, he gave off the gravity and *cojones* of a Hollywood mogul. He even looked the part: sharply angled face, pelt of short-clipped hair, and a wardrobe whose palette veered safely from charcoal to shades of black.

A man of few words, Grey commanded more by silence than rousing speeches, and was a master at keeping things to the point. As to what made him tick, Grey offered few clues. He stayed behind closed doors at the studio, and limited his interaction to a small inner circle. Where there weren't walls, he had them built, such as in the executive dining room, where partitions were erected around his table so that he could dine in private. His own office had a private entrance. He refurbished the studio—or at least the parts that he frequented—to his sleek, museum-like taste, including his office, which was decorated by L.A.-based designer Waldo Fernandez. Gone was the colorfully informal style of Sherry Lansing, who had kept the almost humorously unfashionable green carpet left over from the days when the company was part of Gulf & Western. In came cool tones that offset Grey's rarefied art collection of Ed Ruscha and David Smith originals.

Grey did away with just about everything that had marked Lansing's reign. He was not one to greet anyone he ran into on the lot with a cheerful "Hi, honey!" as Lansing always did. He was far more of an elitist, more sensitive to the hierarchy, and being respected for his place in it. He did not do groupthink or consort much with people outside of his select group of confidants.

The executive makeover at Paramount focused Hollywood's collective attention on the so-called Melrose lot, and Grey was in a rather fierce spotlight. Under such scrutiny, beginner's mistakes quickly became public flare-ups, such as when he unceremoniously fired Paramount president Donald De Line, a popular executive, whom he replaced with Fox network head Gail Berman. (De Line found out he was fired when he received a phone call from a journalist.)

On a macro level there was criticism that Grey wasn't turning things around fast enough at Paramount, where Lansing and her partner, Jonathan Dolgen, chairman of the Viacom Entertainment Group, had left Grey with an empty cupboard. It wouldn't have mattered: Grey, intent on creating his own imprint, was looking to develop his own films, not projects from the previous regime.

Adding to the negative buzz rising at Paramount, in October Grey was mentioned in a *New York Times* story about Anthony Pellicano, the private investigator under investigation by the Feds for wiretapping allegations. Although Grey had not been charged, he was being called to testify and his photo was plastered across newspapers in connection with the biggest scandal to hit Hollywood in decades.

Grey wasn't the only one under hyperscrutiny; Berman, too, was feeling the heat. Although she had spent two decades in television, where she'd built a reputation as a no-nonsense executive with a gutsy instinct for what connected with mainstream audiences (at Fox she'd overseen the mania-stirring series *American Idol* and *24*), she quickly discovered that film was an entirely different world. Complaints call her too harsh; people felt she wasn't coddling the talent or the talent's handlers enough. It was said that she simply didn't "get" the way things were done in film. But if Berman wasn't giving the love, that may have been because she wasn't feeling it from her boss. Not long after she was hired, Grey had also brought on Rob Moore from Revolution Studios, giving him oversight of marketing, distribution, and business affairs. As a result, friends of Berman say that she felt "she had no job." All there was for her to do was green-light movies, and she was having trouble, finding it difficult to get her boss's approval.

To Grey, who even in December was still navigating his tumultuous arrival at Paramount, Spielberg and Co. emerged as a kind of amazing hope. With DreamWorks on the lot, suddenly Paramount's production pipeline would be flush with product—and not just any product, Spielberg-brand product. DreamWorks would also provide Paramount with a ready-made team of seasoned executives, and its splashy purchase would offset all the criticism that Paramount had been attracting. The message would be clear that Grey was serious about revitalizing the slumbering studio.

Grey didn't waste time. After hearing that talks were off between DreamWorks and Universal, he immediately put in calls to Freston in New York, and to Geffen. Freston liked the idea and, after hanging up with Grey, he called Viacom chairman and CEO Sumner Redstone at his home in L.A. A spry octogenarian, Redstone was one of the aging but still all-powerful media titans who never seemed to slow down. For his part, however, Redstone was increasingly prone to odd, even bizarre, bouts of behavior and admissions—such as his daily ritual of swimming nude in his private pool, an anecdote he shared with *Vanity Fair* readers. Or his boast that he had sex as much as four times a day with his much younger (and now ex-) wife.

After hearing Freston's proposition, Redstone expressed concern: he didn't think buying DreamWorks would "fly" with Viacom investors in light of the fact that Viacom was about to be split into two different divisions. (As of the new year, Freston would oversee Viacom, which would consist of Paramount and cable networks like MTV and Nick-elodeon; and CBS CEO Leslie Moonves would head up CBS Corp., which would encompass the CBS network, television and radio sta-tions, Simon & Schuster, and an outdoor advertising business.) In ad-vance of the bifurcation, Redstone reminded Freston, Viacom had told Wall Street that it wouldn't be considering any major acquisitions.

Freston relayed the news to Grey, but they did not give up. Rather, they began to quietly search for investors to reduce the financial bur-den on Viacom in the event of an acquisition.

Meanwhile, back at Universal, Meyer had got wind of Paramount's interest and immediately went back to Wright, convincing him to re-open negotiations. Two weeks after DreamWorks had declared things dead, the studios went back into talks, which continued for several, surprisingly drama-free, weeks. Hollywood observers considered the deal done.

When the December 12 issue of *Time* magazine hit newsstands, its cover featured the very solemn-looking face of Steven Spielberg, alongside the headline "Spielberg's Secret Masterpiece." Inside was an "exclusive" story by Richard Schickel about Spielberg's new movie, which began: "The first and most important thing to say about *Mu-nich* . . . is that it is a very good movie — good in a particularly Spiel-bergian way. By which one means that it has all the virtues we've come to expect when he is working at his highest levels."

Such a media coup should have had publicists at Universal, which was releasing *Munich*, doing cartwheels. But the cover would prove to be a disaster that would damage Spielberg's reputation with the media and hurt *Munich*.

From the very moment Spielberg had become involved with *Mu-nich* — a film about the secret Mossad hit squad that had been ordered to assassinate Palestinian terrorists after the massacre of eleven Israeli athletes at the 1972 Munich Olympics — Spielberg had proceeded with even more secrecy than was customary for the director, due to the project's political implications. Agents at CAA, which first presented him with George Jonas's 1984 book, *Vengeance: The True Story of an Israeli Counter-Terrorist Team,* a major source of inspiration for the movie, were ordered to keep mum about the project and Spielberg's involvement with it. The film's script — whose code name was *Kings*

Cross—written by *Forrest Gump* screenwriter Eric Roth, was closely guarded, shown only to a core group of Spielberg's consultants on the film: a mini state department, including his rabbi, Middle East diplomat Dennis Ross, Bill Clinton, Clinton's press secretary Mike Mc-Curry, and crisis consultant Allan Mayer. When Spielberg sent a copy of *Vengeance* to Clinton, his biggest concern was whether or not the book was factually accurate—he didn't want to put the Spielberg imprimatur on a story of this weight and magnitude if it wasn't true. After reading the script, Clinton said that nothing had come across his desk during his eight years as president that confirmed the story, nor had he seen anything that denied it. This uncertainty made Spielberg hesitate (he'd already been through historical-veracity questioning on *Schindler's List*), and even as Universal executives waited impatiently for dibs on the next Steven Spielberg project, wanting desperately to start shooting in the spring of 2004, the director refused to commit.

Taking its cue from *Vengeance,* Roth's script was procedural, lacking in the way of human emotion and drama, none of which were present in the book. This, too, made Spielberg uneasy. Everything changed, however, when it was discovered that "Avner," Jonas's main source and the alleged head of the hit squad, was not, as had been believed, dead, but living in New York City, running a corporate securities company. His real name was Juval Aviv. Furthermore, Spielberg's brain trust discovered FBI files proving that he and his team were not fictitious. When Aviv was contacted, and agreed to come out to L.A. to meet with Spielberg, the director was beside himself. During a meeting at Amblin, as Aviv chatted away about his story, including details, emotions, anecdotes, Spielberg played the role of the inquisitive schoolboy, at one point asking: "How did you feel after killing somebody?"

Aviv replied that he had a habit of staring into the window of a kitchen supply store in Paris. Those simple symbols of domesticity, which reminded him of his family, were, he said, all that he had, and were what kept him going. (This anecdote would make it into *Munich.*)

Twenty minutes into the conversation, Spielberg knew he finally had his movie. But he also knew that he was going to need more time to get the film where he wanted it, and would not be able to start shooting just yet. "Kristie!" he yelled to his assistant. "Get me a comedy!" (In the end, it would not be a comedy, but *War of the Worlds* that would tide him over before *Munich* was ready to commence.)

Because of this wealth of new material, playwright Tony Kushner (*Angels in America, Homebody/Kabul*)—whom Spielberg was trying to entice to write the script, but who up until that point had been hedging—became interested, and was hired to rework Roth's script, bringing out the human element of Avner's story (he would be played by Eric Bana), as well as that of the Palestinians.

On an intellectual level, Spielberg knew what he was getting into with *Munich.* Everyone would assume, given his ethnicity and politics, that he would be making Israeli propaganda. And yet, when he didn't—in *Munich,* Spielberg wanted to portray both sides of the Israeli-Palestinian dilemma—pro-Israel groups would accuse him of betraying his people. What worried him most was that his beloved Shoah Foundation would be negatively affected, and he confided that if that were truly to be the case, he wouldn't make the movie.

Geffen advised against *Munich,* reasoning that the movie would be bad for Spielberg, bad for the Jews. (Geffen kept up his admonitions, and after getting off the phone with him, Spielberg would appear agitated and flustered.) Even members of the director's family were concerned about the movie, wondering why Spielberg felt compelled to get in the middle of such a sensitive, and personal, debate. But Spielberg persisted, strongly believing this was the thing to do, and presumably, believing he was embarking on a kind of *Schindler's List II.*

Shooting got under way in June of 2005—just as *War of the Worlds* was hitting theaters—at various undisclosed locales, including Budapest, Malta, Paris, and Pinewood Studios in the U.K. The combination of the film's subject matter, plus the fact that it was Spielberg's first foreign shoot since 9/11, made security on the set even tighter than usual. No press was allowed. Even Universal marketing executives, after flying over to Budapest to brief Spielberg, were banned from the set.

By now, those who kept track of such things were aware that Spielberg was making a movie about the assassinations at the Munich Olympics. After Michael Fleming broke the story in *Variety* in April of 2004, bloggers and other media outlets followed suit. But as interest—and assumptions about the movie—heated up, Spielberg was, characteristically, preaching silence. He said he wanted the movie to speak for itself, and, besides, he wasn't sure yet what the film would actually *be*—he would only know that once he'd shot all the footage and assembled it in postproduction.

Universal, meanwhile, was going crazy, wanting desperately to get out ahead of the hype and dictate the terms of the debate. Already there was an abundance of false information—that the movie was about the massacre itself, that Spielberg was either pro- or anti-Israeli.

Finally, Spielberg agreed to release a brief statement about the film to just three media outlets: the *New York Times,* an Israeli newspaper, and an Arab TV network. (Even though this meant burning *Variety;* Fleming had agreed to withhold details he knew about the film when Universal promised him an exclusive at a later date.) The statement was, predictably, short on information, calling the Israeli response to the Munich attack "a defining moment in the modern history of the Middle East."

When, as is the *Times'* wont, reporter David Halbfinger took Spielberg's statement as a jumping-off point to discuss the film and its implications with historians, Middle East experts, and even former Mossad agents (some of whom suggested the film might not be good for Israel), Spielberg, sources say, was furious. He couldn't understand why the *Times* couldn't have just printed the press release.

In December, just weeks before *Munich*'s release, the *Times* again angered Spielberg when Halbfinger, who had been invited to a private screening of *Munich,* brought as his plus-one Ehud Danoch, the Israeli consul general in L.A., an outspoken conservative whom Universal had expressly *not* invited to the screening. Early on in Halbfinger's piece, which ran a few days later, Danoch was quoted describing *Munich* as "a Hollywood movie." Halbfinger noted that Danoch had "promptly fired off a report to his superiors in Jerusalem," and that "he had found plenty to object to."

"He argued, above all," Halbfinger continued, "that the film unfairly drew a moral equivalency between the Israeli assassins and their targets—both explicitly, in dialogue in which the Israelis question their own actions and Palestinians defend theirs, and implicitly, as when the camera shifts from a television broadcast showing the names of the 11 athletes to an Israeli official showing the photographs of the 11 Palestinian targets."

That Danoch's response was being presented as the official Israeli response—which it was not—in the *New York Times,* no less, was too much. Spielberg was beside himself. There would be payback—Halbfinger had been gunning for an interview with Spielberg more than any other reporter. Now, even if Spielberg softened his stance about keeping mum, he would most definitely not be breaking his silence with the *Times*, which was suddenly persona non grata with Steven Spielberg.

By now, Universal was beyond desperate. Politics aside, *Munich* wasn't tracking well, and the studio was increasingly nervous about plunking down a film about violence and terror in the middle of the feel-good Christmas season. Spielberg *had* to talk. There was just too much out there, in the blogosphere, in newspapers, and in magazines. He needed to dictate the spin. An opportunity for Spielberg to get out in front of the story was presented when, in a marketing meeting at Universal, someone suggested he do a Q&A with *Time* magazine. The "10 Questions" format would allow Spielberg to state his case simply without being subject to a reporter's bias. Hearing this, Spielberg said he'd do *Time*—but only if he was on the cover.

Within twenty-four hours, a deal with *Time* was reached. Spielberg would grace the cover (barring a major news event), and Richard Schickel would write the story. It was agreed that if Schickel didn't like the movie, there would be no story. Spielberg signed off on the entire package, and that was that.

Cut to: media maelstrom.

Spielberg hadn't kept his word! He was an elitist—only *Time* was good enough! He got special treatment—Schickel was a friend of Spielberg's who had made a documentary at DreamWorks! Not to mention, everyone knew that appearing on the cover of *Time* was a strategic move when it came to Oscar campaigning. (A month earlier, Universal had wheeled and dealed to get a *Newsweek* cover for its other Oscar candidate, *King Kong*.)

The backlash took Spielberg, and Universal, by surprise, and both camps went into backpedal mode. Spielberg's publicist Marvin Levy explained that the cover had not been planned months in advance as people were claiming, but had come together at the last minute. When, to appease outraged critics—everyone from bloggers to *Variety* was pointing out Spielberg's hypocrisy—Spielberg agreed to sit down with the *L.A. Times*' Rachel Abramowitz, to whom he had promised a *Munich* interview when she'd visited the set of *War of the Worlds*, it only got worse. Now Spielberg was picking more favorites.

Worse than anything was the heightened expectations that the media fuss had caused. The more low-profile Spielberg tried to be, the more attention he attracted, and the same went for his movie. By the time *Munich* was finally screened for critics, the response was not commensurate with its buildup. Reviews were mixed, ranging from the *L.A. Times'* Kenneth Turan's declaration that *Munich* was "the most questioning, provocative film [Spielberg has] ever made" to *Variety's* Todd McCarthy's prediction that the "beautifully made pic will spur newsy media coverage . . . but members of the general public will be glancing at their watches rather than having epiphanies about world peace."

There was indeed coverage, but most of it criticized Spielberg for failing to take a solid stance on the Middle East conflict. Instead of a clear message, went the complaint, there was endless Talmudic debate. *New York Times* op-ed columnist David Brooks observed that "there is, above all, no evil" in *Munich*. "In his depiction of reality there are no people so committed to a murderous ideology that they are impervious to the sort of compromise and dialogue Spielberg puts such great faith in.

"Because he will not admit the existence of evil, as it really exists," continued Brooks, "Spielberg gets reality wrong. Understandably, he doesn't want to portray Palestinian terrorists as cartoon bad guys, but he simply doesn't portray them."

By *Munich's* second week in wide release, it fell out of the top-ten box-office rankings; it was, up to that time, one of Spielberg's worst-grossing movies, ranking somewhere between *Amistad* and *The Terminal*. It would go on to make just $47 million, having cost $70 million to produce. To market the film, one source estimated that Universal spent another $70 million.

When *Munich* failed to garner a Best Picture nomination for the Golden Globes, Terry Press (who was not involved in the film's publicity campaign) was convinced it was because of the *Time* cover story. (*Memoirs of a Geisha*, which Spielberg executive-produced, was also shut out.) Not only had Spielberg not done the customary press interviews with members of the Hollywood Foreign Press Association—the group that votes on the Golden Globes—but at an HFPA screening of *Munich*, issues of *Time* had been handed out, reinforcing Spielberg's snub.

When Patrick Goldstein aired this opinion in the *Los Angeles Times*, his editors received a scathing, three-page-long letter from Universal's Stacey Snider complaining about the piece, which had outlined the bungling of *Munich*'s publicity campaign. Goldstein had always had a good and open relationship with Snider, so he was surprised by the letter. When he aired his confusion with colleagues, he was told that Snider had presumably written the letter knowing that Goldstein's editors weren't going to apologize for the piece. The point, rather, was that Snider could tell Spielberg that she'd stuck up for him, a requisite duty when working for Steven. The letter, as it were, was all about the CC—and in this case, the person who was CC'd was Spielberg.

But no one could adequately protect Spielberg from the debacle that was *Munich*. Hurt, bitterly disappointed—it wasn't just his movie, but his *motives* that were being attacked—and seeking refuge from the press onslaught, he did what he tended to do in these situations: he disappeared, taking off on vacation to heal his wounds. In this case, the healing process would take some time.

32

THE GEFFEN EXPRESS

WE'VE BEEN SOLD TO PARAMOUNT — it's gonna be great! They need us. We're gonna fix them from the inside!"

It was December 9, 2005, and Katzenberg was explaining to Dream-Works executives that, in a last-minute, sleight-of-hand negotiation by David Geffen, DreamWorks had been sold to Paramount. The assumption had been that the studio would be bought by NBC Universal, and now this. What had gone wrong? Paramount, or Viacom, its corporate parent, had offered more money. It was that simple.

Or, almost that simple. As was frequently the case with Geffen, revenge factored in. This time his wrath was directed at Universal. The company's last-minute lowering of its offer had left the DreamWorks negotiator feeling undermined. He was seeking payback.

Katzenberg, revealing no emotion or nostalgia, put the best spin on the news. That was his specialty. If anything, he seemed pumped up, excited. "It's gonna be *fine*," he said, describing DreamWorks and its employees as essential to Paramount, which he presented as in near-terminal shape.

Katzenberg was back in his Moses role, promising his people that he'd lead them to safety. It was the same part he'd played back at the company's inception when he'd led an exodus from Disney to Dream-Works. Only now, the promised land wasn't a sprawling multimedia company set out to redefine how things were done in Hollywood. It was the Melrose lot — Hollywood's oldest movie studio, once run by an ambitious Hungarian immigrant named Adolph Zukor and now owned by Sumner Redstone, who'd breezed through Harvard in two and a half years and spun his father's drive-in-theater business to gold.

One person who didn't seem to share Katzenberg's rosy assessment was his partner, Steven Spielberg, whose satisfaction DreamWorks had once revolved so endlessly around. Though he put on a cheerful face, and said blandly nice things about Redstone to the *Wall Street Journal*, the director was heartbroken that the Universal deal had fallen through. According to sources, he stopped speaking to Geffen, although DreamWorks would deny this. Nothing was working out the way Spielberg had hoped. Geffen was to have been his protector; he was to have ensured that things worked out as Steven wanted.

There had been a shift, a change in the atmosphere. Geffen no longer bowed, as he once had. Katzenberg was a much different, more independent, man. Spielberg, older now and a bit battle-weary, had had his fill of stress and complications. A sentimentalist, he had been anticipating a return to his homeland, the place he associated with calmer, better times. He loathed the notion of joining forces with Paramount, which had been attracting so much negative press as a result of the Pellicano case. The sordid scandal had riveted the town, which was holding its collective breath to see just how many dirty secrets would be revealed in the investigation, and who would be dragged into the spectacle. The fact that Brad Grey might be one of them did not sit well with Spielberg. (Even though, during Katzenberg's Disney trial, his lawyer, Bert Fields, had hired Pellicano to provide security. When Pellicano once showed up in the courtroom, Katzenberg requested that he leave.) Such associations did not complement the notion of himself that he hoped to put forward. Of course, he accepted the Paramount deal; he had to. But he did so grudgingly. He made it clear that he would not move his offices to the Melrose lot, but would continue to work out of the Amblin campus. (He did, however, take a parking spot at Paramount, located right next to Grey's.)

"I remember talking to Steven right after the sale, and he was already [having second thoughts]," one longtime friend of Spielberg's told *Vanity Fair*'s Bryan Burrough. "He had such an emotional reaction. He was leaving his home of twenty years. He refused to move to Paramount. That pretty much says it all."

To the *New York Times*, Spielberg would later say: "I do not like change."

Yet, however opposed he might be to a change of address, Spielberg, along with his partners, did well by Paramount financially. A decade after putting up $33 million each to form DreamWorks, individually they walked away with $175 million from the sale.

The same could not be said for many DreamWorks employees, for whom the dream, finally, was indisputably over. Not all of them would be part of the DreamWorks that would reconfigure on the Paramount lot. Although Spielberg, playing the dad role or trying to save face, assured all that this was a "reverse takeover"—which would become the de facto term used in the press in the weeks following the deal—the extended family was not reassured. Live-action executives were golden; they would remain with Spielberg at Amblin. But what about everyone else? There was talk of a "list" containing the names of DreamWorks employees who would be going to Paramount. People in the know were saying, "I've seen the list, and you're on it!" To others, they weren't saying anything.

For those making it through this episode of *Survivor: DreamWorks,* things weren't much better—in the "integration" (the official term), DreamWorks' distribution and home-video groups displaced Paramount's; half its marketing department made the cut. All told, 250 people from each studio lost their jobs. At their new home, Dream-Works executives bristled within a culture that felt buttoned-down and factory-like. One Paramount executive once described the atmosphere on the lot this way: "It's like everyone saw *The Player* and is trying to act it out—but not as a satire."

The suffering caused by the merger was evident, according to one source, who said that it became something of a sport to watch the stream of people exit the Marathon building (which housed Paramount's marketing department) every day at six o'clock—"They were so beaten down, miserable, pissed off, muttering under their breath."

One person who didn't make it through the process was Terry Press. Spielberg was no longer going to have Jeffrey's Girl handling Dream-Works' movies, particularly after the incident with Adam Goodman. Press would stay on and market DreamWorks Animation films for the next two years, along with a few live-action projects, such as *Dreamgirls,* but that was it.

Given Press's long relationship with Katzenberg, the news was met with shock by observers; those on the inside were less surprised, given the friction that had been building between Press and the live-action studio, culminating in *The Island.* Katzenberg told people he had fought for Press to stay on, but even their relationship was less intense these days. Katzenberg had never seemed to fully recover from the *Sinbad* disaster, and it was no secret that, while he accepted responsibility for the film's failing, he held others—such as Press—equally accountable. One person described the rupture between Katzenberg and Press, which was complete with the break over Paramount, as a "divorce."

Katzenberg, running DreamWorks Animation, would not have an official role at the Paramount-based DreamWorks (the animation studio's movies, however, would now be distributed by Paramount). But he was seen as such an influential player in the integration process that Paramount people used the term "FJK" or, "Friend of Jeffrey Katzenberg," to describe those Katzenberg allies who would be protected in the transition.

True to form, whatever his official duties (or lack thereof), Katzenberg made his presence felt at the Melrose lot, setting up fifteen-minute meetings with Paramount marketing and distribution executives in order to get to know all the new players.

In one such meeting, which commenced once Katzenberg looked up from his BlackBerry, Katzenberg listened to the executive and then concluded the chat by saying, "Well, you know, at least the worst is over," in reference to the merger.

The startled Paramount executive, assuming that a pink slip was inevitable whether or not he kept his cool, exploded: "Maybe to *you* it's over! But to those of us in the trenches, this is only the beginning!"

Katzenberg looked taken aback, but nodded, signaling that he understood. "I hear you," he said. Then he walked away.

By January, the toll of the sale was evident even on the animation lord. On the night of the Golden Globes ceremony, Katzenberg—who was there on behalf of the DreamWorks movies *Munich* (Spielberg had, in the end, received Oscar nominations, for Best Director and Best Picture), *Match Point,* and *Memoirs of a Geisha*—ran into fashion designer Isaac Mizrahi in the elevator of the Beverly Hilton. When Mizrahi inquired what Katzenberg was up to, Katzenberg replied, "Oh, you know. Riding the Geffen Express. Trying to keep up with it."

"That's a wild ride," Mizrahi astutely replied.

"Just make sure you don't get in front of it," Katzenberg clucked wearily as the elevator slowed to a stop. He then excused himself, and, even though it was well before midnight, headed through the gown-and tuxedo-crushed lobby and home to bed.

In fact, the Geffen Express was just starting to pick up speed. In April, Geffen further rattled the delicate power balance between Paramount and DreamWorks by hiring Stacey Snider, a longtime Spielberg ally, to head production at DreamWorks. The notion of the head of Universal giving it all up to head a much smaller entity startled some. It seemed to imply that Spielberg's description of a "reverse takeover" was apt. It also complicated matters at Paramount. Snider had decades of experience over Grey, and the chatter went that she was gunning for his job.

Over at Universal, the move infuriated, and deeply hurt, Ron Meyer, Snider's boss, who remarked to one individual, "Why would she want to go and be Steven Spielberg's D-girl?"

If Geffen thought that Brad Grey would prove to be as facilitating and talent-friendly as Ron Meyer, he was wrong. If he believed that Grey, whom he had helped get the Paramount job, would see him as a kind of mentor, as Meyer had, he was equally wrong. If Universal was all about doing whatever it took to keep its talent happy, Paramount's culture was far more aloof, taking its cues from Redstone, whose philosophy might be summed up in the words "I don't need you." Whether it was wives, children (Redstone's war with his daughter Shari, vice chair of the Viacom board and her father's presumed successor, was about to become fairly epic), or business partners, Redstone had gotten to where he was by not relying on anyone but himself. Eighty-plus years in, this was not about to change.

Over the summer, Redstone showed his supreme indifference to someone else: Tom Cruise. For fourteen years, Cruise and his producing partner, Paula Wagner, had one of Paramount's most prestigious production deals. The studio had paid up to $10 million a year to keep Cruise on the lot, producing blockbusters such as *Mission: Impossible*. But Redstone was all out of love. It was not only that he deemed the star's antics on *Oprah* (jumping on his hostess's couch, raving about Scientology) an embarrassment to the studio, there was also the fact that Cruise was just too damn expensive. Lately his movies, including *Mission: Impossible III*, hadn't been delivering the sort of grosses that justified such a generous outlay.

Cruise might be crazy, as well as expensive, but not even his worst critics thought he deserved such a flogging when Redstone ended Paramount's relationship with the actor, publicly criticizing his behavior. For a moment, Cruise's sagging popularity spiked. One of those offering support was Spielberg, who thought Redstone's behavior was inexcusable. The incident didn't increase Spielberg's estimation of his new home. (Studio chiefs around town, though recognizing that Redstone could have handled the excommunication with more diplomacy, quietly cheered: the move was, fiscally, very smart, and sent the message to talent that, in a lean economy, studios were not going to bend over as much.)

Far worse than the Cruise incident, as far as DreamWorks was concerned, was another Redstone-instigated departure, that of Tom Freston, in September. Freston, who had headed Viacom's cable divisions as co-COO of the conglomerate, had become DreamWorks' major Paramount cheerleader after playing a key role in the deal that had delivered the studio to its new lot. Geffen was furious. He felt that Redstone had disrespected Freston, a popular, well-liked executive who had been at Viacom for twenty-six years.

Geffen considered Redstone's behavior deplorable. Beyond that, there was the fact that the removal of Freston meant that Grey—still busy trying to maintain control both of Redstone and his studio—would handle DreamWorks on a day-to-day level. Despite his years as a manager, Grey was, like Redstone, foremost a businessman. The Paramount culture he was creating reflected that. There was no sense of the old-fashioned gratitude of the sort that studios once showered on their most valuable filmmakers—the one exception to this rule was J. J. Abrams, the onetime Propellerhead whom some considered the next Steven Spielberg (he had created hit after hit, including TV's *Lost* and *Alias* series).

Despite all this, Grey was certainly respectful of Spielberg. When the director showed up at Paramount marketing meetings, Grey deferred to him. He didn't blanch when he—the head of the studio releasing the film—was prevented from reading the script for *Indiana Jones and the Kingdom of the Crystal Skull* until Spielberg finally approved his seeing it. But he stopped short of the complete hero worship that Spielberg seemed to require. He had his limits.

Redstone's relationship with Geffen soured further when the latter called the Viacom chairman to suggest that Katzenberg fill Freston's

job. (Geffen denies making any such call.) On another c͏
fen asked Redstone to buy DreamWorks Animation. It w͏
of thing David Geffen did, as people like Edgar Bronfman Jr.͏
Meyer knew all too well. But Redstone was not amused. He re͏
both offers and a war between Geffen and Redstone was silently
clared—the two men would not speak for a year. To many in Holl͏
wood, the discord was reminiscent of the Geffen/Ovitz face-off. A
friend of Geffen's, who described the Ovitz-Geffen showdown as "The
Hundred Years' War," suggested that Redstone had supplanted Ovitz
as Geffen's latest foe du jour. Ovitz's departure seemed to have created
a vacuum in Geffen's world. "David's got to demonize somebody right
now," this person said.

Redstone, of course, was no Ovitz. He was the billionaire owner of
a sprawling media empire. Ovitz had been a very powerful agent, but
Redstone was a figure who could, simply, care less about Geffen or
any other Hollywood player. What he did need was to keep Viacom's
stock healthy. Said one former Paramount executive: "Sumner will do
anything to help Viacom's stock. It's his only objective. It's his way of
measuring his success or failure in life."

The fact that DreamWorks did not figure largely enough in Redstone's universe was a continuing irritation to Geffen. In the coming
months, as bad press began surfacing about Redstone—regarding his
falling-apart marriage and the feud with his daughter Shari—suspicious glances were cast in the direction of the savvy DreamWorks
dealmaker. How familiar it seemed.

If there was one thing that could bring DreamWorks and Paramount
closer together, or tear them further apart, it was a big, and very special, project. Enter *Dreamgirls,* the movie musical set in the Motown
1960s, set to star an entourage of A-list talent (Beyoncé, Jamie Foxx,
Eddie Murphy). The film, long a passion of Geffen's (he had produced the original Michael Bennett musical in 1981), had been first
developed back in Geffen's movie-producing days, and, years later,
at DreamWorks, before there was any talk of selling the company. In
fact, well before there was any deal between Paramount and Dream-
Works, the former had come aboard as a coproducer of the film (after
Warner Bros. opted out, Paramount had committed to half of *Dreamgirls'* $73 million cost).

·gan shooting, in January of 2006, Dream-
Paramount. The film was one of the first
Press had begun a huge promotional
from the moment she'd first read the
the film's marketing. But Paramount's
om DreamWorks) were also onboard.
ot her start coproducing the Andrew
.... the Amazing Technicolor Dreamcoat
..ok an interest in the film. She could sing every
... show and would do so with writer-director Bill Condon
and producer Laurence Mark when she dropped by the set in downtown Los Angeles, offering notes.

It had all begun in December 2002, at a Christmas party held at the
home of biographer A. Scott Berg and his partner, Kevin McCormick,
an executive at Warner Bros. Condon—who had won an Oscar for
the screenplay for *Gods and Monsters,* which he also directed—and
Mark (*Working Girl, As Good As It Gets*) had begun talking about
musicals they'd like to see turned into films. With the release of Baz
Luhrmann's *Moulin Rouge!* a year earlier, movie musicals were suddenly back in vogue. *Chicago,* which Condon wrote, and which had
just been released by Miramax to much buzz, was also fueling this
momentum.

Speaking off the top of his head, Condon said, "Well, to me, the
great musical that remains unmade is *Dreamgirls.*"

The next day Mark put in a call to Geffen, a friend, who owned the
film rights to the musical. Geffen had tried on more than one occasion to steer *Dreamgirls* to the screen. But each time, fate intervened.
During his short stint as a producer at Warner Bros., in the 1980s, Geffen had begun work on a version starring Whitney Houston as Deena
Jones, the Diana Ross–like diva. But the project ran into problems
when Houston insisted on singing the songs of both Deena and Effie White. (Effie, played by Jennifer Holliday in the original musical,
was the less statuesque member of the Dreamettes. But the character
owned the musical's one, genuinely showstopping tune, "And I Am
Telling You I'm Not Going.") Later, when DreamWorks was formed,
Warner Bros. embarked on a movie starring Lauryn Hill. But when
another one of the studio's Motown biopics, *Why Do Fools Fall in Love,*
tanked at the box office, Warner's pulled the plug on *Dreamgirls.*

When Geffen heard why Mark was calling, he proceeded to lecture him on the difficulties of making *Dreamgirls,* how it hadn't ever worked, despite his efforts.

When he'd finished, Mark said: "Look, David. If you *ever* want to open the door and have a conversation about it, Bill and I, of course, will be happy to try and dazzle you."

Geffen then said, "Fine. Well, what about lunch tomorrow?"

And then he hung up.

The next day, Mark and Condon met in the lobby of the Beverly Hills Hotel to discuss their pitch before driving up to Geffen's estate. Half an hour later, sitting in the informal dining room just off the screening room, with an incredible view of the rolling lawns that surround the historic house, Geffen explained that he felt a duty to protect the musical's legacy, as Michael Bennett, its director and choreographer, had passed away from AIDS in 1987.

"He felt that any inferior film version would destroy the legacy," Condon told me. "He felt that that had happened with [Bennett's other musical] *A Chorus Line*—that it had been hurt by the film version . . . And, with Michael gone, it was up to him to make sure that didn't happen [with *Dreamgirls*]. And that's why, through the years, even though people had developed various projects, he had always sort of stepped in at the last moment and made sure it didn't happen. It was a very precious property for him." Geffen began reminiscing about the old days, amusing Mark and Condon with stories about Bennett and Holliday, and what it had been like back when David Geffen was a plucky music executive with big dreams.

Somewhere between the steamed salmon and the poached pears, the conversation returned to business, and Condon pitched his vision of *Dreamgirls,* saying that the film should embrace the stage show, not turn away from it. Even if modern audiences weren't accustomed to actors breaking out into song in the middle of a dramatic sequence, Condon felt that movie musicals shouldn't shy away from their theatrical conventions. This would be easier to pull off, anyway, because in *Dreamgirls,* virtually everyone in the cast is a musical performer. It wouldn't seem so crazy when they suddenly burst into song. He also wanted *Dreamgirls* to deal more directly with the civil rights movement, which serves as a backdrop to the story, and which, in the musical, had been played down.

As Condon talked, he could see that Geffen was interested. But he wasn't sure that he'd sold him. Then Alan Horn, the president and COO of Warner Bros., called.

As Geffen and Horn chatted, Geffen turned the conversation to *Dreamgirls,* explaining that he was in the middle of yet another pitch for the movie. As Condon listened, he realized Geffen wasn't sounding quite so averse to the project anymore.

"He was saying, 'Yeah, so maybe it's worth developing this, and, you know'—speaking for me—'Bill understands that we've spent all these years, and had all this money against it, so he'll do it for nothing!'" Condon said. "So he was basically there negotiating."

By the time Geffen hung up with Horn, Condon had been hired to write a script—with the promise that if it all worked out, he'd be paid in full. The audition wasn't over. He had passed the first test with Geffen. Now he would have to pass the second: the screenplay.

As it turned out, that wouldn't happen for another year. Condon was about to start shooting *Kinsey.* Cut to fall of 2004. Condon was in the midst of doing publicity for *Kinsey* and close, but not quite finished, with the *Dreamgirls* script. Geffen called, wanting to know where his movie was. By this time, Geffen was playing a more active role in DreamWorks' live-action studio. He was eager to get going with *Dreamgirls.* When Geffen called, Condon was in Seattle, about to go on a radio show. Hearing this, Geffen exploded.

"He was sort of screaming about where the script was," Condon recalled. "And I said, 'Well, I'm here promoting my movie, you're gonna want me to do this in two years when *Dreamgirls* comes out.' And he gave me a nice, long lecture on how I wouldn't sell one more ticket by anything I was doing, that nobody wants to hear from a director . . . that the only thing that mattered was finishing that script.

"It really was a full-formed thesis on how anything that I was doing in this two months of that, like, intense promotional period, was a complete waste of human life."

In January of 2005, Condon handed in his script. Geffen had it picked up at noon, and within a few hours, he called Condon to tell him that he wasn't done reading yet, but what he was reading, he liked. Before six, Geffen called again to say he was finished, he was moved, and he was announcing the movie the next week.

Two weeks later, *Dreamgirls* offices were set up, and the movie was in preproduction.

Next, *Dreamgirls* needed to be cast. While working on the screenplay, Condon had always envisioned Eddie Murphy in the role of James "Thunder" Early, a James Brown–Little Richard hybrid who gives the Dreamettes their first break. When he mentioned this to Geffen, he lit up, and soon enough Condon and Mark were sitting down to lunch at Mr Chow with Murphy and Jim Wiatt, the head of William Morris and Murphy's agent. Murphy admitted he was nervous about the role—he'd never sung or danced before in a movie. He was also not accustomed to not being the lead. But he said he was a fan of the musical, and Mark left the lunch feeling there was a 60–40 chance Murphy would come around.

Money was also an issue (everyone would have to take cuts), but with some persuasive efforts by Katzenberg and Geffen, ultimately, Murphy accepted the role. (Green-lighting *Norbit* helped.)

Costume designer Sharen Davis, who'd worked with Murphy before and knew that the actor was most comfortable as a performer when he was in disguise, would help the cause by suggesting that the gap between Murphy's two front teeth be filled in.

"Sharen knew how much Eddie changes when he's got something to hide behind," Condon said, adding that the first time Murphy performed with his flawless whites, "It was just like you could see he was becoming somebody else, it was really fun to watch."

Casting Jamie Foxx as Curtis Taylor Jr., the Dreamettes' smooth-talking manager and Deena's beau, also took some prodding. Foxx was coming off his Best Actor Oscar for *Ray,* and, now that he was officially one of Hollywood's biggest leading males, he expected to be paid like one. Eventually, thanks to some strong-arming by Geffen, Foxx came around and agreed to work for a reduced fee.

As for Deena, pop superstar Beyoncé Knowles was so eager to land the role that she agreed to do a screen test just like everybody else. For the audition, which was in New York, Beyoncé went out and bought a big, sequined gown at Bergdorf's and performed the movie's title number, live, to the accompaniment of a piano. She also performed two scenes. After returning to L.A., Condon and Mark watched the tape of the screening with Geffen at his home. Geffen didn't waste any time. "Let's have a show business moment!" he said, and then picked up the phone and called Andrea Nelson Meigs, Beyoncé's agent at CAA, on her cell phone. "She's gonna be Deena."

Then there was Effie, the emotional center of the movie. She needed to be raw and vulnerable, but also gutsy; a bit of a wild card. The actress playing her would be faced with the task of stepping into a role that had been owned by Holliday, who had routinely stopped the show on Broadway and whose performance had been seared into audiences' memories for decades. Whoever played Effie needed to be able to sing the hell out of "And I Am Telling You," which Holliday had transformed into a classic.

American Idol winner Fantasia Barrino did a screen test, which Condon loved. "It was a very, very radical rethink of the part," he said. "It would [have been] less about her being the oddball because of her weight, and more about her being the oddball because of being so authentically ghetto and street, and all that—someone you couldn't soften the edges of."

Geffen hated that idea.

More girls were brought in, but no one seemed right. The search continued—far and wide. Just under eight hundred girls, from every corner of the country, gave it a shot. None of them popped. But one hopeful kept coming back to Condon's mind—Jennifer Hudson, another *American Idol* contestant, though one who didn't make it as far as Fantasia. At an audition, she'd been shaky and unprepared (she showed up not knowing she had to sing an entire song and had only rehearsed part); a second audition also proved unmemorable.

With time running out, Condon flew Hudson out to L.A. and spent a day working with her on yet another screen test. This time, Hudson's magic came through; she got the part.

On set, Hudson was raw—she couldn't dance, had trouble remembering her lines, and grew visibly awkward in front of the cameras. Beyoncé, meanwhile, didn't even have to come to dance rehearsals; she'd do a number once, then perform it flawlessly before the cameras. The whole time, Hudson's feet were killing her. Beyoncé couldn't dance in anything less than three-inch heels, and because Condon wanted all the Dreamettes to appear the same height, Hudson—who is five nine—couldn't wear flats. Anika Noni Rose, the third Dreamette, who is only five two, was up on stilts of four inches or higher. Sometimes there were tears, and Hudson would cry, "Lord, I hope they're not all like this! I can't do this again—this is *crazy!*"

Filming had begun in January of 2006, just a month after Dream-Works was bought by Paramount. Over the next few months, as the two studios went through a shaky adjustment, even Condon could feel the stress. "It was an odd moment," he said. "We started the movie in the old DreamWorks, and that changed into something new. We were a little protected from that because this was a David Geffen project, who's a bigger force than any of that stuff, and he was clearly the one who mattered here, but it was odd."

The fact that Gail Berman was laying claim to *Dreamgirls*, talking it up in interviews, did not sit well with DreamWorks. Numerous executives from both studios were deployed to watch over the movie in an ownership struggle. DreamWorks, and Press, in particular, really lost it when Berman proudly showed footage of the film to producer Scott Rudin, who then called Mark and told him how great it looked. To Press, it was a breach in protocol, a big no-no—you never showed material to outsiders, no matter how good it was. She called Geffen, who then called Grey and badmouthed Berman.

The DreamWorks and Paramount marketing forces were also coming to blows. When Press arranged a huge media blowout on the *Dreamgirls* set in downtown L.A., in March, inviting hundreds of journalists and plying them with cocktails, food, and dance numbers from the movie, DreamWorks executives felt that the Paramount marketing team was resentful, feeling outshone.

"Paramount hated us," said one. "It was very poisonous."

The situation was so fraught that the same marketing meetings were repeated multiple times a week because no one could stand to be in a room together.

"There'd be the meeting with Gail without Stacey [Snider], then the same meeting repeated with Stacey," said one former Paramount executive. "I'd be in one meeting and be like, 'Didn't I just say that?' I needed a Chinese checkerboard to figure out the politics."

Press, meanwhile, was invited to marketing meetings on Dream-Works films, but would have to leave once *Dreamgirls* had been discussed.

The Cannes Film Festival provided another opportunity for fireworks. By now Press and Paramount's PR person, Janet Hill—sworn enemies from when Hill worked at Miramax—were feuding. Hill was accusing Press of being responsible for unflattering remarks about Grey that had appeared in the *New York Post;* Press, meanwhile, was trashing Hill to Grey, saying it was her fault his name was being dragged into the Pellicano mess. At Cannes, when Hill accused Press of talking to a gossip columnist, Geffen was dragged in. He stormed into the *Vanity Fair* party at the Hotel du Cap. "Point out Janet Hill," he demanded. He then tore into Rob Moore, who was with his wife, as nearby guests made a run for it.

As the person advising Grey on how to handle the situation with DreamWorks, Hill was proving to be a lightning rod in the disintegrating relations between the two studios. From the beginning, Hill was the mouthpiece for Paramount's stance that DreamWorks wasn't a studio but a label, just like MTV Films and Nickelodeon, an attitude that bred deep resentment among the DreamWorks folks, no one more so than Spielberg. To him, DreamWorks was an identity, a heritage. To treat it as anything else was akin to blasphemy. Spielberg felt so strongly about the matter—and the fact that DreamWorks movies were being referred to as Paramount movies—that he spoke about it in June of 2006 on the AMC show *Sunday Morning Shootout,* saying: "Gail Berman is running Paramount Pictures, and that's separate from DreamWorks Pictures. And that's something we're trying to get the town to understand."

According to one former Paramount executive: "From day one, the Paramount group was being told that DreamWorks is now a boutique label just like MTV Films is a boutique label, or Nickelodeon. Clearly, the guys at DreamWorks never in a million years comprehended, or imagined, that that was the deal they had made."

Things got worse, in October, when Paramount released Clint Eastwood's film, *Flags of Our Fathers,* which was produced by DreamWorks. The film had a weak opening, and when Moore blamed this on Eastwood, telling the *New York Times,* "The biggest draw of the movie is its director, who's not in the movie," Spielberg, who idolized Eastwood, felt, once again, that one of his people was done wrong by a corporate suit. Spielberg was so upset that he demanded a meeting with Moore, who tried to soothe his nerves. Eastwood was also bristling, and said to one person, "Who is this *Rob Moore?*" Even months after the incident, Eastwood would refer to "this *Rob Moore*" in disdainful italics.

Moore felt more heat when, during a Sunday-morning box-office call with Paramount brass, he said, in so many words, that *Flags'* failing was the fault of Press, who'd handled the film's marketing—not knowing that Press was on the call. After indicating that she'd heard what Moore had said, Press hung up and called Snider. Once again, the complaint reached Geffen, who called Grey. Moore then apologized to Press.

If Geffen was fearless in dealing with the "bullies," as he called them, at Paramount, he was less sure of himself when it came to *Dreamgirls*. He was very vocal about the fact that *Dreamgirls* was his swan song to the industry, and he could not conceal his concern about its reception. Since the *Moulin Rouge!*–led revival of movie musicals, a series of musical adaptations, such as *Rent, The Producers,* and *The Phantom of the Opera,* had tanked, suggesting that audiences weren't so keen, after all, to watch actors belting out dialogue and dance-numbering their way through drama.

During the filming of *Dreamgirls,* Geffen's anxiety had surfaced when he asked Condon to try toning down the sequences in which actors spontaneously break into song.

"He asked us to shoot versions of those scenes without singing, so that, for example, when Effie first sings, 'What About How I Feel?' I have a version of it where she speaks it," Condon said. "And to his credit, I went and showed it to him, and he said, 'No, that one moves me.' He understood that the one where she sings was more moving."

At times, Geffen's angst came out in forceful ways. During arguments, he would bellow, "I didn't get to be the thirty-second-richest man in the world for nothing! I know what I'm talking about!" according to a source close to the production.

Although Geffen declined to take a producer credit on *Dreamgirls*—"I see my role as a baby doctor helping people deliver their babies. I felt the same way in the music industry," he told the *Wall Street Journal*—the film was seen as a deeply personal project. When one member of the film's visual-effects crew referred to the film as a "DreamWorks movie," he was corrected by a colleague: "No, it's a *David Geffen* movie."

Geffen's apprehension became especially apparent during test screenings. After a screening in San Diego's Gaslamp Quarter, where *Dreamgirls* tested extraordinarily well, Geffen was fuming. The audience had been presold, and everyone had sung along to all the songs.

When Loretta Devine (who starred in the original Broadway production) made a cameo appearance, the whole place had erupted in cheers.

"Of course it scored well! It was all fags and old people!" Geffen said.

So convinced was he that the audience was a little too predisposed to like a movie musical—and wanting to prove his point—he demanded that, during the discussion session after the movie, the audience be asked who in the crowd was married. When several members of the audience raised their hands, he added another stipulation: who was married *to a man?*

When the movie scored less well in Newport, Rhode Island—the crowd was made up of mostly heterosexual young men—and Geffen was told the numbers, he remained calm. In a perverse way, he almost seemed relieved; as though the universe as he saw it had, at last, been confirmed. "Well, Bill needs to wake up and stop dusting off his mantelpiece, getting ready for his Oscar," he said.

But if Geffen was working hard to temper his confidence in *Dreamgirls,* he was alone in that endeavor. By the fall of 2006, the promotional steam engine that Press had begun masterminding as far back as December of 2005—when a teaser trailer featuring the iconic Jennifer Holliday recording of "And I Am Telling You I'm Not Going," first appeared—was charging full-speed ahead, and the world was happily, dizzily caught up in the ride.

There was, naturally, an *Oprah* appearance (Ms. Winfrey declared *Dreamgirls* "sensational" and "an extravaganza"). Then, on November 21, media screenings of *Dreamgirls* were held at sixty locations around the country. "Media" included theater types, gays, and the sorts of people who would presumably be huge fans of the movie. Unsurprisingly, the events were phenomenally successful. In Philadelphia, the crowd stood and applauded. In Los Angeles, the crowd was palpably energized, ready to fall in love even before the movie started. In New York, people walked out of the theater placing their Oscar bets.

"It's theirs to lose," a "veteran industry insider" said, in reference to the Academy Awards, to the *New York Observer,* which ran a *Dreamgirls*-crazy article subtitled: "David Geffen's Long-Delayed Musical Roused to Life . . . And We Are Telling You They're Going—to the Oscars!"

In the January issue, the film was anointed on the cover of *Vanity Fair,* which featured a photo of Foxx, Beyoncé, and Murphy. Inside the magazine, Peter Biskind began: "Watching *Dreamgirls*-the-movie . . . is like stepping onto a bullet train and seeing the world outside the windows pass by in a breathless blur, one that doesn't end until the film's last frame."

While things were going swimmingly for *Dreamgirls,* the same could not be said for DreamWorks and Paramount. Things reached a head at the New York premiere of *Dreamgirls,* held on the evening of December 4 at the Ziegfeld Theatre. Ironically, earlier that same day, Paramount was blowing kisses at DreamWorks. Speaking at a media conference for investors, newly installed Viacom CEO Philippe Dauman said that "DreamWorks brings a tremendous creative talent" to Paramount, and went on to praise *Dreamgirls,* as well as other upcoming DreamWorks films, such as the Eddie Murphy comedy *Norbit,* and *Transformers,* which, he said, would hopefully become a franchise for the studio.

Later in the evening, all hell broke loose. The cause for the uproar was a one-minute speech that Grey delivered before the film. As Hollywood protocol goes, it was fairly standard. DreamWorks executives, however, were affronted by the notion that Grey would do such a thing, seeing it as a credit-grab for a movie that was not, in their opinion, Paramount's to take credit for. Furthermore, Press had explicitly told Grey—through Hill—that Geffen wanted a "cold opening" to the film (as did Condon and Mark); i.e., no speeches before the curtain rose. When Grey made it clear that he was going to speak, Snider appealed to Hill to change her boss's mind. Then, Geffen had called Grey, who explained to him that it was important for him to say something in front of his Viacom bosses. By the night of the premiere, Press continued to push the matter. When Grey marched up to the front of the theater, DreamWorks executives were aghast.

Grey seemed to be missing, or else choosing to ignore, the most pertinent thing about DreamWorks: This was royalty. Spielberg was the king, and his company the kingdom.

Grey's remarks were short and gracious, both to DreamWorks, and to Geffen, whom Grey praised profusely for getting *Dreamgirls* from the stage to the screen. When the movie ended, and the entire audience stood on its feet applauding, Grey and Geffen even embraced, rather emotionally, according to one witness.

But whatever it looked like, a line had been crossed.

As *Dreamgirls'* release drew nearer, the hype reached a deafening roar. Though when I used that term with Condon, he cringed. "That stuff that was defined as hype early on, I thought was actually genuine," he said. "It seemed like Peter Biskind and other people liked what they saw. Which is not to say that there weren't a lot of other people who saw it and were disappointed in it. But . . . it wasn't a manufactured enthusiasm. We were feeling it from people who would see it. I'm talking about people who were in the culture—journalists and critics, and people like that. We were feeling that enthusiasm."

The publicity drove yet another wedge between DreamWorks and Paramount, which wanted to pull back on promotions, or at least be more measured in spending, which one source put at close to $50 million.

"Paramount was trying to cancel" things, said costume designer Sharen Davis, who was charged with dressing the actresses before their many, many media appearances. "Jennifer was always touring, doing all these Q&As all over. They started cutting those down."

There was "a tug of war" between the studios, Davis said.

Press was leading the publicity charge, and many felt she was even more driven than usual, both because this was her own swan song to DreamWorks and, it was believed, because she was determined to prove to Geffen, the DreamWorks partner with whom she was now the most close, that she was still as untouchable as she'd been back in the *American Beauty* days. But even people involved with the film were beginning to feel the train was going too far, too fast. That it was just too *much* and was going to backfire. Ironically, Press herself had always said that the most dangerous thing to be was the clear front-runner; that once people assumed you were golden, you were anything but. But in the passion and heat of the drama—over *Dreamgirls*, over Dream*Works*—she seemed to be forgetting her favorite adage.

The first pinprick in the balloon of swelling *Dreamgirls* love—or, as Condon put it, the first "thud"—was A. O. Scott's review of the film in the *New York Times*, in which he wrote that "the performances are gratifyingly spirited, but what this movie most obviously lacks is soul."

Scott's critique was quickly overshadowed by many more generous reviews, and by the fact that the film was racking up awards nominations—for the Golden Globes, the Screen Actors Guild Awards, the Directors Guild Awards, the British Academy of Film and Television Awards.

It was at the Globes ceremony, in January, that Grey further incensed DreamWorks brass when he demanded seats at both the *Dreamgirls* table and the table for *Babel,* Paramount's own awards contender. Beyond the presumptuousness of the request, it meant that Jennifer Hudson couldn't bring a date. (In the end, her guest was accommodated by shoving in an extra chair.) When, after both films won Best Picture in their respective categories (and a beaming Grey was pictured with both groups), Grey followed the talent backstage for press interviews, he solidified his image at DreamWorks as a credit whore.

Grey also ruffled feathers at the American Film Institute Awards luncheon, another pit stop on the awards circuit. The lunch was a fairly low-key event as these things go; it was not televised, nor was it black tie. Thus members of the *Dreamgirls* entourage were surprised to show up and find place cards at their table, specifying where everyone should sit. It quickly became clear that the place cards had been Grey's idea and were being enforced by Hill. When Hudson, who'd been placed next to Grey, tried to move her card, Hill swiftly intervened and returned it to its original place.

Both the Golden Globes incident, and the flare-up at the New York premiere of *Dreamgirls,* might have remained behind-the-scenes gossip, only that's not the way DreamWorks played. Suddenly, Nikki Finke's Hollywood news-gossip Web site, Deadline Hollywood Daily, was lighting up with these and other scenarios, all written from the perspective of a wronged DreamWorks being insulted by the power-thirsty idiots at Paramount. At Paramount, everyone assumed Geffen was behind it.

Condon was in London for the U.K. opening of *Dreamgirls.* He watched the nominations from his hotel room.

"I remember watching it, and it's like, the writing [award], that's not happening, and director, that's not happening, and the picture—it didn't hit me, because it happened so fast, it was over, I was like, 'Wow, we didn't get picture!'"

"We'd had all those [award show wins]—PGA, DGA, Golden Globes. Part of the reason it was so surprising was because it was actually an unprecedented turn of events—in terms of having that much leading up to it and then not having it. So, yeah, that was a blow."

Condon gave no credence to the idea that an overload of hype had anything to do with the Oscar oversight.

"I actually, weirdly, believe that, no matter what taste the Academy has, they ultimately take [voting] seriously, and they look and decide whether they like that movie or not," he said.

Even more distraught was Press, who had put her heart and soul into the *Dreamgirls* campaign. When Condon called her in L.A. after the nominations, Press was sobbing.

"I was so touched," Condon said. "I was comforting her. There was something about it that really hurt her. So, Larry and I were kind of like, 'It's OK, it's OK, don't worry.' I was feeling worse for her, in a way, which was a nice way to deal with it."

Geffen, who had always been braced for disappointment, was consoled by the fact that *Dreamgirls* had made more than $100 million at the domestic box office.

"David has been through the vicissitudes of it all, and he takes this sort of thing in stride," said Mark. "He was very good about it. He said something like, 'This does not mean we love the movie any less. The movie's as good as it ever was, and this is nothing.'

"David happens to have a very good bedside manner."

Geffen was less sanguine when he learned—through Nikki Finke's blog—that Sumner Redstone told a dinner guest that Grey had told him that the reason *Dreamgirls* hadn't received a Best Picture Oscar nomination was because "everyone hates David Geffen."

As one DreamWorks source remarked to Bryan Burrough in *Vanity Fair:* "That was big—that was a big mark in the road."

Geffen had a new campaign to focus his energies on. Just weeks before the Academy Awards, he threw the first, very public, punch in the run-up to the 2008 presidential campaign, when he dissed Hillary Clinton to *New York Times* op-ed columnist Maureen Dowd at a fundraiser for Clinton's main opponent for the Democratic ticket— Illinois senator Barack Obama—at his home. "Not since the Vietnam War has there been this level of disappointment in the behavior of

America throughout the world, and I don't think that another incredibly polarizing figure, no matter how smart she is and no matter how ambitious she is—and God knows, is there anybody more ambitious than Hillary Clinton?—can bring this country together," Geffen told Dowd, who wrote it up for a column in the paper, which began, "Hillary is not David Geffen's dreamgirl."

For Geffen to assume the moral high ground against Clinton was somewhat curious for a man whose career had its share of Machiavellian moments. But there was more: Bill Clinton was a "reckless guy." As for the Clintons as a couple, Geffen said, "Everybody in politics lies, but they do it with such ease, it's troubling." The remarks caused sparks to fly in political circles and anointed Obama, who at this point was little known on the Left Coast, as Hollywood's It Boy—no small honor, considering that L.A. was a veritable ATM for the Democrats.

Dowd, and others, sourced Geffen's disillusionment with the Clintons, with whom he had once been so close, to Clinton's 2001 pardon of Marc Rich. (Geffen had requested a pardon for the Native American activist Leonard Peltier, which Clinton had rebuffed.) But people close to Geffen say that his unhappiness with Clinton went farther back, and ran far deeper. They say that Geffen had been disappointed in Clinton by the time he left the White House, feeling that the former president had let the Democratic Party down and, worse, not lived up to his promises. From his weak stance on gays in the military, to losing control of Congress to the Republicans in 1994, to dishonoring the Oval Office over selfish motivations, Clinton was, in the eyes of Geffen, a disgrace. He had supported Al Gore and John Kerry during their presidential campaigns, but not wholeheartedly (and with far less financial support than he'd showered on Clinton, for whom he raised $18 million), seeing them as extensions of their predecessor. By the time Hillary Clinton emerged on the scene as a candidate for the 2008 Democratic ticket, Geffen had had it with the Clintons.

Also influencing Geffen was his friendship with Arianna Huffington, the chameleonic onetime conservative turned liberalish would-be governor of California. In her latest incarnation, she was a mediagenic political pundit and cofounder of her own popular online newspaper *cum* liberal salon, the *Huffington Post*. Huffington owed her fortune to the wealth of her right-wing ex-husband, Congressman Michael Huffington. During his controversial run to become a California senator,

Arianna, always outspoken, always elbowed her way into the lime-light. She was seen as the mastermind behind the campaign, inspir-ing the moniker "Lady Macbeth." Her husband's campaign manager famously described her, in his memoirs, as "beautiful" but "evil."

In the sunshine of L.A., Huffington's past melted away, and she be-came the darling of the left, opening up her $7 million Brentwood palazzo to the town's most powerful and prominent, and jumping to the forefront of liberal causes. Along the way, she met David Geffen, who became a fast friend. Huffington was an early admirer of Obama, and it was she who introduced Geffen to the Chicago senator and fu-eled his interest in the candidate of "change."

Geffen's embrace of Obama put him at odds with his DreamWorks partners, both of whom remained devoted to the Clintons, even as they extended their support to Obama. (Both Spielberg and Katzen-berg supported both candidates in the primary.) The split was sym-bolic of a political fracture that had been growing over the years and that marked a dramatic contrast from DreamWorks' early years, when all three men were united in their support of Clinton as well as other causes. Geffen was going off on his own in other areas, as well, ex-pressing an interest in buying the ailing *Los Angeles Times*, which was on the block.

In the early months of 2007, things grew precipitously worse between DreamWorks and Paramount. In January, when Berman stepped down as president after a wildly tumultuous tenure, Paramount rear-ranged its reporting structure and issued a press release that lumped DreamWorks in with MTV Films and Nickelodeon. It was Grey's at-tempt to manage in the style of Steve Ross, who always believed that multiple fiefdoms under one umbrella made for the best synergy. Sta-cey Snider, who hadn't been given much advance warning about the release, was particularly offended because it insinuated that she was an employee of Grey's, even though she had green-light authority over DreamWorks movies. It was no secret that there was tension between she and Grey; everyone could feel it. Just as things were prickly be-tween Snider and Moore, whom Snider—who at Universal had called all the shots—would have to defer to on marketing dollars spent on DreamWorks films.

Within the next few weeks, a series of articles in the *Los Angeles*

Times and *New York Times* appeared, in which DreamWorks aired its frustrations—again, as Paramount looked on in horror. In the *New York Times* piece, Spielberg, who rarely issues more than a statement through his publicist, sat down with reporters. When Paramount came up, he bent his head down close to the microphone so that his words would not be missed: "I insisted, contractually, on autonomy for DreamWorks if I was going to continue under the Paramount and Viacom funding arrangement. So I take exception when the press is contacted by our friends and partners at Paramount, who refer to every DreamWorks picture as a Paramount picture. It is not the case."

When the denizens of Hollywood woke up to their morning papers and saw that even Spielberg was talking on the record, they knew it was bad. No one doubted that Geffen had a hand in riling him up, but still, when Spielberg was this enraged, things were not cool.

The credit tussle was slowly turning into a low-grade war in which sparks were flying even at the most minute level. The staff working on publicity materials and press kits for upcoming DreamWorks movies were deluged with orders from both sides as to what size the DreamWorks and Paramount logos should be (i.e., whose should be bigger); what side of the page those logos should go on; whether, in some cases, Paramount should even be mentioned at all (an argument made by DreamWorks). Even the live-action studio was taking swipes; if DreamWorks heard that Paramount was pursuing a project, executives would swoop in and take it off the table—agents, picking up on this, would cleverly use the dynamic to play the two sides against each other and try to drive up prices.

Just when things felt like they'd hit a point of no return, Paramount began making amends. Redstone was desperate for the bad press to stop, so Grey made it his mission to placate Spielberg and Geffen. A series of meetings took place between Geffen and Grey, who agreed to give DreamWorks everything it wanted: more green-light authority for Snider (from now on, she could approve movies with a budget up to $100 million, and up to $150 million if Spielberg was directing). DreamWorks was also allowed to hire its own corporate PR person to handle the press. (Janet Hill had left, in part, it was rumored, due to DreamWorks.) Grey went so far as to visit Spielberg on the set of the fourth *Indiana Jones* movie, at his estate in East Hampton. There he offered the director a $1 million check for the Shoah Foundation.

Fueling Paramount's desire to keep the peace was that Dream-
Works—for the first time since its arrival at Paramount—was releasing hit movies. On the heels of *Dreamgirls,* there was *Norbit,* the
make-Eddie-Murphy-happy movie that grossed a surprising $95 mil-
lion; *Blades of Glory* ($118 million); *Disturbia* ($80 million). Then,
over the summer, came *Transformers* ($319 million and $708 million
worldwide), which was the highest-grossing film in DreamWorks'
history. The films were all mainstream and commercial, exactly what
Paramount's marketing and distribution departments were skilled at
handling. It was a chemistry experiment gone oh so right, pleasing
not just to Grey but to higher-ups at Viacom, and nobody wanted it
to end.

Transformers, which Spielberg executive-produced, was the biggest stamp of the Adam Goodman era. (Since his early, somewhat un-
steady, days as DreamWorks' president of production, Goodman had
reformed dramatically as an executive. He was much more even-keeled
and calm, seeming to have benefited from Stacey Snider's example.)
Transformers was an example of a film that likely would never have
been made under the Parkes-MacDonald regime. Based on the Hasbro "more than meets the eye" robot toys, the film had been pitched
to Goodman and Mike De Luca when he was at the studio, by producers Don Murphy and Tom DeSanto. DreamWorks originally passed.
Later, after De Luca's departure, when word got back that Paramount
was pursuing a *Transformers* movie and was negotiating with Hasbro,
Spielberg, who'd always liked the idea, was furious. He was particularly upset that Hasbro, which had signed an early deal with Dream-
Works specifically *because* of Spielberg and his toy fetish, was turning
its back.

The Hasbro deal had been a debacle. One of the first, big hopes
for the marriage had been the low-grossing film *Small Soldiers.* Given
Parkes and MacDonald's sensibilities, it's not surprising that no more
toy movies were green-lighted. Frustrated, Hasbro now told Dream-
Works it wanted to work with a company that "gets things done."
Goodman was determined to become that person. He told Hasbro
that he would be on a plane to Rhode Island, where the company was
headquartered, the next day. Within twenty-four hours, a deal was
struck in which DreamWorks and Paramount joined as partners on
the movie. To remind his boss, Goodman took out a double-truck ad

in *Daily Variety* announcing that DreamWorks and Paramount would be releasing *Transformers* in the summer of 2006. Except for the year, the statement was accurate.

It had been Goodman's idea to hire Michael Bay to direct *Transformers*, back when he was working on *The Island*. Spielberg cast Shia LaBeouf, a scrappy kid who exuded confidence and cool—in a way, he was a mini Steven Spielberg—whom the director had cast as the lead in *Disturbia* as well as in the next *Indiana Jones* installment. (He would play Harrison Ford's sidekick.) Overnight the latest Spielberg "discovery" went from bit parts to gracing the cover of *Vanity Fair*.

Despite the fact that Transformers toys made their mark in the 1980s, Spielberg knew everything about them, and in the first story meeting on the movie, he was the most knowledgeable person in the room, discussing at length the Transformers' "mythology." He knew which robots were which—the difference between, say, Optimus Prime and Megatron—and suggested basing the movie on the Western *The Magnificent Seven,* and having seven "good" robots. (In the end, there were five.)

Production was another Michael Bay–style circus. Bay refused to let Goodman or any other studio executives see dailies other than the ones he approved. All was forgotten when the movie went through the roof. At the *Transformers* premiere, when Brad Grey ran into Bay in the men's room and exclaimed, "The movie's doing well!" Bay replied cockily, from the urinal: "It has been for the last two weeks, in six different countries."

What was really doing well was DreamWorks, which was, in fact, having a better year at Paramount, political turbulence aside, than it had ever had as an independent studio.

It was this success, however, that may have been, and many believed was, Geffen's underlying reason for wanting to pick a fight with Paramount. For it suggested that Geffen had done the thing he never, ever did: made a bad deal. By now, DreamWorks—which was the first studio that year to cross the billion-dollar mark in box-office dollars—had paid for itself and then some. For $1.6 billion, Paramount had gotten a *bargain*. That, to Geffen, was embarrassing.

"They sold for $1.6 billion [what] they could have gotten between $2 and $2.5 billion for—and that's a lot of money to leave on the table," said one source. So, Geffen set things in motion. In July, he let it slip to *BusinessWeek*'s Ronald Grover that he and Spielberg were planning on calling it quits with Paramount when their contracts were up in October of 2008, causing a wave of shock and awe among Paramount brass.

Whatever cage-rattling Geffen was doing, however, Katzenberg needed to maintain good relations with Paramount, seeing as that's who was now releasing DreamWorks Animation films. The next—*Bee Movie,* featuring the voice of Jerry Seinfeld—was coming out in November. Unlike most DreamWorks animated movies, the auteur on this one truly had been Seinfeld, who only agreed to make the movie when he was promised that Katzenberg would not creatively get in his way and that Spielberg would be involved, at least initially.

The partnership between DreamWorks Animation and Paramount was much smoother than the live-action marriage. In marketing DreamWorks' May 2006 release, *Over the Hedge,* Paramount had tapped Nickelodeon resources (DreamWorks and Nickelodeon were also teaming up to produce animated kids' TV programs using DreamWorks characters), and with Katzenberg as a hands-on presence, the two studios worked well together. The only thing that was shocking to Paramount was just how hands-on Katzenberg was, now that he was stripped of his duties at DreamWorks proper, which at one point had included running everything from television to video games to live-action marketing and distribution. Faced with running one studio, which only released two movies a year, Katzenberg's micromanager streak was in overdrive. No tasks were too small, too beneath him.

"He was making sure Cameron Diaz [a voice in *Shrek the Third*] was doing *Leno,*" said one source. "It was crazy the amount of minutiae he got involved in; there'd be a discussion about Hugh Jackman's and Kate Winslet's [voices in *Flushed Away*] schedules, what they were doing. It blew my mind."

Unrelated to Paramount, DreamWorks Animation went through a period of handwringing in the fall of 2006, when the Aardman co-production *Flushed Away* became a $90 million write-off. Paul Allen had so little faith in the movie that he had forced DreamWorks to hold a secondary stock offering in November, when *Flushed Away* was released. In the sale, Allen got about $220 million. A month later, CFO Kris Leslie, who'd shepherded the company through its IPO, was let go. But now, with the release of *Shrek the Third,* in May—which

grossed $322 million domestically and $798 million around the world
—DreamWorks was beginning to regain its footing after its first, very
volatile, years as a public company. DreamWorks Animation stock
was still wobbly, but was up to $32 a share from a *Flushed Away* low of
$20. Still, it was far from its $38 peak during the time of the IPO. And
Paul Allen continued to be cashed out, through another public offering in August. This was Allen's biggest cash-out to date: he sold 15 million shares of DWA stock for $467 million.

Shrek the Third prompted another play by Grey that grated on
DreamWorks' nerves. When Grey sent around a congratulatory e-mail,
saying that in light of the film's success, everyone could leave early
on Friday, it was seen as yet another attempt to take ownership of a
DreamWorks property.

In September, a month before the release of *Bee Movie,* Katzenberg
sat down with DreamWorks' attorney Skip Brittenham to discuss how
the situation could be improved.

As Katzenberg told Burrough: "I think everyone agrees that the
purchase of DreamWorks was both a great coup and a great financial
success. But when you have profited so greatly, it's imperative to find
other ways to reward people, especially people like Steven Spielberg
and David Geffen, who are more interested in how they are treated
than in money. Everyone wants to be appreciated.

"Separate from money, there are ways you can reward talent . . .
make them feel appreciated, valued, respected. That is the crux of the
issue . . . DreamWorks has not been given the proper respect, or credit.
Talent relations is the fuel of this industry. Every day for twenty-five
years, [former MCA/Universal studio chief] Sid Sheinberg made Steven
Spielberg feel like the most important person in the world to him. In
ways large and small, he made it clear to Steven how much he mattered.
The people at Paramount and Viacom haven't done this. Maybe it's out
of intimidation or fear or a lack of understanding of what's at stake, but
when it comes to talent relations, they've simply missed."

But if, up until now, they were missing, in the fall, Viacom started
fighting back. The same day that Katzenberg—following his talk with
Brittenham—had a talk with Geffen, asking him to dial back his vitriol, Viacom CEO Philippe Dauman, speaking at an investors' conference in New York, provided a slap heard round the world—or, at least,
back in Los Angeles at DreamWorks.

When Dauman was asked about the possibility of losing Spielberg, he said: "We're doing everything possible to make him happy . . . Now, Steven and his team have the right to leave if they choose at the end of next year. At that point, if there is someone who steps in with $1 billion, $2 billion, whatever, stepping into the Paul Allen role a decade ago to start a new studio from scratch, that's a possibility. And we're planning for that."

After praising Paramount's upcoming films, Dauman concluded: "So the financial impact to Paramount first and especially to Viacom overall would be completely immaterial in the event somebody shows up to help them start a studio from scratch."

Immaterial! Steven Spielberg! These words had never in the history of time been used in the same context. Here was an opportunity for Geffen and Katzenberg to rev up Spielberg and perhaps take their show on the road again. This time for much more money. Very quickly things were blown even more out of proportion.

The next day, speaking at the same conference, Katzenberg shot back: "As a filmmaker, storyteller, artist, and conscience, Steven Spielberg is nothing short of a national treasure. To suggest that not having Steven Spielberg is completely immaterial seems ill-advised. I think calmer heads need to prevail here."

Geffen was not one of those heads. He fumed to Burrough: "To refer to Steven Spielberg as immaterial is not only disrespectful but it does not entitle them in any way to be in business with him. I've never seen behavior like this in my entire life. Steven Spielberg is anything but immaterial to me and all the people at DreamWorks. We love him!"

Geffen's comments spoke to the symbiotic relationship that always existed between Geffen and Spielberg and that held them together like glue, whatever their many striking differences as individuals. Geffen the Agent and Protector of Steven the Priceless Talent. And now, as Geffen's final service to DreamWorks, he made it his business to extricate Spielberg from Paramount.

There were more flare-ups, albeit less sensational ones. In December, when DreamWorks' *Sweeney Todd: The Demon Barber of Fleet Street* grossed an underwhelming $52 million, Paramount was blamed for marketing the movie like a Johnny Depp blockbuster à la *Pirates of the Caribbean* as opposed to a Tim Burton art-house movie. Paramount countered that the movie cost too much money to market as an art-house film. All the while, there was an underlying rumble that DreamWorks had one foot out the door.

By the spring, Geffen and DreamWorks' financial consultants, including CAA, were closer to finalizing just who that suitor was, just as, in May, Paramount released Spielberg's fourth installment of *Indiana Jones*. The film debuted at Cannes, and the day after, Spielberg hopped on a yacht and didn't check back in until a week and a half later to see how it was doing. The movie was well on its way to grossing $317 million domestically and $786 million worldwide. "You're kidding," he said when he heard the news, sounding genuinely surprised. "That's great."

The success of the film again highlighted just how well Paramount was doing when it came to distributing and marketing DreamWorks' product. Paramount marketing executive Josh Greenstein was considered such a wunderkind, by Spielberg and other top directors, that filmmakers fought to make sure he was working on their films; when he wasn't, they made a fuss. Whatever egos were bruised, the situation was actually working rather well for DreamWorks, and some sensed that if it were up to Spielberg and Snider they might actually stay now that Grey had made the requisite amends. Then there was the fact that, as Geffen was discovering, finding another Paul Allen to cough up millions in financing was not nearly as easy as it had been back in 1994, when the economy was booming and DreamWorks was an untested company with enormous promise, not a mixed track record.

But if there was any hesitation about leaving on Spielberg's part, Geffen was not to be dissuaded. Once he felt he'd been screwed, there was no turning back. He was out to burn bridges and destroy.

Again Geffen turned to the media to trumpet his next move. In June the *Wall Street Journal* reported that DreamWorks was in talks with Reliance Entertainment, the Mumbai-based conglomerate that was beginning to dabble in Hollywood (financing movies for actor-producers such as Tom Hanks, Brad Pitt, and Jim Carrey), to form an independent film studio. (That DreamWorks was continuing to use the press as a soap box and negotiating ploy was maddening to people at Paramount, who likened it to being in the middle of a divorce and having to read about who your spouse was sleeping with.) The hope was to raise $1.7 billion in financing—$500 million of which would come from Reliance—and return to its roots as a privately owned, freestanding studio. The model was more reminiscent of Amblin, Spielberg's original production company, which had produced half a dozen movies a year (as opposed to the dozen that DreamWorks, at least on paper, set out to produce), than the original DreamWorks. In keeping with that model, neither Geffen nor Katzenberg would be a part of the equation; the "new" DreamWorks would be run by Spielberg and Snider. There were complications: Paramount technically owned the films that had been developed at DreamWorks while it was at Paramount. And certain properties, such as the *Transformers* franchise (the sequel was due out in 2009), were jointly owned. But perhaps because of the companies' shared determination to go their separate ways, they were being worked out.

According to the deal, Paramount still technically owned Dream-Works—Viacom would retain DreamWorks' library and projects in development (some of which would be shared with DreamWorks). But Spielberg, Geffen, and Snider were able to contractually exit the company—taking the DreamWorks name with them (a detail that Geffen had cleverly written into the original deal). Basically, the principals, the people who made DreamWorks what it was, were leaving. Geffen was, once again, the mastermind. As for whether it was "good for Steven," as one person put it, "Well, David thinks it is." And David had done a good job of convincing Steven. Left behind at Paramount to serve as an executive *cum* diplomat between DreamWorks and Paramount was Adam Goodman, who'd been replaced by Mark Sourian and Holly Bario to serve as presidents of the "new" DreamWorks.

With the wheels set in motion, Paramount, for once, took control of the situation and, when the deal was finally closed in September—involving far less blood and legal wrangling than anticipated (ironically, the most painless part of the DreamWorks–Paramount marriage was the divorce)—played its own games when it came to spreading the news, leaking its press release to Nikki Finke. DreamWorks was still in the process of finalizing details and wanted to wait and orchestrate its own release, but Paramount stepped on the gas, issuing a statement that made no attempt to make things look friendly. Grey began by saying, "We congratulate Steven, David and Stacey, and wish them well as they start their newest venture. Steven is one of the world's greatest storytellers and a legend in the motion picture business. It has been an honor working closely with him and the DreamWorks team over the last three years and we expect to continue our successful collaboration with Steven in the future."

Then came the rub: "To facilitate a timely and smooth transition, Paramount has waived certain provisions from the original deal to clear the way for the DreamWorks principals and their employees to join their company without delay."

It was those last two words that rang out loud and clear to anyone who had been following the drama on the Melrose lot over those last three years—and that would be everyone in Hollywood. Grey was essentially saying: don't let the door hit you on the way out. What he was also saying was: we don't need you.

"Around town, it was widely considered that Brad Grey won that round," said one source.

Not all was said and done. Reliance's financing was contingent on JPMorgan Chase raising a $700 million credit line. But come October, DreamWorks was free, and DreamWorks 2.0, as it was being referred to, could launch anew. Geffen could finally say goodbye to the movie business, and Katzenberg could continue working with Paramount on his animated movies (DreamWorks Animation was back on a winning streak with *Kung Fu Panda*) without the headache of his noisy ex-partners. Already there was talk of returning "home" to Universal, where the "new" DreamWorks, unsurprisingly, made its distribution deal. All, it seemed, was well with the world.

When I ran into one Paramount executive and asked what it felt like to have DreamWorks on its way out the door, he said: "It's like finding out that you don't have cancer anymore."

Someone from the DreamWorks camp described the departure as "joy," saying that the marriage was "like an organ transplant that didn't work—the arm finally festered and fell off."

The buoyant mood was not to last.

As it happened, the world was on the verge of the worst economic crisis since the Great Depression. But no one knew that yet. Not that anyone in Hollywood would have believed it.

EPILOGUE:
THREE-WAY SPLIT

WHEN STEVEN SPIELBERG took to the lectern on the evening of Sunday, January 11, 2009, at that year's Golden Globe Awards ceremony, the world did not seem so radically transformed. All his friends and loved ones were there in their finery—Kate Capshaw, Tom Hanks, Leo DiCaprio. Even Martin Scorsese was on hand, bestowing on Spielberg what no one doubted he deserved: the Cecil B. DeMille Award, for lifetime achievement. But things were different, for everyone.

As ever, the Globes were a freewheeling, live-it-up evening. There were Brad and Angelina, fresh from a save-the-world pit stop in Afghanistan (a trip that *People* splashed across its pages). Security guards surrounded them as they sauntered, self-consciously un-self-conscious, to the bar. Mickey Rourke, dressed up in biker-boy formal wear, tattoos hidden beneath a black velvet jacket and pinstriped pocket square, was mourning his puppy. After winning Best Actor for his affecting turn in *The Wrestler,* he loitered out onto the smoking patio, where a woman asked to take a picture.

"OK, take off your clothes," Rourke replied with a roguish grin.

The hyperkinetic Ben Silverman, NBC's fresh-faced *enfant terrible,* was everywhere, backslapping, handshaking, air kissing. At the bar, he gushed to Jonathan Rhys Meyers, the sourpuss star of the TV series *The Tudors:* "I just watched the first two episodes of your show and it's . . . amazing. You are my prince. You are my *king.* Amazing."

"Thank you," Meyers replied graciously. "We should get together."

"Yes, we'll play," Silverman replied distractedly as he worked his way back into the throng. "I'll see you later. Goodbye, darling."

Spielberg was in character, looking sheepishly avuncular behind his wire-framed glasses. His speech was what one expected from the filmmaker whom Pauline Kael described as "a boy soprano lilting with joy." Unlike Rourke, the director was not in the business of bleep-filled gratitude. Gracefully settling into storytelling mode, he rewound to Philadelphia, 1952, when his father took him to see De-Mille's *The Greatest Show on Earth*. What struck him was "the biggest train wreck that had possibly ever been put on film."

Afterward, young Spielberg returned to his Super 8, filming his own collisions, using model electric trains. And so began the future king of the blockbusters, who rounded out his remarks by explaining that he judged potential projects' worthiness by asking himself: *Am I going to get away with this?* If a positive response came too readily, he said, he simply wasn't interested. The story was met with warm laughter.

But something was off. Not quite everyone was rapt. As Spielberg spoke, there was an air of distraction. Some lingered on the smoking patio, unmoved to pay their respects to Sir Steven. Something strange was afoot. Not even the master storyteller himself could keep reality from seeping in that evening; lurking on the other side of the ballroom doors was a business already wrought with seismic, balance-sheet-altering shifts. DVDs were no longer saving the studios' asses; movie-ticket sales were down as kids chose iPhone-sized screens over big ones. Everything, it seemed, was going soft, as the United States experienced its worst economic downturn since the Great Depression. For once, Hollywood was not immune. Earnings reports were nose-diving. Agents were flying coach. Seemingly overnight, the era of excess—with its bloated mortgages and loans, designer pooches, and $400 cell phones—was kaput. Salvation was promised in the guise of the "new media," but what happened, people were wondering, to the old?

The world was very different, indeed, from the one in which Spielberg, Katzenberg, and Geffen had first joined forces. Looking back, those early days at DreamWorks seemed almost quaint; like scenes from old black-and-white footage someone had stumbled across in the archives. Something to be studied for clues, lessons: at what point did it start to go wrong?

The new *terra infirma* was affecting Spielberg, even more, perhaps, than anyone else that night. DreamWorks' efforts to launch anew after the departure of two of its partners, and its split with Paramount, were being thwarted by the dismal economy. The bold projection that the recharged and reimagined DreamWorks 2.0 would be another billion-dollar enterprise ($1.4 billion, to be precise) seemed, at this juncture, almost laughable. JPMorgan's bankers had been struggling to raise money—and the investment from DreamWorks' main backer, Mumbai-based Reliance Entertainment, was dependent on the bank's commitment. Reliance itself had taken a hit—its market value was slashed by 60 percent with the stock-market crash—and would no longer be able to put up the promised $500 million. Nothing was clear; everything was on hold. DreamWorks, which had hoped to relaunch on January 1, was stranded, idling in neutral, perhaps remembering Paramount with, for once, fondness. Things were so bad that Spielberg and Stacey Snider—the sole proprietors of the new DreamWorks—had appealed to CAA for help with their woes. Creative Artists had virtually "shut down," according to a rival agent, in order to single-mindedly rescue its star client. Yet not even that had been enough.

This should have been when Geffen—who, in the past, was always DreamWorks' superagent and resident fix-it guy—swooped in, screamed a bit, and dredged up more dough. But Geffen was gone. After detangling DreamWorks from Paramount, he had bid Spielberg adieu, formally ending their professional relationship and perhaps their personal one, at least for a time. Geffen had apparently been offended when Spielberg did not thank him in the press coverage that surrounded the deal. It was a matter of protocol, something that, as the DreamWorks story underscores, matters very much in Hollywood. Especially with David Geffen, who was spending most days "on his boat." That is, in the splendor of his seafaring luxury liner.

It was hard to remember a time when Spielberg was so bereft of protectors and parent figures. Walter Parkes and Laurie MacDonald were, in the new configuration, producers at DreamWorks; stripped even of their company e-mail accounts in the new turn of events. Terry Press remained off the reservation, serving Tom Cruise and his latest rebound effort, *Valkyrie,* as a marketing consultant for MGM. DreamWorks' self-glorifying spins on stories had ground to a halt. Sheltering Spielberg was only Snider, who faced a challenge few in town would have relished—saving DreamWorks.

Even Paul Allen, DreamWorks' long-standing benefactor, was gone.

In February, he finally cashed out his investment in DreamWorks. Fourteen years after he had sunk $500 million into an enterprise he believed was a fantasy (in the end, he would invest $700 million), he was moving on. Certainly, it had not been his wisest investment. Between the money he received from the sale of the live-action studio to Paramount—just under $200 million—and the sale of his DreamWorks Animation stock, Allen ultimately walked away with an amount estimated at more than $1.2 billion. But it was unlikely he would be placing bets on Hollywood again.

Just a few months before, the new plan had all seemed so tenable, so perfect. Reliance had stepped up as DreamWorks' second Paul Allen. A distribution agreement was all but finalized with Universal, which delighted Spielberg. Finally, he would be going home. But by the time the Golden Globes rolled around, everything had changed. Spielberg—for the first time in his career—was paying salaries and overhead out of his own pocket. He had even been forced to cough up $13 million to retain DreamWorks' partnership on seventeen projects left behind at Paramount. Spielberg—an economy of his own, with assets now worth upwards of $3.1 billion—was hardly sending out "Brother, Can You Spare a Dime?" e-mails on his iPhone. But it was an unusual development for someone accustomed to spending other people's money.

With each passing day, Spielberg was losing leverage. Another check was needed to secure DreamWorks' rights to a second batch of projects at Paramount. When DreamWorks failed to produce it, gone were projects such as Peter Jackson's *The Lovely Bones,* based on the best-selling novel. Most painful, Spielberg lost the right to partner on and produce the biopic *Lincoln.* For years, the project—set to star Liam Neeson, who'd cleared his schedule for a spring-summer 2009 shoot—had been Spielberg's passion, his *Schindler*-to-be. But no . . .

When DreamWorks lost the rights to *Lincoln,* Paramount could have hired Spielberg to direct. But the studio passed, tired of the DreamWorks nightmare and unwilling to pay Spielberg's standard fee. *A studio telling Spielberg no?* Quite forcefully. In the wake of the ugliness over DreamWorks' departure and DreamWorks' very public handling of that departure, and its very public playing out, Paramount was pissed. Spielberg might be Hollywood's "national treasure," but not on the Melrose lot. Paramount had recently moved DreamWorks'

The Soloist from a prime late-2008 release date to a no-man's-land date of April 2009. The move had been practical. (Why spend Oscar campaign money on a film whose chances look slim?) But the manner in which the news was delivered to DreamWorks—just three weeks before the film was set to open—was less than courteous. The town took note. As for Spielberg, Paramount's attitude was: If the project made sense, fine. If not: sorry. And as the months wore on, there were more snubs. As for *Interstellar,* the sci-fi thriller that Spielberg hoped to direct for Paramount: sorry. As for *Matt Helm,* a film that had been developed at DreamWorks for years and that now Spielberg was thinking about directing: sorry. (Later, Paramount would reverse its decision on *Matt Helm,* proving that the universe had not *completely* turned inside out.) Meanwhile, Spielberg made his own weight felt by attaching his name to all of the DreamWorks projects that were technically owned by Paramount—a move that one observer called "hysterical." Thus Paramount would actually need Spielberg's blessing if it wanted to move forward on a film.

But ultimately, Spielberg had far less control than was the norm. Universal had opted out of *Tintin,* which Spielberg was about to embark upon with Peter Jackson, citing costs, as well as low awareness on American shores of the plucky Belgian adventurer. (Luckily, Paramount and Sony picked up the slack.)

These problems alone might have felled a mere mortal. But there was more. The WunderKinder Foundation, a charitable organization begun by Spielberg and Katzenberg, had been ensnared in Bernard Madoff's $50 billion epic Ponzi scheme, losing a reported $73 million. (Katzenberg had allegedly lost another $20 million from his and his wife's foundation, but was dealing with it in the way Katzenberg always did: "I'm as lucky and as blessed as I can be. Let's move on," he told Amy Wallace of *Portfolio.*) The men hadn't personally known Madoff, but had become involved when their business manager, Gerald Breslauer, invested on their behalf. Tellingly, Geffen, who was more cautious about how his money was spent and who was spending it, had once been a client of Breslauer's, but had parted ways, fortuitously avoiding the swindle of the century.

The firmament had, indeed, shifted. Not that anyone wanted to admit it. When *Variety* reported that Spielberg was writing personal checks to keep DreamWorks operating, a DreamWorks publicist called, outraged: "You make it sound like we're desperate!" A few weeks later, Snider was dispatched on a PR mission and made an—unprecedented—personal appearance at the *Variety* offices to assure reporters that all was well in Dream Land.

Inside the company, typically fearless employees, who had been steadily fed over the years by DreamWorks' unrelenting pride and pomp, were suddenly anxious. Everyone knew the company was downsizing to the dimensions of a more traditional production company. But nobody knew who would be departing. The private face that DreamWorks had always turned to the public and the media was suddenly turned toward its own employees. Information was doled out on a need-to-know basis. But for the most part, it seemed to have been decided, *no one needed to know.*

In days of old, Katzenberg would have stepped into the leadership vacuum and organized a town hall meeting, as he always did in the wake of major events. But no one was stepping in at this fraught moment. Spielberg was as available as Howard Hughes; behind closed doors, he fretted about how it looked to be rendering people jobless in a time of economic turmoil. Snider remained burrowed in her bunker. The job of messenger was handed to Jeff Small, DreamWorks' chief operating officer. A man barely known to most employees, he delivered their fates matter-of-factly: "You will not be moving forward with DreamWorks."

Just when it looked like things couldn't get worse, they did. In February, DreamWorks—now even more desperate for cash—asked Universal for an investment of $250 million as part of its distribution agreement, which was in the final stages of negotiation. Universal refused, and so DreamWorks turned to Disney, which was hungry for product, having scaled back its output in recent years, and which identified with Spielberg's family-friendly brand. But the situation blew up, rather sensationally. When Universal got wind of what was going on —not by a phone call from either Spielberg or Snider, but by press inquiries—the company, which had been down these roads before, abruptly cut off talks. Anonymous Universal sources in the press lambasted Spielberg and Co. as "pigs" and "the blind leading the blind."

Some suspected it was Geffen (or Geffen via someone) who tipped off the reporter—Ms. Nikki Finke. Why? Why else? Because Dream-

Works' change of heart made it look like Geffen had erred and not made the wisest possible deal. He was still angry that this had turned out to be the case when he turned the company over to Paramount. Curiously, in the days following the blowup, certain sectors were airing the idea that "David always thought Disney was the better deal, anyway. That's where he always thought they should go." As always with DreamWorks, the facts were buried somewhere in the spin. Who ever, really, knew? That was the madness, the fun, the never-dull thing about DreamWorks. The company you either passionately hated or loved. DreamWorks didn't do in between. Whatever anyone in Hollywood felt about the company, it was never, ever indifference. Or boredom. The place kept the town on its toes.

In the weeks following the dust-up, Ron Meyer was angry at DreamWorks, but most of all Snider, who'd betrayed him for the second time now. Spielberg, after all, was talent, a commodity you had to love. Besides, Spielberg and Universal were still attached—there was that pesky theme-park deal. By the spring, Spielberg was over at Meyer's for his annual Easter-egg hunt.

Katzenberg, for one, had to have been flummoxed by the deal with Disney. DreamWorks, after all, had been created as a vehicle in which to exact his revenge on the Magic Kingdom. All of a sudden it was that very kingdom that was opening its gates to his former partner. Disney was a different place in 2009; Eisner, of course, was long gone. Katzenberg actually *liked* Bob Iger. But with Pixar continuing to supply the company with animated hits, and its own animated division retooled and breathed back to life by John Lasseter, who was overseeing both entities, there was no chance DreamWorks Animation would ever be bought by Disney. A reunion of Spielberg and Katzenberg was impossible, at least in the near future. As for Geffen, he had stepped down from the DreamWorks Animation board, cutting his last tie to the movie business. Going forward, for the first time in more than a decade, Katzenberg was truly alone.

Not that Jeffrey didn't have things to do. He'd found a new religion—3-D—and was preaching it with characteristic gusto all over the world. Having been caught behind in the transition from traditional to computer-generated animation, he was not going to be left in the dust on this one. He was leading the charge. From now on, all of DreamWorks Animation's movies would be in 3-D—yes, requiring those awful glasses, though the new kind were cooler than the ones from the 1950s. A revolution, he said, was at hand; the equivalent of the introduction of sound and color, according to Katzenberg.

There were artistic reasons for Katzenberg's latest love: films in 3-D did look a lot neater, the stuff jumped right out at you. But, of course, the financial incentives were even more compelling. Tickets to 3-D movies cost more, which could mean a bump of as much as $80 million to a film's revenues. (They cost more to make, too, but not that much.) However, Katzenberg's stance in the 3-D debate cast him against Spielberg, a traditionalist and purist, who firmly believed that film was *film,* and that that's what movies should be both shot and viewed on. Spielberg's staunch position had caused headaches for Katzenberg, when Spielberg had insisted that *Indiana Jones and the Kingdom of the Crystal Skull* only be viewed on 35mm film. In the end, Paramount ended up releasing both digital and traditional copies of the movie, but it was a reminder of the diametrically opposed motives driving the two men. Commerce versus art.

In Katzenberg's third act, he was building DreamWorks Animation into its own veritable kingdom—a company not just about movies, but TV shows, musicals (*Shrek* had hit Broadway), even theme parks in Dubai and Singapore. The company was looking, curiously, a lot like Disney. Katzenberg had regained some of Wall Street's trust with more successful movies—*Madagascar: Escape 2 Africa* and *Kung Fu Panda,* a film that was lovingly worked on for nearly five years and which had even beaten out Pixar at the Annie Awards (the animation world's version of the Oscars). DreamWorks artists claimed Katzenberg was taking more of a backseat creatively, that he was, more than ever before, letting the artists do their thing. Not that he wasn't multitasking and micromanaging wherever he could, but he seemed to have come to better terms with where his talents lie.

He still had challenges. DreamWorks' stock had taken steps toward recovery but was still, he said, grossly undervalued. With the stock trading at $30 in July, DreamWorks' original stockholders were just barely above water. Longtime DreamWorks employees, at least those who hadn't sold immediately when the stock was briefly flying high, had yet to see their pot at the end of the rainbow. And there would always be Pixar to beat. DreamWorks Animation was a third the valuation of that company, which had been sold to Disney for $7 billion in

2006. In the latest face-off—DreamWorks' *Monsters vs. Aliens* versus Pixar's *Up*—Lasseter had once again come out on top, both at the box office and, especially, in reviews.

Looking back, it had been a siege, since that day in August of 1994, when Katzenberg's ouster had set in motion the birth of Dream-Works. Of the three DreamWorks partners, Katzenberg's experience had been, in many ways, the most dramatic, educational—and painful. He had been forced to face, and come to terms with, enormous failures that rested on his shoulders. There were two of the most disastrous films in his company's history (*The Road to El Dorado* and *Sinbad*). Even worse was the SEC incident over *Shrek 2* DVDs. In the latter case, Katzenberg's supreme confidence had gotten the best of him. As did his desire to beat a rival, and his refusal to recognize his inexperience handling a publicly traded company and defer to someone more seasoned. They were the very qualities Eisner had been wary of all those years ago.

It had all been a rather humbling experience for a man who was not easily humbled, a man who did not believe in self-reflection or taking stock. In time, of course, he got to the glory he was so determined to call his own: *Shrek;* the formation of DreamWorks Animation and its stellar IPO; a much enhanced bank account.

But after all the battles and scary lows, Katzenberg was no longer the kid brother with the unstoppable will and boyish tendencies toward hero worship. He was older, less buoyant, more conscious of other people, his own fallibility, and the presence of circumstances beyond his control. He was on his own, free of elders, free, even, at least for now, of vendettas. He was still relevant in Hollywood, still a king, but the dimensions of his kingdom and his stature were not what he had once imagined.

Speaking to the *New York Times* in 2009, sounding unusually self-reflective, Katzenberg said: "I find myself getting completely comfortable with the idea that if somebody else can do my job as good, let alone better, that's OK. Let me move on and find something else to do.

"That was an interesting transition to make. You know full well I am someone who's spent a very good part of my career as a micromanager. And if you talk about attributes that were my least good attributes, being a micromanager would certainly be on the top of my list. What I have learned recently is to be a selective micromanager.

There are times when it's actually good to be a micromanager, but mostly not."

There was no denying Katzenberg's legacy. Many of the oversize billboards hulking down over L.A.'s Sunset and Sepulveda boulevards were for animated films, a genre that had been all but lost and forgotten until Katzenberg came along and kicked Disney back into shape.

DreamWorks as a whole had left its imprint on Hollywood and beyond. Whatever its financial and management travails, DreamWorks *had* succeeded in being different from the majors, and in working hard to discover and launch artists; in effect, putting art first. Just look at the studio's roster of filmmakers who got their start working for SKG. Gore Verbinski is today one of the most successful directors in Hollywood, having segued from mice to buccaneers. The three *Pirates of the Caribbean* films he's directed—written by *Shrek* scribes Ted Elliott and Terry Rossio—have grossed $2.6 billion. Andrew Adamson gave up ogres for C. S. Lewis, another billion-dollar Hollywood franchise: the third *Chronicles of Narnia* installment was due in theaters in 2010. The screenwriter Alan Ball, whom Spielberg decided to give a shot, has now directed a feature film (*Towelhead*), and is behind two of cable's most critically acclaimed shows: *Six Feet Under* and *True Blood*. The list goes on. Sam Mendes (*Jar Head, Revolutionary Road*). Bill Lawrence (*Scrubs, Cougar Town*). Screenwriters Alex Kurtzman and Roberto Orci (*Mission: Impossible III, Star Trek*). D. J. Caruso (*Disturbia, Eagle Eye*). Not to mention Judd Apatow, Will Ferrell, and Todd Phillips. DreamWorks Records has an impressive artistic legacy as well. Meanwhile, Adam Goodman was promoted to president of Paramount in the summer of 2009, having made a favorable impression on his bosses with his overtly commercial streak of hits, the latest of which, *Transformers: Revenge of the Fallen,* grossed $833 million worldwide in June of that year.

The world changed under DreamWorks' feet almost from the minute the company was formed, as consolidation swept Hollywood; the digital era set in, in earnest; the business contracted. Facing these realities, the partners, all schooled in a distinctly different time, and comfortably middle-aged when DreamWorks was born, did not adapt; at least not enough. Too often DreamWorks looked backwards, whether it was Spielberg longing for a sprawling, physical studio, Katzenberg's dedication to old-fashioned animation, or Geffen's sometimes retro approach to the music division.

At the live-action studio, DreamWorks stumbled onto a winning formula with *American Beauty,* namely, a very modest budget paired with absolute creative freedom for filmmakers. The result was one of the company's most profitable films and a Best Picture Oscar. The idea that smaller is often better could have served DreamWorks well in the long run. But the philosophy behind *American Beauty*—the film "made by mistake" that defined the DreamWorks brand—was never repeated. Even *The Ring,* a "cheap" DreamWorks picture that was very profitable, had a not *so* small budget of $48 million.

Inherent in all of it was hubris, and the idea that DreamWorks didn't need to adapt to any rules, because it was writing them itself. No one was forcing the DreamWorks partners to be accountable, at least no one at their level. Individuals were put in COO roles, but they proved incapable of taming the spending habits and extravagant tendencies of three very rich men. Then there was the power imbalance of the troika. Spielberg, the resident king, handed the live-action studio to Walter Parkes and Laurie MacDonald, inexperienced managers who ultimately drove away much creative talent. Katzenberg, who knew better than anyone how to run a multimedia company, was kept on the sidelines. Geffen, meanwhile, hovered a little too distantly above it all.

Yet in the end, more than anything else, DreamWorks was a failure of expectation, one that resulted from all of the relentless hype. Spectacular success was not so much a goal as an assumption. How could these guys *fail?* DreamWorks itself promulgated this notion through its close relationships with the press, and the company's story is a lesson in the dangers of those staggering expectations. Anything less than delivering the stars and sun and moon (as promised) couldn't help but look like a failure—even to sage Hollywood observers who knew the score in terms of the risky nature of the business. Spielberg had so long been considered infallible that he seemed to believe it himself. Geffen and Katzenberg had so carefully maintained and buffed their public images that they, too, seemed to have forgotten that they were, well: *human.*

In July 2009, finally, Spielberg got his money. He could put away his wallet, having put in a total of $60 million in personal funds to tide DreamWorks over during the last several months. The banks had done their part, Reliance was kicking in, as was Disney. It was a much more modest package than originally envisioned—financing worth $825 million, not $1.4 billion. And Reliance wouldn't be paying half the cost of the five to six films DreamWorks would be making every year, but a much lower 20 percent. This was how it was in the New New Hollywood. DreamWorks, and Spielberg, would have to swallow, and they did. Spielberg, naturally, put a Spielbergian face on the situation, saying that the new venture "opens a new door to our future."

No one doubted there would always be doors open for him. The times may change, but Hollywood still attracts the world's attention, money, and love. As the investors from India and the far reaches of the Middle East are proving, there are always new starry-eyed suitors eager and hungry to be part of the fantasy of it all. The myth, more powerful than any surrounding any other business anywhere, still attracts. The movie called Hollywood never comes to an end, and its kings and knaves still know how to put on a show.

BIBLIOGRAPHY

NOTES ON SOURCES

ACKNOWLEDGMENTS

INDEX

———

BIBLIOGRAPHY

Amis, Martin. *The Moronic Inferno.* London: Jonathan Cape, 1986.

Auletta, Ken. *The Highwaymen: Warriors of the Information Superhighway.* New York: Random House, 1997.

———. *World War 3.0: Microsoft and Its Enemies.* New York: Random House, 2001.

Balio, Tino T. *United Artists, Volume I, 1919–1950.* Madison: University of Wisconsin Press, 1987.

Bart, Peter. *The Gross: The Hits, the Flops: The Summer That Ate Hollywood.* New York: St. Martin's, 2000.

Baxter, John. *Steven Spielberg: The Unauthorised Biography.* London: HarperCollins, 1996.

Biskind, Peter. *Easy Riders, Raging Bulls.* New York: Simon & Schuster, 1998.

———. *Down and Dirty Pictures: Miramax, Sundance, and the Rise of Independent Film.* New York: Simon & Schuster, 2004.

Brillstein, Bernie. *Where Did I Go Right?: You're No One in Hollywood Unless Someone Wants You Dead.* New York: Warner Books, 1999.

Bruck, Connie. *Master of the Game: Steve Ross and the Creation of Time Warner.* New York: Penguin, 1995.

———. *When Hollywood Had a King.* New York: Random House, 2003.

Carter, Bill. *Desperate Networks.* New York: Doubleday, 2006.

Cohen, David S. *Screen Plays: How 25 Screenplays Made It to a Theater Near You—for Better or Worse.* New York: HarperCollins, 2008.

Eisner, Michael. *Work in Progress.* New York: Random House, 1998.

Epstein, Edward Jay. *The Big Picture: Money and Power in Hollywood.* New York: Random House, 2005.

Eszterhas, Joe. *Hollywood Animal.* New York: Vintage, 2004.

Farley, Tom, Jr., and Colby Tanner. *The Chris Farley Show: A Biography in Three Acts.* New York: Viking, 2008.

Foege, Alec. *Right of the Dial: The Rise of Clear Channel and the Fall of Commercial Radio.* New York: Faber and Faber, 2008.

Friedman, Lester D., and Brent Notbohm, eds. *Steven Spielberg: Interviews.* Jackson: University Press of Mississippi, 2000.

Gabler, Neal. *Walt Disney: The Triumph of the American Imagination.* New York: Knopf, 2006.

Griffin, Nancy, and Kim Masters. *Hit and Run.* New York: Simon & Schuster, 1997.

Grover, Ron. *The Disney Touch.* New York: McGraw-Hill Trade, 1996.

Hayes, Dade, and Jonathan Bing. *Open Wide: How Hollywood Box Office Became a National Obsession.* New York: Hyperion, 2004.

Kimmel, Daniel M. *The Dream Team: The Rise and Fall of DreamWorks: Lessons from the New Hollywood.* Chicago: Ivan R. Dee, 2006.

King, Tom. *The Operator: David Geffen Builds, Buys, and Sells the New Hollywood.* New York: Random House, 2000.

Lowenstein, Stephen, ed. *My First Movie: Take Two: Ten Celebrated Directors Talk About Their First Film.* New York: Pantheon, 2008.

Manvell, Roger. *Art and Animation.* New York: Hastings House Publishers, 1980.

Masters, Kim. *The Keys to the Kingdom: The Rise of Michael Eisner and the Fall of Everybody Else.* New York: HarperCollins, 2000.

McBride, Joseph. *Steven Spielberg: A Biography.* New York: Simon & Schuster, 1997.

O'Donnell, Pierce, and Dennis McDougal. *Fatal Subtraction: The Inside Story of Buchwald V. Paramount.* New York: Doubleday, 1992.

Phillips, Julia. *You'll Never Eat Lunch in This Town Again.* New York: Random House, 1991.

Price, David A. *The Pixar Touch: The Making of a Company.* New York: Vintage, 2008.

Rich, Laura. *The Accidental Zillionaire: Demystifying Paul Allen.* New York: John Wiley & Sons, 2003.

Shone, Tom. *Blockbuster: Or, How Hollywood Learned to Stop Worrying and Love the Summer.* New York: Free Press, 2004.

Singular, Stephen. *The Rise and Rise of David Geffen.* Secaucus, N.J.: Carol Publishing Group, 1997.

Sito, Tom. *Drawing the Line: The Untold Story of the Animation Unions from Bosko to Bart Simpson.* Lexington: The University Press of Kentucky, 2006.

Stewart, James B. *DisneyWar.* New York: Simon & Schuster, 2005.

Vogel, Harold. *Entertainment Industry Economics.* New York: Cambridge University Press, 1986.

Wiley, Mason, and Damien Bona. *Inside Oscar.* New York: Ballantine Books, 1986.

NOTES ON SOURCES

A Note to Readers

The discussion of Hollywood's relationship with the press is based on my reporting experience in Hollywood, for *Variety* and other publications and Web sites, as well as on numerous conversations I had with other entertainment journalists and publicists. The meeting between Jeffrey Katzenberg, Terry Press, and editors at the *Los Angeles Times* is based on conversations with sources at DreamWorks and the *Times*, including Claudia Eller. Tom Hanks's comment ("Is that it?") was reported in "More Than a Dream In the Works," by David Cohen, *South China Morning Post*, November 1, 1997.

That fear can accompany an association with DreamWorks and its founders is based on numerous interviews I conducted during the course of researching this book, including with individuals intimately familiar with the company. David Geffen's promise to "destroy" Michael Ovitz was recounted by friends of Geffen's, including Howard Rosenman. Ovitz's comment ("Perception is everything") was reported in "Michael Ovitz Is on the Line," by Lynn Hirschberg, *New York Times Magazine*, May 9, 1999. Maureen Dowd's column, "Obama's Big Screen Test," appeared in the *New York Times* on February 21, 2007.

See the notes for chapter 30 for information on the Securities and Exchange Commision investigation of, and shareholder lawsuits filed against, DreamWorks Animation, as well as Katzenberg's role in the debacle.

Geffen's attempt to buy a small number of equity stakes back from employees before he sold Geffen Records in 1989 is chronicled in Tom King's biography of Geffen, *The Operator*. Information pertaining to how much money Paul Allen made from his investment in DreamWorks is discussed in "Dream Maker," by Richard Morgan, *Deal Magazine*, July 3, 2008. That Spielberg, Katzenberg, and Geffen each netted $175 million in the sale of DreamWorks to Paramount was reported in "The 400 Richest Americans," *Forbes*, September 21, 2006. Employees' unhappiness over not profiting in that sale, as well as in the IPO of

DreamWorks Animation, was recounted in interviews I conducted with former top-level DreamWorks executives. For Spielberg, Katzenberg, and Geffen's profits in the IPO of DreamWorks Animation, see notes in chapter 29.

Peter Guber and Jon Peters's controversial reign at Sony is chronicled in depth in Nancy Griffin and Kim Masters's book *Hit and Run.*

1. THE EMPEROR IN AUGUST

The meeting at Lew Wasserman's house is recounted in Tom King's *The Operator.* For background on Wasserman and his legacy at MCA/Universal and in Hollywood, Connie Bruck's *When Hollywood Had a King* was a bountiful source.

Barbara Johnson, who maintained the Wassermans' koi pond, shared with me Lew Wasserman's comment about his spawning koi. Sources for the tension between Matsushita and MCA include Bruck's book, as well as Kim Masters's *The Keys to the Kingdom,* and Masters's April 1995 *Vanity Fair* article, "What's Ovitz Got to Do with It?"

Details regarding Spielberg's directing and producing contracts—and his deal on *Jurassic Park*—are based on conversations I had with sources at Universal and CAA, and written reports, such as "Dino Soars Again; Why Invest in a Sequel? Tour Spielberg's 'World,'" by Claudia Eller, *Los Angeles Times,* May 30, 1997. Background on Geffen's personal and professional life was drawn from my interviews with sources, as well as *The Operator.*

2. THE END OF MAGIC

Information in this chapter comes from my interviews with Penney Finkelman Cox, Dale Launer, Claudia Eller, and Alan Citron, the source of the quotes attributed to these individuals, as well as a number of Disney executives who worked with Michael Eisner and Jeffrey Katzenberg. Eisner and Katzenberg's history at Disney, their complicated relationship, Katzenberg's break with Disney, and the dispute between the two men with respect to what was contractually owed Katzenberg after he left the company is chronicled at length in James B. Stewart's *DisneyWar* and Kim Masters's *Keys to the Kingdom,* as well as numerous other published reports. Both books also provide details on Katzenberg's personal history, and discuss Geffen's role in encouraging Katzenberg in his battle with Eisner. The characterization of Katzenberg is based on my own reporting, supplemented by written reports in the mentioned sources, as is Geffen's friendship with Katzenberg and the former's contentious relationship with Michael Ovitz.

The tension between Ovitz and Geffen is referenced in Bernie Brillstein's *Where Did I Go Right?* Biographical information on Eisner is drawn from his autobiography, *Work in Progress.* Don Hahn's quote is from the documentary about Disney animation, *Waking Sleeping Beauty,* as is Eisner's quote about Frank Wells ("[He] carried a piece of paper in his pocket . . ."). The description of Katzenberg as "creative but unpolished" appeared in Thomas R. King, "Creative but Unpolished Executive for Hire," *Wall Street Journal,* August 26, 1994.

3. MR. SPIELBERG WILL SEE YOU NOW

My interviews with Scott Frank, Dale Launer, and Sandra Rabins are the source of the quotes attributed to these individuals. Katzenberg's meeting at Spielberg's house, and the ambivalence of Kate Capshaw toward Spielberg's involvement in the new venture, is recounted in Masters's *Keys to the Kingdom.* Details about Spielberg's residence were garnered from sources I interviewed, as well as from published reports, such as "Peter Pan Grows Up But Can He Still Fly?" by Richard Corliss and Jeffrey Ressner, *Time,* May 19, 1997. Capshaw's description of her neighborhood was drawn from "Bad Neighbor Policy," by Catherine Seipp, *Salon,* July 18, 1997. The discussion of Capshaw and Spielberg's relationship is based on an interview I conducted with an individual close to Capshaw.

The phone call from Spielberg to Katzenberg with Robert Zemeckis in the background is recounted in numerous publications, including Masters's *Keys to the Kingdom.* Katzenberg's phone call to Geffen is described in Tom King's *The Operator.* Information about Katzenberg's Maple Drive office, and his arrangement with Price Waterhouse, is based on interviews with Rabins and publicist Harry Clein. Sid Sheinberg's comments about Spielberg, and Spielberg's response, are drawn from "The Man Who Would Be Walt," by Suzanna Andrews, *New York Times,* January 26, 1992. Spielberg's description of himself as a boy are taken from Joseph McBride's biography, as is the quote from Richard Christian Matheson. The discussion of Spielberg's toughness as a businessman, and his scrupulousness about his finances, is based on my interviews with sources at CAA, Universal, and DreamWorks, as well as published reports. The anecdote about negotiations between CAA and Disney is based on my conversation with a former CAA agent. Capshaw's comments about Katzenberg's workaholism are drawn from Masters's *Keys to the Kingdom.*

4. GEFFEN SLEPT HERE

I interviewed Jeff Yarbrough and Howard Rosenman; other associates of Geffen spoke to me on condition of anonymity. The scenario at the Hay-Adams Hotel was recounted in numerous publications, including Tom King's *The Operator,* which also provided the most comprehensive biographical and professional information on Geffen, including his relationship with Steve Ross and his outburst over Warner's falling stock. Other published sources include "Devil in a Bespoke Suit," Leslie Bennetts's *Vanity Fair* piece on Ahmet Ertegun, published in January 1998; and "Marianne's Faithful," by Patrick D. Miller, *Vanity Fair,* June 1991.

Geffen's antagonistic history with Spielberg is based on my conversations with associates of both men, as well as accounts in King's and Masters's books, and Connie Bruck's *Master of the Game,* the source of the Terry Semel quote. Katzenberg's conversation with Geffen about joining his new company is from *The Operator.* Katzenberg's comment to Spielberg about Geffen's wealth is drawn from Masters's *Vanity Fair* piece, "What's Ovitz Got to Do with It?" Background on Ovitz is based on my interviews, accounts in Masters's, Stewart's, and King's books, as well as other published reports, including Hirschberg's *New York Times Magazine* article "Michael Ovitz Is on the Line." Ovitz's letter to Joe Eszterhas threatening to "blow [his] brains out!" was quoted in Eszterhas's book *Hollywood Animal.*

5. THE ANNOUNCEMENT

In my interviews with Alan Citron and Harry Clein, both described the media maneuverings leading up to the announcement of a Spielberg/Katzenberg/Geffen partnership.

Details surrounding Katzenberg's house are drawn from my conversations with associates and friends of Katzenberg's. The meeting at Katzenberg's was described by Clein and reported in Tom King's *The Operator.*

The assumption that Michael Ovitz was angry over being excluded from the initial discussions between the three DreamWorks partners is based on my reporting with sources at CAA, as well as references in Masters's *Keys to the Kingdom,* which is the source of Katzenberg's telling Joe Roth to "get that psycho to call me!"

The description of the press conference at the Peninsula is based on my interviews with Clein and others who attended the event, as well as written reports, including "3 Hollywood Giants Team Up to Create Major Movie Studio," by Bernard Weinraub, *New York Times,* October 13, 1994; and "'Dream Team' Trio Outline Plans for Studio," by Alan Citron and Claudia Eller, *Los Angeles Times,* October 13, 1994. The "What a drama queen!" comment is drawn from Kim Masters's "What's Ovitz Got to Do with It?" (which is also the source of Barry Diller's quote).

6. E.T., PHONE HOME

Quotes from Bruce Cohen, Allen Daviau, Mark Johnson, Peter Hirschmann, and Frank Marshall are from interviews I conducted with these sources. The description of Parkes and the meeting at Amblin on the day the new studio was announced is based on interviews with several Amblin and DreamWorks employees. Spielberg's reaction to the 1976 Oscar nominations is drawn from Mason Wiley and Damien Bona's book, *Inside Oscar*. Parkes and MacDonald's returning home to a message from Spielberg was described in "DreamWorks' Dream Duo: Pair Feted for Blockbuster Year," by Dan Cox, *Daily Variety*, March 11, 1998.

For biographical and professional background on Spielberg, I relied primarily on Joseph McBride's and John Baxter's biographies of the director, along with Peter Biskind's *Easy Riders, Raging Bulls*. The elder Spielberg's quote about his son appeared in the article "Inside Spielberg Inc.," by Julie Salamon, *Wall Street Journal*, February 12, 1987.

The description of Kathy Kennedy and Frank Marshall is based on my reporting; that Spielberg kept Kennedy at Amblin longer than she originally planned is per an Amblin source with direct knowledge of the situation. Descriptions of Amblin, and Spielberg's secrecy at Amblin, is based on interviews with several Amblin sources, and published reports, including Suzanna Andrews's piece, "The Man Who Would Be Walt," in the *New York Times*. Richard D. Zanuck's comments are from an interview I conducted for a *Variety* story.

7. ANIMATED CHARACTERS

Quotes from Penney Finkelman Cox, Sandra Rabins, Marty Katz, Max Howard, Ken Harsha, Floyd Norman, Tom Sito, Bill Higgins, Dylan Kohler, and Andy Waisler are from my interviews with these sources. The description of the DreamWorks offices at Amblin is based on interviews with DreamWorks sources. Information on Gary David Goldberg's deal at DreamWorks was shared with me by agents at UTA. Spielberg's admission that his track record in TV was "lousy" was reported in "S*M*A*S*H," by Rick Marin with Mark Miller, *Newsweek*, October 31, 1994.

Several DreamWorks sources recounted the scenario by which the company's name was arrived at by Spielberg and Walter Parkes. Information about the company's top-secret business plan and the anger that ensued when it was leaked to *Variety* was shared with me by a source directly involved with the plan. DreamWorks' no-bonus policy, Katzenberg's attitude ("Help us grow, and so will you"), and the "multiple hats" approach to jobs at DreamWorks were confirmed by several DreamWorks employees. Katzenberg's comment at the collective-bargaining meeting was conveyed to me by a member of the Animation Guild who was present at the meeting.

Michael Eisner's initial attitude toward Disney's animation division, and Katzenberg's role in reviving it, as well as his controversial relationship with animators, is well documented in Stewart's and Masters's books on Disney. The description of the division's conservative nature is discussed in Tom Sito's *Drawing the Line*. Don Hahn's comment about Katzenberg at Disney is drawn from the documentary *Waking Sleeping Beauty*. The "Some people liked him . . ." comment was relayed to me by a Disney animator, as was Glen Keane's comment to Katzenberg. The meeting between Katzenberg and Pixar is described in David A. Price's book, *The Pixar Touch*.

Rupert Murdoch's quote ("they are about the destruction of Disney") was drawn from "Don't Say No to Jeffrey," by Bernard Weinraub, *New York Times Magazine*, June 30, 1996. Geffen and Eisner's discussion about Katzenberg's bonus is chronicled in King's *The Operator*. Bill Higgins and several associates of Terry Press's shared with me information about Press's relationship with Katzenberg. Rich Frank's departure from Disney, and his promise to Eisner not to work for DreamWorks, is discussed in *DisneyWar*. DreamWorks' proposed profit-participation deal with writers is documented in published reports, such as "Studio Struggles to Build Scribe Tribe," by Andrew Hindes, *Variety*, December 9–December 15, 1996. Geffen's comments to Katzenberg about *The Prince of Egypt* are drawn from "The Subject Was Moses: Jeffrey Katzenberg Tackles a Thing of Biblical Proportions; 'The Prince of Egypt'? No, His Fear," by Lloyd Grove, *Washington Post*, November 29, 1998.

8. LIVE ACTION

Quotes from Peter Dekom and Bruce Jacobsen are from interviews I conducted with these sources. Geffen's statement about calling the new company "Spielberg Brothers" appeared in "The Storyteller," by Ronald Grover, *BusinessWeek*, July 13, 1998. Sources for Katzenberg's live-action record at Disney include Stewart's *DisneyWar* and Masters's *Keys to the Kingdom*. Information on Spielberg's *Men in Black* deal is based on published reports in Peter Bart's book *The Gross*, and "Master Plan," by Giles Whittell, *Times* (London), February 14, 1998. The quote, "It's hard enough to find fifteen decent movies . . ." is from a former Disney executive I spoke with. Geffen's attitude toward Katzenberg's live-action record is based on interviews I conducted with associates of Geffen.

Investors' concerns and skepticism toward DreamWorks is drawn from conversations with financiers involved in raising money for the company, as well as published reports, such as "Hey! Let's Put On a Show! Start Our Own Multimedia Company! Prove the Naysayers Wrong! An Inside Look at the DreamWorks Saga—Act I," by Richard Corliss, *Time*, March 27, 1995, which is also the source of Spielberg's quotes. Discussion of negotiations with Microsoft is based on that piece, Ken Auletta's *World War 3.0*, as well as conversations with Bruce Jacobsen. Information about the inherent riskiness of the movie business is based on my reporting at *Variety*, supplemented by books such as Edward Jay Epstein's *The Big Picture*. Nathan Myhrvold's memo on Katzenberg was printed in "The Microsoft Provocateur," by Ken Auletta, *New Yorker*, May 12, 1997.

The tension between Matsushita and MCA, and Michael Ovitz's and Dream-Works' roles in the drama, is documented in *Keys to the Kingdom*, Bruck's *When Hollywood Had a King*, King's *The Operator*, and Stephen Singular's *The Rise and Rise of David Geffen*. Wasserman's outburst over Ovitz is drawn from Masters's piece, "What's Ovitz Got to Do with It?"

9. Show Me the Money

Quotes from Mike Slade, Howard Rosenman, Howard Weitzman, Ken Solomon, Max Howard, and Bruce Cranston are from interviews I conducted with these individuals. For background on Paul Allen and William Savoy, helpful resources included Laura Rich's book, *The Accidental Zillionaire*, Auletta's *World War 3.0*, and "The Accidental Zillionaire," by Paulina Borsook, *Wired*, August 1994. I also spoke with former associates of Allen's.

Edgar Bronfman Jr.'s negotiations with Matsushita to purchase MCA/Universal is discussed in Bruck's *When Hollywood Had a King*, as well as Bruck's *New Yorker* piece, "Bronfman's Big Deals," which appeared on May 11, 1998, and is the source of the "David Geffen [is] my guardian angel" quote. Ovitz's ambivalence about joining Universal, and his attempt to bring other CAA agents with him, was drawn from conversations I had with former CAA sources, as well as the aforementioned publications, in addition to "Awesome," by Ken Auletta, *New Yorker*, August 14, 1995. The scenes between the DreamWorks partners and Bronfman appeared in King's *The Operator*, and were confirmed in my interviews with knowledgeable sources. The discussion of DreamWorks' distribution deal with Universal is based on my conversations with Universal sources, as is Bronfman's wooing of Meyer. Ovitz's appearance on *Charlie Rose* took place on January 23, 2002.

Geffen's tumultuous history with Mo Ostin is recounted in *The Operator*, which also discusses George Michael's signing with DreamWorks Records. The portrayal of Katzenberg's dealings with Endeavor and the friction between DreamWorks and the agency is based on my interviews with high-level Endeavor sources.

Geffen's comments about Eisner are drawn from "Geffen Ungloved—Round One: 'I'm Not Afraid of Michael Eisner,'" by Robert Sam Anson, *Los Angeles* magazine, July 1995, and "For the DreamWorks Studio, an Unsettling Development," *New York Times*, August 1, 1995. Katzenberg's quotes about Eisner appeared in Auletta's *New Yorker* article "Awesome." Katzenberg's telephone conversation with Eisner was reported in "It's a Small World, After All, Mr. Eisner," by Bernard Weinraub, *New York Times*, August 7, 1995.

10. Culture Clash

My interviews with Bruce Cohen, Mark Johnson, Richie Chavez, Tony Ludwig, Scott Frank, and Keith Critchlow are the source of quotes attributed to these individuals. The culture clash between Amblin and Disney at DreamWorks, and of the sluggish start at the live-action studio, is based on numerous interviews with DreamWorks sources. The Shutters meeting where the confrontation between Parkes and Katzenberg took place was described to me by numerous sources present at the meeting.

Discussion of Walter Parkes and Laurie MacDonald, and their relationship with Spielberg, is based on dozens of interviews with DreamWorks sources, screenwriters, producers, studio executives, and agents. Spielberg's quote about wanting "to be a gentile" appeared in Joseph McBride's biography. Laurie MacDonald's quote ("I do have good instinct") is drawn from "Laurie's Basic Instinct," by Alan L. Gansberg, *Hollywood Reporter,* March 10, 1998. Lawrence Lasker's quote is drawn from "What's Wrong with DreamWorks?" by Kim Masters, *Esquire,* November 1, 2003. The anecdote in which Spielberg asks Parkes to run Amblin is taken from "The Storyteller," by Ronald Grover, *BusinessWeek,* July 13, 1998. Biographical information on Parkes is based on interviews with Parkes's classmates at Beverly Hills High School and Critchlow, as well as information obtained from Beverly Hills High yearbooks. The description of Parkes as "perfect" for Hollywood appeared in "Profile of California's Fourth Reich," by Betty Liddick, *Los Angeles Times,* March 23, 1976. How Parkes and MacDonald first met is mentioned in "Rare Power Couple Keeps Biz in Family," by Jonathan Bing, *Daily Variety,* January 13, 2003.

The discussion of DreamWorks Interactive is based primarily on my interviews with Bruce Jacobsen, Glenn Entis, Noah Falstein, Alan Hartman, and Daniel Kaufman.

11. The Unthinkable Occurs

My interviews with Max Howard, Floyd Norman, Sandra Rabins, and Mark Johnson are the source of quotes attributed to these individuals. Sources for Michael Ovitz's tenure at Disney, and Ovitz's outreach efforts toward Katzenberg over the bonus dispute, include Stewart's *DisneyWar,* Masters's *Keys to the Kingdom,* and "The Mouse Trap," by Bryan Burrough and Kim Masters, *Vanity Fair,* December 1996.

The discussion of competition between studios over animators is based on my reporting, as well as published reports, including "Tooning In: No Longer Bit Players, Animators Draw Fame as Hollywood Stars," by Thomas R. King and Lisa Bannon, *Wall Street Journal,* October 6, 1995. Eisner's remarks to animators at a Disney conference in Orlando are drawn from "Disney Denies Rumors of Talent Drain from Its Animation Unit to Katzenberg," by Tom Brink-moeller, *Orlando Business Journal,* June 30, 1995.

Details surrounding Playa Vista are based on my reporting, as well as published sources, such as "DreamWorks Picks L.A. Site for Studio, City Says; Entertainment: Plan for $70 Million in Incentives Is Prepared for Locating Near Marina Del Rey," by James Rainey, *Los Angeles Times,* December 5, 1995; and "DreamWorks Plans Its Dream Factory," by Claudia Eller, *Los Angeles Times,* December 15, 1995.

12. GEORGE IN SLOVAKIA; JEFFREY IN EXTREMIS

My interviews with Mark Johnson, Mimi Leder, David Rosenbloom, Penney Finkelman Cox, Dylan Kohler, David Silverman, Paul Shardlow, Marty Katz, Zak Penn, and Paul Weitz are the source of quotes attributed to these individuals. Quotes from Leslie Cockburn were obtained via an e-mail exchange. The behind-the-scenes story of the making of *The Peacemaker* is based on interviews with, in addition to Johnson, Leder, and Rosenbloom, producer Branko Lustig, sources at DreamWorks and PDI, and an individual close with George Clooney. I also relied on notes taken by *Variety* reporter David S. Cohen at the *Peacemaker* junket in Los Angeles.

The description of Barry Sonnenfeld as "openly neurotic" is taken from "He's Back—After One Too Many 'Men in Black,'" by John Horn, *Los Angeles Times,* April 16, 2006. Spielberg's comment to Clooney on the set of *ER* is described in "Somebody Has to Be In Control; The Effort Behind George Clooney's Effortless Charm," by Ian Parker, *New Yorker,* April 14, 2008. The DreamWorks presentation of upcoming product held on a Universal sound stage was described to me by a journalist in attendance, and is discussed in "Plenty of Dreams, Not Enough Works?" by Ronald Grover, *BusinessWeek,* July 22, 1996.

Details surrounding Katzenberg's lawsuit against Disney, and Bert Fields's comments about Frank Wells, are drawn from "Katzenberg Sues Disney, Says He Is Owed $250 Million," by James Bates, *Los Angeles Times,* April 10, 1996. Katzenberg's conversation with Eisner at the wake for Don Simpson and the canceled meeting in Aspen are recounted in Masters's *Keys to the Kingdom.* The quote "I've found my love, and it's . . . ," appeared in "Fishing Buddies," by Richard Turner and Corie Brown, *Newsweek,* September 27, 1997.

The discussion of the making of *The Prince of Egypt* is based on interviews with Finkelman Cox, Rabins, and artists who worked on the film, as well as the film's DVD commentary, and published reports, such as "The Prince and the Promoter," by Kim Masters, *Time,* December 14, 1997; and "Revenge of the Zion King," by Sheli Teitelbaum, *Jerusalem Report,* January 4, 1999, which is the source of the quote "This movie would not have been appropriate . . ."

Katzenberg's involvement with *Toy Story* while he was at Disney is discussed in Stewart's *DisneyWar,* as well as *The Pixar Touch,* by David A. Price. Katzenberg's exchange with John Lasseter and Andrew Stanton about *A Bug's Life,* as well as Lasseter's call to Katzenberg, is drawn from "Antz Vs. Bugs," by Peter Burrows, which appeared in the online version of *BusinessWeek,* November 23, 1998. The meeting at PDI during which Katzenberg announced *Antz* was described to me by a person in attendance. Steve Jobs is quoted in "Epics and Insects," by David Hochman, *Entertainment Weekly,* November 20, 1998. The comment from a former Pixar source ("It was pretty mean-spirited") is based on my reporting.

13. THE NOT SO LONG GOODBYE

I interviewed Adam Rifkin and Bruce Cranston. Primary sources for Michael Ovitz's tenure at Disney include Stewart's *DisneyWar,* Masters's *Keys to the Kingdom,* and articles, such as "Ovitz Agonistes," by Bryan Burrough, *Vanity Fair,* August 2002. Ovitz's conversation with Barry Diller, and his subsequent lunch with Geffen, is recounted in King's *The Operator.* Economist Robert Samuelson's *Washington Post* column ("What's $90 Million Between Friends?") appeared on December 25, 1996.

Financial details on where DreamWorks stood in mid-1996 is drawn from "Plenty of Dreams, Not Enough Works?" by Ronald Grover, *BusinessWeek,* July 22, 1996. "The richest and most hyped . . ." quote is taken from "California Dreamin'," by Lisa Gubernick, *Forbes,* July 29, 1996. Spielberg's quote, "It's a question of retaining one's perspective . . ." is taken from Peter Bart's *The Gross.* The DreamWorks party in Santa Monica was described to me by several employees in attendance.

14. OF MEN AND MICE

Quotes attributed to Adi Lieberman, Gore Verbinski, Tony Ludwig, Alan Riche, Bill Lawrence, Ken Solomon, and Bill Higgins are from my interviews with these sources. My conversations with Verbinski, Ludwig, Riche, as well as DreamWorks and agency sources, informed my reporting on the making of *Mousehunt.*

The DreamWorks doll given at the Herb Allen retreat is mentioned in "Top CEOs Make Sweet at Retreat," by Anita M. Busch, *Daily Variety,* July 14, 1997. The discussion of Playa Vista is based on interviews conducted with individuals involved in the negotiations with DreamWorks, as well as Adi Lieberman, and published reports, such as "DreamWorks Can't Escape Publicity, Controversy over Studio Plan," by Lynn Elber, Associated Press, March 14, 1997; and "Getting Swamped," by Jeff Stockwell, *Premiere,* January 1997. I obtained the document citing Katzenberg's communication with the California Transportation Commission. Spielberg's profit from *Men in Black* is reported in "Master Plan," by Giles Whittell, *Times* (London), February 14, 1998. Information about Katzenberg's dealings with Bob Cooper over *Amistad,* and his hiring him as an executive, is per a source with knowledge of the conversations. A source close to Cameron Crowe shared with me Crowe's feelings toward DreamWorks. Spielberg's comment about Robert Zemeckis's student film is drawn from *Blockbuster,* by Tom Shone. Discussion of the friendship between Spielberg and Zemeckis, and ImageMovers' deal with DreamWorks, is based on my conversations with sources with knowledge of the deal. Details about *Ink* and *Arsenio* are drawn from "Next Time Use a Pencil; After Scrapping Four Episodes of Its Big-Money, Big-Name Newsroom Sitcom and Turning the Concept Inside Out, CBS is Finally Delivering 'Ink,' " by Brian Lowry, *Los Angeles Times,* October 20, 1996; and "They Call David Rosenthal Crazy When All He Wants Is Heidi Klum," by Jason Gay, *New York Observer,* August 27, 2001. Discussion of the origins of *Spin City* is based on my interviews with Bill Lawrence and agency sources. Katzenberg's comments regarding the downsizing of DreamWorks TV were reported in "Eye-Opening Experience; Ambitions Still Intact, Studio Copes with Industry Changes," by Claudia Eller and James Bates, *Los Angeles Times,* September 19, 1997.

Discussion of the *Peacemaker* premiere in L.A. is based on descriptions given me by guests in attendance. Details were also drawn from "Clooney Seeks a Niche," by Liz Smith, *Newsday,* September 24, 1997; and "Spielberg Hurt in Shunt; Limo Crash Wrecks Premiere . . . ," by Andy Lines, *Mirror,* September 25, 1997. George Clooney's unwillingness to participate in certain media coverage and Terry Press's comment, "They *will* become collectors' items," are based on a conversation I had with a former DreamWorks publicist. The *Larry King Live* show featuring Clooney and Nicole Kidman aired on CNN on September 26, 1997. Walter Parkes's comments about *Peacemaker* appeared in an article of mine: "Road to Ambition," *Variety,* November 15–November 21, 2004. Katzenberg's comment, "First one in, first one out," appeared in "Fall Sneaks; First the Launch, Then the Mortar," by Bruce Newman, *Los Angeles Times,* September 7, 1997.

15. SLAVES TO THE RHYTHM

My interviews with David Franzoni, Alan Riche, Jill Overdorf, Dylan Kohler, and Bill Villarreal are the source of quotes attributed to these individuals. The discussion of the making of *Amistad* is based on my interviews with Franzoni and DreamWorks sources involved with the film. Spielberg's comments ("I felt very strongly . . .") are taken from "Rescuing a Piece of History; On Location: Spielberg's Children Inspired Him to Recount the Amistad Mutiny of 1839.

For the Record," by Bruce Newman, *Los Angeles Times*, November 9, 1997; the quote, "Comparisons between black slavery and the Holocaust," is from "Master Plan," by Giles Whittell, *Times* (London), February 14, 1998. The reference describing *The Color Purple* as " 'Gone with the Wind' of 1985" is from "Film Clips: Some Blacks Critical of Spielberg's 'Purple,' " by Jack Mathews, *Los Angeles Times*, December 20, 1985.

DreamWorks' marketing concerns over *Amistad*, and discussions on the subject between Spielberg and Terry Press, were relayed to me by DreamWorks sources. Details surrounding Barbara Chase-Riboud's lawsuit against Spielberg appear in "Spielberg Film Faces Charge of Plagiarism," by Bernard Weinraub, *New York Times*, November 13, 1997. Details of the motion filed by Pierce O'Donnell regarding Chase-Riboud's claims against DreamWorks appeared in " 'Amistad' Halt Is Sought," by Adam Sandler, *Daily Variety*, November 19, 1997.

David Geffen's comment ("Steven was in tears this morning . . ."), and his exchange with Terry Press regarding the *Amistad* premiere, appeared in "The Many Lives of David Geffen," by John Seabrook, *New Yorker*, February 23, 1998. Spielberg's comments ("They walked out of *Amistad* . . .") appeared in an interview with Roger Ebert published in the December 23, 2002, edition of the *Chicago Sun-Times*. Spielberg's comments ("The razor could have been used for . . .") appeared in "Spielberg Tells of 'Real' Fear in Testimony at Stalking Trial," *Chicago Sun-Times*, February 27, 1998.

Disney's expansion plans in Glendale were reported in "Disney Seeks Office Tower," by Dave McNary, *Daily News of Los Angeles*, July 22, 1997.

16. SAVING SPIELBERG

My interviews with Robert Rodat, Scott Frank, Mark Gordon, Devra Lieb, and Sherry Lansing are the source of quotes attributed to these individuals. The discussion of the making and marketing of *Saving Private Ryan* was based on my conversations with sources, both on and off the record, as well as Peter Bart's *The Gross*. Terry Press's interactions with Spielberg about the marketing of *Saving Private Ryan* are drawn from *The Gross* as well as interviews conducted with several sources familiar with the conversations.

Discussion of concerns over *Deep Impact* is based on my conversations with sources at DreamWorks and Paramount. The rift between Spielberg, Katzenberg, and Geffen caused by negotiations over *Memoirs of a Geisha* was described to me by sources with knowledge of the situation. Edgar Bronfman Jr.'s comment, "It's a dumb town," appeared in "Bronfman's Big Deals," by Connie Bruck, *New Yorker*, May 11, 1998.

CAA's efforts to put together the *Saving Private Ryan* deal are discussed in "Spielberg, Hanks Hook," by Michael Fleming, *Daily Variety*, June 4, 1996. James

V. Hart's comments ("Steven tends to use writers . . .") appeared in "Spielberg in Neverland," by Clifford Terry, *Chicago Tribune*, December 8, 1991. Janet Maslin's review of *Saving Private Ryan* ("Panoramic and Personal Visions of War's Anguish") appeared in the *New York Times* on July 24, 1998. David Ansen's review appeared in the July 27, 1998, edition of *Newsweek*. DreamWorks' net profit on *Saving Private Ryan* was relayed to me by a source with knowledge of the film's financials.

Geffen's conversation with President Bill Clinton are drawn from "The Many Lives of David Geffen," by John Seabrook, *New Yorker*, February 23, 1998. Geffen's feelings toward Clinton are based on conversations with sources close to Geffen. Geffen's handling of George Michael's PR crisis is discussed in *The Operator*. Discussion of the belt-tightening at DreamWorks Records is based on interviews with former DreamWorks employees. Robert Hilburn's criticism of DreamWorks Records' releases appeared in "'We Can Dream, Can't We?'" by Robert Hilburn, *Los Angeles Times*, August 24, 1998.

17. BUG WARS

Quotes of Noel McGinn, Sandra Rabins, Alicia Ojeda, Alan Ball, Sam Mendes, Marty Bowen, Tom Sherak, Penney Finkelman Cox, and Tony Angelotti are from my interviews with these sources. The race between *Antz* and *A Bug's Life* is based on my conversations with Rabins and McGinn, as well as sources at PDI and Pixar. Steve Jobs's comments ("Jeffrey stole my idea . . .") appeared in "A Survey of Technology and Entertainment: Electronic Anthills," by Emma Duncan, *Economist*, November 21, 1998. Kenneth Turan's review of *Antz* ran on October 2, 1998, in the *Los Angeles Times*.

The story of how *American Beauty* came together is based on my conversations with Ball, Sam Mendes, Dan Jinks, Bruce Cohen, Glenn Williamson, and DreamWorks sources, as well as *My First Movie: Take Two: Ten Celebrated Directors Talk About Their First Film*, edited by Stephen Lowenstein. The relationship between Walter Parkes and Bob Cooper is based on my conversations with DreamWorks sources, agents, and producers.

Katzenberg's comments ("I'm just completely hysterical!") are drawn from "The Subject Was Moses; Jeffrey Katzenberg Tackles a Thing of Biblical Proportions," by Lloyd Grove, *Washington Post*, November 29, 1998.

18. HARVEY BABY

Quotes attributed to Mark Gill, Tony Angelotti, Dale Olson, Mark Gordon, Bruce Cranston, Dan Kaufman, Sandra Rabins, Max Howard, and David Silverman are from my interviews with these sources. Background on Miramax is based on my reporting at *Variety*, as well as on *Down and Dirty Pictures* by

Peter Biskind. The anecdotes involving Terry Press and Spielberg and competing against Miramax are based on conversations with sources close to Press at DreamWorks. Spielberg's reluctance to campaign for an Oscar is also discussed in Peter Bart's *The Gross.*

Harvey Weinstein's comments ("They're trying to take old friends . . .") appeared in "'Shakespeare' Ad Blitz Has 'Ryan' Returning Fire," by Richard Natale, *Los Angeles Times,* March 8, 1999. Press's reaction at the Oscars ("like a ball of fire") is drawn from *Down and Dirty Pictures.* Description of the post-Oscar festivities is based on my reporting, as well as "Sipping Bubbly with Oscar; After the Ceremonies, All Decked Out in Tinseltown," by Sharon Waxman, *Washington Post,* March 23, 1999.

Details surrounding DreamWorks' financial profile at the end of 1998 is drawn from "DreamWorks Wakes Up to Reality," by Claudia Eller and James Bates, *Los Angeles Times,* July 13, 1999. Kim Masters's article reporting that Spielberg was "growing weary" of DreamWorks appeared in *Time* on April 5, 1999. Spielberg's rebuttal appeared in "Changes Afoot at DreamWorks — and Spielberg Will Help Oversee Them," by Claudia Eller, *Los Angeles Times,* April 20, 1999. Discussion of the making of *The Road to El Dorado* and how it was affected by Katzenberg's lawsuits is based on my conversations with people who worked on the film. Animator Marc Lumer's comments are drawn from *The Dream Team,* by Daniel M. Kimmel.

Details surrounding Katzenberg's trial, and the exchange between Geffen and Katzenberg in regards to the sum of Katzenberg's settlement, are drawn from Stewart's *DisneyWar,* as well as numerous reports, including "Let the Games Begin!" by Nikki Finke, *Salon,* April 27, 1999. Spielberg's comments regarding Playa Vista ("[I] wanted to cry") are drawn from the AMC program *Sunday Morning Shootout,* which aired on June 11, 2006.

19. UNEXPECTED BEAUTY

Quotes are from my interviews with Sam Mendes, Dan Jinks, Alan Ball, Scott Frank, Jan de Bont, Gore Verbinski, Penney Finkelman Cox, Ellen Coss, and Paul Lasaine. A. O. Scott's critique of Spielberg appeared in "Do Androids Long for Mom?" *New York Times,* June 29, 2001.

The Claudia Eller quote is from her *L.A. Times* article "Changes Afoot at DreamWorks." Katzenberg's role at DreamWorks' live-action studio is based on conversations with DreamWorks sources, producers, and agents. Katzenberg's comment ("I work for them") appeared in "Katz's New Dream Work," by Nick Madigan, *Daily Variety,* July 29, 1999. Discussion of the origins of *Minority Report* is based on interviews with Jan de Bont, and sources at DreamWorks and Fox, as well as information in *The Operator.*

The depiction of *The Road to El Dorado*'s troublesome development process comes from my conversations with individuals who worked on the film. The discussion between Katzenberg and Finkelman Cox, Rabins, and Ann Daly was relayed to me by several sources with knowledge of the incident.

20. THE BATTLE FOR OSCAR

My interviews with Dale Olson, Sam Mendes, Mark Gill, Paul Feig, Glenn Entis, David Bloom, and Bill Higgins are the source of quotes attributed to these individuals. The discussion of DreamWorks' Oscar campaign for *American Beauty* is based on conversations with Olson, Mendes, Alan Ball, Bruce Cohen, Dan Jinks, Mark Gill, and DreamWorks sources. The studio's campaign spending was reported in "Studio Built Victory 'One Brick at a Time,'" by Amy Wallace, *Los Angeles Times,* March 27, 2000.

The anecdote regarding Justin Falvey was relayed to me by a source at DreamWorks TV. Background on *It's Like, You Know . . .* is based on my interview with Peter Mehlman for a story in the *New York Observer.* The history of *Freaks and Geeks,* and background on Judd Apatow, is based on my conversations with Feig, DreamWorks sources, and published reports, including "Too Good and Weird," by Robert Lloyd, *L.A. Weekly,* May 12, 2000; and "Judd Apatow's Family Values," by Stephen Rodrick, *New York Times Magazine,* May 27, 2007.

The sale of DreamWorks Interactive to Electronic Arts, and the implications for former Microsoft employees, is based on my conversations with sources at DreamWorks Interactive. The discussion of Pop.com is based on conversations with David Bloom, and sources at DreamWorks and Imagine.

21. NOBODY'S BITCH

Quotes attributed to Alan Ball, Sam Mendes, Penney Finkelman Cox, Paul Lasaine, Richie Chavez, Floyd Norman, Bill Villarreal, Noel McGinn, Phillip Nakov, Mike Kelly, Tim Doyle, and Scott Frank are from my interviews with these sources. Frank DiGiacomo's piece, "The Oscars Enter the New Century!" appeared in the *New York Observer* on April 3, 2000.

The depiction of Katzenberg's reaction to the disappointing release of *The Road to El Dorado* is based on conversations with several individuals who worked on the film. Claudia Eller and James Bates's piece, "Animated Features Aren't Studio's Dream Come True," ran in the *Los Angeles Times* on April 28, 2000. DreamWorks' reaction to the story, and retaliation against Eller, is based on my conversations with sources at DreamWorks and the *L.A. Times.* Katzenberg's comment about *El Dorado* being a fiasco "like nothing I've experienced in twenty years" appeared in a Forbes.com Q&A by Peter Kafka and Peter Newcomb on February 20, 2003.

Information on the merger talks between DreamWorks and Imagine was shared with me by sources at Imagine and DreamWorks, as was information about Pop.com and *The Cat in the Hat;* the merger was also reported in articles such as "Union of Imagine, DreamWorks Fails at Prenup Stage," by Claudia Eller, *Los Angeles Times,* May 5, 2000. The comment about Pop.com ("We'd go through the slate of projects . . .") appeared in "Tinseltown Titans Caught in a Web," by Chris Taylor, with Jeffrey Ressner, *Time,* September 18, 2000. The legal battle between Mike Myers and Imagine was reported in articles including "The Dieter Principle," by David Hochman, *Entertainment Weekly,* July 28, 2000; "The Spy Who Emotionally Traumatized Me," *Globe and Mail* (Canada), July 18, 2000 (which excerpts Myers's countersuit); and "Myers Sues U in 'Dieter' Dustup," by Janet Shprintz, *Daily Variety,* July 11, 2000.

Spielberg and Stanley Kubrick's collaboration on *A.I.* is discussed in "Regarding Stanley," by Rachel Abramowitz, *Los Angeles Times,* May 6, 2001. Spielberg's fax machine is mentioned in "Spielberg Takes Extraordinary Measures to Keep *A.I.* a Secret," by Mike Szymanski, *San Diego Tribune,* June 29, 2001. Ron Bass's comment about *Memoirs of a Geisha* appeared in "Steven Spielberg's Giant Step; When This Director Moves, All Hollywood Falls in Behind," by Sharon Waxman, *Washington Post,* April 22, 2000, which also discusses Spielberg's talks with Warner Bros. about *Harry Potter.* That Spielberg claimed to have passed on *Harry Potter,* and then asked to have a producer credit, is based on conversations with individuals familiar with the discussion between Spielberg and Warner Bros. Brad Silberling's reaction to Spielberg's considering directing *Harry Potter* is based on a conversation with a source close to Silberling.

22. Sword Fights

Quotes attributed to Branko Lustig, Douglas Wick, David Franzoni, and Zak Penn are from my interviews with these sources. The behind-the-scenes making of *Gladiator* is based on my conversations with Lustig, Wick, Franzoni, and sources at DreamWorks. Information and anecdotes were also drawn from the BBC documentary *The Hollywood Machine: Shut It Down,* directed by Philip Day, which aired on August 6, 2002, and included commentary from Walter Parkes and screenwriters John Logan and Bill Nicholson.

The screening DreamWorks held for Harry Knowles is discussed in "Hollywood Is More Than Just Browsing; Studios Buy into Internet Marketing . . ." by Patrick Goldstein, *Los Angeles Times,* June 25, 2000. Terry Press's comment about Woody Allen was made at the premiere of an Allen film, which I was covering for *Variety.*

Details regarding Walter Parkes and Laurie MacDonald's renewed contract at DreamWorks and their attitude toward their role at the company are based on conversations with DreamWorks sources. Parkes's comment ("I don't think things are going to change much") appeared in "D'Works Reups Film Co-Toppers," by Paul F. Duke, *Daily Variety*, May 23, 2000.

23. SHREKED

My interviews with Penney Finkelman Cox, Noel McGinn, Phillip Nakov, Bill Lawrence, and Marc Ratner are the source of quotes attributed to these individuals. The story of the making of *Shrek* is based on my conversations with individuals at DreamWorks and PDI who worked on the film, as well as the *Shrek* DVD commentary and production notes, and notes taken by David Cohen at a "Shrekology" presentation at SIGGRAPH on August 7, 2007. Katzenberg's comment ("choke out a yes"), and Ted Elliott's quote ("Farquaad is short because Jeffrey insisted . . .") were taken from "Green Party," by Steve Daly, *Entertainment Weekly*, May 25, 2001.

The description of Ken Wong and the piñata bashing was relayed to me by former Pop employees. The failure of merger talks between Imagine and DreamWorks is based on my reporting as well as published reports, such as "Union of Imagine/DreamWorks Fails at Prenup Stage," by Claudia Eller, *Los Angeles Times*, May 5, 2000. Eller's piece about Katzenberg's behavior at *The Nutty Professor II* premiere, "Katzenberg Aims to Be New Bon Ami," ran in the *L.A. Times* on July 28, 2000. The *L.A. Times* piece examining the paper's entertainment coverage, "Long Soft on Hollywood, Times Seen as Improving," by David Shaw, appeared on February 15, 2001.

The discussion of *Spin City*, and DreamWorks' strategy for replacing Michael J. Fox, is based on my conversations with Bill Lawrence and former DreamWorks TV employees. DreamWorks Records' strategy for Nelly Furtado is based on conversations with Ratner, and "A Warbler Set Aloft by a Dedicated Flock," by Bernard Weinraub, *New York Times*, March 21, 2002. The discussion over Kina is based on conversations with former DreamWorks Records employees.

24. ROCK AND ROLL

Quotes attributed to Scott Frank and Mark Johnson are from my interviews with these sources. Discussion of the making of *Almost Famous* is based on my conversations with sources at DreamWorks and an individual close to Cameron Crowe, as well as published reports, including "Fighting Hollywood's Back-Story Bias; Director Cameron Crowe Likes to Get Characters' Off-Screen Histories Percolating in Your Head and Heart," by Michael Sragow, *Baltimore Sun*, December 16, 2001, which is the source of Crowe's quotes. The lawsuit filed by producer Jerome O'Connor over *An Everlasting Piece* was reported in

"D'Works Faces 'Piece' Lawsuit," by Ian Mohr, *Hollywood Reporter*, February 12, 2001.

Frustration over Walter Parkes's style as an executive is based on dozens of interviews with producers, writers, and agents. Laurie MacDonald's comments about her daughter's reaction to the monster in *Men in Black* appeared in "Laurie MacDonald/Ann Daly: Dynamic Duo Helps Navigate DreamWorks into the Front Ranks," by Christopher Grove, *Daily Variety*, November 29, 2000. The souring relationship between DreamWorks and ImageMovers is based on several conversations with sources at DreamWorks, as well as producers and agents.

25. GOLDEN GLOW

My interviews with Dale Olson, David Franzoni, Carl Rosendahl, Douglas Wick, and Penney Finkelman Cox are the source of quotes attributed to these individuals. Discussion of the marketing of *Gladiator* is based on conversations with Olson and other DreamWorks sources; marketing executives at other studios; and published reports, including "Oscar, Master of Suspense; Some Top Categories are Just Too Close to Call," by Rick Lyman, *New York Times*, March 21, 2001. The cost of double-truck ads in the *L.A. Times* was shared with me by a studio marketing executive. Information about the bonuses Katzenberg gave to the *Shrek* stars was shared with me by an individual with knowledge of the gifts.

Discussion of *Shrek* at Cannes is based on published reports, including "Hollywood Does Cannes," by Dana Thomas, *Newsweek*, May 14, 2001; "Vignettes from the Cannes Film Festival," by Clar Ni Chonghaile, Associated Press, May 15, 2001; and the *Shrek* DVD commentary.

Unhappiness among PDI shareholders at the sale of the company by Carl Rosendahl is based on half a dozen conversations I had with PDI sources, including McGinn. The discussion of DreamWorks' negotiations with Universal over renewing its distribution deal is based on my conversations with sources at Universal, and published reports, including "The Best Little Movie Studio in Hollywood," by Kim Masters, *Esquire*, September 1, 2001.

Financial figures for DreamWorks after the release of *Shrek* are drawn from "So How Does the Dream Work?" by Dade Hayes and Carl DiOrio, *Variety*, June 10, 2002.

26. THE MOTORCYCLE DIARIES

My interviews with Mike Macari, Roy Lee, Dean Zanuck, Rod Lurie, and David Scarpa are the source of quotes attributed to these individuals. The description of and background on Michael De Luca is based on my reporting at *Variety*, as well as conversations with DreamWorks sources and individuals close with De Luca. Jennifer Todd is quoted in the *Variety* article, "So How Does the Dream Work?" by Dade Hayes, June 10, 1002. De Luca's quote ("Some days, I feel like P. T. Barnum . . .") appeared in "Showing His Showmanship," by Bill Higgins, *Variety,* August 30, 1999.

Background on the making of *The Ring* is based on my interviews with Macari, Lee, Gore Verbinski, and DreamWorks sources. Information on *Old School* is based on my conversations with DreamWorks sources and individuals who worked on the film. Background on the making of *The Last Castle* is based on my interviews with Lurie and Scarpa, as well as individuals who worked on the film, and sources at DreamWorks. Background information on Robert Redford's prima donna behavior is available in Peter Biskind's *Down and Dirty Pictures.*

The blow-up between ImageMovers and DreamWorks is based on my interviews with sources with knowledge of the situation, as well as published reports, such as "Zemeckis Migrates to Warner," by Claude Brodesser and Dade Hayes, *Daily Variety,* December 28, 2001; and "ImageMovers Stands Its Ground at DreamWorks," by Michael Fleming and Dade Hayes, *Daily Variety,* April 19, 2002.

27. HARVEY II

My interviews with Sandra Rabins, Joel Madison, and Paul Feig are the source of the quotes attributed to them in this chapter. The confrontation between Harvey Weinstein and Stacey Snider, and the subsequent conversations between Katzenberg and Weinstein, was recounted in Biskind's *Down and Dirty Pictures,* as well as "Beauty and the Beast," by Ken Auletta, *New Yorker,* December 16, 2002. The description of the Oscar campaign for *A Beautiful Mind,* and the tension between DreamWorks and Universal, is based on conversations with sources at both studios, as well as published reports, such as "An Oscar Mantra: Press to Excess," by Patrick Goldstein, *Los Angeles Times,* February 5, 2002; and "Sifting Through the Mud, Looking For a Better Way," by Patrick Goldstein, *Los Angeles Times,* March 26, 2002.

Tensions between DreamWorks and Miramax are based on the above listed sources, as well as my conversations with individuals at the two studios. Weinstein's statement about the financial consequences of a film's being nominated for an Oscar was issued in 2003 in response to the Motion Picture Association of America's decision to ban studios from sending out screener DVDs to anyone but members of the Academy. Brian Grazer's comments ("It's so fucked up") appeared in *Down and Dirty Pictures.* The anecdote about the *60 Minutes* special with John Nash was described to me by a source with knowledge of the episode. DreamWorks' aggressive Oscar campaign for *Shrek* is based on trade ads for the film that ran at the time, as well as published reports, such as Goldstein's piece, "An Oscar Mantra: Press to Excess."

Katzenberg's desire to accept the Academy Award for *Shrek* is based on my conversations with several DreamWorks sources. Steve Jobs's attitude toward *Shrek,* and the Oscar campaign for *Monsters, Inc.,* is based on a conversation with Tony Angelotti. Sting's description of the Miramax pre-Oscar party was relayed to *Washington Post* reporter Sharon Waxman, and was written about by Lloyd Grove in his *Post* column, "The Reliable Source," March 26, 2002. The skit performed at the Mondrian, between Weinstein, Christina Applegate (playing Snider), and Katzenberg, was discussed in *Down and Dirty Pictures,* and reported verbatim in "The Monster's Ball," by Frank DiGiacomo, *New York Observer,* April 1, 2002.

Discussion of the history and making of *Undeclared* is based on my conversations with Feig, Madison, and sources at DreamWorks TV. Apatow's written plea ("pray for us") was reprinted in "Buzz Stop; A Look Back at What Was Happenin' Last Week," by Mike Ross and Steve Tilley, *Edmonton Sun,* February 24, 2002. Apatow's exchange with Mark Brazill appeared in "Brazill, Apatow in Nasty E-Spat," by Josef Adalian, *Daily Variety,* December 6, 2001. Katzenberg's comments about the changing television landscape ("The world has changed") are taken from "D'Works Finds Nest at Peacock," by Michael Schneider, *Daily Variety,* August 8, 2002. His comments about *Spirit* ("It's the difference between an e-mail and a handwritten letter") ran in "Unbridled Enthusiasm: Can DreamWorks' Jeffrey Katzenberg Reinvent the CG-Animated Film?" by Bob Strauss, *Daily News of Los Angeles,* May 26, 2002. The *New York Post* story ("G'Night DreamWorks—Allen Considers Dumping Stake in Studio"), by Dan Cox and Erica Copulsky, ran on May 8, 2002.

28. WHAT SINBAD WROUGHT

The description of the new arrangement at the live-action studio when Walter Parkes and Laurie MacDonald worked out of their home in Santa Monica is based on conversations with former DreamWorks employees. Michael De Luca's behavior at DreamWorks, and his frustration at the studio, is based on conversations with DreamWorks sources, and sources close to De Luca. *The Anchorman* pitch meeting, during which Parkes dismissed Will Ferrell as not being a movie star, appeared in "Despite Success of Shrek, DreamWorks Has Work to Do to Woo Wall Street," by Laura M. Holson and Sharon Waxman, *New York Times,* May 17, 2004.

Michael Ovitz's charges against a "gay mafia" appeared in "Ovitz Agonistes," by Bryan Burrough, *Vanity Fair,* August 2002. Discussion of *Sinbad,* and Katzenberg's reaction to its failing, is based on conversations with DreamWorks sources, artists who worked on the film, as well as Dade Hayes and Jonathan Bing's book *Open Wide,* which discusses the making and marketing of the film. The financial losses at DreamWorks' animation studio are taken from SEC reports that DreamWorks filed before it went public in 2004. Geffen's establishment of a reserve liquidity line for DreamWorks, and Paul Allen's demand for more ownership with his post-*Sinbad* infusion of cash, was shared with me by a source with knowledge of the company's financial arrangements.

The sale of DreamWorks Records as part of Universal's renewed distribution deal with DreamWorks is based on my conversations with individuals familiar with the deal. De Luca's comments ("I was told each and every deal . . .") appeared in "Time for Some DreamWorks Interpretation," by Patrick Goldstein, *Los Angeles Times,* August 9, 2005. Kim Masters's *Esquire* article ("What's Wrong with DreamWorks?") ran on November 1, 2003. Information about Paul Allen's financial losses, and comments by him and Bert Kolde, is taken from "The $12 Billion Education of Paul Allen," by Jay Greene, *BusinessWeek,* May 3, 2004. The depiction of the meeting in which Vulcan investors confronted Katzenberg about DreamWorks is based on information shared with me by an individual who was in the meeting. Katzenberg's comment "If he wants war, we'll fight!" was relayed to me by an individual with knowledge of the conversation.

29. NAKED IN PUBLIC

Eisner's remarks about not having a Pixar sequel in the works is taken from David A. Price's *The Pixar Touch.* The depiction of *Shark Tale*'s troubled production process is based on my conversations with individuals at DreamWorks who worked on the film.

The discussion of Ron Nelson and Helene Hahn's reasons for leaving DreamWorks is based on my conversations with sources with knowledge of the situation. Geffen's suggestion that Katzenberg hire a creative head at the animation studio, and Katzenberg's refusal, was shared with me by a source with knowledge of the conversation. Roger Enrico's comments ("We're done . . .") appeared in "Jeffrey's Wild Kingdom," by Josh Young, *V-Life,* May 16–22, 2005. The string of live-action flops in 2004 and the blame that was put on marketing is based on my reporting at *Variety,* as well as subsequent conversations with DreamWorks sources. Katzenberg's concern about the cost of *The Terminal* is also based on my conversations with DreamWorks sources.

Peter Bart's memo to Spielberg ("The Strivings of Sir Steven Slightly Off Mark") ran in *Daily Variety* on July 19, 2004. Background on Adam Goodman, and his leadership at DreamWorks, is based on my reporting at *Variety,* as well as interviews with several DreamWorks sources. Discussion of the origins of *The Island* is based on my conversations with DreamWorks sources as well as published reports, such as "Attack of the Clones," by Daniel Fierman, *Enter-*

tainment Weekly, July 22, 2005. Dean Zanuck's comment ("That, to me, was the final straw") is from my interview with Zanuck.

Employees' unhappiness over the IPO of DreamWorks Animation and the stock that was allotted, as well as the promises Katzenberg made prior to the IPO, is based on conversations with half a dozen former DreamWorks employees. Ann Daly's stock allotment was documented in SEC filings, and in published reports such as "Studio Discloses Exec Pay," by Jill Goldsmith, *Daily Variety,* July 22, 2004.

30. IN A SNICKET

That Walter Parkes and Laurie MacDonald's hybrid role at DreamWorks provoked the ire of other producers is drawn from my reporting while at *Variety,* and dozens of subsequent interviews I conducted for this book.

Background on the making of *Lemony Snicket's A Series of Unfortunate Events* is based on my conversations with sources who worked on the film, as well as former Paramount executives.

Katzenberg's desire to beat Pixar and ship more DVDs of *Shrek 2* than *The Incredibles* was described to me by a source with direct knowledge of the situation. DreamWorks Animation's projections that *Shrek 2* would go on to sell more than 55 million DVDs was reported in articles such as "DreamWorks Animation Rides 'Shrek 2' to Profit," by Lorenza Munoz, *Los Angeles Times,* December 9, 2004. The meeting at which Katzenberg told executives at DreamWorks Animation that *Shrek 2* DVD sales were off, and the comment that earnings were going to be "as unattractive as its star character Shrek," was reported in "Altered States: Insiders Say DreamWorks Is About to Report Surprisingly Bad Results," by Johnnie L. Roberts, Newsweek.com, May 10, 2005. Katzenberg's comment "I've been sent to the shed . . ." appeared in "Soft Sales of Shrek 2 Hurt Studio," by Lorenza Munoz, *Los Angeles Times,* May 11, 2005. The class-action lawsuits and SEC investigation of DreamWorks Animation following the overestimation of *Shrek 2* DVDs was widely reported in articles including "Katzenberg Catches Heat as Studio Stumbles," by Laura M. Holson, *New York Times,* July 25, 2005. David Baker's comment, "The people running DreamWorks . . ." appeared in a Bloomberg News report printed in the *Los Angeles Times* ("DreamWorks Adds to Chairman's Duties") on July 26, 2005. The description of Katzenberg at the media event for *Wallace and Gromit* is based on my firsthand reporting at the event.

31. NO WHITE SUITS!

Background on the making of *The Island* is based on my conversations with individuals directly involved with the film, as well as written reports, including

"Attack of the Clones," by Daniel Fierman, *Entertainment Weekly*, July 22, 2005; "Early Birds Get to Squirm," by Jonathan Bing, *Variety*, May 30–June 5, 2005; "Helmers Bend Budgets to Save Pricey Tentpoles," by Michael Fleming, *Variety*, November 15–November 21, 2004; and "You Call This Paradise?" by John Horn, *Los Angeles Times*, July 17, 2005. The depiction of tension between the marketing and production teams at DreamWorks is based on several interviews with DreamWorks sources.

Spielberg's unhappiness over Tom Cruise's focus on Katie Holmes and Scientology in interviews, as opposed to on *The War of the Worlds*, was relayed to me by a source with knowledge of Spielberg's complaint. Spielberg's unhappiness with Cruise over the Scientology picketers in front of a doctor's office was reported in "Showdown at Fort Sumner," by Bryan Burrough, *Vanity Fair*, December 2007. That Katzenberg "soft-pedal[ed]" *Wallace and Gromit* was reported in "Toons in Transition," by Ben Fritz and Nicole LaPorte, *Variety*, September 26–October 2, 2005. The piece is also the source of Nick Park's comments. The relationship between Aardman and Katzenberg is based on conversations between myself and former DreamWorks Animation sources. The description of *Wallace and Gromit* as "as English as apple-scrumping . . ." appeared in "An Animated—and Very English—Triumph," by Dominic Wells, *Times* (London), October 10, 2005. The analyst's comment about Katzenberg ("It's like he doesn't realize we write it all down") appeared in "D'Works Draws in Prez," by Ben Fritz, *Daily Variety*, December 6, 2005.

The courtship between Universal and DreamWorks throughout 2005; the meeting between Bob Wright and Geffen; and details surrounding Viacom's subsequent purchase of DreamWorks, were reported in "Hollywood Rewrite: Viacom Outbids GE to Buy DreamWorks," by Merissa Marr, Kate Kelly, and Kathryn Kranhold, *Wall Street Journal*, December 12, 2005. Jeffrey Immelt's comments ("I'm totally the bad guy here") are taken from his appearance on *Charlie Rose*, which aired on November 8, 2007. Details surrounding Brad Grey at Paramount are based on numerous interviews I conducted with former and present Paramount executives, as well as published reports, including, "Experience Required? The Selection of Brad Grey to Run Paramount Was a Shock—the First of Many for Him," by Kim Masters, *Los Angeles* magazine, July 1, 2006. The anecdote regarding Sumner Redstone swimming in the nude was reported in "Sleeping with the Fishes," by Bryan Burrough, *Vanity Fair*, December 2006. Redstone's sexual habits with his wife were reported in "Sumner's Discontent," by Lloyd Grove, *Portfolio*, January 7, 2009.

The discussion of *Munich* and Spielberg's feelings about the film are based on conversations with sources at DreamWorks and Universal, including those who worked on the film, as well as written reports, including "Next: Spielberg's Biggest Gamble," by David Halbfinger, *New York Times*, July 1, 2005; "An Israeli Perspective on New Spielberg Political Thriller," by David Halbfinger,

New York Times, December 9, 2005; and "The 'Munich' Murmurs," by Michael Fleming, *Variety,* July 25–July 31, 2005. Patrick Goldstein's piece about the bungled publicity campaign for Munich ("A Good Film Held Hostage by Bad PR") appeared in the *Los Angeles Times* on December 20, 2005. Stacey Snider's letter to editors at the *Times* was shared with me by Goldstein.

32. THE GEFFEN EXPRESS

My interviews with Bill Condon, Laurence Mark, Ken Solomon, and Sharen Davis are the source of quotes attributed to these individuals. Katzenberg's comments regarding Paramount's purchase of DreamWorks ("it's gonna be great!") were shared with me by two former DreamWorks employees. Spielberg's initial reluctance toward Paramount's purchase of DreamWorks is based on conversations with DreamWorks sources, and was reported in Bryan Burrough's *Vanity Fair* piece, "Showdown at Fort Sumner," which details the unhappy marriage between the two studios, including the anecdotes involving Stacey Snider, Tom Cruise, Tom Freston, and Janet Hill.

Spielberg's aversion to the bad press surrounding Paramount and Brad Grey is based on my conversation with a source close to Spielberg. Spielberg's comment, "I do not like change," appeared in "David Geffen, Savior of Dream-Works, Makes a Sudden Exit," by Michael Cieply, *New York Times,* October 27, 2008. Tension between DreamWorks and Paramount executives in the wake of Paramount's purchase of DreamWorks is based on several conversations I had with individuals at both studios.

The exchange between Katzenberg and Isaac Mizrahi at the Golden Globes was reported in "The Envelope/Golden Globes Postscript," by Richard Rushfield, *Los Angeles Times,* January 18, 2006. Information on the making of *Dreamgirls* is based on conversations with Condon, Mark, and sources at DreamWorks and Paramount. The film's publicity blitz is based on these conversations, as well as my reporting at *Variety.* Press's unhappiness when Gail Berman showed footage from *Dreamgirls* to Scott Rudin was described to me by more than one source with direct knowledge of the incident. Clint Eastwood's reaction to Rob Moore ("Who is this *Rob Moore?*") was relayed to me by a DreamWorks source. Geffen's reactions to test screenings of *Dreamgirls* are based on conversations with sources at DreamWorks and Paramount.

Philippe Dauman's comments ("DreamWorks brings a tremendous creative talent") were reported in "New Mix, Tricks at Par," by Jill Goldsmith, *Daily Variety,* December 5, 2006. The incident at the New York premiere of *Dreamgirls,* as well as Grey's behavior at the Golden Globes, was reported first in Nikki Finke's Deadline Hollywood Daily blog, and later in Burrough's "Showdown at Fort Sumner" piece in *Vanity Fair.* The incident at the AFI luncheon was shared with me by a *Dreamgirls* source. Geffen's comments about Bill and Hillary Clinton appeared in "Obama's Big Screen Test," by Maureen Dowd, *New York Times*, February 21, 2007. The descriptions of Arianna Huffington as "Lady Macbeth" and "beautiful" but "evil," appeared in "Arianna Calling!" by Suzanna Andrews, *Vanity Fair*, December 2005.

Background on *Transformers* and its history at DreamWorks is based on conversations with DreamWorks sources and agents. Michael Bay's refusal to let executives see dailies is based on a conversation with a source involved with the production. The exchange between Bay and Grey at the *Transformers* premiere was described to me by an individual who overheard the conversation. Jerry Seinfeld's demand that he have creative control of *Bee Movie* is based on conversations with former DreamWorks Animation employees.

Dauman's comment that Spielberg was "immaterial," and Katzenberg's rebuttal, was widely reported, and included in "Showdown at Fort Sumner." Spielberg's reaction to the opening weekend box-office grosses of *Indiana Jones and the Kingdom of the Crystal Skull* was described to me by a former Paramount source. The *Wall Street Journal* article that first reported talks between DreamWorks and the Reliance ADA Group—"Spielberg, India Firm Near Deal to Ally with DreamWorks," by Lauren A. E. Schuker and Merissa Marr—ran on June 18, 2008. Paul Allen's decision to force a secondary offering of Dream-Works Animation shares in the wake of *Flushed Away* was reported in "Allen Will Unload DreamWorks Shares," by Jill Goldsmith, *Daily Variety*, October 12, 2006. Allen's $467 million cash-out in August of 2007 was reported in "Dream Maker," by Richard Morgan, *Deal Magazine*, July 3, 2008.

Epilogue: Three-Way Split

The behind-the-scenes anecdotes from the 2009 Golden Globes appeared in "Dispatches from Inside the Golden Globes," by staff writers, "The Envelope," *Los Angeles Times*, January 11, 2009. The impact on Hollywood of the economic downturn that began in 2007 has been widely reported, including in my own stories on TheWrap.com ("Recession Watch: Expense Accounts Out at THR," January 27, 2009).

DreamWorks' struggle to find financial backing for its post-Paramount venture, and Reliance's inability to put up the initially stated $500 million, was widely reported in articles including "DreamWorks Wins Financing for Its Films," by Michael Ciepley, *New York Times*, August 18, 2009. Geffen's anger over Spielberg's not publicly thanking him for arranging the new DreamWorks deal was relayed to me by a DreamWorks source. That Spielberg spent $13 million of his own funds to retain rights to DreamWorks films was confirmed by a source with knowledge of DreamWorks' financial dealings and was reported in "DreamWorks Back in Business after New Funding," WENN Entertainment News Wire Service, July 17, 2009.

Paramount's passing on *Lincoln* is per a source with knowledge of the deal; it was also reported in "Spielberg's Lincoln Troubles," by Kim Masters, *Slate*, February 17, 2009. Spielberg and Katzenberg's connection to Bernard Madoff was reported in "Madoff's Hollywood Connection," by Amy Wallace, *Portfolio*, February 11, 2009. The anecdote involving Stacey Snider and *Variety* was shared with me by a *Variety* source. The atmosphere at DreamWorks when layoffs were announced—including Spielberg and Snider keeping a low profile—was described to me by a number of former DreamWorks employees. Details of Paul Allen's investment return in DreamWorks were reported in Richard Morgan's "Dream Maker." DreamWorks' behind-the-scenes negotiations with Disney were first reported on Nikki Finke's DeadlineHollywoodDaily.com, and followed up in published reports, including "Spielberg's DreamWorks Said to Be Headed to Disney," by Brooks Barnes and Michael Ciepley, *New York Times*, February 7, 2009. A source close to Ron Meyer described to me Meyer's unhappiness with Snider, as well as Spielberg's presence at Meyer's Easter-egg hunt. Katzenberg and Spielberg's divide over the conversion to 3-D cinema was reported in "Digital Leap Divides Trio," by Pamela McClintock, *Variety*, May 5–May 11, 2008.

ACKNOWLEDGMENTS

In many ways, writing this book was an education in the psychology of reporting. What makes people who have little to gain, and potentially much to lose, decide to open up to a reporter? What makes them trust someone who is, in many cases, a virtual stranger? I often asked myself these questions as I listened to individuals who were, as I mention in the preface to this book, often very uneasy about participating in a project that did not have the support of the DreamWorks principals.

When I posed these questions to my sources, answers ranged from the belief that the DreamWorks story was an important one to be told, to the feeling that talking about their experience with the company was somehow therapeutic, even necessary.

I've been told that Jeffrey Katzenberg predicted that a book relying on interviews with DreamWorks insiders would simply be an amalgamation of complaints and criticisms from "disgruntled former employees," but this turned out to be not at all the case. All of my sources had complex feelings about DreamWorks; even those who expressed frustration with the company had many fond memories of working there, as well as a lasting pride in their personal history with the place. Many described working at DreamWorks in terms of a "family"—a work environment they doubted they would ever find again in Hollywood. By the end of these interviews, some individuals who at first had been steely and tough in their analyses became tender and nostalgic, even weepy. And maybe it was this—that DreamWorks had represented for them an ideal that they cherished so deeply—that had brought them to speak with me in the first place.

Whatever their reasons, I am greatly indebted to those who shared with me their views and experiences, whether on the record or not. Without them, this book would not have been possible, and given the circumstances—the potential costs to themselves, personal or professional, of coming forward—my gratitude is mixed with admiration. I thank all of those I interviewed, whether named in this book or quoted here on background—they know who they are—for their courage and candor.

My editor at Houghton Mifflin Harcourt, George Hodgman, was instrumental in this project from the very first time I spoke with him about it. During the planning and research stages, a phone call from George would come in every few weeks—"How's it going? What do you need?"—along with dozens of ideas and thoughts on how I might tackle this complicated assignment. During the editing process, George was as much a partner as an editor, and for those who believe—as I did—that old-fashioned editors who get in the ring and battle it out alongside their writers, and who put considerable care into line-by-line editing, no longer exist, George Hodgman is proof otherwise.

My agent, David Kuhn, got the ball rolling on this book, knowing instinctively where it belonged and how to get it there. In my writing of the proposal, David was a sharp editor, helping me shape the story and tease out crucial scenes, and always holding the bar up high. His always savvy counsel has been a tremendous aid. Many thanks also to Billy Kingsland and Jessi Cimafonte at Kuhn Projects.

I would also like to thank the team at Houghton Mifflin Harcourt, especially publisher Bruce Nichols and editor in chief Andrea Schulz, who always made me feel that this was a project they were excited to invest in, and who have put a considerable amount of energy into doing so. Thanks also to Johnathan Wilbur; the talented marketing team of Bridget Marmion, Lori Glazer, Alia Hanna Habib, and Carla Gray; and Michaela Sullivan and Melissa Lotfy, who were behind this book's handsome design. Copyeditor Melissa Dobson cleaned up my prose and made considerable improvements throughout the manuscript.

The tireless scrupulousness of Lois Wasoff, the legal eye on the text, and Brian Gallagher, who fact-checked, were essential to getting this book to where it needed to be.

Peter Bart, formerly the editor in chief of *Variety*, and now its editorial director, is the reason I left New York and came out to Los Angeles to immerse myself in the fascinating, and never, ever dull, world known as the motion picture business. I thank him for giving me that opportunity.

I am hardly the first person to write about DreamWorks. Many talented journalists came before me. Their work is acknowledged in the text as well as in the notes to this book, but I would like to single out for special praise a few reporters who have written extensively on the subject, and who have inspired my own efforts: Kim Masters, Claudia Eller, Anita Busch, Sharon Waxman, Bernard Weinraub, Nikki Finke, Bryan Burrough, James L. Stewart, Patrick Goldstein, Michael Fleming, Anne Thompson, Ronald Grover, and the late Tom King.

I am also grateful to the journalists and peers who offered their support and advice along the way. I blame Jeffrey Frank for clinching my decision to write this book, and worse, for making it sound easy. To Gerry Degenhardt and Bob Heifetz: my eternal gratitude for taking notice of a kid who liked to read and write. And I thank Alison Rose for, among other things, the best writing advice I have ever received: describe the *hell* out of it.

Finally, and most importantly, family and friends helped keep me sane, even if I was driving them something quite the opposite, and I owe immeasurable gratitude to my parents, the Rushfields, and, most especially, my husband, Richard Rushfield, my everlasting champion and compass.

INDEX